The Laguna Madre of Texas and Tamaulipas

Number Two:
GULF COAST STUDIES
Sponsored by Texas A&M University–Corpus Christi
John W. Tunnell, Jr., General Editor

The Laguna Madre of Texas and Tamaulipas

Edited *by* John W. Tunnell, Jr., *and* Frank W. Judd

Foreword by Richard C. Bartlett

Contributors:

JOHN W. TUNNELL, JR.

KIM WITHERS

ELIZABETH H. SMITH

FRANK W. JUDD

JAMES F. BERGAN

NANCY L. HILBUN

AMY E. KOLTERMANN

SUZANNE J. DILWORTH

SUSAN A. CHILDS

Texas A&M University Press
College Station

Library of Congress Cataloging-in-Publication Data

The Laguna Madre of Texas and Tamaulipas / edited by John W. Tunnell, Jr.
and Frank W. Judd; foreword by Richard C. Bartlett; contributors, John
W. Tunnell . . . [et al.].— 1st ed.
 p. cm.—(Gulf Coast studies; no. 2)
Includes bibliographical references and index.
 ISBN 1-58544-133-3 (cloth : alk. paper)
1. Natural history—Texas—Laguna Madre Region. I. Tunnell, John Wesley. II.
Judd, Frank W. III. Title. IV. Gulf Coast studies; no. 2.
 QH105.T4 L34 2001
508.764´47—dc21
2001002239

Contents

List of Illustrations   **vii**

List of Tables   **xi**

Foreword   **xiii**

Preface   **xviii**

Acknowledgments   **xxi**

Part I   **Overview**   **1**

Chapter 1   Introduction   **3**
JOHN W. TUNNELL, JR.

Chapter 2   Geography, Climate, and Hydrography   **7**
JOHN W. TUNNELL, JR.

Chapter 3   Origin, Development, and Geology   **28**
JOHN W. TUNNELL, JR.

Chapter 4   Tamaulipan Biotic Province   **38**
FRANK W. JUDD

Chapter 5   Ranching Heritage   **59**
NANCY L. HILBUN AND AMY E. KOLTERMANN

Part II   **Natural Resources**   **71**

Chapter 6   The Environment   **73**
JOHN W. TUNNELL, JR.

Chapter 7   Seagrass Meadows   **85**
KIM WITHERS

Chapter 8   Open Bay   **102**
KIM WITHERS

Chapter 9   Wind-Tidal Flats   **114**
KIM WITHERS

Chapter 10   Barrier Islands   **127**
ELIZABETH H. SMITH

Chapter 11   Redheads and Other Wintering Waterfowl   **169**
ELIZABETH H. SMITH

Chapter 12   Colonial Waterbirds and Rookery Islands   182
ELIZABETH H. SMITH

Chapter 13   Shorebirds and Wading Birds   198
KIM WITHERS

Chapter 14   Sea Turtles   211
ELIZABETH H. SMITH AND SUSAN A. CHILDS

Chapter 15   Fish and Invertebrate Fisheries Organisms   223
KIM WITHERS AND SUZANNE J. DILWORTH

Part III   **Special Issues and Concerns**   253

Chapter 16   Red and Brown Tides   255
KIM WITHERS

Chapter 17   The Laguna Madre: A Conservation Framework   259
JAMES F. BERGAN

Chapter 18   Information Gaps and Needs   270
JOHN W. TUNNELL, JR.

Chapter 19   Conservation Issues and Recommendations   275
JOHN W. TUNNELL, JR., KIM WITHERS, AND ELIZABETH H. SMITH

Appendix 1   Contacts   289
Appendix 2   Acronyms   303

Literature Cited   305

List of Contributors   335

Index   337

Illustrations

FIGURES

8	2.1	Laguna Madre of Texas and Tamaulipas
10	2.2	Upper Laguna Madre of Texas
10	2.3	Lower Laguna Madre of Texas
11	2.4	Northern Laguna Madre de Tamaulipas
11	2.5	Southern Laguna Madre de Tamaulipas
29	3.1	Sea level changes related to glacial and interglacial stages
30	3.2	Origin and development of the Texas shoreline
30	3.3	Subsurface late Pleistocene–Holocene valleys below present-day Baffin Bay and Land-Cut
33	3.4	Profile section across typical clay dune overlying Pleistocene Beaumont Clay
36	3.5	Generalized cross sections of Padre Island barrier system
39	4.1	Tamaulipan Biotic Province of Texas and Mexico
39	4.2	Four biotic provinces of Tamaulipas
40	4.3	The approximate boundaries of biotic provinces in Texas and biotic districts of the Tamaulipan Biotic Province in Texas
45	4.4	Vegetational areas of Texas
45	4.5	Transverse profile of South Padre Island showing major topographic zones
48	4.6	The natural regions of Texas
60	5.1	Private ranches in South Texas
62	5.2	South Texas between 1836 and 1848
68	5.3	The Coastal Sand Plains (= South Texas Eolian Sand Sheet)
74	6.1	Diagram of sill or "bulkhead" at the junction of upper Laguna Madre with Corpus Christi Bay
74	6.2	Pattern of surface salinities in the upper Laguna Madre during July–September 1946
76	6.3	Relationship between salinity and annual precipitation in the Texas Laguna Madre
81	6.4	Serpulid reef distribution in Baffin and Alazan Bays
87	7.1	Succession in seagrass meadows in Laguna Madre
88	7.2	Distribution of seagrasses in Texas Laguna Madre between 1965 and 1988
96	7.3	Generalized food web for Laguna Madre seagrass meadows
100	7.4	Distribution of seagrasses in Laguna Madre de Tamaulipas in 1973–74 and 1994–95
104	8.1	Monthly mean abundance of organisms collected in Alazan Bay
104	8.2	Phytoplankton density and diversity in relation to salinity in Alazan Bay
105	8.3	Zooplankton density and diversity in relation to salinity in Alazan Bay
105	8.4	Macrozooplankton abundance and diversity in relation to salinity in Alazan Bay
106	8.5	Benthic invertebrate density and diversity in relation to salinity in Alazan Bay

107	8.6	Invertebrate nekton abundance and diversity in relation to salinity in Alazan Bay
109	8.7	Relationship between salinity and pooled number of phytoplankton and zooplankton taxa in Alazan Bay
109	8.8	Relationship between salinity and pooled number of macrozooplankton, benthic, and nektonic taxa in Alazan Bay
111	8.9	Vertical distribution of major taxa in open bay sediments in upper Laguna Madre
111	8.10	Mean biomass and standard deviation at unvegetated sites in upper Laguna Madre
112	8.11	Conceptual diagram of energy flow and food web of open bay habitats in Laguna Madre
115	9.1	Map of wind-tidal flats adjacent to the Texas Laguna Madre
117	9.2	Horizontal relationship schematic depicting positions of wind-tidal flats in relation to other barrier island and mainland habitat types
117	9.3	Overhead view of tidal flat depicting possible arrangement of microhabitats
119	9.4	Abundance and distribution of the major taxa of blue-green algae and benthic and epibenthic invertebrates
123	9.5	Generalized food chain for tidal flats
126	9.6	Distribution of tidal flats in Laguna Madre de Tamaulipas
129	10.1	Cross-section profiles of barrier island vegetation zonation for Padre Island, Barra El Conchillal, and Barra Jesús María
171	11.1	Salinity and water level fluctuations on Bluff Pond adjacent to upper Laguna Madre of Texas, October–March, 1987–88
171	11.2	Potential changes in vegetation zones in relation to hydrologic conditions
173	11.3	Estimated numbers of redheads from aerial surveys of traditional winter ranges in Texas, Tamaulipas, Florida, and Louisiana, 1980–94
173	11.4	Number of redheads counted during aerial surveys on estuaries and ground surveys on coastal ponds
192	12.1	Nesting habitats for South Bird Island rookery in upper Laguna Madre
192	12.2	Vegetation changes and nesting habitat for Marker 63 Island
193	12.3	Vegetation changes and nesting habitat for Marker 81 rookery
194	12.4	Summary of nesting population dynamics for American white pelicans in upper Laguna Madre
200	13.1	Average monthly total avian abundance north of Malaquite Beach
200	13.2	Shorebirds censused on a blue-green algal flat on north Padre Island
202	13.3	Birds counted on tidal flats between Yarborough Pass and Mansfield Pass during eight surveys in 1992–93
208	13.4	Wading birds censused on blue-green algal flats in upper Laguna Madre or in adjacent shallow waters
214	14.1	Nesting locations of Kemp's ridley sea turtles in Tamaulipas
224	15.1	Mean abundance and diversity of fish in Alazan Bay in relation to salinity
230	15.2	Relative abundances of large fish captured using gill nets during fall, 1975–97
230	15.3	Relative abundances of large fish captured using gill nets during spring, 1975–97
231	15.4	Relative abundances of small fish captured using bag seines, 1975–97
231	15.5	Relative abundances of fish in a shoalgrass bed in upper Laguna Madre
232	15.6	Relative abundances of fish in Baffin Bay
233	15.7	Relative abundances of fish captured in South Bay
234	15.8	Fish landings from Corpus Christi and Port Isabel, 1900–24
237	15.9	Red drum catch rate and mean total length, from gill nets in upper and lower Laguna Madre, 1975–96
238	15.10	Red drum catch rate and mean total length, from bag seines in upper and lower Laguna Madre, 1977–96

239	15.11	Spotted seatrout catch rate and mean total length, from gill nets in upper and lower Laguna Madre, 1975–96
240	15.12	Spotted seatrout catch rate and mean total length, from bag seines in upper and lower Laguna Madre, 1977–96
241	15.13	Black drum catch rate and mean total length, from gill nets in upper Laguna Madre, 1975–96
242	15.14	Black drum catch rate and mean total length, from bag seines in upper and lower Laguna Madre, 1977–96
243	15.15	Brown shrimp catch rate and mean total length, from bag seines in upper and lower Laguna Madre, 1977–96
244	15.16	Brown shrimp catch rate and mean total length, from trawls in upper and lower Laguna Madre, 1982–96
245	15.17	Pink shrimp catch rate and mean total length, from bag seines in upper and lower Laguna Madre, 1977–96
246	15.18	Pink shrimp catch rate and mean total length, from trawls in upper and lower Laguna Madre, 1982–96
247	15.19	White shrimp catch rate and mean total length, from bag seines in upper and lower Laguna Madre, 1977–96
248	15.20	White shrimp catch rate and mean total length, from trawls in upper and lower Laguna Madre, 1982–96
250	15.21	Red drum imports at Port Isabel and Brownsville from the Laguna Madre de Tamaulipas, 1944–62
250	15.22	Spotted seatrout imports at Port Isabel and Brownsville from the Laguna Madre de Tamaulipas, 1944–62
251	15.23	Shrimp catch in the Laguna Madre de Tamaulipas, 1971–78
251	15.24	Commercial landings from Laguna Madre de Tamaulipas, 1990–98
251	15.25	Comparison of Texas Gulf and Laguna Madre de Tamaulipas inshore shrimp landings, 1990–98
261	17.1	The ecoregional planning process as defined by the Nature Conservancy
267	17.2	Critical threats rankings across all systems within the Laguna Madre
268	17.3	Viability rankings for seven conservation targets within the Laguna Madre of Texas
268	17.4	Paradigm for the concept of community-based conservation

COLOR PLATES

138	1	Satellite image of coastline from Copano-Aransas Bays to northern Laguna Madre de Tamaulipas
139	2	Satellite image showing lower Laguna Madre of Texas, Río Grande Delta, and entire Laguna Madre de Tamaulipas
140	3	Aerial view over some of the many natural islands in the northernmost Laguna Madre de Tamaulipas
140	4	Aerial view over Pita Island
140	5	Aerial view over the wind-tidal flats and El Toro "island"
141	6	Vertical high altitude aerial photograph of lower Laguna Madre
141	7	Aerial view of oil and gas channels and dredged material islands, upper Laguna Madre
141	8	Aerial view over Padre Isles development
142	9	Aerial photo of the hotel-condominium zone on South Padre Island
142	10	Vertical high altitude photograph of Mansfield Pass
142	11	Aerial photo over El Mezquital Pass

143	12	Aerial photo over Boca de Catán
143	13	Satellite photo of the Land-Cut area between the upper and lower Laguna Madre
143	14	Demonstration of the impact of salt blowing on vegetation
144	15	Vertical high altitude photograph of the Río Grande Delta
145	16	Aerial photograph over the Río Grande Delta in Mexico
145	17	Clay dune on western edge of Land-Cut wind-tidal flats
145	18	View of clay dune along the "transition zone" between Land-Cut wind-tidal flats and uplands
146	19	Clay dunes encroaching upon uplands in the Land-Cut
146	20	Wind-tidal flats on the eastern side of Laguna Madre
146	21	Wind-tidal flats on the western side of Laguna Madre
147	22	Gulf cordgrass or sacahuiste flats
147	23	Aerial view of banner dune complex on South Texas Eolian Sand Sheet
148	24	Beach rock (coquina) outcrops
148	25	Gypsum crystal found eroded from a dredged material deposit of an oil and gas field channel
149	26	View along eroding clay bluff in northern Laguna Madre de Tamaulipas
149	27	View of sand dunes encroaching on upland habitat
149	28	Aerial view of dense seagrass beds behind barrier peninsula
150	29	Aerial view over extreme northern Laguna Madre de Tamaulipas waters
151	30	Views of the southern part of the northern Laguna Madre de Tamaulipas
152	31	Aerial views of southern Laguna Madre de Tamaulipas
153	32	Fishing boats at Carboneras, southern Laguna Madre de Tamaulipas
154	33	Aerial views of southern Laguna Madre de Tamaulipas
155	34	Aerial views of southernmost Laguna Madre de Tamaulipas
156	35	Seagrasses of Laguna Madre
157	36	South Padre Island wind-tidal flats adjacent to the lower Laguna Madre
158	37	Evidence and impact of high salt content on wind-tidal flats
159	38	Redheads on freshwater pond adjacent to upper Laguna Madre
159	39	Flock of redheads over freshwater pond adjacent to upper Laguna Madre
160	40	Dredge material islands in upper Laguna Madre showing variability in nesting habitat
161	41	Various nesting types seen on Laguna Madre dredge material islands
162	42	Views of nesting colonial waterbirds on Laguna Madre dredge material rookery islands
163	43	Great egret and tricolor heron in freshwater pond habitat on Padre Island
164	44	Dunlin, snowy egret, and reddish egret along the shores of Laguna Madre of Texas
165	45	Dredging activities in Laguna Madre
166	46	Fishing cabins located on dredged material islands
167	47	Numerous long fishing piers extending from the shoreline at Port Mansfield
167	48	Charangas (fish traps) in shallow waters near Mezquital in northern Laguna Madre de Tamaulipas
167	49	*Ixtoc I* oil spill on Padre Island beaches during August 1979
168	50	Impact of Hurricane Allen

Tables

9	2.1	Physiographic data for the Laguna Madre of Texas and Tamaulipas
12	2.2	Population (1990 census) of counties, cities, and towns along the shores of Laguna Madre of Texas
13	2.3	Population (1990 census) of counties, towns, and villages along the shores of Laguna Madre de Tamaulipas
17	2.4	Comparison of precipitation and temperature means among months for Corpus Christi, Brownsville, and Soto la Marina
21	2.5	Major hurricanes affecting the Laguna Madre of Texas and Tamaulipas during the twentieth century
26	2.6	Major channels constructed in the Laguna Madre of Texas and Tamaulipas
45	4.1	Vegetation types in the Texas portion of the Tamaulipan Biotic Province
49	4.2	Comparison of forest and woodland communities among the natural regions
50	4.3	Comparison of herbaceous-dominated communities among the natural regions
51	4.4	Plant associations in Texas recognized by McLendon (1991)
52	4.5	Mammals identified by Blair (1950) as Neotropical species extending northward into the Texas Tamaulipan Biotic Province
53	4.6	Mammals identified by Alvarez (1963) as characteristic of the Mexican portion of the Tamaulipan Biotic Province
54	4.7	Amphibians and reptiles that reach their northern limits of geographic range in the Texas Tamaulipan Biotic Province
55	4.8	List of endangered, threatened, and rare species found in counties adjacent to Texas Laguna Madre
61	5.1	Original Spanish and Mexican land grants bordering the Laguna Madre
68	5.2	Land delineation along the Laguna Madre shoreline
77	6.1	Approximate areal extent of major habitat types in Laguna Madre and Baffin Bay of Texas and Laguna Madre and Laguna el Catán of Tamaulipas
78	6.2	Wetlands and uplands classification surrounding Laguna Madre de Tamaulipas
82	6.3	Number of species found in each plant division and animal phylum within the estuaries of the Texas Coastal Bend, upper Laguna Madre and Baffin Bay, and Laguna Madre de Tamaulipas
83	6.4	Overview of numbers of species in major groups from the Texas Coastal Bend, upper Laguna Madre and Baffin Bay, and Laguna Madre de Tamaulipas
91	7.1	Comparison of the numbers of invertebrate families and species recorded in seagrass meadows in Texas Laguna Madre and Baffin Bay, and Laguna Madre de Tamaulipas
109	8.1	Results of regression analysis for total taxa and mean monthly salinity for biotic assemblages in Alazan Bay, 1978–79
110	8.2	Sediment redox potential and grain sizes in relation to depth and mean benthic invertebrate density, biomass, and diversity

111	8.3	Mean nutrient fluxes in open bay habitats in upper Laguna Madre during April 1992
115	9.1	Areal extent of wind-tidal flats in the Laguna Madre area of South Texas, including Baffin Bay and South Bay
118	9.2	Summary of sedimentary processes affecting wind-tidal flats
132	10.1	Carnivorous reptiles documented from vegetated flat habitats of Padre Island
174	11.1	Time budget assessments of redheads utilizing saltwater and freshwater habitats in geographic portions of their wintering range in southern Texas
176	11.2	Percentages of common waterfowl species recorded along the Gulf Coastal Plain during annual aerial surveys, 1948–65
177	11.3	Percentages of common waterfowl species recorded along the Gulf Coastal Plain during annual aerial surveys, 1970–88
183	12.1	Summary information on all bird colonies surveyed in upper Laguna Madre
185	12.2	Species composition of colonial-nesting waterbirds in upper and lower Laguna Madre and presence documented for each species in colony sites
187	12.3	Summary information on all bird colonies surveyed in lower Laguna Madre
188	12.4	Number of colonial waterbird nesting pairs on northeastern coast of Mexico during May and June, 1973–76
191	12.5	Percentage of nests of three species of herons constructed on each substrate on Island 105 in 1970
199	13.1	Relative abundances of shorebirds in Texas on tidal flats bordering the Laguna Madre
215	14.1	Kemp's ridley sea turtle Rancho Nuevo project summary
217	14.2	Species composition of sea turtle strandings in the northwestern Gulf of Mexico by month, 1986–89
225	15.1	Numbers of families and species of fish found in Corpus Christi Bay and along the Texas Gulf Coast compared with the hypersaline Laguna Madre
226	15.2	Economic role, use as an indicator species, habitat use, trophic level, and qualitative abundances of major life stages of 10 invertebrate and 27 fish species in the Laguna Madre of Texas
249	15.3	General effects of freshwater inflows on fisheries' harvests, 1959–76
263	17.1	Conservation targets and associated communities, guilds, or species within the Laguna Madre of Texas
266	17.2	Identified threats to focal conservation targets within the Laguna Madre of Texas
271	18.1	Summary of literature listed in Laguna Madre Comprehensive Bibliography concerning the Laguna Madre and surrounding areas by geographic area and type of literature
272	18.2	"Information gap matrix" for selected aspects of knowledge concerning the Laguna Madre of Texas and Tamaulipas

Foreword

Some 25 years ago, I mounted the first of many Jeep treks into the *tierra despoblado* of the Laguna Madre ecosystem. *Despoblado* is Spanish for deserted and uninhabited. Technically, Padre Island and the Laguna Madre of Texas were not by then so despoblado, but you could scarcely have convinced me, as on the way south to the Mansfield Channel I saw nary a soul during hours of grinding through albescent sand and slithery shell. Fortunately, the damage from Hurricane Celia's storm surge had healed enough for travel, and Bret was not yet a glimmer in La Niña's eye. A similar four-wheel-drive trip would have been impossible in the fall of 1999.

Hurricane Bret was to visit the Mansfield Channel in August 1999, and its six- to eight-foot storm tidal surge shuffled beach and fore-island dunes like giant dervish dominos. Strong onshore winds coupled with low atmospheric pressure rapidly built the surge so that the storm waves hit the Padre Island beach on an elevated cushion of water. Bret's surge breached the fore-island dune ridge and flooded onto tidal flats through several new channels, including one 150 feet wide and more than five feet deep. Eventually, these storm passes silted up and closed as the island healed itself once again. South of the Mansfield Channel in 1980, an asphalt roadway was pounded into useless chunks by Hurricane Allen. The pavement has been restored. One wonders why.

Now that we have begun a new century, it may be enlightening to reflect on how the Texas coast began the last, with what *National Geographic* described as "a scene of suffering and devastation hardly paralleled in the history of the world." The hurricane that swept over Galveston Island on 8 September 1900 killed 6,000 people on the island and more on the mainland. Coastal developers are quick to point out that since Galveston was "levitated" in 1902—its beach walled, groined, and armored—hurricanes, even the ferocious Carla in 1961, have struck without major damage. They fail to mention that the natural beach is long gone and that without continuous and costly replenishment, there would be no tourist-drawing expanse of sand.

Another landmark event marked that fateful year of 1900, just weeks before that dreadful hurricane. The canescent plumes of snowy and great egrets, pearlescent pink feathers from the roseate spoonbill, and showy plumage from other assorted birds had for many years been plucked off our coasts as raw materials for the New York and London millinery trade. These birds of a feather almost followed their cousin the passenger pigeon into extinction. In May 1900 Congress passed the Lacey Act, which prohibits interstate shipment of wild species killed in violation of state laws. The Lacey Act formed the structure for the Endangered Species Acts (ESAs) of 1966, 1969, and 1973 and back before Congress at the time of writing. I believe the act should be improved to be friendlier to private landowners, but there is no doubt of the ESA's contribution to conservation of biodiversity in America.

A century ago only a few insect-resistant souls lived near beaches. By 2000, 80%

of Americans lived within an hour of the beach. By this same millennial year there were six billion humans and 20 million Texans, increasing numbers of them on their way to the Laguna Madre ecosystem. Cornelia Dean, in *Against the Tide*, points out that "the nation's increasing commitment to living on the beach has created a powerful force against the application of knowledge already in hand. There is a kind of constituency of ignorance, people who have so much invested in coastal real estate that they do not want to hear of how vulnerable it is." Society pays dearly for developing beaches yet seems incapable of breaking the habit. The politics of beach building far outweigh policy based on science and common sense.

This compendium does not address the beachward migration directly. The Nature Conservancy, which funded the project, has as its mission the conservation of biodiversity through protection of habitat. It does not lobby, advocate, or bring lawsuits. In other words, the Nature Conservancy believes in a nonconfrontational, science-based, partnership approach.

The scientists involved in this project are therefore focused on research that allows us to understand the workings of the ecosystem better. Hurricanes are considered part of the natural ecosystem, and with rising sea levels and changing weather patterns, hurricanes can only be expected to have increasing impact. Scientists believe that the best way to protect the barrier islands of Texas and Mexico is to allow them to form and reform, to heal and stabilize through natural revegetation. Hurricane Bret's saltwater bath is creating a mosaic of new dune vegetation, and the sea water exchanges are beneficial for Laguna Madre. These are scientific conclusions, not political judgments.

For years I sailed the Laguna Madre of Texas from Port Isabel to Corpus Christi Bay, and as the wind-tidal flats, scruffy coyotes, and bird-encrusted islands slid slowly by, it was easy to imagine that the land was still as forgotten as when the Spanish explored and settled northeastern Mexico.

My evidence of this lies in a Dutch map I have, reliably dated to 1690 (200 years after Columbus), drawn by one Nicholas Visscher of Amsterdam. It depicts a Tamaulipas–South Texas coastline without barrier islands and an interior without anything much at all: *tierra incognita*. Dutch, English, French, and Spanish explorers and privateers could not sail close enough to shore to do anything but guess at what lay beyond the dunes.

Not much was recorded of the lagunas until 8 March 1687, when Enriquez Barroto and his sailing rowboats *(piraguas)* poked into Río de las Palmas (now Soto la Marina). On 11 March, Barroto rowed into what he called Laguna de Ysmuth, which he identified as a river running parallel to the coast. As he sailed up what we now call Padre Island National Seashore, he made numerous references to the "river that runs within."

In 1854 an entrepreneur named Richard King made one of his first major land purchases north of the Río Grande. He acquired 12,000 Padre Island acres and set up ranch headquarters at an old Spanish camp 26 miles from the south end of the island. (The island is named for Padre Balli, a Portuguese priest who had established ranching operations there exactly two centuries before.) King also acquired mainland acreage, at a creek called Santa Gertrudis, and these two purchases marked the beginning of the most significant contributions to the conservation of the Laguna Madre-those of the ranching families who owned land from Laguna Atascosa to Corpus Christi Bay. A hurricane in 1880 wiped out the Padre Island ranch, but by that time King, his partner Mifflin Kenedy, and their vaqueros had already coaxed the unforgiving mainland ranch into impressive levels of cattle production and created an American legend.

A handful of private landowners still stand guard on the mainland flank of the Laguna Madre: the King, Pinnell, Rockefeller, Armstrong, East, and Yturria families and the Kenedy Memorial Foundation and Kenedy Trust. Some of these holdings are best described by the old Spanish term *latifundios*, ranches of immense size. The largest Laguna segments are those of the King Ranch Laureles and Norias divisions and the Kenedy Ranch. Chapter 5 of this book is devoted to the area's ranching heritage and its ecological importance.

Cina Alexander Forgason, who cochaired the Conservation Committee of the Nature Conservancy of Texas for many years, tells the story of her mother, Helen Groves, collecting seashells along the sandy shore of the Norias Division in the years before midcentury and the Intracoastal Waterway. I was recently on that same shore, now mud. But behind the mud is native coastal prairie, an ecosystem very much intact, thanks to the King family and those of the other "Laguna ranchers." Intact prairie protects the Laguna in many ways.

Cina Alexander Forgason's grandfather was the legendary Bob Kleberg, who loved the wild Norias Division, and this rancher/conservationist family still spends much time at the Norias headquarters. Cina is eloquent about the role of her family and other ranchers in conserving the Wild Horse Desert, the mainland flank of the Laguna: "To many eyes, this land looks like desert, thorns, and brush, but to my grandfather and family it has been the land of milk and honey, sacred hunting grounds, a place to restore your soul."

The trick now is to conserve enough of this dynamic, wildly beautiful, one-of-a-kind ecosystem to ensure that a century hence, our progeny and all the living things of the "river that runs within" will find our hypersaline lagunas alive and well. We cannot ask that they remain unchanged, for that would be not only too much to ask but also ecologically impossible. However, we can continue to work toward the lasting health of this rare and resilient ecosystem. The health of the ecosystem is today challenged as it has not been since the Spanish *entrada*, mainly by the increased threat of major development on South Padre Island, increased agricultural runoff, manufacturing pollutants, and urban wastes piled onto the myriad existing environmental pressures detailed in this work.

During the last five years of the twentieth century, the Nature Conservancy's ecoregional planning process has revealed new conservation opportunities for the Laguna Madre of Texas and Tamaulipas. Scientists have begun to see ways to broaden the conservation agenda, to enhance the natural resource management of this area's rich biodiversity. More windows were opened when the Texas chapter, in 1995, became the first state chapter to fund and manage international conservation efforts jointly with northeastern Mexico. Perhaps the most important opportunity is in pioneering private land conservation in Mexico, which, like Texas, is predominantly privately owned. But the way the Nature Conservancy works is that we *do the science first*. One has to know how all the pieces fit.

That is what drove Chuck Cook and Jim Bergan of the Nature Conservancy, Wes Tunnell of the Center for Coastal Studies at Texas A&M University–Corpus Christi, Frank Judd of the University of Texas–Pan American, and their team of scientists, including Kim Withers, Elizabeth Smith, Nancy Hilbun, Amy Koltermann, Suzanne Dilworth, and Susan Childs. They labored under tight deadlines to research and write this Laguna Madre compendium. All of these talented experts, those they cite, and those who reviewed chapters have devoted significant time to researching the Laguna Madre.

Many of these contributors are concerned that science alone cannot conserve the Laguna, for it is far from forgotten—especially in Texas—by those who would build large-scale resorts on fragile barrier beaches; by those who would profit from land speculation; and by those who would launch amphibious landings across Padre Island and bomb Kenedy county. What seems to have been conveniently forgotten is the *human* havoc wrought by a storm surge.

The Laguna Madre de Tamaulipas has long since been discovered by commercial fishermen, whose thousands of V-shaped *charangas* (traps) dare fish or shrimp to negotiate any channel and whose 2,000-foot-long *chinchorras* net any that do. Flying over this madness plunges one's belief in developing a global conservation ethic to a despairing nadir. But then, just before reaching the Río Grande, one's north-skimming plane sails over the nearly pristine 30,000-acre Rancho Rincón de Anacahuitas of Jorge Martinez, and faith is restored. Rancho Rincón is by far the largest tract of intact native habitat remaining in the entire 130-mile length of the Laguna Madre de Tamaulipas.

Jorge Martinez restores faith in conservation in person, too, for he embodies the ecological wisdom of Leopold and Carson as well as that of his grandfather, Don Ezekiel Reyes, who realized in 1930 that the land along the Laguna Madre was much too fragile for the row-cropping practiced by his neighbors. He knew intensive agriculture would destroy his land, and he sought environmentally sound solutions to make a sustainable living from ranching. Third-generation owner Jorge inherited a conservation ethic that embraces all wild things, as the wealth of waterbirds on his freshwater ponds and the presence of jaguarundis in his rare native brush habitat confirm.

Jorge is but one of many active, involved partners in conserving the Laguna Madre of Texas and Tamaulipas. In Mexico, Ducks Unlimited of Mexico, A.C. (DUMAC), and Pronatura Noreste lead the way. Their work notwithstanding, we are sadly lacking in ecological data for Mexico's lagoon system and are actively seeking yet more partnerships, including with the Mexican academic community and government agencies.

In addition to the scores of current researchers and interested parties listed in appendix 1, other partners include the Robert J. and Helen C. Kleberg Foundation, the National Park Service, Texas Parks and Wildlife Department, University of Texas Marine Science Institute, Texas A&M University–Corpus Christi, the National Fish and Wildlife Foundation, Shell Oil Company, and the Orvis Company.

Has the Nature Conservancy bitten off more laguna than it can swallow? The answer would be yes, unless you factor in community-based conservation. It was a group of local citizens who pushed for establishing Padre Island as the nation's longest national seashore back in 1962. Without question the hard-working employees of U.S. Fish and Wildlife Service at Laguna Atascosa National Wildlife Refuge are members in good standing of the conservation community. They maintain a unique treasure of the national wildlife refuge system and protect its endangered occupants, from aplomado falcon to jaguarundi, species that occur almost nowhere else in the nation.

Communities are made up of concerned individual citizens who make the real difference, such as the late Ila Loetscher of South Padre Island. Ila, the famed "Turtle Lady," almost single-handedly created public awareness of the plight of sea turtles, especially the Kemp's ridley. Some estimates place the female nesting population of Kemp's ridleys at less than 2,000 worldwide. Community organizations are today supporting the creation of a new Kemp's Ridley Marine Reserve stretching 117 miles along the Padre Island coast and 17 miles out to sea.

For more than half the century past I have had an affinity for barrier islands and their lagoons. I grew up in the 1940s fishing, hunting, sailing, swimming with dolphin, turtle-watching, and otherwise absorbing nature's mysteries within the longest lagoon in the world. I would sail for miles on Florida's Indian River Lagoon, never seeing another human, and never dreaming that rockets the length of a football field would blast off from its shores less than 20 years later. Could this happen at Laguna Madre? My guess is that rockets could fly from a spaceport on or near the Kenedy Ranch by sometime early in the twenty-first century, and with the fireworks would come massive change. Forget despoblado. The Laguna and rockets can coexist, as has been learned at Cape Canaveral, but it will take some partnering among natural resource scientists and those involved in aerospace and especially with the communities that would support such a spaceport.

As this volume makes clear, the Nature Conservancy is committed to the immensely complex and financially daunting role of preserving the biodiversity of the Laguna Madre of Texas and Tamaulipas. We invite you to join with us in this, the most significant and challenging conservation effort of the new century in Texas.

RICHARD C. BARTLETT

Preface

As a young marine science student, I took one of my first field trips with Dr. Allan Chaney in the fall of 1965 to the shores of the Laguna Madre de Tamaulipas to collect brine shrimp eggs for our university aquaria at Texas A&I University (now Texas A&M University–Kingsville). Driving in his four-wheel-drive International Scout down the beach 177 km (110 mi) south of the pavement that ended at Playa Washington east of Matamoros, we collected seashells and other marine life, old drift bottles, and glass fishing floats. We "camped" in an old fishing cabin at Boca Jesús María and collected eight one-gallon jars of brine shrimp eggs from windrows on the eastern Laguna shoreline. The remoteness of the area, the unique geological features, and the biological resources were all intriguing to me. It was the sense of scientific adventure and discovery experienced on this trip that made me decide on field-oriented marine science as my career.

The hallmarks of the Laguna Madre (internationally famous as a hypersaline lagoon, with a huge overwintering redhead population, vast seagrass beds, and great fishing grounds) have continued to interest scientists, bird-watchers, fishermen, and nature lovers. Recently, however, concerns about increased population pressures, brown tide impacts, the effects of maintenance dredging on seagrass habitat, non-point source pollution (polluted runoff), and other issues in Texas have focused attention on the long-term health of the ecosystem. In Tamaulipas, environmental concern was recently raised over the possibility of dredging the Gulf Intracoastal Waterway through the Mexican Laguna Madre from Brownsville to Tampico. The international setting and uniqueness of Laguna Madre and concern for its future conservation and protection led the Nature Conservancy (the Conservancy) to name the entire system as one of its four major initiatives in North America in its new Coastal and Marine Program.

In March 1998, Chuck Cook, the Conservancy's director of Coastal and Marine Programs, and Jim Bergan, the Conservancy's South Texas program manager, visited several scientists and other interested parties in South Texas to determine the key issues of concern threatening the Laguna Madre. In April, it was determined that a compendium or synthesis of information was needed as a starting point for their Laguna Madre Initiative. The preferred alternative for the book was to have the experts write each chapter, but this avenue would have taken at least two and possibly three years, and a "faster" edition was desired. As a long-time admirer of the Conservancy and its conservation work, and having a fascination with the natural systems of Laguna Madre, Padre Island, and the great South Texas ranches, I decided to take the challenge. With the agreement of Frank Judd as my coeditor and of Liz Smith and Kim Withers, who made major contributions to the *Current Status and Historical Trends of Estuarine Living Resources within the Corpus Christi Bay National Estuary Program Study Area* report (Tunnell et al. 1996), I proposed that we could meet the Conservancy's nine-month timeline, starting in July 1998 and finishing in March 1999.

Thus almost 35 years after my first visit to the Mexican lagoon and the decision to embark on a career in marine science, I have the opportunity to join with colleagues and to synthesize what is currently known about this unique ecological system. I feel honored and humbled to participate in this work.

Numerous other colleagues reviewed each chapter of the initial draft in February 1999, and each is gratefully acknowledged. During the next year, following initial review, three outside reviewers and a faculty committee, all associated with Texas A&M University Press, then read the draft, and all recommended publication, with certain revisions. This process, although time-consuming, strengthened and tightened the manuscript. Chapters progress from a general overview of the Laguna Madre system and its surrounding lands to major natural resources of the system and the key conservation issues, information gaps, and conservation recommendations.

Since the Conservancy brings to its work in land acquisition and natural resource management an ecoregional planning perspective, and we scientists similarly prefer an ecosystem approach to studying and managing natural resources, we present material on the adjacent Gulf of Mexico, barrier islands, watersheds, and the Tamaulipan Biotic Province. Additionally, since much of the long-term protection of the Laguna Madre in Texas is due to good private-land stewardship by large South Texas ranches, a chapter on the ranching heritage details this unique aspect. Three chapters address three distinct Conservancy target groups of birds: redheads and other waterfowl, colonial waterbirds, and shorebirds and wading birds. A chapter on sea turtles is included at the Conservancy's request due to the conservation needs of this group of animals on the barrier islands and passes immediately east of Laguna Madre.

This compendium is intended as an overview of the Laguna Madre for an audience of both scientists and nonscientists. It is firmly based in science but also for use by others who want to learn about and take care of the Laguna Madre now and in the future. The Nature Conservancy wants the book as an information tool to spark interest and raise awareness for the long-term conservation of Laguna Madre natural resources. For agency personnel and students, this work gathers everything known about the Laguna Madre into one place, and it should be a resource information guide. For scientists, the thorough literature review and listing point out where the strengths and weaknesses are in our knowledge concerning the Laguna Madre. In a few areas, there is enough information to write a solid scientific review or book, for example on seagrass, colonial waterbirds, or fisheries. But in other areas there are great knowledge gaps and substantial research is still needed. As with any work of such size and scope, this one contains many unanswered questions and undoubtedly some errors. But if we can prompt or challenge students and scientists to answer some of these questions and to seek new knowledge, then we have achieved an important goal. In addition, if we have introduced new habitats, biota, or issues within the region that need attention to further the cause of protection and conservation, we have achieved another goal.

Included in the literature cited are more than 650 citations, which are also listed in the Comprehensive Bibliography developed as a companion project of the compendium. The compendium synthesizes over 70 years of literature on the Laguna Madre and surrounding environments. The journals, proceedings, and other titles within the literature cited are spelled out to make acquisition in either language easier. Due to its excessive length (over 1,250 citations), as well as the need to have it in a "searchable" format, the Comprehensive Bibliography is available separately in electronic format from the Center for Coastal Studies at Texas A&M University–Corpus Christi or the Nature Conservancy in San Antonio.

Appendix 1 gives contact information for current researchers and other persons interested in Laguna Madre. All those cited in the text for personal communications or personal observations can be found in appendix 1, with full contact detail. A list of acronyms used in the text is provided in appendix 2.

JOHN W. (WES) TUNNELL, JR.

Acknowledgments

The Laguna Madre of Texas and Tamaulipas compendium was funded by the Nature Conservancy of Texas with grants from the Robert J. and Helen C. Kleberg Foundation and the National Fish and Wildlife Foundation. These organizations are gratefully acknowledged for providing the support necessary to carry out this project. Foremost, we thank Liz Smith and Kim Withers, research scientists at the Center for Coastal Studies at Texas A&M University–Corpus Christi, who led the effort in chapter contributions. They are gifted at sifting through vast amounts of literature and identifying the key elements. Completion of the work in a timely fashion is largely due to their dedicated and untiring efforts. Nancy Hilbun compiled the Comprehensive Bibliography in Reference Manager software and wrote the ranching heritage chapter with Amy Koltermann. Gloria Krause and Linda Simmons assisted with technical aspects of initial manuscript preparation, and Suzanne Dilworth and Susan Childs joined the team to help with the fish/fisheries and sea turtle chapters, respectively. Suzanne Dilworth also ably took charge of the logistics, graphics, and design of the first draft. All of these efforts are sincerely appreciated.

The first draft of the compendium was reviewed during February 1999 by 35 experts, all of whom are gratefully acknowledged (their affiliations are given in appendix 1):

Chapter 1. Introduction: Russ Miget, Warren Pulich
Chapter 2. Geography, Climate, and Hydrography: Bill Longley, Junji Matsumoto, Jim Norwine, Gary Powell, Ruben Solis, Richard Watson
Chapter 3. Origin, Development, and Geology: Jennifer Prouty, Richard Watson
Chapter 4. Tamaulipan Biotic Province: Tim Fulbright, Bob Lonard
Chapter 5. Ranching Heritage: Bruce Cheeseman, Keith Gutherie, Tom Kreneck, Jerry Thompson
Chapter 6. The Environment: Russ Miget, Warren Pulich
Chapter 7. Seagrass Meadows: Mike Beck, Chris Onuf, Warren Pulich, Pete Sheridan, Jim Tolan
Chapter 8. Open Bay: Ed Buskey, Tracy Villareal
Chapter 9. Wind-Tidal Flats: Hudson DeYoe, Chris Onuf
Chapter 10. Barrier Islands: Lynn Drawe, Bob Lonard
Chapter 11. Redheads and Other Wintering Waterfowl: Mark Woodin
Chapter 12. Colonial Waterbirds and Rookery Islands: Allan Chaney
Chapter 13. Shorebirds and Wading Birds: Tim Brush, Allan Chaney, Mike Farmer, Curt Zonick
Chapter 14. Sea Turtles: Donna Shaver, Maurice Renaud
Chapter 15. Fish and Invertebrate Fisheries Organisms: Bob Edwards, Larry McEachron, Kyle Spiller, Randy Blankenship
Chapter 16. Red and Brown Tides: Ed Buskey, Hudson DeYoe, Tracy Villareal

Sandra Alvarado and Gabriela De la Fuente De León reviewed most of the entire compendium. We are thankful for their effort. Chris Onuf was particularly helpful in providing seagrass data, maps, and information about the Texas lagoon. Richard Watson provided two flights over the Texas Laguna Madre to take photographs. Tim Brush, Lee Elliott, and Paul Montagna offered technical information, and Kathryn Harvey and Jace Tunnell redrew a number of figures. In Mexico, Felipe San Martín offered logistical support in Ciudad Victoria, and Ing. Marco Antonio Chapa Martínez, Lic. Gustavo Barroso Hernández, Lic. Mónica Castillo Sagastegul, and Ing. Nora E. Macías Pérez at INEGI-Victoria were very helpful with Tamaulipas data and maps. In Monterrey, assistance was provided by Dr. Ernesto C. Enkerlin Hoeflich, Dr. Diego Fabian Lozano Garcia, Ing. Jorge Brenner Guillermo, and Ing. Julie Noriega Rivera. Especially helpful with data and literature were Biol. Eduardo Carrera González and Ing. Gabriela De la Fuente De León. Dr. Salvador Contreras Balderas assisted with fish literature and provided a draft of the most recent publication on the Laguna Madre in Tamaulipas (Leija-Tristan et al., in press). Three anonymous reviewers for Texas A&M University Press, as well as its Faculty Review Committee, reviewed the entire manuscript. The time, effort, and suggestions offered by all of these persons are gratefully acknowledged. Their assistance and constructive criticisms certainly made the work more accurate and a better product.

Jim Bergan of the Nature Conservancy of Texas was our contact at his organization. He was both supportive and encouraging throughout the preparation of the book and is sincerely thanked. Dick Bartlett of the Nature Conservancy Board of Directors and author of the foreword was also highly supportive of the project and is gratefully acknowledged.

The satellite image on the cover is courtesy of Ducks Unlimited of Mexico, A.C., of Monterrey, Mexico, and Earth Satellite Corporation of Rockville, Maryland.

Finally, we recognize and commend the untiring efforts and long-term dedication of Henry H. Hildebrand to the study of the Laguna Madre ecosystem, particularly in Tamaulipas. His early studies there, starting in 1951, form the basis of our scientific knowledge of that lagoon today. His many trips to the Tamaulipas system, usually self-financed, are testimony to his being a naturalist dedicated to a unique North American natural resource. Because of his efforts and contributions, we dedicate this compendium to Dr. Henry H. Hildebrand.

JOHN W. (WES) TUNNELL, JR.
FRANK W. JUDD

Part I **Overview**

Introduction

JOHN W. TUNNELL, JR.

The rich natural resources of the Laguna Madre of Texas and Tamaulipas are widely known. Competition for these resources, or varied uses of these highly productive and unique ecosystems, has recently generated a greater need for resource management and conservation. Consequently, there are a number of compelling reasons to compile all known information:

1. Although considerable scientific literature is available, it has never been synthesized and compiled into a single source for ready access and use.
2. Because the two lagoons are politically separated in two different countries, the literature is in two languages.
3. Because the two systems are similar, studies completed in one may be applicable to the other.
4. Information gaps need to be identified.
5. Conservation and management issues need to be identified and recommendations presented.

Because effective management must be based on knowledge provided by sound science, the purposes of this compendium are to provide a literature synthesis of major natural resource and conservation issues facing the Laguna Madre of Texas and Tamaulipas and a comprehensive bibliography to stimulate further investigation.

Some historical concepts about the Laguna Madre of Texas have proven false yet continue to persist. For instance, popular lore accounts for the infilling of the Laguna Madre of Texas in the Land-Cut region by "a tropical storm and a tidal wave in 1836 which swept over Padre Island carrying much of the island into the Laguna" (Burr 1945a). This story was related by Captain Mifflin Kenedy, who heard it from a Mexican general. Marine scientists studying the Laguna Madre changed the story somewhat in time but perpetuated the concept by noting that the Laguna Madre was effectively divided in two by the hurricane of 1919 (Gunter 1945a; Hedgpeth 1947). However, more recent research revealed that this land-bridge area was filled by a much slower, long-term process (Miller 1975; Morton and Garner 1993).

Another hotly debated topic is the John F. Kennedy Causeway (Padre Island Causeway until 1968), an earthen or land-fill causeway extending from Corpus Christi to Padre Island, and its impact on water circulation and the "health" of the upper Laguna Madre. Even before its construction in 1950, marine scientists argued that it would likely do great harm or cause death of the entire ecosystem. In regard to the proposed causeway, Gunter (1946) stated that "this proposal is quite likely to turn the Laguna into lifeless brine to the lasting injury of the people of the State." Hedgpeth (1947) makes a similar statement, going on to say that "the whole trouble with the Laguna Madre is that it is dying." Fifty years later, arguments still abound on the effects of the causeway on the overall ecosystem, yet the Laguna continues to be one of the most productive embayments on the Texas coast.

Although the two Laguna Madre systems are separated by the Río Grande Delta, interesting similarities exist between them:

1. Hypersaline conditions (40 to 80 ppt; more in past).
2. Semiarid climate.
3. Shallow, elongate coastal lagoons.
4. Highly productive fisheries (cyclical highs and lows in past).
5. Extensive wind-tidal flats.
6. Clay dunes and/or lomas along mainland shores and in the Río Grande Delta area.
7. Limited freshwater inflow.
8. Divided into upper and lower sections by sand flats.
9. Single embayment within each (Baffin Bay in Texas, Laguna el Catán in Tamaulipas).
10. Predominantly remote, publicly inaccessible shorelines.
11. Extensive overwintering populations of redheads and other waterfowl.
12. Essential habitat for many colonial waterbirds and shorebirds, including protected species, such as piping plover, snowy plover, and reddish egret.

Historical studies on the Laguna Madre of Texas have focused on unique physical features (wind-tidal flats, tidal flat geochemistry, clay dunes, hypersalinity) or biological resources (blue-green or cyanobacteria algal mats, aquatic birds, fisheries productivity, seagrass ecology). In recent times, attention has turned to anthropogenic impacts and concerns, such as dredging of the U.S. Gulf Intracoastal Waterway (GIWW), dredge material disposal, water circulation, causeway elevation, agricultural and other non-point source runoff, boat propeller scarring in seagrass beds, seismic exploration impacts, and vehicular impacts on tidal flats. Natural perturbations such as fish kills from hypersalinity and severe cold spells are well documented, and recently the brown tide algal bloom has received much attention.

The Laguna Madre de Tamaulipas has received much less attention in the past, with early studies focusing on fisheries, hydrography, sediments, and micromolluscs. More recently, with thoughts of extending the GIWW from Texas southward to Tampico (and perhaps beyond), via the coastal lagoons, greater focus has been given to the natural resources and environmental condition of the region. Most recently, a proposal by Ducks Unlimited of Mexico, A.C. (DUMAC), has been submitted to the federal government of Mexico to establish the entire Laguna Madre de Tamaulipas as a protected area (Carrera and De la Fuente 1996). The Laguna Madre de Tamaulipas and several adjacent smaller coastal lagoons are ranked first out of 28 key wetland areas in Mexico that harbor 84% of the wintering waterfowl in the country (DUMAC 1990).

Among all the studies completed on both lagoonal systems, hypersalinity is a common theme. From the earliest writings of Burr (1930, 1945a, 1945b, 1947, 1950) to those of Gunter (1945a, 1945b), Hedgpeth (1947, 1967), Hildebrand (1958, 1969, 1980), Simmons (1957), Breuer (1962), and most recently Quammen and Onuf (1993) and Onuf (1996a), the continuing scientific interest has been hypersalinity or changes related to salinity. Generally, one associates high salinity with low numbers of species and low productivity (Copeland and Jones 1965; Copeland 1967). Yet uniquely, and seemingly in contrast to this idea, many of the studies on the Laguna Madre emphasize the high productivity of seagrasses, fisheries, or waterfowl. This enigma of high productivity in a hypersaline environment appears to be governed in part by water circulation: navigation channels in Texas and hurricane-opened barrier island passes in Tamaulipas. Before the GIWW was dredged, fisheries productivity was high in the Texas Laguna Madre (20% of bay surface in Texas but over 50% of catch; Hedgpeth 1947). However, when salinity reached levels up to two or three times that of oceanic salinity, or when summer or winter temperatures became extreme, there was no escape, and massive fish kills occurred. Today, the GIWW and Mansfield Pass bisecting Padre Island allow for improved circulation and moderated salinities, so that extremes have been eliminated or reduced (Quammen and Onuf 1993). Changes in hypersalinity and productivity have been affected by changes in water circulation. The high productivity also seems to be linked to the extensive seagrass meadows. This seagrass-based ecosystem provides much in the way of food, shelter, and nutrients for the semi-enclosed system; unlike a normal or positive estuary, dependent on freshwater inflow, salt marshes, and phytoplankton for nutrient input, the Laguna Madre appears to recycle its own.

In Mexico, on the other hand, Hildebrand (1980) demonstrated that "boom and bust" fishery cycles were linked to wet hurricanes driving the Laguna Madre de Tamaulipas system. Between hurricanes, passes connecting the Gulf of Mexico with the Laguna closed, and with little or no freshwater inflow, the Laguna became increasingly saline. Several highly productive years were followed by almost no fisheries production in a briny Laguna Madre. The next hurricane would open the Gulf passes, bring much needed rain and flushing of the system, and subsequently stimulate another cycle of high fishery productivity. Hildebrand (pers. comm.) believes that hurricane rainfall floodwaters and El Niño wet cycles, coupled with long-term drought cycles, are more important regulators of change than is channelized circulation in either system. He emphasizes, however, that water storage structures, such as Falcon Lake, now greatly restrict freshwater inflow into either system.

Accessibility and remoteness have played major roles in the study and protection of these two lagoons. Although both systems are somewhat remote, close proximity and accessibility to marine biologists from the Texas Game, Fish, and Oyster Commission (now Texas Parks and Wildlife Department, TPWD) Marine Laboratory in Rockport and marine scientists from the University of Texas Marine Science Institute in Port Aransas aided early studies in the 1940s and 1950s in the upper Laguna Madre. A small field station on lower Laguna Madre aided TPWD work there in early years. In the 1970s, a small Coastal Studies Laboratory on South Padre Island associated with Pan American University (now the University of Texas–Pan American, in Edinburg) increased studies in the lower Laguna. Creation of the Center for Coastal Studies and Conrad Blucher Institute for Surveying and Science at Texas A&M University–Corpus Christi in the 1980s led to increased access and research in the upper Laguna.

In Mexico, accessibility continues to make research difficult. The earliest studies in the Laguna Madre de Tamaulipas necessitated multiday field trips from the University of Texas Marine Science Institute (Hildebrand 1958; Copeland and Jones 1965; Copeland 1967) and the University of Corpus Christi (Hildebrand 1969) or longer expeditions from the Universidad Nacional Autónoma de México in Mexico City (García-Cubas 1968; Yañez and Schlaepfer 1968). Most recently, in the absence of a laboratory facility, marine scientists and biologists continue to make expeditions to the Laguna from Universidad Autónoma de Tamaulipas in Ciudad Victoria and Universidad Autónoma de Nuevo León, Instituto Tecnológico y de Estudios Superiores de Monterrey, Pronatura Noreste, and Ducks Unlimited of Mexico, all in Monterrey. These institutions are at varying distances but many hours' drive from the Laguna Madre de Tamaulipas, and when scientists arrive at the Laguna, accommodations are distant and few.

Remoteness of both Laguna Madre ecosystems has surely limited their scientific study. But this same remoteness has contributed to the protection and conservation of some species and habitats. In Texas, large private ranches along the mainland and two federally protected areas, Padre Island National Seashore and Laguna Atascosa National Wildlife Refuge, limit access and development. In Mexico, large private ranches and the lack of paved roads limit access and settlement along the shores of the Laguna.

The points introduced in this chapter are developed more fully in the pages to follow. Approximately 85% of the literature compiled for this compendium concerns the Texas Laguna Madre and its surrounding area. Of over 1,250 citations compiled for the comprehensive bibliography, approximately 350 are specifically on the two Laguna Madre systems. Unfortunately, much of the most recent and comprehensive information on the Laguna Madre de Tamaulipas, which was generated in regard to the potential GIWW, is owned by the federal government in Mexico and is unavailable, except by permission. The separate comprehensive bibliography, prepared in Reference Manager software (searchable by author, subject, or word), is available from the Nature Conservancy or the Center for Coastal Studies at Texas A&M University–Corpus Christi and will lead interested persons to further information about these two distinctive and dynamic ecosystems.

2 *Geography, Climate, and Hydrography*

JOHN W. TUNNELL, JR.

The Laguna Madre is a bar-built coastal lagoon bordered by barrier islands and peninsulas to the east and by the mainland to the west. Geomorphically, the Laguna Madre is divided into two separate lagunas by the Río Grande Delta: the Laguna Madre of Texas, U.S.A., to the north, and the Laguna Madre de Tamaulipas, Mexico, to the south (fig. 2.1). These two coastal ecosystems form one of only five hypersaline ecosystems in the world (Javor 1989). The other four are (1) the Putrid Sea, or the Sivash, adjacent to the Sea of Azov on the Crimean Peninsula, Ukraine; (2) Laguna Ojo de Liebre, on the Pacific coast of Baja California, Mexico; (3) Spencer Gulf, south Australia; and (4) Shark Bay, western Australia.

Geography

The Laguna Madre of Texas is the largest of seven estuarine systems along the Texas coast (Diener 1975), and the Laguna Madre de Tamaulipas is one of only three coastal lagoons in the State of Tamaulipas and the second largest of all coastal lagoons in Mexico. Together, the Laguna Madre of Texas and Laguna Madre de Tamaulipas form the largest hypersaline system in the world.

Extending along 445 km (277 mi) of coastline, Laguna Madre reaches from Corpus Christi Bay in the north (27° 40.5′ N) to Río Soto la Marina on the south (23° 47′ N). Both the Texas and Tamaulipas lagunas are approximately 185 km (115 mi) each in length, but vary in width, averaging 7 km (4.3 mi) and 12 km (7.5 mi), respectively (table 2.1). The lagunas are separated by 75 km (47 mi) of Río Grande Delta—12 km (7.5 mi) in Texas and 63 km (39 mi) in Tamaulipas—which bulges the Texas-Tamaulipan shoreline over 35 km (28 mi) eastward into the Gulf of Mexico.

Physiographically each laguna is further divided into subunits. In Texas, the upper Laguna Madre (fig. 2.2) is separated from the lower Laguna Madre (fig. 2.3) by a land-bridge extending from Padre Island to the mainland and variously known as the Salt Flats, Saltillo Flats, Kenedy Flats, Laguna Madre Flats, or most commonly as the Land-Cut (fig. 2.2). The latter name was derived when the Gulf Intracoastal Waterway (GIWW) was cut across the extensive tidal flats of the land-bridge in the late 1940s. The upper and lower lagoons in Texas are fairly similar in size, 76 km (47 mi) long by 6 km (3.7 mi) average width and 91 km (57 mi) long by 8 km (5 mi) average width, respectively. In Tamaulipas, however, a shorter, wider northern basin (fig. 2.4) is divided from a longer, narrower southern basin (fig. 2.5) by the Río San Fernando (Río Conchos on some maps) Delta, sometimes referred to as El Carrizal, a barren mudflat (Hildebrand 1969). The northern Laguna in Tamaulipas is approximately 58 km (36 mi) long and averages 20 km (12 mi) in width, and the southern Laguna is about 127 km (79 mi) long and averages only 6 km (3.7 mi) in width (table 2.1). Caution is advised when calculating lengths, widths, and average dimensions of both Laguna Madre systems due to extensive wind-tidal flats and shallows. Normal tides and calm winds leave hundreds of square kilometers of tidal flats exposed, but

Fig. 2.1. Laguna Madre of Texas and Tamaulipas

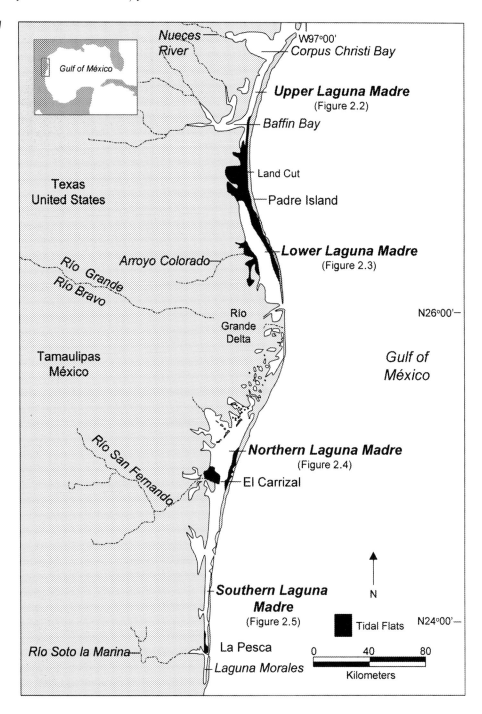

days of strong winds can push water for many kilometers across these flats, inundating vast areas. Elevated tides associated with tropical storm systems also inundate these normally emergent tidal flats.

The lagoon systems in Texas and Tamaulipas are quite similar. Both are very shallow, averaging about 1 meter (3.3 ft) deep, but surface area in Texas is somewhat smaller (table 2.1). Some data in table 2.1 conflict because they were not all obtained using the same method; however, similarities between the two systems are evident. Diener's (1975) work in Texas is the most detailed and frequently cited, but it is reported as Mean Low Water (MLW) and Mean High Water (MHW) and seems quite conservative when compared to data from the Texas Water Development Board

Table 2.1. Physiographic data for the Laguna Madre of Texas and Tamaulipas. See footnotes for data sources.

	Length[a] km (mi)	WIDTH KM (mi)			Depth[b] m (ft)	SURFACE AREA KM² (mi²)		
		Max.	Min.	Ave.		MLW[b]	MSL	MHW[b]
Texas								
Upper Laguna Madre	76 (47)	7 (4.3)	3 (1.9)	6 (3.7)	0.8 (2.6)	191 (74)		277 (107)
Baffin Bay	23 (14)	7 (4.3)	3 (1.9)	5 (3.1)	2.3 (7.5)	219 (85)		247 (95)
Land-Cut	18 (11)	18 (11)	16 (10)	17.5 (11)	+0.6[c] (2.0)			
Lower Laguna Madre	91 (57)	12 (7.5)	6[d] (3.7) 11[e] (7)	8[d] (5) 14[e] (9)	1.4 (4.6)	727 (281)		1,364 (527)
Total Texas Laguna Madre	185 (115)	12 (7.5)	3 (1.9)	7 (4.3)	1.2 (3.9)	1,140 (440) 1,137[f] (439)	1,658[f] (640)	1,888 (729) 2,292[f] (885) 2,142[g] (827)
Tamaulipas								
Northern Laguna Madre	58 (36)	30 (19)	10 (6)	20 (12)	0.7[h] (2.3)		1,100[i] (425)	
Southern Laguna Madre	127 (79)	12 (7.5)	1 (0.6)	6 (3.7)	1.1[j] (3.6)		900[i] (347)	
Total Tamaulipas Laguna Madre	185 (115)	30 (19)	1 (0.6)	12 (7.5)	1 (3.3)		2,000[i] (772) 2,152[h] (831) 2,028[k] (738)	2,728[k] (1,053)

Note: Multiple data are shown in some categories, since there is no consensus on surface area; furthermore, size calculation techniques are uncertain or unknown, so these data, except for DUMAC (1998, from database, Monterrey, N.L.), should be used with caution. MLW = Mean Low Water, MSL = Mean Sea Level, MHW = Mean High Water.

[a] Map calculations (approximate)
[b] Depths and surface area at MLW and MHW from Diener 1975, unless otherwise indicated.
[c] Fisk 1959.
[d] Width across water.
[e] Water width plus wind-tidal flats.
[f] G. Powell, pers. comm.; note that MWH Texas total of 2,292 km² represents "gross surface area" for estimating the input of direct precipitation on the Laguna and includes habitats not normally submerged.
[g] NOAA 1994; MHW Texas total of 2,142 km² represents "total estuary surface area" (= land and water combined?).
[h] Leija-Tristan et al., in press.
[i] Yañez and Schlaepfer 1968.
[j] Jorge Brenner, pers. comm.
[k] DUMAC 1998, from database, Monterrey, Nuevo León.

(TDWR 1983) reported as Mean Sea Level (MSL). Recent remote sensing compilations from satellite data are perhaps the most accurate for Mexico (DUMAC 1996, from database, Monterrey, N.L.).

Islands Natural islands are more common in Laguna Madre de Tamaulipas than in Texas. Over 100 islands are found in the northern portion (plate 3), and slightly fewer than 100 are located in the southern part. Many of the islands, especially in the north, are erosional Río Grande Delta remnants with steep sides and are the sites of small fishing villages (e.g., Isla las Flores, Isla del Vaquero). Others are low sedimentary shoals and spits, especially behind the barrier islands and in the narrow southern Laguna (e.g., Isla la Vaca, Isla la Pita). In Texas, only Crane Island, Pita Island, and

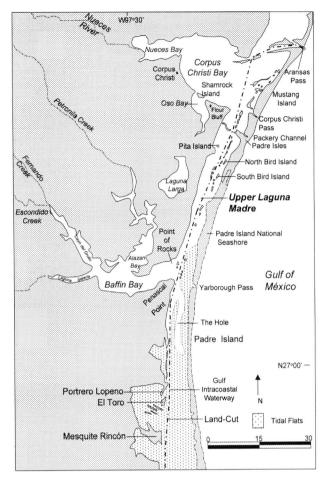

Fig. 2.2. *Upper Laguna Madre of Texas*

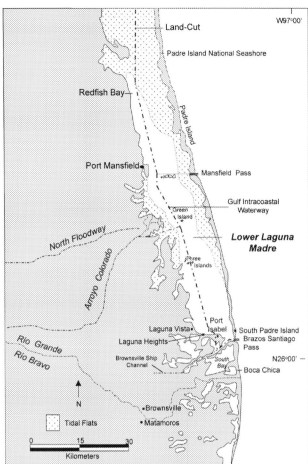

Fig. 2.3 *Lower Laguna Madre of Texas*

North and South Bird islands (plate 4) exist as natural islands in the upper Laguna, and Green Island and Three Islands are found in the lower Laguna. Many other "islands," such as Mullet Island, Hawk Island, and Yucca Island, are located along the mainland shore in the Lower laguna and on the inland side of Padre Island (Deer Island and Los Bancos de en Medio), and others can be found in and just north of the Land-Cut such as Trés Marías, El Toro and Potrero Lopeno (plate 5). These so-called islands are unique in that they are not surrounded by water but by wind-tidal flats except during high wind-tides or storm tides. Locally, these tidal flat islands are referred to as *lomas* (meaning "hill," for those that are round to irregular) or *potreros* ("pasture," for those elongate and parallel to mainland shore). All offer distinctive, is-landlike habitats to their flora and fauna.

Although natural islands are few in the Laguna Madre of Texas, dredge material islands are widespread and abundant along the GIWW (plate 6) and associated oil and gas field channels (plate 7). Many of these islands become vegetated and stabilize over time; some are used as rookery islands for colonial nesting waterbirds, or for oil and gas activities, and small fishing cabins are built on others. In open, more exposed waters, the islands tend to erode faster. Maintenance dredging of the GIWW by the U.S. Army Corps of Engineers requires periodic placement of new materials on old or new sites. Locating new sites for placement has become increasingly difficult because of occupation or use of dredge material islands by humans and birds and the negative impact on aquatic resources caused by open-water placement.

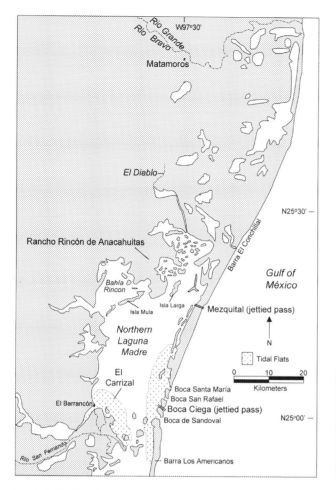

Fig. 2.4. Northern Laguna Madre de Tamaulipas

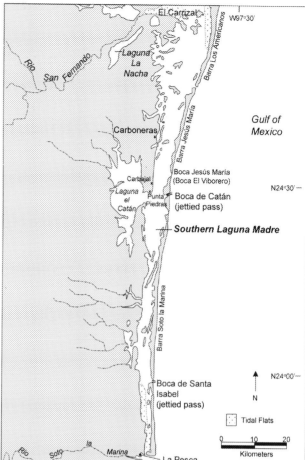

Fig. 2.5. Southern Laguna Madre de Tamaulipas

Counties, Population Centers   Political subdivisions of the Laguna Madre and adjacent lands include five counties in Texas—from north to south, Nueces, Kleberg, Kenedy, Willacy, and Cameron; and three in Tamaulipas—Matamoros, San Fernando, and Soto la Marina. Population centers exist at Corpus Christi in the northernmost upper Laguna Madre; Port Mansfield along the south-central western shore in lower Laguna Madre; and Laguna Vista, Laguna Heights, Port Isabel, and South Padre Island on the southernmost lower Laguna Madre (table 2.2). Only Padre Isles (a subdivision of Corpus Christi; plate 8) and South Padre Island (plate 9) are communities located on the barrier island of Padre Island. Due to the large landholdings of two federally protected areas, Padre Island National Seashore and Laguna Atascosa National Wildlife Refuge, and several large privately owned ranches—King Ranch, Kenedy Ranch, Yturria Ranch, and others—no other communities exist along the shores of the Texas Laguna Madre.

In Tamaulipas, where the Laguna Madre is remote and isolated, there are no large cities located on its shores but only small fishing villages (table 2.3). The city of Matamoros is the nearest large metropolitan area, and it is located over 40 km (25 mi) to the north of the northernmost point of the lagoon. El Mesquital and Higuerillas are the only villages located on the outer coast, and they are situated on the northwestern bank of Mezquital Pass. On the mainland shoreline, east of the town of San Fernando, Carboneras is the largest town on the Laguna and has one of only two good paved roads reaching the Laguna's western shore. The other road, recently

Table 2.2. *Population (1990 census) of counties, cities, and towns along the shores of Laguna Madre of Texas*

County (North to South) City/Town	Total County Population	City/Town Population
Nueces County	302,479	
Corpus Christi		266,958
Kleberg County	31,173	
No towns		
Kenedy County	409	
No towns		
Willacy County	18,775	
Port Mansfield		731
Cameron County	284,392	
Laguna Vista		1,335
Laguna Heights		1,844
Port Isabel		4,801
South Padre Island		1,962
Total	637,228	277,631

Source: From Ramos 1995.

completed, extends through Vergeles to El Barrancón. At its southernmost extent, the fishing and hunting village of La Pesca is located just west of the Laguna on the bank of Río Soto la Marina. Numerous small fishing villages exist on the islands and shores of the Laguna Madre de Tamaulipas.

Population levels around the Laguna Madre are greater in Texas than in Tamaulipas, with 637,228 people in five counties and 444,096 in three counties, respectively (tables 2.2 and 2.3). In cities, towns, and villages immediately adjacent to the Laguna, Texas has 277,631 people compared to 9,738 in Tamaulipas.

Barrier Islands, Peninsulas, and Passes (Tidal Inlets) Barrier islands and peninsulas protect the shallow, calm Laguna Madre from the higher-energy Gulf of Mexico. In Texas, Padre Island extends the entire length of the Laguna Madre, interrupted only by Mansfield Pass, a man-made inlet into lower Laguna Madre (fig. 2.3, plate 10). The northern half of Padre Island is slightly higher in elevation, as well as more vegetated, thus providing more lagoonal protection from storms with fewer washover passes. Brazos Santiago Pass, the entrance to the Brownsville Ship Channel, forms the southern coterminus of the lower Laguna Madre and Padre Island. Brazos Island (now a peninsula, since the small natural pass of Boca Chica closed in 1945) protects South Bay, which was the southernmost part of the lower Laguna Madre before it was cut off by the Brownsville Ship Channel in 1938 (Breuer 1962).

In Tamaulipas, the northernmost Laguna Madre is protected by a barrier peninsula, Barra El Conchillal (fig. 2.4). To the south of this moderately wide peninsula, averaging 2 km (1.2 mi), lie three narrow elongate barrier islands—Barra Los Americanos, Barra Jesús María, and Barra Soto la Marina—500 m (1,640 ft) or less in width. Eight (Hildebrand 1980) to 13 (Leija-Tristan et al., in press) or more inter-

Table 2.3. Population (1990 census) of counties, towns, and villages along the shores of Laguna Madre de Tamaulipas

County Town/Village	Total County Population	City/Town Population
Matamoros County	363,236	
La Bartolina		393
El Huizachal		170
El Tecolote		107
La Amistad		15
San Pedro		8
Las Yesquitas		40
Cinco de Mayo		257
El Caracol		40
Las Flores		17
La Capilla		223
Higuerillas		706
Mezquital		192
San Fernando County	56,650	
Gral. Francisco J. Mujica		466
La Media Luna		220
El Mezquite		49
El Barrancón del Tío Blas		611
Loma del Agua		14
El Carrizal		54
San Isidro Sur		15
Los Ebanos		23
El Arpa		22
Carboneras		2,010
Punta de Alambre		593
Los Legales		16
Carbajal		617
Lavaderos		174
La Florida		149
Soto La Marina County	24,210	
San José de los Leónes		22
Enramadas		339
El Carrizo		227
Las Guayabas		106
Las Flores		11
Benito Juárez		178
La Pesca		1,377
Total	444,096	9,738

Source: DUMAC 1993.

mittent passes (bocas) have been recorded or observed between the Laguna Madre de Tamaulipas and the Gulf of Mexico. These ephemeral passes have been discussed at length by Hildebrand (1958, 1969, 1980, pers. comm.) and are considered a key element governing physical hydrography and hence productivity of the Laguna. Boom (open passes) and bust (closed passes) cycles of fishery productivity have been linked to tropical storms and attendant, or subsequent, heavy precipitation and freshwater inflow into the system. To level out these boom and bust cycles, to stop drying up of the Laguna, and to allow navigation into and out of it, the Mexican government during the 1970s and early 1980s dredged four passes and jettied them: El Mezquital (plate 11), Boca Ciega, Boca de Catán (plate 12) and Boca de Santa Isabel. El Mezquital is located on the Barra El Conchillal Peninsula and is the only pass that can be reached by car. Boca Ciega Pass is located at the southern end of the peninsula in an area of four historical, ephemeral passes: (north to south) Boca Santa María, Boca San Rafael, Boca Ciega, and Boca Sandoval. Southward, the barrier islands of Barra Los Americanos and Barra Jesús María extend to Boca de Catán opposite Laguna el Catán (Bahía Algodones on some maps). The barrier island of Barra Soto la Marina then extends southward to the Río Soto la Marina, and is cut through by Boca de Santa Isabel about 23 km (75 mi) south of Boca de Catán.

Major Lagoon Habitats and Features   Submergent seagrass meadows and emergent wind-tidal flats make up the most extensive habitat types of both lagunas. The two habitats are covered separately within this volume (chapters 7 and 9). Wind-tidal flats are most common on the Padre Island side of Laguna Madre, especially south of the Land-Cut, in the Land-Cut, and along the lower Laguna Madre mainland shore in Texas (plate 13). In Tamaulipas, the broadest flats are located behind the barrier islands in the Boca Ciega Pass area, the El Carrizal or Río San Fernando Delta, and the lowermost southern Laguna Madre near La Pesca. Seagrass beds dominate the shallows of both systems.

Mainland shorelines of both lagunas are typically of low relief, consisting of broad tidal flats or narrow beaches with vegetated berms, but erosional scarps up to 2 m (6.6 ft) above MSL are found in some areas of the northernmost Laguna Madre de Tamaulipas. Two other distinctive shoreline features include clay dunes and beach rock (coquina). Clay dunes are unique geologic features that were first identified and described in South Texas along the lower Laguna Madre mainland shores (Coffey 1909; Price and Kornicker 1961). Beach rock exists along a small segment of both the Texas (Prouty 1996) and Tamaulipan shoreline (Yañez and Schlaepfer 1968). See chapter 3 for details on both of these subjects.

Drainage into Lagoons   Drainage from inland basins into Laguna Madre is minimal. No rivers flow into Laguna Madre in Texas. Within the upper Laguna Madre several ephemeral creeks—San Fernando, Santa Gertrudis, Los Olmos, and others—flow into Baffin Bay only when it rains. In the lower Laguna, Arroyo Colorado, a northern distributary channel of the Río Grande Delta system and a dredge-maintained channel, and the North Floodway (fig. 2.3) drain much of the Río Grande Valley agricultural lands. Although the Río Grande at one time flowed into South Bay, it no longer directly influences any of the Laguna during normal flows but drains directly into the Gulf of Mexico.

In Tamaulipas, besides numerous dry creeks and arroyos, which flow only with substantial rains, the sources of fresh water to the Laguna are the Río San Fernando and drainage from lands irrigated from the Río Grande in the extreme north. Flow from the Río San Fernando has decreased in recent years, as the waters have been diverted for irrigation, and the sediment load has increased due to extensive clearing of lands for agriculture (Yañez and Schlaepfer 1968; Hildebrand 1980; Saunders and Saunders 1981). Most recently, the Río San Fernando has been diverted away from Laguna Madre into Laguna La Nacha (Brenner 1997; DUMAC 1993), then on to the Laguna Madre via a canal. Additionally, in the north, a new channel has been dug to the lagoon to drain irrigation and storm waters from the Río Grande Delta (H. Hildebrand, pers. comm.).

Upland Ecosystems and Features   Landward of Laguna Madre, terrestrial ecosystems are part of the Pleistocene coastal plain, including the Gulf Prairies and Marshes and Río Grande Plains in Texas (Gould 1975) and the Northeast Coastal Plain Province in Tamaulipas (Rzedowski 1978). The Tamaulipan Biotic Province encompasses both lagoon systems (Dice 1943; Blair 1950; see chapter 4, this volume). The topography is gently sloping to rolling. Agriculture is the main land use to the immediate west of the Laguna Madre in both countries, with cattle ranching dominating in most areas. On the Río Grande Plain, however, cultivated lands dominate on both sides of the border. In low areas along the coast, sacahuiste flats of gulf cordgrass *(Spartina spartinae)* are common. Just landward of these flats, the mesquite-grassland association is most common, except where the oak savanna dominates the Coastal Sand Plain in Kenedy County just south of Baffin Bay (Fulbright et al. 1990).

The Río Grande Delta region between the two lagoonal systems forms a complex system of coastal plain uplands and wetlands, lomas, clay dunes, old Río Grande (Río Bravo) distributary channels, oxbow lakes (resacas), playa lakes, wind-tidal flats, and small lagoons. Because of its diverse vegetative communities and migratory birds, this highly complex area of varying geomorphic features and biological habitats has been recognized as important in Mexico, where most of the delta lies—63 km (39 mi) of its 75 km (47 mi) width (DUMAC 1993). The least altered or impacted upland areas along the Laguna Madre de Tamaulipas appear to be Rancho Rincon de Anacahuitas, located on a large peninsula in the northern lagoon (J. Bergan, pers. comm.), the two peninsulas of Laguna el Catán, and the remote mainland areas south of Laguna el Catán toward La Pesca (DUMAC 1993).

Climate

The Laguna Madre region has been classified variously as semiarid (Thornthwaite 1948; Hedgpeth 1953) or subtropical steppe (Norwine et al. 1977). More recently and precisely, the region was characterized as a subhumid-to-semiarid east-coast subtropical climate, with extreme variability in precipitation (Fulbright et al. 1990). Additional characterization includes high temperatures along with deficiencies of moisture and a combination of high humidity and infrequent but significant killing frosts (Fulbright et al. 1990). Interestingly, it has also been classified as a "problem climate" (Trewartha 1961, 1968) in that it is located between two areas of substantially higher rainfall. The coasts of East Texas to the north and Veracruz to the south receive more than double the rainfall of Laguna Madre, which makes the area unique worldwide. Significant coastal drainages are essentially lacking in the Laguna Madre region of the western Gulf of Mexico. Only two rivers, the Río Grande and Río San Fernando, reach the coast along this 445 km (277 mi) of coastline.

Although detailed climatic data are available from long-term NOAA Local Climatological Data stations in Corpus Christi and Brownsville, similar data for Tamaulipas are difficult to access and of shorter duration, and stations have not been continuously occupied on the shores of Laguna Madre de Tamaulipas (Hildebrand 1980). Wind, rainfall, temperature, tropical storms, and hurricanes all have a significant effect on the biota of the area, and they are important influences on the hydrographic and geologic processes of the region (Brown et al. 1976, 1980).

The South Texas region could potentially suffer under global warming during the next century (J. Norwine, pers. comm.) with an increase in the number of hot nights, a reduction in the number of freezes (tending toward "tropical" in the next 100 years), and a sharp increase in evapotranspiration. Likely effects on rainfall are not clear, but it will probably at least become more variable.

Winds　Southeasterly winds from the Gulf of Mexico prevail for most months of the year at Laguna Madre, with northerly winds interrupting southeast winds during winter storms. At Corpus Christi, persistent southeasterly winds blow from March through September and north-northeasterly winds occur with winter frontal passages from October through February (Behrens and Watson 1973; Brown et al. 1976). In Brownsville the persistent southeasterly winds blow from March through November, and short-lived but strong northerly winds occur from December through February (Brown et al. 1980). Conditions are similar for the Laguna Madre de Tamaulipas region (DUMAC 1993). From a hydrographic viewpoint, wind forcing is one of the most important meteorological influences on developing coastal environments. In the inland or isolated reaches of the Laguna Madre, water levels are significantly affected by wind forcing (Ward and Armstrong 1997). Wind stress can cause water level in the lagoon to set down (lower) and set up (rise) on upwind and downwind sides of bays as much as 0.6 to 0.9 m (2–3 ft) (Fisk 1959; McGowen et al. 1977; Morton and McGowen 1980; Weise and White 1980).

Humidity　At the centrally located city of Brownsville the average humidity at 0600 hrs ranges from 85% in December to 90% in July with an annual average of 88%. This high relative humidity causes fairly heavy dew even during drought years. Dense fogs are common at night from December through March (Lonard et al. 1991).

Precipitation　Average annual rainfall decreases slightly along the South Texas coast from Corpus Christi, 70.6 cm (27.8 in), to Brownsville, 68.2 cm (26.9 in), then increases again moving southward along the Tamaulipan coast to Soto la Marina, 74.8 cm (29.4 in), just inland from La Pesca (table 2.4). In Texas, rainfall is typically bimodal with higher values in May–June and August–October, peaking in September (table 2.4). Approximately one-third of the total annual rainfall is received during August–October in Corpus Christi and September–October in Brownsville. Additionally, about two-thirds of the annual rainfall falls during the six-month period from May through October. This division corresponds closely with the "rainy season" that prevails in the tropical region of eastern and central Mexico (Davis 1942). Most of the precipitation results from thunderstorms, and often a single thunderstorm will account for an entire month's rainfall. Flood-producing rains may occur in any season but are most frequent in September and October. Heavy rain is often associated with tropical storms and hurricanes.

Precipitation values alone are not necessarily significant, but the variability among months, years, and long-term cycles (Price 1958; Norwine et al. 1977; Hildebrand 1980) coupled with high evapotranspiration (Carr 1967; Brown et al. 1976, 1980) all make for a complex and highly unpredictable water budget. For example, evaporation averages 147 cm (57.9 in) annually from a free water surface, which is double the average annual precipitation of 68.2 cm (26.9 in) in Brownsville. In Corpus Christi annual rainfall since 1900 has ranged from 13.7 cm (5.4 in) in 1917 to

Table 2.4. *Comparison of precipitation and temperature means among months for Corpus Christi, Brownsville, and Soto la Marina (just inland from La Pesca)*

Month	Corpus Christi[a]	Brownsville[b]	Soto la Marina[b]
Precipitation cm (in)			
January	3.7 (1.4)	3.4 (1.3)	5.3 (2.1)
February	4.1 (1.6)	3.3 (1.3)	1.3 (0.5)
March	3.4 (1.3)	2.6 (1.0)	1.9 (0.7)
April	4.9 (1.9)	3.5 (1.4)	3.4 (1.3)
May	8.3 (3.3)	6.5 (2.6)	4.2 (1.6)
June	7.2 (2.8)	7.0 (2.8)	9.4 (3.7)
July	5.0 (1.9)	4.7 (1.9)	6.9 (2.7)
August	6.3 (2.5)	6.6 (2.6)	10.1 (4.0)
September	12.2 (4.8)	14.0 (5.5)	16.7 (6.6)
October	6.9 (2.7)	8.2 (3.2)	8.7 (3.4)
November	4.3 (1.7)	4.4 (1.7)	2.5 (1.0)
December	4.5 (1.8)	4.0 (1.6)	3.8 (1.5)
Total	70.6 (27.8)	68.2 (26.9)	74.8 (29.4)
Temperature °C (°F)			
January	13.6 (56.5)	15.7 (60.3)	17.0 (62.6)
February	15.2 (59.4)	17.3 (63.1)	19.4 (66.9)
March	18.5 (65.3)	20.2 (68.4)	22.0 (71.6)
April	22.1 (71.8)	23.5 (74.3)	25.0 (77.0)
May	27.7 (81.9)	26.1 (79.0)	28.2 (82.8)
June	28.7 (83.7)	28.0 (82.4)	29.6 (85.3)
July	28.7 (83.7)	28.7 (83.7)	29.1 (84.4)
August	28.8 (83.8)	28.9 (84.0)	29.3 (84.7)
September	27.2 (81.0)	27.3 (81.1)	27.8 (82.0)
October	23.4 (74.1)	24.1 (75.4)	24.7 (76.5)
November	18.5 (65.3)	19.9 (67.8)	21.5 (70.7)
December	14.8 (58.6)	16.6 (61.9)	18.0 (64.4)
Average	22.0 (71.6)	23.0 (73.4)	24.3 (75.7)

Source: U.S. data are from Corpus Christi, Nueces County, and Brownsville, Cameron County, Texas, NOAA Local Climatological Data Annual Summary; Mexico data from Villarreal (2000).

[a] 94-year average.

[b] 40-year average.

127.6 cm (50.3 in) in 1992. Rainfall for the Laguna Madre region should also be characterized as irregular and unpredictable for seasons, years, and decades. Behrens (1966), Price (1968), and Hildebrand (1980) have emphasized this extreme rainfall variability as well as long-term climatic variability. The 1950s drought lasted for 80 months (Price 1968), and dry years and drought years persisted from about 1945 to

1965 (Norwine et al. 1977; Hildebrand 1980; Quammen and Onuf 1993), demonstrating multiple-decade dry periods. Last, recent studies indicate that South Texas experiences increased precipitation in El Niño years, especially in winter.

Temperature   Temperature in the region is characterized by long, hot summers and short, mild winters (table 2.4). In Nueces County, temperatures range from average winter lows of 8.3°C (46.9°F) to average summer highs of 33.3°C (91.9°F), with an average annual mean in the Corpus Christi area of 22.0°C (71.6°F) (Brown et al. 1976). In Cameron County, the average winter low is 8.9°C (48.0°F) and the average summer high is 36.1°C (97.0°F), with an average annual mean in the Brownsville area of 23.1°C (73.6°F). Along the Tamaulipan coast the average annual temperature ranges between 22 and 24°C (71.6 and 75.2°F) (INEGI n.d.), with an overall regional average of 27.7°C (81.9°F) (DUMAC 1993).

The growing season along the South Texas coast varies from 300 days in San Patricio County (just north of Corpus Christi; Everitt and Drawe 1993) to between 330 and 365 days in Cameron County at the extreme southern end of the state (F. Judd, pers. comm.). Although freezes occur only occasionally in Corpus Christi and rarely in Brownsville, two killing freezes occurred in the 1980s throughout South Texas and extended into northeastern Mexico. From 24 to 26 December 1983, 55 consecutive hours below freezing were reported at Brownsville, and a minimum of −6.7°C (19.9°F) was sustained for six hours (Lonard and Judd 1985). During the massive cold wave of 22–24 December 1989, two freezing episodes were reported at Brownsville; one with 33.75 consecutive hours below freezing and a second with 16.75 hours below freezing. A temperature at or below −8.4°C (16.9°F) was recorded for 11.75 hours (Lonard and Judd 1991). Freeze damage to vegetable and citrus production was estimated at $200 million in 1983 and $138 million in 1989 (Lonard and Judd 1985, 1991). The two major freezes in 1983 and 1989 also caused shallow waters to freeze in the upper and lower Laguna Madre, which resulted in major fish kills (Martin and McEachron 1996). In the uppermost Laguna Madre in 1989, surface ice formed from the shoreline of Flour Bluff all the way across the lagoon in the John F. Kennedy Causeway area to the Padre Island shoreline (J. Bronson, pers. comm.). Also during the 1989 freeze, mangrove communities lining the Río Soto la Marina shoreline at La Pesca were killed (J. W. Tunnell, pers. observ.).

Hurricanes   Major hurricanes have caused significant impacts on the natural systems of South Texas (Hayes 1967; Scott et al. 1969; McGowen et al. 1970; McGowen and Scott 1975; Judd and Sides 1983) and northeastern Mexico (Hildebrand 1958, 1969, 1980). Historically, both lagoonal systems were completely (Tamaulipas) to partly (Texas) closed. It appears that they were primarily driven over long-term cycles by being opened and closed due to physical processes of storm surges and torrential rainfall and runoff associated with hurricanes. Tidal inlets and washover passes are widened and deepened by hurricanes and form connections with the open sea (Gulf of Mexico). In time, after the storm, passes begin to close and return to normal conditions. The microtidal coastline in the region does not allow for sufficient water head and scour to maintain more than a few passes in the absence of river outflow. The deeper, artificially maintained (dredged) passes today carry almost all flow, and storm-opened passes close rapidly. In the Laguna Madre of Texas, dredging of the GIWW and Mansfield Pass has permanently altered hydrology, circulation, and salinity. In Tamaulipas, early researchers (Copeland 1967) suggested that study of Mexican hypersaline environments without artificial passes could allow learning by inference of how the Laguna Madre in Texas functioned before channelization.

Since those early studies, however, dredged passes have been cut into the Tamaulipan lagoon.

Tropical storms and hurricanes strike the Texas coast about once every two years (McGowen et al. 1977). Hurricanes are severe tropical storms with cyclonic (counterclockwise) winds, covering thousands—sometimes hundreds of thousands—of square kilometers (Henry et al. 1980). Characteristics of the storms are high-velocity winds, a calm area (eye) at the center, low barometric pressure, torrential rainfall, and tornadoes. Additionally, as the storm approaches land, the tidal surge causes a marked rise in water level, especially on the north side of landfall. Historical records indicate that hurricanes not only differ in intensity (Categories 1–5), but they can also differ in other characteristics. For instance, in South Texas, one hurricane may generate a large storm surge (e.g., Hurricane Carla in 1961), another may be remembered for torrential rainfall (Beulah, 1967), and yet another may be characterized by extreme wind velocities (Celia, 1970) (Brown et al. 1976, 1977, 1980).

Depending upon intensity and other characteristics, tropical storms and hurricanes may cause varying degrees of impacts to coastal geologic processes as well as to local biota and ecology. Geologically, these storms have been shown to accelerate coastal processes so that during the few hours of storm passage, the degree of erosion and deposition in coastal systems might equal what would normally take months or even years to accomplish (Price 1958; Hayes 1967; McGowen et al. 1970; McGowen and Scott 1975; Brown et al. 1976, 1977, 1980; McGowen et al. 1977; Morton and McGowen 1980). Although detailed biological and ecological studies are few, opportunistic studies reveal hurricane impacts on the vegetation of South Padre Island (Judd and Sides 1983), on marshes in the northern Gulf of Mexico (Chabreck and Palmisano 1973; Harris and Chabreck 1958), and on southeastern coastal landscapes (Gardner et al. 1991, 1992).

Within the Laguna Madre of Texas, Hurricane Beulah in September 1967 flushed the system first with marine waters from the Gulf of Mexico due to the storm surge, then with freshwater from rainfall and runoff (Behrens 1969). Prior to this storm, and after several consecutive, dry years, average surface salinities ranged from 63 parts per thousand (ppt) in Baffin Bay to 55 ppt in upper Laguna Madre. Highest salinities exceeded 75 ppt during this time at the upper reaches of Baffin Bay. On 20 September 1967, Hurricane Beulah caused hurricane surges of 1.8–2.1 m (6–7 ft) from Port Aransas to Port Mansfield. Dilution of hypersaline waters with Gulf water gave estimates of 40 ppt in Baffin Bay and 35 ppt in upper Laguna Madre. Accompanying and following the storm's passage, some 51 cm (20 in) of rain fell on most of the area. This rainfall exceeded the all-time monthly records for the area and the total rainfall for some years. For several weeks the water in the system remained stratified, the heavier salt water being overlain by fresher water. After northerly winds promoted mixing, there was essentially no stratification remaining, and salinities in Baffin Bay and Laguna Madre were about 6 ppt and 12 ppt, respectively. Other impacts included sand deposited in the lagoon from the barrier island; mud was carried into the bay by flooded streams and deposited; some carbonate solution took place; and there was a temporary change in fauna. In summary, Hurricane Beulah drastically altered the hydrology of Baffin Bay and Laguna Madre, but it was an almost insignificant event in the depositional history of the system. Both marine and fresh waters were able to drain quickly from the Laguna Madre of Texas due to the GIWW canal system (Behrens 1969).

Most recently, Hurricane Bret made landfall on central Padre Island between Corpus Christi and Brownsville. Before going ashore, Bret had winds of 225 kph (140 mph), traveling up from the Bay of Campeche in the southern Gulf of Mexico.

After the storm, Richard Watson (marine geologist, pers. comm.) made aerial and land surveys along Padre Island, reporting 12 washover passes reopened and extending across the island and onto the wind-tidal flats as washover fans. Watson reported a maximum storm surge on the outer beach of about 1.8 m (6 ft). Within the Laguna Madre in the Land-Cut, the El Toro tide gauge (Blucher Institute of Surveying and Science) recorded a tide height of 1.2 m (4 ft) before it blew over, but it is suspected that the tide height was not much higher (R. Morton, pers. comm.). Chris Onuf (pers. comm.) flew over the Laguna Madre seagrass beds and reported "no evidence of storm damage on the lagoon side in the upper Laguna Madre." Therefore, although threatening great danger as a Category 4 hurricane, Bret had only modest impact on Padre Island and Laguna Madre. Since the storm weakened to Category 3 before landfall and passed over the sparsely inhabited lands of the Kenedy and King ranches, little human impact occurred in the vicinity of the Laguna Madre.

In Laguna Madre de Tamaulipas, major hurricanes are a key force driving the hydrography and fisheries of the system (Hildebrand 1958, 1969, 1980). Although the Mexican lagoon is located on a hurricane coast, major storms are rare events. They seem to be the only weather phenomenon able to reestablish the natural productivity of the lagoon after an extended drought. Hildebrand (1980) suggests that in this sparsely inhabited area, the effects of hurricanes are more positive than negative: major hurricanes open passes through the barrier islands and flush the lagoonal system with rainfall floodwaters, eliminating extreme hypersaline conditions in the lagoon. Fisheries then flourish for several years, until passes close and the system becomes extremely hypersaline and unproductive again, completing the cycle. The hurricanes of 1909, 1933, and 1967 set off major peaks in fisheries productivity, and the *sequias* (droughts) of 1883–1890 and 1960–67 were major negative events (H. Hildebrand, pers. comm.).

Hurricane season lasts from June through November, but most storms occur between August and October. In any given year, the 80 km (50 mi) segment of the southernmost Texas coast has a 9% probability of experiencing a tropical storm, an 8% probability of experiencing a hurricane, and a 2% probability of experiencing a major hurricane (Simpson and Lawrence 1971). During the 20th century, over 50 hurricanes hit or affected the Texas coast, 24 of which were considered major, and nine of those impacted the Laguna Madre of Texas (Henry et al. 1980; Broussard and Martin 1986; Ellis 1986; table 2.5, this volume).

In Tamaulipas, historical records show that 62 hurricanes affected the Mexican Laguna Madre between 1900 and 1979 (Hildebrand 1980). The maximum number of hurricanes in any single year was five in 1933, and the longest period without any hurricanes was 1904 through 1908. Three major storms completely reversed salinity regimes in the Laguna in 1909, 1933, and 1967, before establishment of dredged and jettied passes to the Gulf of Mexico (Hildebrand 1980; table 2.5).

Hydrography

The Laguna Madre of Texas has become a textbook example of a hypersaline or negative estuary (Dyer 1973; Reid and Wood 1976). The unique and characteristic hydrography of Laguna Madre in both countries explains and justifies this longstanding, although now moderated, hallmark: little to no freshwater inflow, evaporation exceeding precipitation, shallow bathymetry, microtidal tide regime, limited circulation, and limited exchange with Gulf waters.

Freshwater Inflow Freshwater inflow is intermittent and is primarily associated with rainfall events and municipal or industrial discharges. In South Texas, the Nueces–

Table 2.5. *Major hurricanes affecting the Laguna Madre of Texas and Tamaulipas during the twentieth century*

Date	Name	Characteristics
		Texas
18 August 1916	Unnamed	Landfall near Corpus Christi
15 September 1919	Corpus Christi storm	116 kph (72 mph) wind
4 September 1933	Unnamed	Landfall just south of Brownsville; 129 kph (80 mph) wind; heavy impact from Corpus Christi into northeastern Mexico
25 July 1934	Unnamed	Landfall near Corpus Christi; 87 kph (54 mph) wind
11 September 1961	Carla	Landfall near Matagorda; 282 kph (175 mph) wind, 12–161 kph (7–100 mph) in Laguna Madre; storm surge affected entire Texas coast, 1.5–3.1 m (5–10 ft) along Padre Island
20 September 1967	Beulah	Landfall near Rio Grande, moved north into Laguna Madre; 175 kph (109 mph) wind; major flooding from torrential rainfall of 38–51 cm (15–20 in)
3 August 1970	Celia	Landfall near Corpus Christi; 261 kph (162 mph) wind
10 August 1980	Allen	Landfall at Port Mansfield; 208 kph (129 mph) wind; 25–38 cm (10–15 in) rain; 3.2 m (10.5 ft) storm surge on Padre Island
17 September 1988	Gilbert	Landfall 201 km (125 mi) south of Brownsville; heavy rainfall and moderate storm surge in South Texas
22 August 1999	Bret	Landfall between Corpus Christi and Brownsville on central Padre Island and the Land-Cut; 225 kph (140 mph) wind; 1.8–2.4 m (6–8 ft) storm surge on Padre Island and about 1.2 m (4 ft) in Laguna Madre; 10–12 washover cuts in Padre Island
		Tamaulipas
28 August 1909	Unnamed	Completely flushed system
5 August 1933	Unnamed	Completely flushed system
20 September 1967	Beulah	Completely flushed system
17 September 1988	Gilbert	Landfall 201 km (125 mi) south of Brownsville near La Pesca; no detailed information available

Source: From Hayes 1967; Henry et al. 1980; Hildebrand 1980; Broussard and Martin 1986; R. Watson, pers. comm. 1999 for Bret.

Río Grande Coastal Basin, 27,045 km² (10,442 mi²), is the contributing drainage basin for Laguna Madre. However, a large portion of the area is noncontributory due to flat terrain and narrow stream channels. The northern part of the coastal basin is drained by a network of intermittent streams flowing into Baffin Bay, whereas the southern part is primarily drained by the Arroyo Colorado (TDWR 1983). There is only sheet-flow, with no channelized drainage within the South Texas eolian sand sheet area (Brown et al. 1977; see fig. 5.3).

Freshwater inflows into the Texas Laguna Madre have varied greatly in both monthly and annual average values as a result of recurrent drought and flood conditions (TDWR 1983). Therefore "average" must be considered with caution. On the average, the total freshwater inflow (excluding direct precipitation) to the lagoon (1941–76 record) consisted of 851 million m³ (690 thousand acre-feet) annually, of which approximately 411 million m³ (330 thousand acre-feet) was contributed from gauged drainages.

To the south, although the Río Grande Basin is very large, it no longer contributes flow directly into Laguna Madre but drains into the Gulf of Mexico by way of the Río

Grande. Today, only runoff from the lowermost reach of the river, below the Anzalduas Dam at Mission, actually contributes to outflow (Orlando et al. 1991). In fact, this lowermost reach is often estuarine, with Gulf of Mexico waters flowing in on flood tides. Under low-flow conditions, the Río Grande is entirely impounded by the Amistad Dam (completed in 1968) and Falcon Dam (completed in 1953), from which waters are diverted for municipal and irrigation use. When rare Río Grande floods do occur, the North Floodway in Texas and the South Floodway in Tamaulipas are activated, diverting flood water away from the normal river channel to the Laguna Madre in Texas and Tamaulipas, respectively (Orlando et al. 1991).

In northeastern Mexico, old distributary channels carry floodwaters toward the Gulf: (north to south) La Pita, Arroyo del Tigre, and Arroyo del Diablo. Only the latter, which drains through Laguna Jasso, flows into the northernmost Laguna Madre. Numerous irrigation and drainage canals interlace the rich agricultural area southwest of Matamoros (INEGI 1980). Most of the drainage influx of fresh water comes from Irrigation Districts 25 and 26 (Hildebrand 1980). Of the seven drains flowing into the northern Laguna Madre, there was an inflow of 9 million m³ (7,344 acre-feet) during a 13-month period between 1 September 1977 and 30 September 1978 (Sanchez 1968). To the south, the Río San Fernando has a drainage area of 13,510 km² (5,216 mi²) and originates in the mountains of Nuevo León, but its runoff is highly variable (Hildebrand 1980). The average annual flow, gauged since 1931, is 665 million m³ (539 thousand acre-feet) and has ranged from 179 million m³ (145 thousand acre-feet) in 1952 to 4.678 billion m³ (3.794 million acre-feet) in 1933 (Anonymous 1967). The Río San Fernando no longer flows directly into the Laguna Madre, because its waters have been diverted into Laguna la Nacha and then to Laguna Madre via a canal (Brenner 1997). Farther south there are a number of small watersheds: Arroyo Chorreras has a drainage basin of 2,273 km² (878 mi²) and average runoff of 386 million m³ (313 thousand acre-feet) per year, and other small watersheds containing an area of approximately 2,432 km² (939 mi²) have an estimated annual freshwater runoff of 377 million m³ (306 thousand acre-feet) (Tamayo 1949). The fresh water in all of these streams is utilized to some extent, with as much as 60–80% of the Río San Fernando being removed, primarily for agriculture, during low-flow years, before it reaches the Laguna Madre.

At the southernmost extremity of the Laguna Madre, the Río Soto la Marina does not contribute waters to the southern Laguna Madre de Tamaulipas due to extensive tidal flats and a road to the beach, which form effective barriers to exchange. Two adjacent lagunas, however, are affected by the Río Soto la Marina: Laguna Almagre, 2,720 ha (6,721 ac), to the west of La Pesca, and Laguna Morales, 3,500 ha (8,649 ac), to the south (Hildebrand 1980). The latter laguna, along with the Laguna Madre de Tamaulipas and the Mexican Río Grande Delta area, are all considered by Mexican scientists as "la sistema Laguna Madre," extending from the mouth of the Río Grande at 25° 52′ N, to the southern end of Laguna Morales at 23° 32′N (Hildebrand 1980).

Evaporation Effects   It is widely understood that evaporation exceeds precipitation in the semiarid region of Laguna Madre in Texas and Tamaulipas. This key climatologic characteristic is one of the primary reasons for the hypersaline condition of both systems, usually with evaporation exceeding precipitation by two to three times. Although there is considerable year-to-year variability, a few direct examples are available for illustration. In the Texas Laguna Madre, precipitation averages only 74 cm/yr (29 in/yr), whereas evaporation considerably dominates, averaging 158 cm/yr (62 in/yr) (TDWR 1983). In Tamaulipas, at the San Fernando weather station, where precipitation is only slightly higher than in Texas, a 34-year record (1932–65) revealed a range from a low evaporation rate in 1941 of 158 cm/yr (62 in/yr) to a high of 230 cm/yr (91 in/yr) in 1946 (Hildebrand 1980). During a 121-month period from July 1960 to February 1966, monthly evaporation rates ranged from a high of 26 cm/mo (10 in/mo) to 6.5 cm/mo (2.6 in/mo), and precipitation exceeded evaporation in only five months during this entire period. Highlighting the high evaporation rate in Laguna Madre de Tamaulipas—coupled with its having little or no freshwater inflow and no permanent connection to the Gulf—water levels of a meter below sea level have been recorded (Anonymous 1967; Yañez and Schlaepfer 1968). Some older newspaper reports have suggested that the entire lagoon has dried up (H. Hildebrand, pers. comm.).

Excessive evaporation over two decades of dry and drought years in both Texas and Tamaulipas focused attention on problems caused by this phenomenon. In Texas, concern and study focused on wind erosion and the impacts of blowing salt (plate 14) on the lands west of the Land-Cut (Coover and Rechenthin 1965; Price 1968). In Tamaulipas, study focused on the evaporation and consequent drying up of the lagoon, physical hydrological characteristics, and a proposed solution to "rehabilitate" the Laguna Madre by cutting passes across the barrier island to the Gulf of Mexico (Anonymous 1967).

Bathymetry Shallowness of the entire lagoonal system is well documented and is an important factor ensuring a well-mixed water column. Although a recent detailed or comprehensive bathymetry map is unavailable for either lagoon, earlier workers mapped each lagoon's depths and contours (Rusnak 1960 for Texas; Anonymous 1967 and Yañez and Schlaepfer 1968 for Tamaulipas). Major bathymetric features are available on Bureau of Economic Geology maps for the Texas lagoon (Brown et al. 1976, 1977, 1980). In Texas, Laguna Madre has a smooth, centrally sloping floor on the eastern side with a few deeper, elongate basins located on the west. Average depth is about 1.0 m (3.3 ft), with upper Laguna Madre slightly shallower and lower Laguna Madre slightly deeper (table 2.1). Deeper areas of 2.4 m (8 ft) occur just south of the Land-Cut in Redfish Bay and just south of the mouth of Baffin Bay.

In Mexico the shorter and wider northern lagoon had a centrally located maximum depth of just over 3.0 m (9.8 ft) when mapped in 1963, whereas the narrower and longer southern Laguna's maximum depth was 1.3 m (4.3 ft) in its northern portion and in Laguna el Catán (Anonymous 1967). In the northernmost Laguna Madre, north of Isla Larga and northwest of Isla Mula, shallow conditions, generally less than 1.0 m (3.3 ft) exist due to erosion of the islands and mainland, both remnants of the Río Grande Delta. Elsewhere, broad washover fans with extensive tidal flats and lagoon shallows exist lagoonward of the four natural intermittent tidal inlets around Boca Ciega.

Channelization in both Texas and Tamaulipas has since altered bathymetry, tides, and hydrology, and subsequently salinity, in these lagoons. Tidal characteristics, water circulation, and salinity are all important environmental parameters that govern the distribution of biota and habitats.

Tides Tides within the Laguna Madre of Texas, even though minimal, have generated intense interest in two divergent subject areas: law and science. In law, tidelines are used to determine ownership boundaries between the privately owned uplands and submerged state-owned lands. Much of the early knowledge about tides in the Laguna Madre of Texas was generated in regard to tidal boundary issues during the 1940s (e.g., Fisk 1949, 1959). Along with Fisk, other early workers in the

Laguna Madre (Hedgpeth 1947; Collier and Hedgpeth 1950; Simmons 1957; Breuer 1957; Rusnak 1960) discovered that meteorological tides, namely wind-tides, were far more important than astronomical tides and thus of unique scientific interest for both geologic and biologic processes.

In the upper Laguna Madre, which is the most studied regarding tides and water levels, three water level components prevail: a dominant semi-annual rise and fall; a meteorological forcing on water levels; and an astronomical component superimposed on the longer-period processes (Smith 1978). Specifically, these components include:

1. Long-period, semi-annual rise and fall of water level in the lagoon; high water occurs in late May and late October, while semi-annual lows occur in late February and late July; this rise and fall in water levels associated with seasons is on the order of 50 cm (20 in).
2. Superimposed on the gradual, seasonal rise and fall are water level variations occurring over time scales of one to two weeks; this rise and fall is quite variable and dependent upon meteorological forcing, and it generally is on the order of 10–20 cm (4–8 in).
3. Diurnal and perhaps semi-diurnal astronomical tides appear as "noise" in the tidal signal, superimposed on the longer-period variations; this component is only on the order of 2–3 cm (0.8–1.2 in).

Additionally, as one travels from the Gulf of Mexico tidal inlet at Aransas Pass south through various channels and ever increasing distance, the tidal amplitude decreases in size. Tidal inlets in the lower Laguna Madre include Mansfield Pass and Brazos Santiago Pass.

Currently nine tide gauges are maintained in the Laguna Madre (Packery Channel, Bird Island, Baffin Bay, El Toro, Rincon de San José, Port Mansfield, Arroyo Colorado, Port Isabel, South Padre Island), as part of an extensive statewide system, the Texas Coastal Ocean Observation Network. This system, operated by the Conrad Blucher Institute for Surveying and Science at Texas A&M University–Corpus Christi, is sponsored jointly by the Texas General Land Office and the Texas Water Development Board. Although initiated in the Laguna Madre in response to tidal boundary issues, it is now widely used by citizens, agencies, industry, and academia, with data collected in near real time via packet radio (similar to Internet), cellular phone, and satellite transmission.

Natural tidal inlets, or bocas, were the avenues for tidal exchange in the Laguna Madre de Tamaulipas before the four jettied channels were dredged. Before dredging, the Laguna's tidal amplitude was only a few centimeters, and a relatively small area around the inlets was influenced by the daily tide (Hildebrand 1980). Astronomic tidal characteristics under today's conditions are not known, but wind-tides are important in mixing and influencing water levels throughout the Laguna.

Wind-Tides   A wind-tide is defined as a rise in water level on the downwind side of a body of water caused by the force of the wind on the water surface (Weise and White 1980). Numerous authors have studied and discussed the importance of wind-tides and their impact on water levels and geologic processes. Fisk (1959) recorded a wind-tide in excess of one meter in the northern part of the lower Laguna Madre. Calculations based on wind velocity and fetch indicate that wind-tides in the 0.3 to 1.2 m (1 to 4 ft) range are common within the Laguna Madre (Rusnak 1960). Copeland and coworkers (1968, p. 199) note that wind-driven water covers "normally dry land" within the Laguna Madre. Within Kenedy and Kleberg counties, "wind driven tides may flood as much as 200 mi² (518 km²) of low-lying lagoonal margin" (Brown et al. 1977, p. 24). Additionally, Brown and colleagues (1977, p. 63) relate that "wind-tidal flats are flooded rapidly, generally by northers or the prevailing southeasterly wind regime," and that flooding from wind-tides can be localized on the flats and is a "function of the duration, intensity, and direction of the wind." McGowen and coworkers (1977) note that strong winds accompanied by spring tides and a barometric low can create tides 0.6 to 0.9 m (2–3 ft) higher than those produced solely by astronomical conditions. And Morton and McGowen (1980, p. 90) note that "wind tides inundate areas not normally affected by astronomical tides."

An excellent example of the regional impact of wind-tides can be seen in their effect on the central portion of the Laguna Madre of Texas. Winds from the south and southeast (1) raise the water level in northern Redfish Bay, which floods a large portion of the Land-Cut; (2) drive water out of The Hole across Middle Ground into the southern part of upper Laguna Madre; and (3) cause water to flow from the Laguna into Baffin Bay, thereby increasing water depth. Conversely, strong north winds produce wind-tides that are low in Baffin Bay and Redfish Bay and high in Middle Ground and The Hole and adjacent northern parts of the Land-Cut (Morton and McGowen 1980).

Channelization

Channelization of both tidal inlets (Mansfield and Brazos Santiago) to the Gulf of Mexico and navigation or access channels within the lagoons have been the key factor in reducing salinities, causing long-term ecosystem change in both Laguna Madre systems (Collier and Hedgpeth 1950; Simmons 1957; Breuer 1962; Hedgpeth 1967; Quammen and Onuf 1993; Onuf 1994). Historically, before channelization, distance from tidal inlets in Texas and lack of continuously open tidal inlets in Tamaulipas led to excessive hypersalinity. In addition, particularly in the upper Laguna Madre of Texas, constrictions to water circulation into The Hole and just north of Baffin Bay caused even higher salinities within and beyond those areas, respectively (Burr 1930; Hedgpeth 1947; Collier and Hedgpeth 1950; Simmons 1957). Shallow water sills between Corpus Christi Bay and upper Laguna Madre (see fig. 6.1; Hedgpeth 1947; Simmons 1957) and between Baffin Bay and upper Laguna Madre (Rusnak 1960) further impeded circulation between those water bodies.

Aside from conditions following storm events, which lowered salinities via rainfall, runoff, or opening tidal inlets, salinities prior to channelization were consistently higher in both Texas and Tamaulipas lagoons. Salinity levels two to three times higher than oceanic levels were common, if not the norm, prior to channelization (table 2.6) in both systems. In Texas, the more restricted upper Laguna Madre had salinities in excess of 100 ppt between 1946 and 1948, prior to dredging of the GIWW (Hedgpeth 1947; Collier and Hedgpeth 1950). In the lower Laguna Madre, salinities over 60 ppt were recorded during this time. After dredging of the GIWW, which was completed in 1949, and before Mansfield Pass was opened in 1962, Breuer (1962) recorded lower Laguna Madre salinities with ppt readings in the 30s to 50s from south to north, demonstrating elevated salinities with increasing distance from the tidal pass (Brazos Santiago Pass). After opening of Mansfield Pass through Padre Island in the northern part of the lower Laguna Madre, a water circulation pattern and exchange of water between the Gulf and lagoon has kept salinities somewhat lower, usually below 40 ppt (Warshaw 1975; Brown et al. 1980; White et al. 1986). Salinities in the upper Laguna Madre have also moderated due to exchange of water through the GIWW Land-Cut connection with the lower Laguna Madre.

Table 2.6. *Major channels constructed in the Laguna Madre of Texas and Tamaulipas*

Channel	Date	Width × Depth m (ft)	Reference
Texas			
Brownsville Ship Channel	1938	? × 8.5 (? × 28)	Breuer 1962
	1980	61 × 11 (200 × 36)	Orlando et al. 1991
Murdoch's Landing (= Yarborough Pass)	1941–44	24 × 2.4 (80 × 8)	Gunter 1945a
GIWW	1944–49	38 × 3.6 (125 × 12)	Warshaw 1975; Orlando et al. 1991
Channel to Harlingen	1951	38 × 3.6 (125 × 12)	Orlando et al. 1991
Mansfield Pass	1962	90 × 4.2 (295 × 14)	Kieslich 1977
Tamaulipas			
El Mesquital	1976	no data	
Boca Ciega	?	no data	
Boca de Catán	?	no data	
Boca de Santa Isabel	?	no data	

Quammen and Onuf (1993) have graphically illustrated these moderating conditions by plotting salinities over the 44-year period between 1945 and 1988 (see fig. 6.3).

An earlier interesting but failed attempt to reduce salinities in the upper Laguna Madre prior to the dredging of the GIWW involved cutting a pass through Padre Island opposite Baffin Bay. The Texas Game, Fish, and Oyster Commission (now Texas Parks and Wildlife Department), after recording numerous fish kills due to excessive hypersalinity and after considerable public outcry, sent its own dredge on four separate occasions to dredge a pass at Murdoch's Landing (now Yarborough Pass; Burr 1945, 1950; Gunter 1945a). Between 1941 and 1944 the dredge cut its way through the upper Laguna to and from the site, coming each time from its docking place in Rockport, taking several months each way. The pass silted in rapidly after each dredging, staying open only 10 months during the four-year period. When it was open, salinities were reduced only 0.5–1.0 ppt and only in the immediate area of the pass (Gunter 1945a).

Using the same notion that dredged passes to the Gulf would reduce excessive salinities, the Mexican government began cutting and jettying passes into the Laguna Madre de Tamaulipas in 1976. The first one was El Mezquital Pass (Hildebrand 1980). Subsequently, three other passes were dredged and jettied to allow permanent connection between the Gulf of Mexico and the Laguna: (north to south) Boca Ciega, Boca de Catán, and Boca de Santa Isabel. The first two connected into the northern basin and the second two into the southern basin.

Historically in Tamaulipas, there were no continuously open tidal inlets. However, several remained in the same area, called by their place names in Spanish but given numbers by Americans fishing the area (e.g., Boca Sandoval = 5th Pass). Several of these tidal inlets are observed on maps of the region, and they opened and closed depending upon prevailing climatological conditions. The greatest number opened immediately after hurricanes, and all might be closed during prolonged droughts and might remain closed for years. In the region of the current jettied Boca Ciega there was a cluster of four inlets in a 13 km (8 mi) stretch of barrier island: (north to south) Boca Santa María, Boca San Rafael, Boca Ciega, and Boca Sandoval. These passes varied in depth from a few centimeters to 1.8 m (6 ft), and the yearly cycle involved shoaling in summer and deepening in winter as north winds piled water in the southeastern part of the northern Laguna Madre (Hildebrand 1980). South of this area, two other passes existed, Boca San Antonio and Boca Jesus María, passing into the southern Laguna. Little is known of Boca San Antonio, but Boca Jesus María, also known as 8th Pass, had a substantial fishing village and was the most stable and deepest of all the passes into the Laguna, with average depths of 1.8 to 2.4 m (6 to 8 ft). Boca El Viborero existed to the south of Boca Jesus María and became the dominant pass after Hurricane Beulah in 1967. Since there is not enough tidal prism to maintain multiple passes, it is assumed, as in Texas, that most of the time the natural passes no longer function due to tidal dominance by the maintained passes. However, on 14 February 1999, after a winter storm with strong north winds, Boca Sandoval was observed open (J. W. Tunnell, pers. observ.).

Like historical salinity levels in the Texas Laguna Madre, salinities in the Mexican lagoon no longer seem to reach the excessive hypersaline values recorded prior to channelization (dredging of barrier island inlets). Except for periods after major wet hurricanes, the Tamaulipas laguna generally had salinities two to three times greater than oceanic salinity and frequently had recordings in the mid-100s ppt (Copeland and Jones 1965; Copeland 1967; Hildebrand 1969). Extreme salinities of 175 ppt in 1961 (Hildebrand 1969) and 295 ppt in 1965 (Copeland and Jones 1965) were recorded during the drought of the 1960s.

3 *Origin, Development, and Geology*

JOHN W. TUNNELL, JR.

To understand distribution and ecology of present day biota and habitats, it is important to understand both the influence of current physical processes (e.g., temperature, salinity, wind, precipitation, etc.) and the effects of origin, development, and geology on the landscape. The geomorphological structures that we see today in the Laguna Madre of Texas and Tamaulipas are expressions of historical development as well as present-day processes. The vast Río Grande Delta separating the U.S. and Mexican lagoons, the further division of both lagoons into smaller subunits (Land-Cut and El Carrizal), and the lagoonal protection provided by the barrier islands and peninsulas all have profound effects on the contemporary expression of living resources. Most major present-day coastal features formed over the past several thousand years, and they are continually in the process of long-term, dynamic change (McGowen et al. 1977; Brown et al. 1976, 1977, 1980; Morton and McGowen 1980).

A wealth of geologic information exists about the Texas coastline due to two factors: (1) vast oil and gas reserves and the consequent studies associated with this industry, and (2) the University of Texas Bureau of Economic Geology. Since publications on the geological aspects of the Laguna Madre de Tamaulipas are rare and those about the Texas lagoon are common, focus here is on the Texas system, with the assumption that most processes are similar for Tamaulipas. Many of the earlier ideas and concepts about South Texas geology and the Laguna Madre belong to Dr. W. Armstrong Price, pioneering coastal geologist (e.g., 1933, 1958, and many more).

Origin and Development

The Laguna Madre of Texas, like the entire Texas coastline, is primarily a product of Pleistocene and Recent (Holocene and Modern) geologic history. The Pleistocene ice age included over one million years of complex glacial and interglacial periods and corresponding fluctuations in sea level (Brown et al. 1976, 1977, 1980; fig. 3.1). Four major glacial episodes, during which sea level fell, were separated by warmer interglacial periods, when sea level rose.

According to the model of LeBlanc and Hodgson (1959) (fig. 3.2a), about 18,000 years before present (YBP), near the end of the final glaciation period (Wisconsin) and the end of the Pleistocene, sea level was some 91 to 137 m (300 to 500 ft) lower than today (Curray 1960), and the shoreline was about 80 km (50 mi) east of its present position. During this time period, streams cut deep valleys into underlying deposits in Baffin Bay (Behrens 1963), the Land-Cut area (Fisk 1959; fig. 3.3), and the Río Grande (Fulton 1976). These river valleys were flooded or drowned as the sea transgressed the land with the continued melting of glacial ice, and sediment began filling these drowned river valleys. At the end of the Holocene, about 5,000 to 4,500 YBP, sea level reached about 4.6 m (15 ft) below its present level, and modern geologic processes became active, including the formation of sand bars and shoals

Fig. 3.1. Sea level changes related to glacial and interglacial stages. (A) Generalized Pleistocene sea level variations and associated erosional and depositional episodes. (B) Generalized sea level changes during Late Wisconsin glaciation. (C) Proposed sea level changes during last 20,000 years (From Brown et al. 1977)

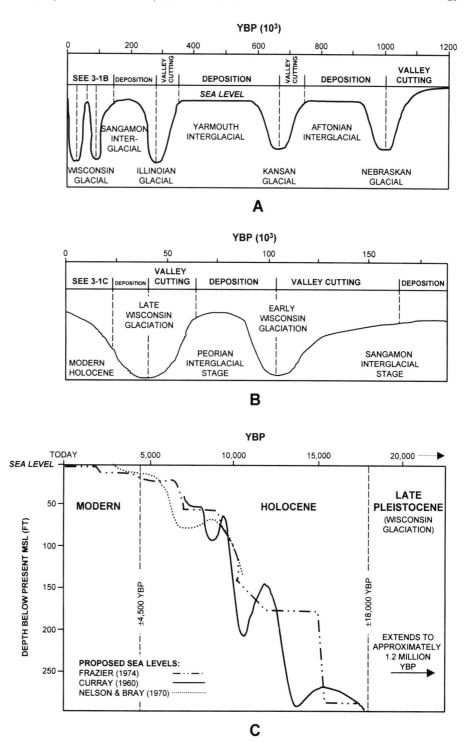

parallel with the coast (fig. 3.2B). When the sea reached its present level, about 2,800 to 2,500 YBP, those shoals and bars coalesced to form Padre Island and other barrier islands (LeBlanc and Hodgson 1959; fig. 3.2B). Thus, the origin of Laguna Madre is related to the formation of Padre Island and its enclosure of the lagoonal system. Other developmental processes during the last several thousand years are responsible for certain shapes and forms of Laguna Madre features today. Baffin Bay, for instance, is believed to have become hypersaline prior to Laguna Madre, sometime between 5,000 to 4,300 YBP (Behrens 1974).

Fig. 3.2. Origin and development of the Texas shoreline: (A) Late Pleistocene falling sea level stage about 18,000 YBP; (B) Early Modern sea level stage with barrier islands forming about 4,500 years YBP; (C) Present standing sea level stage (From Le Blanc and Hodgson 1959)

Fig. 3.3. Subsurface late Pleistocene–Holocene valleys below present-day Baffin Bay and Land-Cut. Valleys were incised during last glaciation (low sea level) and progressively filled by Holocene to Modern fluvial, estuarine, and open marine sedimentation. (Modified from Brown et al. 1977)

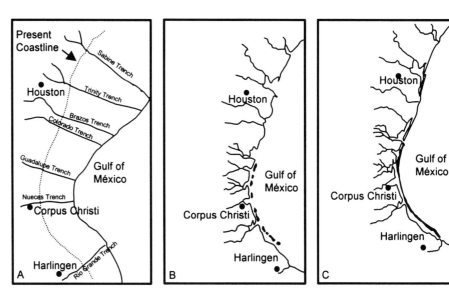

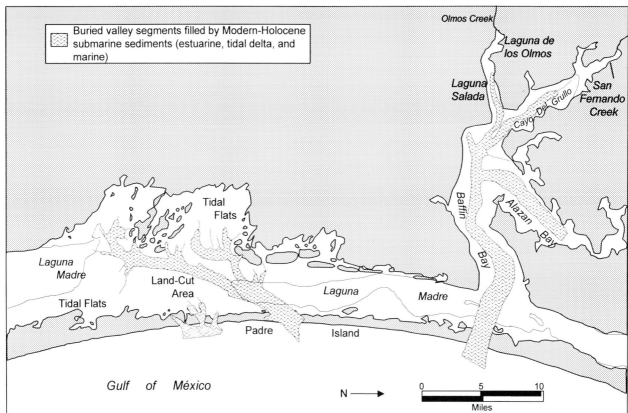

Over the past several thousand years, hurricanes and tropical storms, in conjunction with eolian processes, have transported sediment from Padre Island landward into Laguna Madre (Morton and McGowen 1980). These processes caused development of extensive tidal flats on the lagoon side of southern Padre Island and northward. In the Land-Cut area these same processes have caused the slow but continual infilling of Laguna Madre until a land-bridge was formed connecting Padre Island with the mainland (see plate 13). Scientists first proposed that this infilling occurred due to the massive 1919 hurricane (Gunter 1945a; Hedgpeth 1947). However, Fisk (1959), through extensive coring in the area, demonstrated that it was a much more gradual process, with final closure possibly occurring in the early 19th century. Most recently Watson (1989) and Morton and Garner (1993), through investigations on rates of wind-tidal flat accumulation, indicate that closure of the Land-Cut area occurred hundreds of years ago. Even in the more vegetated area of northern Padre Island, the island has slowly migrated into the Laguna Madre, particularly during periods of drought and overgrazing, which exposed bare sand (Prouty and Prouty 1989).

Certain distinctive mainland features also relate to geological development of the area: the Río Grande Delta; the Arroyo Colorado Delta; clay dunes; wind-tidal flats; the South Texas Eolian Sand Sheet; beach rock (coquina) at Penascal Point and Punta Piedras; and serpulid reefs in Baffin Bay.

Río Grande Delta   The predominant feature of the South Texas and northeastern Mexico shoreline is the bulge caused by the Río Grande Delta. This segment of the coast occupies more than 1,550 km^2 (600 mi^2) of deltaic plain in Texas and Mexico over what were formerly shallow waters of the Laguna Madre and inner continental shelf (Lohse 1958). This highly complex segment of coast forms a unique system of meander streams, oxbow lakes (resacas), playa lakes, wetlands, mudflats, lomas, and clay dunes (plates 15, 16). Some of these features, like Bahía Grande, Laguna Larga, and San Martín Lake, are remnants of the Laguna Madre (LeBlanc and Hodgson 1959). Little is known of the biology and ecology of these habitats.

Sediment discharge from the Río Grande has continually diminished during the past 4,500 years, and during the past 50 to 60 years, discharge has almost ceased due to extensive irrigation and dam construction along the river and its main tributaries (Brown et al. 1980). Consequently, the modern Río Grande Delta is undergoing erosion, and South Padre Island and Laguna Madre are retreating landward over the subsiding delta. Coring, seismic studies, and carbon-14 dating conservatively indicate that the delta shoreline stood about 16 km (10 mi) gulfward of the present shoreline 3,500 YBP (Morton and Pieper 1975; McGowen et al. 1977). The current prognosis for this area is continued subsidence and gradual retreat of the Gulf and mainland shoreline (Brown et al. 1980).

Arroyo Colorado   The highly irregular western Laguna Madre shoreline in the vicinity of the Arroyo Colorado is attributed to the earlier drainage and deposition of this system into the area as well as to current erosional and depositional processes. Although most waters of the Arroyo Colorado flow into the Laguna Madre via the dredged Arroyo Colorado Cut-Off, floodwaters from the northern and western part of the Río Grande Valley flow via the North Floodway into the old Arroyo Colorado Delta area. A faint or remnant bird's-foot delta can still be observed in this area on geologic/environmental maps and aerial photographs (Brown et al. 1980). Additional sediments are added via Cayo Atascosa, which drains Laguna Atascosa within the Laguna Atascosa Wildlife Refuge, although flow is minimal due to small dams on the drainage system. The complexity of the shoreline here is due to continued compaction and subsidence of deltaic sediments, erosion of remnant deltaic deposits, and the formation by deposition of wind-blown clay dunes.

Distinctive clay-sand dunes, such as Yucca Island, Horse Island, Hawk Island, Mullet Island, and numerous unnamed dunes exist on wind-tidal flats in this area of the Laguna Madre. Furthermore, several true islands within the waters of the Laguna Madre, such as Three Islands, Rattlesnake Island, and Green Island, were formed on these western wind-tidal flats but were subsequently isolated by subsidence of the flats beneath lagoonal waters (Brown et al. 1980). "Islands" on the wind-tidal flats on the lagoon side of southern Padre Island—La Punta Larga, Los Bancos de en Medio, and Deer Island—are thought to have a similar origin (McGowen et al. 1977).

Clay Dunes   Well-developed clay dunes are present all along the South Texas coast, from St. Charles Bay (28° 13′ N) southward into northeastern Mexico, along the coast of Tamaulipas to Rancho Tepehauje (23° 30′ N), about 24 km (15 mi) south of the Río Soto la Marina at La Pesca (Price 1933; Huffman and Price 1949; Price and Kornicker 1961). As unique depositional structures, they were first described in the Port Isabel area of South Texas (Coffey 1909). Like their more common and better known sandy counterparts (sand dunes), clay dunes are formed when blowing clay particles or pellets accumulate as topographic features downwind of saline flats. Clay dunes, however, only form in dry climates (dry subhumid to semiarid). Although known from a few dry inland areas in the western United States and southwestern Australia, clay dunes are most widespread and best known from coastal South Texas and Tamaulipas in the western Gulf of Mexico (Huffman and Price 1949; Price and Kornicker 1961). Like Padre Island, the longest barrier island in the world, and Laguna Madre, the largest hypersaline system in the world, clay dunes are possibly more extensive here than in any other coastal region of the world.

Clay dunes in the Laguna Madre region of Texas and Tamaulipas are even-topped, ridge-shaped eolian deposits that form on the lee, or northwest, side of clay-floored saline playas or wind-tidal flats (Price and Kornicker 1961). Dunes grow primarily with the strong southeast winds but only during the drier months of the year when the soil is not wet (plate 17). In South Texas dune growth extends from March through November but is most active during the drier months of the summer and during droughts. Growth is arrested during the winter with precipitation associated with northers and with reduced evaporation (Huffman and Price 1949). The highest clay dunes, at 10.7 m (35 ft), are located in the Río Grande Delta area, becoming lower in elevation (1 m [3 ft]) in the more humid climates to the north and south. Erosion of these structures occurs during heavy rainfall and hurricane storm surges with associated wave action.

The distribution of clay dunes in South Texas can be observed easily on the "environmental geology" maps of the Kingsville area (Brown et al. 1977) and the Brownsville-Harlingen area (Brown et al. 1980) in the *Environmental Geologic Atlases.* The most extensive area of clay dunes exists as a transition zone, or western border, between the wind-tidal flats and uplands between Baffin Bay through the entire Land-Cut (plates 18, 19). Other concentrations are in the Río Grande and Arroyo Colorado deltas. Inland, throughout the coastal zone, clay-sand dunes are widely scattered on the South Texas Eolian Sand Sheet, primarily associated with saline ponds or playas. A typical clay dune profile overlying the Pleistocene Beaumont Clay is illustrated in figure 3.4 (Huffman and Price 1949).

In addition to being unique depositional features, clay dunes have importance in archaeology, paleoecology, and plant distribution. Archaeological evidence (Price 1958), consisting of shell middens, indicates that early human occupants of the South Texas coastal area may have favored habitation on clay dunes at times, perhaps due to elevated viewing of the surrounding area and adjacent lagoonal location. The presence of dwarf surfclam *(Mulinia lateralis)*, a widespread and common lagoonal clam, interbedded in clay at 2.4 to 10.0 m (8–33 ft) above sea level in clay dunes near Laguna Vista in South Texas demonstrates the interrelationship of wind and the adjacent lagoon on the depositional history of the area (Price and Kornicker 1961). Finally, certain plants such as saltbush *(Atriplex* spp.) prefer the clayey, salty soils of clay dunes. Kleberg saltbush *(Atriplex klebergorum),* located on clay dunes in Kleberg

Fig. 3.4. Profile section across typical clay dune overlying Pleistocene Beaumont Clay. Top figure, vertically exaggerated; bottom, to scale (Modified from Huffman and Price 1949)

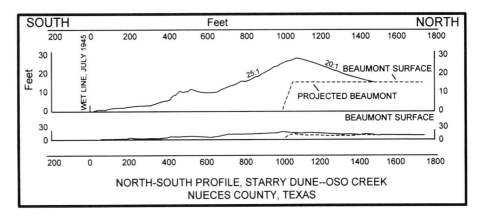

County along Baffin Bay, is apparently found only in this specific habitat and is listed as rare because of a limited distribution in this habitat and only in Kleberg County.

Wind-Tidal Flats   Like clay dunes, wind-tidal flats are unique and widespread within the Laguna Madre of Texas. These broad, low tidal flats developed over the past several thousand years and cover an area of over 900 km² (350 mi²) along the margins of Laguna Madre and Baffin Bay and in the Río Grande Delta (Brown et al. 1976, 1977, 1980). The regional semiarid climate and the hypersaline and microtidal characteristics of the waters are all necessary ingredients for producing these extensive flats.

Wind-tidal flats on the eastern side of Laguna Madre are primarily composed of sand washed or blown lagoonward from Padre Island (plate 20). Western or mainland side wind-tidal flats, on the other hand, developed where wind deflation extensively eroded the shoreline. Therefore, they are mainly clay in composition (plate 21). The broad embayment or indention into the mainland along the western edge of the Land-Cut, clearly visible on both maps and satellite images of the area (see fig. 2.2, plate 2), is a unique and graphic demonstration of the immensity of wind deflation that has taken place in this area. The largest and most extensive flats are located in the Land-Cut area, on the lagoon side of southern Padre Island from the Land-Cut southward, and in the mainland area around the Arroyo Colorado Delta. In Tamaulipas, tidal flats are most common leeward of the four tidal inlets (Boca Santa María, Boca San Rafael, Boca Ciega, and Boca Sandoval) in the northern Laguna, and also in the area of the Río San Fernando Delta, termed El Carrizal flats by Hildebrand (1980). Most early studies focused on the geology or geological processes of the tidal flats (Price 1933; Fisk 1959). Later interest focused on the geochemistry of the flats (Amdurer and Land 1982; Long and Gudramovics 1983). Until the 1970s, these wind-tidal flats were considered of little ecological value, but studies in recent decades have shown that they have multiple ecological values and functions as well as linkages to surrounding habitats. Chapter 9 is therefore dedicated to the wind-tidal flats of the Laguna Madre.

South Texas Eolian Sand Sheet (Coastal Sand Plain)   The predominant sand ridge that extends along the mainland coast today from Matagorda Bay to Baffin Bay has been interpreted as a former shoreline, representing a sea level high-stand during the Sangamon Interglacial Stage. This large sand body, which averages about 4.8 km (3 mi) wide and occupies a major portion of the peninsulas parallel to the Texas Coastal Bend, extends along the western margin of the northernmost upper Laguna Madre. Although interpreted differently—as either a barrier island (Price 1933) or barrier strand plain (Wilkinson et al. 1975)—this Ingleside Barrier (Price 1933) represents a system similar to our present-day landscape. Further, it has been suggested that several parallel water bodies and lowland flats behind the barrier represent a former lagoonal system (Ingleside Lagoon). The parallel-to-the-coast orientation of Copano Bay, Port Bay, Oso Bay, Laguna Larga (a freshwater lake south of Corpus Christi on the King Ranch), and Alazan Bay all seem to support this concept. The extensive coastal sacahuiste flats (mainly gulf cordgrass *[Spartina spartinae]* flats; plate 22) occupy the ancient, infilled Ingleside Lagoon and now form the Ingleside Terrace (Price 1933).

During the Holocene, the South Texas climate became progressively more arid, and persistent southeasterly wind systems began to develop (Brown et al. 1977). Eolian (wind) deflation or erosion of coastal plain sediments began and increased with intensity. The old Ingleside Barrier south of Baffin Bay was blown inland, along with sands from Padre Island, to form the South Texas Eolian Sand Sheet (Price 1933) or system (Brown et al. 1977). Additionally, this area is located at a convergence of longshore drift due to winds (creating waves) and a bend in the coastline (Watson 1971; McGowen et al. 1977). The area has probably been a location of excessive sand accumulation for tens of thousands of years or more. Today this vast sand sheet covers parts of five counties, from Baffin Bay in the north to the Río Grande Delta in the south and extending approximately 120 km (75 mi) inland. Recently, due to the unique soil and vegetative characteristics of the sand sheet, researchers have suggested that it deserves recognition as a unique area of rangeland, the Coastal Sand Plain of southern Texas (Fulbright et al. 1990). The extensive barren and vegetated sand dunes, and especially the widespread banner dune complexes (plate 23) within the region, certainly mark this area as unique (Price 1958; Brown et al 1977, 1980).

In Tamaulipas, Behrens (1966) suggested that an ancient beach ridge, located on the southward-projecting peninsula (south of Carbajal) enclosing the northern part of Laguna el Catán, is the same geologic structure as the Ingleside Barrier deposits of Price (1933). The orientation of Laguna el Catán parallel to this ridge and the coastline possibly represents an extension of the old Ingleside Lagoon of Price (1933) and adds support to Behrens's contention.

Beach Rock (Coquina)   Beach rock (coquina) outcrops discontinuously along the mainland shoreline of Laguna Madre from Baffin Bay at Penascal Point southward for approximately 10 km (6 mi) (Prouty 1996; plate 24, left). This beach rock correlates with the Ingleside Barrier already mentioned (Price 1933) and represents the only lithified bedrock exposure along the South Texas coast. Additionally, it contains well-developed late Pleistocene–early Holocene karst features (solution pipes and caliche crusts), unknown elsewhere on the Texas coast (Prouty and Lovejoy 1992; Prouty 1996). The coquina appears to have accumulated in a localized zone of converging longshore Gulf of Mexico currents along a Gulf beach, similar to Little Shell and Big Shell today on Padre Island (Watson 1971). Carbon dating and karst features provide evidence of regional late Pleistocene–early Holocene climate changes from more humid during the Wisconsin sea level low-stand 18,000 YBP to more arid at the commencement of the Holocene approximately 11,000 YBP (Prouty 1996). The beach rock in this location extends as scattered rocks seaward of the shoreline (Prouty 1996) and forms part of the shallow sill across the mouth of Baffin Bay (Rusnak 1960). It has been suggested that this sill has restricted water circulation and caused elevated salinities higher than in upper Laguna Madre in the past (Collier and Hedgpeth 1950), before dredging of the GIWW and a Baffin Bay channel.

In Tamaulipas, the beach rock outcrop at Punta Piedras (Yañez and Schlaepfer

1968) located at the tip of the northern peninsula enclosing Laguna el Catán in the southern Laguna Madre (plate 24, right), probably correlates with the Penascal Point coquina. Shelly beach sediments, similar to Little Shell on Padre Island, begin just south of Boca Jesús María, on the Gulf beach opposite Punta Piedras, and extend southward to the Río Soto la Marina (J. W. Tunnell, pers. observ.). Additionally, some scattered coquina is located in places along this stretch of beach.

The lagoonal beach rock in Texas and Tamaulipas provides natural hard substrate habitat that is rare in both systems. Serpulid worm reefs provide another natural hard substrate.

Serpulid Reefs   Relict serpulid worm reefs exist in a scattered distribution around Baffin Bay (Breuer 1957; Andrews 1964; Behrens 1974; Cole 1981; Hardegree 1997). These reef rock structures are composed of the calcareous external tubes of serpulid polychaetes (Phylum Annelida, marine segmented worms), which no longer live in the area. These remnant skeletal structures indicate a past less saline environment for these colonial, suspension-feeding marine or estuarine organisms. Although some living serpulid worms are found on the reefs today (Cole 1981; Hardegree 1997), they no longer build reef structure in the hypersaline environment. Two different types of serpulid reefs are recognized within the shallow waters of Baffin Bay: patch reefs and reef fields (Andrews 1964). They are predominantly found along bay margins, but some are distributed across the mouths of Baffin and Alazan bays. Patch reefs are small, isolated structures, whereas reef fields are comparatively large expanses of reef rock. These reef rock areas provide rare natural rocky habitat in this typically soft substrate region. Many of these structures are undergoing degradation from being hit by outboard motors driven by uninformed or unknowing boaters in the area, causing a reduction of this unique habitat (Hardegree 1997).

Geology

The Laguna Madre of Texas is a linear, coastal lagoon that developed on the pre-Holocene (Pleistocene) erosional surface by the buildup and enclosure of a barrier island, Padre Island (Rusnak 1960). The sediment buildup and lagoonal enclosure were caused by the slowing of postglacial rise in sea level. The Holocene deposits average 3 to 6 m (10 to 20 ft) in thickness, although low areas in the Pleistocene surface may have much thicker deposits. The majority of the Holocene sediments consist of fine sands (Rusnak 1960). Sands are more common in the shallow eastern lagoon near the barrier island, where storm surges and southeasterly winds are filling the lagoon, and clays and silts are more common along the mainland western shore and in the west-central basins. The Laguna Madre de Tamaulipas is characterized as a Gilbert–de Beaumont Barrier Lagoon (Lankford 1977), which has the same or similar features and processes (Yañez and Schlaepfer 1968). Figure 3.5 shows two generalized cross sections of Padre Island from the Gulf of Mexico into the Laguna Madre, demonstrating the thicker island and lagoonal sediments north of Mansfield Pass compared to the thinner sediments to the south of La Punta Larga.

In addition to the generalized geological setting given here, as well as some of the geomorphic features and processes given earlier in this chapter, there are several other geochemical processes occurring in the Laguna Madre of Texas that are unique to the region. Two of these are quiet-water oolite formation and gypsum crystal formation. Oolites (laminated accretionary grains of calcium carbonate) are forming on the Laguna Madre shoreline just north of the Point of Rocks at the mouth of Baffin Bay (Shepard and Rusnak 1957; Rusnak 1958, 1960; Freeman 1962) and near two submerged sand bars between Baffin Bay and Padre Island (Behrens 1966). The

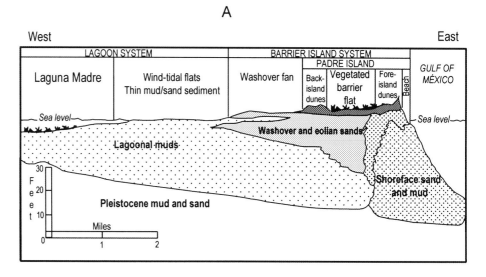

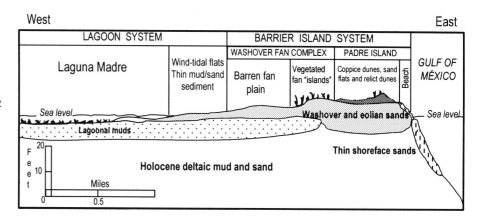

Fig. 3.5. *Generalized cross sections of Padre Island barrier system: (A) Central Padre Island north of Mansfield Channel exhibits 9 m (30 ft) of Modern barrier island sand; (B) South Padre Island between La Punta Larga and Brazos Santiago Pass illustrates the thin, sand-deficient character of the island. In the south the island rests upon Holocene Río Grande deltaic sediments. The poorly developed barrier south of La Punta Larga is susceptible to extensive breaching by hurricane tidal surge. (Modified from Brown et al. 1980)*

quiet-water shoal areas defied the classic theory that water agitation was necessary to form the distinctive accretionary layers of oolites. High energy does seem essential for the development of symmetrical oolites, but the rough, irregular, oolites found in Laguna Madre suggest that agitation is not critical for the accretionary development of carbonate coatings on grains.

Bladelike crystals and rosettes—that is, clusters of crystals resembling a rose—composed of the mineral gypsum (calcium sulfate) are unique structures found in the wind-tidal flats of Laguna Madre in Texas (Weise and White 1980). They have been found on both sides of the GIWW in the Land-Cut area as well as along Mansfield Channel. Crystals apparently form when high salinity waters periodically flood the wind-tidal flats and seep into the underlying sediments. These mineral-laden waters precipitate gypsum, forming the crystals, which grow larger with each successive flooding, infiltration, and precipitation (Masson 1955). When channels are dredged across the flats, the crystals, along with other dredge material, are deposited in piles. In time, wind and rain erode the sediments away, leaving the crystals and rosettes exposed on the surface. Three different types have been observed: clear amber-colored blades/crystals; gray sand-textured blades/crystals (plate 25); and small, light-colored, sand-textured rosettes. The clear forms and smaller rosettes have been found on dredged material deposits along oil field channels of the Land-Cut, and the larger gray forms, presumably created in a hydrogen sulfide environment that produced the grayish color, have been found in dredged material along the Mansfield Channel as well as in the Land-Cut (J. W. Tunnell, pers. observ.).

As demonstrated briefly here but far more extensively by many publications of the Bureau of Economic Geology, when consideration is given to conserving or preserving coastal natural resources, it is imperative to consider geologic history and process. The origin and development of the coastal zone, as well as the current physical processes affecting the area, can help determine the probable success or failure of proposed efforts. There is great variety in Laguna Madre and Padre Island features. Variability results from such factors as Pleistocene depositional and erosional history, sand availability, climatic conditions, density of vegetation, water circulation, sediment transport, and others (McGowen et al. 1977). When human activities are superimposed upon the natural landscape, the long-term dynamic balance tips toward disequilibrium. Coastal processes that have interacted for thousands of years to create the coastal features can become agents of destruction. Therefore, understanding these processes is imperative to regional coastal planning and management.

Coastal problems caused by interrupting natural geologic processes have been clearly elucidated in the three *Environmental Geologic Atlases* covering the Laguna Madre in Texas (Brown et al. 1976, 1977, 1980). Observations of the effects of increased development are presented, and recommendations for orderly development compatible with the capacity and capability of natural systems are suggested. Interestingly, many of the recommendations given some 20 years ago—about how to proceed in an orderly fashion on such items as channelization, devegetation, shoreline construction, waste disposal, filling and land reclamation, artificial passes, and natural catastrophes—are still largely ignored today. Reasons for not following these guidelines are unclear but may include lack of communication between scientists and decision makers or perhaps a lack of enforcement or dollars for implementation.

4   *Tamaulipan Biotic Province*

FRANK W. JUDD

The identification, description, and mapping of the geographic extent of biotic provinces constitute one method of organizing the biotic diversity of North America. This approach was introduced by Dice (1943). It focuses on the ranges and centers of distribution of plant and animal species in physiographic regions. As defined by Dice (1943), a biotic province is a considerable and continuous geographic area. Thus, it never occurs as discontinuous fragments. A biotic province may include more than one major ecological association. It includes freshwater communities but excludes marine communities (Dice 1943). Consequently, focus is on upland and freshwater communities in this chapter. Current scientific names are used because there have been many taxonomic changes since the publication of many of the papers cited: plant names follow Everitt and Drawe (1993), Lonard (1993a), Richardson (1995), and Everitt and colleagues (1999); amphibian and reptile names follow Dixon (2000); and mammal names follow Davis and Schmidly (1994).

Geographic Extent and Initial Characterization

Dice (1943) identified, mapped, and described 29 biotic provinces in North America. The southern boundary of the Tamaulipan Biotic Province (TBP), as mapped by Dice (1943), begins at the Río Panuco and extends northward from a line connecting Tampico and San Luis Potosí through those portions of the Mexican states of Tamaulipas, Nuevo León, and Coahuila east of the Sierra Madre Oriental into southern Texas (fig. 4.1). Dice (1943) limited the distribution of the TBP to the southern tip of Texas, but Blair (1950) extended it northward to the Balcones fault line in the north and the line separating pedocal from pedalfer soils on the northeast (fig. 4.1). This northeastern boundary marks the area where the vegetation changes from thorny brushlands to prairie and oak-hickory "alternes" (Blair 1950) and is about at the San Antonio River. Throughout its length the Gulf of Mexico forms the eastern boundary of the province.

Alvarez (1963) draws the southern U-shaped boundary of the TBP in Tamaulipas beginning in the southeast at La Pesca, 180 km (112 mi) north of Tampico, and looping down to Acuña and Santa Isabel at the bottom then northward to Ciudad Victoria in the southwest (fig. 4.2). Regardless of whether the southern boundary is drawn at Soto la Marina (Alvarez 1963) or at Tampico (Dice 1943), all of the Laguna Madre of Texas and Mexico is included in the TBP.

Dice (1943) pointed out that most of the province is confined to the Gulf Coastal Plain, but he also emphasized that it includes numerous rolling hills, some limestone ridges, and a few mountains. The highest are the San Carlos Mountains in Tamaulipas (fig. 4.1), which rise to an elevation of about 1,524 m (5,029 ft).

Dice (1943) states that generally biotic provinces are characterized by peculiarities of vegetation type, ecological climax, flora, fauna, climate, physiography, and soil. In his brief description of the TBP, the province is said to be characterized by a dense

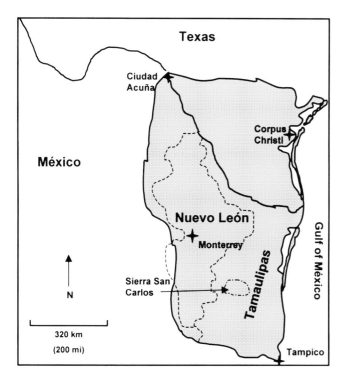

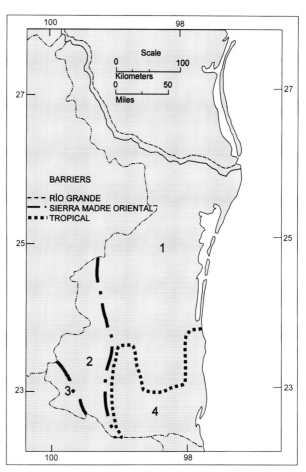

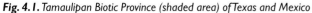

Fig. 4.1. Tamaulipan Biotic Province (shaded area) of Texas and Mexico

Fig. 4.2. Four biotic provinces of Tamaulipas, Mexico, recognized by Alvarez (1963): 1 = Tamaulipan; 2 = Potosian; 3 = Chihuahuan; 4 = Veracruzian

growth of shrubs and small trees (Dice 1943). The absence of true forest, except on mountains, is attributed to the limestone substrate, which does not hold moisture well, and to high summer temperatures that produce high evaporation. The Gulf Coastal Plain portion of the province is reported to be characterized by a dense growth of thorny shrubs and numerous cacti. The foothills of the Sierra San Carlos also support thorny shrubs as the dominant life form, but the species comprising the vegetation are different from those of the coastal plain. The upper elevations of the mountains are said to support an oak and pine forest (Dice 1937). Blair (1950) reports that thorny brush is the dominant life form in the vegetation of the TBP in Texas.

Dice (1943) says little about the fauna of the TBP but cites Allen (1892, 1893), Nelson and Goldman (1926), and Dice (1937) for mammals and birds characteristic of the region. Smith (1939) is cited as reporting typical reptiles. Dice (1943) notes that the fauna and flora of the TBP contain many Central American and South American elements, citing parrots and palms as examples of these. Mammals that range little north of the province are said to include the white-nosed coati *(Nasua narica)*, jaguar *(Felis onca)*, jaguarundi *(Felis yagouaroundi)*, Mexican spiny pocket mouse *(Liomys irroratus)*, nine-banded armadillo *(Dasypus novemcinctus)*, and collared peccary *(Tayassu tajacu)*. We now know that the latter two species extend beyond the TBP in Texas. Additional information on the vertebrate fauna of the TBP is provided in a later section of this chapter.

Climatic Factors Climate is a crucial aspect in the designation of a biotic province (Dice 1943; Blair 1950). Climate of this area is covered in detail in chapter

2, but it is addressed briefly here to help clarify the nature of the TBP. Blair (1950) pointed out that the climate of the TBP is semiarid and megathermal. This means that temperature is sufficiently high to support plant growth throughout the year, but at times there is insufficient moisture to permit growth.

Southeasterly winds from the Gulf of Mexico prevail in every month except December, when a northwest wind is common. The average relative humidity at Brownsville, Texas (about midway through the province on a north-south axis), at 6:00 A.M. ranges from 85% in December to 90% in July, with an annual average of 88%. This high relative humidity causes fairly heavy dew even during drought years. Dense fogs are common at night from December through March. Precipitation is highest near the Gulf of Mexico and decreases westward. For example, in the northeastern corner of the province, total annual precipitation is 91 cm (35.8 in) and in the northwestern corner it is 51 cm (20.1 in). The normal annual rainfall at Brownsville, Texas, is 68.2 cm (26.9 in), and the peak of precipitation occurs in September and October (Lonard et al. 1991). About one-third of the total annual rainfall occurs during this period. Sixty-nine percent of the annual rainfall is received during the six-month period from May through October. This division corresponds closely with the "rainy season" that prevails in the tropics of eastern and central Mexico. Most precipitation results from thunderstorms, and often a single thunderstorm accounts for an entire month's rainfall.

Temperatures in summer and early fall are fairly constant in the middle 30s (°C) during the day and middle 20s (°C) at night. Freezes occur on a regular basis in the northern portion of the province, but from the Lower Río Grande Valley southward the mean length of the frost-free period is 330 to 365 days.

Subdivisons in Texas

In Texas, the Tamaulipan Biotic Province is bounded to the north by the Balconian Biotic Province and to the northeast by the Texan Biotic Province (fig. 4.3). Blair (1950) subdivided the TBP into two districts, the Matamoran Biotic District and the Nuecian Biotic District (fig. 4.3). The Matamoran Biotic District was separated from the Nuecian because of the unique flora and fauna of the Lower Río Grande

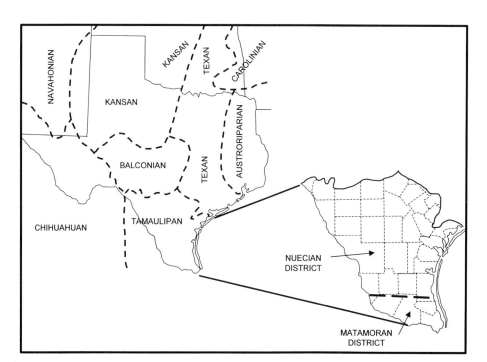

Fig. 4.3. The approximate boundaries of biotic provinces in Texas and biotic districts of the Tamaulipan Biotic Province in Texas

Valley of Texas (Cameron, Hidalgo, Starr, and Willacy counties). The extent of the Matamoran Biotic District in Mexico has not been delineated, and no subdivisions of the province have been named in Mexico.

Matamoran Biotic District   The Matamoran Biotic District as defined by Blair (1950) corresponds to the Lower Río Grande Valley of Texas (Lonard et al. 1991). Clover (1937) and Johnston (1955, 1963) have discussed the vegetation of the entire area in considerable detail. Blair (1950, 1952) provided an overview and identified important woody species. Judd and coworkers (1977), Lonard and coworkers (1978), and Lonard and Judd (1980) reported on the flora and vegetation of South Padre Island. Davis (1942) discussed the vegetation of Texas palmetto groves in Cameron County. Based on this information, Lonard and colleagues (1991) partitioned the natural vegetation of the Lower Río Grande Valley into four major habitats: River Floodplain, Coastal Prairies and Marshes, Barrier Islands, and Brush-Grasslands.

Blair (1952) briefly described the vegetation at four sites in the Matamoran Biotic District. About 10 km (6 mi) south of McAllen, Hidalgo County, Texas, the dominant plants were large cedar elms *(Ulmus crassifolia)* mixed with various thorny brush species including Texas ebony *(Chloroleucon ebano)*, granjeno *(Celtis pallida)*, mesquite *(Prosopis glandulosa)*, huisache *(Acacia minuata)*, and retama *(Parkinsonia aculeata)*. Texas prickly pear *(Opuntia engelmannii)* was scarce and confined primarily to disturbed areas.

At La Gloria Ranch, 27 km (17 mi) northwest of Edinburg, Hidalgo County, Texas, near the northern limit of the district, Blair (1952) reported the principal brush species to be mesquite, granjeno, retama, Texas ebony, Texas silverleaf *(Leucophyllum frutescens)*, guayacan *(Guaiacum angustifolium)*, goatbush *(Castela texana)*, huisache, common lantana *(Lantana horrida)*, lime pricklyash *(Zanthoxylum fagara)*, anacahuita *(Cordia boissieri)*, desert yaupon *(Schaefferia cuneifolia)*, leatherstem *(Jatropha dioica)*, and coyotillo *(Karwinskia humboldtiana)*. The most common grass was red grama *(Bouteloua trifida)*. He noted that the soil was sandy at this site. On another site with deep, loose sandy soil, about 16 km (10 mi) northwest of Raymondville, dense thickets of brush and prickly pear and savanna-like clumps of mesquite were scattered over grasslands dominated by threeawn *(Aristida* spp.). Just west of Port Isabel, Cameron County, Texas, on a black clay soil, the principal plant species were gulf cordgrass *(Spartina spartinae)* and goatbush.

Brush-Grasslands   This vegetation type extends throughout the upland areas away from the river and the coast. It is the most widespread habitat in the Matamoran Biotic District. The vegetation is characterized by a great variety of low trees, shrubs, cacti, and yuccas of variable density with small grassy areas in open sites (Lonard et al. 1991). Species richness is due to the overlap of western desert, northern plains, and tropical floras. Presence or absence of woody species is largely determined by soil and moisture conditions. The communities are usually stratified into an overstory of species such as mesquite, huisache, or Texas ebony, with an almost impenetrable understory that includes Texas silverleaf, coyotillo, granjeno, guajillo *(Acacia berlandieri)*, guayacan, common lantana, leatherstem, lime pricklyash, lotebush *(Ziziphus obtusifolia)*, narrowleaf forestiera *(Forestiera angustifolia)*, border paloverde *(Parkinsonia texana* var. *macra)*, prickly pear, anacahuita, and blackbrush *(Acacia rigidula)*. On sandy to gravelly soils where drainage is good, numerous cacti are present. Prominent species include pencil cactus *(Opuntia leptocaulis)*, prickly pear, pitaya *(Echinocereus enneacanthus)*, lace echinocereus *(Echinocereus reichenbachii)*, hedgehog cactus *(Ferrocactus setispinus)*, and pichilinga *(Mammillaria heyderi* var. *hemisphaerica)*. In areas transected by arroyos, shrubs usually are larger near the banks where water stands after rains. Huisache and retama are often abundant in these places. In areas of deep sands, grasses are more abundant and the vegetation is usually a savanna type with large mesquite scattered in small clumps (mottes) or occurring as single individuals. Areas such as irrigation- and drainage-canal banks, railroad rights-of-way, and highway rights-of-way typically support a dense cover of buffelgrass *(Pennisetum ciliare)*. Buffelgrass is introduced from India and is widely planted in "improved" pastures. It establishes quickly in cleared areas and becomes dominant.

River Floodplain   Vegetation of the river floodplain includes riparian forest along the banks of the river and along resaca banks. Dominant species may be cedar elm, mesquite, Texas ebony, sugar hackberry *(Celtis laevigata)*, anacua *(Ehretia anacua)*, or a combination of two or more of these species. Perhaps the most important community in the eastern section of the river floodplain is the native Texas palmetto *(Sabal texana)*.

Blair (1950) stated that characteristic plant species of the Matamoran Biotic District included retama, Texas ebony, anacahuita, and anacua. He noted that cedar elm was dominant in the floodplain forest of the Río Grande at some localities, and at others there was an alternation of cedar elm and brush species. Blair (1950) reported that Texas palmetto reached its northern limit at Southmost, below Brownsville on the Río Grande, but Lockett and Read (1990) found an isolated population in Jackson County on the central coast of Texas.

Shelford (1974) includes the Matamoran Biotic District in the Southern Temperate Grassland Biome and maps the vegetation as an acacia-grassland community. Odum (1971) recognized the "Broad-leaved Evergreen Forest" as a distinct biome that is represented in the hammocks of Florida and in the live oak forests along the Gulf and South Atlantic coasts of the United States. Benson (1979) characterized the vegetation of the southern portion of this biome as the "American Subtropical Flora" and stated that this vegetation is represented in the United States chiefly in the hammocks and everglades of southern Florida and to a slight extent in the swampy regions along the Gulf of Mexico, particularly near Brownsville, Texas. Odum (1971) reported that palms such as sabal or cabbage palm are often prominent members of the community and that vines and epiphytes are characteristically present.

The Texas palmetto community has been recognized as distinct by Clover (1937), Davis (1942), Odum (1971), Benson (1979), and Diamond and colleagues (1987). In 1852 stands of Texas palmetto extended along the Río Grande from a point near its mouth to about 130 km (81 mi) inland from the Gulf of Mexico (Clover 1937). By the late 1930s, clearing for agriculture had reduced the extent of this palm forest in the United States to a small reach of the Río Grande from a point 16 km (10 mi) below Brownsville, Cameron County, Texas, upriver 6.4 km (4 mi) (Clover 1937). The most extensive growth of palms was at Rabb Ranch, located approximately 16 km (10 mi) southeast of Brownsville at a bend where the river reaches its southernmost point (Clover 1937; Davis 1942). A 70 ha (172 ac) tract of the ranch was purchased by the Audubon Society in 1971 to establish the Sabal Palm Grove Sanctuary. Today about 13 ha (32 ac) of palm forest are present with the remaining land consisting of abandoned farm fields.

Clover (1937) included the Boscaje de la Palma as a coastal climax association of the Lower Río Grande Valley of Texas. She pointed out that this is one of only four arborescent palm communities in the continental United States outside Florida, the other three being located in the southeastern Atlantic area, the Mississippi Delta area, and the southern California desert. Clover (1937) provided a list of 81 species associated with the Texas palmetto community. Davis (1942) focused on the Boscaje de la Palma in Cameron County, Texas, and she also provided a description of the distribution of Texas palmetto in the Río Grande Delta area. Diamond and col-

leagues (1987) recognized the "Texas Palmetto Series" (dominated by Texas palmetto) as a distinct late seral-stage forest in Texas, and they identified it as endangered. Indeed, it was one of only three communities (of 78) in Texas to be listed as endangered. The Texas Organization for Endangered Species (Carr et al. 1993) considers Texas palmetto a threatened species in the state.

Everitt and colleagues (1996) used remote sensing and spatial information technologies to map Texas palmetto in the Lower Río Grande Valley. Future censuses may be compared with their map (and imagery) to quantify changes in population densities. The map may also prove useful to resource managers in identifying land for acquisition for conservation and reestablishment of Texas palmettos. For example, the map may be useful in assessing the feasibility of developing corridors connecting presently fragmented populations.

Resacas are often selected as sites for housing developments, but native vegetation remains along the banks of many such sites. Important woody species include retama, huisache, Texas ebony, black willow *(Salix nigra)*, and black mimosa *(Mimosa pigra)*.

In the western section of the river floodplain, important woody species along the banks of the Río Grande that are subject to flooding include: huisache, black willow, retama, sugar hackberry, and Mexican ash. Floodwaters disturb or destroy the smaller vegetation along the river, leaving stretches of deep sand. These stretches are often covered by almost pure stands of groundsel tree *(Baccharis* spp.). On terraces that are rarely flooded, the dominant woody species are huisache, mesquite, and granjeno.

Nuecian Biotic District Blair (1952) listed the plant communities of the Nuecian Biotic District: (1) live oak-dominated; (2) mesquite-cactus; (3) mesquite savanna with the grasses red threeawn *(Aristida purpurea* var. *longiseta)*, hairy grama *(Bouteloua hirsuta)*, and hooded windmillgrass *(Chloris cucullata)*; (4) sugar hackberry-retama-blackbrush; (5) creosote bush *(Larrea tridentata)*–prickly pear; (6) a mixed community containing mesquite, granjeno, guayacan, bluewood *(Condalia hookeri)*, leatherstem, and mountain laurel *(Sophora secundiflora)*; (7) a mixed community containing mesquite, granjeno, huisache, guayacan, Texas silverleaf, common beebush *(Aloysia gratissima)*, and Texas ebony; and (8) a community in which la coma *(Bumelia celastrina)* is the characteristic tree, with red grama as the dominant grass.

Jones (1975) published on the flora (exclusive of grasses) of the Texas Coastal Bend, which includes the northeastern portion of the Nuecian Biotic District. Gould and Box (1965) published the companion volume on the grasses of the Texas Coastal Bend, and Gould (1975) published the *Grasses of Texas.* Jones (1975) reports that at the time of initial settlement by European peoples (about 1800), this area was largely treeless prairie that varied from flat and poorly drained to undulate or rolling. Grasses prevailed, but there were nongrassy herbs and probably a scattering of shrubs including mesquite and prickly pear. Trees were generally scarce but occurred wherever there was a steady supply of moisture. There were extensive woods along the Nueces and San Antonio rivers and smaller wooded areas along the Mission and Aransas rivers. Tree species Jones (1975) identifies as dominants are consistent with extant communities identified in the South Texas Plains and Gulf Prairies and Marshes vegetation areas discussed in considerable detail in a later section of this chapter.

Plant Communities and Characteristic Plant Species

Blair (1950) identified the species characteristic of thorny brush communities throughout the TBP in Texas as mesquite, various species of *Acacia, Mimosa,* and *Condalia,* granjeno, guayacan, Texas silverleaf, common beebush, prickly pear, pencil cactus, and goatbush.

Coastal marshes dominated by gulf cordgrass were identified by Blair (1950) as a distinct plant community. Vegetative patterns identified by Blair (1950) were:

1. From the coast westward the brush thins out (becomes sparser) as available moisture decreases.
2. The brush on sandy soils differs in species and aspect from that on clay soils. Mesquite in open stands and mixed with various grasses is characteristic of sandy soils. Clay soils support a variety of species, including mesquite.
3. The brushlands of the Lower Río Grande Valley in Cameron, Hidalgo, Starr, and Willacy counties are more luxuriant than the brushlands farther south (in Mexico) and they are characterized by several plant species that decrease in abundance northward.
4. The most luxurious brush occurs in the immediate floodplain of the Río Grande.

Gould (1969) recognized two major vegetational areas in the Texas portion of the TBP, the Gulf Prairies and Marshes and South Texas Plains. This distinction is largely based on the presence or absence of trees and shrubs. The Gulf Prairies and Marshes area is primarily grassland, whereas the South Texas Plains area is thought originally to have supported a savanna grassland. Johnston (1963) discussed the past and present grasslands of the TBP. He objected to allegations that woody vegetation had encroached on grassland in southern Texas and particularly that the brush species had invaded from Mexico. He maintained that the brush species already occupied their present ranges when the first collector visited the region in 1828. Johnston (1963) emphasized that many grasslands were infested with mesquite long ago but that the growth of mesquite was stunted due to recurrent fires. He argued that the rapid takeover of the mesquite brush resulted from fire control and involved increase in the stature of the aerial parts of the plant and increase in density of stands, rather than invasion by mesquite into previously brushless areas.

McMahan and colleagues (1984) followed Gould (1969) in recognizing two major ecological areas in southern Texas—the Gulf Prairies and Marshes and the South Texas Plains (fig. 4.4). Within these two ecological areas 12 "vegetation types," excluding crops, were recognized (table 4.1). The Laguna Madre is bordered throughout its length by communities of the Gulf Prairies and Marshes ecological area. Consequently, we focus attention on these barrier island and mainland communities that border on the Laguna Madre. The Marsh–Barrier Island Vegetation Type occurs on the eastern margin of the Laguna Madre, and this vegetation type and all others identified in the Gulf Prairies and Marshes ecological area (table 4.1) occur on the western margin of the Laguna Madre.

Barrier Islands   The vegetation of barrier islands bordering the eastern margin of the Laguna Madre is essentially one-layered, and species richness is relatively low compared to that on barrier islands of the Atlantic Coast of the United States. Judd and colleagues (1977) point out that the major difference between the vegetation of South Padre Island, Texas, and that of the barrier islands on the eastern coast of the United States is the absence of shrub or tree zones on South Padre Island. Virtually all species on South Padre Island are herbaceous. Mesquite and prickly pear occur on the island, but only as rare, low-growing, isolated individuals. Except for trees and shrubs planted by residents, the only conspicuous woody vegetation consists of the black mangrove (*Avicennia germinans)*, which is abundant on the margin of the Laguna Madre near the Queen Isabella Causeway. On North Padre Island there is a small grove of live oak (*Quercus virginiana)* on the Laguna Madre side of the island (Weise and White 1980).

An idealized profile of South Padre Island includes the following topographic zones and vegetation (fig. 4.5): (1) a bare foreshore zone; (2) a backshore zone with a

Table 4.1. *Vegetation types recognized by McMahan and colleagues (1984) in the Texas portion of the Tamaulipan Biotic Province (exclusive of crops)*

Vegetation Type	South Texas Plains	Gulf Prairies and Marshes
Bluestem grassland *Schizachyrium scoparium*		X
Texas silverleaf–blackbrush–creosotebush brush *Leucophyllum frutescens–Acacia rigidula–Larrea tridentata*	X	
Mesquite–blackbrush brush *Prosopis glandulosa–A. rigidula*	X	X
Mesquite–granjeno parks *P. glandulosa–Celtis pallida*	X	X
Mesquite–granjeno woods	X	
Mesquite–live oak–bluewood parks *P. glandulosa–Quercus virginiana–Condalia hookeri*	X	X
Live oak woods/parks *Q. virginiana*	X	X
Post oak woods, forest and grassland mosaic *Q. stellata*	X	
Post oak woods/forest	X	
Bald cypress–water tupelo swamp *Taxodium distichum–Nyssa aquatica*	X	
Marsh-barrier island Variety of dominants depending on salinity, substrate, and elevation		X
Native or introduced grasses Occurs where brush has been cleared	X	X

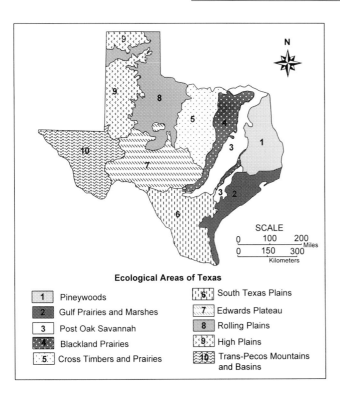

Ecological Areas of Texas

1 Pineywoods
2 Gulf Prairies and Marshes
3 Post Oak Savannah
4 Blackland Prairies
5 Cross Timbers and Prairies
6 South Texas Plains
7 Edwards Plateau
8 Rolling Plains
9 High Plains
10 Trans-Pecos Mountains and Basins

Fig. 4.4. *Vegetational areas of Texas (Adapted from Gould 1969 and McMahan et al. 1984)*

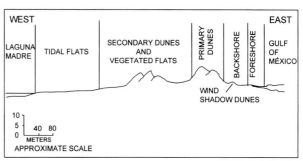

Fig. 4.5. *Transverse profile of South Padre Island, Texas, showing major topographic zones*

belt of sea purslane *(Sesuvium portulacastrum)* nearest the Gulf and a landward zone dominated by sea-oats *(Uniola paniculata)*; (3) a primary dune ridge supporting fiddleleaf morningglory *(Ipomoea imperati)* and sea-oats as dominants; (4) a zone of either secondary dunes or vegetated flats or a mosaic of both, in which seacoast bluestem *(Schizachyrium scoparium)* is dominant; and (5) a tidal flat zone that is largely bare but supports typical halophytic vegetation in a narrow zone bordering the vegetated flats. Species of importance include seashore dropseed *(Sporobolus virginicus)*, camphor daisy *(Haplopappus phyllocephalus)*, sea-lavender *(Limonium carolinianum)*, and shoregrass *(Monanthochloe littoralis)*. This profile is also typical for North Padre Island, but Weise and White (1980) use slightly different terms for the topographic zones: (1) forebeach rather than foreshore, (2) backbeach rather than backshore, (3) fore-island dunes rather than primary dunes, (4) vegetated barrier flat and back-island dunes rather than secondary dunes and vegetated flats, and (5) back-island sand flats and wind-tidal flats rather than tidal flats. Weise and White (1980) do not give dominant species in each of the topographic zones, but the lists of associated species they provide suggest that the dominants may be similar to those on South Padre Island.

Coastal Prairies and Marshes   On the Texas mainland, the vegetation of the Gulf Prairies and Marshes ecological area includes three distinct habitats (Lonard et al. 1991): salt flats, marshes, and lomas (clay dunes). Salt flats are characterized by periodic inundation by salt water from storms and high tides. The soils are very saline and are largely barren except at the margins of outwash slopes of lomas. Most of the plants are halophytic herbaceous species. Dominant species are shoregrass, saltwort *(Batis maritima)*, annual seepweed *(Suaeda linearis)*, bushy sea-ox-eye *(Borrichia frutescens)*, and glasswort *(Salicornia* spp.). Mainland coastal marshes are dominated by gulf cordgrass. A few shrubs such as mesquite, huisache, or retama may be scattered through the marsh.

Auffenberg and Weaver (1969) described the vegetation of lomas in eastern Cameron County as a chaparral association consisting of several species of thorny shrubs and low trees. Dominant woody species include lotebush, coyotillo, mesquite, and huisache. Prickly pear, pencil cactus, lime pricklyash, and Spanish dagger *(Yucca treculeana)* grow along the edges of the dense shrubs and trees and in open patches. Buffalograss *(Buchloe dactyloides)* is dominant in open areas on the top or crest of lomas. At the periphery of the slope and extending in a narrow band almost around the entire loma is a zone composed of seepwillow *(Baccharis salicifolia)* and gutta-percha *(Maytenus texana)*.

Bluestem Grassland   Bluestem grasslands occur on the Texas mainland coast between the Mission and San Antonio rivers (McMahan et al. 1984). This community is particularly manifest in Goliad, Victoria, and Refugio counties, Texas. Seacoast bluestem is dominant. Associated species include bushy bluestem *(Andropogon glomeratus)*, slender bluestem *(Schizachyrium tenerum)*, silver bluestem *(Bothriochloa laguroides* subsp. *torreyana)*, threeawn, buffalograss, bermuda grass *(Cynodon dactylon)*, brownseed paspalum *(Paspalum plicatulum)*, gulfdune paspalum *(Paspalum monostachyum)*, smutgrass *(Sporobolus indicus)*, gulf cordgrass, windmillgrass *(Chloris* spp.), and dewberry *(Rubus riograndis)*. Woody species scattered in the grassland include live oak, mesquite, huisache, and groundsel tree.

Mesquite-Blackbrush Brush   This community type occurs primarily in the South Texas Plains, but it is present in the Gulf Prairies and Marshes of Texas in Goliad, San Patricio, Nueces, Willacy, and Cameron counties (McMahan et al. 1984). A small portion of one population borders on Corpus Christi Bay, north of the mouth of the Nueces River. The dominant species are mesquite and blackbrush. Associated species include lotebush, Texas silverleaf, guajillo, narrowleaf forestiera, allthorn *(Koeberlinia spinosa)*, common beebush, bluewood, granjeno, guayacan, leatherstem, prickly pear, pencil cactus, Texas kidneywood *(Eysenhardtia texana)*, yucca *(Yucca* spp.), desert yaupon, goatbush, purple threeawn *(Aristida purpurea* var. *purpurea)*, pink pappusgrass *(Pappophorum bicolor)*, tridens *(Tridens* spp.), slim tridens *(Tridens muticus* var. *muticus)*, hairy grama *(Bouteloua hirsuta)*, mat euphorbia *(Euphorbia serpens)*, coldenia *(Tiquilia* spp.), common dogweed *(Thymophylla pentachaeta)*, knotweed leaf flower *(Phyllanthus polygonoides)*, and twoleaf senna *(Senna roemeriana)*.

Mesquite-Granjeno Parks Mesquite-granjeno parklands occur primarily on sandy or loamy upland soils in the South Texas Plains (McMahan et al. 1984), but this vegetation type is also common in the Gulf Prairies and Marshes south of Corpus Christi Bay. It is the principal community in Kleberg and Kenedy counties. A small population occurs in Refugio County and reaches the shores of Copano Bay.

Associated species include bluewood, lotebush, coyotillo, guayacan, Texas colubrina *(Colubrina texensis)*, pencil cactus, prickly pear, Pan American balsamscale *(Elionurus tripsacoides)*, gulfdune paspalum, hooded windmillgrass, tanglehead *(Heteropogon contortus)*, purple threeawn, tumble lovegrass *(Eragrostis sessilispica)*, Lindheimer tephrosia *(Tephrosia lindheimeri)*, Texas bullnettle *(Cnidoscolus texanus)*, croton *(Croton* spp.), slender evolvulus *(Evolvulus alsinoides)*, common lantana, silverleaf nightshade *(Solanum elaeagnifolium)*, and indian blanket *(Gaillardia* spp.).

Mesquite-Live Oak-Bluewood Parks This community type comes within 25 km (15.5 mi) of Aransas Bay in San Patricio County, Texas. The dominant species are mesquite, live oak, and bluewood. Associated species include huisache, twisted acacia *(Acacia schaffneri* var. *bravoensis)*, common beebush, granjeno, lotebush, Berlandier wolfberry *(Lycium berlandieri)*, blackbrush, desert yaupon, prickly pear, coma *(Bumelia lanuginosa)*, pencil cactus, agarito *(Mahonia trifoliata)*, Texas persimmon *(Diospyros texana)*, purple threeawn, pink pappusgrass, Halls panicum *(Panicum hallii)*, slimlobe poppymallow *(Callirhoe involucrata* var. *lineariloba)*, sensitive briar *(Schrankia* spp.), twoleaf senna, and mat euphorbia (McMahan et al. 1984).

Live Oak Woods and Parks This community type occurs mainly on sandy soils, and it borders portions of Copano Bay in Refugio and San Patricio counties. It is most abundant in Kenedy County, where it borders on the south shore of Baffin Bay and the lower Laguna Madre of Texas. The dominant species is live oak, and associated species include prickly pear, lime pricklyash, greenbriar *(Smilax* spp.), sunflower *(Helianthus* sp.), tanglehead, crinkleawn *(Trachypogon secundus)*, gulfdune paspalum, fringed signalgrass *(Urochloa ciliatissima)*, Lindheimer tephrosia, croton, silverleaf nightshade, Texas bullnettle, common lantana, dayflower *(Commelina* spp.), silverleaf sunflower *(Helianthus argophyllus)*, and shrubby oxalis *(Oxalis berlandieri)*.

Native or Introduced Grasses Native and introduced grasses occur in the South Texas Plains where brush has been cleared but are also represented abundantly in Willacy and Cameron counties along the lower mainland coast of the lower Laguna Madre. Buffelgrass, an introduced species, is commonly planted to create "improved" pasture.

Fig. 4.6. The natural regions of Texas recognized by Diamond and colleagues (1987)

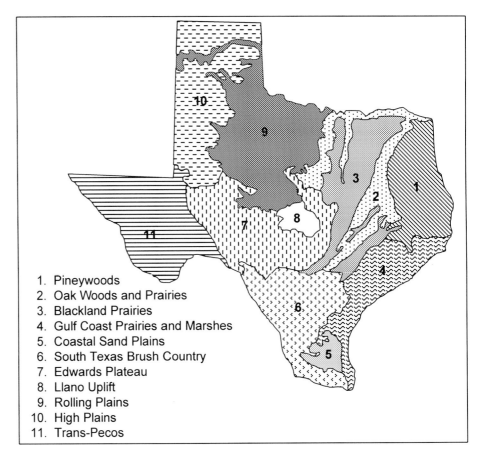

1. Pineywoods
2. Oak Woods and Prairies
3. Blackland Prairies
4. Gulf Coast Prairies and Marshes
5. Coastal Sand Plains
6. South Texas Brush Country
7. Edwards Plateau
8. Llano Uplift
9. Rolling Plains
10. High Plains
11. Trans-Pecos

Community Classifications and Dominant Species

Diamond and colleagues (1987) provided a classification of community types in Texas. They divided the state into 11 natural regions, which were subdivided into community types. In keeping with Gould (1969) and McMahan and colleagues (1984), they included as natural regions in the Texas TBP the South Texas Brush Country (= South Texas Plains of Gould [1969] and McMahan and colleagues [1984]) and the Gulf Coast Prairies and Marshes. However, they added a third natural region called Coastal Sand Plains (fig. 4.6).

The South Texas Brush Country natural area was subdivided into three vegetative types: the Brush Country, Bordas Escarpment, and Subtropical Zone. The Gulf Coast Prairies and Marshes natural area was similarly divided into three vegetative types: Dunes/Barrier, Estuarine Zone, and Upland Prairies and Woods. The Coastal Sand Plains natural area was not subdivided.

Table 4.2 shows the communities and dominant species of forests and woodlands recognized in the Texas TBP by Diamond and colleagues (1987). Eight different forest and woodland communities are identified. Two of the communities occur in both the Gulf Prairies and Marshes and the South Texas Brush Country natural areas. The Coastal Live Oak–Seacoast Bluestem community is limited to the Coastal Sand Plains.

Communities where shrubs constitute the dominant vegetation are identified only in the South Texas Brushlands (Diamond et al. 1987). In the Brush Country subdivision, three communities are recognized: (1) an Evergreen Shrubland consisting of a Cenizo Series dominated by Texas silverleaf; (2) a Deciduous Shrubland including a Blackbrush Series where blackbrush is dominant; and (3) a Deciduous Shrubland with a Fern Acacia Series where guajillo (*Acacia berlandieri*) is dominant. This is the only

Table 4.2. *Comparison of forest and woodland communities among the natural regions recognized by Diamond et al. (1987)*

Area of Region	Community	Dominant Species
Gulf Prairies and Marshes		
Throughout	**Deciduous Forest**	
	Sugarberry–elm series	*Celtis laevigata/C. reticulata–Ulmus* spp.
Upland Prairies and Woods	**Deciduous Forest**	
	Water oak–coastal live oak series	*Quercus nigra–Q. virginiana*
	Deciduous Woodland	
	Coastal live oak–pecan series	*Q. virginiana–Carya illinoensis*
	Coastal live oak–post oak series	*Q. virginiana–Q.stellata*
	Mesquite–huisache series	*Prosopis glandulosa–Acacia minuata*
Coastal Sand Plain		
Throughout	**Evergreen Woodland**	
	Coastal live oak–seacoast bluestem series	*Q. virginiana–Schizachyrium scoparium* var. *littoralis*
South Texas Brush Country		
Throughout	**Deciduous Forest**	
	Sugarberry–elm series	*C. laevigata/C. reticulata–Ulmus* spp.
Brush Country	**Deciduous Woodland**	
	Mesquite–huisache series	*P. glandulosa–A. minuata*
Subtropical Zone	**Evergreen Forest**	
	Texas palmetto series	*Sabal mexicana*
	Evergreen Woodland	
	Texas ebony–anacua series	*Chloroleucon ebano–Ehretia anacua*

community recognized in the Bordas Escarpment region. The Subtropical Zone includes a Deciduous Shrubland comprised of a Texas Ebony–Snake-eyes Series, where the dominant species are Texas ebony and snake-eyes *(Phaulothamnus spinescens)*.

A comparison of herbaceous-dominated communities occurring in the natural regions of southern Texas reported by Diamond and colleagues (1987) is provided in table 4.3. Swamps (wetlands with woody dominants) identified by Diamond and colleagues (1987) include a Black Mangrove Series dominated by black mangrove, which occurs in the Subtropical Zone of the South Texas Brushlands, and a Buttonbush Series dominated by common buttonbush *(Cephalanthus occidentalis)*, which occurs on Upland Prairies and Woods of the Gulf Coast Prairies and Marshes natural area.

Marshes (wetlands with herbaceous dominants) identified by Diamond and colleagues (1987) include a Rush-Sedge Series dominated by rushes *(Juncus* spp.), which occurs in all of the natural regions. A Gulf Cordgrass Series dominated by gulf cordgrass occurs in each of the subdivisions of the Gulf Prairies and Marshes and the South Texas Brush Country. A Smooth Cordgrass Series dominated by smooth cordgrass *(Spartina alterniflora)* occurs in the Dunes/Barrier and Estuarine zone of the Gulf Prairies and Marshes. A Saltgrass Series dominated by saltgrass occurs in the Coastal Sand Plains and South Texas Brush Country.

Table 4.3. *Comparison of herbaceous dominated communities among the natural regions recognized by Diamond et al. (1987)*

Area of Region	Community	Dominant Species
	Gulf Prairies and Marshes	
Dunes/Barriers	**Tall Grassland**	
	Seacoast bluestem series	*Schizachyrium scoparium* var. *littoralis*
	Forb-Dominated Vegetation	
	Cenicilla–beach morning glory series	*Sesuvium portulacastrum–Ipomoea imperati*
Upland Prairies and Woods	**Tall Grassland**	
	Gamagrass–switchgrass series	*Tripsacum dactyloides–Panicum virgatum*
	Little bluestem–brownseed paspalum series	*Schizachyrium scoparium–Paspalum plicatulum*
	Little bluestem–indiangrass series	*Schizachyrium scoparium–Sorghastrum nutans*
	Coastal Sand Plain	
Throughout	**Tall Grassland**	
	Seacoast bluestem series	*Schizachyrium scoparium* var. *littoralis*
	South Texas Brush Country	
Brush Country	**Medium-Tall Grasslands**	
	Cane bluestem–mesquite series	*Bothriochloa barbinodis–Prosopis glandulosa*

A focus of the work by Diamond and colleagues (1987) is the identification of the conservation status of the communities they identified. These are ranked in four categories ranging from endangered (1) to secure (4). Communities occurring in the Texas TBP considered endangered are the Texas Palmetto Series, Texas Ebony–Anacua Series, Gamagrass-Switchgrass Series, and Little Bluestem–Indiangrass Series. The Texas Ebony–Snake-eyes Series is considered threatened. It is significant that only three forest and woodland community types are considered endangered in Texas, and two of these occur in the Río Grande Delta region of the Texas TBP.

Diamond and Fulbright (1990) examined the grassland communities of the Coastal Sand Plains in detail and found that seacoast bluestem is the prevailing dominant species. Gulfdune paspalum was a dominant species in swales and on moderately drained flats. Camphorweed *(Heterotheca subaxillaris)* was important on dune ridges and well-drained flats. Principal component analysis showed that there were two community types. A gulfdune paspalum–seacoast bluestem community occupied swales and moderately drained flats, while a camphor daisy–seacoast bluestem community occurred on dune ridges and well-drained flats. They conclude that the composition of climax communities prior to human disturbance is problematic. However, they suggest that the prevailing dominant was likely seacoast bluestem.

McLendon (1991) classifies the vegetation of South Texas but omits coastal wetlands and the Lower Río Grande Valley. He divides the vegetation into grasslands, woodlands, and shrublands and identifies associations and communities within associations, recognizing 29 communities within ten associations. The ten associations and their dominant species are shown in table 4.4.

Table 4.4. *Plant associations in Texas (exclusive of the Lower Río Grande Valley and coastal saline areas) recognized by McLendon (1991)*

Associations	Dominant Species
Grasslands	
Little bluestem–trichloris	*Schizachyrium scoparium–Trichloris pluriflora*
Seacoast bluestem–balsamscale	*S. scoparium var. littoralis–Elionurus tripsacoides*
Woodlands	
Sugar hackberry–huisache	*Celtis laevigata–Acacia minuata*
Live oak–post oak	*Quercus virginiana–Q. stellata*
Shrublands	
Mesquite–granjeno	*Prosopis glandulosa–Celtis pallida*
Huisache–prickly pear	*A. minuata–Opuntia engelmannii*
Mesquite–prickly pear	*P. glandulosa–O. engelmannii*
Guajillo–cenizo (Texas silverleaf)	*A. berlandieri–Leucophyllum frutescens*
Blackbrush–twisted acacia	*A. rigidula–A. schaffneri*
Creosotebush–prickly pear	*Larrea tridentata–O. engelmannii*

Communities of the Mexico Portion of the TBP

Much less is known of the Mexican portion of the TBP than the Texas portion. The bulk of the province is in Tamaulipas. Alvarez (1963) reports that the vegetation of the TBP in Tamaulipas is, in general, Mesquite Grassland except for the vegetation of the Sierra San Carlos and Sierra de Tamaulipas. Two plant formations are identified in the Mesquite-Grassland: Mesquite Scrub and Gulf Bluestem Prairie (Alvarez 1963). The dominant species of the Mesquite Scrub is mesquite, and associated woody species include anacahuita, Spanish dagger, prickly pear (*Opuntia* spp.), and several species of *Acacia*. The dominant grasses are of the genera *Bouteloua* and *Andropogon*. In the Gulf Bluestem Prairie, bluestems are the dominant grasses on well-drained sites, whereas sloughs and depressions are occupied by cordgrass (Alvarez 1963). Alvarez (1963) notes that in many areas the Gulf Bluestem Prairie has been invaded by mesquite and other shrubs.

In the foothills of the Sierra de Tamaulipas and in the area between it and the Sierra San Carlos, the vegetation is Thorn Forest (Alvarez 1963), where Alvarez identifies the dominant genera as *Acacia, Ichthyomethia, Ipomoea, Prosopis,* and *Cassia*. At 300 m (984 ft) and 700 m (2,297 ft) elevation in the Sierra de Tamaulipas, the trees reach heights of 20 m (66 ft) and the canopy averages 8 m (26 ft) high (Alvarez 1963). This community is identified as Tropical Deciduous Forest. Common tree species are identified as belonging to the genera *Tabebuia, Ipomoea, Bombax,* and *Conzattia*. Species of *Bursera, Acacia,* and *Cassia* are less abundant (Alvarez 1963). In low canyons *Bursera, Ceiba,* and *Psidium* are draped with lianas and epiphytes.

A Pine-Oak formation is present above 800 m (2,625 ft) in the Sierra de Tamaulipas. It is characterized by Mexican pinyon *(Pinus cembroides)*, Nelson pine *(P. nelsoni)*, Aztec pine *(P. teocote)*, and Arizona white oak *(Quercus arizonica)*. Montane scrub vegetation occurs at elevations between 600 and 900 m (1,969–2,953 ft). This vegetation is formed by huisache along with a few oaks and some trees of the Tropical Deciduous

Table 4.5. *Mammals identified by Blair (1950) as Neotropical species extending northward into the Texas Tamaulipan Biotic Province*

Common Name	Scientific Name
Virginia opossum*	*Didelphis virginiana*
Leaf-chinned bat*	*Mormoops megalophylla*
Northern yellow bat*	*Lasiurus intermedius*
White-nosed coati	*Nasua narica*
Eastern hog-nosed skunk	*Conepatus leuconotus*
Jaguar	*Felis onca*
Ocelot*	*F. pardalis*
Margay	*F. wiedii*
Jaguarundi	*F. yagouaroundi*
Mexican spiny pocket mouse	*Liomys irroratus*
Fulvous harvest mouse*	*Reithrodontomys fulvescens*
Pygmy mouse*	*Baiomys taylori*
Coues' rice rat	*Oryzomys couesi*
Collared peccary (javelina)*	*Tayassu tajacu*
Nine-banded armadillo*	*Dasypus novemcinctus*

* = species known to extend north of the TBP.

Forest (Alvarez 1963). Vegetation of the Sierra San Carlos is similar to that of the Sierra de Tamaulipas and has been described in some detail by Dice (1937).

Amphibians, Reptiles, and Mammals

Blair (1950) confined his treatment of the vertebrate fauna of the Texas TBP to the groups he knew best: mammals, amphibians, and reptiles. He noted that the vertebrate fauna of TBP includes a considerable element of Neotropical species, a considerable element of primarily grassland species that range northward into the Texan and Kansan biotic provinces, some Austroriparian species, and some species in common with the Chihuahuan Biotic Province.

The Neotropical element is what distinguishes the TBP from other biotic provinces in Texas. Since the publication of Blair's (1950) paper, three additional Neotropical mammal species have been added to the mammal fauna of the Texas TBP (Davis and Schmidly 1994): Mexican long-tongued bat *(Choeronycteris mexicana)*, southern yellow bat *(Lasiurus ega)*, and Gulf Coast kangaroo rat *(Dipodomys compactus)*. The Texas pocket gopher *(Geomys personatus)* is reported to be endemic to the TBP. Blair (1950) noted that 15 of 61 species of mammals in the TBP have Neotropical affinities (table 4.5) and that six of these are limited in Texas to the Matamoran Biotic District. These species are the ghost-faced bat *(Mormoops megalophylla)*, northern yellow bat *(Lasiurus intermedius)*, eastern hog-nosed skunk *(Conepatus leuconotus)*, jaguarundi, Mexican spiny pocket mouse, and Coues' rice rat *(Oryzomys couesi)*. The leaf-chinned bat has now been found farther north than the TBP in western Texas, and the northern yellow bat extends northeastward past the TBP.

Alvarez (1963) lists the mammal species characteristic of the Mexican (= Tamaulipas) portion of the TBP (table 4.6). All of the species except for the Tamaulipan mole *(Scalopus inflatus)* and black-eared rice rat *(Oryzomys melanotis)* have populations in

Table 4.6. *Mammals identified by Alvarez (1963) as characteristic of the Mexican portion of the Tamaulipan Biotic Province*

Common Name	Scientific Name
Tamaulipan mole*	*Scalopus inflatus*
Eastern cottontail	*Sylvilagus floridanus connectens*
Desert cottontail	*S. audubonii parvulus*
Black-tailed jackrabbit (2 subspecies)	*Lepus californicus curti,* L. c. merriami*
Spotted ground squirrel*	*Spermophilus spilosoma oricolus*
Yellow-faced pocket gopher*	*Cratogeomys castanops tamaulipas*
Merriam's pocket mouse	*Perognathus merriami merriami*
Gulf Coast kangaroo rat (2 subspecies)	*Dipodomys compactus compactus, D. c. parvabullatus**
Black-eared rice rat	*Oryzomys melanotis carrorum*
Fulvous harvest mouse	*Reithrodontomys fulvescens intermedius*
Brush mouse	*Peromyscus boylii ambiguus*
Hispid cotton rat*	*Sigmodon hispidus solus*
Coyote (2 subspecies)	*Canis latrans texensis, C. l. microdon*
Gray wolf	*Canis lupus monstrabilis*
American badger	*Taxidea taxus berlandieri*
Striped skunk	*Mephitis mephitis varians*
Ocelot	*Felis pardalis albescens*
West Indian manatee	*Trichecus manatus latirostris*
White-tailed deer	*Odocoileus virginianus texanus*

* = species or subspecies endemic to the TBP.

Texas. Tropical pocket gopher *(Geomys tropicalis)* is not included because Alvarez (1963) places it in the Veracruzian Biotic Province. All of the Neotropical mammals in the Texas portion of the TBP also occur in Tamaulipas, Mexico.

Blair (1950) reported that the amphibian fauna of the Texas TBP consisted of three species of salamanders and 19 frog species. The reptilian fauna included 19 lizard species and 36 snake species. He did not identify the number of turtle species but referred to the two species of terrestrial turtles present: ornate box turtle *(Terrapene ornata)* and Texas tortoise *(Gopherus berlandieri)*. Blair (1950) noted that the northern and northeastern distribution limits of the Texas tortoise correspond closely to the boundaries of the TBP.

As with mammals, the distinctiveness of the amphibian and reptile fauna is determined by the tropical species that reach their northward limits of distribution in the TBP and do not occur elsewhere in Texas or the United States. A list of these species is provided in table 4.7. There are seven species of amphibians, none extending north of the Matamoran Biotic District except the black-spotted newt and the sheep frog. Ten reptilian species reach their northern limit of distribution in the TBP. Six species (blue spiny lizard, rose-bellied lizard, black-striped snake, speckled racer, Mexican hook-nosed snake, and cat-eyed snake) do not range north of the Matamoran Biotic District. Two reptiles, the Texas tortoise and reticulated collared lizard, are endemic to the TBP. Indeed, the geographic range for the Texas tortoise is a virtual match of the geographic extent of the TBP. It is the species that best characterizes the province.

Table 4.7. Amphibians and reptiles that reach their northern limits of geographic range in the Texas Tamaulipan Biotic Province

Common Name	Scientific Name
Amphibians	
Black-spotted newt	*Notopthalmus meridionalis*
Mexican burrowing toad	*Rhinophrynus dorsalis*
Sheep frog	*Hypopachus variolosus*
Giant toad	*Bufo marinus*
Mexican treefrog	*Smilisca baudinii*
Rio Grande chirping frog	*Syrrhophus cystignathoides campi*
White-lipped frog	*Leptodactylis fragilis*
Reptiles	
Texas tortoise*	*Gopherus berlandieri*
Reticulated collared lizard*	*Crotaphytus reticulatus*
Keeled earless lizard	*Holbrookia propinqua*
Blue spiny lizard	*Sceloporus cyanogenys*
Rose-bellied lizard	*S. variabilis*
Black-striped snake	*Coniophanes imperialis*
Speckled racer	*Drymobius margariterferus*
Indigo snake	*Drymarchon corais*
Mexican hook-nosed snake	*Ficimia streckeri*
Cat-eyed snake	*Leptodeira septentrionalis*

* = endemic species.

Ward and colleagues (1990) used cluster analysis and detrended reciprocal averaging to analyze the distribution of terrestrial reptiles in Texas. They found that cluster analysis produced seven regions that corresponded closely to the biotic provinces proposed by Blair (1950).

Biogeographic Importance of the Tamaulipan Biotic Province

The TBP is an area of great biodiversity (Blair 1950, 1952; Alvarez 1963). Indeed, in Texas, the TBP exhibits greater faunal diversity than any of the other biotic provinces in the state. The TBP is also important as a dispersal route for tropical species moving northward and for temperate forest and grassland species moving southward. These movements have often resulted in isolation of populations and subsequent speciation (Blair 1952).

The massive movements of bird species that breed in temperate or boreal North America and winter in the tropics have been studied for more than 50 years. At least half of the avifauna of North America winters in the Neotropics—338 of the approximately 650 species that regularly occur north of Mexico migrate south of the Tropic of Cancer for the winter (Rappole 1995). Another 80 to 90 species breed in the subtropics of southern Texas, Arizona, New Mexico, and northern Mexico, and migrate into the tropics, but their movements are poorly known (Rappole 1995). In

Table 4.8. List of endangered, threatened, and rare species found in counties adjacent to Texas Laguna Madre

Common Name	Scientific Name	Federal	State	Nueces	Kleberg	Kenedy	Willacy	Cameron
		STATUS		COUNTY				
Plants								
Texas windmillgrass	*Chloris texensis*		R	X				
Bailey's ballmoss	*Tillandsia baileyi*		R		X	X	X	X
Elmendorf's onion	*Allium elmendorfii*		R	X		X		
Chandler's amberlily	*Anthericum chandleri*		R	X				X
Mexican mud-plantain	*Heteranthera mexicana*		R					X
Runyon's huaco	*Manfreda longiflora*		R					X
Roughseed sea-purslane	*Sesuvium trianthemoides*		R			X		
Lundell's nailwort	*Paronychia lundellorum*		R			X		
Slender rushpea	*Hoffmannseggia tenella*	E	E	X	X			
South Texas rushpea	*Caesalpinia phyllanthoides*		R		X			
Vasey's adelia	*Adelia vaseyi*		R					X
Texas ayenia	*Ayenia limitaris*	E	E					X
Black-laced cactus	*Echinocereus reichenbachii var. albertii*	E	E	X	X			X
Runyon's cory cactus	*Coryphantha macromeris var. runyonii*		R					X
Star cactus	*Astrophytum asterias*	E	E					X
Tharp's rhododon	*Rhododon ciliatus*		R	X				
Runyon's justicia	*Justicia runyonii*		R					X
South Texas ambrosia	*Ambrosia cheiranthifolia*	E	E	X	X			X
Plains gumweed	*Grindelia oolepis*		R	X				X
Welder machaeranthera	*Machaeranthera heterocarpa*		R	X				
Molluscs								
Texas hornshell	*Popenaias popei*		R					X
Insects								
Superb grasshopper	*Eximacris superbum*		R				X	
Los Olmos tiger beetle	*Cicindela nevadica olmosa*		R			X		
Smyth's tiger beetle	*Cincindela chlorocephala smythi*		R					X
Maculated manfreda skipper	*Stallingsia maculosus*		R	X	X			
Fishes								
Opossum pipefish	*Microphis brachyurus*		T	X	X	X	X	X
Texas pipefish	*Syngnathus affinis*		R	X				
River goby	*Awaous tajasica*		T					X
Blackfin goby	*Gobionellus atripinnis*		T					X

Table 4.8. (continued)

Common Name	Scientific Name	STATUS		COUNTY				
		Federal	State	Nueces	Kleberg	Kenedy	Willacy	Cameron
Amphibians								
South Texas siren, large form	*Siren* sp. I		T	X	X	X	X	X
Black-spotted newt	*Notophthalmus meridionalis*		T	X	X	X	X	X
White-lipped frog	*Leptodactylus labialis*		T					X
Mexican treefrog	*Smilisca baudinii*		T					X
Sheep frog	*Hypopachus variolosus*		T	X	X	X	X	X
Reptiles								
Texas diamondback terrapin	*Malaclemys terrapin littoralis*		R	X				
Green sea turtle	*Chelonia mydas*	T	T	X	X	X	X	X
Atlantic hawksbill sea turtle	*Eretmochelys imbricata*	E	E	X	X	X	X	X
Kemp's ridley sea turtle	*Lepidochelys kempii*	E	E	X	X	X	X	X
Leatherback sea turtle	*Dermochelys coriacea*	E	E	X	X	X	X	X
Loggerhead sea turtle	*Caretta caretta*	T	T	X	X	X	X	X
Texas tortoise	*Gopherus berlandieri*		T	X	X	X	X	X
Gulf saltmarsh snake	*Nerodia clarkii*		R	X	X			
Speckled racer	*Drymobius margaritiferus*		T					X
Indigo snake	*Drymarchon corais*		T	X	X	X	X	X
Scarlet snake	*Cemophora coccinea*		T	X		X		
Black-striped snake	*Coniophanes imperialis*		T			X	X	X
Northern cat-eyed snake	*Leptodeira septentrionalis*		T		X	X	X	X
Mexican blackhead snake	*Tantilla atriceps*		R		X			
Keeled earless lizard	*Holbrookia propinqua*		R	X	X	X	X	X
Spot-tailed earless lizard	*Holbrookia lacerata*		R	X	X	X		
Texas horned lizard	*Phrynosoma cornutum*		T	X	X	X	X	X
Birds								
Brown pelican	*Pelecanus occidentalis*	E	E	X	X	X	X	X
Reddish egret	*Egretta rufescens*		T	X	X	X	X	X
Wood stork	*Mycteria maericana*		T	X	X	X	X	X
White-faced ibis	*Plegadis chihi*		T	X	X	X	X	X
Common black hawk	*Buteogallus anthracinus*		T				X	X
Zone-tailed hawk	*Buteo albonotatus*		T		X			X
White-tailed hawk	*Buteo albicaudatus*		T	X	X	X	X	X
Northern aplomado falcon	*Falco femoralis septentrionalis*	E	E		X	X	X	X

Table 4.8. *(continued)*

Common Name	Scientific Name	STATUS		COUNTY				
		Federal	State	Nueces	Kleberg	Kenedy	Willacy	Cameron
Birds *(continued)*								
American peregrine falcon	*Falco peregrinus anatum*	DL	E	X	X	X	X	X
Arctic peregrine falcon	*Falco peregrinus tundrius*	DL	T	X	X	X	X	X
Whooping crane	*Grus americana*	E	E					
Snowy plover	*Charadrius alexandrinus*		R	X	X	X	X	X
Piping plover	*Charadrius melodus*	T	T	X	X	X	X	X
Eskimo curlew	*Numenius borealis*	E	E	X				
Interior least tern	*Sterna antillarum athalassos*	E	E		X	X	X	
Sooty tern	*Sterna fuscata*		T	X	X		X	X
Cactus ferruginous pygmy owl	*Glaucidium brasilianum cactorum*		T			X	X	X
Northern beardless tyrannulet	*Camptostoma imberbe*		T			X	X	X
Rose-throated becard	*Pachyramphus aglaiae*		T					X
Tropical parula	*Parula pitiayumi*		T			X		X
Brownsville common yellowthroat	*Geothlypis trichas insperata*		R					X
Texas Botteri's sparrow	*Aimophila botterii texana*		T	X	X	X	X	
Henslow's sparrow	*Ammodramus henslowii*		R	X				
Sennett's hooded oriole	*Icterus cucullatus sennetti*		R	X		X	X	X
Audubon's oriole	*Icterus graduacauda audubonii*		R		X	X		X
Mammals								
Yuma myotis	*Myotis yumanensis*		T					X
Southern yellow bat	*Lasiurus ega*		T	X	X			X
Maritime pocket gopher	*Geomys personatus maritimus*		R	X	X			
Coues' rice rat	*Oryzomys couesi*		T			X		X
Black bear (extirpated)	*Ursus americanus*	T	T			X		
White-nosed coati	*Nasua narica*		T					X
Plains spotted skunk	*Spilogale putorius interrupta*		R	X	X			X
Jaguarundi	*Felis yagouaroundi*	E	E	X	X	X		X
Ocelot	*Felis pardalis*	E	E	X	X	X		X
Jaguar (extirpated)	*Panthera onca*	E	T		X			X
West Indian manatee	*Trichechus manatus*	E	E				X	X

Source: TPWD 1998a, b; 1999a, b, c.
Note: E = endangered; T = threatened; DL = delisted (federal); R = rare.

general, it is known that some bird species migrate through the length of the TBP as they travel around the Gulf of Mexico through the coastal zone, while other species travel through the width of the TBP as they migrate across the Gulf (Rappole et al. 1979). Thus large flocks of hawks, shorebirds, and passerine birds move through the TBP in spring and fall each year. Riparian forests, such as those along the Río Grande, may be particularly important stopover sites because of the more abundant food, cover, and fresh water there. Beach grasslands and wooded areas along the coast are especially important during storms, when birds migrating over the Gulf of Mexico attempt to make the nearest landfall. Because the TBP is the first landfall for many birds migrating northward across the Gulf, it is crucial that this area continues to provide necessary habitats and sufficient resources in these habitats to ensure the continued existence of the migrating bird species. Degradation of habitats in the TBP could lead to extinction of many migrating species.

Lands comprising the five counties (Nueces, Kleberg, Kenedy, Willacy, Cameron) bordering the Texas Laguna Madre provide habitat for 87 species of rare, threatened, and endangered species of plants and animals (table 4.8). Federal preserves such as Laguna Atascosa National Wildlife Refuge and Padre Island National Seashore contribute significantly to the protection of these species. Many of these rare, threatened, and endangered species continue to persist because of the large ranches that occur in the area, such as the King, Kenedy, Armstrong, and Yturria ranches. These ranches preserve native habitat and restrict entry so that there is little disturbance by humans. And there is little or no development on these lands. Structures are mainly a few homes and barns. There are no towns or commercial enterprises. Clearly, the wise stewardship provided by governmental agencies and ranch owners is responsible for the continuing high species diversity in the Texas TBP.

The TBP as a whole, however, has suffered serious human perturbation. For example, Jahrsdoerfer and Leslie (1988) report that since the 1920s, more than 95% of the original native brushland in the Lower Río Grande Valley has been cleared and converted to agricultural and urban use. In the past decade the value of the biodiversity of the lands along the Río Grande and in other areas of the Matamoran Biotic District have been recognized by a variety of private and governmental organizations, and these entities have been purchasing lands and working to reestablish native habitat. Wise planning and stewardship are helping to maintain and increase the important resource known as the Tamaulipan Biotic Province.

5 *Ranching Heritage*

NANCY L. HILBUN AND AMY E. KOLTERMANN

Both the eastern and western shores of the Laguna Madre have extensive ranching histories. Padre Island is no longer devoted to ranching, but the western shore consists primarily of large ranches (fig. 5.1). Ranching has affected the lands bordering the Laguna Madre and, consequently, the structure, health, and productivity of the lagoon. By limiting access to the Laguna Madre, ranching enterprises have kept human perturbations at a markedly lower level than they might otherwise have been. In this chapter we chronicle the history of ranching on lands bordering the lagoon and discuss the effects ranching has had on the ecology of the Laguna Madre.

Early History

The first European arrival in South Texas was Alonso Alvarez de Pineda in 1519. While searching for a water passage to the Orient, Pineda mapped the Gulf of Mexico coastline from Florida to Veracruz, Mexico. Pineda stopped at a small river south of the Río Grande and claimed the land for Spain (Thompson 1997).

Prior to Pineda's voyage, the coastal areas of South Texas and northern Mexico were inhabited by various groups of Indians. The Karankawa and Coahuiltecan Indians were the predominant groups along the Texas and northern Mexico coasts. The Coahuiltecans consisted of many subgroups, such as the Katuhanno, Bobole, Carrizo, Payaya, Aránama, Tamique, Oregón, Pachal, and Kesale-Terkodam (Thompson 1997). Other noted Indian groups of the area included Malaguitas, Manos De Perro, Pasnacas, Patún, Piguisas, Pimaraqui, Comecrudos, and Tanaquiapemes (Salinas 1990).

Significant Spanish influence on coastal southern Texas and northern Mexico and their inhabitants did not occur until the seventeenth century when missionaries brought cattle into South Texas to supply the missions near San Antonio. These missions served as some of the first formal ranches in Texas. The livestock provided a dependable food supply that fed the priests, and it was also used to attract Indians to the missions and hold them there (Jackson 1986). Due to the harsh living conditions, the area between the Nueces River and the Río Grande was thought unfit for habitation. During this time Spain controlled Mexico, while the French and English were building colonial empires in other parts of North America. The threat of the expanding English and French empires prompted Spain to send José Escandon to the Río Grande area and initiate colonization (Weise and White 1980; Cruz 1988). Escandon named the area Colonia del Nuevo Santander in 1746 and sent seven units to investigate its resources the next year. Escandon reported there were large numbers of wild horses and cattle. In 1749 Escandon was appointed governor of the new Spanish province, and settlements were erected along both sides of the Río Grande. Several establishments along the Río Grande were successful, including Camargo, Reynosa, Revilla, Mier, Laredo, and Dolores. Colonization was successful from the mouth of the Río Grande to the Nueces River by the late 1700s (Smylie 1964a).

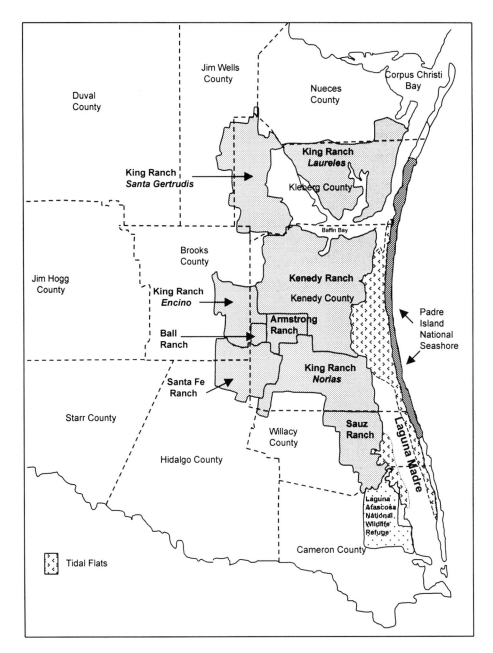

In the 1760s, Spain sent Juan Armando de Palacio and José de Ossorio y Llamas to survey towns, allocate land to individual settlers, and establish clear title to the land from the Crown of Spain. The colonists were classified as original, old, or recent, and land was divided on the basis of merit and seniority. Settlers of these early colonies began requesting individual allocations of land as early as 1753; however, bureaucratic delays postponed land distribution for over a decade (TGLO 1988). Spanish land grants were divided into three different groups. The first group consisted of elongated quadrangles or *porciones* (Scott 1966; Jackson 1986). This type of grant provided settlers with a long strip of land having narrow frontage on a river, so that crops and livestock could have dependable water. About 170 porciones were located within present-day Texas, most consisting of about 2,023 ha (5,000 ac) with a small area bordering the Río Grande.

The second group of grants involved much larger tracts of land issued for ranching or grazing purposes. Most of these grants were given to influential citizens of Ca-

Table 5.1. Original Spanish and Mexican land grants bordering Laguna Madre

Original Grantee	Name of Property	Size	County	Date	Country
Cabazos, José Narciso	San Juan de Carricitos	243,487 ha (601,657 ac)	Hidalgo, Kenedy	1792	Spain
José Salvador de la Garza	Espiritu Santo	115,102 ha (284,416 ac)	Cameron	1781	Spain
José Francisco Ballí	La Barreta	50,303 ha (124,297 ac)	Kenedy	1804	Spain
José Perez Rey, José María Perez Rey, and José Manuel García	Rincón de los Laureles	40,813 ha (100,848 ac)	Kleberg, Nueces	1807	Spain
Ramón de Ynojosa	El Rincón de Corpus Christi	32,945 ha (81,407 ac)	Nueces	1832	Mexico
Alvino de la Garza and Domingo de la Garza	La Parra*	26,882 ha (66,426 ac)	Kenedy	1833	Mexico
Nicolas Ballí and Juan José Ballí	Padre Island	20,609 ha (50,926 ac)	Cameron, Kenedy, Kleberg, Nueces, Willacy	1829	Mexico
Enrique Villarreal	Rincón del Oso	17,337 ha (42,840 ac)	Nueces	1831	Mexico
Rafael Ramirez	Rincón del Penascal	15,941 ha (39,390 ac)	Kenedy	1833	Mexico
Rafael García	Santa Isabel	13,094 ha (32,355 ac)	Cameron	1828	Mexico
Manuel de la Garza y Soza	El Potrero de Buena Vista	12,229 ha (30,218 ac)	Cameron	1828	Mexico
Gabriel Treviño	Rincón de la Boveda*	11,649 ha (28,785 ac)	Kleberg	1834	Mexico
José Ygnacio de Treviño	San Martin	11,044 ha (27,290 ac)	Cameron	1827	Mexico
Juan Antonio Ballí (Cabazos)	El Paistle*	10,437 ha (25,790 ac)	Kenedy	1834	Mexico
Ygnacio Villarreal	Rincón de Mirasoles	9,647 ha (23,837 ac)	Kenedy	1833	Mexico
Leonardo Salinas	La Barreta	8,960 ha (22,140 ac)	Kenedy	1834	Mexico
García Bernardo	El Infiernillo*	8,689 ha (21,471 ac)	Kleberg	1834	Mexico
Teodora Garza	El Alazan*	5,476 ha (13,532 ac)	Kenedy	1834	Mexico

Source: TGLO 1988.
* Land grants that border only Baffin Bay.

margo and Reynosa. This land was usually bordered by the Gulf of Mexico or the Laguna Madre and often backed up to the porciones. At least 35 of these grants were made, the largest being San Juan de Carricitos (table 5.1). It comprised 243,487 ha (601,657 ac) and was granted to José Narciso Cavazos (TGLO 1988). The third group of land grants was for vacant land and was used to prevent settlement by the French or English (Scott 1966; Jackson 1986).

Two influential families at the time, the Hinojosa and Valli families, acquired large amounts of land through the land grant process. The latter name has been written in numerous ways, including Valli, Vallin, and most recently Ballí. These two families established pioneer ranches in South Texas (Scott 1966; Jackson 1986). Captain Juan José de Hinojosa was chief justice of Reynosa during this time. His influence in the government, classification as a Primitive Settler, and personal wealth allowed him to acquire large amounts of land. Don José María Ballí was a local surveyor who began working with Captain Hinojosa (Robertson 1985). Many of the porciones and larger land grants went to the Hinojosa and Ballí family members. The bond between families was further strengthened when Don José María Ballí married Doña Rosa María Hinojosa, the daughter of Captain Hinojosa. As many as 11 large land grants and three porciones were acquired by the families from 1770 to 1829, making the Hinojosa and Ballí families the

Fig. 5.2. *South Texas between 1836 and 1848. Texas and Mexico both claimed the Nueces Strip, the land between the Nueces River and the Río Grande (Adapted from Weise and White 1980)*

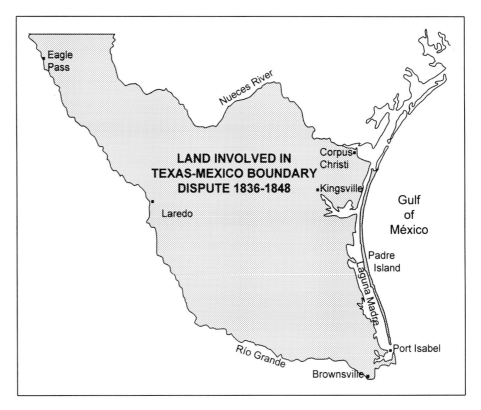

largest landowners in the Lower Río Grande Valley. These influential families used the land to graze large herds of cattle and sheep (García 1979; Jackson 1986).

In 1821 Mexico gained independence from Spain and the land south of the Nueces River became part of the State of Tamaulipas (Calvert and DeLeón 1990). Mexico continued to grant land for grazing purposes. However, by 1836 the First Congress of the Republic of Texas claimed all land north of the Río Grande (Weise and White 1980). Therefore, the land between the Nueces River and the Río Grande was claimed by both Texas and Mexico (fig. 5.2). This area became known as the Nueces Strip and was considered a no-man's-land where thievery, smuggling, and cattle stealing were rampant. Indians were recorded attacking the area in the first half of the nineteenth century and forcing many people to abandon their ranches, further promoting a no-man's-land (Smith 1986). Throughout this time Mexico continued to issue land grants in the area. Texas was annexed by the United States in 1845, and in 1846 General Zachary Taylor was dispatched to South Texas to establish the United States' claim on all land north of the Río Grande (D. S. Smith 1986; Thompson 1997). Mexico broke diplomatic relations with Texas after the annexation, and the Mexican Army was driven south of the Río Grande by Taylor's army. In 1848 the Treaty of Guadalupe Hidalgo was signed and the Río Grande was established as the border between Texas and Mexico. The treaty stated that land grants made by Spain or Mexico until 1848 were valid (Robertson 1985). A committee was then established to confirm these grants. Commissioners William Bourland and James Miller were in charge of the operation, and in 1852, 152 grants were confirmed (TGLO 1988).

King and Kenedy Dynasty

During the 1840s, two men arrived in South Texas who would forever change the ranching history of the world. Richard King was born to Irish immigrant parents in New York City in 1824. He was apprenticed to a Manhattan jeweler at the age of nine and ran away at the age of eleven. King stowed away on a boat headed for Mobile, Alabama, and then worked his way from cabin boy to steamboat pilot. King then enlisted to fight in the Seminole wars, where he met his future business partner Mifflin Kenedy (Cheeseman 1997). Kenedy was from a Quaker family in Pennsylvania and had held various jobs, including teaching school. When King and Kenedy met, Kenedy already had a plan to captain a U.S. Army boat to help move supplies for Gen. Zachary Taylor (Douglas 1968). In 1847 King joined Kenedy, who by that time had founded a small shipping enterprise on the Río Grande. King and Kenedy were successful moving supplies for the U.S. Army (Cheeseman 1994). After the end of the Mexican War in 1848, King and Kenedy joined other residents of Matamoros and Brownsville and purchased the boats from the army. Kenedy and King formed a thriving business under the name M. Kenedy and Company and soon bought out the other partners. At one point Kenedy and King owned and operated 26 boats along the Río Grande (Rowe 1953).

In 1852 King made a trip on horseback from Brownsville to the Nueces River and back. He was impressed by the vast potential of the land, and upon returning to Brownsville, he inquired about the area surrounding Santa Gertrudis Creek (Rowe 1953). Known as Rincón de Santa Gertrudis, the land was part of a grant from Mexico to Juan Mendiola, dated 21 December 1832, and was then owned by the Mendiola heirs (TGLO 1988). King formed a partnership with a friend, Texas Ranger Captain Gideon K. ("Legs") Lewis, to establish and maintain a livestock operation on Rincón de Santa Gertrudis (McCampbell 1952; Nixon 1986). King purchased 6,273 ha (15,500 ac) of land for less than two cents an acre and started to import Mexican cattle to stock his land (Lea 1957a). As his ranching enterprise grew, King continued to buy land and cattle. In 1855, Lewis, was shot and killed, leaving no heirs (Nixon 1986).

By 1860 the King Ranch had become a major cattle enterprise and Kenedy offered to buy an interest in the holdings. A three-way partnership was formed under the name R. King and Company (Cheeseman 1994). Richard King and Mifflin Kenedy each received three-eighths, and James Walworth, another investor, received two-eighths (Lea 1957b). Cattle, sheep, goats, and horses were the principal livestock King and Kenedy raised. Their successful steamboat operation allowed them to keep in close contact with market demand, resulting in a thriving ranching business (Rowe 1953).

Ranching became an obsession with Captain King, leading him to hire attorneys to research old land grants of the area, locate the owners, and purchase the lands. Stephen Powers, and later James Wells, were responsible for many of King's land acquisitions (Lea 1957b). Although King was an ambitious man, he also demonstrated great compassion. During a trip to Mexico to purchase stock, King traveled to a poor village where many people were hungry. He purchased their livestock and offered to relocate the entire village to his ranch. These people became his work force, and their descendants have continued to work the King Ranch; they became known as Kineños, King's men (Nixon 1986; Monday and Colley 1997). In contrast, Kenedy hired skilled Mexican vaqueros from the Río Grande area, who became known as Kenedeños. King and Kenedy both developed close relationships with their employees, and this helped to form a loyal and dedicated work force (Crimm 1997).

After the onset of the Civil War, the steamboat business was once again booming. Working under the Confederate flag, King and Kenedy supplied the Confederacy with meat and horses. They also imported lead from Mexico and carried cargo, mainly cotton, upriver. Later in the war, Brownsville was taken by the Union Army; being Confederates, King and Kenedy were forced to move across the river and operate under the Mexican flag (McCampbell 1952). King and Kenedy were, however, able to continue ranching during this time (Rowe 1953). In 1865 Walworth's share of the ranching enterprise was sold back to King and Kenedy for $50,000. King had accumulated 59,082 ha (146,000 ac) by the end of the Civil War and branded his cattle for the first time with the Running W (its origin is still unknown). By 1867 King and Kenedy had decided to dissolve the partnership in the interests of their heirs. King kept the Santa Gertrudis and Agua Dulce ranches, while Kenedy maintained the Laureles Ranch (Lea 1957a, b). In 1882 Kenedy sold the Laureles Ranch to a Scottish firm, the Texas Land and Cattle Company, and began to purchase the La Parra Ranch (Cheeseman 1994). Mrs. Henrietta King later bought the Laureles from the Scottish firm. King and Kenedy remained in the steamboat business until it was no longer profitable and sold the company in 1874 (Kelley 1986).

The two separate ranches continued to operate successfully. Captains King and Kenedy were the first in the state to fence large tracts of land. They both believed that this was the only means to protect their livestock (Rowe 1953). King and Kenedy were the recognized leaders of the cattle industry in the West, doing more than any others to stabilize the industry in the United States (Rowe 1953). Captain Kenedy continued in many profitable business ventures, such as the building of a railroad from San Antonio to Aransas Pass. Kenedy also established the Kenedy Pasture Company with his son John, and this company owned 1,554 km^2 (600 mi^2) of rangeland in Cameron County (Daniell 1892). Captain Kenedy and Petra Vela de Vidal had six children. Their daughter Sarah J. Kenedy married Dr. E. A. Spohn of Corpus Christi, for whom Spohn Hospital in Corpus Christi was named. Today the Kenedy Ranch covers over 202,347 ha (500,000 ac) in Kenedy County, Texas (Fulbright et al. 1990), and is divided between two ownership entities, the John G. Kenedy Charitable Trust and the John G. and Marie Stella Kenedy Memorial Foundation.

In the early 1880s, Robert Kleberg came to the attention of Richard King by beating him in a lawsuit. King was impressed with Kleberg's potential and hired him. Kleberg later married King's youngest daughter, Alice Gertrudis King (Rowe 1953; Nixon 1986). With the death of Richard King in 1885, Robert Kleberg was made manager of the King Ranch by King's widow Henrietta. In 1888 the town of Alice, named after King's daughter, was settled; located at the railway 32 km (20 mi) north of the King Ranch, it became the largest cattle shipping point in the world (Nixon 1986). Kleberg was one of the first to recognize the effects of overgrazing and the encroachment of mesquite. He also recognized the connection between Texas fever and the ticks on the cattle in South Texas and pressed the government into research that confirmed his belief. Kleberg designed the first dipping vat to treat cattle for ticks and other parasites (Nixon 1986). In 1899, Richard King's successor, Robert Kleberg, dug the first water well in South Texas at a depth of 162 m (532 ft). This well was an indicator of sufficient and reliable water in the area and led to more extensive settlement in South Texas (Nixon 1986). Just as driven as Richard King, Kleberg continued to increase the wealth of the King empire through purchase of new lands, selective breeding of cattle and horses, development of farms and orchards, and the introduction of a railroad to the area (Nixon 1986).

With the death of Henrietta King in 1925 and the death of Robert Kleberg in 1932, many felt that a chapter in South Texas ranching history was closed. Kleberg represented the last of the true cattle barons who made fortunes and history (Nixon 1986). He is recognized as a driving force in the development of South Texas, including Kingsville, Bishop, and Corpus Christi (Nixon 1986). To keep the empire alive during the depression, Bob Kleberg focused on renewing oil leases with Humble Oil and Refining Company (now Exxon). This partnership will not expire until 2013 (Nixon 1986).

From the beginning, Richard King had wanted to improve the cattle stock on his ranch, which needed to be able to withstand the heat and short water supply of South Texas while nevertheless maintaining beef quality for the consumers. His descendants fulfilled his dream with the development of the Santa Gertrudis stock, which is a cross between the Brahman and Shorthorn breeds. Caesar Kleberg, cousin to Richard and Robert Kleberg, saw the potential of crossing a Brahman on a visit to Ed Lasiter's ranch. Dick Kleberg first saw their dream realized in a bull calf they eventually called Monkey (Nixon 1986). In 1940 the Department of Agriculture recognized the Santa Gertrudis as the first beef breed developed in the United States.

In addition to the dream of developing quality cattle, there was the desire to produce quality horses, and Robert Kleberg, Jr., was the driving force for development of the King Ranch Quarter Horse program (Nixon 1986). Bob Kleberg's breeding endeavors eventually produced the prize racehorse Assault, which claimed the Triple Crown in 1946 (Toland 1996). Improvements on the King Ranch continued under the management of Dick and Bob Kleberg (Nixon 1986).

By 1935 Alice Kleberg and her children created a corporation and divided the stock equally. They decided that the ranch would not be split but would stay together under family ownership (Hollandsworth 1998). During the 1970s and early 1980s, the ranch corporation was run by a committee of various family members. In the late 1980s, the King Ranch Corporation voted to hire executives outside the family to lead the company and serve on its board of directors. The King Ranch Corporation is now run from its new corporate headquarters in Houston, Texas, under the leadership of Jack Hunt (Grant 1998).

Today the King Ranch covers approximately 333,873 ha (825,000 ac) of South Texas and consists of four divisions. About half of it is leased for hunting, and 24,300 ha (60,000 ac) are used as farmland for cotton and grain sorghum. The ranch carries only about 50,000 head of cattle on its Texas divisions. The King Ranch also owns a cattle operation in Brazil; a St. Augustine sod, citrus, and sugar cane operation in Florida; and an alfalfa, onion, and honeydew melon farm in Arizona (Ford 1998). Through these and other activities, the King Ranch Corporation continues to thrive.

Padre Island

Indians known as the Camones lived on Padre Island during the sixteenth century. In the seventeenth century the Negro and Malaquito Indians inhabited the island. These people were thought to be closely related to or subtribes of the Coahuiltecans, who occupied the adjacent mainland (WRT 1950). By the nineteenth century, Karankawa Indians inhabited many of the barrier islands and much of the coastal plain of Texas, including Padre Island (Reese 1938; WRT 1950; Ricklis 1996). The Karankawa lived a nomadic life along the South Texas coast. Their diet consisted mostly of fish, shellfish, birds, and bird eggs obtained from the Laguna Madre and surrounding areas (Weise and White 1980; Ricklis 1996).

Alonso de Pineda was the first European to explore and name Isla Blanca, now Padre Island (Weddle 1985; Thompson 1997). The island was ignored until Spain initiated the land grant program in response to the expanding English and French empires (Weise and White 1980). In 1800, Padre José Nicolas Ballí, son of Don José María Ballí, applied for a Spanish land grant for Padre Island, then called Corpus Christi Isla or Isla Santiago. The first application was not clear, and another one was made in 1829. This time Nicolas Ballí included his nephew Juan José Ballí in the application as his business partner (García 1979). Padre Ballí wanted to establish missions on the island and convert Indians, while Juan José Ballí wanted to establish a ranch. Rancho Santa Cruz, meaning Holy Cross, was built 42 km (26 mi) north of the island's southern tip. The Ballís successfully imported large herds of cattle, sheep, and horses to the island. The land was officially granted to Nicolas Ballí by Mexico in 1829 (Reese 1938)—also the year of Padre Ballí's death (Smylie 1964a). The Ballí family continued to ranch on Padre Island until 1840; however, they began selling parts of the island as early as 1830. The last of the Ballí descendants had fled the island by 1844 in response to U.S. threats to annex the region (Weise and White 1980).

The Singer family came to Padre Island in 1847, after being blown off course on their way to Port Isabel. John Singer and his family chose to stay on Padre Island. Although the island was unoccupied, the northern half was still owned by José María Tovar and the southern half by Ballí's heirs. The Singers purchased one-seventh of the southern half of Padre Island in 1851, which was the beginning of a profitable ranching business (Weise and White 1980). During this time it is believed that John Singer funded his brother Isaac, who was the inventor of the Singer sewing machine, suggesting that Padre Island is the location for the first use of the sewing machine. But John Singer's ranching success was short-lived; he was forced to leave the island in 1861 by Confederate forces because of his sympathies toward the Union. Prior to his hasty departure, he buried $80,000 in silver in a jar near his home. After the Civil War Singer was unable to find his treasure, giving rise to one of the island's most famous treasure stories (Smylie 1964b; Weise and White 1980).

For a time it seemed that Padre Island was unoccupied; however, it was never overlooked as an important strategic area for the military and for smugglers such as Colonel H. L. Kinney. Kinney had established squatters rights near Corpus Christi, later focusing on the development of Corpus Christi as a major port city (Smylie 1964a; Weise and White 1980).

During the confusion of the Civil War, King and Kenedy continued to purchase ranch land. As early as 1854, King acquired 4,856 ha (12,000 ac) on Padre Island from a niece of Padre Ballí. In the 1870s King and Kenedy leased additional land and established a thriving ranch operation on Padre Island. A major storm in 1880 greatly reduced their ranching operations on the island, and by 1886 the operation was completely abandoned (Smylie 1964b).

In the late nineteenth century Patrick Dunn moved to the forefront of Padre Island's ranching history. Dunn was the son of Irish immigrants and had become a successful rancher by taking advantage of the open range. After the invention of barbed wire, Dunn turned his interest to Padre Island, which was bounded by "natural fences." Dunn first leased land on the island in 1879, and by 1926 he owned nearly the entire island—52,610 ha (130,000 ac; Weise and White 1980). Dunn ranched the island efficiently by building four major line camps placed about 24 km (15 mi) apart, the distance a herd of cattle could be driven in one day. Dunn's men would start rounding up cattle at the southern end of the island and drive them northward and eventually across the shallow Laguna Madre, near Flour Bluff, to market (Smylie 1964b). Known as the Duke of Padre or Don Patricio, Dunn became a legend of the time. He not only ranched the island but also conducted experiments with native grasses. Furthermore, Dunn was elected to the state legislature, where he served from 1910 to 1916. In 1926 he sold the surface rights of the island to real estate developer Colonel Sam Robertson, retaining the mineral and grazing rights. Dunn ranched on the island until his death in 1937. The Dunn ranching business continued through his son, Burton Dunn, until 1971, when grazing was terminated within the Padre Island National Seashore (Rabalais 1977; Weise and White 1980).

Recreational interest in Padre Island dates back to the 1930s (NPS 1974). Between 1930 and 1950 development on Padre Island was scarce. After World War II interest in the island's recreational potential revived. Senator Ralph Yarborough proposed the first Padre Island Bill in 1958. In 1962, the land was purchased by the government for $17 million, and Padre Island National Seashore was established (Sheire 1971).

Other Significant Ranches

While the King and Kenedy ranches are the largest and best known in South Texas, other large ranches are present. The Armstrong Ranch, located in Kenedy County, was founded by Major John H. Durst. Major Durst was a close friend of Richard King and Mifflin Kenedy and an influential citizen of the time. In 1852, for 1,600 pesos, Durst purchased almost 37,637 ha (93,000 ac) of the La Barreta land grant held by the Ballí family (Smith 1986). The Santa Fe Ranch, located in Brooks, Kenedy, and Hidalgo counties, consists of more than 60,704 ha (150,000 ac). Today, the ranch is owned by the heirs of Alice East, granddaughter of Captain Richard King (Rowe 1953). Likewise, the Sauz Ranch—45,326 ha (112,000 ac) in Willacy County—is owned by the heirs of Nettie King Atwood, who was the daughter of Captain Richard King (Douglas 1968).

The San Juan de Carricitos Spanish land grant, originally made in 1790, is the source of many large ranches in Willacy County. The La Becerra Ranch, approximately 316 ha (781 ac), is owned by the descendants of José Narciso Cavazos (also spelled Cabazos), the original grantee of a large land grant. Other ranches that stemmed from the San Juan de Carricitos grant were started by Francisco Yturria, who was a powerful figure of the late nineteenth century in Matamoros. At the time of his death in 1912, Yturria owned over 55,038 ha (136,000 ac). These lands have since been divided among heirs into separate ranches: Santa Berta Ranch, Tres Mesquites–Thomas Ranch, and F. Yturria Ranch (TDA 1983). The El Devisadero Ranch in Kenedy County is also owned by Yturria's heirs. The Tres Norias Ranch in Willacy County can be traced back to the San Juan de Carricitos land grant as well. Abundio García purchased land from the wife of José Narciso Cavazos during the nineteenth century, and the land, about 177 ha (437 ac), is still owned by García heirs today (TDA 1985).

Ranching and the Laguna Madre

What roles have historical and present-day ranching played on the ecology of Laguna Madre? As early as the middle of the nineteenth century King built dams across dry creeks to save rainwater, thus altering the freshwater flow into the Laguna Madre (Nixon 1986). This probably did not have a major effect on the Laguna Madre, since drainage was minor and intermittent, but it was the beginning of human impact on the environment. As ranching in the area increased, so did changes in the landscape. Although cattle ranching was a major enterprise at the time, it was not the only form of ranching in South Texas. Other livestock also significantly impacted the native grasslands of South Texas in the nineteenth century. In some locations sheep outnumbered cattle 2:1 (Lehmann 1969). It has been said that when Mifflin Kenedy first saw Padre Island it was "as green as a garden" (Price and Gunter 1942). However, Padre Island became denuded of vegetation shortly after 1870, and the fauna changed (Rabalais 1977). This phenomenon also occurred throughout South Texas from the blackland prairies to the coast with the expansion of the cattle industry from 1870 to 1880. Because of this loss of vegetation, infilling of the Laguna Madre increased due to sand blowing in from Padre Island, carried by hurricanes and the relatively constant southeast winds (Price and Gunter 1942). Cattle ranching continued

Fig. 5.3. *The Coastal Sand Plains (= South Texas Eolian Sand Sheet), covering parts of six counties in South Texas (Fulbright et al. 1990)*

on Padre Island until 1971 (Rabalais 1977). The Laguna Madre was also experiencing the effects of increased sedimentation caused by erosion due to less vegetated terrain. Price and Gunter (1942) concluded that faunal and floral changes throughout South Texas were primarily due to cattle ranching on Padre Island and the mainland, and farming to the northwest and southwest of Laguna Madre. Severe droughts and storms also contributed to increased sedimentation in the Laguna Madre caused by these human-induced alterations to the landscape.

Studies also have been conducted on the effects of cattle on the shoreline vegetation of the natural and man-made ponds in South Texas (Whyte 1978). To provide water for cattle during summer or drought, man-made ponds ("tanks") are constructed. These ponds exhibit an "edge effect," creating an ideal microecosystem for waterfowl and other birds. Although constant grazing by cattle damages vegetation on the edges of watering ponds, fencing modifications can limit damage (Whyte 1978).

Despite these changes, the land management of South Texas has greatly benefited the Laguna Madre ecosystem. The lack of urban development in the area has had the effect of preserving numerous critical ecosystems in the Laguna Madre and surrounding uplands, the ecosystems continuing to thrive because of the absence of human pressures. Rappole (1993) states that on the King Ranch alone, at least 18 threatened or endangered species are known or suspected to be present.

The Coastal Sand Plains (= South Texas Eolian Sand Sheet) make up a unique ecosystem protected by large ranches and lack of urban development (fig. 5.3; see chapter 4). Two of the four King Ranch divisions are located in the Coastal Sand Plains, consisting of more than 809,356 ha (2 million ac) of rangeland in South Texas. Active sand dunes make up 5% of the entire region (Fulbright et al. 1990). Several habitats exist on the Sand Plains, including extensive uplands, which are home to open grasslands with large live oak mottes; honey mesquite mottes; and coastal wind-tidal flats and saline habitats (Fulbright et al. 1990). The diversity of the wildlife found on the Coastal Sand Plains is attributed to the diversity of habitats.

Mottes are especially important for Neotropical migrant songbirds; during spring migration, bird densities within mottes can be up to 20 times higher than at other times of the year (Anonymous 1993). The Sand Plains area is also important to endangered and threatened species such as the ocelot *(Felis pardalis)* and the cactus ferruginous pygmy owl *(Glaucidium brasilianum cactorum)* (Fulbright et al. 1990; Rappole 1993). Tewes (1993) reports that the King and Kenedy ranches are major habitats for the endangered ocelot. Research is ongoing at the Caesar Kleberg Wildlife Research Institute, located at Texas A&M University–Kingsville, regarding the importance of habitat conservation for these and many other threatened species (Nixon 1986).

Table 5.2. *Land delineation along the Laguna Madre shoreline*

Land Use	Approximate Distance along Shoreline	%
King and Kenedy Ranches	142 km (89 mi)	34
Laguna Atascosa Wildlife Refuge	26 km (16 mi)	6
Padre Island National Seashore	112 km (70 mi)	27
Other	141 km (88 mi)	33
Total Laguna Madre Shoreline	421 km (263 mi)	100

Wetlands located on the King Ranch are prime breeding habitats for many species of waterfowl. Some of these wetlands are in danger of being drained and filled for Gulf Intracoastal Waterway dredge material placement by the Army Corps of Engineers (Lonard 1993b; Rappole 1993). Since wetlands serve an important ecological function, they are protected areas. The ranch wetlands provide habitats for many species of ducks and other waterfowl as well as being an important rest stop for migratory birds (Rappole 1993). Rappole (1993) has noted that any destruction of coastal habitat bordering the Laguna Madre and on the King and Kenedy ranches would be detrimental to many species, including the Texas tortoise *(Gopherus berlandieri)*, brown pelican *(Pelecanus occidentalis)*, black skimmer *(Rhynchops niger)*, least tern *(Sterna antillarum)*, white-tailed hawk *(Buteo albicaudatus)*, and white-faced ibis *(Plegadis chihi)*.

Although overgrazing by ranch livestock has not been a positive influence on the ecology of the Laguna Madre, the remoteness of the large ranches has sustained many habitats for plants and animals (Anonymous 1993). Between the large privately owned ranches and federally protected lands, approximately 67% of the Texas Laguna Madre shoreline is protected from development or other human encroachment (table 5.2). Setting aside these lands has preserved many habitats that might otherwise have been destroyed long ago through commercial development (Simmons 1957). With responsible land management, the Laguna Madre and its surrounding ecosystems should continue to benefit from protection provided by large ranches and federally conserved lands.

Laguna Madre de Tamaulipas

Remoteness and inaccessibility, chiefly because of the lack of roads, has played an even larger role in Tamaulipas than in Texas in protecting much of the shoreline of Laguna Madre. As a result of this lack of development, some large expanses of mainland remain intact and mostly undisturbed. Two areas of note include mainland areas south of Laguna el Catán and Rancho Rincón de Anacahuitas in the northwest. The property of Rancho Rincón de Anacahuitas is the largest conservation project in northeastern Mexico. Including 12,141 ha (30,000 ac) of native thornscrub brushland, 51 km (30 mi) of shoreline, considerable wetland acreage, nesting colonies of American white pelicans *(Pelecanus erythrorhynchos)* and roseate spoonbills *(Ajaia ajaja)*, 400 species of birds, and 170 species of plants, the ranch is an ideal land conservation model. The land, located 48 km (30 mi) south of Matamoros, has been owned by the Jorge Martinez family for many generations. The long-term family land management philosophy has been to leave the native brush intact. At present, with funds from the Ford Foundation and with the efforts of Pronatura Noreste, the leading conservation organization in northeastern Mexico, the Texas Center of Policy Studies, and the Nature Conservancy of Texas, the ranch is moving from being mainly a cattle operation to ecotourism (camping, sailing, hiking, bird-watching) and fishing (J. Martinez, pers. comm.). This model is encouraged for other ranches along the Tamaulipan lagoon.

Part II   *Natural Resources*

6   *The Environment*

JOHN W. TUNNELL, JR.

The Laguna Madre of Texas has been characterized as a negative estuary or hypersaline lagoon (Hedgpeth 1947, 1967; Carpelan 1967; Gunter 1967). Rather than being a typical estuarine ecosystem, characterized by freshwater inflow, phytoplankton, and saltmarsh productivity, it is a system characterized by lack of freshwater inflow, with clear and normally phytoplankton-free waters, barren shorelines, and hypersaline conditions, where seagrass meadows predominate. The food chain in the upper Laguna Madre is predominantly based on submerged benthic (bottom-dwelling) plants rather than on free-floating phytoplankton, and most animals then feed via an abbreviated food chain dependent on decomposition of dead seagrass (Fry and Parker 1979). This abbreviated detrital food chain in an enclosed lagoon system makes the transfer of carbon (energy) from seagrass to higher trophic levels highly efficient compared to the phytoplankton-based food chain in typical, positive estuaries (Pulich 1980). This mechanism of high productivity is undoubtedly what explains the observations of earlier workers that the Laguna Madre supplied about 60% of the total Texas bay finfish production, even though it comprised only 20% of the total Texas bay area (Hedgpeth 1947; Simmons 1957). Complementing these data during an early study of upper Laguna Madre productivity, Hellier (1962) calculated the efficiency of conversion of plant production into fish production at 0.074% on a dry weight basis, which is higher than that calculated for offshore fishing banks or coral reefs (Pulich 1980).

Today, we know that the Laguna Madre of Texas and Tamaulipas consists of ecosystems in a state of long-term (decadal) change due primarily to anthropogenic influences. Historically, both systems were driven more by natural climatic events, such as droughts and hurricanes, which produced salinities ranging from brackish (or mixosaline = 0.5–30 ppt) after major wet hurricanes to eusaline (= 30–40 ppt) or hypersaline (= 40–80 ppt) during "normal" climatic conditions, to brine (= more than 80 ppt) during severe droughts (Hedgpeth 1947; Hildebrand 1958, 1969; Copeland 1967). In both Texas and Tamaulipas, increased water circulation and the consequent moderating of salinities appears to be responsible for recent, ongoing ecosystem changes (Hildebrand 1980; Quammen and Onuf 1993). H. Hildebrand (pers. comm.) thinks hurricane rainfall floodwaters and El Niño wet cycles, coupled with long-term drought cycles, are more important regulators of change than circulation changes due to channelization in either system. He also emphasizes, however, that water storage structures, such as Falcon Lake, now greatly restrict freshwater inflow into both systems.

Prior to the hydrologic changes in the Texas Laguna brought about by dredging the Gulf Intracoastal Waterway (GIWW), few studies were conducted that characterized the ecosystem completely, but early works by Gunter (1945a), Hedgpeth (1947), and Collier and Hedgpeth (1950) paint an interesting picture of the upper Laguna Madre. Underwater sills occurring between upper Laguna Madre and Corpus

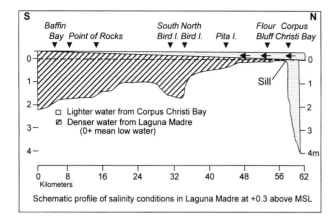

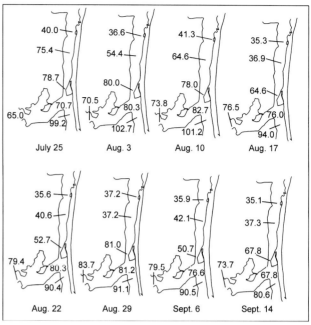

Fig. 6.1. *Diagram of the sill or "bulkhead" at the junction of upper Laguna Madre with Corpus Christi Bay (Adapted from Hedgpeth 1947)*

Fig. 6.2. *Pattern of surface salinities in the upper Laguna Madre during July–September 1946, before completion of the GIWW (Adapted from Hedgpeth 1947)*

Christi Bay (fig. 6.1), a similar one at the mouth of Baffin Bay, and shallow water constrictions across the lagoon combined to result in higher salinities in Baffin Bay and southward toward the Land-Cut. Twenty-eight months of salinity samples, taken weekly by light seaplane, offer the best data set of pre-GIWW conditions (Hedgpeth 1947). Figure 6.2 gives an example of a three-month period (July–September) in 1946 when water exchange between Corpus Christi Bay and upper Laguna Madre reduced salinities due to the autumnal rise in tides (Hedgpeth 1947). Besides droughts and hurricanes, this seasonal exchange seemed to be the only regular moderation in salinities. Frequent fish kills caused by excessive salinities and freezes are well documented prior to channelization, which now allows an escape route for fishes that would formerly have been trapped (Gunter 1945a; Hedgpeth 1947; Simmons 1957; Gunter 1967).

After completion of the GIWW in Texas, and the beginning of the moderation of Texas Laguna salinities, some Texas researchers studied the Laguna Madre de Tamaulipas as a hypersaline ecosystem, providing information about fisheries and hydrography (Hildebrand 1958, 1969), community metabolism (Copeland and Jones 1965), and environmental characteristics (Copeland 1967). Hildebrand (1958, 1969) presented a model of "boom or bust" cycles of fisheries production tied to wet cycles, due to hurricane rainfall and opened Gulf passes, and subsequent dry, excessively hypersaline conditions, respectively. Copeland and Jones (1965) revealed very sparse plant and animal populations and low community metabolism, similar to those of polluted environments. Five years of salinity data, ranging from 51 ppt in 1961 to 295 ppt in 1965 (Copeland 1967), graphically demonstrate the relationship between increasing salinity and decreasing fish species richness. At 51 ppt, 29 species of fishes were encountered; at 95 ppt, there were eight species; and at 110 ppt, only five species were present. When salinities remained between 110 and 120 ppt for almost one year, only sheepshead minnow *(Cyprinodon variegatus)* and tidewater silverside *(Menidia beryllina)* remained. When salinity reached 140 ppt, both of these fishes disappeared, and after 150 ppt, only brine shrimp *(Artemia salinas)* existed. At 295 ppt, brine shrimp had disappeared and sodium chloride was precipitating, although there were large windrows of brine shrimp eggs on the windward shore

(Copeland 1967). In the late fall of 1965, extensive windrows of these eggs were observed on the barrier island lagoonal shores of Boca Jesús María (J. W. Tunnell, pers. observ.). (Please see plates 26 through 32 for a visual characterization of Laguna Madre de Tamaulipas habitats, islands, waters, and surrounding landscapes.)

During the major drought of the 1950s, Hildebrand (1958) was the first to present preliminary information on the biology of the Laguna Madre de Tamaulipas. The northern and southern parts of the lagoon were distinctively different, with the larger northern area exhibiting salinities in excess of 100 ppt (108–117 ppt in March 1955) and no fish or plant communities. These briny waters supported only a brine fly *(Ephydra)* community. In contrast, the southern lagoon around Punta Piedra supported a dense meadow of submerged vegetation, composed primarily of shoalgrass *(Halodule beaudettei* [= *wrightii])* and mermaid's wine glass *(Acetabularia* sp.) of between 0.3 and 1.5 m (1–5 ft). Salinities in this southern area were 41–48 ppt (March 1953 and 1954), and an intense fishery existed. A review of fishery records provided the information for Hildebrand to develop his concept of productive and nonproductive cycles for this ecosystem. Records since the first commercial fishery in 1911 indicate a boom and bust fishery for this northern lagoon, which during the mid-1950s was no more than a shallow brine pool. The presence of oyster shells a few inches down in the northern Laguna Madre sediments was also evidence of a wetter past climate, trending toward a drier one (Hildebrand 1958).

In 1967, Hurricane Beulah struck the northeastern Mexico coastline with subsequent extensive rainfall and provided strong support for Hildebrand's model of boom and bust. In November 1967, three months after the storm, he measured a salinity of only 9 ppt and dragged a minnow seine that yielded 15 species of fishes, including carp *(Cypinus carpio)* and mosquito fish *(Gambusia affinis)*, both freshwater species. Within two years, commercial landings of spotted sea trout *(Cynoscion nebulosus)* went from zero to over a 453,000 kg (1,000,000 lb) (Hildebrand 1969).

Through these and other early studies, several basic principles and concepts were developed about biota in hypersaline ecosystems. Hypersaline environments tend to have fewer species but a larger number of individuals per species (Parker 1959; Gunter 1967). Gunter suggests that the reduced number of species in hypersaline environments follows from the well-known biogeographic principle that impoverishment of species takes place as physical environmental factors vary from optimum. Additionally, vertebrate species (fish) tend to be larger in hypersaline environments (Gunter 1967) and invertebrates tend to be smaller (Parker 1959). Hypersaline "optimum" conditions for vertebrate and invertebrate species appear to be between 40 and 50 ppt, as numbers of red drum *(Sciaenops ocellatus)*, for example, were severely limited in the upper Laguna Madre in salinities greater than 50 ppt. Additionally, year-one juveniles avoided entering the upper Laguna when salinities were greater than 54 ppt (Gunter 1967). Simmons (1957) considered a salinity of 80 ppt or greater to be a lethal concentration for most species.

In this stressed hypersaline environment, trophic-level interactions are simplified, and this type of ecosystem has been described as "pioneer climax" (Pulich 1980). Resident species of plants and animals compete not so much with one another as with the severe physical and chemical conditions of their environment. As salinities increase to the brine level, the reduction in species continues until what are essentially monocultures are achieved.

Organisms that thrive under hypersaline conditions are not those especially adapted to this environment but rather are euryhaline species able to tolerate both high and low salinities (Carpelan 1967). Tremendous osmoregulatory abilities are found within the hearty species that can survive.

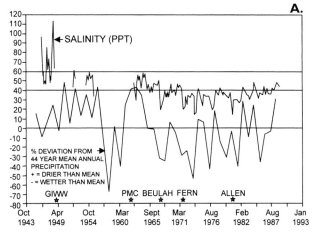

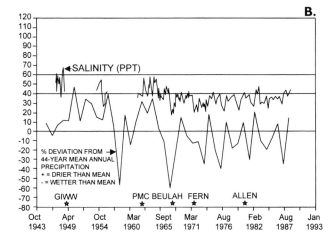

Fig. 6.3. *Relationship between salinity and annual precipitation in the Texas Laguna Madre at stations with the highest salinities before completion of the GIWW: (A) Upper Laguna Madre, south of Baffin Bay; (B) Lower Laguna Madre, north end. Reference lines at 40% and 60% are included to facilitate comparisons over time and between locations. Precipitation is expressed as % deviation from mean annual precipitation over the 44-year period 1945–88. Years drier than the long-term mean are above the 0 line, years wetter than the long-term mean are below the 0 line. GIWW = Gulf Intracoastal Waterway completed; PMC = Port Mansfield Channel made permanent; Hurricanes Beulah, Fern, and Allen were responsible for massive freshwater inputs over short periods of time. (From Quammen and Onuf 1993)*

Convincing evidence is now available that anthropogenic-induced hydrologic changes (dredging of channels in Texas and of tidal inlets in Tamaulipas) have caused moderation of excessive hypersaline conditions and have set in motion long-term ecosystem changes (Hildebrand 1980; Pulich 1980; Quammen and Onuf 1993). Although far more evidence and data exist for the Texas Laguna, information is sufficient for both systems to surmise that the lethal concentrations of salinity of over 80 ppt, and certainly the briny waters of over 100 ppt, are environments of the past. Unless dredge maintenance of barrier island passes and inland channels is halted, those excessive salinities and briny waters may never be reached again.

In Texas, dredging of the GIWW has had the greatest effect on moderating salinities (Simmons 1957; Breuer 1962; Hedgpeth 1967; Quammen and Onuf 1993). Although data prior to dredging the GIWW are sparse and some segments are missing, a salinity time-series graph ranging from the mid-1940s to 1990 clearly shows the ameliorating conditions caused by GIWW dredging and the subsequent increased water circulation (fig. 6.3). Continuing long-term succession of the Laguna seagrass ecosystem (see chapter 7 for details) also seems to be in progress (Quammen and Onuf 1993). Three factors working in concert appear to be responsible for moderating the Texas Laguna Madre hypersaline conditions: (1) increased water exchange with the Gulf of Mexico resulting from channel dredging; (2) increased precipitation since 1965 compared to the previous 20 years; and (3) increased flow into the Laguna from Arroyo Colorado and North Floodway, the two principal drainage systems of the Río Grande Valley agriculture and municipal areas (Quammen and Onuf 1993).

Habitats

The Laguna Madre ecosystems in both Texas and Tamaulipas are similarly dominated by seagrass and bare bottom habitats in the aquatic system, while wind-tidal flats and shallow sandy margins comprise the shoreline. The Laguna Madre of Texas has a larger areal extent of both seagrass and tidal flat habitat, while the Tamaulipas lagoon has more bare open-bay bottom (table 6.1). This last condition is probably related to the fact that drastic environmental fluctuations characterized the Mexican lagoon until more recently, prior to channelization of barrier island passes (inlets), than in Texas. Seagrasses may currently be expanding due to moderated salinities and less frequent extreme salinity fluctuations between brackish and brine.

Calculation of areal extent of habitat types has recently been accomplished for the Tamaulipas system by Ducks Unlimited of Mexico, which classified all wetlands and upland habitats within and around the Laguna Madre of Tamaulipas (DUMAC unpubl. data). This digitized dataset covers 39 quadrangle sheets at a scale of

Table 6.1. *Approximate areal extent of major habitat types in Laguna Madre and Baffin Bay of Texas and Laguna Madre and Laguna el Catán of Tamaulipas*

	LAGUNA MADRE AND BAFFIN BAY, TEXAS			**LAGUNA MADRE AND LAGUNA EL CATÁN, TAMAULIPAS**		
	Areal Extent km² (mi²)	**% MSL**	**% GSA**	**Areal Extent[a] km² (mi²)**	**% MSL**	**% GSA**
Mean sea level (MSL)[b]	1,235 (477)			2,028 (783)		
Gross surface area (GSA)[b]	2,160 (834)			2,728 (1053)		
Tidal flats	917[c] (354)	—	42	508 (196)	—	19
Vegetated bottom	753[d] (291)	61	35	420[e] (162)	21	15
Emergent marsh	8[c] (3)	—	<1	192 (74)	—	7
Bare bottom	482[f] (186)	39	22	1,609 (621)	79	59
		100	100		100	100

Source: Texas data are compilations from C. Onuf (pers. comm.) and Brown et al. (1976, 1977, 1980) unless otherwise noted.

[a] Unpublished data provided by DUMAC.

[b] See table 2.1 for details on MSL and GSA. MSL = vegetated bottom + emergent marsh + bare bottom; GSA = tidal flats + MSL.

[c] Brown et al. (1976, 1977, 1980).

[d] Quammen and Onuf (1993), Laguna Madre seagrass = 732 km² (283 mi²); Pulich (1998) Baffin Bay seagrass = 21 km² (8 mi²); therefore, total Laguna Madre (732 km²/283 mi²) and Baffin Bay (21 km²/8 mi²) = 753 km² (291 mi²).

[e] 338 km² (131 mi²) seagrass, 82 km² (32 mi²) algae = 420 km² (162 mi²) total vegetated bottom (see table 6.2).

[f] Unvegetated lagoonal bottom; 284 km² (110 mi²) Laguna Madre (C. Onuf, pers. comm.); 198 km² (76 mi²) Baffin Bay; total = 482 km² (186 mi²).

1:50,000—the entire northeastern region of Mexico surrounding the Laguna Madre de Tamaulipas (table 6.2). A similar digitized dataset is not available for the entire Laguna Madre of Texas. However, Pulich and Hinson (1996) have produced a classified habitat map from November 1992 TM (Thematic Mapper) imagery for the northern portion of the upper Laguna Madre southward to the Middle Ground region.

In Texas, submerged habitat in the Laguna Madre is predominantly vegetated bottom at 61%, whereas bare bottom occupies 39% (table 6.1). In Tamaulipas, bare bottom is more widespread (79%) than vegetated bottom (21%). When considering the gross surface area (all submerged areas plus emergent marsh and tidal flats), the Texas lagoon has more tidal flats (42%) than the Tamaulipas lagoon (19%). Conversely, the Texas system has less than 1% emergent marsh, whereas in Tamaulipas, this occupies 7% of the area.

In addition to the three major habitats (seagrass beds, bare bay bottom, and wind-tidal flats), several other habitats have small areal coverage but are important and unique to the Laguna Madre ecosystem: jettied tidal inlets, coquina (beach rock), serpulid worm reefs, oyster reefs, and mangroves. Because the major habitat types of seagrasses (see chapter 7) and wind-tidal flats (see chapter 9) are covered in detail later, these smaller habitats are discussed only briefly here. For the most part, other artificial hard substrates besides jetties—including petroleum platforms, riprap, pier pilings, navigation buoys, floating debris, causeway bridges, and channel markers—have not been studied.

Jettied Tidal Inlets Jettied tidal inlets (passes) between the Gulf of Mexico and the Laguna Madre include Mansfield Pass and Brazos Santiago Pass in Texas and Mezquital, Boca Ciega, Boca el Catán, and Boca Santa Isabel in Tamaulipas. There

Table 6.2. *Wetlands and uplands classification surrounding Laguna Madre de Tamaulipas*

	Class	Ha	Ac
M1OW	Marine Subtidal Open Water	275,948	681,868
M2BB	Marine Intertidal Beach/Bar	1,567	3,872
E1OW	Estuarine Subtidal Open Water (bare bottom)	160,850	397,460
E2ABP	Estuarine Intertidal Aquatic Bed (seagrasses)	33,776	83,460
E2AB	Estuarine Intertidal Aquatic Bed (algae)	8,199	20,260
E2FL	Estuarine Intertidal Flat	49,884	123,263
E2EM	Estuarine Intertidal Emergent	19,170	47,369
E2FLMD	Estuarine Intertidal Flat Modified	965	2,385
L1OW	Lacustrine Limnetic Open Water	15,788	39,012
L2OW	Lacustrine Littoral Open Water	7,188	17,762
L2AB	Lacustrine Littoral Aquatic Bed	2,770	6,845
POW	Palustrine Open Water	55	136
PAB	Palustrine Aquatic Bed	199	492
PEMWT	Palustrine Emergent Wetland	36,330	89,771
PEMMD	Palustrine Emergent Modified	5,970	14,752
RIVER	Riverine	5,384	13,304
RVEG	Riverine Vegetated	1,392	3,440
RX	Riverine Artificial	543	1,342
UPAGR	Upland Agriculture	1,082,482	2,674,813
UPBAR	Upland Barren	28,733	70,999
UPDEV	Upland Developed	5,520	13,640
UPHAL	Upland Halophyte Vegetation	87,187	215,439
UPSS	Upland Scrub/Shrub	933,290	2,306,160
CLOUDS	Clouds (cloud cover)	5,122	12,656
Total		2,768,312	6,840,499

Source: DUMAC unpubl. data. Digitized data from Earth Observation Satellite Corporation image (Landsat Thematic Mapper), 18 March 1990, covering 39 1:50,000 scale quad sheets in northeastern Mexico surrounding Laguna Madre de Tamaulipas.

are also jetties at the southern extremity of the Mexican lagoon at the mouth of the Río Soto la Marina at La Pesca. Jetties are made of granite in Texas and of sandstone in Tamaulipas, where they are typically higher, wider, and shorter than their Texas counterparts. Jetties provide an artificial hard-substrate habitat lining these tidal inlets. Introduction of these structures created a stable, hard-substrate habitat within a region of predominantly unstable, soft sediments. As this new ecological environment was introduced, new hard-bottom communities were thus established where they did not previously exist in nearshore coastal waters (Hedgpeth 1954; Britton and Morton 1989).

No information is available on the jetty habitat in Tamaulipas, and little is available for Texas except for Aransas Pass on the north end of Mustang Island, located just north of Padre Island and Laguna Madre. Ecology of the Aransas Pass jetties at Port Aransas, Texas, has been studied since the 1940s (Whitten et al. 1950; Hedgpeth 1954; Hoese et al. 1968; Edwards and Kapraun 1973; Kapraun 1980; Rabalais

1982; Britton and Morton 1989) and continues to undergo investigation (Whorff 1992; Hicks and Tunnell 1993, 1994; Alvarado 1996).

Ecological zonation of biota is readily evident on the Texas jetties, where organisms can attach firmly to the granite surface. In Tamaulipas, however, zonation is not quite as evident nor as distinct, possibly because organisms find it more difficult to attach to the weathering, softer surface of sandstone. Moreover, the Texas jetties at Port Aransas are more than 100 years old, while those in Tamaulipas are only about 20 years old. A distinctive pattern does exist, although it is somewhat simple in terms of typical natural rocky shore biotic zonation. This may be a function of the jetties' relative newness compared to natural rocky shores and/or of the low tidal range of less than 0.5 m (1.5 ft) (Britton and Morton 1989; Alvarado 1996). The supratidal (supralittoral) zone is characterized by blue-green algae (Cyanobacteria) and the sea roach *(Ligia exotica)*. Next, the supratidal fringe is dominated by the lined periwinkle *(Nodilittorina lineolata)*, sometimes in great abundance. In the intertidal (midlittoral or eulittoral) zone, the fragile barnacle *(Chthamalus fragilis)* and the false limpet *(Siphonaria pectinata)* are characteristic inhabitants. Below this, in the subtidal fringe, macroscopic and epiphytic algae predominate and clearly distinguish this zone. Over 100 species of algae have been reported from the Port Aransas jetties, and a distinctive seasonal succession has been noted (Hedgpeth 1953, 1954; Edwards and Kapraun 1973; Britton and Morton 1989; Alvarado 1996; Lehman 1999). Temperate species dominate in the winter and tropical ones are prevalent during the summer. Common genera include green algae (Chlorophyta) such as *Enteromorpha*, *Cladophora*, and *Ulva*; brown algae (Phaeophyta) such as *Padina*, *Ectocarpus*, and *Petalonia*; and red algae (Rhodophyta) such as *Gelidium*, *Bangia*, and *Gracilaria*. Lowest on the jetties, the subtidal (sublittoral) zone is more diverse than its shallower counterparts and includes numerous algae, sponges, hydrozoans, the warty anemone *(Bunodosoma cavernata)*, sea whips (soft corals, *Leptogorgia setacea* and *L. virgulata)*, ivory bush coral (stony coral, *Occulina diffusa)*, numerous bivalves and gastropods, the common octopus *(Octopus vulgaris)*, numerous crabs, the purple sea urchin *(Arbacia punctulata)*, and the Caribbean rock-boring urchin *(Echinometra lucunter)* (Alvarado 1996).

Although the jettied inlets provide a migratory route between the Gulf and the bays and lagoon for many species of shellfish and finfish, certain fishes are characteristic of the jetty habitat. Jetty-associated species include herbivorous blennies *(Labrisomus nuchipinnis, Blennius cristatus,* and *Hypleurochilus geminatus)*, sergeant-major damselfish *(Abudefduf saxitilis)*, Atlantic spadefish *(Chaetodipterus faber)*, and carnivores such as spotted jewfish *(Epinephalus itajara)*, Atlantic needlefish *(Strongylura marina)*, halfbeak *(Hyporhampus unifasciatus)*, and toadfish *(Opsanus beta)* (Alvarado 1996). The most common bird groups using the jetties for resting, and using adjacent waters for feeding, are gulls and terns. Additionally, some sea turtles and Atlantic bottle-nose dolphin, *(Tursiops truncatus)* use the jettied tidal inlets for passage and feeding areas (Shaver 1990a; Schmidly and Shane 1978).

Due to their proximity to navigation lanes, jetties are vulnerable to introduction of exotic or non-indigenous species from foreign shipping traffic. In February 1990, the invasive, edible brown mussel *(Perna perna)* was discovered on the Port Aransas jetties (Hicks and Tunnell 1993). Within four years, it spread a short distance north to the Matagorda jetties and expanded southward all the way to southern Veracruz, Mexico, a distance of over 1,300 km (807 mi) (Hicks and Tunnell 1994). Due to the major macrofouling characteristics of the species in other parts of its range (e.g., Venezuela and Brazil), there was potential for major disruption to the established jetty community and its ecology. Densities of 10,000–12,000/m² were commonly found on South Texas jetties, and densities of up to 27,200/m² of small individuals were recorded (Hicks and Tunnell 1993). Although some species were displaced by the fouling mat of *P. perna*, other species—such as nestling, burrowing, sedentary, and clinging organisms—took advantage of the protective properties of the mussel beds and increased in diversity and abundance during the early to mid-1990s (Smith 1996). By 1996, the mussel beds began to decline, and by 1998, they were difficult to find except in preferred high-energy habitats near the seaward end of jetties. The reason for this decline is as yet not fully understood.

The jetty habitat provides an interesting ecological and biogeographical environment where bay and Gulf species as well as temperate and tropical species mingle. For example, among the oysters, eastern oyster *(Crassostrea virginica)*, the common estuarine species, can be observed adjacent to the crested oyster *(Ostrea equestris)*, an offshore species. Using tree oysters (Isognominidae) as a biogeographic example, the temperate bicolor purse-oyster *(Isognomon bicolor)* is found on Texas jetties, whereas at La Pesca, the tropical flat tree oyster *(I. alatus)* is present. Analogous to the seasonality of macrobenthic algae already mentioned, jetty fish populations, which are predominantly warm temperate, can attract tropical reef species during the summer months when warm tropical waters from the southern Gulf move up along the Texas shoreline (J. W. Tunnell, pers. observ.).

Thus in addition to providing for water and migratory exchange between the lagoons and Gulf, jettied inlets also provide a hard-substrate habitat for a variety of estuarine, Gulf, temperate, and tropical species that normally would not be present, or abundant, in a region dominated by soft substrates.

Beach Rock (Coquina)   Natural rocky coquina outcrops are located in both the Texas and Tamaulipas lagoons at the mouths of their respective bays: Penascal Point at Baffin Bay and Punta Piedras at Laguna el Catán (Prouty 1996; Yañez and Schaepfer 1968). The origin of these unique, natural hard-substrate areas is discussed in chapter 3, but unfortunately there is no biological or ecological information about their role or functioning in the lagoonal ecosystem. Although nothing is known of their biology or ecology today, their presence indicates that a Gulf beach environment occurred at these localities with a previous high-stand of the sea during the Pleistocene and before the existence of the present Laguna Madre.

Serpulid Worm Reefs   Standing today as an indicator of a wetter past climate are the relict serpulid worm reefs of Baffin Bay. Like the beach rock, they provide rare, naturally occurring hard-substrate habitat (Breuer 1957; Andrews 1964; Behrens 1974; Cole 1981; Hardegree 1997). Described as patch reefs and reef fields (Andrews 1964) scattered in various localities around the Baffin Bay system (fig. 6.4), the reefs are composed of the calcareous tubes of serpulid polychaete worms. Although some serpulid polychaetes, such as *Hydroides dianthus*, can be found alive today on the reefs, serpulids no longer appear to be building reef structure.

Approximately 16 km² (6 mi²) of serpulid reefs have been recorded in the Baffin Bay system (Brown et al. 1977). Patch reefs are found near the mouth of the bay and vary in shape and size from small circular structures about 8 m (26 ft) in diameter to larger ellipsoidal ones approximately 40 m (131 ft) in length (Andrews 1964). Height ranges from 0.5 to 2 m (1.5–6.6 ft) above the sediment. Reef fields, on the other hand, are large expanses of reef rock, protruding only slightly above the bay bottom and scattered across the upper reaches of the bay.

Serpulid worm reefs have long been favorite fishing grounds on Baffin Bay because of their generally high level of catch success. Recently, an ecological study was

Fig. 6.4. *Serpulid reef distribution in Baffin and Alazan Bays, Texas (Modified from Andrews 1964)*

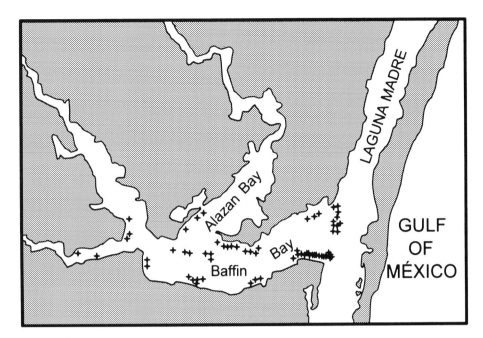

conducted on these reefs to determine if there were more or larger fish around the reefs and if productivity was increased because of them (Hardegree 1997). Neither ichthyofaunal diversity nor catch rate differed significantly between reef and nonreef areas in the study. Likewise, little evidence was found to support the hypothesis that fish congregate and are larger around the reef structures, although the selective sampling technique used (trammel net) would not allow a conclusive answer. Additionally, high species richness (29) and abundance of invertebrates were noted on the reefs, along with biomass and photosynthetic rates of epiphytic algae comparable to those in the upper Laguna Madre seagrasses (Hardegree 1997).

The serpulid reefs of Baffin Bay are now apparently degrading in size and being reduced in distribution. Comparing their reduced distribution and size from earlier works (Breuer 1957; Brown et al. 1977), Hardegree (1997) suggests reef degradation by a combination of natural wave energy, increased boat traffic (prop damage), and fishermen (trampling). Further, even though his work did not show increased size and abundance of fishes around the reefs, the high historical catch rates for the Baffin Bay system indicate that the entire system may be more productive because of the reefs. The serpulid worm reefs, therefore, appear to be a fragile and important component of the Baffin Bay–upper Laguna Madre system and to merit protection from anthropogenic degradation.

Oyster Reefs Oyster reefs are natural accumulations of shells, primarily of the eastern oyster, in the same locality for successive generations over time (Norris 1953). Oyster shell and living oysters provide a hard substrate for settlement of a wide variety of sessile organisms as well as protective habitat for many mobile ones. Although the eastern oyster is broadly euryhaline, oyster reefs thrive best in salinities of 10–30 ppt. However, a population of oysters in South Bay in the southernmost lower Laguna Madre has recently drawn attention because of its survivability in normal to hypersaline conditions. These oysters are of interest because they have been reported to be physiologically (Breuer 1962) and genetically (Groue and Lester 1982; Buroker 1983) divergent from other populations (King et al. 1994). Oysters in the lower Laguna Madre are atypical in that they have adapted to hypersaline

82

JOHN W. TUNNELL, JR.

Table 6.3. *Number of species found in each division (plants) or phylum (animals) within the estuaries of the Texas Coastal Bend, upper Laguna Madre and Baffin Bay (Tunnell and Alvarado 1996), and Laguna Madre de Tamaulipas (Leija-Tristan et al., in press; DUMAC 1993).*

Taxon	Texas Coastal Bend[a]	Upper Laguna Madre and Baffin Bay	Laguna Madre de Tamaulipas
Division Cyanophyta	9	2	23
Division Bacillariophyta	341	177	57
Division Pyrrhophyta	43	19	14
Division Chlorophyta	33	5	37
Division Phaeophyta	17		18
Division Rhodophyta	68	1	65
Division Spermatophyta	6	6	6
Phylum Sarcomastigophora	31		
Phylum Ciliophora	13	6	
Phylum Porifera	11		
Phylum Cnidaria	36	7	17
Phylum Ctenophora	2	2	
Phylum Platyhelminthes	3		
Phylum Nemertea	33	5	
Phylum Gastrotricha	2		
Phylum Nematoda	50	3	
Phylum Rotifera	8		
Phylum Kinorhyncha	1		
Phylum Gnathostomulida	1		
Phylum Annelida (Class Polychaeta)	289	73	28
Phylum Mollusca	230	72	86
Phylum Arthropoda	343	110	96
Phylum Sipunculida	3		
Phylum Echiurida	1		
Phylum Tardigrada[b]	1?		
Phylum Bryozoa	19	4	
Phylum Phoronida	2	1	
Phylum Brachiopoda	1		
Phylum Echinodermata	29	9	16
Phylum Chaetognatha	4	3	

conditions (Breuer 1962). The South Bay population is probably a remnant of when the Río Grande flowed into that area (White et al. 1986). Recent research has shown that Laguna Madre oysters are genetically divergent from oysters inhabiting other parts of the Texas coast and areas farther eastward (King et al. 1994). If the eastern oysters in Laguna Madre of Texas are unique, they warrant protection.

In Laguna Madre de Tamaulipas, oysters are harvested commercially. The amount harvested varies greatly (see fig. 15.24) and is probably governed by lagoon

Table 6.3. (continued)

Taxon	Texas Coastal Bend[a]	Upper Laguna Madre and Baffin Bay	Laguna Madre de Tamaulipas
Phylum Chordata			
Subphylum Urochordata	14	1	
Subphylum Hemichordata	2	1	
Subphylum Vertebrata			
Class Elasmobranchiomorphi	23	7	18
Class Osteichthyes	211	79	122
Class Reptilia	3	3	3
Class Aves	157	130[c]	98
Class Mammalia	4	2	2
Total	2,043	938	706

[a] The Texas Coastal Bend includes three estuaries: Mission-Aransas Estuary (Copano and Aransas Bays); Nueces Estuary (Nueces and Corpus Christi Bays); and upper Laguna Madre and Baffin Bay.

[b] Not in literature but known to exist.

[c] This is an arbitrary number and should be used with caution. The Chaney et al. (1996) checklist does not list geographic distribution for birds, so 130 of 157 aquatic birds from the Coastal Bend was estimated for upper Laguna Madre and Baffin Bay.

Table 6.4. *Overview of numbers of species in major groups from the Texas Coastal Bend, upper Laguna Madre and Baffin Bay (Tunnell and Alvarado 1996), and Laguna Madre de Tamaulipas (Leija-Tristan et al., in press)*

Group[a]	Texas Coastal Bend[a]	Upper Laguna Madre and Baffin Bay	Laguna Madre de Tamaulipas
Phytoplankton and Microalgae	393	198	94
Macroalgae	118	6	120
Vascular Plants	6	6	6
Total Plants	517	210	220
Invertebrates	1,112	505	243
Protochordates	16	2	0
Vertebrates	398[b]	221[b]	243
Total Animals	1,526	728	486
Total Plants and Animals	2,043	938	706

[a] See table 6.3 for breakdown of species within each group.

[b] Aquatic birds are listed in these numbers of vertebrates from Texas Coastal Bend and upper Laguna Madre and Baffin Bay only for comparative purposes with aquatic bird list from the Tamaulipas lagoon. Since Chaney et al. (1996) did not separate bird distribution in their checklist, 130 of 157 aquatic birds from the Coastal Bend were estimated to occur in upper Laguna Madre–Baffin Bay.

salinities. These oysters may also be genetically distinct, but no research has been conducted on these populations.

Mangroves   Mangrove forests *(mangal,* an international term denoting a mangrove community) are the tropical shoreline equivalent of temperate smooth cordgrass *(Spartina alterniflora)* salt marshes: northern Gulf of Mexico estuarine shorelines are dominated by cordgrass marshes and southern estuaries and lagoons by mangroves. In the Texas Laguna, cordgrass is limited by hypersalinity and is only sparsely distributed in the northernmost and southernmost extremities. Only one mangrove species, black mangrove *(Avicennia germinans),* is sufficiently tolerant of Texas winters to form a substantial mangal in Laguna Madre (Sherrod and McMillan 1981). This species is most common and widely distributed along the southernmost shores of the Texas Laguna, but plants are scattered along shorelines throughout the Laguna Madre. Texas black mangroves rarely exceed 2 m (6.5 ft), unlike their tropical counterparts, which may reach 10 m (33 ft). Because they are at the extreme northern limits of their range, catastrophic mortality due to winter freezes may occur, as in the severe freezes in 1983 and 1989. McMillan (1975) suggested that the Texas population belongs to a genetic race capable of surviving colder temperatures. The red mangrove *(Rhizophora mangle)* was observed at South Padre Island before the 1983 freeze (J. W. Tunnell, pers. observ.). Within the Laguna Madre de Tamaulipas, black mangroves have been observed scattered along the shoreline between Carboneras and Punta Piedras (J. W. Tunnell, pers. observ.). Several buttonwoods *(Conocarpus erectus)* were also seen during December 1998. The most northerly extent of the typically zoned tropical mangal is within the Río Soto la Marina at the southernmost extremity of the Laguna Madre de Tamaulipas. Although zonation is narrow due to steep riverbanks, red, black, and white mangroves *(Laguncularia racemosa)* are present in the subtidal, intertidal, and supratidal zones, respectively. Interestingly, the riverbanks of the Río Soto la Marina in the La Pesca area also have smooth cordgrass growing riverward of the mangal.

Biota

No comprehensive surveys or checklists exist for the biota of the two Laguna Madre systems combined. However, two recent works allow an overview of what is known and what information gaps exist. In Texas a recent comprehensive checklist of all species occurring within the estuarine waters and islands of the Texas Coastal Bend included the upper Laguna Madre and Baffin Bay system (Tunnell and Alvarado 1996). There is no such compilation for the lower Laguna Madre, although such a compilation for major taxonomic groups was recently completed for the Tamaulipas lagoon (Leija-Tristan et al., in press). Table 6.3 and table 6.4 compare the Texas Coastal Bend, the upper Laguna Madre–Baffin Bay complex, and the Laguna Madre de Tamaulipas. Review of the table reveals two important matters: less work has been done on some taxonomic groups in Tamaulipas, and species richness is dramatically lower in both hypersaline lagoon systems than in the more diverse normal or positive estuaries to the north—about one-third the number of species. A third consideration is that tabulation or listing of species has not been accomplished for some groups. With further research, it is thought that the Tamaulipas lagoon may prove to have greater species richness due to the presence of tropical species within that system. Greater numbers of macroalgae, molluscs, and fish species in the present list are indicators that this is probable.

7   *Seagrass Meadows*

KIM WITHERS

Seagrass meadows are among the most common coastal ecosystems and are extremely valuable because of their diverse roles within the landscape. The fundamental role seagrasses play is to provide complex structure in both water column (leaves) and sediments (roots and rhizomes). Physically, this structure baffles waves, reduces erosion, and promotes water clarity by removing suspended sediments. Seagrasses increase bottom area as a result of leaf surfaces allowing complex epiphytic communities to develop. Dense meadows may consist of more than 4,000 plants per square meter with an associated increase in bottom area of 15 to 20 times (McRoy and Helfferich 1977). Biologically, seagrasses provide nursery areas, refuge, and rich foraging grounds for a variety of estuarine fish and invertebrates, including a number of commercially and recreationally important species. Although consumed by few organisms, seagrasses are essential food sources for some waterfowl and sea turtles. Seagrasses play a major role in nutrient cycling within the water column and sediments, and their detritus is an important source of organic material to adjacent coastal and nearshore ecosystems.

Seagrass habitats are typically among the most productive submerged habitats. Annual production of seagrasses and associated primary producers (i.e., epiphytes, benthic algae, and phytoplankton) in subtropical areas such as Texas ranges from 1,000 to 4,000 grams Carbon per square meter (gC/m^2) (McRoy and McMillan 1977), with daily productivity in upper Laguna Madre of up to 3 g C/m^2 (Tomasko and Dunton 1995). At these values, seagrass communities rank with the most productive terrestrial monocultural crops such as corn and often exceed productivity of coral reefs and oceanic upwelling areas. Only salt marshes are more productive than seagrasses. Entire fisheries may depend directly or indirectly on production by seagrass habitats (McRoy and Helfferich 1977). Historically, they have supported over 50% of the Texas inshore finfish catch (Hedgepeth 1967).

Five seagrass species in three families are found in bay systems along the Texas and Mexico coast (taxonomy follows Jones et al. 1997): shoalgrass *(Halodule beaudettei* [= *wrightii*]) and manatee-grass *(Cymodocea* [= *Syringodium*] *filiforme)* in the family Cymodoceaceae; wigeon grass *(Ruppia maritima)* in the family Ruppiaceae; and clover grass *(Halophila engelmannii)* and turtle-grass *(Thalassia testudinum)* in the family Hydrocharitaceae (plate 35). In the Texas Laguna Madre, seagrass meadows are the most common submerged habitat type. Although permanent meadows of perennial species (e.g., shoalgrass, turtle-grass) and/or wigeon grass (an annual species) occur in nearly all bay systems along the Texas Gulf Coast, the majority (79%) of the state's seagrass cover is found in Laguna Madre (Pulich 1998). The concentration of Texas' seagrass resources in Laguna Madre is primarily the result of geographic and climatic factors rather than impacts or other disturbances on the upper coast. Seagrasses dominate in areas where rainfall is low and evaporation is high, with average salinities above 20 ppt. Seagrasses are largely excluded from bays north of

Pass Cavallo, where rainfall and inflows are high and salinities average less than 20 ppt, as well as from the upper, fresher portions of most estuaries. Thus, seagrasses in the Laguna Madre constitute a unique resource that cannot be duplicated elsewhere on the Texas coast.

General Seagrass Ecology

Factors Affecting Species Composition and Zonation The presence of seagrass species and their community zonation are determined by substrate composition, wave energy, water depth (related to light penetration and exposure tolerance), salinity tolerance, and successional stage. Although shoalgrass and turtle-grass may be found on sandy substrates, both grow better on muddier substrates. The other species are found almost exclusively on muddy substrates, with clover grass able to tolerate practically liquid mud as well as highly polluted areas (den Hartog 1977). Seagrasses typically colonize fairly low energy, shallow water areas with restricted circulation.

Most seagrasses require a minimum of 11–25% surface irradiance (SI; the light present at the water's surface relative to the plant surface) to maintain themselves (Duarte 1991; Kenworthy and Haunert 1991; Fonseca 1994). However, 41–46% SI provided ideal growing conditions for shoalgrass at an average depth of 1.25 m (4.1 ft), whereas 17–19% SI resulted in signs of light stress (Dunton 1994). Neither shoalgrass nor turtle-grass were able to tolerate light levels below 14–16% SI, particularly during spring and summer when increased water temperatures increase the metabolic demands of growth and tissue maintenance (Czerny 1994; Czerny and Dunton 1995). In turbid waters, seagrasses are usually restricted to areas shallower than 1 m (Thayer et al. 1975).

Seagrasses must be submerged in water and are not tolerant of prolonged exposure. Shoalgrass and clover grass have the widest range of depth tolerances, extending from mean highest high water (MHHW) to considerable depths (McNulty et al. 1972; den Hartog 1977). However, clover grass is mostly found in deeper water and is tolerant of low light situations. Wigeon grass is typically found in shallow water only, between mean lowest high water (MLHW) and mean lowest low water (MLLW) (McNulty et al. 1972). Turtle-grass is found below MLHW to depths of 10–12 m (32.8–39.4 ft) (McNulty et al. 1972; den Hartog 1977). Manatee-grass is not tolerant of desiccation, so it is restricted to areas below MLLW (den Hartog 1977).

Salinity tolerances of seagrass species are important determinants of species composition and growth. Shoalgrass has the widest salinity tolerance (3.5–70 ppt), with an optimum around 45 ppt; death occurred after 28 days at 70 ppt in the laboratory (McMahan 1968). Dwarfing was noted at about 60 ppt (Simmons 1957), although growth continued in laboratory experiments (McMillan and Moseley 1967). Clover grass has the narrowest range (13–50 ppt). Turtle-grass and manatee-grass are intermediate in their tolerances. Turtle-grass tolerates salinities of 0–60 ppt (optimal 20–36 ppt). Manatee-grass tolerates 3.5–50 ppt (optimal 35 ppt) but ceased growth at 45 ppt in laboratory experiments and died within 21 days at 52.5 ppt (McMillan and Moseley 1967). Rates of photosynthesis declined in turtle-grass and manatee-grass when salinities decreased below 35 ppt (Zieman 1975). Wigeon grass is essentially a freshwater species with marked salinity tolerance (0–70 ppt) (McMillan and Moseley 1967; Kantrud 1991).

Succession Succession in seagrass communities is determined by species size, tolerance of environmental variability and disturbance, and competitive ability (den

Fig. 7.1. Succession in seagrass meadows in Laguna Madre (Modified from Zieman 1982)

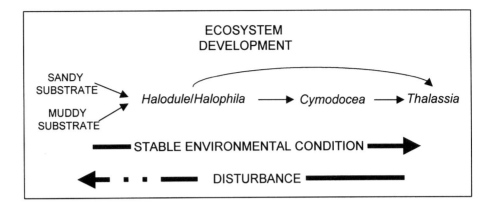

Hartog 1977; Zieman 1982). Shoalgrass and clover grass are small and have little capacity to compete with larger, more aggressive species; they are typically found in habitats unsuitable for other species. Turtle-grass and manatee-grass are medium-sized species with fairly high tolerance to environmental variability and high competitive ability. These differences in ecological capacities determine how succession will proceed (fig. 7.1). Shoalgrass and wigeon grass are pioneer species that can rapidly colonize bare areas either by seed or vegetative branching. They stabilize sediments and help to protect the integrity of sediment surfaces by buffering effects of currents. Shoalgrass colonizes bare or algae-covered substrate, possibly with clover grass in the understory or at the edges of meadows in deeper water. Although frequently absent, manatee-grass may appear next, often intermixed with shoalgrass in earlier successional phases, and later with turtle-grass as climax is approached. As sediments become very stable, turtle-grass begins to colonize the area, eventually constituting the climax.

As succession in seagrass meadows proceeds toward climax, structural changes occur. The most obvious change is increased leaf area, which allows epiphyte colonization (Zieman 1982). Communities characterized by shoalgrass and/or clover grass develop rapidly after disturbance and are generally a simple mosaic of species. Epiphytic flora is composed mainly of diatoms. On the larger leaves of turtle-grass and manatee-grass, epiphytic communities may contain hundreds of species of algae (den Hartog 1977). Grazing probably controls epiphytic community composition to some extent. Dominance of tightly adhering and/or encrusting species are, at least in part, the result of selective grazing (van Montfrans et al. 1984).

Seagrass Distribution and Meadow Community Composition

Upper Laguna Madre and Baffin Bay In upper Laguna Madre, seagrasses currently cover about 243 km^2 (94 mi^2) (Quammen and Onuf 1993; fig. 7.2). Shoalgrass is the dominant species, but all species have been reported. Three distinct species associations are common: sparse, monotypic shoalgrass in higher energy environments like the mainland shoreline near the entrance of Baffin Bay; dense meadows of shoalgrass with clover grass as subdominant vegetation in shallow, low energy areas; and clover grass–dominated areas with shoalgrass as subdominant vegetation, primarily in deeper and/or more turbid areas such as along the edges of channels (Brown et al. 1976; Merkord 1978; Quammen and Onuf 1993). Turtle-grass, manatee-grass, and wigeon grass occur locally (Phillips 1974; Merkord 1978; McMillan 1979; Williamson 1980). Wigeon grass can be abundant locally and seasonally (C. Onuf, pers. comm.) and has been found in channels paralleling the John F. Kennedy Causeway, east of Marker 21, near Pita Island, and at the northern end of

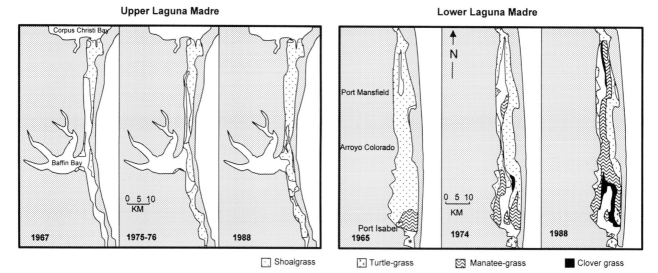

Fig. 7.2. *Distribution of seagrasses in Texas Laguna Madre between 1965 and 1988. * = No samples taken from South Bay in 1965 (Redrawn from Quammen and Onuf 1993)*

The Hole (Merkord 1978). Seeds of wigeon grass were common in sediments, suggesting that it may be more common than is documented (McMillan 1985). Turtle-grass may be found in deeper water (>0.5 m) with moderate salinities (Brown et al. 1977). No turtle-grass meadows have been mapped in the upper Laguna Madre (Merkord 1978; Quammen and Onuf 1993), but one fairly large meadow was observed near Humble Channel in 1989 (Withers 1996a). Manatee-grass cover has increased since 1988 surveys and is becoming dominant in some areas (C. Onuf, pers. comm.) Seagrass density decreases south of Baffin Bay, with only poorly developed meadows found near the Land-Cut and within The Hole (Brown et al. 1977).

Seagrass meadows within Baffin Bay and its secondary bays covered only about 21 km² (8 mi²) in 1992 (Pulich 1998). Shoalgrass is the dominant species with lesser amounts of clover grass and wigeon grass. Dense, marginal meadows grow on the narrow, shallow shelf along the north shore of Baffin Bay, along the southeast shore of Alazan Bay, and in Cayo del Grullo and Cayo del Infiernillo (Kreuz 1973; Dokken 1981; Cornelius 1984).

Lower Laguna Madre   Seagrasses cover about 480 km² (185 mi²) in lower Laguna Madre (Pulich et al. 1997). Although shoalgrass once dominated the system, diversity has increased over the last 30 years. Once only a minor member of the community, manatee-grass has come to dominate the system, and both clover grass and turtle-grass coverage has increased (Quammen and Onuf 1993). Wigeon grass may be found locally, particularly along the Gulf Intracoastal Waterway (GIWW) north of Three Islands (Chin 1978; Brown et al. 1980). Turtle-grass had been largely confined to South Bay and southerly portions of the lower Laguna Madre near passes (Brown et al. 1980; Quammen and Onuf 1993) but has become more widespread since 1988 (C. Onuf, pers. comm.). Clover grass is also found mostly in the southern portion of the bay, in deeper water where meadows transition to bare bay bottom (Quammen and Onuf 1993).

Algae and Phytoplankton   Various species of algae are common components of seagrass meadows. In upper Laguna Madre, attached algae are uncommon, although several species of green and red algae may be found in soft bottoms or attached to shell or other solid substrates within meadows. Mermaid's wine glass (*Acetabularia*) was abundantly distributed in lower Laguna Madre, particularly east of GIWW

(Chin 1978). Unattached or "drift" algae may be found in large quantities. Communities composed largely of red algae were common in shoalgrass meadows of both upper and lower Laguna Madre (Chin 1978; Merkord 1978; Williamson 1980). Drift algae tends to accumulate in depressions, in the taller leaves of manatee-grass associated with shoalgrass, or wherever movement is hindered. Drift algae was found at over 70% of stations sampled in both upper and lower Laguna Madre. Drift algae contributed more to baywide biomass than any single seagrass species (Onuf 1996a). Leaves of seagrasses provide substrate for a wide variety of epiphytic micro- and macroalgae in Laguna Madre (Humm and Hildebrand 1962; Conover 1964). These algae are highly productive, sometimes contributing over 50% of total productivity per unit area of seagrass meadow (Morgan and Kitting 1984). In addition, they are palatable and have a more important trophic role than their seagrass hosts, because they are directly grazed by a wide variety of invertebrates (Kitting et al. 1984). Diatoms dominate the phytoplankton community associated with seagrass meadows in Laguna Madre, and dinoflagellates are common (Simmons 1957; Breuer 1962; Hildebrand and King 1978; Chaney 1988).

Successional Change Extreme hypersalinity prior to completion of GIWW probably excluded seagrasses from much of the Laguna Madre (Quammen and Onuf 1993). However, in the mid-1920s, the bottom of upper Laguna Madre north of Baffin Bay was described as grassy or muddy "depending on proximity to sediment-laden rivers or creeks" (Pearson 1929). Although this description seems incongruous since no rivers or creeks run into upper Laguna Madre, I think Pearson may have been describing water flowing across the large sandy flat that almost completely separated Corpus Christi Bay from the lagoon shown on the map in his report. No other information concerning former seagrass extent or species composition is available until TPWD surveys of the late 1950s. It seems logical that seagrass populations waxed and waned in Laguna Madre prior to completion of GIWW in response to changing salinities caused by drought and tropical storms and hurricanes. In this disturbance-dominated regime, it is probable that only shoalgrass and wigeon grass were present in upper Laguna Madre. Manatee-grass and turtle-grass may have been found in lower Laguna Madre, particularly near Brazos Santiago Pass where salinities would have been tolerable, but shoalgrass and wigeon grass likely dominated.

In 1965, shoalgrass dominated in both upper and lower Laguna Madre and was the only species present in upper Laguna Madre (see fig. 7.2). Both manatee-grass and turtle-grass were present near the pass at Port Isabel in lower Laguna Madre (McMahan 1966; 1967a). By 1974, manatee-grass had expanded considerably in lower Laguna Madre, displacing shoalgrass (Merkord 1978). Shoalgrass coverage had increased in upper Laguna Madre, with areas of clover grass noted where meadows transitioned to bare bottom. By 1988, manatee-grass extended nearly the length of lower Laguna Madre at intermediate depths but had been replaced by turtle-grass in the extreme south (Quammen and Onuf 1993).

Between 1965 and 1988, shoalgrass in upper Laguna Madre increased and covered nearly the entire basin. Manatee-grass was not found in samples taken from upper Laguna Madre in 1988, but patches were observed in transit between stations (Quammen and Onuf 1993) as well as north of the JFK Causeway (J. W. Tunnell, Jr., pers. comm.). Manatee-grass cover has increased dramatically since 1988 and currently constitutes about 17% of total seagrass cover (C. Onuf, pers. comm.).

Succession appears to be proceeding toward a turtle-grass climax in lower Laguna Madre, with little further expansion of manatee-grass expected (Quammen and Onuf 1993). Manatee-grass is already established in areas with suitable depth and water clarity, but there is ample room for expansion of turtle-grass. Small patches of turtle-grass were observed as far north as Arroyo Colorado and will probably expand and coalesce, displacing manatee-grass, as has already occurred farther south. However, at its present rate of expansion, it is unlikely that turtle-grass will dominate in lower Laguna Madre for another 50 years (Onuf 1996a). In upper Laguna Madre, the spread of manatee-grass suggests that succession is proceeding slowly to the turtle-grass climax (Quammen and Onuf 1993). Manatee-grass patches appear to be expanding rapidly, suggesting that in the next few decades composition of upper Laguna Madre meadows will become similar to present composition of lower Laguna Madre meadows (Onuf 1996a).

Seasonality (Phenology)   With the exception of wigeon grass, seagrasses are generally perennial, but populations of both shoalgrass and clover grass may appear or disappear quickly (Phillips and Meñez 1988) and probably did so prior to completion of GIWW. In Laguna Madre, seagrasses are dormant between December and March and begin growing in April (Conover 1964). Luxuriant growth is typically observed between May and August, although biomass tends to diminish in late July and early August when air and water temperatures peak. Shoalgrass biomass typically peaks in early summer and again in early fall after temperatures have moderated (Morgan and Kitting 1984).

Animal Communities

Invertebrates   The invertebrate community associated with seagrass meadows is diverse and consists of epibenthic, benthic, epiphytic, and nektonic organisms. Most studies have been confined to upper Laguna Madre, and most studies of benthic organisms have concentrated on molluscs, so there is little information concerning distribution or abundance of annelids or epibenthic crustaceans (e.g., crabs, amphipods). Invertebrate nekton have been almost completely ignored. Table 7.1 shows numbers of invertebrate families and species that have been collected. The low numbers for lower Laguna Madre reflect the lack of studies there rather than a lack of diversity. It is likely that communities in lower Laguna Madre are just as diverse as in upper Laguna Madre, and they may be more diverse, since seagrass community composition is more diverse and the likelihood of finding tropical species is also increased. The potential for increased diversity in lower Laguna Madre is reflected by increased numbers of bivalve families and species collected in the few studies conducted there. Low numbers for Baffin Bay reflect the lack of seagrass habitat within the bay but are also affected by other factors. Extreme salinity fluctuations combined with low recruitment due to lack of circulation between Baffin Bay and upper Laguna Madre may prevent establishment of an abundant and/or diverse benthic community.

It is probable that polychaetes are the most abundant benthic invertebrates in seagrass meadows in Laguna Madre. In studies where polychaetes were collected and identified (for upper Laguna Madre: Rickner 1979; White et al. 1983c, 1989; Montagna 1992, 1993; Rocha et al. 1995; for lower Laguna Madre: White et al. 1986), they were often the most abundant member of the community, and always had higher species richness than the molluscan component. Members of the families Spionidae, Ampharetidae, Capitellidae, and Maldanidae were typically dominant. Most members of these families are deposit feeders, although some spionids are suspension feeders.

Gastropods typically outnumber bivalves in seagrass meadows but have lower species richness. Ceriths (Family Cerithiidae), slippershells (*Crepidula* spp.), and

Table 7.1. Comparison of the numbers of invertebrate families and species recorded in seagrass meadows in Texas Laguna Madre (ULM = upper; LLM = lower) and Baffin Bay, and Laguna Madre de Tamaulipas

Taxon	ULM	LLM	Baffin Bay	Tamaulipas
Phylum Bryozoa	X	X	?	?
Phylum Platyhelminthes	X	?	?	?
Phylum Rhynchocoela				
Families	2	3	0	?
Species	2	3	0	?
Phylum Annelida				
Class Oligochaeta	X	?	?	?
Class Polychaeta				
Families	20	6	3	?
Species	47	9	3	?
Phylum Mollusca				
Class Gastropoda				
Families	19	10	?	4
Species	33	13	?	4
Class Bivalvia				
Families	16	20	?	7
Species	26	30	?	11
Subphylum Crustacea				
Class Malacostraca				
Order Ostracoda	X	?	?	?
Order Cumacea				?
Families	1	1	?	?
Species	2	1	?	?
Order Amphipoda				
Families	8	2	?	?
Species	11	2	?	?
Order Isopoda				
Families	3	2	?	?
Species	4	2	?	?
Order Tanaidaceae				
Families	1	1	?	?
Species	1	1	?	?
Order Decapoda				
Families	11	?	?	?
Species	14	?	?	?
Class Cirripedia				
Order Thoracica				
Families	1	?	?	?
Species	1	?	?	?

Table 7.1. (continued)

Taxon	ULM	LLM	Baffin Bay	Tamaulipas
Subphylum Chelicerata				
Class Pycnogonida	I	?	?	?
Phylum Echinodermata				
Class Holothuroidea	4	?	?	?
Class Ophiuroida	I	?	?	?
Class Asteroida	X	?	?	?

Note: X = present but no other information; ? = unknown.

caecums (Family Caecidae) were common in seagrass meadows throughout Laguna Madre (Cornelius 1975; Rickner 1979; Powell et al. 1982; Wilhite et al. 1982; Williamson 1980; White et al. 1983c, 1986, 1989; Rocha et al. 1995). The dominant species are deposit feeders, but a number of predators (Family Pyramidellidae), scavengers (e.g., bruised nassa, *Nassarius vibex*), and herbivores (e.g., striate bubble, *Bulla striata*) are also common.

Atlantic papermussel *(Amygdalum papyrium)* and Morton eggcockle *(Laevicardium mortoni)* are bivalves considered indicator species of shoalgrass meadows (Parker 1959). Other common species in seagrass meadows throughout Laguna Madre include tellins and macomas (Family Tellinidae), dwarf Atlantic surfclam *(Mulinia lateralis)*, and—particularly in turtle-grass meadows—lucines (Family Lucinidae) (Cornelius 1975; Rickner 1979; Powell et al. 1982; Wilhite et al. 1982; Williamson 1980; White et al. 1983c, 1986, 1989; Rocha et al. 1995). Bay scallops *(Argopecten irradians)* are commercially important members of the seagrass bivalve community. These bivalves exhibit cyclical population levels, appearing in large numbers at irregular intervals, then disappearing. All bivalves are filter feeders.

When benthic and epiphytic crustaceans (i.e., amphipods, isopods, cumaceans, and tanaids) within seagrass meadows in Laguna Madre were studied (White et al. 1983c, 1986, 1989; Rocha et al. 1995), they were conspicuous and often abundant members of the invertebrate community. These organisms are typically herbivores or detritivores and are trophically important because they link primary producers with higher consumers.

Shrimp and crabs are the most prominent of the epibenthic and/or nektonic crustaceans. Some of these organisms are also important commercial species, notably penaeid shrimp—brown shrimp *(Farfantepenaeus aztecus)*, pink shrimp *(F. duorarum)*, and white shrimp *(Litopenaeus setiferus)*—and blue crab *(Callinectes sapidus)*. Although both Simmons (1957) and Breuer (1962) included invertebrate nekton in their surveys, only Chaney (1988) addressed invertebrate nekton in the Laguna Madre in detail. Shrimp dominated the assemblage, followed by blue crabs. Grass shrimp *(Palaemonetes* spp.) were the most abundant species recovered. Jellyfish (Phylum Cnidaria), comb jellies (Phylum Ctenophora), mantis shrimp (Phylum Crustacea, Order Stomatopoda), and squid (Phylum Mollusca, Class Cephalopoda) were also collected. Shrimp and crabs are typically omnivorous, eating everything from other invertebrates to detritus and carrion. Jellyfish, comb jellies, and squid are carnivorous predators.

Echinoderms are not typically abundant but may constitute a significant proportion of animal biomass in seagrass meadows because they are large (Rocha et al.

1995). Sea cucumbers (Class Holothuroidea) are most frequently encountered, and brittle stars (Class Ophiuroidea) may also be found (Rickner 1979; Montagna 1993; Rocha et al. 1995). Sea cucumbers are typically deposit or suspension feeders, whereas brittle stars may use several feeding modes including deposit, filter, and suspension feeding as well as carnivory and scavenging. Ribbon worms (Phylum Rhynchocoela) are also common deposit feeders and predators in seagrass beds (Rickner 1979; Montagna 1993; Rocha et al. 1995; Wern 1995).

Fish Fish in seagrass meadows can be categorized based on their life history and temporal use (Kikuchi 1980). Permanent residents are generally small, cryptic, less mobile species that spend their entire life in the meadow, such as pipefishes, gobies, blennies, and eels. Seasonal residents spend their juvenile or subadult stages or spawning season in seagrass meadows. This group includes many important commercial or sport species such as drums, mojarras, grunts, and porgies. Transients are present infrequently and unpredictably and include large carnivores of offshore or oceanic origin, such as jackfish and mackerel (Zieman 1982). Many fish found in seagrass meadows are carnivores that prey on the abundant fish and crustacean inhabitants. Several species include seagrasses in their diets, such as sheepshead *(Archosargus probatocephalus)*, black drum *(Pogonias chromis)*, cownose ray *(Rhinoptera quadriloba)* (Carangelo et al. 1975); pinfish *(Lagodon rhomboides)* (Darnell 1958; Carr and Adams 1973); Atlantic needlefish *(Strongylura marina)* (Darnell 1958); and striped mullet *(Mugil cephalus)* (Pullen 1960).

Simmons (1957) surveyed the fish fauna of upper Laguna Madre without noting which species occurred within seagrass meadows. Twenty-nine species of small fish in 18 families were collected from mixed wigeon grass and shoalgrass meadows between the JFK Causeway and Bird Island Basin (Hellier 1962). The most abundant species were striped mullet, pinfish, spot *(Leiostomus xanthurus)*, and bay anchovy *(Anchoa mitchelli)*. Yearly production of fishes in the area was calculated at 156 kg/ha (139 lb/ac). In a single shoalgrass meadow near Bird Island Basin, 26 species of small fish in 16 families were collected (Chaney 1988). Tidewater silversides *(Menidia peninsulae)* and rainwater killifish *(Lucania parva)* were the most abundant species (see fig. 15.5). Juvenile spotted seatrout *(Cynoscion nebulosus)* were collected from midsummer to early winter, while juvenile red drum *(Sciaenops ocellatus)* were collected from winter to early spring. Postlarval and juvenile spotted seatrout prefer seagrass meadows during warm weather (Lassuy 1983). Red drum juveniles remain in estuaries for at least six months (Reagan 1985) and many remain in the bays for up to five years before moving offshore (L. McEachron, pers. comm.).

Although a number of studies have addressed the fish fauna of Baffin Bay, and particularly Alazan Bay (Breuer 1957; Fuls 1974; Tinnin 1974; Krull 1976; Dokken 1981; Cornelius 1984; Dokken et al. 1984; Hardegree 1997), none included seagrass meadows in the sampling protocol.

In lower Laguna Madre, Breuer (1962) surveyed the fish fauna without differentiating which species were collected from seagrass meadows. In South Bay, spot and tidewater silversides dominated in seagrass habitats (Hook 1991). Larval fish communities of manatee-grass meadows, shoalgrass meadows, and bare areas were compared during summer, fall, and winter spawning periods using cluster analysis (Tolan 1994; Tolan et al. 1997). Larval anchovies *(Anchoa spp.)* dominated vegetated areas during summer and fall spawning periods. Tidewater silversides were also important members of the shoalgrass ichthyofaunal assemblage during fall. During winter spawning, Gulf menhaden *(Brevoortia patronus)* dominated in manatee-grass areas, whereas densities of pinfish and Gulf menhaden were nearly equal in shoalgrass meadows. Overall, members of the families Engraulidae and Clupeidae dominated in vegetated areas, and juveniles generally preferred shoalgrass meadows to manatee-grass meadows.

Sea Turtles   Turtle canneries along the Texas coast in the mid-1800s processed many tons of turtle meat before the industry collapsed around 1900 (Shaver 1990a; USFWS and NMFS 1992). Many turtles came from lower Laguna Madre, where green turtles were the leading marine product by weight (Hildebrand 1981; Doughty 1984). In a three-year study of sea turtle strandings along the southern Texas coast (Rabalais and Rabalais 1980), loggerhead turtles *(Caretta caretta)* were most abundant, followed by Kemp's ridley turtles *(Lepidochelys kempii)*, green turtles *(Chelonia mydas)*, and leatherback turtles *(Dermochelys coriacea)*. Green turtles were the only sea turtles reported from within Laguna Madre. More recently, in lower Laguna Madre, more than 20 sea turtles have been captured in gill nets during TPWD's fishery monitoring program (R. Blankenship, pers. comm.), whereas only one has been captured in upper Laguna Madre (K. Spiller, pers. comm.). Large numbers of live and dead sea turtles stranded in lower Laguna Madre during a severe cold spell in February 1989, when water temperatures dropped to as low as 3°C (Shaver 1990b).

Leaves of seagrasses comprise up to 100% of the diet of juvenile green turtles and hawksbill turtles *(Eretochelys imbricata)* (Bustard 1972; Hirth et al. 1973; Rebel 1974). Habitat preferences of one loggerhead and four green turtles were determined using radio and sonic telemetry in the South Bay area of the lower Laguna Madre (Renaud et al. 1992). The loggerhead spent approximately 50% of its time in seagrass bed habitats north of the Queen Isabella Causeway, whereas the green turtles spent about 60% of their time associated with seagrasses. Additional observations were made on turtles that were not radio-tagged. Loggerheads were observed only north of the Queen Isabella Causeway, which is primarily shallow and vegetated with seagrasses, whereas green turtles were observed in vegetated, unvegetated, and jetty habitats. Turtle-grass was the dominant component of fecal samples from 12 green turtles with carapace lengths >40 cm (15.7 in) captured near seagrass meadows. Algae was the main component of feces of green turtles of carapace lengths <40 cm (15.7 in) captured near jetties. Smaller turtles appeared to prefer jetty habitats, while larger turtles were most often found in seagrass and channel habitats. These distributions were attributed to changes in feeding preferences of turtles as they grow.

Birds   Although many birds use seagrass meadows as feeding and resting areas (Zieman and Zieman 1989), only waterfowl, particularly redhead *(Aythya americana)* use of meadows has been studied in Laguna Madre. The majority of the North American population of redheads winters in the Laguna Madre in Texas and Tamaulipas (Weller 1964). Intensive use of these lagoons is likely related to presence of extensive and nearly homogeneous stands of shoalgrass (Cornelius 1977). Redheads are typically found feeding over shallow shoalgrass meadows along the perimeter of Laguna Madre (McMahan 1970; Cornelius 1975, 1977; Adair et al. 1990a). Shoalgrass rhizomes were the most common food found in stomachs of redheads wintering in upper Laguna Madre, as well as in those of American wigeons *(Anas americana)* and northern pintails *(A. acuta)* (Koenig 1969; Woodin 1996).

Marine Mammals   There is no information concerning marine mammal use of seagrass meadows in Laguna Madre. Bottlenose dolphins *(Tursiops truncatus)*, which are common in the area, feed over seagrass meadows in Florida (Zieman and Zieman 1989). This animal migrates between bays and the Gulf of Mexico (Schmidly 1981;

Shane and Schmidly 1978; Brager 1993), and seagrass meadows within Laguna Madre are likely used as foraging habitat.

Community Structure Seagrass meadows provide an important refuge from predators for a wide variety of aquatic animals. This is usually attributed to "macrophyte structural complexity," a measure of both plant biomass and plant architecture or configuration. The effect of this phenomenon on prey habitat choice and predator foraging efficiency is viewed by most scientists as one of the key mechanisms organizing animal communities associated with seagrass meadows (Leber 1985). In lower Laguna Madre, seagrass habitat complexity (expressed as a function of computed leaf aggregate index) in shoalgrass meadows decreased from east to west, and shoalgrass meadow complexity was generally higher than that of manatee-grass meadows (Tolan et al. 1997). The more complex shoalgrass habitats typically held more species of fish as well as more individuals.

The nursery role of seagrasses for young fish has been questioned since their protective value would be greatest for those individuals able to orient to the blades (Olney and Boehlert 1988). The apparent nursery function of seagrass beds in upper Laguna Madre for numerous species has been noted (Hildebrand and King 1978). Tolan et al. (1997) found that both unvegetated, open water areas and seagrass meadows serve as primary nursery areas for early-stage larvae of many species in lower Laguna Madre, but some species, notably tidewater silversides, showed marked preference for shoalgrass meadows. These researchers concluded that seagrass meadows did not serve as the exclusive nursery area for early larval stages for either estuarine-spawned fishes (e.g., tidewater silversides) or estuarine-dependent, marine-spawned fishes (e.g., red drum) in Laguna Madre. However, postlarval and young juveniles of a number of species were strongly associated with seagrass habitats, and shoalgrass meadows were the preferred nursery habitat for these life stages.

Ecosystem Processes

Energy Flow and Food Web Traditionally, seagrass-meadow food webs have been considered detritus based, but the relative roles of detrital and microalgae-epiphytic pathways are largely dependent on local conditions and consumer community composition (Zieman and Zieman 1989). Seagrasses and associated epiphytes transfer energy to higher trophic levels by direct grazing, detrital food webs, or export of material to other systems. Often, little of seagrass primary productivity is used directly by consumers, either alive or as detritus, although the importance of shoalgrass to redhead and other waterfowl wintering in Laguna Madre suggests that this pathway is important seasonally. Epiphytic primary productivity often contributes more carbon to consumer diets than do the seagrasses themselves (Morgan and Kitting 1984), but this pathway has not been studied in Laguna Madre. Much of the carbon fixed by seagrasses in Laguna Madre may be transported out of meadows by currents and storms. Large rafts of shoalgrass are often seen along the banks of Laguna Madre, particularly during winter as well as following storms and high tide events.

Many consumers in seagrass meadows are opportunistic (omnivorous), so trophic structure is dynamic and fluctuates, depending on changes in densities and species composition of both predator and prey compartments. Predation pressure on prey species may change as relative abundances of other prey species increase or decrease. Diets of many fish change as they grow and often change diurnally in response to changes in prey availability resulting from circadian rhythms of invertebrate prey

Fig. 7.3. *Generalized food web for Laguna Madre seagrass meadows (Modified from Withers 1996a)*

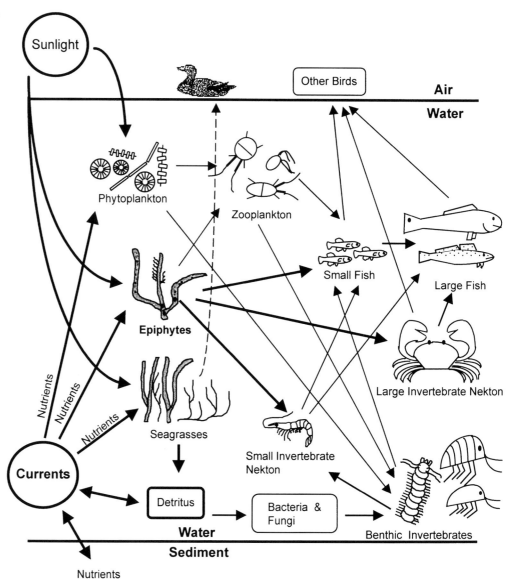

species (Kikuchi and Pérès 1977). A generalized food web for Laguna Madre seagrass meadows is presented in figure 7.3.

Nutrient Cycling   Although seagrasses are highly productive, they are often found in low-nutrient environments and probably recycle and conserve most of the nutrients needed for growth and maintenance (Capone and Taylor 1980). There is controversy over the relative importance of nutrient uptake out of the water column by leaves and nutrient uptake out of sediments by roots. Studies in upper Laguna Madre and nearby Redfish Bay suggest that both nitrogen and phosphorus uptake by shoalgrass and wigeon grass are primarily through roots (Pulich 1985). Neither species appeared to derive many nutrients from the water column. Shoalgrass required sediments rich in organic material to obtain nutrients. Wigeon grass was adapted to low nutrient conditions and would be outcompeted by shoalgrass in organic-rich sediments. Microbial recycling of organic material was much more significant in shoalgrass meadows than in wigeon grass meadows. No other studies of seagrass nutrient cycling have been conducted in Laguna Madre.

Current Issues   Seagrass cover and community composition have been changing and will likely continue changing for the foreseeable future. Changes in species composition are mostly the result of natural processes (i.e., succession) but were set in motion by moderation of salinity resulting from dredging of the GIWW and Mansfield Pass. However, decreases in cover and biomass have also been occurring. In upper Laguna Madre, shoalgrass cover decreased by 3.8%—or 9.4 km^2 (3.6 mi^2)—between 1988 and 1994, and shoalgrass biomass at depths greater than 1.4 m (4.6 ft) decreased by 60% (Onuf 1996b). These decreases have been attributed to the brown tide that started in 1990 and continues in at least some parts of the system today. Changes in species composition due to succession have been most pronounced in lower Laguna Madre, but a more troubling change is increased bare area. Overall, bare area has increased to 190 km^2 (73 mi^2), up 280% between 1965 and 1988 (Quammen and Onuf 1993). Turbidity caused by maintenance dredging has been implicated in the decline of shoalgrass and the increased bare area in lower Laguna Madre (Onuf 1994). Light attenuation is responsible for most landscape-level losses, but scarring by boat propellers is also of concern. Changes in species composition may result in reduced resource availability for some fish and waterfowl.

Effects of Long-Term Light Reduction   Amount of light reaching the bottom is the crucial factor determining seagrass meadow extent and productivity. Reduced light has been linked to reductions of both seagrass cover and productivity (Orth and Moore 1983; Kenworthy and Haunert 1991; Dunton 1994; Czerny and Dunton 1995; and others). In Laguna Madre, there are two causes of light reduction that have resulted in changes in seagrass cover and biomass: dredging and brown tide.

Despite the fact that dredging and dredge material disposal have immediate and direct effects on water clarity, until recently few seagrass losses were attributed to these activities. Turbidity caused by dredging has been viewed as short-lived, often because background turbidity levels are already high, and as limited to areas within 5 km (3 mi) of the discharge (Cronin et al. 1970; Nichols et al. 1990). However in lower Laguna Madre, loss of shoalgrass in deep areas and close alignment of newly denuded areas with navigational channels between 1965 and 1974 led Merkord (1978) to hypothesize that turbidity resulting from maintenance dredging of GIWW was the cause.

Onuf (1994) tested the hypothesis that light reduction caused by dredging in lower Laguna Madre resulted in changes in seagrass cover. He postulated that seagrasses are able to tolerate the short periods of light reduction that occur during dredging because seagrasses survive frequent episodes of light reduction from natural causes. Therefore, he reasoned that dredge-related light reduction must persist for weeks or months to impact seagrass distribution. Intensive monitoring of the underwater light regime before and after maintenance dredging of GIWW near the Mansfield ship channel determined that light reduction attributable to dredging and dredge material disposal persisted for 10–15 months after the dredging project in half of the areas studied. Wind-generated waves were primarily responsible for resuspension and dispersion of dredged material within affected areas. Such events occurred so frequently that elevated turbidity levels were long-lasting and transported over long distances. Onuf outlined a scenario in which frequent resuspension, long-term susceptibility of deposited dredge material to resuspension, and long-distance transport of turbidity result in loss of seagrasses, particularly on the edges of meadows. Given that maintenance dredging is necessary every two to three years in this part of the lagoon (Onuf 1994), light reduction is chronic, and the loss of seagrass will continue until dredge disposal practices are modified to reduce the amount of sediment resuspension. The integrative model of seagrass distribution and productivity produced by Dunton et al. (1998a) also strongly suggests that light attenuation due to dredging operations will negatively impact seagrass health.

The sudden appearance of the brown tide in upper Laguna Madre in 1990 resulted in a nearly immediate light reduction (50%; Dunton 1994) that persisted through 1997. Although changes in seagrass cover were not noted in the first two years following initiation of the bloom (1991–92), approximately 2.6 km² (1.0 mi²) were lost between 1992 and 1993, and by 1995, 9.4 km² (3.6 mi²) had been lost (Onuf 1996b). Biomass in the deepest areas (>1.4 m; 4.6 ft) decreased two years before declines in cover and increases in bare area were noted. Overall, biomass decreased by 60% in the deepest areas but did not decrease in the shallowest waters. Utilization of stored reserves allowed seagrasses to persist throughout the study at intermediate depths and for two years in deeper areas, but the trend toward loss in deeper areas was apparent. Based on light attenuation measures, Onuf predicted that when seagrass distribution reached steady-state with the brown tide–influenced light regime, 24% of upper Laguna Madre would be bare compared to only 6% before. However, in 1996, clover grass began revegetating about half the area where shoalgrass had been lost, and shoalgrass retreat slowed (Onuf, in press). Although water clarity improved briefly, and shoalgrass began to recover, return of brown tide to bloom concentrations in spring and summer 1998 caused most regrowth to die.

Effects of Changes in Cover and Community Composition on Fish and Waterfowl Although seagrasses were not the only habitats used by larval and juvenile fish, many species were strongly associated with seagrass meadows, and some exhibited preferences for shoalgrass in lower Laguna Madre (Tolan et al. 1997). Widespread replacement of shoalgrass by manatee-grass suggests a concomitant decrease in preferred nursery habitat for juveniles. The effect of manatee-grass replacement by turtle-grass as succession proceeds in Laguna Madre is unknown; however, turtle-grass meadows in other areas typically have higher densities of fish than do manatee-grass meadows (Martin and Cooper 1981). In upper Laguna Madre, loss of cover due to brown tide may also have impacted available nursery habitat for juvenile fish. Since succession appears to be proceeding slowly, it is likely that the same loss of preferred nursery habitat noted by Tolan et al. (1997) in lower Laguna Madre will occur in upper Laguna Madre in the future.

The Laguna Madre of Texas and Tamaulipas is the primary wintering area for redheads, which feed almost exclusively on shoalgrass. About 75% of the world population of redheads winter in these lagoons (Weller 1964). Other traditional wintering areas such as Chesapeake Bay, Pamlico Sound, and Galveston Bay have been abandoned because seagrasses declined or disappeared, leaving upper Laguna Madre and Laguna Madre de Tamaulipas to support nearly the entire wintering population. Degradation and loss of shoalgrass meadows are of particular concern in the Texas Laguna Madre (e.g., Onuf 1995), especially if the trend continues or escalates, since that would leave Laguna Madre de Tamaulipas as the only area with suitable habitat. As of 1995, most seagrass losses were confined to the deepest waters (>1.4 m; 4.6 ft), which may not be used frequently by redheads; they typically dabble in shallow water. In addition, deeper water may be avoided since many of the deepest areas are near navigational channels. Redheads choose habitats based not only on food availability but also on disturbance and potentially on proximity to the freshwater ponds they require for drinking water. However, if losses of seagrasses in shallow water have occurred, this represents a potentially serious impact.

Scarring Recreational boating has been recognized as a source of negative impacts to seagrass habitats through destruction of both above- and below-ground tissues by propellers (Phillips 1960; Zieman 1976; Eleuterius 1987; Dunton et al. 1998b). The scar itself is not the end of the damage. Erosion of the scar by wave action causes the disturbed area to deepen, and scouring within the scar may result in widening, with additional losses along the edge of the scar (Zieman 1982; Eleuterius 1987). In addition turbidity may increase, resulting in light attenuation and inhibition of seagrass growth and/or recovery in the vicinity of the scar (Zieman 1982). Most scarring occurs in areas less than 1 m (3.3 ft) deep at low tide (Zieman 1976). Scarring lasts longer in turtle-grass meadows and is more likely to become permanent, since turtle-grass is a slower-growing, perennial species and does not recover as quickly as shoalgrass, a colonizing species. Scarring may be an important factor in loss of seagrasses in densely populated areas and is contributing to seagrass loss in shallow areas of the Redfish Bay/Harbor Island complex just north of Corpus Christi (Pulich et al. 1997).

Dunton et al. (1998b) determined extent of seagrass scarring in upper Laguna Madre around the JFK Causeway and north to the mouth of Corpus Christi Bay. This area is probably one of the most heavily used by recreational boaters, since there are few boat launches available between the causeway and Port Mansfield. Excluding the GIWW and other channels, water depth ranged from 0.3 to 0.5 m (1.0–1.6 ft) and seagrass cover totaled about 2,850 ha (7,042 ac). Seagrass scarring was categorized based on density of scars (% seagrasses impacted: light (<5%); moderate (5–20%); and heavy (>20%). A total of 493 ha (1,218 ac) or 34.6% was scarred, with the majority of scarring in the moderate category. Although seagrass beds are heavily used by anglers, all recreational boaters are thought to be responsible to some degree. Four explanations accounted for the moderate to severe scarring observed in the area: (1) proximity of seagrass meadows to densely populated areas including waterfront homes; (2) shortcuts taken at channel junctions, around shallow areas, and between islands as well as accidental straying out of channels; (3) entry to shallow meadows from blind channels dredged for gas well or pipeline access; and (4) channels that are illegally marked and maintained through frequent and intensive boat traffic directly through meadows.

Laguna Madre de Tamaulipas

Seagrass Distribution and Species Composition Seagrass meadows (*pastos marinos*) cover about 340 km² (131 mi²) in the Laguna Madre de Tamaulipas (DUMAC 1996). Another 82 km² (32 mi²) are vegetated by attached algae. All five seagrass species may occur within the lagoon (Cornelius 1975; Martínez and Novelo 1993; Leija-Tristan et al., in press; Garcia-Gil et al. 1993; DUMAC 1996). Based on species associations, seven communities have been described: monotypic shoalgrass; monotypic manatee-grass, monotypic wigeon grass, mixed shoalgrass and manatee-grass, mixed shoalgrass and wigeon grass, mixed shoalgrass and turtle-grass (DUMAC 1996); and mixed shoalgrass and clover grass (Cornelius 1975). Red drift algae was widespread, especially in areas where wave action was reduced by dense manatee-grass beds (Cornelius 1975).

Extensive meadows of shoalgrass were reported in the southern portion in the late 1950s and 1960s (Hildebrand 1958, 1969). Cornelius (1975) prepared a map of the distribution and composition of seagrass meadows from the northernmost portion of the lagoon to just south of Laguna el Catán (fig. 7.4). His surveys of the area between Carboneras and Punta Algodones in 1974–75 showed that much of the area was covered with submerged vegetation, and shoalgrass was the most common

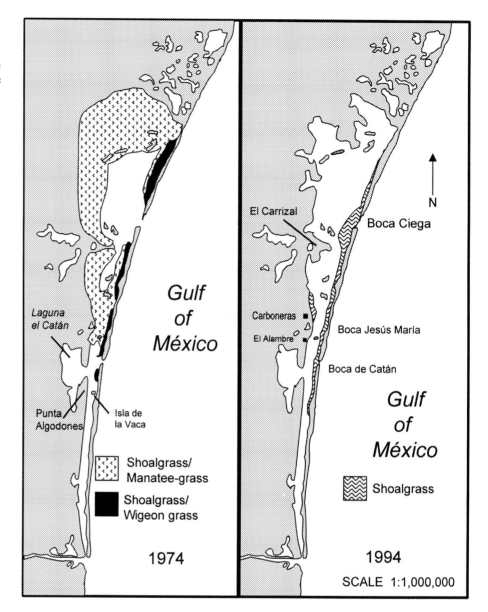

Fig. 7.4. *Distribution of seagrasses in Laguna Madre de Tamaulipas in 1973–74 (redrawn from Cornelius 1975) and 1994–95 (redrawn from DUMAC 1996). Only shoalgrass was mapped by DUMAC in 1994–95.*

species encountered. Clover grass was often found growing in association with shoalgrass on the lee side of the barrier island. Scattered patches as well as extensive homogeneous beds of manatee-grass were located south of the old 8th Pass (Boca Jesús María or Boca Viborero). Sand shoals paralleling the barrier island created shallow, protected lagoons that were dominated by wigeon grass but that are not shown on the map. Aerial surveys suggested that the narrow band of wigeon grass extended from Boca Jesús María to Isla de la Vaca, with a second band extending from Boca Ciega to the northern limit of the bay. Although no sampling was done north of Carboneras, commercial fisherman reported a band of grass beds 1–2 km (0.6–1.2 mi) wide extending from just south of Laguna el Catán to the northern limit of the bay. This was confirmed by aerial reconnaissance, which also found spotty beds on the mainland shore from El Alambre north to El Carrizal and extensive beds north of El Carrizal along the western and northern shorelines. The map shows these areas as mixed shoalgrass and wigeon grass, but since no sampling was done, it is possible that these areas consisted of shoalgrass alone. It is likely that coverage and distribution of seagrasses in the area north of El Carrizal was highly variable, since water exchange with the Gulf of Mexico was limited, as were freshwater inflows, and salinities often soared to over 100 ppt (Hildebrand 1958, 1969). However, the four jettied passes (north to south: El Mezquital, Boca Ciega, Boca de Catán, and Boca de Santa Isabel; for locations see figures 2.4 and 2.5) that are now being maintained open have probably ameliorated salinities, and seagrass populations may become more stable in the future.

Recent mapping by DUMAC (1996) using satellite imagery (30 m × 30 m pixels) shows only a thin band of seagrasses limited mostly to the back of the barrier islands (see fig. 7.4). Species composition was not delineated, but monotypic shoalgrass was most commonly found. Most seagrasses were concentrated in the shallow, clear waters. In 1988, only small patches of shoalgrass were reported growing near Boca Jesús María (Martínez and Novelo 1993).

Shoalgrass biomass ranged from a high of 527.5 ±394 g/m^2 in April 1974 to a low of 153.4 ±60 g/m^2 in January 1975, with an annual mean of 413.7 ±341.8 g/m^2 (Cornelius 1975). DUMAC (1996) reported an annual mean shoalgrass biomass of 154 g/m^2, only 37% of the annual mean reported by Cornelius (1975) but within the range of mean values (72–756 g/m^2) for 1974–75. DUMAC (1996) expressed concern about this apparent decrease, citing water pollution and decreased salinity as probable causes. However, since there are no data for the years between 1975 and 1995, it is unknown if this decrease is the result of a downward trend or a natural low in cyclical populations. More study is needed to determine the nature of the decline.

Invertebrates   Almost nothing is known about invertebrate communities associated with seagrass meadows in Laguna Madre de Tamaulipas (see table 7.1). Cornelius (1975) collected 14 species of molluscs (3 gastropods, 11 bivalves) but thought his sampling methods were inadequate to describe the community properly. The species he collected were all common in shoalgrass meadows in both upper and lower Laguna Madre in Texas. The most abundant bivalves were tellins, and the most abundant gastropods were virgin nerites *(Neritina virginea)*. Variable bittiums *(Bittium varium)* were the most abundant macroinvertebrates collected between 1994–95 (DUMAC 1996).

Waterfowl   Several hundred thousand waterfowl, primarily redheads and pintails, wintered in Laguna Madre de Tamaulipas prior to 1960, and the lagoon had more wintering waterfowl than any other lagoon between the Río Grande and Tampico Delta (Saunders and Saunders 1981; see chapter 11, this volume). During the January 1947 survey, 447,000 redheads and 379,000 pintails were counted. However, declines in the extent of shoalgrass meadows after 1949 due to closing of passes and extreme hypersalinity resulted in sparse populations of waterfowl. Only about 2,000 were recorded in 1962, and none were seen during 1966. Resurgence of shoalgrass during the late 1960s and early 1970s resulted in return of redheads to the lagoon, but numbers were lower than previously estimated (Cornelius 1975). Between October and December 1973, numbers ranged from 500 to 48,065; between December 1974 and February 1975, numbers ranged from 34,685 to 75,000. Maintenance of passes will likely result in more stable populations of both shoalgrass and redheads in the near future; however, it is probable that amelioration of salinities may also set succession into motion, and replacement of shoalgrass by manatee-grass may impact habitat suitability for waterfowl.

Open Bay

KIM WITHERS

Open bay habitats are unvegetated subtidal areas with soft sediments and are typically one of the most extensive and productive habitats in estuarine systems. As their name implies, open bay habitats are open systems; that is, they interact strongly with overlying waters and adjacent habitats such as seagrasses, tidal flats, marshes, tidal inlets, and riverine systems (Armstrong 1987). Benthic invertebrate communities of open bay habitats play an important role in recycling and regenerating nutrients from the sediments back into the water column for use by phytoplankton (Zeitzschel 1980). Regenerated nutrients may supply 30–100% of phytoplankton nutrient requirements in coastal euphotic zones (Rowe et al. 1975; Rowe and Smith 1977; Hargrave and Connolly 1978). The activities of benthic organisms appear to regulate flow of nutrients from sediments into overlying waters (Rhoads 1974; Aller 1978) and may also greatly modify sediment biological, physical, and chemical attributes. Benthic invertebrates are important primary consumers in the open bay habitat and often regulate phytoplankton standing crop in shallow water. They also function as secondary producers, converting primary productivity (often in the form of detritus) into available biomass for use by higher consumers. The main issue associated with open bay habitats within Laguna Madre is recent increases in bare areas at the expense of seagrasses primarily because of turbidity associated with dredging and light attenuation due to brown tide, as discussed in detail in chapter 7.

Extent, Distribution, and Trends in Texas

Extent of unvegetated bay bottoms in Laguna Madre varies depending on extent of seagrass cover. A recent estimate of unvegetated habitats at or below MSL in Laguna Madre found that such habitat covers about 482 km^2 or about 39% of nonemergent estuarine habitats (see table 6.1). In upper Laguna Madre, the majority of open bay habitat is found in Baffin Bay (198 km^2), restricted to the deeper waters of the GIWW and the fairly turbid waters of The Hole (see fig. 7.2). It is likely that open bay habitats dominated upper Laguna Madre prior to completion of the GIWW, although seagrass cover probably increased in response to freshening of the system and decreased as hypersalinity became severe. Open bay habitat decreased dramatically from 1967 to 1988 as seagrass cover, primarily shoalgrass (*Halodule beaudettei* [= *wrightii*]), increased by 110% in response to long-term salinity declines brought about by dredging of GIWW (Quammen and Onuf 1993). Between 1988 and 1994, unvegetated bottom increased as seagrass cover decreased by about 4%, probably due to light attenuation caused by brown tide (Onuf 1996b). Although seagrass cover has increased slightly in Baffin Bay over the last few years, unvegetated bay bottom constituted over 89% of the area in 1992 (Pulich 1998).

Open bay habitats probably also dominated in lower Laguna Madre prior to completion of the GIWW, but it is likely that seagrass cover was more widespread and persistent, since salinities were not as extreme due to tidal exchange with the Gulf of

Mexico via Brazos Santiago Pass and some freshwater inflow via Arroyo Colorado. In 1965 seagrasses, primarily shoalgrass, dominated the entire lower lagoon, but by 1988 bare bottom areas had expanded by 95% (Quammen and Onuf 1993; see fig. 7.2). Unvegetated habitat in the lower lagoon is found primarily in the deepest portions and was aligned with the GIWW during 1974–75 surveys. Expansion of bare areas in lower Laguna Madre has been attributed to turbidity caused by maintenance dredging of the GIWW (Merkord 1978; Onuf 1994; Dunton et al. 1998b).

Plant Communities

Phytoplankton are the dominant plants in the open bay habitat, although drift macroalgae may also be present. Benthic microalgae are found on and within bottom sediments. In upper Laguna Madre, Hildebrand and King (1978) identified 135 species of phytoplankton. Between 1972 and 1978, diatoms (116 species) comprised 97–99% of total phytoplankton. The four most abundant genera were *Chaetoceros*, *Nitzschia*, *Thalassionema*, and *Thalassiothrix*. Dinoflagellates (19 species) comprised the remainder of observations. The most abundant dinoflagellate was *Ceratium furca*. Phytoplankton densities were generally lowest during spring and summer and highest between December and March. Greater winter densities were attributed to more favorable temperature and rainfall conditions. Major diatom blooms were most often characterized by *Chaetoceros affinis*, *Thalassionema nitzschoides*, *Asterionella japonica*, and *Skeletonema costatum*. Most blooms occurred after salinity changes, but they never occurred when salinities exceeded 40 ppt. Phytoplankton were nonexistent in salinities greater than 60 ppt (Simmons 1957).

In Alazan Bay (Baffin Bay), 93 species of phytoplankton in six divisions were identified (Cornelius 1984). Diatoms (46 species) dominated collections and accounted for 69% of the total cells counted. Three species, *Nitzschia closterium*, *Rhizosolenia setigera*, and *Thalassionema nitzschioides*, accounted for more than half of the total cells. Diatoms dominated collections in April–June, September, and December. Dinoflagellates (25 species) were the next most abundant division and constituted 15% of the total cells. Dinoflagellates dominated collections during August only. Phytoplankton density peaked in April and September, with a smaller peak in June, and was lowest in February–March and October–November (fig. 8.1). Mean densities were greatest at salinities of 11–20 ppt and 41–50 ppt, whereas diversity was greatest at salinities of 31–40 ppt (fig. 8.2).

Diatoms also dominated phytoplankton collections made by Breuer (1962) and EHA (1977) in lower Laguna Madre. Seventy species in seven divisions were collected during July 1977 (EHA 1977) from stations within the lower Río Grande Basin, including lower Laguna Madre. Diatoms constituted 95% of collections from Laguna Madre stations. Phytoplankton densities were highest in two stations with salinities of 19 ppt and 21 ppt and lowest in stations with salinities greater than 30 ppt.

The drift macroalgal community of the upper Laguna Madre is dominated by red algae, primarily *Gracilaria* and *Laurencia* (Hildebrand and King 1978). In lower Laguna Madre, red algae are also common, as is the phaeophyte *Sargassum*, which enters the lagoon through passes during spring and drifts throughout the system (Breuer 1962).

The diatom flora of sediment surfaces in Laguna Madre and Baffin Bay has been described in some detail (Ferguson-Wood 1963). In upper Laguna Madre, 102 species were collected. *Amphora* was frequently dominant, *Rhodpalodia* was abundant, and *Achnanthes*, *Actinoptychus*, and *Grammatophora* were common. In Baffin Bay, only 29 species were collected and numbers of individuals were low. Near the mouth of

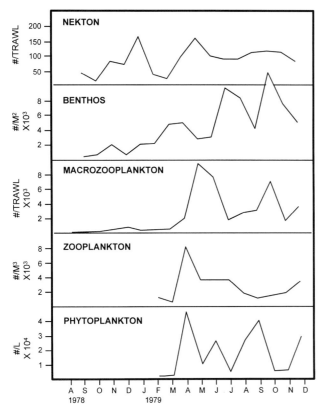

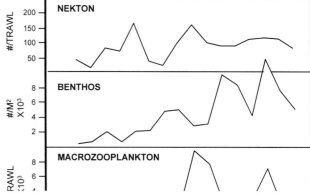

Fig. 8.1. *Monthly mean abundance of organisms collected in Alazan Bay (Cornelius 1984)*

Fig. 8.2. *Mean density (bars) and Shannon diversity (line) of phytoplankton in relation to salinity in Alazan Bay (Data from Cornelius 1984)*

the bay the community resembled that of the upper Laguna Madre. In lower Laguna Madre, 82 species were collected. *Cocconeis* was usually dominant, and as in the upper lagoon, *Rhodpalodia* was abundant and *Grammatophora* was common. In general, cell counts were greatest in sediments where the water depth was less than 1 m and lowest in water depths of 2 m or more (Oppenheimer and Wood 1965).

Animal Communities

Zooplankton   Zooplankton are divided into two types: holoplankton, animals that spend their entire lives in the plankton, and meroplankton, animals with life cycles that include a planktonic stage. These organisms graze directly on phytoplankton and/or other zooplankton. Holoplankton communities in the Laguna Madre and Baffin Bay are typically dominated by the copepod *Acartia tonsa* (Simmons 1957; Hedgepeth 1967; Hildebrand and King 1978; Cornelius 1984), although it was not present in large numbers during July 1977 in lower Laguna Madre (EHA 1977). Meroplankton communities are dominated by trochophore larvae, bivalve larvae, gastropod veligers, and barnacle nauplii (Hildebrand and King 1978; Cornelius 1984).

In upper Laguna Madre, zooplankton population densities were erratic between 1972 and 1978 but generally peaked during spring (Hildebrand and King 1978). *Acartia tonsa* made up about 50% of the total organisms in each year of the study, with peak abundances of copepods occurring in fall and spring. Other important calanoid copepods were members of the genera *Pseudodiaptomus* and *Centropages*. Cyclopoid copepods, primarily *Oithona* and *Saphirella*, were only about one-tenth as abundant as the calanoid copepods. Meroplankters contributed heavily to spring peaks, and most declined during summer.

In Alazan Bay, 37 zooplankton taxa were identified (Cornelius 1984). Only ten

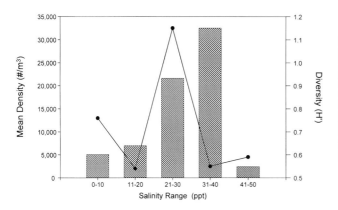

Fig. 8.3. *Mean density (bars) and Shannon diversity (line) of zooplankton in relation to salinity in Alazan Bay (Data from Cornelius 1984)*

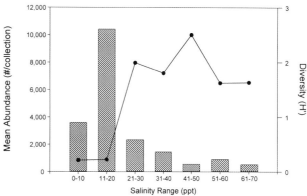

Fig. 8.4. *Abundance (bars) and Shannon diversity (line) of macrozooplankton in relation to salinity in Alazan Bay (Data from Cornelius 1984)*

taxa constituted nearly 99% of all collections. Copepods made up 92% of the ten most abundant taxa and were dominated by *Acartia tonsa* adults and copepodids (73%). Overall plankton abundance peaked in April then declined through September; copepod abundance followed the same pattern (fig. 8.1). Seasonal variation in the meroplankton appeared to be correlated with reproductive periods of the non-planktonic adults. For example, bivalves appeared to have a spring spawning event, with bivalve larvae peaking during May, followed by a protracted spawning period beginning in July and continuing through December, when the greatest numbers of bivalve larvae were collected. Polychaetes spawned three times during the study period, with March and July being the most important. Barnacle larvae were found during midsummer. Mean zooplankton abundance was greatest in salinities from 21 to 40 ppt, with greatest diversity in salinities of 21–30 ppt (fig. 8.3).

Cornelius (1984) also characterized the "macrozooplankton" community of Alazan Bay. These organisms have some limited abilities to swim and are sometimes categorized as micronekton. Forty-two invertebrates and 26 vertebrates (larval and juvenile fish) were collected. Of the 20 most abundant taxa, invertebrates made up 97%. Mysids, primarily *Americamysis* (= *Mysidopsis*) *almyra*, dominated, occurring in over 88% of all samples. Two peaks in macrozooplankton populations were noted, May-June and October 1979 (fig. 8.1). Larval and postlarval fish abundance peaked during May. Mysid populations in particular fluctuated rapidly and dramatically in response to changes in salinities, generally increasing as salinities decreased. Overall, mean numbers of all macrozooplankton were greatest in salinities between 0 and 30 ppt, whereas species richness and diversity were greatest at salinities between 21 and 50 ppt (fig. 8.4).

Benthic and Epibenthic Invertebrates   In upper Laguna Madre, the benthic fauna of unvegetated areas is typically dominated by molluscs and/or polychaetes and is often relatively low in diversity, but abundances of individuals may be high (Parker 1959; White et al. 1989; Montagna 1993). In the shallow, central portion of the lagoon Parker (1959) collected only four mollusc species: dwarf surfclam (*Mulinia lateralis*), Tampa tellin (*Tellina tampaensis*), pointed venus (*Anomalocardia auberiana*), and variable cerith (*Cerithium lutosum*). Although diversity was very low, numbers of individuals were high. He concluded that with the exception of oyster reefs, this assemblage represented the largest living molluscan assemblage along the northern Gulf Coast. White et al. (1989) recognized two assemblages in unvegetated areas, the relatively depauperate bay margin assemblage and the more diverse bay center assemblage. In the shallow, sandy bay margin, polychaetes dominated. Characteristic species were the polychaetes *Heteromastus filiformis*, *Axiothella mucosa*, *Haploscoloplos foliosus*, and the Tampa tellin. The bay center assemblage was found in deeper, muddier areas of the lagoon and was dominated by molluscs, primarily bivalve species. Characteristic mollusc species were pointed nutclam *(Nuculana acuta)*, Texas tellin *(Tellina texana)*, glassy lyonsia *(Lyonsia hyalina)*, dwarf surfclam and beautiful caecum *(Caecum pulchellum)*. Characteristic polychaete species were *Magelona pettiboneae* and *Clymenella torquata*. Four unvegetated areas were sampled during a study of the success of seagrass mitigation projects in upper Laguna Madre (Montagna 1993). In the natural area, dwarf surfclam was the most abundant mollusc, but syllid polychaetes and oligochaetes dominated. In three scrapedown areas where seagrass establishment had been unsuccessful, dwarf surfclams and tellins were the most abundant molluscs, but assemblages were dominated by colonizing capitellid and spionid polychaetes and by oligochaetes, generally considered indicative of disturbance.

In soft bottoms of Baffin Bay, dwarf surfclams are the dominant mollusc (Cornelius 1984; White et al. 1989, Montagna 1993). In Alazan Bay, 51 taxa from seven phyla were identified (Cornelius 1984). Dwarf surfclams constituted 41% of organisms collected and occurred in 98% of samples. Benthic abundance was generally high and peaked during July and October (fig. 8.1). Mean abundance was highest at salinities of 0–10 ppt and 21–40 ppt; diversity was also greatest in salinities of 21–40 ppt (fig. 8.5). The bay center and bay margin habitats described by White et al. (1989) encompassed the greatest area and contained an assemblage dominated by dwarf surfclams and the amphipods *Ampelisca abdita* and *Grandidierella bonnieroides*. Dwarf surfclams and capitellid polychaetes dominated the assemblage in the mouth of Baffin Bay (Montagna 1993).

A unique, unvegetated, hard substrate also exists in Baffin Bay. Serpulid reefs, composed of the calcareous tubes of serpulid polychaetes, are found throughout the bay. However, these reefs currently contain few, if any, reef-building serpulid worms. Crustaceans, polychaetes, and molluscs are the most abundant organisms associated with this habitat (Mackin 1971; Martin 1979; Cole 1981; White et al. 1989; Hardegree 1997). Both Mackin (1971) and Hardegree (1997) described polychaete/amphipod assemblages dominated by amphipods in the genus *Corophium*. Organisms found at all sites in Cole's (1981) study of black drum feeding habits were nemerteans, scorched mussels *(Brachiodontes exustus)*, acorn barnacles *(Balanus balanus)*, and the polychaetes *Diopatra cuprea*, *Polydora* spp., *Mediomastus californiensis*, *Pectinaria gouldii*, *Marphysa sanguinea*, and *Hydroides dianthus*. The serpulid reef assem-

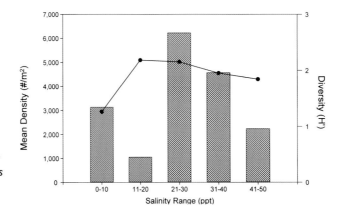

Fig. 8.5. Density (bars) and Shannon diversity (line) of benthic invertebrates in relation to salinity in Alazan Bay (Data from Cornelius 1984)

blage described by White et al. (1989) was dominated by scorched mussels and the polychaete *Nereis succinea*. Other abundant species in this assemblage were dwarf surfclams, glassy lyonsia, and the isopod *Edotea montosa*.

Open bay bottom benthic communities in lower Laguna Madre were divided into three different types depending on habitat (White et al. 1986). At the bay margin along extensive wind-tidal flats, characteristic species were the bivalves Tampa tellin and pointed venus, the polychaete *Haploscoloplos foliosus*, and the tanaid *Leptochelia rapax*. The open bay center assemblage was characterized by bivalves including dwarf surfclam, pointed nutclam, glassy lyonsia, and minor jackknife clam *(Ensis minor)* and the polychaete *Mediomastus californiensis*. In inlet-influenced areas of the Mansfield Channel and Brazos Santiago Pass, a bivalve, Atlantic abra *(Abra aequalis)*, and the polychaetes *Armandia maculata, Cossura delta, Sigambra tentaculata*, and *M. californiensis* were characteristic. Parker (1959) also described an inlet-influenced assemblage in lower Laguna Madre characterized by greedy dovesnail *(Costoanachis avara)* and the cross-barred venus *(Chione cancellata)*.

Within South Bay are the only living oyster reefs within the Texas Laguna Madre ecosystem. These reefs are composed of eastern oysters *(Crassostrea virginica)* of a genetically distinct population that appears to be adapted to high salinities (King et al. 1994). Other molluscs associated with this habitat are scorched mussels and impressed odostomes *(Boonea impressa)* (White et al. 1986). Characteristic polychaetes include *Tharynx marioni, Hydroides dianthus,* and *Prionospio heterobranchia*.

Nekton Since an entire chapter has been devoted to fish (chapter 15), only invertebrate nekton are discussed here. Because so much of the bottom of Laguna Madre is vegetated, it is often difficult to determine which species are associated with unvegetated areas. Generally speaking, the most abundant invertebrate nekton are shrimp, crabs, and jellyfish. In upper Laguna Madre, the two most abundant invertebrates were blue crab *(Callinectes sapidus)* and brown shrimp *(Farfantepenaeus aztecus)*, although it is not clear that these species were collected from unvegetated areas (Hildebrand and King 1978). In Alazan Bay, 14 nektonic invertebrate taxa were identified (Cornelius 1984). Of the 20 most abundant species (vertebrate and invertebrate), only three were invertebrates—brown shrimp, mud crab *(Neopanope texana)*, and bay squid *(Lolliguncula brevis)*—and together they constituted only about 1% of the total nekton collected. Of the 20 predominant nekton by weight, blue crab constituted 38%, and brown shrimp and bay squid together comprised less than 1%. Abundance of all nekton peaked in January and May (see fig. 8.1). Abundance of invertebrate nekton was greatest at salinities less than 10 ppt, whereas diversity was greatest at salinities of 21–30 ppt (fig. 8.6). There is little information concerning

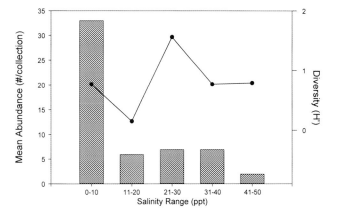

Fig. 8.6. *Abundance (bars) and Shannon diversity (line) of invertebrate nekton in relation to salinity in Alazan Bay (Data from Cornelius 1984)*

invertebrate nekton use of unvegetated areas of lower Laguna Madre. In a study of the distribution of penaeid shrimp in lower Laguna Madre, white shrimp *(Litopenaeus setiferus)* were taken most commonly in areas with little or no vegetation, and brown shrimp abundance was greatest in areas devoid of vegetation (Stokes 1974). Pink shrimp *(Farfantepenaeus duorarum)* were taken from channels but otherwise never from areas without vegetation.

Birds and Marine Mammals   Birds and mammals can be important higher consumers in open bay habitats. Floating and diving birds such as ducks and cormorants forage for fish and both benthic and nektonic invertebrates in deep and shallow waters. Scaup, in particular, make use of benthic molluscs such as dwarf surfclam. Wading birds, such as great blue herons, often forage for fish and crustaceans along bay margins. Aerial hunters, such as gulls, terns, pelicans, and osprey, also find prey in the deeper waters of the bay center. Bottlenose dolphins *(Tursiops truncatus)*, although not abundant, often frequent the deeper waters of channels and inlets.

Community Structure

Salinity Effects   Salinity is the chief factor affecting biotic communities in any open bay habitat but particularly in Laguna Madre, where hypersalinity is the rule, not the exception. Salinity affects both abundance and diversity of organisms. Depending on the temporal scale of changes in salinity (sudden, drastic vs. gradual, long-term), communities may respond in different ways, particularly the benthos (Armstrong 1987). For example, in Corpus Christi Bay, numbers of benthic organisms as well as benthic production increased dramatically following record rainfalls that decreased salinity and increased nutrient inputs. More subtle, prolonged increases in salinity resulted in substantial changes in the benthic species assemblage, but these changes also appeared to stimulate benthic production.

In Alazan Bay, the effects of the gradual decline in mean salinity over the study period had no universal effects on abundance except for the benthos (Cornelius 1984; fig. 8.1). The response was not immediate but lagged one to two months behind decreases in salinity, with an overriding upward trend during the latter part of the study when salinities remained below about 36 ppt. Phytoplankton and macrozooplankton appeared to respond positively in the short term to freshening in early summer (May–June) and fall (September–October) but tended to decline fairly rapidly with short-term salinity increases (1–2 months). Nekton numbers declined between April and May when salinities declined and remained stable throughout the latter part of the study. Highest diversity typically occurred in salinities of 21–40 ppt (see figs. 8.2–8.6). With the exception of macrozooplankton, animal numbers were also highest between 21 and 40 ppt, whereas phytoplankton numbers were lowest in the same range. Macrozooplankton was most abundant in brackish waters (11–20 ppt). Overall, there was a significant negative linear relationship between the total taxa and salinity for all assemblages except zooplankton (figs. 8.7, 8.8, table 8.1).

Sediment Effects on Benthic Invertebrate Communities   Sediment characteristics greatly affect the structure of benthic invertebrate communities because the organisms have limited mobility (Rhoads 1974). Sediment grain size is usually considered the most important factor determining species distribution, but other factors that directly or indirectly influence distribution patterns include sedimentation rates, sediment stability, food availability, and depth of oxygenation.

A general pattern of low diversity with high density in sediments with high clay contents and high diversity with low density in sediments with high sand content has

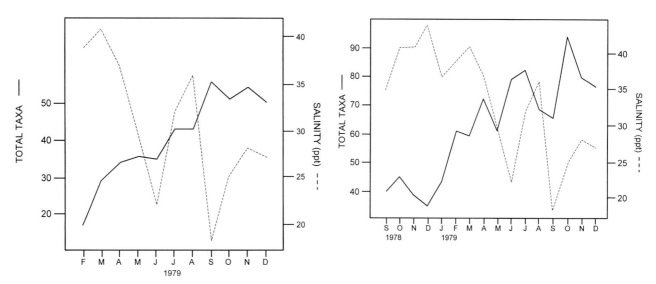

Fig. 8.7. Relationship between salinity and pooled number of phytoplankton and zooplankton taxa in Alazan Bay (Cornelius 1984)

Fig. 8.8. Relationship between salinity and pooled number of macrozooplankton, benthic, and nektonic taxa in Alazan Bay (Cornelius 1984)

Table 8.1. Results of regression analysis for total taxa and mean monthly salinity for biotic assemblages in Alazan Bay, 1978–79

Assemblage	n	Intercept	Slope	r²
Phytoplankton	11	65.04	1.19	−0.748
Zooplankton	11	10.69	0.04	0.090
Macrozooplankton	16	50.82	0.62	−0.610
Benthos	16	34.40	0.45	−0.520
Nekton	16	29.40	0.50	−0.807

Source: Cornelius 1984.

been postulated (Whitlach 1982) and was noted in Corpus Christi Bay (Flint et al. 1982). In Laguna Madre, sediments grade from muddy with high clay content on mainland shorelines to sandy on barrier island shorelines. Although diversity was lowest in sediments with the highest clay content (Baffin Bay), mean density was not high (see BB in table 8.2; Montagna 1993). Mean density was greatest in the samples from sediments with 31% clay (Genesis Petroleum, GES), and biomass was greatest in samples from sediments having only 1.1% clay (Transco scrapedown, TSS). No consistent pattern was exhibited in this limited study of open bay habitats in Laguna Madre.

Depth of oxygenation of sediments is also an important factor determining distribution of benthos, especially those that do not maintain burrows or tubes providing a consistent connection with the sediment surface (Armstrong 1987). Oxygenation is typically measured as the oxidation redox potential (Eh), with voltages of zero indicating the beginning of anoxic conditions. In general, as the depth of oxygenated sediments decreases, both species richness and benthic biomass decrease. No clear pattern emerges with regard to sediment Eh in Laguna Madre (table 8.2). Severely anoxic sediments contained high densities of organisms with relatively high biomasses in most cases. However, the highest biomass was noted at TSS (10 cm depth) in only slightly anoxic sediments, with a mean biomass of 0.016 g/indi-

Table 8.2. Sediment redox potential (Eh, millivolts) and grain sizes in relation to depth and mean benthic invertebrate density, biomass (dry weight), and Shannon diversity

Station	Depth (cm)	Eh (mV)	Rubble (%)	Sand (%)	Silt (%)	Clay (%)	Density (#/m²)	Biomass (g/m²)	Diversity (H)
BB	3	21	1.4	3.3	14.7	80.6	3,403	2.436	0.87
	8	−240	3.9	8.4	19.8	67.9	946	0.085	
189	3	−363	20.9	47.7	7.4	15.2	6,902	1.300	2.38
	10	−352	10.9	50.3	5.2	33.6	2,175	3.291	
GES	3	−388	0.5	62.7	5.8	31.0	18,248	0.509	1.39
	10	−399	1.7	94.2	0.1	4.0	8,510	2.007	
GIS	3	−10	5.0	90.7	2.1	2.1	4,349	1.815	1.79
	10	−319	4.5	90.3	1.8	3.3	1,702	2.327	
TSS	3	−1	2.4	94.5	1.0	2.0	2,458	1.220	2.09
	10	−5	3.7	93.9	1.3	1.1	1,230	20.082	

Source: Data from Montagna 1993.

Note: BB = mouth of Baffin Bay; 189 = Marker 189, GIWW; GES, GIS, TSS = scrapedown areas in northern upper Laguna Madre.

vidual. The most aerobic sediments (BB at 3 cm depth) contained only moderate numbers of organisms, with a mean biomass of 0.0007 g/individual.

Montagna's (1993) study was limited and focused mostly on unvegetated sites where attempts to establish seagrass communities after the areas had been scraped down had failed. However, the lack of pattern associated with either sediment grain size or redox potential suggests that salinity of the overlying water column or other sediment factors (e.g., organic matter) had a greater influence over benthic abundance and distribution than did either grain size or Eh.

Spatial Distribution of Benthic Invertebrates   In open bay habitats in Laguna Madre, benthic invertebrates are horizontally distributed primarily as a function of the distance from inlets and of water depth. Parker (1959) and White et al. (1986, 1989) recognized inlet-influenced communities, bay margin communities, and bay center communities. Benthic invertebrates are also distributed vertically within the sediments, with the majority occurring within the top 0–3 cm (Montagna 1993; fig. 8.9). Polychaetes dominated regardless of depth but were virtually the only organisms found in sediments 3–10 cm below the surface. Biomass was typically greater in the 3–10 cm section than in the 0–3 cm section (table 8.2) due to larger individuals.

Ecosystem Processes

Benthic Community Function   The function of benthic invertebrate communities in open bay habitats is extremely important to the entire estuarine system, especially in areas that support major commercial fisheries (Mills 1975). Benthos convert primary productivity into animal biomass and provide food for a variety of organisms, including fisheries species. Perhaps more important, the benthos regulate dynamics of the ecosystem as a whole through benthic-pelagic coupling processes, especially through nutrient recycling and regeneration. Through their contribution to both energy transfer and nutrient conservation, they help maintain and stabilize the base of estuarine food webs (Armstrong 1987).

As primary consumers, benthic invertebrates "trap" energy from phytoplankton

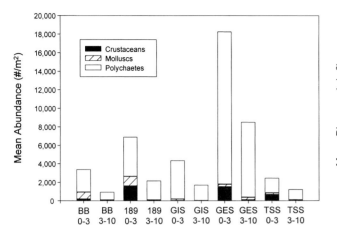

Fig. 8.9. Vertical distribution of major taxa in open bay sediments in upper Laguna Madre (Data from Montagna 1993)

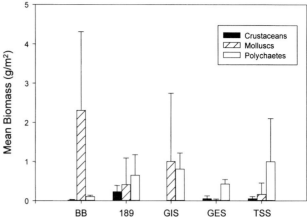

Fig. 8.10. Mean biomass and standard deviation at unvegetated sites in upper Laguna Madre. BB = mouth of Baffin Bay; 189 = GIWW Marker 189; GIS, GES, TSS = unvegetated scrapedown sites (Data from Montagna 1993)

Table 8.3. Mean nutrient fluxes (mmol/m^2/h) in open bay habitats in upper Laguna Madre during April, 1992

Site	O$_2$	DIN	NH$_4$	NO$_2$	NO$_3$	PO$_4$	SiO$_4$
BB	−1.4	−26.3	−26.0	1.12	−0.37	−0.7	6.9
189	−1.7	−1.0	0.1	−0.04	−1.06	−1.03	34.4
GES	−0.9	−1.6	−1.4	−0.06	−1.06	−1.0	1.9
GIS	0.1	−5.7	−0.2	0.02	−5.33	0.15	−1.4
TSS	−1.9	1.2	2.3	−0.03	−1.08	−0.3	0.8

Source: Data from Montagna 1993.

Note: BB = mouth of Baffin Bay; 189 = GIWW Marker 189; GES, GIS, TSS = scrapedown sites in upper Laguna Madre.

and from terrestrial and estuarine detritus and concentrate it into biomass for consumption by secondary consumers (Armstrong 1987). Biomass varied greatly at unvegetated sites in upper Laguna Madre (fig. 8.10). Molluscan biomass was greatest at the site in the mouth of Baffin Bay, reflecting the overall importance of phytoplankton as primary producers within that subsystem of the lagoon. Polychaetes generally contributed the most biomass at the other sites, reflecting the importance of detritus, primarily from seagrasses, in the food web of the rest of the lagoon.

Nutrient inputs from freshwater inflow are low in Laguna Madre, accounting for only about 50% of the areal loading of carbon, nitrogen, and phosphorus in the system (Armstrong 1987). Lack of significant freshwater inflows or exchanges with Gulf waters suggests that recycling of regenerated nutrients must be important over the long term. Within the lagoon proper, seagrasses produce a tremendous amount of organic carbon, whereas in Baffin Bay, phytoplankton produce most of the organic carbon. Recycling of inorganic nutrients seems necessary to support the high level of primary productivity exhibited by both open bay and seagrass habitats in Laguna Madre. However, sediment nutrient fluxes during April 1992 generally showed uptake rather than regeneration of all nutrients except silicate (table 8.3; Montagna 1993). There was a small amount of ammonia and nitrate regeneration. These results may not be typical,

Fig. 8.11. *Conceptual diagram of energy flow and food web of open bay habitats in Laguna Madre. Weight of boxes and arrows shows relative importance of each component and pathway.*

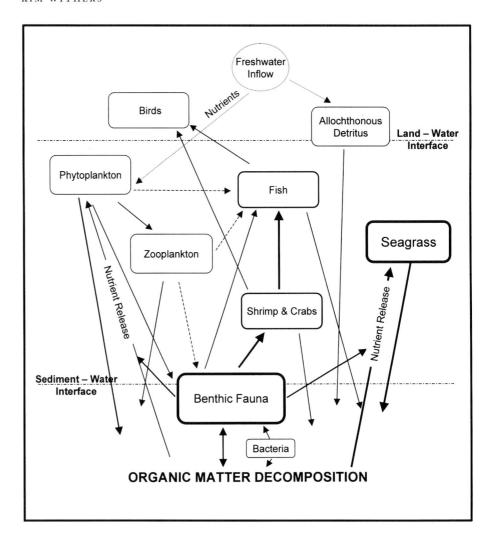

since April is a month of active growth of submerged vegetation as well as peak abundances of phytoplankton, and nutrient demand is likely very high during this month.

Energy Flow and Food Web   There are two potential primary carbon sources for food chains within open bay habitats, phytoplankton and detritus (fig. 8.11). Due to the large areal coverage of seagrasses in the lagoon proper and the lack of significant allochthonous detrital inputs, the primary carbon source within open bay habitats is seagrass detritus. However, within Baffin Bay, seagrasses are not prominent, and a grazing food chain based on phytoplankton, dwarf surfclam, and black drum has been postulated (Street et al. 1997).

Laguna Madre de Tamaulipas

Unvegetated habitats at or below MSL in Laguna Madre de Tamaulipas are estimated to cover about 1,609 km² or about 79% of nonemergent estuarine habitats (see table 6.1). Open bay habitat has expanded considerably since 1974 (see fig. 7.4) when seagrasses covered most of the northern lagoon. Until recently when passes were dredged open and stabilized with jetties, the "boom or bust" character of Laguna Madre de Tamaulipas resulted in a great deal of variability in the coverage of seagrasses and bare bottom. During wet years and for several years after a wet hurricane or tropical storm, seagrasses increased until they covered much of the bottom;

during dry years and as the length of time since a hurricane or tropical storm increased, seagrass coverage declined. As overall salinity declines due to more exchange with Gulf waters, bare area will likely decrease as seagrass coverage expands and stabilizes.

In the mid-1960s, much of Laguna Madre de Tamaulipas was unvegetated and nearly dry (Anonymous 1967). Sediment composition of the bay bottom was described by Yañez and Schlaepfer (1968). Three types were recognized: (1) well-sorted fine sands distributed along the back of the barrier islands; (2) clay-mud sediments with abundant shell and shell fragments distributed parallel to the mainland; and (3) poorly sorted fine sediments (clay-mud) found primarily in the bay center of the lagoon and Laguna el Catán.

García-Cubas (1968) described the live and dead micromolluscan fauna of Laguna Madre de Tamaulipas. His study sites encompassed the entire lagoon during a period when it is probable that little or no submerged vegetation was present, although he gives no information concerning its presence or absence. Seventeen species of bivalves and 16 species of gastropods were identified. Overall, numbers of individuals ranged from 0 to 675 per 10 cc of sediment, with lowest numbers found at stations near mainland and barrier island shorelines. Numbers fluctuated greatly in the northern lagoon depending on collection site; in the southern lagoon, molluscs tended to be more numerous, especially in and near Laguna el Catán and Punta Piedras. Bivalves, principally pointed venus and dwarf surfclam, dominated collections and constituted over 50% of the molluscs at all stations except two. Hildebrand (1958) also noted dominance by these species. Other important bivalves were broad-ribbed carditid *(Carditamera floridana)*, cross-barred venus, yellow eggcockle *(Laevicardium mortoni)*, and Tampa tellin. Gastropod numbers were low except at one station in the northern lagoon and at the station near the mouth of Río San Fernando. The species with the most widespread distribution and highest relative abundance were pitted baby-bubble *(Rictaxis punctostriatus)* and an odostome *(Odostomia canaliculata)*. No other information concerning invertebrates of unvegetated bottoms is available.

9 Wind-Tidal Flats

KIM WITHERS

Tidal flats are nearly featureless sand and/or mud habitats found in many estuarine areas. They are neither terrestrial nor aquatic but fall somewhere in between and are harsh, unpredictable environments. Tidal flats of Laguna Madre are unique because wind and storm tides, rather than astronomical tides, are primarily responsible for flooding and exposure; thus the flats are called "wind-tidal flats." Worldwide, extensive wind-tidal flats are found only adjacent to hypersaline lagoons, and they cover vast expanses of land adjacent to Laguna Madre in Texas and Tamaulipas. Moving southward along the Texas coast, wind-tidal flats replace salt marshes as both freshwater inflow and annual precipitation decrease, and eolian erosion, especially from barrier islands, increases (White et al. 1983c).

To the casual observer, wind-tidal flats in Laguna Madre appear unproductive and devoid of life (plate 36). Irregular flooding, prolonged exposure, extreme summer temperatures, low freshwater inflow, and high soil salinities (plate 37) do not allow marsh plant communities to develop (Pulich et al. 1982). Plant communities, when present, are usually restricted to felts or mats of blue-green algae (Cyanobacteria) that form over and intermix with sediments, binding them. Despite lack of readily recognizable plant communities, primary productivity by algal mats may be nearly as high as that of seagrass meadows and is about 20–40% that of a typical cordgrass (*Spartina*) marsh (Pulich and Rabalais 1982, 1986; Pulich et al. 1982). On Laguna Madre flats that are frequently flooded, persistent benthic invertebrate communities develop (Withers 1994, 1996b, 1998; Withers and Tunnell 1998). These invertebrates convert primary productivity into animal biomass that is used by higher consumers like shorebirds when flats are exposed and by wading birds, crabs, and demersal fish when flooded. Laguna Madre wind-tidal flats are one of the most significant feeding areas for aquatic birds on the Texas coast (Senner and Howe 1984; Haig and Plissner 1993; Withers 1994; Brush 1995). They are essential foraging habitats for wintering and migrating shorebirds and wading birds and are important to several state or federally listed endangered or threatened species or "species of concern": piping and snowy plovers (*Charadrius melodus, C. alexandrinus*), reddish egrets (*Egretta rufescens*), white-tailed hawks (*Buteo albicaudatus*), and peregrine falcons (*Falco peregrinus*).

Texas Laguna Madre

Distribution, Status, and Trends   Wind-tidal flats cover approximately 114 km² (44 mi²) in upper Laguna Madre and over 820 km² (317 mi²) in lower Laguna Madre (including the Land-Cut). Areal coverage of wind-tidal flats increases from Yarborough Pass southward (fig. 9.1, table 9.1). Very large wind-tidal flats are found on lagoon sides of barrier islands, particularly in lower Laguna Madre (see plate 36), with smaller expanses on mainland shorelines and at the mouths of creeks or other drainages. The largest flats, often known as the Laguna Madre Flats, are found in the Land-Cut, a land-

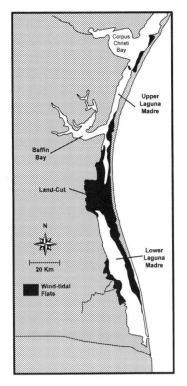

Fig. 9.1. Map of wind-tidal flats adjacent to the Texas Laguna Madre (Modified from Pulich and Rabalais 1986)

bridge between the mainland and central Padre Island and the separation between upper and lower Laguna Madre.

Tidal flat area throughout the Coastal Bend decreased markedly between the 1950s and 1992 (White et al. 1998). In the region of the upper Laguna Madre that was studied (north Padre Island from JFK Causeway to South Bird Island), tidal flat area decreased by 71%. About 45% of the loss occurred between the 1950s and 1979. During this period, accelerated sea level rise caused permanent inundation of flats and their conversion either to open water or to seagrass meadow (White et al. 1983c, 1989; Pulich et al. 1997). Sea level rise was also implicated in losses caused by conversion of tidal flats to marsh. Relative sea level rise slowed between 1979 and 1992 (W. White, pers. comm.), but losses were still substantial. Other causes of loss included dredge and fill activities associated with navigational channels and conversion of some flats to uplands.

There is little information concerning changes in tidal flat area in lower Laguna Madre. An estimated 90 km^2 (35 mi^2) have been lost due to dredge and fill activities associated with channelization (Brown et al. 1980; Farmer 1991). No other loss estimates exist, but it is likely that losses associated with relative sea level rise have occurred. Losses of small flats have occurred due to commercial development (M. Vega, pers. comm.) and conversion resulting from mitigation projects (Cobb 1987), but the cumulative impact of these losses is unknown.

The Physical Environment   Unlike in most terrestrial communities and many aquatic communities, abiotic rather than biotic characteristics and processes drive the dynamics of Laguna Madre wind-tidal flats. As their name implies, wind determines hydrology of wind-tidal flats and is the primary force shaping topographic and sedimentological features. Blue-green algae and algal mats, if present, also influence microrelief, sediment type, and moisture content of flats. Elevation, orientation, flooding/exposure,

Table 9.1.   Areal extent of wind-tidal flats in the Laguna Madre area of south Texas, including Baffin Bay and South Bay; all values are in square kilometers

Type of Tidal Flat	COUNTY (NORTH TO SOUTH)					
	Nueces	**Kleberg**	**Kenedy**	**Willacy**	**Cameron**	**Total**
Wind-tidal flat, sand, loose, rarely flooded	0.0	0.0	59.8[a]	0.0	0.0	59.8
Wind-tidal flat, sand and mud, firm	37.2[b]	70.2	162.5	12.5	150.3	432.7
Wind-tidal flat, sand and mud, extensive algal mats, alternatively emergent/submergent	0.0	2.6	93.6	51.5	78	225.7
Wind-tidal flat, mud and sand, algal-bound mud, gypsiferous, firm	3.1	0	104.0	11.7	0.0	118.8
Wind-tidal flat, mud and sand, extensive algal mats, depressed relief, wet and soft	0.0	0.0	33.8	9.9	2.1	45.8
Total wind-tidal flat by county	40.3	72.8	419.9	85.6	230.4	849.0
Percent of total	4.7	8.6	49.5	10.1	27.1	100
Transitional zone, wind-tidal flat to eolian sand sheet, wind deflation, concentrated clay dunes, sand	0.0	1.3	172.1	19	0.0	192.4

Source: Compiled from Brown et al. 1976, 1977, 1980.

[a] To convert km^2 to mi^2, multiply by 0.386.

[b] Nueces County figures also include wind-tidal flats outside of Laguna Madre. Square kilometers are not separable by bay system in Brown et al. (1976).

sediment type, microrelief, physiography, and changing sea levels determine extent and persistence of biologic development, not just from year to year but from day to day and even from hour to hour. The physical environment of wind-tidal flats can change dramatically in a matter of hours if winds shift or temperatures increase or decrease.

Hydrology   Astronomical changes in water level play only a minor role in day-to-day flooding and exposure of wind-tidal flats in Laguna Madre. Seasonal increases in systemwide water levels (September–October, April–May) result in fairly long periods when many flats are completely inundated with little or no exposure. Seasonal decreases in water levels in July–August usually expose flats completely with little or no flooding, but during the winter low (January–February), flooding of lower flats ranges from rare to frequent, depending on winds. For the most part, winds drive the hydrology of wind-tidal flats, and flooding or exposure occurs mainly when winds are aligned to blow directly along the axis of the estuary (Brown et al. 1977). Occurrence and persistence of both flooding and exposure are irregular, and either may occur rapidly (within a few hours) depending on wind speed and direction (Fisk 1959; Hayes and Scott 1964; Hayes 1965; Brown et al. 1977; White and Galloway 1977; Weise and White 1980; Withers 1996b). Flooding of flats in upper Laguna Madre and the upper reaches of Baffin Bay occurs at rates directly related to wind strength and persistence. Southeasterly winds of 13–17 kph (8–11 mph) forced water over flats in the Land-Cut at 0.5–1 km/day (0.3–0.6 mi/day) (Fisk 1959). When wind speeds increased to 30–50 kph (19–31 mph), the wind-tidal surge moved 4.2–6.1 km/day (2.6–3.8 mi/day). Strong northerly winds pushed water completely across the Land-Cut in 36 hours at rates of 12 km/day (7.5 mi). During a 24-hour period with north winds of 8–20 kph (5–12 mph), Amdurer (1978) noted a 6 cm (15 in) rise in water level and when wind direction changed, floodwater receded rapidly, with a drop of 3 cm (5 in) in four hours.

Physiography   Wind-tidal flats in Laguna Madre are found at elevations between mean sea level (MSL) and 1 m above MSL (fig. 9.2) and slope gently lagoonward at 10 cm/km (16 in/mi) (Herber 1981). Herber (1981) classified the entire wind-tidal flat as intertidal, with low, middle, and upper zones. The lower intertidal was flooded nearly daily and was dry only during extreme summer low tides. The upper intertidal was flooded for only about 20 days annually (5% of the year), and the middle intertidal was flooded for an intermediate number of days, usually during winter storms and extreme high tides. Although Herber's observations concerning the timing and length of flooding are correct, his classification of the entire flat as "intertidal" was not. By strict astronomical tide definitions, most of the flat should be considered supratidal.

Because effects of astronomical tides on barrier island wind-tidal flats in Laguna Madre are negligible, a mosaic of microhabitats often occurs (Withers 1994; fig. 9.3), rather than traditional zonation defined as bands of environmental conditions with an associated fauna. This mosaic is composed of three essentially emergent microhabitats defined by water depth and substrate saturation and reflecting shorebird foraging ability (Baker and Baker 1973; Withers and Chapman 1993; Withers 1994): (1) Intertidal—areas at the edge of a body of water (usually the lagoon) covered with 2–5 cm (0.8–2 in) of water; (2) Wet—usually saturated but always wet areas, often covered with water ranging in depth from a "film" to about 2 cm (0.8 cm) deep; and (3) Damp—areas that may appear dry on the surface but are damp to wet below the surface, occasionally with standing water (up to 2 cm deep) in depressions. The intertidal microhabitat is the only habitat that is always analogous to a "zone" since it occurs in a band of varying width at the edge of the water; however, shallow depressions filled with 5 cm (2 in) of water or

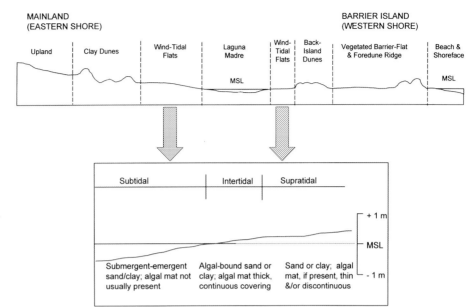

Fig. 9.2. Horizontal relationship schematic depicting positions of wind-tidal flats in relation to other barrier island and mainland habitat types. A close-up view of the flat at MSL (mean sea level) shows gentle slope, sediment type, and position of algal mat, if present.

Fig. 9.3. Overhead view of tidal flat depicting a possible arrangement of microhabitats

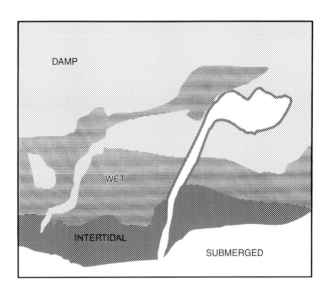

more also have an intertidal microhabitat along their edges. The existence of the remaining microhabitats as either a mosaic or as zones is largely determined by wind speed and direction and by microrelief within the tidal flat.

Although microhabitats may be arranged in a manner analogous to zones, it is not unusual for the wet microhabitat to occur at a distance farther from the water than the damp microhabitat, or for there to be patches of microhabitats with no obvious arrangement. Areal coverage of microhabitats differs with water levels, and sometimes microhabitats are nonexistent. A typical back island flat is generally dry and sandy at the highest elevations near back island dunes, where flooding is rare. As elevations decrease, bare sand and/or mud grade into sand and/or mud covered with a blue-green algal mat, particularly at and just above MSL, where flooding and exposure normally occur, if somewhat irregularly. There is a sharp textural boundary between the rarely exposed sandy or muddy areas below MSL and the blue-green algal flat, with a "step up" onto the algal bound areas (Withers 1994).

Table 9.2. *Summary of sedimentary processes affecting wind-tidal flats*

Type of Process	Process Description	Effect
Biological	Trapping or binding by blue-green algae	Major
	Addition of detritus by plants (esp. seagrasses)	Major/Minor
	Disruption by plants	Minor
	Addition of detritus from shell	Minor
Physical	Wind transport	Major/Minor
	Currents—wind tides (seasonal)	Major/Minor
	Desiccation	Major
	Currents—storms	Minor
Chemical	Precipitation of carbonates	Major

Source: Modified from Herber 1981.

Geology and Geomorphology   Wind-tidal flats in Laguna Madre are geologically young features that began forming about 2,500 years ago when sea level reached approximately its present level. The significant process that contributed to formation of tidal flats on the bay side of barrier islands was development of flood-tidal deltas and washover fans (Brown et al. 1976). Wind-tidal flats cover vast areas on the bay side of Padre Island and are composed primarily of medium and fine sands (63–250 μm) (Withers 1994). On the mainland, wind-tidal flats typically develop on fluvial deltaic deposits, where erosion by streams diminishes as they flow into upper reaches of bays or where winds have deflated older eolian, barrier-strandplain, or deltaic deposits. Mainland flats are composed primarily of clays and are generally small and scattered. The largest mainland flat in all of the Laguna Madre is the Land-Cut located between the upper and lower lagunas. This flat causes a distinct indentation of the mainland coastline (see fig. 9.1) and is about 20 km (12 mi) long and 10 km (6 mi) wide. The western side of the flat is deflated and the eastern and central portions are infilled by wind-blown sand to form a land-bridge. Another large mainland flat is found in the delta of the Arroyo Colorado in lower Laguna Madre. In upper Laguna Madre, mainland flats are best developed in the upper reaches of Baffin Bay (Brown et al. 1976, 1977).

A number of sedimentary processes affect wind-tidal flats in Laguna Madre (table 9.2). Deposition was basically complete about 200 years ago when Laguna Madre tidal flats became subaerial (Long and Gudramovics 1983). Flats increase in size primarily through accretion of wind-transported sand from barrier islands. Wind-blown sand may adhere to wet or damp blue-green algal mats, and when these are flooded for extended periods, algal filaments extend into the water column, trapping clays (Fisk 1959). The process of accretion is typically incredibly slow. Vertical accretion in the Land-Cut gradually decreased during the last 2,500 years from 0.5 to 0.25 mm/yr (0.1 to 0.006 in/yr) or less (Miller 1975). However, rapid shoreline progradation of wind-tidal flats near Bird Island Basin was noted between 1941 and 1969 (Prouty and Prouty 1989). Progradation was attributed to greater amounts of wind-blown sand caused by drought-induced devegetation of dunes. Floodwaters carry suspended sediments, especially to mainland flats. Prevailing southeasterly winds force sediment-laden waters away from Padre Island and into Baffin Bay, and the waves generated may erode tidal flat margins. Seasonally, northers carry sediments back to barrier islands, but these events are infrequent and relatively unimportant (Fisk 1959; Herber 1981).

Plant Communities

Vascular plants are rare to nonexistent on wind-tidal flats in Laguna Madre, primarily because sediment salinities are extremely high and there is little freshwater inflow. Scattered saltmarsh vegetation may be found, primarily glasswort (*Salicornia* spp.) and saltwort *(Batis maritima)*, particularly in or around depressions within the flat and during wet years. Occasionally sparse smooth cordgrass *(Spartina alterniflora)* is found along lagoonal edges of flats and black mangroves *(Avicennia germinans)* along tidal channels (Herber 1981; White et al. 1983c; Pulich and Scalan 1987).

Benthic microalgae are the major primary producers found on tidal flats. Filamentous blue-green algae (Cyanobacteria) are the most common and abundant microalgae found on wind-tidal flats in Laguna Madre, forming feltlike or leathery mats from 1 to 3 cm thick (fig. 9.4). *Lyngbya confervoides* (= *Microcoleus lyngbyaceus*) typically constitutes at least 70% of the living community (Fisk 1959; Sorenson and Conover 1962; Armstrong and Odum 1964; Dykstra 1966; Zupan 1971; Gotto et al. 1981; Herber 1981; Pulich et al. 1982; Pulich and Rabalais 1986). Pennate diatoms are common, especially at salinities less than 60 ppt, but usually constitute less than 10% of total algal biomass (Simmons 1957; Pulich et al. 1982).

Succession Succession from unvegetated salt flat to a saltwort-glasswort marsh may occur under conditions of adequate fresh water (Brogden et al. 1977). Under optimal conditions the following sequence may occur: (1) colonization of salt flat by blue-green algae and development of algal mat; (2) stabilization of surface by algal mat promoting deposition, accumulation of organic material, and fixation of atmospheric nitrogen; (3) germination of glasswort seeds at higher elevations in depressions where water accumulates; (4) burrowing by fiddler crabs (*Uca* spp.), which allows rainwater to penetrate sediments, ameliorating high soil salinities; and (5) colonization by other saltmarsh plants such as saltwort, shoregrass *(Monanthochloe littoralis)*, and saltgrass *(Distichlis spicata)*. Because this sequence of events is totally dependent on adequate freshwater inflow, the process may be halted or reversed by extended periods of drought or by

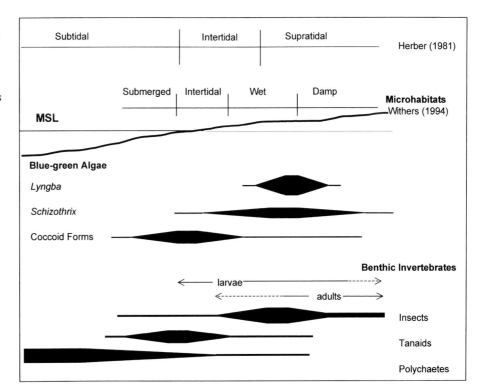

Fig. 9.4. *Abundance and distribution of the major taxa of blue-green algae and benthic and epibenthic invertebrates. Blue-green algal distribution from Herber (1981); invertebrate distribution from Withers (1994). Weight of lines reflects relative abundances of different groups.*

extremely high tides. This process may be occurring on some flats north of the JFK causeway (Withers and Tunnell 1998) and in the Horse Island area of lower Laguna Madre (C. Onuf, pers. comm.), where dense stands of glasswort have vegetated large areas of some tidal flats. In general, succession on most flats in Laguna Madre appears arrested in the algal mat stage.

Animal Communities

Invertebrates   Where flats are more than 1 m (3.3 ft) above MSL or are not frequently inundated, saltwater–adapted insects that live on the surface are the only invertebrates able to survive (Pulich et al. 1982). The most abundant insect families collected from drier areas of two flats (Yarborough Pass and South Bay) were Corixidae and Saldidae (Order Hemiptera), Limnichidae (Order Coleoptera), and Sphaeroceridae (Order Diptera).

Flooding is necessary for abundant benthic and epibenthic invertebrate communities to develop and persist (Withers 1994). Invertebrates have the opportunity to colonize many, if not most, wind-tidal flats during fall high tides. Persistence and stability of the community on the flat is largely dependent on flooding frequency, and communities are usually more ephemeral in some areas than in others. Abundance and community composition may also be modified locally as shorebirds deplete patches of organisms. On flats that are frequently flooded, invertebrate communities can exist between late fall and midsummer. Organisms are usually most abundant during winter and spring, although a brief summer flush may be observed during June. Summer low tides extirpate communities on most flats, which become hot, dry, and hypersaline.

The most common and abundant members of the invertebrate community associated with algal flats in the upper Laguna Madre are dipteran larvae, polychaetes, and tanaids (Withers 1994, 1996b, 1998; Withers and Tunnell 1998). Of these three common taxa, polychaetes are typically the most diverse, with as many as 65 species. The assemblage of invertebrates associated with each of the previously described microhabitats (i.e., damp, wet, and intertidal), as well as with submerged areas 5–10 cm (2–4 in) deep adjacent to emergent microhabitats, constitutes a subset of the community as whole (fig. 9.4). Although semi-terrestrial organisms (e.g., insect larvae, insects) may be found in all microhabitats, they dominate only in the damp microhabitat. Likewise aquatic-adapted organisms (e.g., polychaetes, tanaids) may be found in all microhabitats, but their numbers and dominance increase as sediment saturation and/or water depth increases (Withers 1994).

The invertebrate community of wind-tidal flats in lower Laguna Madre has not been studied extensively. Withers (1998) described the invertebrate community of a flat located just south of the Land-Cut between December 1997 and April 1998. Assemblages associated with microhabitats were not differentiated. This flat differed from most flats in upper Laguna Madre in that the blue-green algal mat was not well developed. Polychaetes, molluscs (primarily Tellinidae), and insect larvae were the most common and abundant organisms recovered. No crustaceans of any kind were collected. Organisms were collected during all months of the study, with greatest abundances during late winter and early spring.

The fiddler crab, *Uca subcylindrica*, is endemic to the supralittoral zone of South Texas south to Tampico (Thurman 1984). This species is common along the upland margins of wind-tidal flats in Laguna Madre and the upper reaches of Baffin Bay and is typically the only fiddler crab found in these environments. *Uca subcylindrica* is more terrestrial than other members of the genus; it is rarely found closer to a water source than 20 m and is often found more than 70 m inland on dry soil. It is able to tolerate hypersalinity better than other members of its genus due to a combination of excellent osmotic and ionic regulatory abilities and tolerance to desiccation (Rabalais and Cameron 1985a). In addition, its early development is abbreviated, and larval and early postlarval stages are far more tolerant to salinity extremes and desiccation than in other fiddler crabs (Rabalais 1983; Rabalais and Cameron 1985b).

Invertebrate nekton such as shrimp may be present on flats when they are flooded. However, no study has addressed the occurrence or composition of this ephemeral community.

Fish Fish can be present on wind-tidal flats only when these are flooded, and this community has not been well documented. Sheepshead minnows *(Cyprinodon variegatus),* silversides (*Menidia* spp.), and Gulf killifish *(Fundulus similis)* were the most common and abundant fishes collected on flooded flats in South Bay, whereas only sheepshead minnows were collected at Yarborough Pass (Pulich et al. 1982). Sheepshead minnows were the only fish consistently observed on several other flooded flats in upper Laguna Madre (Withers 1996b) and are probably the only fish that could be considered regular residents of flooded flats. Sheepshead minnows feed on algae and detritus when they are small—<30 mm (7.6 in)—and on crustaceans, insects, and small fish when they are larger (Harrington and Harrington 1972; Pfeiffer and Wiegert 1981). When flats become exposed, sheepshead minnows may congregate in depressions, becoming stranded and easy prey for birds, or they move into deeper water where they are preyed upon by a variety of fish (Pulich et al. 1982). Occasionally, southern flounder *(Paralichthys lethostigma)* were disturbed in the shallow water adjoining flats in upper Laguna Madre, and "finger" striped mullet *(Mugil cephalus)* were also observed sporadically either on flooded flats or in shallow adjacent waters (Withers 1996b). Large bottom-feeding fish such as black drum *(Pogonias cromis),* red drum *(Sciaenops ocellatus),* and striped mullet may also be found if waters are deep enough (Fisk 1959).

Birds Whether flooded or exposed, wind-tidal flats provide foraging habitat for birds. Shorebirds (Charadriiformes) use flats when they are exposed or covered with less than 5 cm (2 in) of water, whereas wading birds (Ciconiiformes) and occasionally ducks use flats when they are flooded with deeper water. Peregrine falcons and white-shouldered hawks, both listed as endangered and/or threatened, also forage on or near flats during winter.

Seasonal abundance and habitat use of wind-tidal flats by shorebirds has been studied extensively in upper Laguna Madre (Withers 1994, 1996c, 1998; Withers and Tunnell 1998; see chapter 13). Fewer studies of the entire community exist in lower Laguna Madre (Ecoservices 1993a; Brush 1995; Withers 1998). At least 32 species of shorebirds occur in the Laguna. The majority observed during Ecoservices (1993a) surveys on the lagoon side of Padre Island were found on frequently flooded wind-tidal flats, although adjacent habitats, particularly washover areas, may be important, especially to breeding and roosting birds. In upper Laguna Madre, numbers of shorebirds on tidal flats generally increase in late fall after seasonal high tides drop, peak during winter, then decline through spring as migrants return to northern breeding grounds. The most common and abundant species migrating through or wintering in Laguna Madre are sandpipers (*Calidris* spp.), but banded plovers (*Charadrius* spp.), black-bellied plovers (*Pluvialis squatorola),* dowitchers (*Limnodromous* spp.), and willets *(Catoptrophorus semipalmatus)* are also common. Shorebird numbers fluctuate widely during early summer. Shorebirds present are either species that breed in the area, such as Wilson's plovers *(Charadrius wilsoni)* or snowy plovers, or nonbreeding, often immature individuals that did not complete the migration to northern breeding grounds. Tidal flats in the Coastal Bend and upper Laguna Madre may not be heavily used by shorebirds during southward fall migration (late July–October) due to the lack of invertebrate prey following summer low tides coupled with lack of adequate exposed area during fall high tides (Withers and Chapman 1993; Withers 1994).

Shorebird communities of blue-green algal flats can be divided into three guilds based on their apparent preferences for tidal flat microhabitats (Withers 1994). Sandpipers and black-bellied plovers preferred the wet microhabitat. The wet and damp habitats were used in nearly equal proportions by piping, snowy, and semipalmated (*Charadrius semipalmatus*) plovers, whereas adjacent shallow waters were used by a number of long-legged, long-billed shorebirds, such as dunlin (*Calidris alpina*). Only western sandpipers (*Calidris mauri*) exhibited any preference for the intertidal microhabitat, but they used it in nearly equal proportion to use of the wet microhabitat. Brush (1995) also defined guilds based on habitat preference. The shallow water guild contained birds that forage exclusively in water, such as American avocets (*Recurvirostra americana*). The exposed mudflat guild contained plovers, some sandpipers, and ruddy turnstones (*Arenaria interpres*) and was similar in composition to the wet/damp guild described by Withers (1994) on upper Laguna Madre flats. The water/mudflat guild contained western sandpipers, which showed a preference for the intertidal microhabitat in upper Laguna Madre, as well as long-legged, long-billed shorebirds like dowitchers and dunlins, which preferred submerged habitats in upper Laguna Madre.

Herons and egrets forage on flooded tidal flats or in adjacent shallow water areas, but there are few quantitative studies addressing their seasonal abundance or habitat use. Nearly all common wading bird species may be found, but great blue heron (*Ardea herodias*), great egret (*Ardea alba*), and reddish egret are most common (Pulich et al. 1982; Ecoservices 1993; Brush 1995; Withers 1996b). During 1991–93, wading birds in upper Laguna Madre were most abundant from April to November (Withers 1996a).

Ecosystem Processes

Energy Flow and Food Web   Lack of readily recognizable vegetation on wind-tidal flats conveys a false impression of insignificant primary productivity. However, as noted, primary production by benthic algae on wind-tidal flats can be nearly as high as that of seagrasses. Primary production on wind-tidal flats in Laguna Madre has been estimated at from 222 g C/m²/yr to over 500 g C/m²/yr (Odum and Wilson 1962; Brogden et al. 1977; Pulich and Rabalais 1982, 1986), with an algal turnover rate of about 10.8 times/yr (Pulich and Rabalais 1982, 1986). Systemwide, this represents a substantial amount of production because of the vast areas occupied by wind-tidal flats and the lack of salt marshes.

It is likely that both grazing and detrital food chains are found on tidal flats in Laguna Madre. There is strong evidence that grazing pathways are the principal means by which primary productivity associated with benthic algae moves to higher trophic levels (Pulich and Scalan 1987). Carbon isotope studies (δ^{13} C) on insects collected from Yarborough Pass indicated that blue-green algae from the algal mat was the source of organic carbon. Studies in other systems have also shown benthic microalgae to be much more important than expected in nutrition of primary consumers in estuaries (Haines and Montague 1979). Seagrass detritus and moribund algae likely form the basis of detrital food chains.

Regardless of the source of organic matter (microalgae vs. detritus), wind-tidal flats in Laguna Madre are important sites where primary productivity is converted to animal biomass for use by larger estuarine predators. In higher, drier areas of wind-tidal flats, an abbreviated food chain based on microalgae and saltwater-adapted insects has been suggested (Pulich and Rabalais 1982; Pulich and Scalan 1987). On algal flats that are frequently flooded, polychaetes, crustaceans, and insect larvae are the primary consumers.

Fig. 9.5. Generalized food chain for tidal flats. Weights of arrows and boxes reflect the relative importance of each compartment and pathway. (From Withers 1996b)

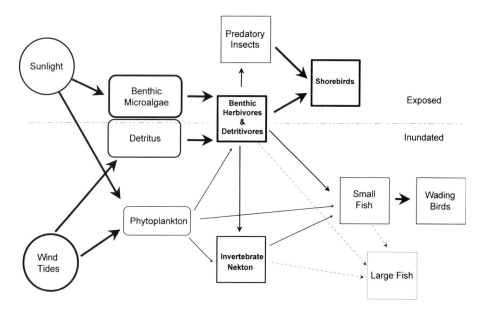

A generalized food web is depicted in figure 9.5. The presence of vertebrate predators (i.e., shorebirds, wading birds, or fish) is dependent on flooding and exposure of flats. Shorebirds are the only predators that can use flats when they are either exposed or covered with shallow water. Flooding with shallow water allows small fish to come up onto the flats, providing wading birds with prey, but waters must be fairly deep before predatory fish can forage. Thus, presence of predators is determined seasonally by systemwide water level fluctuations and daily by flooding and exposure by wind-tides.

Nutrient Cycling   Nitrogen is typically considered a limiting nutrient in marine systems, but phosphorus appears to fill that role in many hypersaline systems, including Laguna Madre (Villareal et al. 1998). Nitrogen is generally available, if not abundant, on wind-tidal flats in Laguna Madre. Blue-green algae fix much of the nitrogen they need; nitrogen is also fixed by anaerobic bacteria in sediments below algal mats. Average annual nitrogen inputs from mats in Laguna Madre to adjacent shallow waters ranged from 4 to 89 kg N/ha/yr (Pulich and Rabalais 1982, 1986), which represents a considerable contribution to the system. In addition, substantial amounts of dissolved ammonia were always detected leaching out of flooded algal mats, representing an important source of "new" nitrogen to adjacent waters. There is also evidence that dissolved ammonia percolates down through sediments to the water table (R. Hay, pers. comm.).

Phosphate may accumulate in blue-green algal mats in Laguna Madre. After algal mats had been exposed to the point of desiccation and dormancy, reflooding resulted in leaching of accumulated phosphate from the mat (Pulich and Rabalais 1982, 1986). There was also evidence that phosphate was lost through downward percolation. When mats were wet or flooded and actively growing, net uptake of phosphorus was observed.

Current Issues

In Laguna Madre, tidal flats occupy the space that marshes fill in other areas. Salt marshes convert plant biomass to animal biomass at the place where the seawater meets the land; tidal flats do the same. To most people, "wetlands" means marshes, not tidal flats. People understand "no net loss" when the idea is applied to marshes but are not as easily convinced that tidal flats deserve the same consideration. Even scientists and resource agency personnel were uninterested until about the last 20 years, when the uniqueness and importance of such habitat was revealed. Although awareness of the needs of piping plovers goes some of the way toward developing advocates for tidal flats, there is no easily seen, readily understood component like cordgrass as a focal point in this habitat; thus the value of tidal flats is difficult to convey to people outside the circle of scientists and resource agencies involved in their management. Birders aside, most people do not understand why they should care, and this poses a distinct challenge for the long-term protection and conservation of tidal flats as an important coastal natural habitat.

Wind-tidal flats in Laguna Madre represent the most important habitat for wintering shorebirds at the northernmost extent of most species' wintering range. Those same flats are being impacted by a variety of natural and human disturbances, some of which are serious and long-lasting. Dramatic reductions in areal extent, largely due to relative sea level rise, means that the remaining flats may be essential to shorebirds in general and critical to populations of some species. Reduction of serious, long-lasting human disturbances is the most important challenge facing managers today, since little can be done to stop sea level changes.

Tidal Flat Losses   Tidal flats are lost as rises in sea level, plant community succession, or mitigation converts them to other habitats or through destruction due to residential or commercial development. These losses carry potential for both long- and short-term reductions in shorebird carrying capacities. There is evidence that competition may already limit numbers of shorebirds in microhabitats they prefer (Withers 1994); reductions in current carrying capacity could result in negative impacts on shorebird populations.

At the landscape level, losses of tidal flat habitat due to conversion associated with sea level rise or plant community succession might be permanent, but they could also be relatively short-lived, lasting perhaps decades. Relict tidal flats in nearby Copano Bay provide evidence the habitat may reform at higher elevations when sea level increases (Ricklis 1995; Ricklis and Blum 1997). Rapid progradation of Padre Island tidal flats during periods of drought (Prouty and Prouty 1989) indicates that increased accretion rates associated with drought might also be enough to offset some losses. Conversely, sea level rise combined with normal or increased rainfall may decrease sediment salinities enough to allow plant community succession to proceed. Recent expansion of glasswort on a number of flats in upper and lower Laguna Madre may be the result of these conditions, but return to drought conditions may arrest or reverse the expansion as quickly as it began.

Vegetating tidal flats with cordgrass, black mangroves, or seagrasses in mitigation projects is often viewed as enhancing existing habitat (Withers and Tunnell 1998). In view of the growing awareness of the productivity and importance of tidal flats, it is ironic that these flats are themselves frequently targeted for vegetating to mitigate losses of vegetated wetlands, and further that impacts to tidal flats are routinely mitigated by vegetating unvegetated habitats. Mitigation projects in lower Laguna Madre have converted several tidal flats to black mangrove and/or cordgrass habitats. With few exceptions, there has been no "in kind" mitigation for tidal flats lost to development in Laguna Madre.

Tidal flat habitat has been completely destroyed by commercial or residential development in a number of areas in both upper and lower Laguna Madre (Withers and Tunnell 1998; M. Vega, pers. comm.). Large tracts of wind-tidal flats have already been protected from further development. Some of the largest expanses of flats are found within the boundaries of Padre Island National Seashore, where they are safe from all but oil and gas development. In addition, two areas north of JFK Causeway have recently been set aside. Under the Adopt-A-Habitat program begun by the Texas General Land Office and U.S. Fish and Wildlife Service, about 405 ha (1,001 ac) of tidal flats and salt marshes in the Packery Channel–Newport Pass area were set aside as the Mollie Beattie Coastal Habitat Community in 1996. Another 3 ha (7.4 ac) were set aside in late 1997 at Corpus Christi Pass as mitigation for impacts to tidal flat habitat associated with development around the JFK Causeway.

The key to preventing and/or mitigating losses of flats due to human activities depends on adequate evaluation of flats before impacts occur. Support of migrating and wintering shorebirds is the primary management issue. One difficulty with evaluating tidal flats in Laguna Madre is the extreme temporal variability that may be exhibited by populations of both shorebirds and benthic invertebrates; another difficulty is the lack of multi-year baseline studies. Withers and Tunnell (1998) have proposed an evaluation strategy specifically designed for blue-green algal flats in Laguna Madre and surrounding bay systems. Because shorebirds are mobile and their presence on a given flat can and does change rapidly, this strategy evaluates tidal flat productivity based on measures of more "permanent" parameters such as sediment chlorophyll and benthic invertebrate density and biomass in addition to shorebird density. The strategy also measures all parameters over five to 12 months rather than relying only on the presence or absence of piping plovers during specific months. When applied to three flats within Padre Island National Seashore (Withers 1998), the results identified one flat as an essentially untapped resource for shorebirds, with high benthic productivity, and one flat as a productive site for both shorebirds and benthic invertebrates. It was clear from the evaluation that these two sites warranted additional study as well as preservation from impacts. The third site evaluated was not productive for either shorebirds or benthic invertebrates during the evaluation period. Managing these types of flats is less clear-cut. Short time periods for evaluation do not allow evaluation of the possibility that flats such as these are merely experiencing temporary or cyclical decreases in productivity. In addition, primary productivity in these areas may be high, and they may contribute indirectly to productivity of surrounding habitats through their role in nutrient cycling.

Tidal Flat Degradation   Although there are many ways tidal flats may be degraded by human activities, development, tracking by vehicles, oil spills, dredging, and dredge material disposal constitute major threats to tidal flats in Laguna Madre.

Scars of tracking, probably due to cattle, are evident on Mustang Island tidal flats in 1938 aerial photos. Today, tracking by vehicles and propeller scars from boats are evident on nearly all tidal flats in Laguna Madre, and these scars can persist for decades. Impacts from vehicles are much more serious when flats are wet or saturated. Studies in other areas have concluded that only a few passes by a vehicle were sufficient to cause maximum damage to benthic invertebrate communities and that all vehicles should be banned from tidal flats (Leatherman and Godfrey 1979). However, there do not appear to be any significant long-term effects on benthic communities once tracking stops (Withers 1996c). In fact, old tire tracks on tidal flats within Padre Island National Seashore appeared to act as refugia for benthic organisms since they retained water after surrounding areas began to dry. They may also act as recolonization pools. Although there do not appear to be any long-term biological impacts of tracking, driving on flats should not be encouraged. If driving is necessary, it should only occur when flats are dry.

Lack of daily tidal flushing on Laguna Madre tidal flats means there is little or no potential for self-cleaning if oil spills occur (Withers and Tunnell 1998). An environmental sensitivity index for South Texas coastal environments gave sensitivity ratings of 5 or 7 (on a scale of 1 to 10) to most exposed tidal flats in Laguna Madre (Hayes et al. 1980). Sheltered flats in the upper reaches of Baffin Bay were assigned a sensitivity of 9. Biological effects were predicted as slight to severe on exposed flats, depending on tidal flushing, and severe on sheltered flats that are flushed infrequently. Use of mechanical cleanup equipment was not recommended due to soft sediments. These indices were assigned prior to listing of piping plovers as an endangered species and should probably be higher now for exposed flats (Withers and Tunnell 1998). Piping plovers use both exposed and sheltered flats throughout Laguna Madre and could be seriously affected by oil spills on these sites.

Dredging impacts tidal flats when channels are cut through them, and when they are used as disposal areas (Withers and Tunnell 1998). Both activities have occurred in numerous places throughout Laguna Madre. Channelization destroys benthic faunas, reduces area for birds, and changes hydrology by blocking floodwaters from inundating flats or by causing flats to drain more quickly. Dredge material disposal buries benthic organisms, reduces foraging area for birds but may increase roosting area, and changes hydrology by blocking wind-tides and isolating remaining flats from inundation. At a minimum, either practice may change hydrology to the point that most function ceases. Proliferation of navigational channels and marinas with associated dredge material disposal on tidal flats has been implicated in rapid and more extensive flooding and erosion of vegetated barrier flats, subaerial spoil, and made-land (Morton et al. 1977; White and Brogden 1977).

Laguna Madre de Tamaulipas

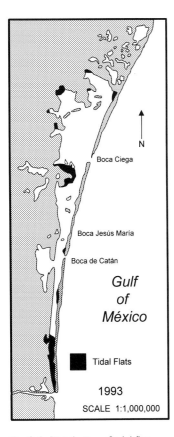

Fig. 9.6. Distribution of tidal flats in Laguna Madre de Tamaulipas (Redrawn from Farmer and Carrera Gonzalez 1993)

Virtually nothing is known about the ecology of wind-tidal flats in Laguna Madre de Tamaulipas. Using the Cowardin Wetland Classification System (Cowardin et al. 1979), DUMAC (unpubl. data) estimated that approximately 508 km² (196 mi²) of wetlands in Laguna Madre de Tamaulipas were either Estuarine Intertidal Flat (E2FL) or Estuarine Intertidal Flat Modified (E2FLMD), the two designations corresponding to wind-tidal flats. Very large expanses of tidal flat are found within the system. In the delta of the Río San Fernando, a large flat known as El Carrizal divides the Laguna into northern and southern parts. The La Pesca flat extends from Río Soto la Marina at the village of La Pesca to as far north as 25 km (15 mi) south of the entrance of Laguna el Catán, ranging in length from 15 to 50 km (9–31 mi), depending on the source consulted (Cornelius 1975; Britton and Morton 1989). Both of these flats have extensive blue-green algal mats (Farmer and Carrera Gonzalez 1993). The La Pesca flat is flooded only during strong northerly winds and tropical storm tides (J. W. Tunnell, pers. comm.)

Farmer and Carrera Gonzalez (1993) mapped tidal flats in Laguna Madre de Tamaulipas (fig. 9.6) and described their hydrology as part of a study of wintering ecology of reddish egrets. They described flats as either narrow or broad, broad meaning wider than 1 km (0.6 mi). Few broad flats were found other than those at El Carrizal and La Pesca. One of the larger broad flats was found on the bay side of the barrier island near Tres Bocas. Although similar in width to flats on the bay side of Padre Island, it was only about 10 km (6 mi) long, or about one-tenth the length of Padre Island flats. Small areas of broad flat were found on the mainland associated with various coves in the northern basin. For the most part, tidal flats ranged from only a few meters to a few hundred meters wide.

The flats in Tamaulipas are important winter foraging habitat for reddish egrets, with potential to support large numbers of shorebirds when exposed. When flats were flooded, numbers of reddish egrets ranged from fewer than 20 on narrow flats to over 500 on the La Pesca flat (Farmer and Carrera Gonzalez 1993). Several hundred piping and snowy plovers have been found during recent winter censuses of barrier island tidal flats conducted by a multi-agency group (C. Zonick, pers. comm.). Wintering snowy plovers used mainland flats extensively during surveys of the northern lagoon, but few piping plovers were found (J. Bergen, pers. comm.). To date, no nesting birds have been found on tidal flats (Zonick 1997a).

10 *Barrier Islands*

ELIZABETH H. SMITH

The geomorphic position of barrier islands between the open Gulf of Mexico and adjacent mainland bays and lagoons of Texas and Mexico delineates the protective importance of these island systems to sustainability and dynamics of tidal flats, lagoons, and bays. River sediments discharged into the Gulf of Mexico function as a primary source for barrier islands. Sand and shell deposited on Gulf beaches provide necessary material for coppice dune and foredune ridge formation and maintenance. Dune stability produced by vegetation establishment provides protection of leeward habitats during storm surges. Vegetation composition is influenced by salt spray from the Gulf of Mexico, thus affecting soil salinity, fresh water, and availability of nutrients. A unique plant assemblage is associated with each topographic zone across a barrier island. Extreme high tides from storm surges may flood vegetated flats, and plant and animal community dynamics are influenced by these events for several years afterward. Sand deposition on tidal flats is increased during droughts, when areal coverage of unvegetated, active dunes increases. Seagrass meadows benefit from the physical protection of barrier islands but may become shallower due to sediment deposition from adjacent island dune fields. Open bay habitats are indirectly affected by barrier islands as a protection from the Gulf of Mexico and directly affected by transport of marine waters and organisms through island passes.

Physical Setting and Processes

Barrier islands are elongate landforms positioned parallel to the coastline and typically isolated from the mainland by bays and lagoons. Longshore currents, low tidal range, and wave energy work together to form and maintain barrier island systems (Britton and Morton 1989). These islands function as protective barriers to the adjacent Texas mainland and shallow bays and lagoons. Padre Island is part of a barrier island chain extending from the central Texas coast to the southernmost extent of Texas. A similar barrier island chain is located along the northeastern coastline of Tamaulipas. Unique flora and fauna inhabiting islands contribute to Tamaulipan Biotic Province diversity.

The geological formation of all Texas barrier islands is similar (chapter 3); however, slight differences in topography, vegetation, and animal composition are evident on each island, due to combinations of physical factors and degree of isolation from the mainland and adjacent barrier islands. Barrier islands are formed by deposition of sands via Gulf currents parallel to the mainland—longshore currents. Constant redistribution of sands, driven primarily by prevailing southeasterly winds, contributes to formation of distinct topographic features across the islands. These dynamic, eolian forces continue to erode some areas and build up others, as can be observed with active dune migration across islands. Abrupt changes in topography occur as a result of hurricanes and storm surges. These events may reopen passes through an island, denude and/or flatten active dune areas, and erode beachfronts (Price 1933; Weise and White 1980).

Natural passes separate barrier islands from each other and, in turn, the Laguna Madre of Texas and Tamaulipas separate barrier islands from the mainland (see fig. 2.1). Both natural and artificial passes connect lagoonal systems to the Gulf of Mexico. Padre Island is separated from Mustang Island to the north by an intermittently open washover pass, Packery Channel (historically known as Corpus Christi Pass). Other washover passes occur in this area as well (Newport and Corpus Christi passes), but they are connected to the Gulf only during and after tropical storms or hurricanes (Brown et al. 1976). Padre Island extends 181 km (113 mi) south to Brazos Santiago Pass and is generally isolated from the mainland by Laguna Madre. An artificial pass, Mansfield Pass, connects lower Laguna Madre to the Gulf. Several shallow passes are located along the Tamaulipas barrier island chain, but most were closed historically except during and following hurricane storm surges and subsequent freshwater inflow. During the past two decades, four passes have been dredged and jettied (see chapters 2 and 3).

North Padre Island is quite wide, and has extensive fresh to brackish marshes within the vegetated barrier flats in the island interior. Padre Island becomes narrower with similar marsh complexes in the Padre Island National Seashore boundaries. South of Mansfield Pass, the island becomes even narrower, and washover passes and wind-tidal flats prevail over well-established dune zones (Brown et al. 1980). Tamaulipas barrier islands are much narrower than Padre Island and have few marshes in the island interior (Britton and Morton 1989). Expansive wind-tidal flats occur along the lagoon side of Padre Island, the Land-Cut, and the South Bay–Laguna Larga–San Martin Lake area of Texas (Brown et al. 1976, 1977) and bordering much of the Laguna Madre de Tamaulipas shorelines (Saunders and Saunders 1981; see chapters 3 and 9).

Barrier islands along the southern Texas and northern Tamaulipas coasts are elongate in shape and typically wider at their northern end (Selander et al. 1962; Brown et al. 1976, 1977, 1980). Several habitat types occur across the islands and are related to elevation, physical forces, and geomorphology of the adjacent Gulf of Mexico and lagoons. Physiographic zones extend the island length and include foreshore (swash zone), backshore (from high tide line to dunes), foredunes, vegetated flats with ponds and marshes, and wind-tidal flats with back-island dunes and coastal marshes in some places (fig. 10.1). Foreshore habitat, wind-tidal flats, and coastal marshes are affected more by hydrologic and eolian forces than are terrestrial dunes and vegetated flats. Ponds and marshes in vegetated flats form an integral component of the ecological relationships of barrier island systems.

The highest elevations on barrier islands in Texas occur along foredune ridges landward from Gulf beaches. Padre Island has the highest dunes along the Texas coast, some as high as 15.2 m (50 ft) above sea level (Weise and White 1980), although average dune heights range from 6.1 to 7.6 m (20–25 ft) on North Padre Island (Brown et al. 1976). Most dune heights on Tamaulipas barrier islands are lower than on Padre Island (Britton and Morton 1980), although some dunes were estimated to be 6 m (20 ft) in elevation (Hall 1951) and others up to 10.7 m (35 ft; J. W. Tunnell, Jr., pers. observ.). A unique island profile begins north of Mesquital and extends southward to Boca Ciega Pass, where coppice dunes vegetated with sea purslane *(Sesuvium portulacastrum)* prevail across most of the island, extending from 1 to almost 3 km (0.6–1.8 mi) wide. Large unvegetated dunes 13–15 m (43–49 ft) high are located near the lee side of the peninsula or barrier island, covering shrubs (primarily mesquite) and grasses (gulf cordgrass *[Spartina spartinae]*) (J. W. Tunnell, Jr.,

Fig. 10.1. Cross-section profiles of barrier island vegetation zonation for Padre Island, Texas, and in Tamaulipas, Barra El Conchillal near Mezquital (northern), and Barra Jesús María near Boca de Catán (southern)

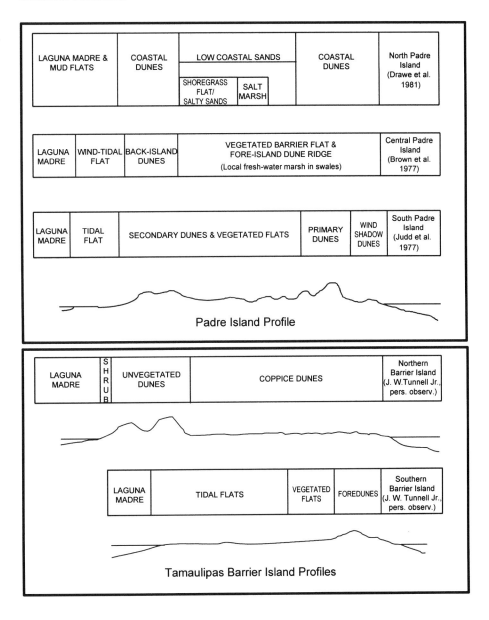

pers. comm.). Foredunes are less vegetated from north to south in Texas due to lower average precipitation rates (Weise and White 1980).

In many areas immediately seaward of foredunes, lower dunes termed coppice dunes may occur. These dunes typically have low, spreading vegetation that collects sand migrating up the beach face. In addition, wind-shadow dunes may form behind coppice dunes due to sand accumulation in wind-protected areas (Weise and White 1980). Coppice and wind-shadow dune elevations typically average 1 m (3.3 ft) tall; however, taller dunes were noted due to sand accumulation in vegetation over extended periods. If these dunes are not eroded by storm surges or high tides, they may coalesce with the foredune ridge or form a new ridge.

Elevations within central parts of barrier islands are not uniform due to formation of ridges and swales resulting from east-to-west dune migration across the island (Prouty and Prouty 1989). Ridge and swale topography forms during alternating wet and dry periods. During wet periods, vegetation growth stabilizes the active dune; during droughts, the active dune migrates ahead of the stabilized ridge and produces a long, linear depression or deflation trough (Hunter et al. 1972). These troughs typically have standing water during years of high precipitation and support a diversity of wetland flora and fauna (Prouty and Prouty 1989). Increases in vegetative cover will stabilize the deflation flat area, but migrating dune fields may locally cover flats, increase elevation, and bury vegetation (Longley et al. 1989).

In low areas, where wind scours the surface down to the water table, sediment moisture eliminates further erosion. Average water table depth depends on precipitation, so erosion rates vary from year to year. During wet years, these troughs hold water and are important to barrier island ecology. The number and size of ponds and marshes vary from island to island; and due to variability in rainfall from north to south and from year to year, areal extent of these habitats is difficult to quantify. Ridge and swale topography within vegetated flats is oriented longitudinally along northern Padre Island; thus, ponds and marshes often exhibit a linear configuration. Ponds and marshes located immediately leeward of foredune ridges exhibit more elliptical shapes. These low areas are formed by erosion of fore-island dunes (Weise and White 1980).

Foredune ridge orientation is parallel to the Gulf beach, but dune migration occurs from southeast to northwest. Back-island dunes on northern Padre Island are aligned east to west (Hunter et al. 1972), while back-island dune fields are more obliquely oriented in relation to prevailing southeast wind. These dunes typically are not as tall as foredunes and are generally <3 m (10 ft) high, but they may reach about 7.5 m (25 ft) in protected areas on northern Padre Island (Weise and White 1980) and about 9 m (30 ft) on southern Padre Island (Brown et al. 1980). Vegetation density tends to increase with increased rainfall, and dune stabilization typically occurs under these conditions. During droughts, sediment from devegetated dunes migrates across the island in a net west-northwest direction on Padre Island (Prouty and Prouty 1989). Back-island dunes averaging about 5 m (~15 ft) on Tamaulipan barrier islands were stabilized with shrub vegetation bordering Laguna Madre de Tamaulipas flats in some places (Selander et al. 1962).

Sediment composition on the barrier islands is predominantly sand with high to very high permeability and low water-holding capacity (McGowen et al. 1976). Shell fragments are intermixed with sand during periods of high wave and wind energy. Sediment composition changes from north to south, due to various sources of river sediment, and from east to west as a result of Gulf and bay processes. Offshore bars and older submerged sand bodies deposited by ancient river systems serve as sediment reserves. Longshore currents and waves resuspend and deposit sediments on beaches. As sediments dry, finer particles are transported by wind to backshore and dune ridges. Short-term sediment transfer from beach to foredune ridges occurs by southeasterly wind transport throughout most of the year. Larger sediment amounts are transported during hurricanes, tropical storms, and spring tides (Weise and White 1980). The longshore current along the Texas coast generally runs north to south until it converges with the northward longshore current of eastern Mexico and southernmost Texas around Big and Little Shell beaches on Padre Island (Watson 1971). The beach face is more steeply angled, and loosely sorted shell fragments predominate on the foreshore and backshore for several kilometers (Britton and Morton 1989).

Foredune ridges are typically composed of fine, well-sorted sands transported up the beach face. Migrating dunes in vegetated flats leeward of the foredune ridge and back-island dunes have similar composition (Weise and White 1980), although some finer sediments may be transported from unvegetated deflation-flat areas (Longley et al. 1989). Sediments in the vegetated flats are generally composed of sand and shell deposits, whereas some finer sediments and organic matter may accumulate and overlay sand and shell in ponds and marshes (Weise and White 1980).

Average annual rainfall decreases and average temperature and evaporation increase from north to south along Padre Island. Permanent freshwater sources may be lacking during droughts, although some fresh water collects temporarily in low depressions following rainfall. These water sources usually become brackish or evaporate completely. The shallow, perched aquifer below the surface provides some water and the only freshwater source from rain percolating through sands before it evaporates. The freshwater lens is situated above the saltwater table due to lower density and is located about 2.4–3.0 m (8–10 ft) below the surface of the island interior (Brown et al. 1976). In a survey of three ponds on Padre Island National Seashore, Sissom (1990) reported that water levels were lowest during September 1989 from summer dry-down. Water levels measured over the study were used to assess potential changes of wetland to upland vegetation composition. Pond level fluctuated during the study, increasing in depth to about 0.6 m (2 ft) as a result of heavy rains in March 1990, increasing volumes and surface areas. Water levels eventually returned to preflood conditions as excess water percolated through surrounding sands. High levels of relative humidity provide an additional water source as dew collects on plants at night. Relative humidity is an important aspect of the barrier island climate regime and typically is high throughout the year as a result of moist Gulf air mediating air temperatures.

Trophic Levels within Barrier Island Systems

Vascular plants are the predominant primary producers in barrier island habitats. Vascular plant species richness is substantial and comparable to that in grassland-dominated mainland systems. Species diversity changes within habitats across the barrier island and among barrier islands (Drawe et al. 1981). Fresh water and nutrient availability influence primary production. Prevailing southeasterly winds transport sand, silt, and salts up the beach face (Whelan 1975) and may also affect coppice and foredune vegetation productivity (Britton and Morton 1989). Due to high soil porosity, available nutrients are quickly leached out, particularly in the dunes (Drawe et al. 1981). Fires may temporarily reduce standing biomass, but often productivity increases the following growing season (Drawe and Kattner 1978).

Dune plants are specially adapted to tolerate high salinities, low water availability, and sediment accretion. Conditions in the barrier flat zone are less stressful (e.g., lower salinities, more water availability, and more available nutrients), so plant species richness often is higher. Plants adapted to periodic flooding and drying are primary producers in ponds and marshes located within barrier vegetated flats (Britton and Morton 1989).

Little information is available concerning decomposition processes in South Texas barrier islands; but litter decomposition was described as a gradual process (Longley et al. 1989), accelerated only by fire (Kattner 1973; Drawe and Kattner 1978). No information is available on roles of bacteria and fungi in barrier island vegetation dynamics.

Invertebrates—from herbivores to primary and secondary carnivores, scavengers, and detritivores—perform every type of consumer role in a barrier island system. Importance of invertebrates as part of the food web has not been quantified for Texas and Tamaulipas barrier island chains, but extensive species lists and habitat preferences have been compiled for Padre Island (Ortiz 1976).

An ecological study of fish communities in three earthen ponds within Padre Island National Seashore reported only three species, occurring in variable abundance (Caudle 1992). The sheepshead minnow (*Cyprinodon variegatus*) was the most abundant fish species in two of the ponds examined. The mosquitofish (*Gambusia affinis*)

Table 10.1. *Carnivorous reptiles documented from vegetated flat habitats of Padre Island*

Common Name	Scientific Name
Mediterranean gecko	*Hemidactylus turcicus*
Keeled earless lizard	*Holbrookia propinqua*
Six-lined racerunner	*Cnemidophorus sexlineatus viridus*
Great Plains skink	*Eumeces obsoletus*
Ground skink	*Scincella lateralis*
Slender glass lizard	*Ophisaurus attenuatus*
Diamondback water snake	*Nerodia rhombifera*
Texas brown snake	*Storeria dekayi texana*
Eastern checkered garter snake	*Thamnophis marcianus marcianus*
Gulf Coast ribbon snake	*Thamnophis proximus orarius*
Eastern hognose snake	*Heterodon platyrhinos*
Eastern yellowbelly racer	*Coluber constrictor flaventris*
Bullsnake	*Pituophis melanoleucus sayi*
Mexican milk snake	*Lampropeltis triangulum annulata*
Western massasauga	*Sistrurus catenatus tergeminus*
Western diamondback	*Crotalus atrox*

Source: PINS 1984.

was the dominant species in the third pond, and Gulf killifish *(Fundulus grandis)* abundance was low in all ponds.

The keeled earless lizard *(Holbrookia propinqua)* is abundant in dune habitats on Padre Island (PINS 1984) and Tamaulipas barrier islands (Selander et al. 1962), feeding predominantly on insects (Judd 1976; Garrett and Barker 1987). The six-lined racerunner *(Cnemidophorus sexlineatus)* in Texas (F. W. Judd, pers. comm.) and the Texas spotted whiptail *(C. gularis)* in Tamaulipas (Selander et al. 1962) are also found in dune habitats and prey on an assortment of invertebrates (Garrett and Barker 1987). One herbivorous tortoise is listed for this habitat, although undoubtedly other turtles and terrapins cross when migrating from pond to pond on the island interior. The Texas tortoise *(Gopherus berlandieri)*, listed as rare on Padre Island National Seashore (PINS 1984), is herbivorous, feeding on grass, on the pads, flowers, and fruits of prickly pear *(Opuntia engelmannii)*, and on other vegetation (Auffenberg and Weaver 1969; Conant 1975). This species was also documented in stabilized dunes on a Mexican barrier island (Selander et al. 1962). Several carnivorous reptiles were documented on Padre Island (table 10.1).

The green tree frog *(Hyla cinerea)*, Hurter's spadefoot toad *(Scaphiophus holbrooki hurteri)*, and Río Grande leopard frog *(Rana berlandieri)* were listed as uncommon in Padre Island National Seashore during an inventory in the early 1980s (PINS 1984); green tree frogs have increased in relative abundance in recent years (A. H. Chaney, pers. comm.). All three species prey upon a variety of small insects (Garrett and Barker 1987). No ecological studies were conducted on Padre Island or Tamaulipas barrier islands. The breeding season and life history stages of two species of toads, the Gulf coast toad *(Bufo valliceps)* and Texas toad *(B. speciosus)*, were examined in a pond on northern Mustang Island, correlating reproduction to high rainfall (Moore 1976). This ecological strategy may be similar along South Texas and Tamaulipas barrier islands.

Gulf beaches are essential resting and feeding habitats for both resident and migratory shorebirds as well as other bird species. Use and importance of this habitat to shorebirds is described in chapter 13. Seed-eating birds probably utilize the seasonal abundance of several plant species within the foredune zone as well as those within the vegetated barrier flat. However, no study has been conducted identifying and quantifying the importance of dunes to resident and migrant herbivorous birds. No information was found for herbivorous bird use in the vegetated flats zone. Northern mockingbirds, cardinals, and bobwhites were documented within clay dune habitat at the margins of Laguna Madre de Tamaulipas (Selander et al. 1962).

Barrier islands along the Texas and Tamaulipas coast are important stopovers for migrating peregrine falcons *(Falco peregrinus)* (Hunt and Ward 1988); the islands support large concentrations of fall and spring migrating peregrine falcons, which use Padre Island for hunting and foraging (Hunt et al. 1975). During spring migration, four falcons were monitored on Padre Island; they moved up to 70 km/day on the island, but usually returned to a roosting site near that of the previous night. During fall migration, three falcons were located in the same general area, moving less than 10 km (6.2 mi) from the point of capture.

Gulf coast kangaroo rats *(Dipodomys compactus)* are dominant rodents in the sparsely vegetated dunes on Padre Island (E. H. Smith 1986; Davis and Schmidly 1994) and were collected in similar habitats on Tamaulipas barrier islands, although listed as uncommon (Selander et al. 1962). Based upon collecting information, lower abundance may be attributed to common occurrence of land crabs (Hall 1951). Kangaroo rats are primarily herbivorous but occasionally feed on insects. The spotted ground squirrel *(Spermophilus spilosoma)* inhabits Padre Island and Tamaulipas barrier islands (Selander et al. 1962) and is an opportunistic feeder. Most forage analyses list tender forage, seeds, and roots as primary food sources. Insects and remains of an occasional vertebrate (keeled earless lizards) were found in burrows. Spotted ground squirrels utilize two main zones on Padre Island, active dunes and vegetated flats (Segers and Chapman 1984). In dunes, the spotted ground squirrel forages in barren areas, where it can more readily identify and escape from terrestrial predators (e.g., snakes). However, aerial predators such as raptors are able to spot ground squirrels in these open areas. Therefore, this animal constructs several refuge burrows throughout its home range for rapid escape in both dune and vegetated areas. Home burrows are typically located high in dunes and are constructed with varying complexity, containing a nest chamber and food cache chambers. The spotted ground squirrel also forages in vegetated flats, traveling via runways between and underneath vegetation. This species is opportunistic in a harsh environment, and extensive foraging efforts and food cache reserves are important for survival. The Texas pocket gopher *(Geomys personatus)* was documented on both northern Padre Island and Tamaulipas barrier islands (Selander et al. 1962; Davis and Schmidly 1994), inhabiting vegetated flats to dune margins, but it has not been documented for southern Padre Island (F. W. Judd pers. comm.).

Blacktail jackrabbits *(Lepus californicus)*, coyotes *(Canis latrans)*, white-tailed deer *(Odocoileus virginianus)*, feral hogs *(Sus scrofa)*, and badgers *(Taxidea taxus)* utilize dunes to some extent but primarily inhabit vegetated flats on Padre Island (PINS 1984). These species, with the exception of feral hogs, were also recorded in Tamaulipas barrier island habitats (Selander et al. 1962). Blacktail jackrabbits and white-tailed deer are herbivorous, badgers are carnivorous, and coyotes and feral hogs are opportunistic omnivores. The rice rat *(Oryzomys palustris)*, fulvous pocket mouse *(Reithrodontomys fulvescens)*, and hispid cotton rat *(Sigmodon hispidus)* occur on Padre Island, are primarily herbivorous, and are important prey items in the food web. Several omnivores including the Virginia opossum *(Didelphis virginiana)*, nine-banded armadillo *(Dasypus novemcinctus)*, and raccoon *(Procyon lotor)* were recorded on Padre Island (Selander et al. 1962; Baker and Rabalais 1975). The pygmy mouse *(Baiomys taylori)*, Merriam's pocket mouse *(Perognathus merriami)*, white-footed mouse *(Peromyscus leucopus)*, and eastern cottontail *(Sylvilagus floridanus)* are additional herbivores listed as inhabiting Padre Island (Baker and Rabalais 1975). Merriam's pocket mouse and the southern plains woodrat *(Neotoma micropus)* were collected on Tamaulipas barrier islands in 1961 (Selander et al. 1962); the hispid cotton rat was listed as well in 1950 (Hall 1951). Turning to insectivores, the least shrew *(Cryptotis parva)* and eastern mole *(Scalopus aquaticus)* were documented on Padre Island (Thomas 1972; Baker and Rabalais 1975; Yates and Schmidly 1977; Harris 1988), as were two insectivorous bat species, the Mexican free-tailed bat *(Tadarida brasiliensis;* Harris 1988; Chapman and Chapman 1990) and Georgia bat *(Pipistrellus subflavus;* Zehner 1985). Among carnivores, the striped skunk *(Mephitis mephitis)* and Gulf coast hog-nosed skunk *(Conepatus leuconotus)* were also reported on Padre Island (Bailey 1905 in Blair 1952; Baker and Rabalais 1975; Harris, 1988).

Rice rats typically nest over water in their natural range, although no studies have been conducted on island ponds. Most mammals probably utilize freshwater sources on islands. Sissom (1990) identified the following species by track around ponds within PINS: bobcat *(Lynx rufus)*, coyote, badger, raccoon, and white-tailed deer. In addition, several blacktail jackrabbits were observed adjacent to pond margins.

Community Structure and Zonation

Carls et al. (1990) reviewed the literature regarding designations of Padre Island plant communities and listed the following: Gulf Prairies and Marshes of Texas (Thomas 1975), Marsh/Barrier Island vegetation type (McMahan et al. 1984), and Dune/Barrier Island subregion of the Gulf Coast Prairies and Marshes natural region (Diamond et al. 1987). The following zonation descriptions are a composite of several habitat designations and associated vegetation.

The backshore zone is located west of the berm crest in the Gulf beach community to the seaward base of the primary dunes (Judd et al. 1977). Two species may predominate within the backshore, sea purslane and sea oats *(Uniola paniculata)*, although they occur in sparse patches on Padre Island. The mat-forming ground cover of sea purslane is important in formation of embryonic dunes by capturing wind-blown sand and ameliorating wave forces for leeward dunes (Lonard and Judd 1980). Infrequent inundation by seasonal spring and storm tides precludes establishment of many species in this zone. Isolated patches of seashore dropseed *(Sporobolus virginicus)* may also occur in the backshore zone. Vegetation structure impedes movement of sand across the beach face; subsequently, low coppice dunes are formed.

Primary dunes are located upslope from the backshore zone. This zone is rarely inundated by tides (Judd et al. 1977); however, high seasonal tides and winter storm surges may inundate bases of primary dunes, uproot vegetation, and remove sand. Prevailing winds and air-blown salt influence vegetation type in the primary dune zone. Drawe et al. (1981) described the zone (classified as Coastal Dunes) for North Padre Island and listed the dominant grass species as sea oats, gulfdune paspalum *(Paspalum monostachyum)*, and thin paspalum *(P. setaceum)* and predominant forbs as Gulf croton *(Croton punctatus)*, beach evening primrose *(Oenothera drummondii)*, goat-foot morningglory *(Ipomoea pes-caprae)*, fiddleleaf morningglory *(I. imperati)*, and prairie senna *(Chamaecrista fasciculata)*.

The vegetated flats zone is typically grass dominated, with sandy soils and low relief interspersed with low vegetated dunes, ponds and marshes, and active dune fields. Topography of this zone is a result of various environmental and geologic factors, and the zone can be quite diverse in vegetation. Primary dune protection ameliorates prevailing winds most of the year; therefore, density of vegetation and areal vegetative coverage increases in the vegetated flats. An occasional group of stunted oak (*Quercus* spp.) trees occurs at higher elevations of vegetated flats, but their occurrence decreases from north to south along barrier islands. Judd et al. (1977) noted that although several woody species inhabit the adjacent mainland and have potential to disperse seeds, low colonization and establishment rate is due to harsh environmental conditions.

Low vegetated dunes described within vegetated flats by Judd et al. (1977) were analyzed separately by Drawe et al. (1981) on northern Padre Island and classified as low coastal sands. Plant diversity and vegetative cover increased in these areas, and grass and forb compositions were slightly different than in primary dunes. Gulfdune paspalum, red lovegrass *(Eragrostis secundiflora)*, seashore dropseed, sea oats, thin paspalum, and fimbry *(Fimbristylis castanea)* were predominant grasses and sedges; dominant forbs included woolly stemodia *(Stemodia tomentosa)*, seaside heliotrope *(Heliotropium curassavicum* var. *curassavicum)*, frogfruit *(Phyla nodiflora)*, largeleaf water-pennywort *(Hydrocotyle bonariensis)*, and Corpus Christi fleabane *(Erigeron procumbens)*. Additionally, plant litter and mulch increased in low dunes areas and were effective enough to reduce photosynthetic activity in some areas.

Final sere or climax vegetation on barrier islands is described as a mid-grass prairie; however, due to the dynamic nature of barrier islands, potential climax communities may not be exhibited (Drawe et al. 1981). Inhibiting factors include continual coastal dune migration, variable soil salinities in relation to storm surge, limited nutrient availability, and high evapotranspiration rates in the region. Extensive vegetation studies in the 1970s and 1980s were valuable in determining successional dynamics. Climax vegetation is postulated as slowly progressing toward a mid-grass or even a tallgrass prairie climax dominated by seacoast bluestem *(Schizachyrium scoparium* var. *littorale)*, bushy bluestem *(Andropogon glomeratus)*, and bitter panicum *(Panicum amarum)*.

No quantitative studies were found on invertebrate community structure within South Texas and Tamaulipas barrier islands, although these species form an important component of grassland structure and function. Many insects—grass- and planthoppers, beetles, flies, and wasps—form an integral part of invertebrate communities, although ghost crabs *(Ocypode quadrata)* often inhabit dunes. Vertical zonation within this area is typically related to wind speed and direction, as most species are found within or beneath the plant canopy and in the soil on leeward and windward sides of dune ridges. Ortiz (1976) investigated the insect fauna on Padre Island through four seasons and counted 245 species (nine orders) in backshore primary dunes (coppice dunes), foredunes, and vegetated flat zones. Onshore winds, blowing sand, and vegetation density for both food and shelter were the primary factors affecting distribution; more species were found on the leeward sides of dunes than the windward sides due to these factors.

Spatial zonation of the vertebrate community is related primarily to prey distribution, abundance, and degree of feeding specialization. Barrier islands are very dynamic systems and are influenced by physical factors and processes; therefore, a generalist strategy is an advantage over a selective feeding mode. Most resident vertebrates are either generally herbivorous or omnivorous; home ranges typically correspond to body size. Small rodents usually inhabit vegetated areas of islands and feed on seeds, leaves, and stems characteristic in a particular zone. Mode of locomotion through vegetation and ability to burrow in sand further defines each group's range. Cricetids (e.g., hispid cotton rat, white-footed mouse, fulvous harvest mouse) use runways underneath vegetation for foraging and for protection from predators. They feed on herbaceous plants, seeds, and small invertebrates. Primary food items of Gulf coast kangaroo rats include seeds, some herbaceous vegetation, and small invertebrates as available in the dune zone and along edges of dune-vegetated flats (Davis and Schmidly 1994). Larger mammals use most, if not all, vegetated zones to search for prey items; most common species feed opportunistically on both vegetation and animals (e.g., coyote). Badgers are specialists on ground squirrels.

Island resource utilization varies seasonally, as with peregrine falcons and Neotropical passerine migration in spring and fall or, in spring and summer, as invertebrate populations increase. Migrating peregrine falcons use sparsely vegetated dune fields and adjacent tidal flats to ambush low-flying avian prey. Neotropical passerines are found in all zones during migration, using islands for food and protection. Some resident bird species may nest in vegetated flats yet feed in more open dune areas, particularly on the leeward, less windy sides (Rappole and Blacklock 1994).

The ephemeral nature of inland ponds within vegetated flats may limit community structure complexity. Most amphibian species are opportunistic breeders, taking advantage of wetland habitat and food following heavy rains (Moore 1976). Increases in adult frog and toad abundance surrounding ponds during breeding, and the subsequent population boom of tadpoles, is capitalized upon by several vertebrate predators including other adult frogs, snakes, birds, and mammals. Fish population dynamics and community structure have not been investigated in natural island ponds. Studies of three earthen ponds within PINS reported that environmental pond conditions (i.e., salinity, water temperature, and dissolved oxygen vs. pond depth) have an important impact on species diversity and habitat complexity. All physical parameters varied widely among ponds and within ponds during the study, and this may have been the cause of low species richness and the dominance of one fish species in each pond (Caudle 1992).

The barrier island food web is similar to that in a grassland-dominated system and probably follows a grazing pathway. Most resident and migratory species are dependent upon root, rhizome, plant part, nectar, and seed production for survival. Herbivorous invertebrate and vertebrate species are numerous and are utilized as prey items for primary and secondary consumers, ranging in size from spiders, lizards, and toads to snakes, raptors, and larger mammals. Productivity of the barrier island system is influenced by physical factors including variable rainfall, high evaporation and temperatures, and tropical storm surge events. Therefore, population dynamics of most species cycles are closely correlated with environmental variability. Omnivory may give a consumer the advantage to survive in this stressful habitat.

Color Plates

138

Plate 1. *Satellite image of South Texas and northeastern Mexico coastline from Copano-Aransas Bays to northern Laguna Madre de Tamaulipas. Scale 1:250,000 (Katie Nolan and Owen Martin, TAMU-CC Planetary Image Processing Lab, Corpus Christi, Texas)*

Plate 2. Satellite image of South Texas and northeastern Mexico coastline showing lower Laguna Madre of Texas, Río Grande Delta, and entire Laguna Madre de Tamaulipas. Scale 1:250,000; TM Bands 3,4,5; Path 26/Rows 42–43; 18 March 1990 (used with permission, DUMAC and Earth Satellite Corporation, Rockville, Maryland)

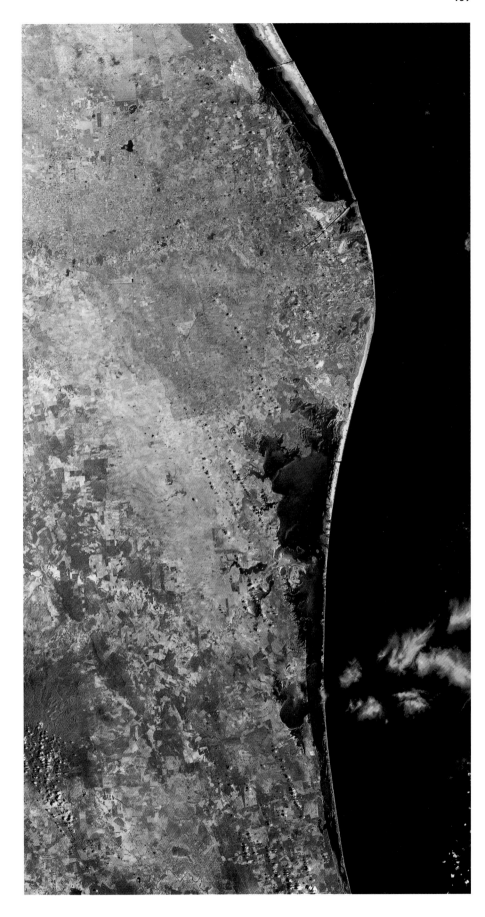

Plate 3. *Diagonal aerial view to the south over some of the many natural islands in the northernmost Laguna Madre de Tamaulipas (February 1999; J. W. Tunnell)*

Plate 4. *Diagonal aerial view to the north over Pita Island (right, midground),* one of the few natural islands in the upper Laguna Madre of Texas *(January 1999; J. W. Tunnell)*

Plate 5. *Diagonal aerial view to the northeast over the wind-tidal flats and El Toro "island" in the Land-Cut, Kenedy County, Texas; GIWW in background. Vegetated islands in foreground are dredged material from oilfield channel. (July 1987; J. W. Tunnell)*

Plate 6. Vertical high altitude (18,288 m/60,000 ft) aerial photograph of lower Laguna Madre over the Arroyo Colorado. Note numerous dredged material islands adjacent to GIWW and oilfield channels. (1973; USGS)

Plate 7. Aerial view of oil and gas channels and dredged material islands just south of John F. Kennedy Causeway, upper Laguna Madre, Texas (January 1999; J. W. Tunnell)

Plate 8. Diagonal aerial view to the northwest over Padre Isles development on northern Padre Island (January 1999; J. W. Tunnell)

142

Plate 9. Diagonal aerial photo to the north over the hotel-condominium zone on South Padre Island, Texas (September 1992; J. W. Tunnell)

Plate 10. Vertical high altitude (18,288 m/60,000 ft) photograph of Mansfield Pass cutting through Padre Island from the Laguna Madre to the Gulf of Mexico (1973; USGS)

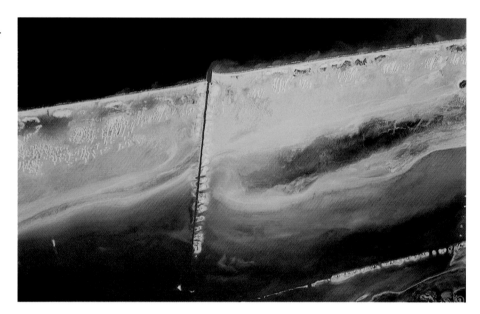

Plate 11. Diagonal aerial photo to the east over El Mezquital Pass, Tamaulipas (February 1999; J. W. Tunnell)

Plate 12. Diagonal aerial photo to the east over Boca de Catán, Tamaulipas (February 1999; J. W. Tunnell)

Plate 13. Satellite photo from the Space Shuttle of the Land-Cut area between the upper and lower Laguna Madre, Texas. Wind-tidal flats are the most common habitat type in the Land-Cut and extend southward along the backside of Padre Island. (NASA)

Plate 14. Demonstration of the impact of salt blowing on vegetation (live oak, Quercus virginiana). Tree is "pointing" to northwest due to strong and persistent southeast winds laden with salt and clay. Located on upland just west of Land-Cut wind-tidal flats and clay dunes (May 1989; J. W. Tunnell)

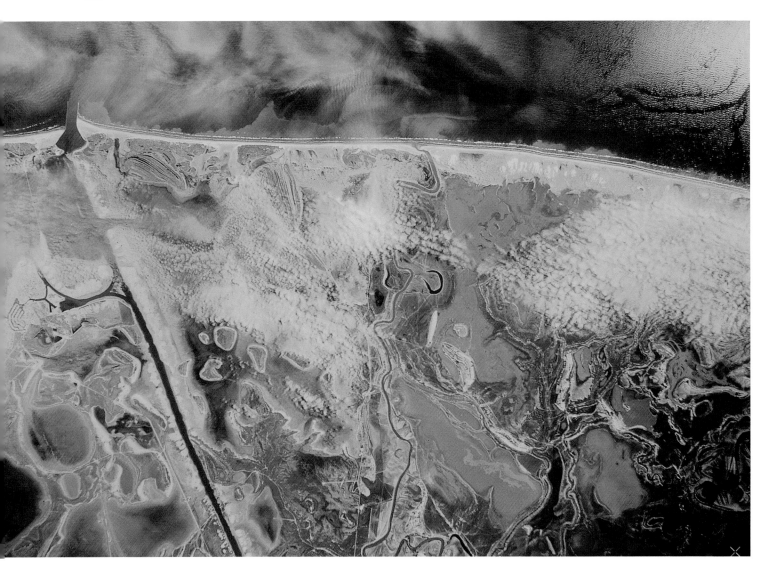

Plate 15. *Vertical high altitude (60,000 ft) photograph of the Río Grande Delta, showing extreme southern lower Laguna Madre of Texas, Brazos Santiago Pass, and Brownsville Ship Channel (left), Río Grande (middle), and highly complex surrounding lands of playas, lakes, resacas (oxbow lakes), wetlands, mudflats, lomas, and clay dunes (1973; USGS)*

Plate 16. *Diagonal aerial photograph to the north over the Río Grande Delta in Mexico. The town of South Padre Island can be seen on the horizon in the upper part of the photo. (February 1999; J. W. Tunnell)*

Plate 17. *Clay dune on western edge of Land-Cut, Kenedy County, Texas, wind-tidal flats. Note clay deposition on lower slopes and wind erosion on upper parts. (May 1989; J. W. Tunnell)*

Plate 18. *View of clay dune to the south along "transition zone" between Land-Cut, Kenedy County, Texas, wind-tidal flats and uplands. Seasonal high tides and strong southeast winds pushed water into the cayos (flat-bottomed valleys between clay dunes). (May 1989; J. W. Tunnell)*

Plate 19. *Clay dunes encroaching upon uplands in the Land-Cut:* (left) *small clay dunes in the north;* (right) *large clay dune in the southwest (May 1989; J. W. Tunnell)*

Plate 20. *Wind-tidal flats on the eastern side of Laguna Madre, primarily composed of sand blown or washed over the barrier islands into the lagoon:* (left) *sandy wind-tidal flat just north and west of*

Mansfield Pass on Padre Island (December 1982; J. W. Tunnell); (right) *sandy wind-tidal flat on the western side of South Padre Island (July 1980; J. W. Tunnell)*

Plate 21. *Wind-tidal flats on the western or mainland side of Laguna Madre are characteristically composed of clay. Blue-green algal (Cyanobacteria) mats are common in areas that are irregularly but*

consistently flooded: (left) *the "Basin" (Fisk 1959) in north-central Land-Cut (March 1993; J. W. Tunnell);* (right) *close-up of algal mat (August 1982; J. W. Tunnell)*

Plate 22. Gulf cordgrass or sacahuiste flats dominated by Spartina spartinae *are common coastal plain habitats in South Texas and northern Tamaulipas landward from Laguna Madre. Price (1933) suggested gulf cordgrass flats occupy the ancient, infilled Ingleside Lagoon that now forms the Ingleside Terrace. (July 1988; J. W. Tunnell)*

Plate 23. Diagonal aerial view of banner dune complex on South Texas Eolian Sand Sheet, Kenedy County, Texas (July 1987; J. W. Tunnell)

Plate 24. *Beach rock (coquina) outcrops:* (top) *Penascal Point, western shore of upper Laguna Madre, Texas, at Baffin Bay (July 1987; J. W. Tunnell);* (bottom) *Punta Piedras, western shore of southern Laguna Madre de Tamaulipas at Carbajal (December 1998; J. W. Tunnell)*

Plate 25. *Gypsum crystal found eroded from a dredged material deposit of an oil and gas field channel in the Land-Cut, Kenedy County, Texas (August 1982; J. W. Tunnell)*

Plate 26. View to the east along eroding clay bluff just off the highway leading to Mezquital in northern Laguna Madre de Tamaulipas (March 1991; J. W. Tunnell)

Plate 27. View to the east of sand dunes encroaching on upland habitat along highway to Mezquital (September 1982; J. W. Tunnell)

Plate 28. Oblique aerial view of dense seagrass beds behind barrier peninsula just south of Mezquital (February 1999; J. W. Tunnell)

Plate 29. *Oblique aerial view over extreme northern Laguna Madre de Tamaulipas waters isolated by Mezquital highway (top) and abandoned salt ponds (salinas) along the same highway (bottom) (February 1999; J. W. Tunnell)*

Plate 30. *Views of the southern part of the northern Laguna Madre de Tamaulipas: (top) eroding clay dune bluff line at El Barrancón (note clay dunes in far background; October 1999; J. W. Tunnell); (center) Río San Fernando Delta and tidal flat (El Carrizal; February 1999; J. W. Tunnell); (bottom) Boca Ciega pass west across tidal flats and seagrass beds (February 1999; J. W. Tunnell)*

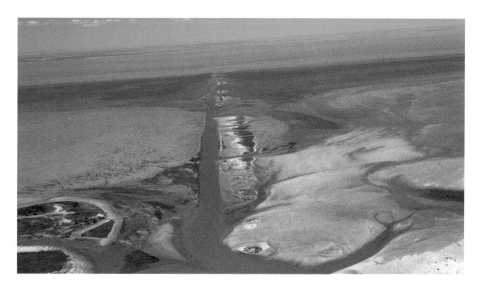

Plate 31. Oblique aerial views of southern Laguna Madre de Tamaulipas: (top) seagrass beds and islands north of Carboneras; (center) coastal fishing village of Carboneras; (bottom) coastal fishing village of Carbajal (note freshwater ponds on peninsula and Laguna el Catán in background). Punta Piedras begins at immediate lower left of photo. (February 1999; J. W. Tunnell)

Plate 32. *Fishing boats at Carboneras, southern Laguna Madre de Tamaulipas: (top) modern fiberglass outboard boats; (bottom) a restored old sailing skiff, once used to pull chinchorros (a large bag seine) (December 1998; J. W. Tunnell)*

Plate 33. *Oblique aerial views of southern Laguna Madre de Tamaulipas:* (top) *Boca de Santa Isabel, the southernmost jettied pass into the lagoon;* (bottom) *seagrass beds behind the narrow barrier island (Soto la Marina) and two washover passes (February 1999; J. W. Tunnell)*

Plate 34. *Oblique aerial views of southernmost Laguna Madre de Tamaulipas:* (top) *Río Soto la Marina and fishing village of La Pesca. Tidal flat in foreground is southernmost extent of lagoon where it empties into river (during storm tides only) (February 1999; J. W. Tunnell);* (bottom) *Soto la Marina barrier island extending northward from La Pesca showing the southernmost Laguna Madre de Tamaulipas (February 1999; J. W. Tunnell)*

Plate 35. *Seagrasses of Laguna Madre:* (top) *shoalgrass mixed with widgeon grass (the floating branched ones);* (center) *dense stand of shoalgrass;* (bottom) *turtle-grass (flat blade) mixed with some manatee-grass (thinner, round blade) (J. W. Tunnell)*

Plate 36. South Padre Island wind-tidal flats adjacent to the lower Laguna Madre: (top) to southwest from eastern side of flats near vegetated dune area of Padre Island; (center) middle of flats; (bottom) western edge of flats with wind-tidal flat to right, "intertidal" sand margin zone in middle, and seagrass bed of lagoon to left (July 1980; J. W. Tunnell)

Plate 37. *Evidence and impact of high salt content on wind-tidal flats: (top) salt rim around drying pond (July 1980; J. W. Tunnell); (center) dead fish around salt pond, probably died from excessive salinity (August 1993; J. W. Tunnell); (bottom) dried salt in tracks left by seismic vehicles (July 1980; J. W. Tunnell)*

Plate 38. *Redheads on freshwater pond adjacent to upper Laguna Madre (Photograph by Marc Woodin)*

Plate 39. *Flock of redheads over freshwater pond adjacent to upper Laguna Madre (males with red head, females with brown head) (Photograph by Marc Woodin)*

Plate 40. Dredge material islands in
upper Laguna Madre showing
variability in nesting habitat: (top)
Island 81 with dense vegetation;
(bottom) Island 72 showing sparse
vegetation due to newly deposited
dredge material (Photographs by
Allan H. Chaney)

Plate 41. *Various nesting types seen on Laguna Madre dredge material islands:* (top left) *royal and sandwich terns;* (top right) *least tern;* (center left) *gull-billed tern;* (center right) *Forster's tern;* (bottom left) *great blue heron young;* (bottom right) *great egret nestlings (Photographs by Allan H. Chaney)*

162

Plate 42. *Views of nesting colonial waterbirds on Laguna Madre dredge material rookery islands:* (top) *American white pelicans;* (center) *Caspian terns;* (bottom) *black skimmers (Photographs by Allan H. Chaney)*

Plate 43. *Great egret* (top) *and tricolor heron* (bottom) *in freshwater pond habitat on Padre Island, adjacent to Laguna Madre (Photographs by Allan H. Chaney)*

164

Plate 44. *Dunlin* (top); *snowy egret* (center); *and reddish egret* (bottom) *along the shores of Laguna Madre of Texas (Photographs by Allan H. Chaney)*

Plate 45. Dredging activities in Laguna Madre: (top) dredge in lagoon (September 1999; A. H. Chaney); (center) open water dredge material disposal from GIWW into upper Laguna Madre (November 1983; J. W. Tunnell); (bottom) dragline building dredge material containment area (J. W. Tunnell)

Plate 46. *Fishing cabins located on dredged material islands:* (top) *northern part of the Land-Cut between GIWW (upper part of photo) and "The Hole" (October 1995; J. W. Tunnell);* (bottom) *upper Laguna Madre, Texas (November 1983; J. W. Tunnell)*

Plate 47. Numerous long fishing piers extending from the shoreline at Port Mansfield, Texas, into lower Laguna Madre, Texas (July 1987; J. W. Tunnell)

Plate 48. Charangas (fish traps) in shallow waters near Mezquital in northern Laguna Madre de Tamaulipas (February 1999; J. W. Tunnell)

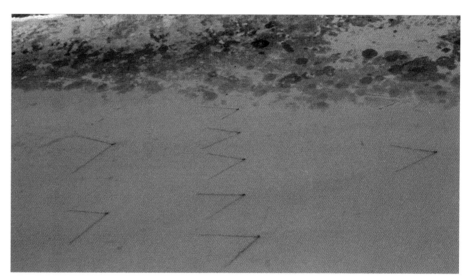

Plate 49. Ixtoc I oil spill on Padre Island beaches during August 1979 (Brian R. Chapman)

168

Plate 50. *Impact of Hurricane Allen:
(top)* foredunes eroded 33.5 m (110
ft) on northern Padre Island
*(September 1980; J. W. Tunnell);
(bottom)* the park road highway cut
in numerous places by hurricane
washover on South Padre Island
(October 1980; J. W. Tunnell)

11

Redheads and Other Wintering Waterfowl

ELIZABETH H. SMITH

The Texas coast is essential to millions of waterfowl as migration and wintering habitat (Bellrose 1980). Each year, more than two dozen waterfowl species funnel southward from all over continental North America, converging upon Texas coastal wetlands to winter on coastal prairies, bays, and lagoons rich with food, water, and roosting resources: white-fronted geese *(Anser albifrons frontalis)* from Alaska; Canada geese *(Branta canadensis)* from the Arctic, lesser snow geese *(Anser caerulescens)* from Hudson Bay; and mallards *(Anas platyrhynchos)*, redheads *(Aythya americana)*, northern pintails *(Anas acuta)*, gadwalls *(Anas strepera)*, American wigeons *(Anas americana)*, lesser scaup *(Aythya affinis)*, greater scaup *(Aythya marila)*, and canvasbacks *(Aythya valisineria)* from parkland and prairie potholes. Texas supports more waterfowl than any other state in the Central Flyway. Some species, such as blue-winged teal *(Anas discors)*, rest briefly along the coast before continuing their migration to Central and South America. Others, such as redheads (plates 38, 39), typically end their migration in saltwater bays and lagoons along the western Gulf of Mexico (TPWD 1982).

The Texas coast encompasses diverse wetland types, ranging from estuarine bays, ephemeral freshwater ponds, extensive rice fields along coastal prairies, and deep marshes of the upper coast to hypersaline lagoons, stock tanks, and freshwater ponds of the lower coast. This habitat diversity satisfies unique requirements of wintering waterfowl. Historical and continuing wetland losses in Texas (Dahl and Johnson 1991) have increased the necessity to preserve remaining habitat to ensure continued survival of continental waterfowl populations. Existing habitats may be reaching carrying capacity, particularly during drought periods (TPWD 1982).

Lagoonal systems of the lower Texas and northeastern Mexico coast have unique hydrologic attributes as a result of low average precipitation, high evaporation rates, and limited freshwater inflow. Alternating wet and dry periods create a dynamic environment in coastal depressions located on mainland areas adjacent to the lagoons (McAdams 1987). Coastal ponds fill with fresh water typically as a result of tropical storm activity and are valuable habitats for migrating and wintering waterfowl. This resource for drinking water is especially critical for those wintering waterfowl species feeding exclusively in hypersaline lagoons (Saunders and Saunders 1981).

Waterfowl research in North America was historically directed at breeding population dynamics and associated breeding ground issues. Only recently has the focus been redirected toward wintering waterfowl ecology (Reinecke 1981). The relationship between quality of wintering habitat and breeding population dynamics is important, as reproductive success can be influenced by previous winter habitat conditions (Milne 1976; Fredrickson and Drobney 1979; Heitmeyer and Fredrickson 1981; Kaminski and Gluesing 1987). Waterfowl habitat selection is governed by a number of factors including isolation from predators; however, distribution of food resources appears to be the most important parameter (Bergman 1973; Hobaugh and Teer 1981; Talent et al. 1982; Baldassarre and Bolen 1984; Mulhern et al. 1985).

Each waterfowl species exhibits characteristic migration patterns and wintering habitat use, which are driven primarily by resource requirements. Those species wintering in estuarine habitats are restricted to available resources within a given geographic region. Redhead and lesser scaup are species that feed almost exclusively on estuarine food items along the western Gulf of Mexico (Bellrose 1980; Weller 1964; Woodin 1996). Redheads are entirely dependent on shoalgrass (*Halodule beaudettei* [= *wrightii*]) rhizomes found in estuarine subtidal environments. This seagrass species is found in greatest abundance in Laguna Madre of Texas, with lesser amounts along the rest of the Texas, Mexico, Louisiana, and Florida coasts. Hypersaline conditions in Laguna Madre often prevail, therefore coastal ponds with low salinities are critical to reduce osmotic stress for these wintering waterfowl. Lesser scaup feed primarily on molluscs and winter in greatest concentrations in coastal Louisiana and Florida (USFWS 1987). The combination of estuarine food resources and inland freshwater ponds is particularly important for waterfowl in South Texas and Mexico (Adair 1990; Adair et al. 1990a, b; Weller 1964). With the exception of redheads, limited information exists on populations of wintering waterfowl in Laguna Madre of Texas, Laguna Madre de Tamaulipas, the Río Grande Delta, and coastal depressional wetlands. Census data collected along Texas and Mexican coasts are not easily correlated with existing quantity and quality of winter habitats.

This chapter is organized to summarize information on each lagoonal system, adjacent coastal ponds, and the Río Grande Delta in regard to importance to wintering waterfowl. An ecological summary for most species documented in surveys and literature is given, with particular emphasis on redheads. Key issues and conservation recommendations are included from the literature to form a basis for long-term strategies to conserve wintering waterfowl populations.

Key Waterfowl Habitats

Seagrass meadows constitute a large proportion of bay bottom habitat in Laguna Madre of Texas but are currently less widely distributed in Laguna Madre de Tamaulipas (see chapter 7). Five seagrass species are present in varying amounts and distributions: shoalgrass, manatee-grass (*Cymodocea* [= *Syringodium*] *filiforme*), turtle-grass (*Thalassia testudinum*), clover grass (*Halophila engelmannii*), and wigeon grass (*Ruppia maritima*). Seagrasses provide an important food resource for plant-feeding waterfowl and as invertebrate prey habitat used by animal-feeding waterfowl.

Changes in seagrass dominance and distribution are important to those waterfowl species dependent upon a particular seagrass. Redheads feed primarily on shoalgrass during winter (Cornelius 1977; Woodin 1996). A loss of shoalgrass meadows may limit the use of Laguna Madre by this species and may have long-term impacts on breeding population dynamics. Seagrass distribution in Laguna Madre is related to water depth and salinity, and long-term changes of these two driving factors have altered seagrass meadow composition (Merkord 1978; Quammen and Onuf 1993). Decreases in salinity over the past several decades have resulted in decreased shoalgrass dominance relative to other species less palatable to redheads. Dredged material placement during channel maintenance in Texas has altered water depths, covered seagrass meadows entirely, or limited light penetration through the water column from suspended sediments (Onuf 1994). These factors have contributed to losses of seagrass meadows in Laguna Madre of Texas.

Coastal ponds in South Texas and Tamaulipas are dynamic systems due to alternating wet and dry climatic cycles (McAdams 1987). Many ponds are quite shallow.

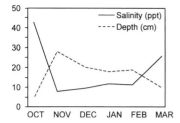

Fig. 11.1. *Salinity and water level fluctuations on Bluff Pond adjacent to upper Laguna Madre of Texas during October–March 1987–88 (Adapted from Adair 1990)*

Fig. 11.2. *Conceptual model depicting potential changes in vegetation zones in relation to hydrologic conditions (Adapted from Adair 1990)*

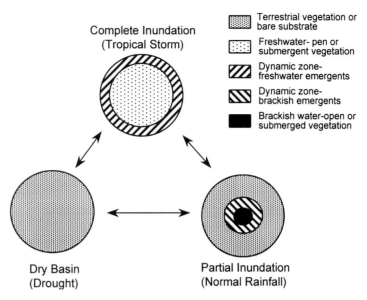

The presence, depth, and physicochemical characteristics of surface water determine habitat availability and quality for waterfowl. Following significant rainfall, ponds fill with fresh water and either reduce existing water salinities or provide a new freshwater resource (fig. 11.1). Depending on basin topography and size, wetland plant communities may develop and persist for extended periods. Ultimately, pond water evaporates, increasing soil salinities and changing wetland vegetation composition. Vegetational changes in relation to water level and salinity fluctuations were predicted based on two-year surveys of coastal ponds in South Texas (fig. 11.2). Local rainfall variability throughout South Texas may result in ponds exhibiting varying stages of vegetation composition, salinity, and water depth (Adair 1990; Adair et al. 1990b). The amount of freshwater emergents changes within the dynamic zone (see fig. 11.2) in relation to the timing of drawdown and reflooding events. During complete inundation, salinities are lowered, emergent vegetation develops in the dynamic zone, and submerged vegetation may develop in the pond center. During long-term drying periods, water levels recede and salts are concentrated. During partial inundation, basin perimeters may become exposed mudflats, or terrestrial vegetation may invade. Salinity-tolerant emergent and submerged vegetation also may develop during partial inundation. If drought conditions occur, basins may dry completely and become exposed mudflats or be covered by terrestrial vegetation. Other water quality parameters, such as pH and conductivity, fluctuate with local weather conditions and generally decrease following moderate rainfall events (McAdams 1987). All these factors interact to provide dynamic habitats for migrating and wintering waterfowl.

Climatic extremes in northern Tamaulipas determine amount and quality of habitat available for waterfowl. Although documentation is limited on the relationship, historical field notes during preliminary aerial surveys in 1938, and continuing in 1947–64, recorded habitat availability and proportion of wintering populations utilizing the Río Grande Delta, Laguna Madre de Tamaulipas, and coastal freshwater ponds (Saunders and Saunders 1981). An extended drought occurred from 1945 to 1951, limiting the amount of freshwater inflow to coastal bays and lagoons and reducing water levels in freshwater ponds. Although 1952 precipitation was higher, the following year was very dry. Little flow was observed in the Río Grande, and many basins where waterfowl usually wintered were dry. In 1954, rainfall increased and habitat improved slightly. Several months of rainfall in 1955 increased habitat availability, and hundreds of wetlands in the Río Grande Delta were filled with freshwater. A population increase to 30,000 ducks was recorded that year, as compared to only 2,500 in 1954. Little rainfall in 1956 meant that only larger depressions retained water, so waterfowl numbers were very low (Saunders and Saunders 1981).

Conditions improved considerably by 1959, and wetland habitat quantity and quality were the highest since surveys began in winter 1947. Although only half of the areas were surveyed in 1959, overall habitat availability increased along the Tamaulipan coast, and waterfowl populations were more than twice the totals reported since 1948. Drought conditions prevailed in 1960, and even more permanent lagoons exhibited very low water levels. Extensive windrows of dead shoalgrass were observed along western shallows of Laguna Madre de Tamaulipas. As the drought continued in 1961, no freshwater inflow was observed along Laguna Madre; every river between the Río Grande and Tampico was landlocked. Only Boca Jesús María (8th Pass) was still open to the Gulf, and tidal flow was negligible. Water levels within the Laguna were low and salinities high. The lowest waterfowl numbers since the survey began were documented. Although the Río Grande Delta remained dry during 1962, rainfall from Hurricane Carla filled many coastal ponds. Duck and goose populations were the highest since 1959 in these inland areas, as Laguna Madre water levels remained low and continued to be highly saline.

Drought conditions persisted in 1963 for the Río Grande Delta and Laguna Madre; almost all waterfowl populations were concentrated on coastal ponds. Goose numbers were the highest ever recorded during the surveys, and redhead numbers also increased substantially. In 1964, freshwater habitats continued to support even higher waterfowl populations, whereas Laguna Madre numbers continued to be low (Saunders and Saunders 1981). All Gulf passes were closed and lagoon salinities were high (see chapter 2). Conditions began to improve in 1967, when storm surges and freshwater inflow associated with Hurricane Beulah reopened many Gulf passes (Baldassarre et al. 1989). Wintering redhead populations also began increasing through 1988. Two to three passes remained open throughout this period, ameliorating high salinity levels and supporting shoalgrass meadows in Laguna Madre de Tamaulipas. Although no recent data exist, fluctuations in water availability and waterfowl response are probably similar.

Waterfowl in Texas Laguna Madre

About 38 waterfowl species have been documented along the lower Texas coast (Rappole and Blacklock 1994), although several species are reported as casual, rare, or accidental. Aerial waterfowl surveys conducted along U.S. Fish and Wildlife Service refuges on the Texas coast document 14 duck species in varying abundances. During the 1997–98 survey, in which duck totals were counted monthly and reported as cumulative totals over the six-month period, redheads were documented as the most numerous (cumulative total = 2,399,487 from September through March), followed by green-winged teal (*Anas crecca*), northern pintails, gadwalls, blue-winged teal, and northern shovelers (*Anas clypeata*) (cumulative total estimate range for all species = 139,852–268,197). Population estimates from Laguna Atascosa National Wildlife Refuge demonstrated the importance of lagoonal and coastal habitat to redheads and northern pintails (cumulative total = 206,588 and 104,806, respectively), northern shovelers, green-winged teal, gadwalls, American wigeons, and canvasbacks (cumulative total estimate range = 19,761–30,088).

Gulf of Mexico coastal habitats are the primary wintering destination for wintering redheads. Over 80% of the North American breeding population winters in the

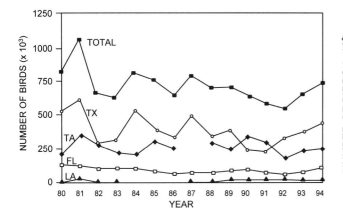

Fig. 11.3. *Estimated numbers of redheads from aerial surveys of traditional winter ranges in Texas (TX), Tamaulipas (TA), Florida (FL), and Louisiana (LA) in the Gulf of Mexico region, 1980–94 (Adapted from Woodin 1996)*

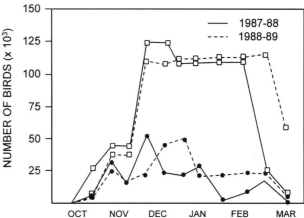

Fig. 11.4. *Number of redheads counted during aerial surveys (□) on estuaries and ground surveys (•) on coastal ponds from Corpus Christi to the Land-Cut during October–March, 1987–88 (Adapted from Adair 1990)*

western Gulf of Mexico region (Weller 1964; Bellrose 1980), with Laguna Madre of Texas and Tamaulipas generally comprising 77% of that wintering population. The spatial distribution of redheads in the Gulf of Mexico has been evaluated from 1980 to 1994 (Woodin 1996). Although wintering estimates in each state varied proportionally among years, Texas supported more redheads almost every year (fig. 11.3). In addition, these estimates closely followed total numbers estimated for the entire region. In contrast, Florida and Louisiana wintering population estimates remained much lower during that period. The temporal distribution also varies throughout the migration and wintering period (fig. 11.4). Monthly surveys conducted within a portion of the upper Laguna Madre, Texas, characterize redhead migration, wintering, and emigration patterns for two consecutive periods. Redheads began their migration around early October, with peak wintering populations observed in December, January, and February. Northward migration began in late February, and generally most redheads were gone by the end of March.

Redheads used Laguna Madre of Texas primarily for feeding and resting, spending 40 and 42% of their time on these activities, respectively, in northern areas of the lagoon system and in Redfish Bay farther north (Woodin 1994). Less than 20% of their time was spent on comfort, swimming, or other behaviors. An examination of their behavioral use of coastal pond habitat on the adjacent mainland showed that use varies along the length of Laguna Madre of Texas (table 11.1). These habitats appear quite important to redheads for drinking, particularly in a study conducted in the late 1980s (Adair 1990). Drought conditions prevailed during 1988–89, and salinities were high in the Laguna; therefore, redheads may have depended more on coastal ponds for dietary fresh water.

The first documentation of pond use in 1987–88 in lower Laguna Madre did not support previous conceptions that redheads also fed in these habitats (Mitchell et al. 1992). The importance of these freshwater habitats appeared more important when the ducks first arrived, probably assisting the birds' osmoregulatory response to hypersaline conditions of Laguna Madre.

Redheads feed primarily on one seagrass species, shoalgrass, concentrating on the belowground plant parts or rhizomes. Their wintering distribution within Laguna Madre is closely tied to shallow shoalgrass meadows (McMahan 1970; Cornelius 1975; 1977; Adair et al. 1990a). Estimates of the prevalence of shoalgrass consump-

Table 11.1. *Time budget assessments of redheads utilizing saltwater and freshwater habitats in geographic portions of their wintering range in southern Texas*

Area	SALTWATER			FRESHWATER		
	Feed %	Drink %	Rest %	Feed %	Drink %	Rest %
Northern[a]	41	<1	40	<1	8	52
Central[b]	25	<1	33	<1	31	42
Southern[c]	46	<1	41	<1	<1	78

Source: From Woodin 1996.
[a] Woodin 1994.
[c] Adair 1990.
[c] Mitchell et al. 1992.

tion range from about 70 to 85%, with molluscs and other items completing the diet of redheads (Saunders and Saunders 1981; McMahan 1970; Cornelius 1977; Woodin 1996).

Extensive feeding in certain shoalgrass meadows affected productivity the following year, suggesting that redheads may have a pronounced effect on seagrass meadow sustainability. Redheads did not remain in areas that had been grazed to the extent that feeding efficiency was compromised. However, areas were selected in relation to moderate salinities rather than dense shoalgrass areas (Mitchell et al. 1992). Water depth of 12–30 cm (4–12 in), in conjunction with extensive shoalgrass meadows, has also been used as a tool for predicting areas of concentration of wintering redheads in lower Laguna Madre (Mitchell 1992).

Changes in abundance and distribution of shoalgrass meadows in Laguna Madre of Texas may have long-term effects on redheads and, to a lesser extent, other waterfowl species (Mitchell et al. 1992; Woodin 1996). These habitats provide nearly all the food for redheads and are the most extensive in areal coverage along the southern Texas and northern Mexico coasts. Heavy grazing in smaller areas may result in substantial reduction of shoalgrass recovery the following year (Mitchell et al. 1992). Loss or degradation of this habitat through dredging activities (changing the salinity regimes of the lagoon and increasing turbidity in the water column) will ultimately reduce the extent of shoalgrass available and affect the value of the ecosystem to redheads (Onuf 1994; Woodin 1996).

Waterfowl in Coastal Ponds of Texas

Waterfowl select wetlands in relation to a variety of characteristics, including water depth and submergent vegetation (White and James 1978), water clarity, wetland surface area, submergent vegetation (Hobaugh and Teer 1981), physiography, and food resources (Bailey and Titman 1984). Their ability to move from pond to pond allows them to capitalize on optimum wetland habitats as conditions change (Swanson et al. 1974; Serie and Swanson 1976). Extensive coastal pond use by redheads in fall months has been documented for several decades (Kiel 1957; McMahan 1967b; Koenig 1969; Cornelius 1975; Adair 1990; Moore 1991), although use varies (Clark 1961; Briggs and Everett 1983; McAdams 1987; Adair 1990). Coastal ponds are used throughout the winter, and numbers of ducks on the ponds vary among months and years (see fig. 11.4).

Redheads and scaup eat estuarine foods and require dietary fresh water to reduce osmotic stress, therefore coastal ponds are essential components of their wintering habitat. During 12 ground surveys conducted on coastal ponds in 1987–88 and 1988–89, redheads comprised the largest estimates (192,014 and 239,666, respectively) using these habitats, followed by scaup (155,079 and 32,674). Nine other waterfowl species were documented but in much lower numbers. Because redheads and scaup compete for this resource with other species, such as bay-feeding northern pintails, American wigeons, and buffleheads *(Bucephala albeola)*, all of the ponds containing water at salinities lower than 15 ppt may not be available. This often resulted in ponds being used by only one or two species during a survey. Large numbers of scaup on a pond appeared to prevent redheads from using the same pond. Therefore, a number and diversity of coastal ponds with varying food resources and dietary water are essential to support the entire waterfowl community (Adair 1990).

Diving ducks select ponds with water depths >10 cm (4 in) and salinities <15 ppt. In addition, interactions among the following factors are important: current biological demands, an individual's physical abilities, existing conditions as modified by weather factors, interspecific interactions with sympatric wintering waterfowl species, and responses to human disturbances. Continued use of a given pond is not interpreted as evidence of site fidelity but rather as a combination of ecological requirements and interspecific interactions. Particular pond use by a high number of ducks over time might tend to decrease if increased concentrations of ammonium nitrogen from duck excrement degraded water quality. Therefore, spatial diversity of coastal ponds is necessary to accommodate shifting waterfowl usage (Adair 1990).

Heavy utilization of coastal ponds by redheads and scaup is tied to estuarine resources available in Laguna Madre and Baffin Bay. Redheads feed primarily on shoalgrass rhizomes in shallower lagoon margins, and lesser scaup eat molluscs and other invertebrates from deeper lagoon sites. These seagrass habitats and mollusc/invertebrate populations in the estuarine system, in conjunction with coastal ponds adjacent to the estuary, comprise ecosystem diversity essential to continued survival of these wintering populations. Reduction in either food or dietary freshwater resources ultimately changes waterfowl distribution within the lagoonal ecosystem. Therefore, an ecosystem approach to conservation is critical for these and other wintering waterfowl.

Waterfowl along the Mexican Gulf Coast

Waterfowl declines in North America became a serious concern and priority for conservation biologists early in the 1930s. Habitat loss in conjunction with extensive drought conditions in breeding areas was documented. Preliminary work in wintering areas highlighted the importance of continuous, long-term surveys to evaluate waterfowl trends. George B. Saunders, who surveyed Mexico in 1937–38, estimated waterfowl species using the Central Flyway in North America. Based upon his recommendations to conduct yearly, low-level aerial surveys, these surveys began in 1947 along both Mexican coasts and concluded in 1964 (table 11.2). Surveys were reinitiated in 1970 and continued through 1988 (Baldassarre et al. 1989; table 11.3). The extensive field notes and observations synthesized within Saunders and Saunders (1981), and additional comments in Baldassarre et al. (1989), provide the following information for waterfowl use of the Tamaulipan Río Grande Delta, Laguna Madre, and coastal ponds.

The percentage of species composition of waterfowl wintering along the east

Table 11.2. *Average percentages of common waterfowl species recorded along the Gulf Coastal Plain during annual aerial surveys from 1948 to 1965, unless otherwise noted (Saunders and Saunders 1981). Percentages in bold highlight the locations representing the highest and second-highest values for each species.*

	Rio Grande	Laguna Madre	Tampico/ Tamiahua	Alvarado	Tabasco	Campeche/ Yucatán
Lesser Canada goose[a]	**55.6**	**40.5**	3.8			
Lesser Canada goose[b]	**68.6**	**30.7**	0.7			
White-fronted goose	**40.6**	15.9	**21.2**	17.5	4.8	
White-fronted goose[b]	**77.8**	9.4	**10.6**	1.1	1.1	
Lesser Snow goose	**34.6**	21.1	**33.0**	11.2		
Black-bellied whistling duck	1.1	<1.0	15.4	**19.5**	**63.4**	<1.0
Mottled duck	25.6	17.4	**31.1/25.4**	<1.0	<1.0	
Gadwall[a]	9.3	3.6	**37.8/30.2**	4.1	14.8	
Pintail	9.2	15.8	**22.2**	**21.3**	10.5	21.0
Green-winged teal	**22.2**	6.2	**55.8**	12.9	2.2	<1.0
Blue-winged teal	<1.0	<1.0	11.2	20.3	**30.2**	**36.7**
American wigeon	2.6	3.4	11.2	16.7	**22.9**	**43.2**
Northern shoveler	**20.3**	16.4	**37.9**	15.3	2.7	7.4
Redhead	<1.0	**93.7**	1.5	<1.0	1.9	**2.1**
Ring-necked duck	5.0	1.1	**38.0**	13.4	15.4	**27.1**
Canvasback	2.3	12.1	**41.7**	19.9	3.4	**20.6**
Lesser scaup	<1.0	3.7	**21.1**	7.6	9.1	**57.7**
Ruddy duck	1.2	**25.9**	**56.8**	13.2	<1.0	2.5

[a] 1951–65.

[b] 1961–65.

coast of Mexico did not change dramatically between the two survey periods (1948–65 and 1970–88), with the following exceptions. A larger percentage of lesser snow goose and white-fronted goose wintering populations shifted from Tampico/Tamiahua area to the Lower Laguna Madre in the later survey, utilizing the Río Grande area similarly in both surveys. Mottled duck *(Anas fulvigula)* and gadwall populations shifted from Tampico/Tamiahua area to increased percentages using Río Grande and Lower Laguna Madre in later years. Northern pintail percentages shifted from a large percentage occupying both Tampico-Tamiahua and Alvarado lagoons in earlier years to Laguna Madre and the Río Grande in later surveys. American wigeon percentages shifted from Campeche-Yucatán and Tabasco in early survey estimates to Laguna Madre and Río Grande areas. Percentages of northern shovelers decreased from Tampico lagoons in the early survey to increases in Río Grande and Tabasco areas. Ring-necked ducks *(Aythya collaris)* decreased from Tampico lagoons in earlier surveys to Campeche-Yucatán areas in the later surveys. Canvasback percentages shifted from Tampico lagoons to Laguna Madre and, to a lesser extent, Río Grande areas. Scaup decreased in the Campeche-Yucatán area from earlier years to increases in Laguna Madre in later surveys. Ruddy duck *(Oxyura jamaicensis)* percentages shifted from Tampico-Tamiahua lagoons to Río Grande areas, increasing slightly in Laguna Madre.

Table 11.3. *Average percentages of common waterfowl species recorded along the Gulf Coastal Plain during annual aerial surveys from 1970 to 1988 (Baldassarre et al. 1989). Percentages in bold highlight the locations representing the highest and second-highest values for each species.*

	Rio Grande	Lower Laguna Madre	Tampico/ Tamiahua	Alvarado Lagoons	Tabasco Lagoons	Campeche/ Yucatán
Lesser Canada goose	**68.0**	**27.3**	4.7/0.0	0.0	0.0	0.0
White-fronted goose	**60.7**	**28.6**	6.6/4.1	0.0	0.0	0.0
Lesser Snow goose	**68.4**	**21.2**	0.0/10.4	0.0	0.0	0.0
Whistling ducks	8.7	0.1	20.2/0.4	**30.3**	**40.1**	0.1
Mottled duck	**64.4**	**26.7**	5.4/0.4	2.6	0.5	0.0
Gadwall (1951–65)	**33.4**	**28.2**	15.0/7.8	11.1	3.7	0.8
Northern pintail	18.2	**61.1**	4.3/3.9	5.0	4.8	2.7
Green-winged teal	**56.7**	13.4	**21.3/4.0**	3.7	0.8	0.1
Blue-winged teal	0.6	0.4	2.2/2.2	17.8	**47.9**	**28.9**
American wigeon	**19.8**	**42.8**	4.0/6.8	11.9	6.8	7.9
Northern shoveler	**40.5**	9.4	6.1/3.4	8.2	**25.0**	7.5
Redhead	0.1	**97.5**	0.0/2.1	0.0	0.0	**0.2**
Ring-necked duck	1.1	2.9	1.9/0.3	14.4	**17.5**	**62.0**
Canvasback	11.4	**55.2**	**7.9/17.7**	7.5	0.1	0.2
Scaup	1.1	**36.7**	6.3/12.7	5.6	5.4	**32.2**
Ruddy duck	**31.8**	**33.8**	14.9/7.2	7.5	4.9	0.0

Waterfowl in the Río Grande Delta

Prior to damming and water diversion of the Río Grande, waterfowl use of the delta probably was much higher (Baldassarre et al. 1989). However, high numbers of migrating and wintering waterfowl used this habitat in 1938, 1947–64 (Saunders and Saunders 1981), and 1970–88 (Baldassarre et al. 1989). This continued usage illustrates the importance of Río Grande Delta wetlands in comparison with other Gulf of Mexico areas. This wetland complex supports higher goose populations than any other area along the Mexican Gulf Coast, and the proportion of all wintering goose populations increased in Tamaulipas over other Gulf areas during 1970–88. Over half of lesser Canada goose populations along the Mexican Gulf Coast were documented in the Río Grande Delta from 1951 to 1964 (Saunders and Saunders 1981), and they increased even more in the later surveys (Baldassarre et al. 1989). White-fronted goose populations were highest in the delta as well, with over 75% of the entire wintering population documented along the Gulf Coast during 1961–64. Prior to the 1950s, only a few thousand of this species were present, but numbers increased as land use was converted to sorghum fields. As more geese were observed in the Río Grande Delta, aerial survey coverage also intensified. As a result, more numbers were documented for the delta. One-third of lesser snow geese documented along the Mexican Gulf Coast were counted within the Río Grande Delta in 1947–64 and 1970–88.

Mottled duck, green-winged teal, and northern shoveler numbers were substantial (>20% of total Mexican Gulf Coast population) in the delta during 1947–64 (Saunders and Saunders 1981). The proportion of these species wintering in the delta more than doubled in 1970–88 (Baldassarre et al. 1989). Mottled ducks were first documented in Tamaulipas in 1937 and were found chiefly in lagoons and marshes of the Río Grande Delta (Saunders and Saunders 1981). More mottled ducks have been documented in this area than anywhere else along the Mexican Gulf Coast (Baldassarre et al. 1989).

For ring-necked ducks, northern pintails, and gadwalls, 5 to 10% of Mexican Gulf populations used the delta. Northern pintails are the most abundant duck in Mexico, where they migrate through Tamaulipas from September through November and return in January during their spring migration (Saunders and Saunders 1981). As compared to other areas of the Mexican Gulf Coast, less than 3% of black-bellied whistling duck *(Dendrocygna autumnalis)*, blue-winged teal, American wigeon, red-head, canvasback, lesser scaup, and ruddy duck populations were documented in the Río Grande Delta. Blue-winged teal are often the earliest migrants to reach Mexico in fall, but most continue to Central America and northern South America. American wigeons are one of the most common and widely distributed duck species in Mexico. Lesser scaup is the most abundant species on the Gulf Coastal Plain (Saunders and Saunders 1981).

Waterfowl in Laguna Madre de Tamaulipas and Coastal Ponds

Redheads are one of the most abundant duck species using the Mexican Gulf Coast, and a large proportion of the population winters in Laguna Madre de Tamaulipas. Historic wintering grounds of redheads documented along the Mexican Gulf Coast include Laguna Madre de Tamaulipas, Laguna Morales, and Laguna San Andres. Wintering populations were estimated as 469,000 in January 1947 and decreased to 219,000 the following year. Declines continued through 1950 (21,000 wintering population). An increase in survey estimates occurred through the 1950s to 240,000 in 1959, then wintering populations declined precipitously to 23,000 by 1964 (Saunders and Saunders 1981).

Population estimates from aerial surveys conducted from 1980 to 1994 exhibited less dramatic fluctuations (see fig. 11.3) (Woodin 1996). Although no quantitative trend evaluations on seagrass distribution and availability have been conducted in Laguna Madre de Tamaulipas, a baseline database was generated during the 1970s (Cornelius 1975) and continued in the 1990s (DUMAC 1996; see chapter 7). Recent studies in Texas showed a decline (Merkord 1978; Quammen and Onuf 1993). Closing and opening of Gulf passes into Laguna Madre de Tamaulipas resulted in changes in lagoonal salinities and probably influenced shoalgrass abundance (Saunders and Saunders 1981; Baldassarre et al. 1989). Proportions of redhead populations wintering in Laguna Madre de Tamaulipas actually decreased from the early surveys (1947–64) to later years (1970–88; Baldassarre et al. 1989).

The majority of wintering lesser Canada geese along the Mexican Gulf Coast utilized Laguna Madre de Tamaulipas and adjacent coastal ponds and wetlands in 1938 and from 1947 to 1964. Access to cultivated fields adjacent to wetland areas is cited as the primary reason. Lesser snow geese and white-fronted geese represented 21% and 16% of total Gulf population, respectively, in the Laguna Madre area. Lesser snow geese are fairly common west of Laguna Madre, but not as numerous as in the Río Grande Delta. Blue-phase individuals were documented with white-phase groups in the Río San Fernando Delta. White-fronted geese are the most widely distributed goose in Mexico, but they were found in lower numbers on Laguna Madre and adjacent freshwater ponds (Saunders and Saunders 1981).

Mottled ducks, northern pintails, northern shovelers, and canvasbacks also used Laguna Madre and coastal ponds during the 1938 and 1947–64 surveys, each representing from 10 to 20% of Mexican Gulf Coast wintering populations (Saunders and Saunders 1981). Mottled ducks have been observed in the Río San Fernando Delta (Saunders 1953) and on small ponds and marshes west of Laguna Madre. A flock of 16 was seen at Rancho Anacahuitas at the northern end of Laguna Madre (Saunders and Saunders 1981). Mottled ducks wintering along the Mexico Gulf Coast increased in Laguna Madre in the 1970–88 surveys in proportion to other Mexican Gulf areas (Baldassarre et al. 1989). Northern pintails are one of the most abundant ducks in Mexico; this species was documented as having the second highest wintering population along the Mexican Gulf Coastal Plain. Large concentrations of northern pintails have been documented on Laguna Madre; in 1955, over 97,000 northern pintails were observed on Laguna Madre during the January survey. More than one million northern pintails have been seen with large rafts of redheads feeding on shoalgrass rhizomes (Saunders and Saunders 1981). Proportions of this species wintering in Laguna Madre in relation to the entire Gulf Coast did not change from the 1947–64 period to the 1970–88 period (Baldassarre et al. 1989). Northern shovelers rank eighth in abundance on the Gulf Coastal Plain and winter in low numbers along the Gulf Coast (Saunders and Saunders 1981). Proportions of this species decreased between the two survey periods (Baldassarre et al. 1989). Canvasbacks are ranked ninth on the Gulf Coastal Plain and historically were numerous south of Laguna Madre de Tamaulipas (Saunders and Saunders 1981).

Wintering populations of green-winged teal, American wigeon, lesser scaup, gadwall, ring-necked duck, black-bellied whistling duck, and blue-winged teal in the Laguna Madre system consisted of less than 10% of the Gulf Coast estimates in 1938 and from 1947 to 1964. Although green-winged teal are ranked seventh in abundance along the Gulf Coastal Plain, they were documented in highest numbers south of Laguna Madre de Tamaulipas near Tampico (Saunders and Saunders 1981). A higher proportion of green-winged teal used Laguna Madre in recent years (Baldassarre et al. 1989). American wigeons frequent both saltwater and freshwater habitats in Mexico and are a common and widely distributed species there. This species ranks fourth in abundance on the Gulf Coastal Plain, peaking in 1948, 1956, and 1961. Lesser scaup ranks first, and is often the most abundant duck every year. Abundance estimates showed a southward shift as more lesser scaup were counted south of Laguna Madre (Saunders and Saunders 1981). Later surveys grouped both scaup species and reported a significant increase in the proportion of wintering scaup using Laguna Madre (Baldassarre et al. 1989). Gadwalls are more numerous on the Gulf Coastal Plain south in Tampico lagoons. Decline of this species has been attributed to decreased abundance of naiad; this plant species may have experienced a decline due to increased brackishness of lagoonal and coastal pond waters during 1947–64 (Saunders and Saunders 1981). However, higher proportions of the wintering populations appear to have shifted to Laguna Madre de Tamaulipas in 1970–88 (Baldassarre et al. 1989).

Rare Waterfowl Species Documented in the Río Grande Delta and Laguna Madre de Tamaulipas

Swans (*Cygnus* spp.)   Trumpeter swans (*C. buccinator*) are reported to be rare winter visitors to northeastern Mexico. This species was documented only once in Tamaulipas south of Matamoros, on 21 January 1909 (Phillips 1911). Whistling swans (*C. columbianus*) also are extremely rare in Tamaulipas, and the only documented observation in Tamaulipas occurred on 11 January 1964 near Laguna Madre. Six adults and five immature swans were seen during an aerial survey on a small freshwater lake 104 km (62 mi) south of Matamoros (Saunders and Saunders 1981).

Muscovy Duck *(Cairina moschata)*   These ducks are found along heavily wooded habitats associated with rivers and have been documented along the Río Soto la Marina (Saunders and Saunders 1981).

Mallard   The most abundant duck in North America and the Northern Hemisphere, the mallard has wintering range extending into northern Mexico, although population numbers are low (Bellrose 1980). Mallard numbers and distribution in Mexico have increased since cultivated land use practices were altered and reservoir numbers increased in the midwestern and western United States and Tamaulipas (Saunders and Saunders 1981). Slight increases in mallard wintering populations were attributed to greater grain sorghum acreage and less acreage in cotton production between Matamoros and San Fernando.

Cinnamon Teal *(Anas cyanoptera septentrionalium)*   This species is common locally on both coasts and in the interior of Mexico during winter, with 95% of the population migrating from breeding grounds in Utah, California, and the Pacific Northwest (Bellrose 1980). The cinnamon teal has been reported to breed in Tamaulipas (Friedmann et al. 1950; Leopold 1959).

Wood Duck *(Aix sponsa)*   These ducks are found primarily within Canada and United States, but winter from the southeastern United States (Bellrose 1980) south to northeastern Mexico (Friedmann et al. 1950; Rappole and Blacklock 1994). Individuals were documented rarely at wooded lagoons of the Río Grande Delta. A flock of 25 was recorded in the delta during an aerial survey in January 1963 (Saunders and Saunders 1981), and Evendon (1952) documented a female wood duck on a roadside pond 117 km (73 mi) southwest of Matamoros.

Greater Scaup   Although greater scaup were collected in the Corpus Christi area, no individuals were documented in Mexico (Saunders and Saunders 1981). These ducks typically winter along the Atlantic and Pacific coasts as well as on the Great Lakes and along the northern Gulf of Mexico coast (Bellrose 1980).

Common Golden-eye *(Bucephala clangula)*   This species breeds across northern Canada and winters along the Alaskan and western Canada coasts. Fewer than 2,000 migrate to Texas, and the majority of this minor population winters on large interior lakes. Less than 100 are estimated to reach the coast (Bellrose 1980). Common golden-eyes are rarely documented in Tamaulipas, but small flocks have been recorded in the Río Grande Delta and Laguna Madre (Saunders and Saunders 1981).

Bufflehead   Buffleheads breed in northwestern Canada and Alaska and migrate southward in the winter as far as the northern Gulf of Mexico coast. Buffleheads are listed as very scarce along the Mexican Gulf Coast and occur primarily on or near Laguna Madre de Tamaulipas. Flocks ranged from 12 to 132 during surveys in 1938 and during 1947–64 (Saunders and Saunders 1981). Two interior locations in Mexico are also documented wintering areas (Bellrose 1980).

Mergansers *(Mergus* spp.)   Hooded mergansers *(M. cucullatus)* migrating southward along the Mississippi Flyway utilize appropriate wintering habitat in Louisiana, Mississippi, Tennessee, and Arkansas (Bellrose 1980). This species may even winter as far south as northern Mexico (Rappole and Blacklock 1994) and was first recorded in Tamaulipas by Berlandier at Matamoros (Baird et al. 1884). Two males were documented on Laguna Culebron near Matamoros in January 1943 (Saunders and Saunders 1981). Common mergansers *(M. americanus)* generally winter throughout the United States (Bellrose 1980) but are an uncommon winter resident in the Texas Panhandle and rare to casual in South Texas (Rappole and Blacklock 1994). Tamaulipan sightings are even rarer; several individuals were reported on inland reservoirs near Reynosa in 1940 and two birds were recorded in January 1941 on Laguna Madre. Red-breasted mergansers *(M. serrator)* are a more common winter visitor along the Mexican Gulf Coast, but numbers have never been high. Small flocks were observed on Laguna Madre, near passes, and on the Gulf (Saunders and Saunders 1981).

Whistling Ducks (*Dendrocygna* spp.)   Several Mexican and Central American species are found in northern Mexico at the northernmost extension of their range. Black-bellied whistling ducks were reported as a regular resident in Tamaulipas (Saunders and Saunders 1981), using Mexican coastal habitats as breeding areas and as migration corridors from breeding areas in southern coastal Texas (Bellrose 1980). Fulvous whistling ducks *(Dendrocygna bicolor)* are a Mexican species, typically rare in the United States, with higher numbers in breeding areas in Louisiana and Texas (Bellrose 1980). In Mexico, they occur on both coasts in brackish and freshwater marshes and along lagoon shorelines, utilizing these areas as breeding and wintering areas (Saunders and Saunders 1981). This species breeds in marshes associated with the Río San Fernando and Río Soto la Marina.

Masked Duck *(Oxyura dominica)*   These ducks are a Central American species that ranges into northern Mexico lowlands and the Texas Coastal Plain (Rappole and Blacklock 1994). They prefer densely vegetated marshes (Saunders and Saunders 1981). No individuals were recorded during aerial surveys, although a pair was observed near Brownsville and Harlingen in June 1941 and another pair on Laguna Atascosa National Wildlife Refuge in 1942 (Saunders and Saunders 1981).

European Wigeon *(Anas penelope)*   This species may be present as a single individual within flocks of American Wigeon or other duck species. Sightings along the Atlantic and Gulf coasts were explained partially as winter visitors from Iceland (Bellrose 1980). An adult drake European wigeon was documented at Culebron reservoir near Matamoros in a flock of American wigeons and gadwalls (Saunders and Saunders 1981).

12 Colonial Waterbirds and Rookery Islands

ELIZABETH H. SMITH

Several hundred islands were created in the late 1940s in the Laguna Madre of Texas from deposition of dredged material during the excavation of the Gulf Intracoastal Waterway (GIWW). Plant succession has occurred over time and most of the islands with sufficient elevation support a diversity of grass, forb, and shrub vegetation assemblages (Coover and Rechenthin 1965; Chaney et al. 1978). In turn, many islands are used by colonial waterbirds as rookeries, or breeding grounds, from early January through September each year (plates 40, 41, 42). Essential feeding areas are available in the shallows around the islands and shorelines of the Laguna Madre.

The larger dredge material islands are located adjacent to the GIWW, and active disposal areas are used within the system. Smaller dredged material islands are present to a lesser extent as a result of excavation and maintenance of boat channels, marinas, and residential canals. Active dredging to construct and maintain artificial channels has occurred for over 100 years within the Texas Coastal Bend (Soots and Landin 1978).

Most colonial waterbirds are dependent upon estuarine habitats for both foraging and reproduction. They typically feed on fish and crustaceans in shallow and open water areas. Natural and artificial islands for nesting, if isolated from disturbance, are critical for these birds' continued survival. Therefore, colonial waterbirds are excellent indicators of ecosystem health (Soots and Landin 1978). Islands in Texas are used in varying degrees depending upon one or more of the following factors: accessibility of islands to predators; human disturbance and activities; size of islands; and presence of vegetation, topography, or elevation suitable to support one or more nesting species (Chaney et al. 1978). Most lagoonal islands in the Texas Coastal Bend support fairly similar vegetation communities that include salt-tolerant high-marsh species above flats; a variety of shrubs, cacti, and small trees (hereafter grouped within "shrub" categories); and unvegetated shell and sand beaches (see plates 40, 41, 42). Islands may also be important to nonbreeding birds (e.g., resident and migratory waterbirds, shorebirds, songbirds, and raptors) for resting, roosting, and feeding (Soots and Landin 1978).

Nesting History

Upper Laguna Madre of Texas   Early investigations of colonial waterbird rookeries in the Laguna Madre of Texas reported breeding colonies of tricolored herons (*Egretta tricolor*), snowy egrets (*Egretta thula*), reddish egrets (*Egretta rufescens*), and great blue herons (*Ardea herodias*) on islands suitable for a variety of nesting species (Bent 1926). Tricolored herons, reddish egrets, and great blue herons were documented on Bird Island in upper Laguna Madre (Carroll 1927).

Thirty-four colonies have been variously surveyed in the upper Laguna Madre from 1973 to 1996 (table 12.1; TCWS 1982; TCWC 1998), and Texas Colonial Waterbird censuses continue. Sizes of both dredged material islands and natural islands range from <0.5 ha to 5.6 ha (13.8 ac) (A. H. Chaney, pers. comm.). Species richness for each colony also is variable (1–21) and is probably dependent upon size, nesting

Table 12.1 Summary information on all bird colonies surveyed in upper Laguna Madre from 1973 to 1980 (TCWS 1982) and 1981 to 1996 (TCWC 1998); modifications by A. H. Chaney (pers. comm.) contributed greatly to three categories of data: number of islands, their sizes, and extent of human disturbance.

Colony Number	Name	Total Number of Islands in Colony	Size (1980)	Human Disturbance (1980)	Species Richness (total)	Cumulative Survey Total (1973–96)	Number of Years	Average Pairs per Year
614-221	Naval Air Station Islands	30ᵃ DMI & NI	3–5 ha or less	Med–Low	19	42,070	19	2,214
614-222	Kennedy Causeway Islands	27 DMI & NI	2–0.5 ha or less	Med	16	48,541	19	2,555
614-240	Mkr 2–17 (13–35) Spoil Islands	14ᵇ DMI	2–0.5 ha or less	Med, Low	14	7,934	14	567
614-300	Pita Island/Humble Channel Spoil	NI, 2 DMI; 8 DMI	10.5 ha	High, Med	18	27,302	24	1,138
614-301	Mkr 31–33 (34) [65–71 (72)] Spoil Island	4 (5) DMI	5.6, 5.0 ha	Med	8	652	18	36
614-302	Mkr 37–38 (75) Spoil Island	1 (2) DMI	4 ha	High	7	1,565	21	75
614-303	Mkr 39–41 (79–85) Spoil Islands	2 DMI	4.4, 3.9 ha	Med	4	198	20	10
614-304	N of Bird Island Mkr 43 (87–91)	4 (5) DMI	24 ha	Low	14	2,550	22	116
614-305	W of North Bird Island (93–103)	7 DMI	33 ha	Low	8	603	19	32
614-306	North Bird Island	NI	6 ha	Low	9	4,023	21	192
614-307	West Side Spoil Island	3 DMI	16.9 ha		3	53	16	3
614-320	Padre Island Development Fill	Residential site	8 ha	Med	1	24	3	8
614-340	South Bird Island	NI	5.0 ha	Low	19	84,019	23	3,653
614-341	South of South Bird Island	4 DMI	3.7–7.4 ha	Low	21	136,006	24	5,667
614-342	Mkr 63–65 (127–131) Spoil Island	2 (1) DMI	0.4 ha each	Low	14	2,056	21	98
614-343	Mkr 69 (141) Spoil Island	1 DMI	1.6 ha	Med	13	2,892	21	138
614-344	Mkr 72 (152) Spoil Island	1 DMI	1.5 ha	High	9	1,711	20	86
614-345	Mkr 81 (163) Spoil Island	1 DMI	1.7 ha	Low	20	24,455	24	1,019

Table 12.1 (continued)

Colony Number	Name	Total Number of Islands in Colony	Size (1980)	Human Disturbance (1980)	Species Richness (total)	Cumulative Survey Total (1973–96)	Number of Years	Average Pairs per Year
614-346	Mkr 77A (155) Spoil Island	1 DMI	1.2 ha	Low	9	418	16	26
614-347	Mkr 85A (165) Spoil Island	1 DMI	0.5 ha	Low	11	584	15	39
614-348	Yellow House Spoil (162)	1 DMI	0.5 ha	High	2	55	1	55
614-360	Mkr 91 (185) Spoil Island	2 DMI	0.3 ha each	Low	14	593	17	35
614-361	Mkr 103–117 (207–221)	7 DMI	0.5–4.2 ha	High	19	41,153	24	1,715
614-362	South Baffin Bay Islands	4 DMI	one 1.8 ha; others 0.6 ha each	Unknown (Med)	17	15,377	24	641
614-363	Diked Island (178)	1 DMI	1.7 ha	High	5	849	16	54
614-364	Side Channel Island (199)	3 DMI	18 ha	Low	3	71	7	10
614-380	Mkr 139–149 (21–35) Spoil	8 DMI	3.0 ha	High	12	15,194	20	760
614-381	Yarborough Pass	1 DMI	0.5 ha	Low	10	1,358	12	113
614-382	North Yarborough Pass (37–39)	1 DMI	1.5 ha	High	9	2,353	17	138
614-383	South Yarborough Pass (41–47)	>1 DMI	0.5 ha	Med	10	1,688	18	94
614-384	The Hole	4 DMI	1 ha	Med	11	961	16	60
614-385	Padre Island Spoil	9 DMI	3 ha	Low	12	745	15	50
614-400	East Potrero Grande				5	599	8	75
614-401	East Potrero Cortado				5	435	8	54

Note: DMI = dredged material island; NI = natural island.
[a] 25 islands currently checked.
[b] 15 islands currently checked.

Table 12.2. *Species composition of colonial-nesting waterbirds in upper and lower Laguna Madre and presence documented for each species in colony sites*

Species	UPPER LAGUNA		LOWER LAGUNA	
	Colonies[a]	%	Colonies[b]	%
Black skimmer (Rhynchops niger)	32	94.1	19	90.5
Gull-billed tern (Sterna nilotica)	31	91.2	18	85.7
Great blue heron (Ardea herodias)	26	76.5	14	66.7
Tricolored heron (Egretta tricolor)	26	76.5	13	61.9
Laughing gull (Larus atricilla)	25	73.5	17	81
Reddish egret (Egretta rufescens)	23	67.7	14	66.7
Caspian tern (Sterna caspia)	23	67.7	0	0
Snowy egret (Egretta thula)	22	64.7	12	57.1
Least tern (Sterna antillarum)	22	64.7	11	52.4
Forster's tern (Sterna forsteri)	20	58.8	9	42.9
Royal tern (Sterna maxima)	19	55.9	15	71.4
Little blue heron (Egretta caerulea)	15	44.1	9	42.9
Great egret (Ardea alba)	14	41.2	11	52.4
White-faced ibis (Plegadis chihi)	14	41.2	8	38.1
Sandwich tern (Sterna sandvicensis)	14	41.2	14	66.7
Cattle egret (Bubulcus ibis)	11	32.4	12	57.1
Black-crowned night heron (Nycticorax nyticorax)	10	29.4	5	23.8
Roseate spoonbill (Ajaia ajaja)	8	23.5	6	28.6
Sooty tern (Sterna fuscata)	8	23.5	9	42.9
American white pelican (Pelecanus erythrorhynchos)	4	11.8	0	0
White ibis (Eudocimus albus)	4	11.8	9	42.9
Neotropic cormorant (Phalacrocorax brasilianus)[c]	1	2.9	0	0
Yellow-crowned night heron (Nyctanassa violacea)	0	0	2	9.5

Source: Data summarized from TCWC 1998.

[a] Number of colonies (out of 34) where species were documented during the survey period (1973–96).

[b] Number of colonies (out of 22) where species were documented during the survey period (1973–96).

[c] Probably miscounted as nester, more likely loafing (A. H. Chaney, pers. comm.).

habitat complexity, and degree of disturbance. Twenty-three species have been documented on a rookery island at least one year during the surveys (table 12.2). Some species nested in most rookeries almost every year; for example, black skimmers *(Rhynchops niger)* nested on over 90% of rookery islands in upper Laguna Madre of Texas at some point during the surveys. Nesting pair estimates of all birds totaled 503,761 from 1973 to 1996 (summarized from TCWC 1998 data).

In a recent evaluation of the status and trends of 25 species documented as nesting colonially on rookery islands in the Texas Coastal Bend (including upper Laguna Madre), Texas Colonial Waterbird Surveys were deemed sufficient and fairly accurate data suitable for analysis (Chaney et al. 1996). Trends were calculated for each species by grouping data of 91 rookeries by year (1973–90) and conducting regression analysis. Colonial waterbirds that typically nest in shrubs all exhibited declining populations (some degree of negative trend), with the exception of little blue herons *(Egretta caerulea)* (Chaney et al. 1996). The increase of little blue heron breeding pairs was explained as potential loss of habitat in inland areas and subsequent movement to nesting islands in upper Laguna Madre. Great blue heron, great egret *(Ardea alba)*, and tricolored heron populations may have declined as a result of habitat degradation (including an increase in predators) or habitat loss in the Texas Coastal Bend. Reddish egret declines may be attributed to the same factors and/or to emigration out of the area as a result of habitat degradation or loss. These species may also be experiencing increased competition for remaining nest space, a potential causative factor for the snowy egret as well.

Cattle egrets *(Bubulcus ibis;* exotic) have declined in recent years, possibly due to migration inland during wet years to nest around freshwater ponds with emergent shrubs. In addition, this species nests later than other herons and egrets; therefore, breeding pair numbers may not accurately reflect count estimates. Black-crowned night-heron *(Nycticorax nycticorax)* numbers also may not represent actual trends because earlier counts may have included bird groups at day roosts. Recent counts may underestimate the breeding population, as this species nests lower in the vegetation and is difficult to detect during surveys. Apparent declines in roseate spoonbill *(Ajaia ajaja)* breeding populations may be a function of loss of habitat in some areas negatively affecting this species overall, though increased numbers have been documented on some islands, or may reflect the fact that early surveys counted individuals instead of nesting pairs (A. H. Chaney, pers. comm.).

Breeding white-faced ibis *(Plegadis chihi)* declines were attributed to reduced habitat and to competition with laughing gulls *(Larus atricilla)* for nest sites or nest destruction by laughing gulls whenever disturbance flushed white-faced ibis off nests (Chaney et al. 1996). This species is particularly susceptible to disturbance, often being the first group to leave nests when disturbed and the last to return. This response has probably caused nesting failure and decreased populations. Laughing gull populations have remained stable throughout the Texas Coastal Bend.

Colonial waterbirds that require unvegetated shell and sand substrates include black skimmers and several gull and tern species. Least terns exhibited the greatest decline in numbers of breeding pairs in the Texas Coastal Bend (Chaney et al. 1996). However, colonial waterbird counts may not accurately reflect numbers of this species, as they often nest in isolated pairs. Location of nests could be affected by high tides, and pairs could be missed during surveys. In addition, they may nest anywhere new dredged material is deposited or outside a recognized rookery area. Black skimmers also are described as having a sharply declining trend, due to loss and degradation of nesting habitat over time and high tides that negatively affected nesting success in recent years (Chaney et al. 1996). Caspian and royal tern nesting pair numbers may have been overreported in early survey years; therefore, the decline may be exaggerated. Gull-billed terns also require unvegetated substrate and may move from island to island searching for new nesting locations; trends appeared stable, but declining slightly. Declines in Forster's terns were attributed to nest placement on berms susceptible to high tides; in addition, this species prefers to nest apart from other species. These two factors may be responsible for the downward trend. Royal and sandwich terns exhibited positive trends from 1973 to 1990. These species have similar nesting requirements and frequently nest together; consequently it is often difficult to get accurate separate counts (Chaney et al. 1996; A. H. Chaney, pers. comm.).

Lower Laguna Madre of Texas   Twenty-two colonies have been variously surveyed in the lower Laguna Madre from 1973 to 1996 (table 12.3; TCWS 1982;

Table 12.3. Summary information on all bird colonies surveyed from 1973 to 1996 in lower Laguna Madre, Texas (TCWS 1982; TCWC 1998).

Colony Number	Name	Total Number of Islands in Colony	Size (1980)	Human Disturbance (1980)	Species Richness (total)	Cumulative Survey Total (1973–96)	Number of Years	Average Pairs per Year
618-100	South Land Cut	8 DMI	5 ha	Low	18	34,136	21	1,626
618-120	East Flats Spoil	1 DMI	0.5 ha	Low	11	5,572	13	429
618-121	Mansfield Odd Spoil	Several DMI	0.5 ha	Low	10	7,992	16	499
618-122	East Mkr 265 Spoil	1 DMI	0.5 ha	Low	4	191	9	21
618-140	NE Mansfield Intersection	1 DMI	2.0 ha	Med	15	39,285	24	1,637
618-141	SW Mansfield Intersection	1 DMI	2.0 ha	Low	11	5,049	24	210
618-142	SE Mansfield Intersection	1 DMI	0.5 ha (eroding)	Low	2	334	12	28
618-143	Green Hill Spoil Island	1 (discontinuous) DMI	3.2 km long, 2 ha	Med	20	31,035	24	1,293
618-144	Mansfield Channel Spoil				2	80	6	13
618-160	Green Island Cut Spoil	7 DMI	8 ha	Med, High	16	32,715	21	1,558
618-161	Green Island	NI	10 ha	Low	15	54,652	21	2,602
618-162	Spoil SW of Green Island				1	60	8	7
618-180	Arroyo Colorado Int. Spoil	1 (discontinuous) DMI	8 km long, 250 ha	Med	17	40,168	19	2,114
618-181	East Arroyo Spoil	8 DMI	4 ha	Low	9	4,135	13	318
618-182	Three Island Spoil	1 (discontinuous) DMI	10 km long, 180 ha	Med	18	193,187	21	9,199
618-183	South Three Islands	5 DMI	3 ha	Low	15	5,311	14	379
618-184	Four Islands				8	8,334	10	833
618-200	Port Isabel Spoil	1 (discontinuous) DMI	5 km long, 6 ha	Med	13	13,996	18	77
618-201	Padre Beach Estates	sand beach	2 ha	High	1	71	3	24
618-220	Laguna Vista Spoil	9 DMI	7 ha	Med	16	42,139	17	2479
618-240	Dead Pecker Hill	black mangrove island	5 ha	Med	11	4,522	14	323

Note: DMI = dredged material island; NI = natural island.

Table 12.4. Number of colonial waterbird nesting pairs on northeastern coast of Mexico during May and June 1973–76

Species	1973	1974	1975	1976
American white pelican	404	490	250	290
Olivaceous (neotropic) cormorant		30		
Great blue heron	770	448	417	507
Reddish egret	32	67	52	69+
Cattle egret		120	450+	1,145
Great egret	1,040	1,138	692	410
Snowy egret	1,875	1,055	870+	165
Tricolored heron	600	637	362	59+
Black-crowned night heron	25	36	22	226
Unspecified ibis species (dark colored)				10
White ibis		172	10+	10
Roseate spoonbill	51	60	11	20
Total	4,792	4,253	3,136	2,900
Number of Colonies	9	13	11	10

Source: Sprunt and Knoder 1980.

TCWC 1998), and Texas Colonial Waterbird censuses continue. Sizes of both dredged material islands and natural islands are recorded as total hectares for all islands and range from 2 to 250 ha (5–618 ac). Species richness for each colony also is variable (1–20) and is probably dependent upon island size, nesting habitat complexity, and degree of disturbance. Twenty-three species have been documented on a rookery island in at least one year during the surveys (see table 12.2). Some species nested within most of the colonies at some point during the survey. Nesting pair estimates totaled 488,828 from 1973 to 1996 (summarized from TCWC 1998 data; A. H. Chaney, pers. comm.).

Laguna Madre de Tamaulipas   Population surveys of wading birds and other colonially nesting species were conducted from the Río Grande south to Laguna de San Andreas in 1973–76 (Sprunt and Knoder 1980; table 12.4). Bird colonies in the Laguna Madre de Tamaulipas were not extensive; however, American white pelicans and reddish egrets were documented in significant numbers. The only coastal breeding colony of American white pelicans in Mexico is located in the northern Laguna.

Factors Affecting Nesting Success

Vegetation Dynamics on Rookery Islands   Soil texture influences stability of island structure and configuration (Chaney et al. 1978). The soil used in island deposition ranges from sand to reef material, clay, and silt in the Baffin Bay area (DePue 1974). Fine materials are more prone to redistribution by wind, rainfall, and tidal action. Vegetation colonizes on finer soils more slowly; however, succession may be faster once the pioneer community is established due to increased water-holding soil capacities (Chaney et al. 1978). Saline-alkali soils predominate throughout the Laguna Madre, and vegetation must be tolerant of limited fresh water availability (Barnes 1971). Higher salinities predominate in lagoonal waters around South Texas islands, resulting in more expansive zones of salt-tolerant species at higher eleva-tions. Hypersaline conditions in upper Laguna Madre are a result of lower precipi-tation and higher evaporation rates; this phenomenon favors perennial forb and grass species. In addition, shrub zones are less developed than on islands farther north (Chaney et al. 1978).

Other factors that may influence vegetation type and succession rate include the proximity to seed and propagule sources (carried by wind, water, or animals), distur-bance event frequency (storms or trampling by animals), and overfertilization by bird excrement. Many plant species that colonize bay islands are disseminated by water or wind or brought in via bird or mammal droppings. No quantitative data were found that evaluated storm effects on vegetation succession. Studies in other areas have determined that colonial waterbirds may have an effect on vegetation composition, density, and/or succession. Larger terns (i.e., royal or Caspian terns) arrive early in the season on dredged material islands in North Carolina and may impact annual veg-etation establishment by trampling and overfertilization. Plant species too large to trample and/or tolerant of fertilization continued to dominate the site with luxuriant growth. If the dominant species continued to flourish, royal terns would not select the site in following years. Increased plant density also limited site selection by other ground-nesting species. Most other ground nesters—including gull-billed terns, common terns (S. hirundo), and black skimmers—did not nest in high densities char-acteristic of royal terns and did not defecate in the nesting site. As a result, fertiliza-tion did not occur until later in the season, when young birds enriched the soil by on-site defecation. Arboreal nesters also appeared to have an effect on vegetation dy-namics by reducing herbaceous growth underneath shrubs and trees and even killing taller vegetation by overfertilization in old heronries (Soots and Parnell 1975).

Temporal Nesting Dynamics   Reproductive behavior has been observed on rook-ery islands throughout most of the year (January through October), although timing of island use may vary from year to year depending on weather conditions. In general, most species are active from March through September, although species such as great blue heron may initiate courtship and nest building in early January. Because the nesting season peak varies among species, colonial waterbird censuses may not repre-sent accurately those species that have completed nesting or those that initiate nest-ing later in the year. However, because censuses are typically conducted at the same time each year, bias should be consistent. Each phase of the breeding cycle is impor-tant, and any disruption may impact nesting success for that year (Chaney et al. 1996).

Spatial Nesting Dynamics   Habitat type provided by rookery islands determines types of species that may utilize the islands, based on the species' nesting substrate preferences. In general, species may be categorized as ground nesters, for which the substrate may be bare to densely vegetated with herbs and shrubs, or arboreal nesters, which place nests above the ground in supporting vegetation. A species may require one specific type of nesting substrate or have preferences for one type but may use an alternate if necessary. Generally, pelicans, skimmers, gulls, and terns are ground nesters, and spoonbills, herons, egrets, and ibises are shrub nesters. Species that nest in forest habitat types will nest in herb-shrub or shrub thicket where forest canopies do not occur. Some species also seem to prefer to have available a certain amount of dead vegetation, litter, or drift line material to line nests. Nesting densi-ties among species and colonies may involve closely arranged nests, as in royal and Sandwich terns, or widely scattered nests, as documented for least terns.

Some ground-nesting species establish territories only with other pairs of their own species, and some interspecific associations have been documented. Generally, those species that nest in loosely packed colonies may be interspersed with other species; and those that have nests in high densities are typically found in single-species colonies. However, Sandwich terns only rarely nest without the presence of royal terns. Understanding the positive and negative associations is helpful in determining potential habitat partitioning among species in a managed or restored rookery (Soots and Parnell 1975; Soots and Landin 1978).

Great blue herons constructed over half of their nests on bushy sea-ox-eye daisy *(Borrichia frutescens)* on four dredged material islands near Baffin Bay. Average height of nests was 0.20–0.46 m (0.66–1.5 ft). Sea-ox-eye daisy is typically found in low-lying areas and is usually the tallest plant in the vegetative assemblage. The stems are thick and sturdy, and regrowth occurs from vegetative propagation. The patchy occurrence of this species determined the great blue heron nest groupings. Many nests were constructed along the perimeters of inland ponds, and this species did not attempt to renest in these areas when dredged material was deposited within the ponds. Several nests were constructed in common cattail *(Typha latifolia)* stands around the ponds and were between 0.9 and 1.2 m above the ground. One island supported a stand of mesquite *(Prosopis glandulosa)*, and great blue heron used this habitat for nesting. Average height of nests was 1.3 ±0.3 m (0.9–1.8 m; 2.9–5.9 ft) in both tree clusters and isolated individual trees. No nests were constructed in 1971, presumably because drought resulted in absence of foliage. Several advantages were noted for tree nesters: nests had sturdy support; foliage provided shading and seclusion for nestlings; and trees gave additional protection from high winds (Simersky 1971).

Reddish egret nests were located either in common ragweed *(Ambrosia artemisiifolia)* stands in large, low depressions or in bushy sea-ox-eye daisy stands located at slightly higher elevations. Average height for both areas was 0.23 m (0.76 ft). Initiation of nesting is determined by availability of preferred vegetation, and few individuals nested in these areas when drought conditions limited new growth in 1971. Common ragweed is a seasonally abundant species with peak growth occurring in spring. Several individual plants must be located in densities high enough to support reddish egret nests (Simersky 1971).

Tricolored herons nested in common ragweed in a large depressional area of the island and in bushy sea-ox-eye daisies and false indigo *(Baptisia bracteata)* on the island slopes. Average height of the nests was 0.20 ±0.07 m (0.10–0.31 m; 0.33–1.1 ft). Snowy egrets nested primarily in common ragweed in a large depression, and many nests were built so that the crowns of the plant shaded eggs and young. The nests were located in proximity to other species in 1971, when preferred nesting vegetation was limited (Simersky 1971).

Great blue herons begin selecting nest sites earlier than other species, possibly to avoid competition, and prefer tall, shrubby vegetation. The same nest may be used several years in succession (Palmer 1962; Simersky 1971). Several other shrub-nesting species arrive on the islands at about the same time, and competition for sites may occur. These species did not nest in proximity to great blue herons. On dredged material islands 103 and 105, snowy egrets nested in isolated areas, whereas reddish egrets and tricolored herons nested adjacent to each other. It appeared that reddish egrets were more concentrated in dense vegetation (common ragweed; Simersky 1971; McMurry 1971), and tricolored herons nested in more open areas of common ragweed and marginal stands of bushy sea-ox-eye daisy (Simersky 1971; table 12.5). This evidence of spatial partitioning was explained as deriving from reddish egrets being more successful in competing for premium nest sites. Threat displays and territory defense appeared to be directed against birds of the same species (Simersky 1971).

Table 12.5. *Percentage of nests of three species of herons constructed on each substrate on Island 105 in 1970*

Substrate	Snowy egret	Reddish egret	Tricolored heron
Common ragweed (Ambrosia cumanensis)	84.6	46.4	25.4
Bushy sea-ox-eye daisy	0.0	25.0	30.2
Camphor daisy (Haplopappus phyllocephala)	0.0	3.6	3.6
Sea purslane (Sesuvium portulacastrum)	7.7	3.6	2.4
Common ragweed and bushy sea-ox-eye daisy	0.0	3.6	8.4
Bushy sea-ox-eye daisy and camphor daisy	7.7	7.1	8.4
Bushy sea-ox-eye daisy and sea purslane	0.0	0.0	9.6
Camphor daisy and sea purslane	0.0	3.6	1.2
Bushy sea-ox-eye daisy, camphor daisy, and sea purslane	0.0	7.1	10.8
Number of nests	13	28	83

Source: From Simersky 1971.

Early reports of nesting failure in herons and egrets were attributed to great-tailed grackles *(Quiscalus mexicanus)* and vultures (Bent 1926). Egg predation, primarily by laughing gulls, occurred throughout the incubation phase and increased when human disturbance drove away skimmer pairs (DePue 1974).

Adjacent Feeding Habitats   The importance of feeding areas adjacent to rookeries was documented in studies in upper Laguna Madre adjacent to Baffin Bay. Great blue herons were observed feeding in groups near the islands, whereas reddish egrets foraged individually in adjacent areas as well. Both species appeared to defend small feeding territories. Variation in feeding strategies allowed spatial partitioning of the feeding area. Reddish egret pellets contained mostly sheepshead minnows *(Cyprinodon variegatus;* Simersky 1971) or longnose killifish *(Fundulus similis;* McMurry 1971) along with pinfish *(Lagodon rhomboides)* and striped mullet *(Mugil cephalus).* Tricolored herons also preferred sheepshead minnows, and snowy egret diets are primarily composed of sheepshead minnow, anchovies *(Anchoa* spp.), and gulf menhaden *(Brevoortia patronus).* Stomach contents of recently deceased great blue heron nestlings included sheepshead minnows and anchovies, and 12 large brown shrimp *(Farfantepenaeus aztecus)* were regurgitated by a fledgling during banding. Increased water turbidity caused by deposition of dredged material prior to the 1971 breeding season appeared to inhibit feeding by adults around the islands (Simersky 1971). However, when waters cleared at the end of the breeding season, fledged young were seen feeding in areas that had previously been too turbid.

Key Rookery Islands

Upper Laguna Madre   Pita Island/Humble Channel Spoil rookery includes two portions of a natural island of 5.4 ha (13.3 ac) and ten dredged material islands of 1.8 ha (4.4 ac) (A. H. Chaney, pers. comm.). The natural island has been modified for oil production, which has limited available nesting habitat. The dredged material islands include shrubs and herbaceous vegetation.

South Bird Island is located south of North Bird Island in upper Laguna Madre

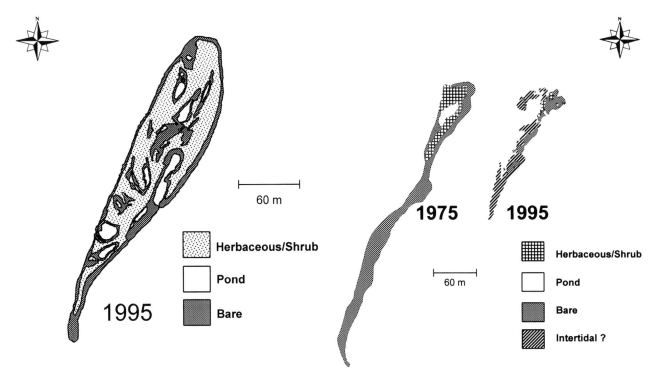

Fig. 12.1. *Nesting habitats for South Bird Island rookery in upper Laguna Madre (Smith and Cox 1998)*

Fig. 12.2. *Vegetation changes and nesting habitat for Marker 63 (New Marker 127) Island, part of Marker 63–65 (New Marker 127–131) rookery (1975 map modified from Chaney et al. 1978; 1995 map from Smith and Cox 1998)*

and encompasses about 5 ha (12.4 ac) of yucca, prickly pear, subshrubs, grasses, and loose sand/shell hash habitat. The island is relatively similar to North Bird Island but has several interior ponds with some tidal connections (fig. 12.1; Smith and Cox 1998); it is within the Padre Island National Seashore boundary but is managed by the National Audubon Society (TCWS 1982). This island has experienced prolonged and extensive colonial waterbird nesting usage (A. H. Chaney, pers. comm.).

LM 63A (New Marker 127) dredged material island (located within Padre Island National Seashore boundaries) is an elongated island that has undergone significant erosion since 1975 (fig. 12.2). This island is part of the Marker 63–65 Island (New Marker 127–131) rookery. The southwestern spit documented in 1975 was used by ground-nesting species that prefer shell or sand berms. In 1995, vegetation at the northern tip was composed of bushy sea-ox-eye daisy, common ragweed, and camphor daisy, all in small relict patches. Although the bare and intertidal areas to the south are probably at elevations too low to support nesting species during high tides (Smith and Cox 1998), ground-nesting species still attempt to nest in this area (A. H. Chaney, pers. comm.).

Marker 81 (New Marker 163) Spoil Island is located in upper Laguna Madre adjacent to the Gulf Intracoastal Waterway within the boundary of Padre Island National Seashore. The dredged material island encompassed about 1.7 ha (4.2 ac) in the 1970s (TCWS 1982) but decreased to about 1.1 ha (2.8 ac) by 1986 (Coste and Skoruppa 1989). Nesting habitats include shrubs, subshrubs, and bare sand (TCWS 1982). The entire island has continued to decrease in areal extent from erosion (fig. 12.3). The bare habitat suitable for ground nesters in the 1970s has become intertidal flats along the southern portions, and the northern perimeter exhibits an abrupt terrace from herb-shrub habitat to a narrow bare beach, then becomes intertidal

Fig. 12.3. *Vegetation changes and nesting habitat for Marker 81 (New Marker 163) rookery (1975 map modified from Chaney et al. 1978; 1995 map from Smith and Cox 1998)*

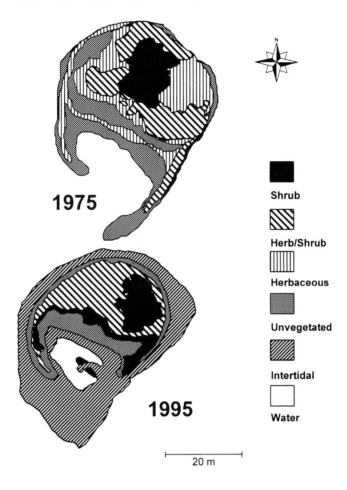

habitat. A narrow herbaceous area is located downslope from the higher, herbaceous/shrub habitat primarily composed of seashore paspalum *(Paspalum vaginatum)*. The herb-shrub habitat includes saline aster *(Aster tenuifolius)*, common ragweed, and bermudagrass *(Cynodon dactylon)* (Smith and Cox 1998).

Lower Laguna Madre of Texas   Green Island Cut Spoil is located east of Laguna Atascosa National Wildlife Refuge. In 1980, it had a total area of 8 ha (20 ac) with a maximum elevation of 4 m (13 ft) (TCWS 1982). The island is primarily unvegetated, with patches of low vegetation, and supports large colonies of Sandwich and royal terns. An increase in tricolored herons and other shrub-nesting species was documented in mid-1980s, but they declined thereafter (TCWC 1998). The rookery is under management of the Texas Audubon Society sanctuary program.

Green Island is a natural island adjacent to Laguna Atascosa National Wildlife Refuge and south of Green Island Cut Spoil. The area of the colony was estimated at 10 ha (24.7 ac) or less in 1980, with a maximum elevation of 5 m (16.5 ft). Most of the island is densely vegetated with thorny shrubs, small trees, and cactus. The rookery has supported a diversity of shrub-nesting wading birds since the surveys began (TCWS 1982; TCWC 1998). The Texas Audubon Society sanctuary program oversees management of the rookery island.

Three Island Spoil encompasses about 7.2 km (6 mi) of discontinuous, dredged material islands adjacent to the GIWW. The low sand and shell beaches and grass/subshrub zones have supported high numbers of laughing gull pairs (ranging from 2,000 to 10,000 most years), and royal and Sandwich terns (>1,100 and 300 pairs, respectively). This rookery is also managed by Texas Audubon Society sanctuary program.

Laguna Madre de Tamaulipas   Numerous small islands with low relief are located in northern Laguna Madre de Tamaulipas. Most are sparsely vegetated and a few have supported colonial waterbirds (Chapman 1988). American white pelicans nested under low, dense blackbrush *(Acacia rigidula)*. Other species (great blue herons, snowy egrets) also were documented in 1977.

Selected Species of Concern

American White Pelican   American white pelicans have maintained a viable nesting population in the upper Laguna Madre for many years, moving from island to island in the past 20 years (fig. 12.4). Overall, counts have not varied much throughout the survey period, remaining at an average of 262 birds (A. H. Chaney, pers. comm.). From the 1880s until 1980, pelicans maintained a nesting population on South Bird Island (A. H. Chaney, pers. comm.). The nesting population was documented on South Bird Island rookery from 1973 to 1975. In 1976–77, 120 nests were established at nearby South of South Bird Island rookery. The movement was attributed to tick infestation and predator visitation by coyotes (A. H. Chaney, pers. comm.). No birds nested in South Bird Island rookery in 1978, and few were recorded in 1979. Total pair numbers were lower in these years, then 100 pairs nested on South of South Bird Island in 1980. In 1981, two nesting populations were documented: on South of South Bird Island and at East Potrero Grande in the Land-Cut

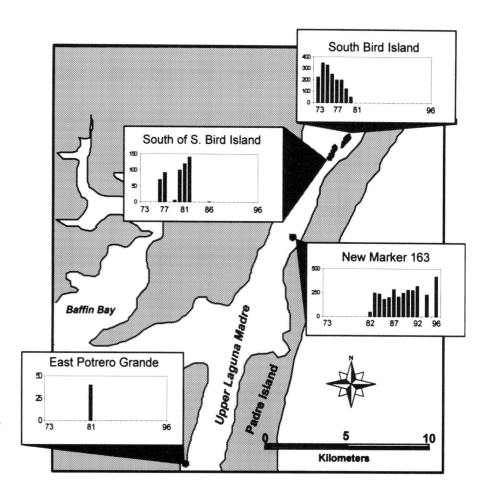

Fig. 12.4. Summary of nesting population dynamics for American white pelicans in upper Laguna Madre, documented from rookeries at South Bird Island; South of South Bird Island; Marker 81 (New Marker 163); and East Potrero Grande spoil island (Modified from Smith and Cox 1998)

area (this was the only year the latter site was used). The birds moved southward in 1982 to Marker 81 (New Marker 163) Island rookery. The entire nesting population have been documented as nesting in this rookery since 1983, although one nesting pair was documented in South of South Bird Island rookery in 1986 and four pair in 1990 (A. H. Chaney, pers. comm.).

Several explanations have been postulated in an effort to understand this species' migration among the islands, including elevated ectoparasite populations in established rookeries, storms, predator disturbance, and brood reduction (Chapman 1988). A coyote was removed from the area west of South Bird Island and a badger was observed on the island in 1978 (A. H. Chaney, pers. comm.). Since the islands are located within the Padre Island National Seashore, the rookeries have had limited human disturbance. The island's location in proximity to the bay shoreline of Padre Island, and the shallow lagoon between this shore and the rookeries could be a corridor for predators (e.g., coyotes, raccoons, feral hogs). Although no documentation is available of storm tides decimating the nests and young, it is possible that the birds moved due to repeated nest failures. Additionally, it was noted that although nesting pairs are an indirect indicator of nest success, years were documented when pairs produced eggs or young that were abandoned prior to fledging (1930, 1978, 1981).

Reddish Egret   Wading birds have used the dredged material islands in the Laguna Madre of Texas for many years (Bent 1926). As early as the 1950s, scientists became concerned about decreases in nesting populations of some species (Allen 1954; Cottam 1970). Reddish egrets have been described as a species of extremely restricted distribution (Oberholser 1974), utilizing coastal bays and marshes along the Gulf of Mexico and Caribbean coastlines (Bent 1926; Palmer 1962). Populations of reddish egrets have been recovering along the Texas coast following a precipitous decline at the turn of the century. The dramatic decrease in numbers was attributed to impacts from plume hunters, and no rookeries were documented from around 1900 to 1918 along the Texas coast.

Reddish egrets were recorded in the Second Chain of Islands in Mesquite Bay north of Laguna Madre in 1918 (Pearson 1922), and in 1922 they were found on Big Bird Island and Green Island in the Laguna Madre. A population decline was reported from 1939 to 1950 along the central coast; numbers decreased from 4,000 to 2,800 on Green Island, the largest known colony. Increased human activity near rookeries was the suspected cause of the declines (Allen 1954). About 40–50% of the world population is now located in the Laguna Madre of Texas and other Texas bays to the north (Paul 1991, in Farmer and Carrera Gonzalez 1993).

Reddish egrets were present along the east coast of Mexico in Laguna Madre de Tamaulipas and on the Campeche/Yucatán coasts during surveys in 1971 and 1973–76 (Sprunt and Knoder 1980). Colonies were not large in the Laguna (see table 12.4), and the total population was estimated <500 pairs. This geographic area is important for wintering reddish egrets (Allen 1954, 1955), presumably migrating from Laguna Madre of Texas to use foraging habitat in Laguna Madre de Tamaulipas (Farmer and Carrera Gonzalez 1993). Lagoonal waters flood the flats during successive north fronts, providing excellent winter habitat for this species. Individuals begin southward migration from rookeries in Laguna Madre of Texas to Laguna Madre de Tamaulipas in early fall (Farmer 1991). More information on wintering ecology of reddish egrets is provided in chapter 13.

Black Skimmer   Black skimmers typically nest in low-lying areas of loose sand and shell, depositing 3–5 eggs in shallow depressions (Sprunt 1925; Tomkins 1933;

DePue 1974). DePue (1974) studied a colony of black skimmers on dredged material islands at the mouth of Baffin Bay in 1972–73. He found that sediment composition in skimmer colonies was sand and shell (83–91%), silt (6–9%), and clay (2–11%). Sparse vegetation may be present, usually accounting for <30% cover of less than 25 cm height. Vegetation included prairie bluet *(Hedyotis nigricans)*, camphorweed *(Heterotheca subaxillaris)*, annual seepweed *(Suaeda linearis)*, and sea purslane. Under normal circumstances, nests with eggs were rarely left unattended. If neither parent is incubating, at least one stands nearby. Only when disturbance occurred did the pair leave the eggs. The role of the mate not incubating the eggs involved defending the nest from both ground and aerial intruders. The male provides whole fish to the young, delivering the meal to the nest. Most of the fish were identified as sheepshead minnow, striped mullet, ladyfish *(Elops saurus)*, and tidewater silverside *(Menidia beryllina* [= *peninsulae]*). Two to three weeks after hatching, the nests were abandoned and the young moved to the protective cover of dense vegetation.

Black skimmers nest on unvegetated shell hash berms subject to tidal inundation. Such locations place the nest and eggs in danger from storm tides and waves, often resulting in reproductive failure. If this event occurs early in the breeding season, the skimmers may reestablish the nest and successfully raise young in the same year (Bent 1921; Tomkins 1933). It is unclear why these birds nest in vulnerable areas; possibly they are poor competitors for nest sites (Pearson 1922), though capable of repeated reproductive investment (Bent 1921). They also may prefer to nest away from other species and therefore may not nest in established rookeries. However, they are particularly susceptible to human disturbance, selecting low-lying areas used by humans later in the nesting season (e.g., on bay beaches, along causeway frontage areas). Human disturbance in black skimmer rookeries may result in detrimental exposure of eggs or nestlings to the sun; prolonged separation from the parents; disruption of feeding; egg theft by gulls, particularly laughing gulls; or nest abandonment (DePue 1974; Chaney et al. 1996).

Black skimmers may nest in association with terns, especially least terns and gull-billed terns; however, skimmers usually maintain separate areas on islands with sufficient space for partitioning. Black skimmer colonies were located at lower, less vegetated areas, whereas gull-billed terns nested in mats of dead vegetation at slightly more elevated locations (DePue 1974). When interspecific colonies were documented, skimmers appeared to be more restrictive in habitat selection and terns more flexible, nesting in both bare areas and dead vegetation mats. This nesting association seemed advantageous to both species, as they combined their defenses against intruding laughing gulls.

Declining nesting populations of black skimmers in upper Laguna Madre and other rookeries in the Texas Coastal Bend have been attributed to erosion and loss of suitable habitats protected from disturbance (Chaney et al. 1996). Recommendations for ensuring nesting skimmer and tern population recovery include: (1) periodic redeposition of dredged material on eroding islands; (2) periodic creation of new small to moderate-sized dredged material islands with sufficient elevation to prevent inundation from storm tides and with little vegetation (to minimize laughing gull nesting habitat); (3) prohibiting construction of new cabins and limiting human use; (4) establishing cabin use rules to reduce disturbance during nesting season; and (5) initiating a public awareness program to educate visitors about the sensitivity of rookeries to disturbance (DePue 1974).

Laughing Gull Laughing gull nesting colonies typically have negative impacts on other colonial waterbird species, particularly ground-nesting skimmers, gulls, and terns. Laughing gull nesting populations have been relatively stable since 1973 and they constitute half to three-quarters of the total population of many rookeries. Although nesting pairs have declined in some rookeries, particularly at Marker 81 (New Marker 163) Island, numbers of pairs have increased in other rookeries (e.g., Pita Island/Humble Channel Spoil). In most cases, laughing gulls are abundant, but the range of variability indicates that there may be large population fluctuations both between and within years among rookeries (TCWC 1998).

13 Shorebirds and Wading Birds

KIM WITHERS

The Laguna Madre in Texas and Mexico contains some of the largest expanses of undisturbed wetland complexes in the Western Hemisphere (Baldassarre et al. 1989) and is one of the most significant areas for aquatic bird life on the Gulf of Mexico coast (Senner and Howe 1984; Morrison et al. 1993). For migrating and wintering shorebirds (Charadrii) using the Central Flyway, the wind-tidal flats and barrier beaches of the Laguna Madre represent the largest continuous expanse of suitable habitats between northern breeding grounds and more distant wintering grounds in South America. Laguna Madre de Tamaulipas held 65% of all shorebirds counted on the Mexican Gulf/Caribbean Coast during 1993 (Morrison et al. 1993). It is probable that most of the threatened Great Plains population of piping plover (*Charadrius melodus*) winter in Laguna Madre (Haig and Plissner 1993), and both barrier islands and tidal flats appear to be essential habitats (Withers 1994; Zonick and Ryan 1994). Washover passes are used as nesting habitat by a few shorebirds such as snowy plovers *(C. alexandrinus)* and are important roost sites (Rupert 1997; Zonick 1997a, b). Other habitats that may be used are coastal ponds and wetlands farther inland (Chaney 1981; Bacak-Clements 1988; Bauer 1993) and dredged material placement areas (EHA 1997; Zonick et al. 1998). For wading birds (Ciconiiformes), the Laguna Madre provides plentiful shallow water habitats where they feed on fish and invertebrates (plates 43, 44). Flooded tidal flats, seagrass meadows, shallow bay margins, and coastal ponds are used as foraging habitats. In addition, many species breed on natural and dredge material islands in the region (see chapter 12).

Shorebird Abundance and Distribution in Texas

Barrier Island Beaches Shorebirds, gulls, and terns use barrier island beaches for foraging, resting, nesting, and roosting. On Padre Island National Seashore, 30 shorebird species (table 13.1), and 20 gull and tern species have been documented (Chapman 1984; Ecoservices 1993b). The most common and abundant shorebird, gull, and tern species were sanderlings *(Calidris alba)*, laughing gulls *(Larus atricilla)*, and royal terns *(Sterna maxima)*. Total abundance appears bimodal (fig. 13.1), with a large peak during fall migration (August–September) and a smaller peak during spring (March–April). Numbers were lowest in early winter (December–January) and June. Gulls and terns constituted at least 50% of the total during all seasons except spring, when shorebirds dominated (Chapman 1984). Birds concentrated in the damp foreshore, where shorebirds foraged for benthic invertebrates and gulls and terns loafed. Piping and snowy plovers, ruddy turnstones *(Arenaria interpres)*, and a few other species foraged along the berm, picking at debris. The backshore was rarely used as either foraging or resting habitat. Barrier island beaches in Texas do not appear to support nesting shorebirds.

Table 13.1. Relative abundances of shorebirds in Texas on tidal flats bordering the Laguna Madre (Ecoservices 1993a; Withers 1994, 1996b, c, 1998; Withers and Tunnell 1998), beaches of Padre and Mustang islands (Chapman 1984; Ecoservices 1993b), and Padre Island washover passes (Ecoservices 1993a).

Species	Tidal Flats	Beach	Passes
Peeps (Calidris mauri, C. semipalmatus)	A	R	A
Dunlin (Calidris alpina)	A	*	A
Least sandpiper (Calidris minutilla)	A	R	A
Dowitchers (Limnodromous spp.)	C	R	A
Willet (Cataptrophorus semipalmatus)	C	A	C
Sanderling (Calidris alba)	C	A	A
Black-bellied plover (Pluvialis squatorola)	C	A	C
Piping plover (Charadrius melodus)	C–U	A	U
Snowy plover (Charadrius alexandrinus)	C–U	C	C
Long-billed curlew (Numenius americanus)	C–U	C	R
Ruddy turnstone (Arenaria interpres)	C–U	A	U
Red knot (Calidris canutus)	C–U	A	A
Semipalmated plover (Charadrius semipalmatus)	C–U	R	R
American avocet (Recurvirostra americana)	C–U	*	C
Marbled godwit (Limosa fedoa)	U	R	R
Lesser yellowlegs (Tringa flavipes)	U	R	U
Black-necked stilt (Himantopus mexicanus)	U	R	R
Greater yellowlegs (Tringa melanoleucus)	U	R	R
Wilson's plover (Charadrius wilsonia)	U	A	U
Stilt sandpiper (Calidris himantopus)	U–R	R	U
Baird's sandpiper (Calidris bairdii)	R	*	
Wilson's phalarope (Phalaropus tricolor)	R	*	R
American oystercatcher (Haematopus palliatus)	R	R	
Spotted sandpiper (Actitis macularia)	R	R	R
Killdeer (Charadrius vociferus)	R	*	
Whimbrel (Numenius phaeopus)	R	*	R
Pectoral sandpiper (Calidris melanotus)	R	*	
White-rumped sandpiper (Calidris fuscicollis)	R	*	U
Solitary sandpiper (Tringa solitaria)	R	*	
Lesser golden plover (Pluvialis dominica)		*	
Upland sandpiper (Bartramia longicauda)		*	
Buff-breasted sandpiper (Tryngites subruficollis)		*	

Note: A = abundant; C = common; U = uncommon; R = rare; * = present but no abundance data available.

Fig. 13.1. Average monthly total
avian abundance along an 8.1 km
(5 mi) stretch of beach north of
Malaquite Beach (Padre Island
National Seashore), October 1979–
June 1981 (Chapman 1984)

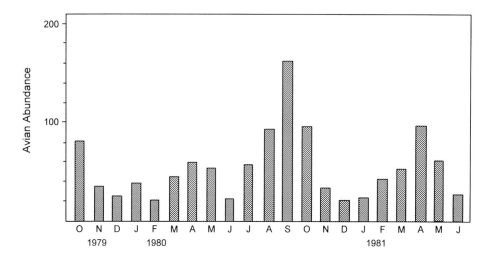

Fig. 13.1. Average monthly total avian abundance along an 8.1 km (5 mi) stretch of beach north of Malaquite Beach (Padre Island National Seashore), October 1979–June 1981 (Chapman 1984)

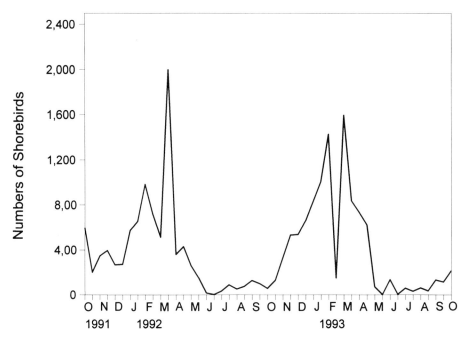

Fig. 13.2. Total number of shorebirds censused on a blue-green algal flat on north Padre Island, October 1991–93 (Withers 1994)

Wind-Tidal Flats   Large numbers of shorebirds use exposed tidal flats in Laguna Madre as foraging habitat during winter and migratory periods (Senner and Howe 1984; Bauer 1993; Ecoservices 1993a; Haig and Plissner 1993; Withers 1994, 1996b, 1998; Brush 1995; Lee 1995; Withers and Tunnell 1998). A few shorebirds nest on the flats, notably snowy and Wilson's *(Charadrius wilsonia)* plovers. Most wind-tidal flats in Laguna Madre are at least partially covered with a mat of blue-green algae, but vegetated and unvegetated sand flats are also present. Shorebird abundance and habitat use, as well as prey abundance and biomass, have been studied extensively on a number of blue-green algal flats in upper Laguna Madre, but nonalgal flats have received little attention. There have been few studies of shorebird ecology in lower Laguna Madre.

As many as 37 species of shorebirds have been documented on tidal flats on the central Texas Gulf Coast (Rappole and Blacklock 1985). During 1991–93, large numbers of shorebirds used mainland mudflat areas from August to May (Bauer 1993). On barrier island blue-green algal flats (Withers 1994, 1996b, c, 1998; Withers and Tunnell 1998), shorebirds are most abundant from late fall (November) through early spring (March–April; fig. 13.2). Overall, sandpipers *(Calidris* spp.), notably least sandpipers *(C. minutilla)* and dunlins *(C. alpina)*, were the most common and abundant species (see table 13.1), followed by piping and snowy plovers. Highest populations of shorebirds were observed after the February low tide through March, when flats were exposed and used as a staging area for northbound migrants. Peak densities of the most abundant species were often staggered throughout winter and spring, and many individual species peaks were offset from one another (Withers 1994). This suggested that movements by the largest flocks of a particular species or species group were timed to avoid being present in the same place at the same time as large flocks of other behaviorally similar species, analogous to the pattern reported by Recher (1966) on the California coast. Numbers of shorebirds were typically low but variable between May and October, with few birds using the flats during fall (Withers 1994). Rising water levels through fall limit space available to birds for foraging. Sandpipers, particularly western sandpipers *(C. mauri)*, were the only short-legged shorebirds that were relatively abundant on algal flats during fall.

Most shorebirds using blue-green algal flats in upper Laguna Madre are broadly grouped into a shallow-probing, surface-feeding guild, relying primarily on visual cues to locate prey. However, this guild can be further divided into three microhabitat guilds based on apparent microhabitat preferences (Withers 1994; for a more detailed explanation microhabitats see chapter 9). Sandpipers and black-bellied plovers *(Pluvialis squatorola)* were the dominant members of a guild that preferred the wet microhabitat, or areas with wet or saturated sediments. Piping, snowy, and semipalmated *(Charadrius semipalmatus)* plovers used the damp microhabitat, or areas that appear damp or dry on the surface, in nearly equal proportions with the wet microhabitat. Longer-legged, longer-billed shorebirds like dunlins, dowitchers *(Limnodromous* spp.), and willets *(Catoptrophorus semipalmatus)* preferred open water microhabitats, or areas covered with at least 5 cm (2.0 in) of water. The western sandpiper was the only bird showing a preference for the intertidal microhabitat, or areas less than 4 cm (1.6 in) deep at the water's edge, but was found most often in the wet microhabitat, so was included in that guild.

Lee (1995) conducted weekly censuses of shorebirds on a vegetated sandflat just south of Corpus Christi Bay on Mustang Island. The site was not heavily used by shorebirds. Willets and black-bellied plovers were the most common and abundant species. Total numbers of birds were greatest during November–December 1990 and March–April 1991. Few birds were observed in June or July, but fall migrants were evident during late summer. Willets used submerged habitats on the flat most frequently. Falling tides, resulting in increased exposed sandflat habitat, often resulted in significantly more birds using the sandflat when compared to nearby beach habitats.

The entire lagoon side of Padre Island National Seashore from Yarborough Pass to Mansfield Pass was surveyed to determine shorebird habitat use and numbers during eight months in 1992–93 (Ecoservices 1993a). Thirty-two species were observed. In July and October 1992, a pulse of fall migrants was evident; however, the 320 individuals observed during the October survey were less than 1% of the maximum of 86,776 observed during February 1993 (fig. 13.3). Few individuals were seen in November or December. Although the area surveyed was about 80 km (50 mi) long, birds were mostly found in the area between Yarborough Pass and Mile 32 due to a lack of suitable flat habitat within the boundaries of Padre Island National Seashore. The majority of shorebirds were observed in wind-tidal flat habitats, but washover channels that contained water were also used by a number of birds, particularly in the area south of Mile 32.

A number of tidal flat habitats in and near Laguna Atascosa National Wildlife Refuge were surveyed in lower Laguna Madre during November–February 1992–93 and 1993–94 (Brush 1995). Four habitats were censused about every two weeks dur-

Fig. 13.3. *Total numbers of birds counted on tidal flats between Yarborough Pass and Mansfield Pass during eight surveys in 1992–93 (Data from Ecoservices 1993a)*

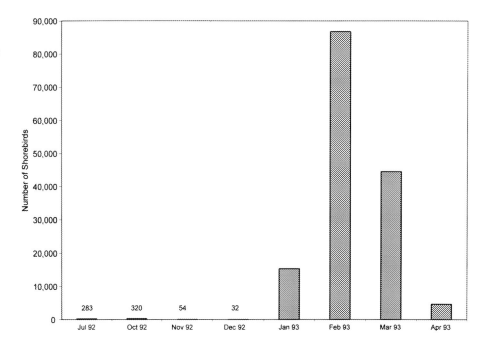

ing the study: high mudflat/pool—a complex of enclosed shallow water and exposed, firm mudflats with poorly developed algal mats; high algal flat—wind-tidal flats with well-developed algal mat; low mudflat—shoreline and frequently flooded mudflats and seagrass areas; and low seagrass flat—low mudflats with about 50% coverage by turtle-grass *(Thalassia testudinum)* that were inundated and exposed by daily tides. The total number of species observed was 23, and 11 species were recorded in all four habitats. Numbers varied between years and months but were highest during December and January. The highest numbers for both species and individuals were found in the high mudflat/pool habitat; only limited numbers of shorebirds used the low seagrass flat. Numbers of some species, notably western sandpipers, fluctuated in response to changing water levels in all study areas, with overall shorebird use declining as habitats dried out due to prolonged exposure.

Brush (1995) grouped the shorebirds in his study into three guilds based on habitat preferences: shallow water; exposed mudflat; and water/mudflat. The species in the shallow water and exposed mudflat guilds were seen foraging in those habitats in at least 95% of observations. Long-legged, long-billed shorebirds such as American avocets *(Recurvirostra americana)* and stilt sandpipers *(Calidris himantopus)* used the shallow water exclusively. Visual foragers such as ringed plovers, ruddy turnstones, black-bellied plovers, least sandpipers, and sanderlings constituted the exposed mudflat guild. The water/mudflat guild was composed of shorebirds that are primarily tactile foragers, such as willets, dunlins, and dowitchers, or that at least include a tactile component in their foraging strategy, such as western sandpipers.

Shorebird density was determined on a tidal flat just south of the Land-Cut (Mile Marker 45) during December 1997–April 1998 (Withers 1998). This wind-tidal flat was much different than similar habitats in upper Laguna Madre because the algal mat was poorly developed. Only seven shorebird species were observed. Densities ranged from under 5/ha (2/ac) during December, March and April to nearly 10/ha (4/ac) during January and February.

Other Habitats   Washover passes were used regularly by a number of shorebird species, including piping and snowy plovers (Ecoservices 1993b; Zonick 1997a, b;

see table 13.1). Passes were most commonly used by shorebirds when bayside tides were high and during spring migration (Zonick 1997a, b). Passes supported large breeding colonies of snowy plovers as well as smaller breeding populations of a few other shorebirds, notably Wilson's plovers.

Habitat in dredged material placement areas range from well-developed uplands to mudflats and open water. Seventeen shorebird species were observed in dredged material placement areas in lower Laguna Madre during February 1997 (EHA 1997). Willets and sanderlings were the most frequently observed species. Snowy plovers and several other shorebird species nested within dredged material placement areas during 1997 (Zonick et al. 1998).

Over 100 species of birds have been documented using coastal ponds and wetlands near Laguna Madre (Chaney 1988). At least 15 species of shorebirds use these habitats, and peak abundances coincided with fall and spring migratory periods (Bacak-Clements 1988; Bauer 1993). Bauer (1993) classified the majority of shorebirds he observed as winter residents.

Shorebirds of Laguna Madre de Tamaulipas

Laguna Madre de Tamaulipas supports more wintering shorebirds than any other coastal wetland or lagoon system on the Mexican Gulf/Caribbean Coast (Morrison et al. 1993). Twenty-four species were documented. The only substantial numbers of small shorebirds (sandpipers and banded plovers) found on the Mexican coast were found within the lagoon. The area was also important to dowitchers. The majority of shorebirds were found on extensive mainland and barrier island tidal flats.

Sanderlings were the most abundant shorebird wintering on barrier island beaches adjacent to Laguna Madre de Tamaulipas (Morrison et al. 1993). Several species of shorebirds, including snowy and Wilson's plovers, nest in the broad coppice dune zone on beaches between the Río Grande and Mezquital, Tamaulipas (Zonick 1997a).

Seasonality and residency status of some of the more common species have been described. Perales Flores and Contreras Balderas (1986) divided the lagoon into three zones. The northern zone, consisting of isolated mudflats and ephemeral wetlands between the Río Grande and the northern Laguna Madre, was used by many species of shorebirds. Farmer and Carrera Gonzalez (1993) describe this area as broad tidal flat but without regular tidal inundation, with most flooding occurring after heavy rainfall and only persisting if rainfall was regular. The northern lagoon was designated as the central zone, and the southern zone consisted of the southern lagoon. Few shorebirds were specifically listed as occurring in either the central or southern zone; however, they undoubtedly use extensive mudflats found in these zones. A number of species occurred throughout the lagoon, including black-bellied plovers, willets, sanderlings, western sandpipers, and least sandpipers. A few species were found only in the southern zone, including snowy and Wilson's plovers. Eleven of the 18 species were listed as year-round residents. With the exception of Wilson's plovers, the remaining six species were resident during winter and spring. Wilson's plovers breed in the area and were found only during summer. All 16 shorebird species observed between La Carboneras and La Pesca were found during fall, but only nine were also found during winter (Contreras Balderas et al. 1990).

Nonbreeding Ecology of Shorebirds

Since most shorebirds are found in Laguna Madre during winter and migratory periods, this section of the chapter is focused on nonbreeding ecology. The breeding ecology of snowy plovers in the area is fairly well known but is described later in the chapter.

Shorebirds spend the majority of the year in migratory staging areas or stopovers or on their wintering grounds. In general, shorebirds concentrate in a few stopover sites that are separated by fairly large distances (Goss-Custard and Durrell 1990), and individuals of many species return to the same staging areas and wintering grounds year after year, exhibiting remarkable site fidelity (Pitelka et al. 1980; Johnson and Baldassarre 1988). Migrating and wintering shorebirds spend most of their time foraging (Senner and Howe 1984). There is evidence that most mortality occurs during winter, and it is largely related to food shortages (Goss-Custard 1979, 1985). Shorebirds may starve or suffer increased predation or disease due to malnutrition, and even small increases in winter mortality due to habitat loss or degradation have the potential to result in large declines in shorebird populations (Goss-Custard 1979; Goss-Custard and Durrell 1990).

The primary food source for wintering and migrating shorebirds is macrobenthic invertebrates inhabiting intertidal flats. Densities of shorebirds and their prey exist as a mosaic or gradient at several levels of temporal and spatial scale (Goss-Custard and Charman 1976). Variability in food supply appears to cause shorebirds to concentrate in areas of resource abundance (Goss-Custard 1983). Densities and distributions of shorebirds have been linked to distribution and density of their prey in Europe (e.g., Wolff 1969; Goss-Custard 1970; Goss-Custard et al. 1977; Bryant 1979; Goss-Custard 1983; Meire and Kuyken 1984) and North America (e.g., Hicklin and Smith 1984; Kelsey and Hassall 1989; Wilson 1990; Colwell and Landrum 1993; Withers 1994). In fact, the circular or elliptical migration patterns exhibited by many shorebird species are thought to have evolved in response to spatial and temporal changes in resource (food) abundance and availability (Cooke 1910; McNeil and Burton 1977; Williams et al. 1977; Harrington and Morrison 1979; Morrison 1984; Hicklin 1987; Myers et al. 1987, 1990; Withers and Chapman 1993). Wunderle and colleagues (1989) noted that northbound birds appeared to bypass the Caribbean, possibly because the January–May dry season limits invertebrate populations on mudflats dependent on rainfall runoff.

As shorebirds concentrate in areas of resource abundance, habitat quality may decrease due to interference (Goss-Custard and Durrell 1990) or declines in prey availability. Interference may cause agonistic or competitive interactions between birds, often resulting in younger, inexperienced birds being forced into marginal feeding habitats. Direct interference between morphologically similar species (i.e., those with similar bill sizes and/or similar foraging behavior) may be prevented by timing migratory movements to avoid being present in the same area at the same time (Recher 1966). Concentration of birds in areas may also affect prey availability, either by driving prey organisms deeper into the substrate and out of reach of probing bills (Goss-Custard 1970) or through depletion. Numerous studies have demonstrated that shorebirds are capable of depleting the supply of prey organisms (e.g., Baker and Baker 1973; Bengtson et al. 1976; O'Conner and Brown 1977; Schneider 1973; Evans et al. 1979; Schneider and Harrington 1981; Quammen 1984; Withers 1994). They typically remove 20–40% of invertebrate standing crop in temperate areas of Europe and North America (Goss-Custard 1980).

Importance of Laguna Madre Tidal Flats   Flooding and exposure of wind-tidal flats determines extent of biological development, especially abundance and persistence of benthic invertebrate communities (chapter 9). Frequent flooding is necessary to maintain invertebrate communities, but flats must be exposed for shorebirds to use them (Withers 1994). On flats that are frequently flooded, invertebrates are usually most abundant during winter and spring, although a brief summer flush may occur during June. Summer low tides extirpate communities on most flats, which become very hot, dry, and hypersaline. Abundance of benthic organisms mirrors shorebird abundance within the system but may be modified locally as shorebirds deplete patches of organisms. Numbers of shorebirds also fluctuate in response to local and seasonal changes in water levels. Few shorebirds are present on tidal flats during fall, not only because fall high tides reduce foraging area but also due to summer low tides causing a lack of invertebrate prey. Barrier island beaches are typically used by shorebirds when preferred bayshore habitats are unavailable (Zonick 2000). Withers and Chapman (1993) suggested that high resource availability during winter and early spring on tidal flats of the central Texas coast were logistically important in the evolution of migration routes of some shorebird species.

Within any given tidal flat, relative abundance and community composition of prey communities varies by microhabitat (for a detailed explanation of microhabitats, see chapter 9). Shorebirds foraging on wind-tidal flats in Laguna Madre can be broadly grouped into a shallow-probing, surface-feeding guild but can be further subdivided into microhabitat guilds based on microhabitat preferences (Withers 1994; see "Shorebird Abundance and Distribution in Texas" earlier in this chapter for a brief description). Despite the fact that the most prey was found in the intertidal microhabitat, it was used very little, suggesting that shallow-probing, surface-feeding shorebirds are inefficient foragers in areas covered by water. The western sandpiper was the only species that exhibited a preference for this microhabitat, suggesting that it includes a tactile element in its foraging strategy. This may help explain its presence during fall high tides, when flat microhabitats were essentially reduced to the intertidal microhabitat only. The wet and damp microhabitats were used more than were expected based on prey availability. These data suggest that resources may be limiting, and competition for space and resources may be intense in preferred microhabitats, since interference tends to be more pronounced among visual foragers (Goss-Custard 1980). These results were contrary to the lack of competition inferred from large niche breadths and overlaps among the most abundant species in nearby Oso Bay (Withers and Chapman 1993).

Association analysis (X^2) revealed significant associations between the wet guild and tanaid density and between the damp-wet guild and adult insect density (Withers 1994). Regression analysis of benthic variables, tide height, and shorebird numbers resulted in a number of strong relationships at several levels of spatial and temporal scale. Models at the spatial scale of site and temporal scale of season were the most predictive. Typically, bird numbers appeared more strongly dependent on benthic density than on benthic biomass. Tide height, an indirect measure of the area available for foraging, was often another important variable in significant models. At the spatial scale of estuary, tide height was negatively related to bird numbers, reflecting decreasing foraging area estuarywide as tide height increased. The landscape-level models suggested that sufficient area as well as adequate numbers of prey were important determinants of shorebird densities within the estuary. At the spatial scale of site, tide height was often positively related to shorebird density, a seemingly contradictory finding. However, on individual sites, shorebirds appeared to be responding to the frequency and extent of flooding, the primary means by which benthic organisms are recruited to flats, and the primary factor governing invertebrate community persistence. Seasonally, the best predictors of shorebird numbers were densities of aquatic-adapted organisms such as polychaetes. Taken together, these results indicated that overall shorebird numbers on tidal flats were determined by adequate total area estuarywide containing well-developed invertebrate communities as well as adequate seasonal flooding of sites to maintain local populations of invertebrates.

Shorebird Species of Concern

Piping Plover   In 1991, 55% of the population of the federally protected piping plover wintered in Texas, with over 43% on tidal flats (Haig and Plissner 1993). Piping plovers have been found on tidal flats and barrier island beaches throughout the Texas Laguna Madre and were documented during most of the previously cited studies. An atlas of piping plover sightings from 1992 to 1998 on the Texas coast has recently been completed (White and Elliott 1998). It is likely that many of the plovers "missing" from the wintering portion of the International Piping Plover censuses may be found in Laguna Madre de Tamaulipas. During recent winter censuses in Tamaulipas, several hundred piping plovers were counted on barrier islands and tidal flats adjacent to the lagoon (C. Zonick, pers. comm.).

Piping plovers were prominent members of shorebird communities of blue-green algal flats in the upper Laguna Madre (Withers 1994). They typically appeared on flats in late September, increased to a peak in December or January, then declined steadily until April when they left for the breeding grounds. They exhibited significant associations (X^2) with polychaetes, tanaids, and insect larvae. Regression analysis revealed that benthic variables, primarily polychaete density or biomass and/or density of insect larvae or tanaids, were the best predictors of piping plover abundance on blue-green algal flats.

On South Padre Island, piping plovers were present during all months but were most abundant between September and January (Garza 1997). They used a variety of habitats, but densities were highest on mudflats, followed by algal flats. They preferred to forage within 20 m (66 ft) of the water's edge, and most foraging activity occurred on mudflats, followed by algal flats and sandflats. Sandflats were used mostly for roosting.

Zonick (2000) compared ecology of piping plovers wintering in Laguna Madre to that of plovers wintering in the more estuarine northern Texas coast. Piping plovers occurred at higher densities on the upper coast than in Laguna Madre. Prey types differed markedly between the two systems (upper coast dominated by polychaetes vs. lower coast dominated by crustaceans and insect larvae), but foraging efficiency was similar. Piping plovers were more gregarious in Laguna Madre and exhibited lower levels of intraspecific aggression and territoriality than their upper coast counterparts. The greatest densities of piping plovers occurred where three habitat types (tidal flats, washover channels or passes, and beaches) were in close proximity. These birds were more common on barrier island tidal flats than on mainland tidal flats.

Zonick (2000) found that tidal amplitude was a strong determinant of piping plover use of tidal flats, with numbers decreasing as tides inundated flat areas. He also found strong relationships between total benthic density and flock size on individual sites. A multiple regression model comparing the relative effects of prey availability, bayshore habitat availability, beach habitat availability, and human disturbance on piping plover site abundance indicated that although piping plovers used bayshore flats when all habitat types were available, the factors most strongly associated with depressed site abundance along the Texas coast were linked to beach habitat quality and availability. The model suggests that overall barrier island carrying capacity is presently limited more by availability of protected beach habitat than the availability of tidal flats or other bayshore habitats.

Wintering piping plovers in lower Laguna Madre had relatively large home ranges, with most moving among a suite of widely spaced locations (Zonick et al. 1998). Dredged material disposal areas were rarely used. Piping plovers regularly moved between habitats, largely in response to flooding and exposure of preferred bayshore habitats. Although beaches were preferred secondary habitat on the upper and middle coast, mainland flats and washover passes were preferred over beaches in lower Laguna Madre. Barrier island beaches, mainland flats, and washover passes in lower Laguna Madre were critical high tide refuges and roosting areas. A complex of bayshore habitats (e.g., sandflats, mudflats) with small inlets (e.g., washover passes) and beaches appears essential to piping plovers in their wintering range (Johnson and Baldassarre 1988; Nicholls and Baldassarre 1990; Zonick 2000; Zonick et al. 1998). These findings underscore the need for a comprehensive, landscape approach to preserving habitat for piping plovers in Laguna Madre.

Snowy Plover Wintering snowy plover abundance and habitat use on tidal flats and adjacent habitats in Laguna Madre are similar to those of piping plovers (Ecoservices 1993a; Withers 1994, 1996b, 1998; Brush 1995; Withers and Tunnell 1998). Snowy plovers in lower Laguna Madre roosted almost exclusively in high flat habitats and appeared to require multiple roosts because they moved among multiple feeding areas (Zonick et al. 1998).

Nesting snowy plovers were found in a variety of habitats, including high sand flats, washover passes, and dredged material placement areas (Rupert 1997; Zonick 1997a; Zonick et al. 1998). Nesting begins in late March (Rupert 1997). Snowy plovers appeared to prefer nesting in shell-covered areas and lined their nests with shell fragments (Zonick 1997a). They often nested in association with least terns *(Sterna antillarum)* and may experience less predation due to the association (Rupert 1997; Zonick 1997a). Many plover nests in dredged material placement areas were found on the sides of bermlike perimeter levees, often in areas with accumulations of stones and shell fragments (Zonick et al. 1998). In Tamaulipas, snowy plovers appear to nest primarily on the beach in broad coppice dune fields bordering the shoreline (Zonick 1997a). Hatch rates and nest success were generally low (Rupert 1997; Zonick 1997a). High rates of mammalian predation were the primary cause of nest failure.

Wading Bird Abundance and Distribution

Although nonbreeding distribution of the most common wading bird species in Laguna Madre has been described to some extent, reddish egrets *(Egretta rufescens)* have received the most attention. There have been no studies of wading bird nonbreeding ecology or use of resources other than habitat within the system. Information concerning breeding ecology of some species (primarily colonial nesters) appears in chapter 12.

Wading bird use of flooded wind-tidal flats and adjacent shallow water areas has been quantified throughout the system, but their use of other habitats such as seagrass meadows has received only cursory attention. Nearly all common species may be found on tidal flats, but reddish egrets, great blue herons *(Ardea herodias)*, and great egrets *(Ardea alba)* are most frequently observed (Pulich et al. 1982; Farmer 1991, 1996; Ecoservices 1993a; Brush 1995; Withers 1996b). The reddish egret is the most abundant species. Great blue herons and reddish egrets are residents in the system, and most other species are highly migratory and move south during winter (Farmer 1991).

On or around algal flats in upper Laguna Madre, wading birds were most abundant from April to November (Farmer 1996; Withers 1996b; fig. 13.4). In surveys on the lagoon side of Padre Island between Yarborough Pass and Mansfield Pass, reddish egrets were the most common and abundant species, making up from 55 to 100% of all wading bird observations (Ecoservices 1993a). Overall, wading birds were most abundant in July 1992 and least abundant during October 1992; populations remained fairly steady from November to February then increased slightly to the end of the study in April 1993. Wading birds used flooded wind-tidal flat habitats, lagoon margins, grassflats, and washover channels containing water. Habitat availability for reddish egrets in upper Laguna Madre is reduced during late fall and

Fig. 13.4. *Total numbers of wading birds censused on blue-green algal flats in upper Laguna Madre or in adjacent shallow waters (Withers 1996b)*

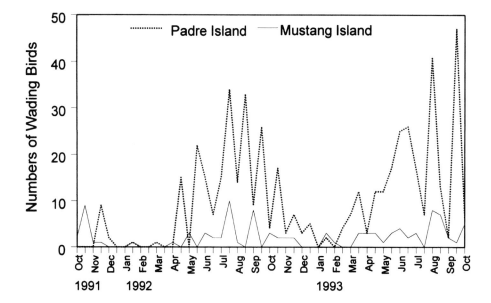

winter because persistent north winds raise water levels above these birds' preferred foraging depth (Farmer 1996).

During his study of shorebird habitat use in lower Laguna Madre, Brush (1995) noted that reddish egrets and snowy egrets *(Egretta thula)* "often occurred in large numbers" in the high mudflat/pool habitat and "some" reddish egrets and tricolored herons *(Egretta tricolor)* were found in the low seagrass flat. Great blue heron and reddish egret abundance in lower Laguna Madre increased from March to early December then declined sharply in late December (Farmer 1991). Little blue herons *(Egretta caerulea)* and great egrets were present only in low numbers and appeared to be resident species. The other three common species observed, snowy egrets, tricolored herons, and white ibis *(Eudocimus albus)*, were most abundant during summer (May–August).

Fourteen species of wading birds have been documented in Laguna Madre de Tamaulipas (Perales Flores and Contreras Balderas 1986; Contreras Balderas et al. 1990). The only quantitative study addressed reddish egret distribution (Farmer and Carrera Gonzalez 1993; see later discussion). Of the 14 species known to occur, eight were considered residents (Perales Flores and Contreras Balderas 1986). Seasonal occurrence of the other species varied with their migratory ecology, but none was found during summer. The eight resident species—great blue herons, great egrets, snowy egrets, tricolored herons, reddish egrets, little blue herons, cattle egrets *(Bubulcus ibis)*, white ibis, and white-faced ibis *(Plegadis chihi)*—were distributed throughout the lagoon. Green herons *(Butorides virescens)* were found only in the northern zone of wetlands between the Río Grande and the northern Laguna Madre. Black-crowned and yellow-crowned night herons *(Nycticorax nycticorax, Nyctanassa violacea)* and roseate spoonbills *(Ajaia ajaja)* were found only in the northern lagoon. No wading birds were found exclusively in the southern lagoon. Of the 11 species documented by Contreras Balderas and colleagues (1990), all but little blue herons were present during fall. They found no reddish egrets or black-crowned night herons during winter, but the remaining nine species were present.

Wading Bird Species of Concern

Reddish Egret　　Reddish egrets are more dependent on coastal areas than are other wading birds (Bent 1926; Palmer 1962; Oberholser 1974). The largest concentration of reddish egrets in the world is in the western Gulf of Mexico (Farmer and Carrera

Gonzalez 1993), where they are the most common wading bird throughout Laguna Madre in both Texas and Tamaulipas (Farmer 1991, 1996; Ecoservices 1993a; Farmer and Carrera Gonzalez 1993). They are relatively uncommon elsewhere. In general, most reddish egrets winter in Laguna Madre de Tamaulipas, with lower numbers in the lower Laguna Madre of Texas and upper Laguna Madre. Reddish egrets prefer tidal flat habitats and use the broad wind-tidal flats of the Laguna Madre at all water levels. These habitats are not used extensively by other wading bird species, which largely use flats as "traps" when pools form after water levels recede and leave fish behind (Farmer 1991). In lower Laguna Madre and Laguna Madre de Tamaulipas, most reddish egrets were found on broad tidal flat areas, with fewer than 1/km (1/0.6 mi) recorded in narrow bay-margin habitats (Farmer 1991, 1996; Farmer and Carrera Gonzalez 1993).

In Texas, reddish egrets began arriving during March in lower Laguna Madre, with most arriving in April (Farmer 1991). Numbers on tidal flats increased from March to December as adults and fledged young left breeding islands and as birds emigrated in from upper Laguna Madre during late fall, apparently because north winds reduced foraging habitat in the lagoon (Farmer 1996). Numbers declined sharply in late December (Farmer 1991). During January and February 1993, more than twice the number of reddish egrets found in upper Laguna Madre (379) were found in lower Laguna Madre (957; Farmer 1996). Aerial surveys in Laguna Madre de Tamaulipas during January 1992 and January 1993 (including Laguna Morales) estimated the population at about 1,500 birds (Farmer and Carrera Gonzalez 1993). The majority of the birds surveyed were found on the large wind-tidal flats at La Pesca and Laguna Morales (surveyed during 1993 only). These estimates combined with the estimated 2,000 birds in Texas Laguna Madre account for the combined total nesting pairs and their fledged young (≈3,500 birds). It appears that the great majority of adult breeding reddish egrets depend on tidal flats within these systems year-round, and postbreeding adults are weakly migratory between Texas and Tamaulipas to take advantage of changing habitat availability due to changing water levels.

Reddish egrets in lower Laguna Madre displayed an inclination to feed in flocks, a characteristic not previously noted in the literature (Farmer 1991). The tendency for birds to form flocks (to aggregate) as well as the number and size of flocks varied by site and by season. In spring, there were few flocks on any given site (12–30), consisting of an average of 30–38 birds, with less than 55% of all reddish egrets aggregated into flocks. In contrast, during fall, 59–83% of birds aggregated into flocks, flocks consisted of an average of 93–207 birds, and there were 17–64 flocks on a site. Results were variable during summer, but in areas where birds aggregated, the majority of birds were in flocks, and flocks were relatively large, averaging 98–203 birds.

Numbers at specific sites varied seasonally as birds moved throughout the system, probably in response to changing water levels and their effect on prey availability (Farmer 1991). Over 95% of reddish egrets fed in water of a depth less than half leg length or up to 15 cm (5.91 in) deep. Farmer (1991) formulated a simple, intuitive model to predict foraging habitat availability. The model tested the hypothesis that areas of extensive wind-tidal flats preferred by foraging reddish egrets are uniform, slightly sloping habitats where the area available for foraging remains more or less constant throughout the semi-annual water level cycle. As systemwide water levels rise or fall, the area between the water's edge and depths of ≤15 cm (5.91 in) remains about the same, simply moving higher up the slope or lower down the slope. Thus, foraging reddish egrets simply move "inland" as water levels rise and "bayward" as water levels fall. However, Farmer (1991) rejected the intuitive model because in reality, and despite their uniform appearance, most tidal flats in Laguna Madre do not slope enough for preferred foraging area to remain constant. Areas of broad tidal flat are, in fact, flat or shallow bowls that vary by only a few centimeters over hundreds of meters. The combination of wind-tidal flat topography and hydrology and the bird's narrow water depth requirement restricts available habitats even during seasonal high tides or in areas that are frequently flooded. Consequently, very small changes in water depth can greatly increase or decrease the amount of foraging habitat available for reddish egrets. However, despite the fact that tidal flat topography did not conform exactly to the tested hypothesis, significantly greater numbers of egrets occurred in test areas only when the model predicted that more habitat of the preferred depth was available.

Farmer (1996) summed up his views on reddish egret distribution in Texas and Tamaulipas in the following statements:

Reddish egrets are found mostly on broad wind-tidal flats, habitats that are rarely used by other wading bird species.

Use of tidal flats changes seasonally with water depths, reflecting the semi-annual rise and fall of systemwide water levels as well as wind-tides.

The combination of tidal flat hydrology and water depths preferred by foraging reddish egrets restricts the amount of available habitat even in areas that are regularly flooded.

Year-to year distribution of seasonal habitat availability, and thus of reddish egrets, should be at least as predictable as the semi-annual water-level cycle and predominant winds.

Conservation Issues

The primary conservation issue is habitat preservation. Tidal flats are the preferred habitat for wintering and migrating shorebirds as well as for reddish egrets, and issues pertaining to their loss and degradation are discussed fully in chapter 9. Habitat preservation cannot be limited to sites used by large numbers of birds. Both shorebirds and reddish egrets move throughout the system as changing water levels cause changes in foraging space and prey availability. For shorebirds in general, habitats exhibiting a wide range of "quality," defined as amount of foraging space and quantity of prey, are needed for populations to remain stable. In high quality areas where both space and prey are abundant, crowding and prey depletion cause habitat quality to decline, so there is a need for lower quality and even marginal areas into which the birds can move. Thus, preserving the gradient of habitat quality is just as important as preserving habitats that are consistently used by birds year after year. For piping plovers, this appears to require preserving habitat complexes containing tidal flat or other bayshore and beach habitats for foraging as well as washover passes for resting and roosting.

For reddish egrets, maintaining hydrology of broad tidal flats is the most important issue, since the presence of broad tidal flats appears to account for the high densities of reddish egrets, especially in lower Laguna Madre and Laguna Madre de Tamaulipas (Farmer 1991, 1996; Farmer and Carrera Gonzalez 1993). Replacement of broad tidal flats with narrow foraging habitat would result in a substantial decline in the system's ability to support large numbers of reddish egrets. Activities such as channelization and dredge material disposal have altered hydrology of broad flats significantly in some parts of lower Laguna Madre (Farmer 1991). Only about 40% of the 1920s area of tidal flats remains in the South Bay region. The timing of construction of ship channels in lower Laguna Madre and a 40% decline of breeding reddish egrets between 1934 and 1951 appear to coincide. Much of the loss of habitat seen in lower Laguna Madre is the direct result of dredge material placement and its effect on tidal flat hydrology.

14 Sea Turtles

ELIZABETH H. SMITH AND SUSAN A. CHILDS

Five species of marine turtles are documented in the western Gulf of Mexico: Kemp's ridley sea turtle *(Lepidochelys kempii)*, loggerhead sea turtle *(Caretta caretta)*, green sea turtle *(Chelonia mydas)*, leatherback sea turtle *(Dermochelys coriacea)*, and hawksbill sea turtle *(Eretmochelys imbricata)*. Kemp's ridley sea turtle has the most restricted distribution of the five species, occurring mainly in coastal waters of the Gulf of Mexico and northwestern Atlantic Ocean. Adults of the species are usually confined to the Gulf of Mexico, but they have been documented on the Atlantic Coast of the United States. Young individuals are usually found dwelling over crab-rich sand or mud bottoms, inhabiting bays, river mouths, coastal lagoons, and Gulf coastal habitats. Most Kemp's ridley adult females concentrate annually (in spring and early summer) along the northeastern Mexico coast, primarily at Rancho Nuevo, Tamaulipas, to use Gulf beach nesting grounds (USFWS and NMFS 1992).

Loggerhead sea turtles are the most common marine turtles in the southeastern United States (USFWS 1991). Their geographic distribution includes temperate and tropical waters of the world; they often inhabit continental shelves and estuarine environments along the margins of the Atlantic, Pacific, and Indian oceans (USFWS and NMFS 1991). Historically, green sea turtles were described as the most important species in Texas, with numbers reported in the thousands during the early 1800s (Hildebrand 1981). Historic accounts substantiate reports of large numbers of green sea turtles once occupying Texas bays (Shaver 1990b, c). One hundred years ago, the Atlantic form of this species (known for its green fat) was common in Texas waters (Doughty 1984). In 1915, John K. Strecker noted that "if all the green turtles shipped from the coast country are captured in Texas waters, the animal must be quite abundant." In 1980s aerial surveys over Texas and Louisiana waters, green turtle sightings were described as infrequent, probably a function of low abundance in the western Gulf of Mexico and difficulty in proper identification (Fritts et al. 1983).

Information on the leatherback sea turtle is limited in the western Gulf of Mexico, with very few individuals reported (Hildebrand 1981). Leatherback sea turtles are widely distributed in Mexican waters, with aggregations concentrated off Barra de San Pedro from August to November. In the 1980s an estimated 115,000 adult female leatherbacks remained worldwide, about 50% of them nesting in western Mexico (Pritchard 1982). The hawksbill sea turtle is the rarest marine turtle in the Gulf of Mexico with few records from Texas (Hildebrand 1981).

Species Descriptions

Marine turtles vary greatly in size, weight, and physical description. Kemp's ridley is the smallest sea turtle (USFWS and NMFS 1992), ranging in weight from 36 to 45 kg (79–99 lb; USFWS 1991). Color changes significantly during development, from the gray-black dorsum (back) and venter (belly) of hatchlings to the lighter gray-olive carapace (back shell) and cream-white or yellowish plastron (belly shell) of adults (USFWS and NMFS 1992).

Adult and subadult loggerhead sea turtles possess a large reddish brown carapace; dorsal (back) scales along the shell edge are reddish brown but with light yellow margins (USFWS 1991; USFWS and NMFS 1992). Adults in the southeastern United States weigh up to 113 kg (248 lb). Hatchlings differ from adults, possessing three dorsal and two plastral keels (ridges), lacking the reddish tinge, and varying from light to dark brown on the back (USFWS and NMFS 1991). The green sea turtle is a medium to large, brownish sea turtle with radiating or mottled patterns on the shell (USFWS 1991). In comparison to other sea turtles, its head is small, and the biting edge of the lower jaw is serrated. Adult weights average 440–660 kg (200–300 lb) (USFWS 1991).

The leatherback sea turtle is the largest living marine turtle worldwide and can attain a weight up to 3,080 kg (1,400 lb). The black shell is covered with white blotches, without scales, and covered by a firm, rubbery skin with seven longitudinal ridges or keels (USFWS 1991). The front flippers are proportionally longer than in other sea turtles and in adult leatherback sea turtles may measure 270 cm (106 in). Hatchlings are covered with tiny polygonal beadlike scales and are black dorsally. Flippers are margined in white, and rows of white scales resembling stripes occur along the length of the carapace (USFWS and NMFS 1992). The hawksbill sea turtle is a small to medium sea turtle with a colored shell of thick overlapping scales, from which the term "tortoise shell" is derived. Adults weigh approximately 45–90 kg (100–200 lb) (USFWS 1991).

Ecological Requirements

Kemp's ridley sea turtle hatchlings, post-hatchlings, and juveniles are found in pelagic (open ocean) environments foraging on the surface, whereas subadults and adults are described as benthic, or bottom dwellers (Ogren 1989). Hatchling Kemp's ridleys are presumed to feed on *Sargassum* and associated epifauna in the Gulf of Mexico (USFWS and NMFS 1992). As they develop, Kemp's ridleys are carnivorous, primarily foraging on portunid crabs (Ogren 1989; Dobie et al. 1961). Gut content analyses from wild subadult and adult turtles identified crabs as the primary food item, followed by molluscs, fish, and vegetation. Although high numbers of portunid crabs were taken from the turtles examined, large quantities of other crabs were also eaten. The Kemp's ridley may be an opportunistic forager rather than selective for a particular crab species (Shaver 1991). Additional studies of stomach contents of dead turtles suggest that this species is a shallow water, benthic feeder (Dobie et al. 1961; Ernst and Barbour 1972; Hildebrand 1981; Lutcavage and Musick 1985). Results of a tracking study suggest that Kemp's ridley turtles move along the Gulf shoreline, usually within 15 km (9.3 mi) of shore in waters of <18 m (<60 ft) (Renaud 1995).

The greatest concentrations of loggerhead sea turtles are found along the Atlantic Coast from North Carolina to southern Florida (Hildebrand 1981). Smaller populations have been observed along the entire Gulf Coast from the Florida Keys to Quintana Roo, Mexico. Although no reliable population estimates in the Gulf of Mexico are available (Hildebrand 1981), the eastern U.S. population was estimated at 25,000 to 50,000 adults (Lund 1974), but these figures should be used with caution (D. Shaver, pers. comm.). Loggerhead sea turtles were documented in Gulf waters adjacent to Texas throughout the summer months around oil platforms, rock reefs, and other obstructions (Hildebrand 1981), where they forage on a variety of crabs, jellyfish, and molluscs (USFWS 1991). A feeding ecology study of loggerheads identified pen shells (*Atrina* sp.) as the highest ranked prey, occurring in 56.1% of the samples and accounting for 58.7% of total prey dry weight (Plotkin et al. 1993). Hatchlings are thought to feed on macroplankton, gastropods, small fish, and *Sargassum* spp. associated with the *Sargassum* mats. Juveniles of less than 40 cm (15.7 in) in carapace length (CL) feed on various benthic organisms, such as crabs, barnacles, gastropods, and other molluscs (Dodd 1988).

Green sea turtle juveniles are generally found along the Florida coast and are especially abundant in seagrass meadows (USFWS 1991). Historically, this species was reported in high numbers in Texas bays (Shaver 1990b, c). Little is known about the ecological requirements of the species. Movement patterns and behavior of juvenile green sea turtles were investigated in Brazos Santiago Pass from August through September (Renaud et al. 1995). Jetties were used more than other available habitats, suggesting that juveniles congregate in this area for algal food resources. Individuals were observed grazing on algal growth, particularly around dusk. Tagged individuals exhibited site fidelity to the jetty area, rarely moving far from this habitat during the study. This area was used for resting at night; therefore movement away from the jetties was not necessary. Movement along and within the ship channel was limited and was related to migration to other feeding areas along the jetties or as escape from human disturbance. One individual was also tracked throughout the eastern portion of South Bay in the lower Laguna Madre (Renaud et al. 1993). Individuals larger than 40 cm CL (15.7 in) were captured in seagrass meadows in lower Laguna Madre. Turtle-grass *(Thalassia testudinum)* was the principal component in fecal samples (Landry et al. 1992; Renaud et al. 1993).

Adult leatherback sea turtles are migratory and are believed to be the most pelagic of all sea turtles; however, habitat requirements for juveniles and post-hatchling leatherbacks are not known. In Texas, an estimated 100 leatherbacks were recorded in December 1956, ranging in length from 1–2 m (3.3–6.6 ft), along a 50 km (31 mi) line extending north from Port Aransas, Texas (Leary 1957). Dixon (1987) documented leatherback sea turtles for six Texas coastal counties—Jefferson, Galveston, Brazoria, Aransas, Nueces, and Kenedy—and Judd and colleagues (1991) added Cameron County. No ecological habitat information could be located for this species.

The hawksbill sea turtle is a tropical, reef-dwelling turtle that forages principally on sponges (USFWS 1991). During a study of the occurrence of sea turtles on the South Texas coast, four small (<20 cm CL) (<7.9 in) hawksbills were observed off the Aransas Pass Inlet jetties in late summer from 1970 to 1975 (Rabalais and Rabalais 1980). Throughout 25 years studying sea turtle nesting habits, Hildebrand (1981) observed only two hawksbills captured in healthy condition. Other observations made on this species were on small individuals that washed up dead on the beach.

Nesting History

Kemp's ridley sea turtles were abundant in the Gulf of Mexico less than 50 years ago. Most current nesting occurs on a 20 km (12.4 mi) length of beach at Rancho Nuevo, Tamaulipas, Mexico, located approximately 322 km (193 mi) south of Brownsville (fig. 14.1; Marquez et al. 1989). Prior to 1958, this nesting area was not known to sea turtle biologists (Hildebrand 1963). During his investigation of the nesting area, Hildebrand (1963) obtained an amateur film made on the beach in 1947. The film showed at least 40,000 females nesting between 9:00 A.M. and 1:00 P.M. in a daytime aggregation or *arribada* (synchronized diurnal landing). By 1961, the population was severely depleted due to exploitation of both eggs and adults. In 1966, protective strategies at this nesting beach were implemented. However, in May 1968, only 3,000 to 5,000 females were found nesting (Pritchard 1969).

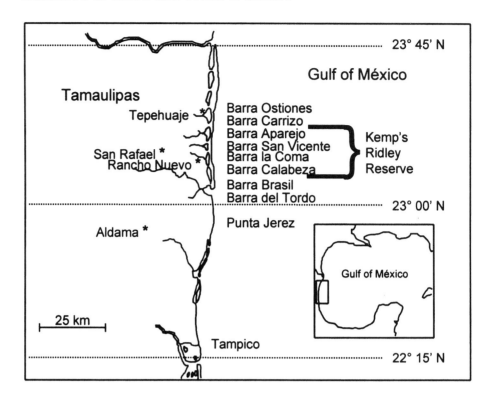

The entire Kemp's ridley sea turtle nesting population (adult females) in the early 1990s was estimated to be fewer than 700 (Shaver 1992). This estimate excludes males, immature turtles, and smaller breeding groups or single nesters located between Padre Island, Texas, and Isla Aguada, Campeche (USFWS and NMFS 1992). More recent figures estimate 3,000 adults in the population for 1996–97, assuming a 1:1 sex ratio (TERG 1998). This species is capable of producing multiple clutches (≈3) in one reproductive season (Rostal et al. 1997). One female sea turtle was tracked from Cameron, Louisiana, in August, arriving in the Rancho Nuevo area in March. Two successful nesting events occurred with 103 eggs hatching (85% success) on 14 June 1995 and 98 eggs hatching (76% success) on 5 July 1995 (Renaud et al. 1996). Table 14.1 gives a summary of the number of nests per season at the Rancho Nuevo nesting beach, and estimates of the percentage of hatchlings from 1978 to 1991 (table 14.1) (USFWS 1991). Thirteen confirmed Kemp's ridley sea turtle nests were recorded along the Texas coast in 1998 (Shaver 1999); 16 were found in 1999 and 12 in 2000 (D. Shaver, pers. comm.). Several of the females were already tagged, confirming their return (in some cases, multiple returns) to nest on Texas beaches. One female tagged in Texas was found nesting in Tepehuajes, Tamaulipas, Mexico, and was the first confirmed female to nest in both the United States and Mexico.

Loggerhead sea turtles nest in temperate zones and subtropical areas (Carr 1986). Only 11 confirmed nests were documented on the Texas coast from 1979 through 1996. In 1997, one nesting emergence of loggerhead young was reported. In addition, one female was recorded nesting, and four sets of loggerhead tracks were located (Shaver 1998). Two loggerhead nests were found along the Texas coast in 1998, both within the PINS boundary. Since the female was not documented during egg laying, the two nests may have involved the same female or two different females (Shaver 1999).

Green sea turtles currently nest in Mexico on Cayos Arcas, Cayo Arenas, Arrecife

Table 14.1. Kemp's ridley sea turtle Rancho Nuevo project summary

Year	Known Nests[a]	Protected Nests[b]	Eggs Protected	Hatchlings Produced	% Hatch
1978	924	834	85,217	48,009	56
1979	954	954	98,211	63,996	65
1980	868	796	82,374	37,378	45
1981	897	897	89,906	53,282	59
1982	750	750	77,745	48,007	62
1983	746	746	77,432	32,921	43
1984	798	798	80,798	58,124	72
1985	702	677	67,633	51,033	75
1986	744	675	65,357	48,818	75
1987	737	714	72,182	44,634	62
1988	842	830	83,229	62,218	75
1989	878	826	84,802	66,752	79
1990	992	973	93,937	74,795	79
1991	1,155	1,107	107,134	75,953	71
1992	1,275				
1993	1,241				
1994	1,562				
1995	1,930				
1996	2,080				
1997	2,387				
1998	3,845				
1999	3,648				
2000	+5,000				

[a] Includes all known nests; nests protected, nests left in situ, and nests raided or destroyed. Data prior to 1991 from USFWS (1991). After 1991 from USFWS unpublished data, D. Shaver, pers. comm.; no other data available.

[b] Nests moved from the site of oviposition for incubation. All data in columns ending in 1991 are from USFWS (1991).

Alacránes, and Arrecife Triángulos on Campeche Bank, with an occasional sighting at Rancho Nuevo. Historical nesting grounds of green sea turtles are not known. Nesting populations may be increasing, or there may merely be more nests reported. Increased individual sightings were attributed to "head-starting" efforts in Isla Mujeres resulting in emigration to Texas (Hildebrand 1981); however, the current extent of this program is unknown. The first confirmed nesting of green sea turtles on the Texas coast was in 1987. On 13 July 1987, two turtle eggs were collected from a nest in Kenedy County, Texas, at PINS (Shaver 1988). Tracks of the nesting female extended from the high tide line to the embryonic dune area, where a depression and mound of sand were located at the termination of the tracks. After imprinting was performed at the Kemp's ridley incubation laboratory, one of the hatched eggs was sent to the University of Texas Marine Sciences Institute (UTMSI) in Port Aransas for seven months of head-starting. Unfortunately, the turtle died after only a few weeks (D. Shaver, pers. comm.). In 1998, five green sea turtle nests were confirmed on the Texas coast (Shaver 1999).

Nesting grounds of leatherback sea turtles are distributed around the world (Sternberg 1981); the Pacific coast of Mexico supports the world's largest known concentration of nesting leatherbacks. In Caribbean regions, the largest nesting colony is found at Yalima po–Les Hattes, French Guiana, where the estimated total number of adult females is from 14,700 to 15,300 (Fretey and Girondot 1989). In the past, this species has nested at Rancho Nuevo, Tamaulipas (Hildebrand 1981). No nesting has been reported on the west coast of Florida since the year the state began keeping records in 1979; however, in 1974, a nest was reported on St. Vincent Island off the northwest coast of Florida (LeBuff 1976). Nesting was documented on the Texas coast in the vicinity of Little Shell Beach on PINS in the 1920s and 1930s, but no records exist since the 1940s (Hildebrand 1981).

Records of hawksbill sea turtles nesting on the Texas coast are rare and few have been confirmed. In August 1987, a live hawksbill hatchling was found stranded on the beach at Mustang Island near Port Aransas (Shaver 1988). The hatchling measured 5.46 cm (2.15 in) straight CL by 4.47 cm (1.76 in) straight carapace width (CW), weighed 28 g (1 oz), and possessed an egg tooth, indicating a recent hatching. It is uncertain whether this hatchling emerged from a Texas nest. The first confirmed nest was found in 1998 on PINS; however, the only beach patrolled along the coast for nesting is at PINS, so other nests may go undetected (Shaver 1999). In addition, nest searching is conducted for Kemp's ridley sea turtles, and portions of the nesting season for other species may be missed (D. Shaver, pers. comm.). Thus while there may be a few nestings, South Texas beaches are at present insignificant as hawksbill nesting beaches, as they probably were in the past (Hildebrand 1981). A small population of hawksbill sea turtles was reported near Veracruz, Mexico. Fishermen reported nests from Isla de Lobos in northern Veracruz southward to Anton Lizardo. The northern part of the state around Cabo Rojo and the area from Isla de Lobos to Alvarado have been reported to be good nesting and feeding grounds for sea turtles, including hawksbills (Hildebrand 1981).

Status and Trends

Fewer than 2,000 adult Kemp's ridleys remained in the early 1990s, and it was the most endangered sea turtle species (Shaver 1992). However, recently the population appears to have increased substantially, based on the increased numbers of nests reported annually (TERG 1998). Historical exploitation is responsible for the past decline (Magnuson et al. 1990). The Texas coast supported turtle canneries at four different sites during the mid-1800s (USFWS and NMFS 1992; Shaver 1990c). It is suspected that the cannery commerce involved mainly green sea turtles, but given the Tamaulipas Kemp's ridley population mentioned in excess of 40,000 females as late as the 1940s, it is probable that Kemp's ridley sea turtles also were captured along the Texas coast (Doughty 1984). Most turtles were caught in Aransas Bay, Matagorda Bay, and lower Laguna Madre. Nets and seines were set in shallow lagoons and channels, and fishing vessels were equipped with trawls. By 1900, the catch had declined to the extent that turtle fishing and the processing industry ceased (Hildebrand 1963). Activities such as dredging, boating, and recreational and commercial fishery operations have recently threatened sea turtles occupying Texas inshore waters, and whether turtles inhabiting these areas are receiving adequate protection is unknown (Shaver 1990b).

Direct egg exploitation occurred at the Rancho Nuevo nesting beach during the 1940s and continued through the early 1960s. During that time, eggs were taken out

Table 14.2. *Species composition of sea turtle strandings in the northwestern Gulf of Mexico by month, summed over years 1986–89*

Species	J	F	M	A	M	J	J	A	S	O	N	D	Total
						MONTH							
Loggerhead	9	10	46	146	95	33	40	37	31	29	19	20	515
Kemp's ridley	0	6	36	82	48	36	27	51	23	22	17	9	357
Hawksbill	0	1	2	0	1	5	4	15	18	14	2	5	67
Green	1	0	5	7	6	6	2	2	0	4	1	4	38
Leatherback	0	0	1	8	5	3	0	1	0	2	3	0	23
Unknown	0	0	6	6	2	5	10	4	5	6	1	2	47
Total	10	17	96	249	157	88	83	115	77	78	43	40	1,047

Source: After Caillouet et al. 1991.

in mule trains, by truck, and on horseback (Hildebrand 1963). Hildebrand cautioned that continued exploitation would lead to the decline of the species and documented the disappearance of arribadas on various beaches along the coast near Rancho Nuevo. Presently, the most important factor affecting the reproductively valuable large juveniles and adults is growth of the shrimp trawling industry in the Gulf (Crouse et al. 1987). An estimated 9,047 commercial boats under 7.8 m (25 ft) in length and 5,439 vessels greater that 7.8 m (25 ft) in length trawled for shrimp in the Gulf during 1987 (NOAA 1989). These estimates do not include recreational or weekend trawlers, which probably account for another 40,000 vessels. In addition to nest-poaching activities, the decline of the Kemp's ridley sea turtle population coincided with the buildup of the fishery industry during the late 1940s and 1950s. Intensification of shrimping in the United States and Mexico, in conjunction with consequent entrapping of turtles in trawls, was identified as a major cause for the decline of Kemp's ridley sea turtle (USFWS and NMFS 1992).

Sea turtle strandings along coastal shorelines of the southeastern United States are used as an indicator of mortality due to shrimping (Magnuson et al. 1990). Increases in sea turtle strandings during commercial shrimping seasons and decreases with the closing of these seasons have been observed on the Atlantic and Gulf of Mexico coasts (Hillestad et al. 1978; Magnuson et al. 1990; Renaud et al. 1997). There is unequivocal documentation that sea turtles are caught in shrimp trawls (Murphy and Hopkins-Murphy 1989; Magnuson et al. 1990). Sea turtles probably congregate in shrimping areas to feed on discarded bycatch. Sea turtle strandings (all species) were analyzed in the northwestern Gulf of Mexico during 1986–89. Loggerhead and Kemp's ridley sea turtles stranded most frequently, followed by hawksbill, green, and leatherback turtles (table 14.2). Results did not include strandings of head-starts (captive-reared animals) because distribution may be affected by location of release (Caillouet et al. 1991).

A three-year survey of sea turtles on South Texas beaches revealed an increase in strandings in 1978 and 1979. No definite cause was established, but increased trawling activity in nearshore waters has occurred in conjunction with periods of high incidence of strandings (Hillestad et al. 1978). A greater frequency of turtle strandings occurred along certain portions of the coast (Little Shell and Big Shell beaches, northern Padre Island and Mustang Island), where increased trawling activity in nearshore waters was also documented (Rabalais and Rabalais 1980). Alternatively, the data may reflect variable amounts of coverage along the barrier island beaches (D. Shaver, pers. comm.). To determine causes and consequences of strandings, year-round coverage is necessary to monitor stranding frequency and to provide biological data, tissue samples, specimens for necropsy, and other information related to human activities and to oceanographic shifts.

On 28 July 1978, the loggerhead sea turtle was listed as threatened under the Endangered Species Act of 1973 (USFWS and NMFS 1991). The stock of nesting females in the southeastern United States had been reported to be declining (Ehrhart 1989). Some fishery activities threaten loggerheads in Texas, but they most likely suffer mortality from various other causes attributable to the activities of humans. Dead turtles were observed on the beaches of South Texas, but no counts were made prior to or during the early 1950s (Hildebrand 1981). Strandings of marine turtles on the coast of Texas from Cedar Bayou to Brazos Santiago Pass were examined from September 1976 to 1 October 1979, with 202 dead loggerheads recorded. Strandings were greatest during fall and spring, corresponding with peak inshore and nearshore shrimping (Rabalais and Rabalais 1980).

Between 1980 and 1989 the Texas Sea Turtle Stranding and Salvage Network (STSSN) database documented 166 sea turtles (30 loggerheads) stranded alive or dead within Texas state inshore waters (Shaver 1990a). Considerably more wild turtles were stranded during 1989, with loggerhead strandings occurring primarily during April and June. A severe and widespread hypothermic stunning event occurred in February 1989, when water temperatures in lower Laguna Madre dropped to as low as 3°C. Stranded live and dead sea turtles, including loggerheads, were found immediately after the drop in temperature (Shaver 1990a), but green turtles appeared to be affected the most (D. Shaver, pers. comm.). The number of wild turtles stranded during the first five months of 1994 (227) exceeded numbers for the entire year of 1991 (176; Shaver 1994). More turtles were documented stranded within Texas waters during 1994 than in any year on record with the STSSN, established in 1980. Out of the 527 turtles found stranded, 194 were loggerheads (D. Shaver, pers. comm.).

The green sea turtle is listed as endangered in Florida and in eastern Pacific breeding populations and threatened elsewhere within its range (USFWS 1991). Nesting locations and local populations congregating in and around beaches made green sea turtles easy targets. The sea turtles were slaughtered for meat, oil, skins, and shells. The Karankawa Indians hunted turtles, which they boiled in earthen pots or roasted in ashes (Doughty 1984). Large numbers of green sea turtles were exploited along the Texas coast early in the nineteenth century. By 1890, turtles ranked tenth among forty-six fishing products caught in the Gulf states and fifth in Texas. Between 1880 and 1900, about 10,909 kg (24,000 lb) of green sea turtles were landed in Texas; in Louisiana, 13,636 kg (30,000 lb) were landed, valued at $1,200. The turtle catch in Texas reached a record high in 1890, with the take of green turtles that year increasing more than twentyfold over that of 1880. A cannery was established on Aransas Bay at Fulton in 1881. Many turtles probably came from local feeding grounds of seagrass in Aransas Bay. The green sea turtle was the leading marine product by weight in the Laguna Madre and lower Río Grande tidal zone. In Texas, overall weight of turtles landed was vast, substantiating the considerable volume of readily available, cheap turtle meat. In turn, this commodity led to the establishment and expansion of canneries for processing green sea turtles in the late 1800s (Doughty 1984).

Ten green sea turtles were among the 259 turtles stranded between September 1976 and September 1979 (Rabalais and Rabalais 1980). In recent years, occurrence of these strandings has been recorded formally as part of a long-term study of bird populations utilizing Mustang Island beach (Amos 1989). From 1983 to 1985, 120 individuals from five species stranded on Mustang Island, including green sea turtles. Between January and June 1994, 246 sea turtles were documented stranded along the Texas coast, including 14 green sea turtles (Shaver 1994). Fisheries operations, including shrimping, menhaden fishing, and illegal gill netting were suspected as probable causes. Improperly installed and malfunctioning turtle excluder devices (TEDs) also were implicated in the strandings (D. Shaver, pers. comm.).

The leatherback sea turtle is considered endangered throughout its global range and was listed as endangered under the authority of the Endangered Species Act by the United States Department of the Interior on 2 June 1970. Declines in the number of nesting females were documented and reported worldwide, and it is not known at present whether leatherback sea turtle populations within the United States are stable, increasing, or declining. Leatherback sea turtle strandings on U.S. shores are generally of animals adult or subadult in size, which may indicate the importance of pelagic habitat under U.S. jurisdiction to turtles breeding in tropical and subtropical latitudes (USFWS and NMFS 1992). Evidence currently available from tag returns and strandings in the western Atlantic suggests that adults engage in routine migrations between boreal, temperate, and tropical waters (Pritchard 1976). From 1980 to 1991 there were 816 reported strandings along the continental U.S. coastline. Thirty-six leatherback strandings were recorded in Texas coastal counties from January 1981 through December 1989 (Judd et al. 1991).

Leatherback sea turtles were never harvested to any great extent along coasts of the southeastern United States, but there are reports of turtle shootings in Florida and harvesting along the eastern coast of Mexico. In February 1980, Hildebrand noted evidence of meat removed from an individual left on the beach near Veracruz (Hildebrand 1981). Residents had rendered this species for oil on more than one occasion. The oil is reputed to have medicinal value, particularly for skin and lung disorders, and one leatherback may yield up to 30 liters of oil (Hildebrand 1981).

Currently, the hawksbill sea turtle is listed as endangered, with populations facing significant threats in the marine environment from human pressure and exploitation. There is little scientific information concerning this species. Its eggs are gathered for food, and turtles of all sizes are captured and mounted for the curio trade. Few hawksbill sea turtle strandings have been reported from inshore waters along the Texas coast, and most individuals found stranded along the Texas coast are post-hatchlings and small juveniles. Other small individuals are found entangled in marine debris or injured but are usually alive (Amos 1989); entanglement and young washing ashore with strong currents are cited as most common reasons for hawksbill strandings (D. Shaver, pers. comm.). From 1 January to 31 May 1994, one hawksbill sea turtle was included among 227 turtles reportedly stranded along the Texas coast (Shaver 1994). Of the 120 sea turtles of five species already mentioned as having been stranded from 1983 to 1985, 12 were juvenile hawksbills (Amos 1989). The STSSN recorded stranded turtles, dead or alive, within state inshore waters between 1980 and 1989 (Shaver 1990c). Of the 166 stranded sea turtles documented, eight were hawksbills. The hawksbill sea turtle was initially listed as third highest, with 67 stranded animals (Caillouet et al. 1991), but subsequent analyses reduced this number (D. Shaver, pers. comm.).

Future Threats

All five sea turtle species are susceptible to perturbations in their marine and estuarine habitats, including via dredging, pollution, oil and gas exploration, increases in marine debris resulting in ingestion or entanglement, loss or degradation of habitat and food resources, beach armoring, beach management strategies, and expanding development pressures. Localized impacts from gill netting (illegal in Texas), shrimping, hook and line fisheries, longline fisheries, and improperly installed or absent turtle excluder devices result in death and injury of sea turtles (Hildebrand 1981; USFWS and NMFS 1991, 1992). Other threats identified as harming sea turtles include the explosive removal of obsolete oil platforms (Klima et al. 1988), collisions with boat hulls or propellers, power plant entrapment, and disturbance in foraging grounds (Magnuson et al. 1990).

Nesting habitat is constantly in danger from development pressures and human disturbance. Continued human population growth and expanding development pressure will undoubtedly increase threats to turtle nest success on some beaches in Mexico. Current threats to nesting survival include egg poaching by locals for food and hatchling predation by gulls and mammalian scavengers that frequent urban settlements. As development increases along the shorelines (especially in Texas), maintenance activities to maintain the beach may negatively impact nesting success. Mechanical beach cleaning is usually accomplished by scraping the beach of trash and debris and depositing it in nesting areas along the high tide line. Nests may be destroyed during the scraping process or compaction of the debris may increase difficulty of the female turtle to dig into the substrate to deposit her clutch. Destruction of nesting habitat may also occur from remediation techniques to offset beach erosion by armoring or renourishing beaches. Human encroachment and access along the entire nesting area are serious concerns at the primary nesting beach in Rancho Nuevo, Tamaulipas, for Kemp's ridleys. Plans for massive expansion of La Pesca (north of the nesting area) as a fishing center or for dredging the Gulf Intracoastal Waterway (GIWW) from Brownsville, Texas, to Barra del Tordo (at the southern part of the nesting beach) were being considered for over a decade (USFWS and NMFS 1992; M. A. Cruz-Nieto, pers. comm.).

Currently, motorized equipment and non-native dune vegetation do not pose an immediate problem at Rancho Nuevo, nor do erosion, nest depredation, or other nest loss agents. However, when increasing numbers of nests necessitate leaving the nests in situ and unprotected outside the conservation area, these factors must be addressed. One threat that may occur due to management practices at Rancho Nuevo involves concentration within corral enclosures of eggs from collected nests. These eggs may have reduced viability due to their movement, concentration of disease vectors, and inundation by tides (USFWS and NMFS 1992).

Conservation and Management

In 1978, the Kemp's Ridley Sea Turtle Restoration and Enhancement Project was undertaken by the Instituto Nacional de Pesca (INP) of Mexico, U.S. Fish and Wildlife Service, National Marine Fisheries Service, National Park Service, and Texas Parks and Wildlife Department (TPWD) in accordance with Section II of the Endangered Species Act (Shaver 1990d). Establishment of a secondary breeding population at Padre Island was one of several project goals. PINS was chosen because the species had been known to nest there historically and because the NPS would be able to provide some protection in the event that a new breeding population became established.

A portion of the restoration program included a 10-year experimental attempt to establish a secondary breeding colony at PINS through "imprinting" (Shaver 1990d). Each summer, from 1978 to 1988, about 2,000 eggs were collected at Rancho Nuevo as they were laid. They were placed in styrofoam boxes containing Padre Island sand and transported via aircraft to PINS. The styrofoam boxes were placed in a predator-proof, screen-enclosed outdoor incubation shed. During 11 years, the overall hatching rate of the 22,507 eggs sent to Padre Island was 77.1%. Hatchlings were released on the beach at Padre Island to crawl down the beach, enter the surf, and swim approximately 10 m (33 ft), whereupon they were recaptured using aquarium dip nets. From 1978 through 1988, 15,875 recaptured hatchlings were transported to the NMFS laboratory in Galveston, Texas, for one year of head-starting. Overall, approximately 80% of the hatchlings survived head-starting, and most of these head-started turtles (some 12,000) were released offshore from Mustang and Padre islands.

Through 1998, five turtles released from this project were found nesting in South Texas. A mating pair of Kemp's ridley sea turtles was sighted within the Mansfield Channel, located at the southern end of the PINS on 3 June 1991 (Shaver 1992). Unfortunately, the turtles could not be identified as either wild or head-started, and nests were not found following mating. Although PINS no longer receives eggs from Rancho Nuevo, Tamaulipas for incubation, PINS continues active conservation projects conducted on behalf of this species, including an extensive program to detect nesting on northern Padre Island. Operation of the PINS incubation facility continues, and PINS incubates most sea turtle eggs found on the Texas coast. Public education programs, beach patrols, and protection and monitoring of nesting sea turtles and nests will continue at the park for the foreseeable future (D. Shaver, pers. comm.).

Nesting beach protection in the vicinity of Rancho Nuevo has increased significantly over the past two decades. Other beaches in Tamaulipas and Veracruz are now being used as nesting areas, and nest detection programs are under way (D. Shaver, pers. comm.). Collaboration of Mexican and U.S. conservationists under INP and USFWS is now used as a model for an international multi-agency effort (USFWS and NMFS 1992). For adult females, a downward trend in population numbers continued through 1985, in spite of efforts to stop egg poaching and harm to nesting females on the beach since 1966. Over one million hatchlings have been released at the nesting beach, with an increase in the number of nests documented at Rancho Nuevo since 1985. Wider coverage of the nesting beach by the binational protection team is partially responsible, in addition to increased numbers of nests. Poaching of adult turtles on the nesting beach has not been documented since 1980 due to intensive vigilance of the binational protection team, adequate motorized beach patrols, and the presence of armed marines. This has resulted in large increases in nesting turtle numbers, with over 5,000 Kemp's ridley nests documented in 2000 (see table 14.1).

Since the leatherback sea turtle was listed as endangered on 2 June 1970, conservation efforts have greatly improved. Lighting ordinances designed to control light pollution on nesting beaches have been passed by nine counties and over 20 towns, cities, and parishes in Florida (USFWS and NMFS 1992). In 1986 it became illegal to drive vehicles or ride horses on beaches in the U.S. Virgin Islands. In December 1990, the governor and cabinet of the State of Florida approved a beach-armoring policy restricting armoring (seawalls, riprap, revetments, groins, and sandbags) to structures threatened by a five-year return-interval storm event.

Another important management effort is the implementation of the requirement that the U.S. shrimp fleet use turtle excluder devices. Publication in 1987 of regulations requiring TEDs was a major accomplishment in protecting sea turtles in their foraging and migratory habitats. Use of these devices reduces mortality for most of the sea turtles captured, although leatherback adults are so large that they are not normally excluded (D. Shaver, pers. comm.). TED trials were conducted in Mexico, and use of TEDs aboard the Mexican shrimp fleet is now mandatory. In addition to

TEDs, future management efforts include habitat research, continued protection at the nesting beach at Rancho Nuevo in Mexico, and enforcement of the Marine Pollution Treaty (MARPOL).

A number of education activities and efforts are under way to expand public awareness and understanding of sea turtle conservation. Personnel conducting turtle projects are in touch daily with tourists on how to minimize disturbance to nesting turtles. In addition, state and federal parks that conduct programs for awareness of sea turtle status provide information to visitors, and signs have been posted on many beaches informing people of the laws protecting turtles (USFWS and NMFS 1991). Public support for sea turtle conservation efforts is essential for long-term success.

Investigations of suggested and known stranding factors are ongoing. Government agencies and their personnel, in addition to private organizations, have cooperated to document and investigate strandings. Personnel conducting turtle projects on the Atlantic Coast often advise tourists on what can be done to minimize disturbance to nesting turtles, to protect nests, and to rescue disoriented hatchlings (USFWS and NMFS 1991). Agencies included in conservation and management efforts are the STSSN, NMFS, NPS, U.S. Geological Survey (USGS), TPWD, University of Texas at Austin Marine Sciences Institute (UTMSI), and University of Texas–Pan American Coastal Studies Laboratory. Signs have been posted on many beaches informing people of the laws protecting sea turtles and providing either a local or a hotline telephone number to report violations.

Fishery regulations of the early 1980s were amended in Puerto Rico to ban nets with mesh greater than 10 cm (7.9 in), and in 1985 regulations were passed for the management and regulation of endangered species, with fines assessed as high as $5,000. A substantial effort is being made by government and nongovernment agencies and private individuals to increase public awareness of sea turtle conservation. Recovery objectives are designed to protect and manage habitats so that the U.S. population of leatherbacks can be downlisted from endangered or delisted completely (USFWS and NMFS 1992).

One of the most difficult issues in habitat management is to minimize or eliminate installation of seawalls, riprap, groins, sandbags, and improperly placed drift or sand fences (USFWS and NMFS 1991). Several state and federal laws have been designed to protect beach and dune habitat, some of which have had varying degrees of success at maintaining stable nesting sites for loggerhead sea turtles.

Conservation efforts for the protection and restoration of all sea turtle populations have been implemented both nationally and internationally. One of the most significant measures achieved is the ratification of Protocol to the Cartagena Convention concerning areas and wildlife needing special protection. Parties to the Convention for the Protection and Development of the Marine Environment of the Wider Caribbean Region (Cartagena Convention) adopted the Protocol for Specially Protected Areas and Wildlife in January 1990. Annex II of the protocol includes all six sea turtle species found in the wider Caribbean. It prohibits taking, possession, killing, or commercial trade in sea turtles and their eggs, parts, or products as well as prohibiting disturbance, particularly during periods of breeding, incubation, aestivation, and migration and at other times of biological stress (USFWS and NMFS 1992).

15 Fish and Invertebrate Fisheries Organisms

KIM WITHERS AND SUZANNE J. DILWORTH

Early descriptions of the fish and fisheries of the Laguna Madre depict an isolated and hypersaline yet remarkably productive system linked to the Gulf of Mexico via mostly ephemeral barrier island passes. Historically, productivity of fish and fisheries in Laguna Madre was driven by hurricane-opened passes and/or accompanying heavy rainfall that lowered salinities, after which production of fish and shrimp would surge for several years (Hildebrand 1958, 1969, 1980). Early observers reported seasonal movements of fish ready to spawn heading toward the Gulf and great schools of tiny red drum *(Sciaenops ocellatus)* moving into inside waters through passes (Higgins and Lord 1926). Today we know that many species spawn within the Laguna in addition to, or in place of, spawning in the Gulf (K. Spiller, pers. comm.). However, before hypersalinity was moderated by human activities, temporary linkage to the Gulf of Mexico and lowering of salinities due to wet hurricanes and tropical storms were probably the main reasons for the uncharacteristic productivity in the Laguna Madre.

The boom or bust character of the fisheries has been altered as an incidental result of navigational development. Although salinities in Laguna Madre still cannot typically be characterized as "estuarine," they are lower now than they were prior to the completion of dredging of the GIWW in Texas (1949) and pass stabilization with jetties in both Texas and Tamaulipas. Despite human interference, the fisheries resource has demonstrated remarkable resilience. Although there is no question about our role in the decline of some species, especially red drum, efforts to repair the damage have been at least moderately successful. Upper and lower Laguna Madre remain the most productive bays in Texas for finfish and support important recreational fisheries for spotted seatrout *(Cynoscion nebulosus)* and red drum as well as a large commercial black drum *(Pogonias cromis)* fishery. Baffin Bay, extending off upper Laguna Madre, has a well-deserved reputation among recreational anglers for producing trophy spotted seatrout.

Data available about the fish and fisheries organisms of the Laguna Madre de Tamaulipas are few. Poor record keeping and lack of scientific studies have resulted in uncertainty about the health and resources of the Mexican lagoon; however, evidence of overfishing and habitat alteration has led to development of fishing regulations and restrictions. Unfortunately, Mexico does not have the resources to enforce these laws, so the fate of the ecosystem currently lies primarily in the hands of commercial and recreational fisherman.

Effects of Hypersalinity on Fish and Fish Communities

Hypersalinity may affect fishes directly by disturbing their osmotic balance and indirectly by decreasing dissolved oxygen content of water, especially during summer, and preventing water from freezing during winter cold spells. Most fish found in Laguna Madre are euryhaline and are probably better able to cope with the harsh conditions because they are able to osmoregulate in salinities varying from fresh water to marine levels (Gunter 1967). For example, Gunter (1945a) seined sheepshead

Fig. 15.1. Mean abundance (bars) and diversity (line) of fish in Alazan Bay in relation to salinity (Data from Cornelius 1984)

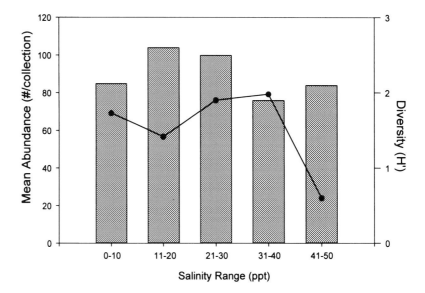

minnows *(Cyprinodon variegatus)* and tidewater silversides (*Menidia beryllina* [= *peninsulae*]) from Baffin Bay at 71.5 ppt, and the same fish were still present two and a half months later after heavy rains reduced salinities to 2.2 ppt. Strictly marine fish are rarely encountered despite the fact that they are able to withstand fairly high (35 ppt) but relatively stable salinities (Gunter 1967). In addition, salinities over 70 ppt are not strictly comparable to sea water because several compounds precipitate out, significantly altering both the ionic environment and the osmotic pressure (Copeland 1967). Salinities in the range of 40–50 ppt appeared optimum for many species in upper Laguna Madre (Simmons 1957). Larger individuals of a species occurred at higher salinities than smaller individuals (e.g., spotted seatrout; Gunter 1961), and at nonlethal salinities the average size of fishes was larger (Simmons 1957). Although stunting due to hypersalinity has frequently been documented in invertebrates (Simmons 1957; Hallam 1965), it does not appear to occur in fishes (Gunter 1967).

Higgins and Lord (1926) were the first to document mortality in fishes, especially food fishes, in upper Laguna Madre due to extreme hypersalinity (80–110 ppt; Gunter 1967) during summer. Prior to the 1940s, catastrophic summer fish kills that killed nearly all fish in upper Laguna Madre occurred about every ten years (Gunter 1967). Although fish often went blind and their eyes took on a "cooked" appearance even during normal years, extreme hypersalinity compounded the effects of high water temperatures on dissolved oxygen content, causing the massive kills. The last catastrophic kill due to hypersalinity occurred in the late 1930s, but small kills were documented into the 1960s and may still occur locally, particularly in Baffin Bay.

Effects on Diversity in Laguna Madre   Faunas of hypersaline lagoons are usually derived from local brackish waters rather than the sea (Hedgpeth 1967). In both high and low salinity environments, depauperate faunas are the rule, and in stable hypersaline areas the number of species is generally small, but the numbers of individuals may be extremely large (Parker 1959). However, as salinities decrease (up to a point), species richness increases and abundances decrease. In addition, when low water temperatures coincided with high salinity, species not normally tolerant of hypersalinity were present. In upper Laguna Madre, total species richness was greatest at salinities between 40 and 50 ppt and decreased below 40 ppt (Simmons 1957). In Alazan Bay, abundance was greatest at between 11 and 30 ppt, whereas diversity and species richness were greatest at between 21 and 40 ppt (fig. 15.1; Cornelius 1984).

Table 15.1. Numbers of families and species of fish found in Corpus Christi Bay and along the Texas Gulf Coast compared with the hypersaline Laguna Madre

	ELASMOBRANCHIOMORPHI		OSTEICHTHYES	
	Families	**Species**	**Families**	**Species**
Texas Gulf Coast	21	50	116	498
Corpus Christi Bay	9	13	47	102
Upper Laguna Madre and Baffin Bay	5	7	37	79
Lower Laguna Madre and South Bay	4	5	54	89
Laguna Madre de Tamaulipas	5	18	44	122

Sources: Coastwide (including bays and shallow nearshore environments): Murdy (1983); Corpus Christi Bay, Upper Laguna Madre and Baffin Bay: Tunnell and Alvarado (1996); Lower Laguna Madre and South Bay: Breuer (1962), Hook (1991); Laguna Madre de Tamaulipas: Leija-Tristan et al. (in press).

The effect of hypersalinity on diversity can be seen by comparing the numbers of families and species present in Texas Laguna Madre and Laguna Madre de Tamaulipas to Corpus Christi Bay, which has more estuarine salinities, and to coastwide totals from Texas (both estuarine and shallow nearshore environments; table 15.1). Fewer families are found in the Laguna Madre than in Corpus Christi Bay or coastwide. Within the Laguna, Tamaulipas has more species than the other lagoons, probably due to presence of 24 strictly tropical species (Leija-Tristan et al., in press). Laguna Madre de Tamaulipas is a transition zone, with most species (54%) widely distributed in temperate and tropical waters of the Atlantic Ocean and Gulf of Mexico. Although there have been few studies of the fish fauna in lower Laguna Madre, recent reports indicate that numbers are not substantially lower than in upper Laguna Madre. About half of all families—two Elasmobranchiomorphi (sharks and rays), and 19 Osteichthyes (bony fishes)—were found in all bay and lagoon categories listed in table 15.1, but nine families were found only in Corpus Christi Bay (three Elasmobranchiomorphi, six Osteichthyes). Two families were restricted to lower Laguna Madre, Chaetodontidae (butterflyfishes) and Pomocentridae (damselfishes), and two to Laguna Madre de Tamaulipas, Ephippidae (spadefishes) and Ostraciidae (boxfishes). The family Sciaenidae (drums) was the most diverse family, with 10 species from the Laguna Madre of Texas and 13 in Laguna Madre de Tamaulipas.

Ecology of Important Fish Species in Texas

Twenty-six of the 31 species of fish identified from Gulf of Mexico estuaries by NOAA's Estuarine Living Marine Resources program (Nelson 1992; Patillo et al. 1997) as having ecological, commercial, or recreational value have been found within the Laguna Madre in Texas (table 15.2). Ecological value is defined by an organism's habitat use and trophic level. For example, spotted seatrout are top-level carnivores, ecologically categorized as an as estuarine-dependent species that migrates through passes to use the seagrass beds of the Laguna Madre as nursery areas. Both ecological habitat and trophic level provide critical information describing the importance of the Laguna Madre in a species' life cycle as well as the species' position within the ecosystem. Equally important are the commercial and recreational values of many species found within the Laguna Madre. These values are categorized as commercially important species, recreationally important species, forage or bait species, and incidental commercial or recreational use species. Of the 26 species listed in table

Table 15.2. *Economic role, use as an indicator species, habitat use, trophic level, and qualitative abundances of major life stages for 10 invertebrate and 27 fish species in the Laguna Madre of Texas*

Common Name	Scientific Name	Economic Role[a]	Indicator[b]	Habitat[c]/ Trophic Level[d]	ABUNDANCE[e]				
					A	S	J	L	E
Invertebrates									
American oyster	*Crassostrea virginica*	CR	FPM	R/FW-f	+	+	+	+	+
Bay scallop	*Argopecten irradians*	C*R	H	G/FW-f	+	+	+	+	+
Bay squid	*Lolliguncula brevis*	I		W/C	++	++	++	++	++
Blue crab	*Callinectes sapidus*	CR	PMO	W/FW-o	+++	++	+++	+++	+++
Brown shrimp	*Farfantepenaeus aztecus*	CR	HPMO	GP/FW-o	+		+++	+	
Grass shrimp	*Palaemonetes* spp.	F	HPMS	G/FW-d	++++	++++	++++	++++	++++
Gulf stone crab	*Menippe adina*	CR	TB	ST/FW-p	+	+	+	+	+
Pink shrimp	*Farfantepenaeus duorarum*	CR	PMO	GP/FW-o	++		+++	+	
Spiny lobster	*Panilirus argus*	I		N/C	+		+		
White shrimp	*Litopenaeus setiferus*	CR	PM	GP/FW-o	++		+++	+	
Fish									
Atlantic croaker	*Micropogonias undulatus*	CR	MO	NP/C	+++		+++	+++	
Bay anchovy	*Anchoa mitchilli*	I	W	W/FW-c	++++	++++	++++	++++	++++
Black drum	*Pogonias cromis*	CR		NP/C	++	++	++	++	++
Bull shark	*Carcharhinus leucas*	R	M	O/P			+		
Code goby	*Gobiosoma robustum*	F		S/P	+++	+++	+++	+++	+++
Crevalle jack	*Caranx hippos*	R		NP/P	++		++		
Florida pompano	*Trachinotus carolinus*	R		NP/C	+		+		
Gizzard shad	*Dorosoma cepedianum*	I		O/FW-o	+				
Gray snapper	*Lutjanus griseus*	CR		NP/C	+		++		
Gulf flounder	*Paralichthys albigutta*	CR		O/C	+		+		
Gulf killifish	*Fundulus grandis*	F	HOA	S/FW-po	+++	+++	+++	+++	+++
Gulf menhaden	*Brevoortia patronus*	CF	MO	NOP/FW-f	++		+++	++	
Hardhead catfish	*Arius felis*		M	W/C	+++	+++	++++	+++	+++
Pinfish	*Lagodon rhomboides*	IF	H	SO/FW-po	+++		++++		
Red drum	*Sciaenops ocellatus*	C*R	M	NP/P	+		++		
Sand seatrout	*Cynoscion arenarius*	C*R		W/P	+		+		
Sheepshead	*Archosargus probatocephalus*	IR		NP/P	++		+++		
Sheepshead minnow	*Cyprinodon variegatus*	F	O	S/FW-c	++++	++++	++++	++++	++++
Silversides	*Menidia* spp.	F	HI	S/FW-c	++++	++++	++++	++++	++++
Silver perch	*Bairdiella chrysoura*	I	P	W/C	++	++	+++	++	++
Snook	*Centropomus undecimalis*	C*R		W/P	+	+	++	+	+
Southern flounder	*Paralichthys lethostigma*	CR		O/P	++		+++		
Spot	*Leiostomus xanthurus*	I	PMOI	W/C	+++		++++		

Table 15.2. (continued)

Common Name	Scientific Name	Economic Role[a]	Indicator[b]	Habitat[c]/ Trophic Level[d]	ABUNDANCE[E]				
					A	S	J	L	E
Fish (continued)									
Spotted seatrout	*Centropomus nebulosus*	C*R	POI	NGP/P	++	++	++	++	++
Striped mullet	*Mugil cephalus*	CRF	HP	W/FW-h	++	++	+++	++	++
Tarpon	*Megalops atlanticus*	R	P	NOP/C	+		+		

Source: Nelson 1992; Patillo et al. 1997.

[a] Economic roles:
    C = commercial importance
    C* = historical fishery species
    R = recreational
    F = forage or bait
    I = incidental commercial or recreational use

[b] Use as indicator species for:
    H = hydrocarbons
    F = fecal coliform
    P = pesticides
    M = metals
    O = organics
    I = inorganics
    W = water quality
    T = toxicity
    A = acidified water

[c] Habitat:
    N = nursery
    G = grassbeds
    R = reef
    W = widespread, depending on life stage
    O = open waters, including offshore

    P = estuarine-dependent organisms that migrate through passes
    S = shallow waters, widespread

[d] Trophic level:
    FW = food web linkage
      f = filter feeder
      d = detritivore
      h = herbivore
      o = omnivore
      c = generalized carnivore
      p = predator
    C = generalized top-level carnivore, often demersal feeder
    P = top trophic-level predator

[e] Abundance:
    A = adults
    S = subadults
    J = juveniles
    L = larvae
    E = eggs
    + = rare
    ++ = common, frequently encountered
    +++ = abundant, substantial numbers
    ++++ = very abundant, numerically dominant

15.2, 11 are or have been commercially important, 15 are recreationally important, five are forage or bait species, and six are incidental species. A more detailed overview of life history and abundance is provided for red drum, spotted seatrout, and black drum, the most important of the commercial and/or recreational species.

Red Drum   Red drum are estuarine-dependent. Spawning occurs in nearshore and inshore waters near barrier island passes from summer to early winter (Patillo et al. 1997). Larvae and postlarvae are carried by tides into shallow, inside waters, where they settle in quiet areas with muddy bottoms and patchy submerged vegetation that will protect them from predators until they are able to swim actively. Juveniles are widely distributed in shallow, protected, open waters from secondary bay margins to quiet backwaters. Subadults move into deeper, more open water in primary bays and then migrate offshore after first spawning.

All free-swimming life stages are carnivorous. Food consists of copepods, mysid shrimp amphipods, decapods, and fish, depending on life stage as well as size and availability of prey (Patillo et al. 1997). Red drum are long-lived (up to and over 37 years) top predators that feed opportunistically on the bottom or in the water column at dawn and dusk. Although larvae and juveniles are potential prey for other fish and wading birds, little is known about the effects of predation on red drum populations. Natural mortality occurs due to red tides, parasitism, disease, and old age. Destruction of nursery habitat and overfishing seriously impact red drum populations.

In general, juvenile and subadult red drum (<700 mm; Patillo et al. 1997) are frequently encountered throughout the year in Laguna Madre and Baffin Bay (Nelson 1992). Red drum appear to be fairly evenly distributed throughout upper Laguna Madre (Lacson and Lee 1997).

Spotted Seatrout Spotted seatrout are estuarine-dependent but, unlike red drum, complete their entire life cycle within inshore waters and exhibit little migratory movement (Patillo et al. 1997). Spawning occurs at dusk within bays and lagoons. Eggs are often released in shallow, grassy areas, near passes or in deeper water where they can drift into grassy areas. Moderate to high salinities appear necessary for spawning, but excessive hypersalinity may lower recruitment of young fish into the population. Other factors influencing timing of reproduction may be related to increasing water temperatures or changing photoperiods. Spotted seatrout may be found in a wide variety of underwater habitats ranging from unvegetated sandy, muddy, or shelly substrates to oil platforms and shell reefs, but juveniles and adults are often associated with seagrasses, particularly shoalgrass (*Halodule beaudettei* [= *wrightii*]) and turtle-grass *(Thalassia testudinum)*. Adults, spawning adults, juveniles, larvae, and eggs of spotted seatrout are frequently encountered and are widely distributed in Laguna Madre and Baffin Bay throughout the year (Nelson 1992; Lacson and Lee 1997).

Spotted seatrout are top-level carnivores that probably play a significant role in structuring prey communities, especially in seagrass beds (Patillo et al. 1997). These visual predators feed almost entirely on free-swimming organisms at the surface and mid-depths. Prey choices change as fish grow and seasonally with abundance of prey organisms. Copepods are favored by larvae, shrimp by small juveniles; larger juveniles and adults consume mostly shrimp in warmer months and fish in cooler months when shrimp are not as readily available. Juveniles are preyed upon by a variety of fish including larger trout, red drum, hardhead catfish, and Atlantic croaker. A number of environmental conditions can result in catastrophic mortalities, including severe cold, hurricanes, very low salinities, and high turbidities. Destruction of seagrass habitats may have serious consequences and has been implicated as a cause of declining populations in some areas.

Black Drum Like red drum and spotted seatrout, black drum are estuarine-dependent. Most spawning occurs in deeper nearshore waters and passes, with peak activity from January to mid-April and sometimes a second peak in fall (Patillo et al. 1997). Juveniles and young adults prefer unvegetated estuarine habitats with muddy substrates but often move into the more open waters of passes and the nearshore Gulf as they mature. Adults frequent unvegetated sandy or muddy areas and oyster or worm reefs. Although in the past it has been thought that mature individuals typically stay within bays until ripe, move into passes to spawn, then return quickly to their preferred bay habitats, recent observations indicate that spawning takes place in both the Gulf and the bays. In addition, spawning occurs in almost all areas of upper Laguna Madre, including creeks, during seasons other than spring, and by smaller individuals. Migratory movements are limited in fish less than four years old except during adverse environmental conditions.

Black drum are carnivores throughout their lives with prey ranging from zooplankton to molluscs, depending on life stage (Patillo et al. 1997). Proportions of soft-bodied benthic organisms in the diet decrease as pharyngeal teeth develop. Adults are demersal feeders, preying primarily on bivalves and crabs. Sensitive chin barbels help them find organisms burrowed into the bottom, and powerful pharyngeal teeth crush molluscs and crabs. Foraging black drum often dig pits into the surface of flooded tidal flats in Laguna Madre (Fisk 1959). Filter-feeding fish are potential predators on black drum eggs and larvae, and larger larvae and juveniles are probably preyed upon by various drums and other large fish (Patillo et al. 1997).

Black drum are long-lived fish, implying extremely low natural mortality rates and little surplus yield to support an intensive or even a moderate fishery (Patillo et al. 1997). Rapid and extreme temperature fluctuations often cause mortalities. Black drum constituted the majority of fish killed by freezing weather in Laguna Madre in 1983 and 1989 (Martin and McEachron 1996). Population growth is thought to be limited by amount of preferred habitat containing adequate food resources, and black drum may sometimes compete with other fish for benthic resources (Patillo et al. 1997).

Black drum adults and juveniles are frequently encountered in Laguna Madre throughout the year, whereas spawning adults, larvae, and eggs are found during spring (Nelson 1992). The temporal pattern is similar in Baffin Bay, but abundances are higher, with substantial numbers of individuals encountered regardless of time of year or life stage. Adult and subadult fish (>300 mm total length [TL]; Pearson 1929; Simmons and Breuer 1962) are caught throughout upper Laguna Madre, with concentrations noted within Baffin Bay and north along the lagoon side of Padre Island.

Fish Community Structure in Texas

Using 22 years (1975–97) of fisheries-independent data collected by TPWD (summarized in Hensley and Fuls 1998), relative abundances of important fish species within Texas bays can be determined and compared. TPWD uses a variety of methods to collect data, and in the following two sections, fish community structure in Laguna Madre is described and compared with community structure in Corpus Christi Bay and coastwide (all bays along the coast) using gill net data for large fish and bag seine data (1.3–1.9 cm [0.5–0.75 in] mesh) for small fish. Using other data sources, community structure for Baffin Bay, South Bay, and a seagrass bed in upper Laguna Madre are also summarized.

Large Fish (Gill Net Data)   TPWD collects gill net data in fall and spring, so comparisons can be made both between bay systems and between seasons (figs. 15.2, 15.3). Regardless of season, marked differences in community structure can be seen when relative abundances of species in Laguna Madre are compared with coastwide and Corpus Christi Bay values. Although the commercially and recreationally important members of the drum family (red drum, black drum, spotted seatrout, and Atlantic croaker) constitute a large proportion of fish captured coastwide (39–45%), they dominate in Corpus Christi Bay (44–48%), and both upper (60–63%) and lower (59–63%) Laguna Madre. The most striking difference is the dominance of black drum in upper Laguna Madre. Black drum may be as much as three times more abundant in upper Laguna Madre than either coastwide or in Corpus Christi Bay and about 15% more abundant than in lower Laguna Madre. Another important difference is the low proportion of menhaden in lower Laguna Madre, especially during fall. Lack of diversity in both lagoons is seen in the small proportion of "other" species. Seasonally, community structure in upper Laguna Madre is fairly stable with little difference between fall and spring. Overall, the proportion of spotted seatrout increases from fall to spring in both lagoons, doubling during spring in lower Laguna Madre.

Fig. 15.2. *Relative abundances of large fish captured using gill nets during fall, 1975–97 (Data from Hensley and Fuls 1998)*

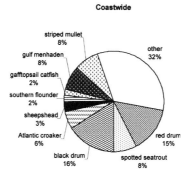

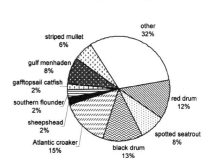

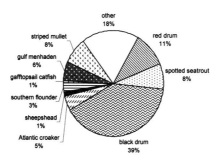

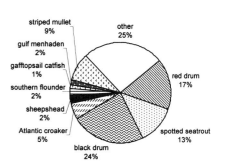

Fig. 15.3. *Relative abundances of large fish captured using gill nets during spring, 1975–97 (Data from Hensley and Fuls 1998)*

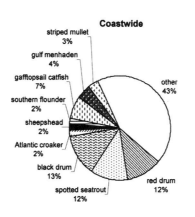

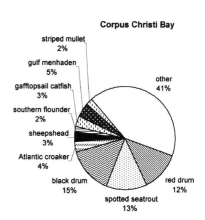

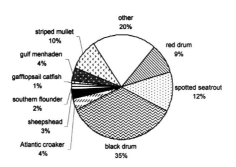

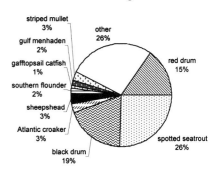

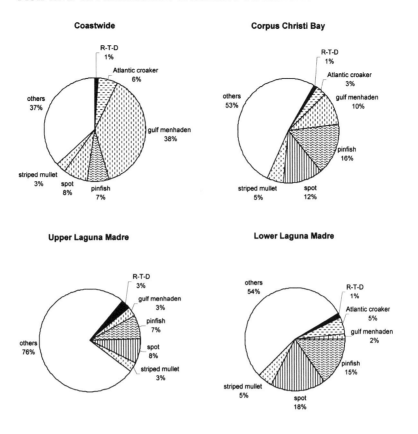

Fig. 15.4. Relative abundances of small fish captured using bag seines, 1975–97. R-T-D = aggregate of red drum, spotted seatrout, and black drum (Data from Hensley and Fuls 1998)

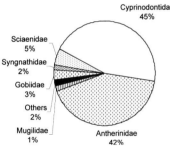

Fig. 15.5. Relative abundances of fish in a shoalgrass bed in upper Laguna Madre (Data from Chaney 1988)

Small Fish (Bag Seine) Coastwide, menhaden dominate the small fish fauna (fig. 15.4), but they constitute only a small proportion in southerly bays and lagoons. Overall, the small fish fauna appears to be more diverse than the large fish fauna, as indicated by dominance of the "other" category, especially in upper Laguna Madre. Among the drum, the combined proportion of red drum, spotted seatrout, and black drum (R-T-D) is generally low. Spot and Atlantic croaker are the most important drum, especially in lower Laguna Madre. Overall, the small fish faunas of lower Laguna Madre and Corpus Christi Bay are similar, differing mainly in the combined proportion of commercially important drum (red drum, black drum, spotted seatrout, Atlantic croaker, and spot) and proportion of menhaden.

Shoalgrass Bed, Upper Laguna Madre Using a 6 mm (0.25 in) seine, Chaney (1988) surveyed the fish associated with shoalgrass beds near Bird Island Basin in upper Laguna Madre. A total of 24 species in 15 families was collected. Killifish, primarily rainwater killifish (*Lucania parva*, 39.1%), dominated (fig. 15.5) along with tidewater silversides in all seasons. Four species of drum were collected, including both spotted seatrout and red drum, but spot (4%) were the most numerous. More fishes were collected during the day than at night, although the relative abundances of families were similar. More fish were caught during low tides in February, May, and August, and few fish were collected during fall and winter.

Baffin Bay Baffin Bay fish have received more study than fish in any other part of the Laguna Madre system. The number of species in the resident fauna ranges from six to ten (Breuer 1962; Fuls 1974; Krull 1976), most commonly including striped mullet, gulf menhaden, gizzard shad, spot, Atlantic croaker, black drum, and spotted seatrout. Tinnin (1974) and Fuls (1974) studied the fish fauna in Laguna Salada (Alazan Bay) using trammel nets (bag mesh size 3.75 cm [1.5 in]; fig. 15.6). Relative

Fig. 15.6. *Relative abundances of fish in Baffin Bay. Trammel net data for 1971–74 from Tinnin (1974) and Fuls (1974); for 1990–91 from Hardegree (1997). Bag seine data for 1971–72 from Krull (1976); for 1990–91 from Hardegree (1997). Trawl data from Cornelius (1984)*

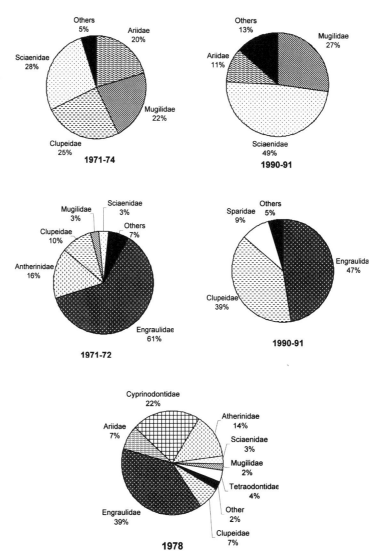

abundance of and number of species (8–9) of drum was greatest, but dominance of the moderately sized fish fauna was fairly evenly split among four families: Sciaenidae, Clupeidae (menhaden), Mugilidae (mullet), and Ariidae (sea catfish). Spot and spotted seatrout were the most abundant drum species (18–19% of total). Using larger trammel nets (bag mesh size 9 cm [3.5 in]), the relative abundance of drum captured in association with serpulid reefs throughout Baffin Bay (fig. 15.6) was more than double that captured in smaller trammel nets (Hardegree 1997). Three species dominated the fauna: black drum (20%), spotted seatrout (15%), and spot (12%). During the year after heavy rainfall associated with Tropical Storm Fern (September 1971) reduced salinities to as low as 1 ppt, the small fish fauna (5 mm [0.2 in] bag seines) in Laguna Salada was dominated by anchovies (Engraulidae; fig. 15.6; Krull 1976). It was much more diverse than the community described using similar gear throughout Baffin Bay during a period of normal hypersalinity (fig. 15.6; Hardegree 1997). The most striking difference between the faunas is the dominance of gulf menhaden (Clupeidae) in Hardegree's collections and their relative unimportance in Krull's. Although silversides (Antherinidae) were present throughout Baffin Bay, they were much more abundant in Laguna Salada at lower salinities. Likewise, pinfish (Sparidae) were present in Laguna Salada but were more abundant at "nor-

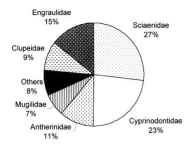

Fig. 15.7. Relative abundances of fish captured in South Bay (Data from Hook 1991)

mal" salinities. Trawl and beach seine collections from Alazan Bay (Cornelius 1984) were much more diverse than collections with other gear (fig. 15.6). Although anchovies, silversides, and menhaden constituted 60% of the fish collected, killifish (Cyprinodontidae) were important in these collections but not in the others. In addition, puffers (Tetraodontidae) were more abundant than either drum or mullet. Gobies (Gobiidae, 64%) and anchovies (35%) dominated the larval assemblage in Alazan Bay (Dokken 1981).

South Bay   The fish assemblage in South Bay was described using an otter trawl (25 cm [10 in] cod end mesh) in deep water at the entrance and a bag seine (8 mm [0.35 in] outside mesh, 4 mm [0.16 in] inside mesh) in shallow environments around the bay margin (Hook 1991). A total of 90 species in 55 families was collected, of which ten species were collected only in trawl samples. Overall, the assemblage was fairly diverse but dominated by drum (fig. 15.7), particularly spot (25.6%), and killifish, primarily sheepshead minnows (19.8%). Other important species were bay anchovy (12.7%) and tidewater silversides (*Menidia beryllina* [= *peninsulae*]; 10.8%). Seagrass habitats were dominated by spot or tidewater silversides, a black mangrove (*Avicennia germinans*) channel by sheepshead minnows, a steeply sloping unvegetated shoreline by tidewater silversides, and a shallow turbid area surrounding oyster beds by striped mullet. In addition to differences between sites, seasonal differences were also noted, with greatest abundances recorded at all sites during January. Seasonally, dominance shifted among the four most important species: winter—Gulf menhaden; spring—spot; summer—sheepshead minnow; and fall—bay anchovy. Decreased abundances of some species at some sites were associated with major changes in temperature and salinity.

Ecology of Important Invertebrate Fisheries Organisms in Texas

The economic and ecological attributes as well as general abundance patterns of ten nvertebrate fisheries organisms found in the Laguna Madre of Texas are summairized in table 15.2. Because penaeid shrimp are the most important commercial species, a more detailed overview of their ecology and abundance follows.

Penaeid Shrimp   Brown, pink, and white shrimp species are frequently encountered as adults, with substantial numbers of juveniles throughout the Laguna Madre (Nelson 1992). Adults of all three species are present primarily between March and May. Although shrimp species overlap as regards presence of juveniles during fall, major recruitment events for pink shrimp are temporally separated from those for brown and white shrimp. Juvenile pink shrimp are present September–April but are most abundant during late winter–spring, whereas juvenile brown and white shrimp are present June–November and are most abundant late summer–fall. In upper Laguna Madre, larger juvenile and subadult shrimp of all species taken in trawls appeared concentrated in Baffin Bay but were fairly evenly distributed throughout the rest of the system (Lacson and Lee 1997). Smaller shrimp taken in bag seines were concentrated at the mouth of Corpus Christi Bay. In lower Laguna Madre, pink and brown shrimp were most widely distributed, with white shrimp limited to areas along and west of the GIWW from Port Mansfield to South Bay (Stokes 1974).

Shrimp are neritic to estuarine, pelagic to demersal, depending on life stage and species (Patillo et al. 1997). Most adults are found offshore, where spawning occurs. Eggs and early larval stages are planktonic or demersal. Postlarval and early juvenile stages migrate through passes during incoming tides and disperse into shallow, often vegetated areas, where they transform into juveniles. Pink shrimp are notable in their preference for seagrass habitats in general and shoalgrass in particular, with optimum habitat consisting of dense seagrass meadows that are flushed daily by tides. Postlarvae actively select seagrass habitats, and juveniles are commonly found burrowed into the substrate of seagrass meadows during the day. Juveniles of all species migrate into open bays, where they are typically associated with shallow vegetated habitats, but they may also be found over silty sand and nonvegetated mud bottoms. Subadults migrate into coastal waters then emigrate to offshore spawning grounds during full moons and ebb tides. Most shrimp activity takes place at night.

Shrimp play an important role in estuarine food webs because they transfer a great deal of energy to top-level consumers like finfish and large crustaceans (Patillo et al. 1997). Shrimp are generally omnivorous, but their consumer roles vary with age from carnivore to detritivore and herbivore, making them important biomass converters, linking a variety of food chains together. Brown shrimp are more carnivorous than white shrimp, possibly as a result of interspecific competition. Juvenile shrimp are particularly important because they appear to support the majority of juveniles of some commercially important fish species. Predation by fish is the cause of most direct natural mortality in nursery areas. Environmental conditions, particularly habitat alteration, changing food availability, and substrate type, may affect distribution as well as mortality. Although shrimp generally prefer vegetated substrates, salinity, turbidity, and light conditions may cause them to move into nonvegetated areas where they may be more vulnerable to predation. Episodic natural catastrophes (drought, freezes, red tide) and disease are the other major causes of natural mortality.

Fisheries Stocks and Commercial Harvest: Texas

Historical Perspective Although Laguna Madre is a productive and flourishing ecosystem providing an excellent resource for commercial and recreational fishing, overfishing has long been a concern. Early in the twentieth century, Texas relied chiefly on size limits and closures to conserve fisheries resources (Pearson 1929). Higgins and Lord (1926) reported that sport fisherman believed commercial fishermen were depleting fish supplies along the Texas coast as early as 1890. In 1925, scarcity of certain fish in the markets aroused fear that fish supplies were being exhausted. Conversely, fishermen complained that regulations prevented them from supplying the markets. This brought demands from the state fishery administration, fishermen, fish dealers, state representatives, and others for an investigation of Texas fisheries. Upon studying limited records and talking with local fisherman and dealers, Higgins and Lord (1926) determined that coastwide yields were level or rising slightly between 1901 and 1924. However, yields from Corpus Christi (primarily Nueces Bay and upper Laguna Madre) and Port Isabel generally increased until WWI (1916), when no local statistics were kept (fig. 15.8). All fisheries regulations were suspended between 1916 and 1918 (WWI), after which the overall state yield increased; therefore, it is likely that local yields increased as well. In annual production, Corpus Christi ranked second from 1901 to 1924, and Port Isabel ranked fourth from 1901 to 1910 but increased to the most productive port on the coast between 1912 and 1924.

The Texas finfish fishery was concentrated on spotted seatrout and red drum between 1890 and the end of WWI, when black drum, previously considered an inferior species, equaled or slightly exceeded red drum in landings (Higgins and Lord 1926). Spotted seatrout and red drum both declined after WWI, and the fact that black drum was marketed was evidence of the scarcity of both in markets. However, the record was inadequate to determine if this was a true decline or an artifact of reg-

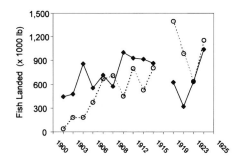

Fig. 15.8. Fish landings from Corpus Christi and Port Isabel, 1900–24 (Data from Higgins and Lord 1926)

ulations. Higgins and Lord (1926) emphasized the need for studies of the life history of several species since most regulations of the time were based on incomplete knowledge. They recommended a program of conservation including establishment of a system of fishery statistics, initiation of biological investigations, and reorganization of the Game, Fish, and Oyster Commission (now Texas Parks and Wildlife Department).

As a result of Higgins and Lord's report, a detailed study of the life history of red drum and other commercial sciaenids was initiated, as was investigation of fish kills due to hypersalinity in upper Laguna Madre and Baffin Bay. Pearson's (1929) work in the waters between Copano Bay and the Land-Cut is the earliest work on many aspects of the life histories of red drum, black drum, spotted seatrout, Atlantic croaker, and spot. He recommended reopening closed waters to drum fishing but restricting legal size to 20.3–50.8 cm (8–20 in). It is interesting to note that size limits were not enacted for black drum until 1988. Pearson especially recommended reopening upper Laguna Madre to both drum and seatrout fishing because either cold or hypersalinity "destroys great quantities of fish with no benefit whatsoever to the State of Texas." He called for closure of waters in the vicinity of passes, especially the area around Corpus Christi Pass (now Packery Channel). He reiterated previous calls to collect fisheries statistics and continue biological research. However, it was 1934 before the first biologist was hired and legislation was enacted requiring record keeping by fishermen and dealers (Ponwith and Dokken 1996). The Texas Game, Fish, and Oyster Commission began keeping records in a fairly consistent format in 1942.

Gear   A variety of methods and kinds of gear are used to harvest fish and shrimp in Texas coastal waters. Advances in technology and implementation of restrictions caused changes in the equipment used.

In the 1890s and early 1900s, most fish were harvested using seines pulled by crews in thigh-deep water (Higgins and Lord 1926). The efficiency of this method resulted in the summer seining ban in 1914, and fishermen changed to other gear types (e.g., gill and trammel nets) as a result of the regulation. Although the ban on seining was lifted in 1922, the change from seines to other nets was permanent. Another factor contributing to continued use of gill nets was the availability of cracked ice to preserve gilled fish that would formerly have spoiled before reaching market. Hook and line, cast nets, and gigs were also used to harvest fish commercially.

With the decline of red drum and spotted seatrout stocks in the late 1970s, a number of new gear restrictions were implemented to prevent further depletion and to promote recovery of the populations. Currently, nine methods can be used to harvest nongame fish: hook and line, cast net, gig, spear, minnow seine, perch trap, purse seine (menhaden only), trawls, and trotline; however restrictions apply to all. Gamefish such as red drum can only be harvested using hook and line and sail line methods. Size, bag, and possession limits are in place for selected species.

Commercial shrimping in Texas bays is closely regulated. Commercial shrimping vessels use either an otter trawl or beam trawl for harvesting shrimp. Strict laws regulate net length, trawl door size, and net mesh size. In addition, shrimping hours and bag limits are enforced for each shrimping season for all commercial shrimp (including table and bait shrimp). In addition to the large commercial shrimping vessels, small pushnet boats are used to harvest bait shrimp. However, they are illegal in all areas except a small portion of upper Laguna Madre located within Nueces County (J. Tolan, pers. comm.). Both upper and lower Laguna Madre are designated as bait bays, therefore only regulations related to bait bays apply.

Status of Important Fisheries Species   Data on species abundances and sizes since 1975 used in this section were compiled from fisheries-independent data collected by TPWD's Coastal Fisheries Management Program as summarized in Hensley and Fuls (1998).

Red Drum   Red drum is highly prized by anglers for its fight and as excellent table fare. Currently, commercial harvest of wild stocks is nonexistent in U.S. waters, but historically, the red drum was probably the most important sciaenid species harvested (Patillo et al. 1997). It remains one of the most important sciaenid sportfish and one of the seven most sought gamefishes in the Gulf of Mexico. Red drum were second only to oysters in amount and value of commercial harvest during 1890 in Refugio, Aransas, and Nueces counties and generally ranked fourth behind shrimp, spotted seatrout, and black drum in pounds harvested in Aransas and Laguna Madre districts (Rockport to Brownsville) between 1942 and 1970 (Ponwith and Dokken 1996).

Size restrictions on red drum have existed since at least the early 1920s (Pearson 1929). Fish of 36–81 cm (14–32 in) were the only salable fish between the 1920s and 1981, when the commercial fishery closed and sales were banned (Ponwith and Dokken 1996). Slot limits on sportfish have existed since that time and currently stand at 51–71 cm (20–28 in), although up to two oversized fish may be kept each year if properly tagged.

TPWD began working to restore depleted red drum populations in Texas after the commercial fishery was closed in 1981. Conventional management practices such as net bans and bag and size limits, along with a stocking program that began in earnest in 1983, started a recovery in the fishery after the mid-1980s (McEachron et al. 1998). After recovery began, management strategies emphasized maintaining populations: (1) to ensure sustainable recruitment; (2) to satisfy anglers with quality fish in sufficient numbers; and (3) to add fish to the Gulf of Mexico spawning group to maintain stocks and genetic diversity. Since 1983, over 618 million fry and 34 million fingerlings have been released into upper Laguna Madre, resulting in increased numbers of subadult fish (Lacson and Lee 1997). Since 1990, subadult red drum have become about twice as abundant as they were in the 1980s because of TPWD's long-term management efforts (McEachron et al. 1998). In addition, recreational catches increased 18% and numbers of adult red drum (>711 mm [28 in] TL) increased by more than 750%.

Mean gill net catch rates for red drum were higher in lower Laguna Madre during both fall and spring than in upper Laguna Madre (fig. 15.9). However, catch rates in both the upper and lower Laguna peaked at similar levels and at intervals of two to five years, with a general upward trend in numbers and size. Mean bag seine catch rates for upper Laguna Madre were low in the 1980s but have shown a sustained increase since 1990 (fig. 15.10). In lower Laguna Madre, mean catch rates have fluctuated widely, with peak intervals about every four to six years, with every other peak interval similar in magnitude. Mean length from bag seine collections followed the same general trend in both upper and lower Laguna Madre; however, in 1987, red drum mean length in upper Laguna Madre was nearly twice that in lower Laguna Madre. Modeled gill net catch per unit effort (CPUE) indicated a curve upward after 1982, with modeled bag seine CPUE curving upward after 1985 (Lacson and Lee 1997). Relatively few young-of-year were caught during 1983–86 as a result of the severe freeze in 1983. Overall, long-term increases in CPUE of subadult fish were attributed to effects of the netting ban, more restrictive slot limits, and stocking by Texas Parks and Wildlife Department.

Fig. 15.9. Red drum mean catch rate (number/hour; top) and mean total length (millimeters; bottom) during spring (solid line) and fall (broken line) in gill nets (all mesh sizes combined) between 1975 and 1996 in upper and lower Laguna Madre. LL = lower Laguna Madre; UL = upper Laguna Madre (Data from Hensley and Fuls 1998)

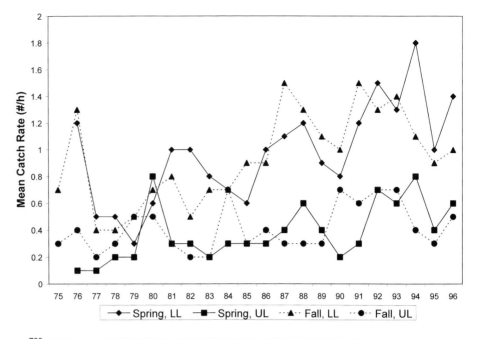

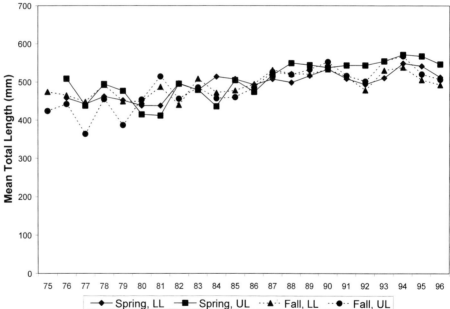

Spotted Seatrout

Spotted Seatrout Although the commercial fishery for spotted seatrout was closed in Texas in 1981, commercial landings still occur throughout the year in a few Gulf states (Patillo et al. 1991). Spotted seatrout is one of the top seven species sought by anglers, and recreational catch far exceeds commercial catch. The commercial harvest ranked third behind oysters and red drum in Refugio, Aransas, and Nueces counties in 1890 and ranked second with black drum behind shrimp between 1942 and 1970 in the Aransas and Laguna Madre districts (Ponwith and Dokken 1996). In the 1920s the spotted seatrout was described as "the most valuable marine food fish in Texas" (Pearson 1929). As in the case of red drum, seatrout size restrictions have been in place since the early 1920s, with minimum size limits for salable fish set at 30.5 cm (12 in). Today, the minimum size for retained sportfish is 38.1 cm (15 in).

In the upper Laguna Madre, gill net mean catch rate declined markedly in 1984

Fig. 15.10. Red drum annual mean catch rate (number/ha; top) and mean total length (millimeters; bottom) in 18.3 m (60.4 ft) bag seines between 1977 and 1996 in upper and lower Laguna Madre. LL = lower Laguna Madre; UL = upper Laguna Madre (Data from Hensley and Fuls 1998)

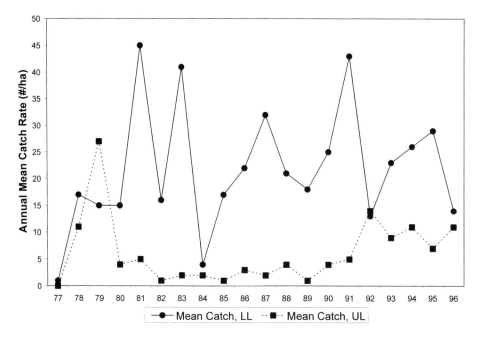

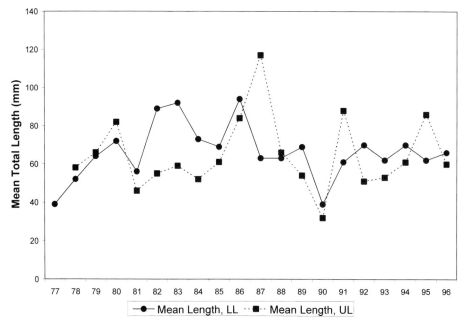

after the severe December 1983 freeze, then increased slightly in 1986 (fig. 15.11). The freeze of 1989 again decreased catch rates in the upper Laguna, but rates have shown a sustained increase since 1991. Catch rates for spotted seatrout are highest in lower Laguna Madre during spring but highest for upper Laguna Madre during fall. Mean total length of spotted seatrout varied little, with only a slight upward trend in size. Bag seine catch rates were generally low during the 1980s but increased in the 1990s, particularly in upper Laguna Madre (fig. 15.12). Mean catch rates were three to four times higher in the upper than in the lower Laguna. Mean length for spotted seatrout peaked during the 1980s, with a decreasing trend in size in the 1990s. Trend analysis indicated stability or slight improvement in CPUE, particularly after the 1986 red tide (Lacson and Lee 1997). Recovery can be attributed to removal of spotted seatrout from the commercial market, improved management measures

Fig. 15.11. Spotted seatrout mean catch rate (number/hour; top) and mean total length (millimeters; bottom) during spring (solid line) and fall (broken line) in gill nets (all mesh sizes combined) between 1975 and 1996 in upper and lower Laguna Madre. LL = lower Laguna Madre; UL = upper Laguna Madre (Data from Hensley and Fuls 1998)

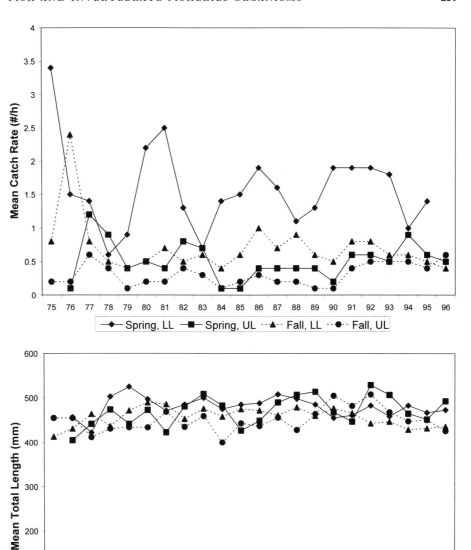

(i.e., increased minimum size limits and decreased bag and possession limits), and removal of nets from coastal waters.

Black Drum   Black drum are harvested commercially from the upper and lower Laguna Madre, primarily with trotlines. Currently, Texas supplies up to 71% of the U.S. commercial black drum landings and has supplied about the same percentage since the 1920s (Pearson 1929). Although black drum were not tallied in the commercial harvest of 1890, they represented the majority of finfish harvested in the Aransas and Laguna Madre districts in 18 of 28 years between 1942 and 1970 (Ponwith and Dokken 1996). During the 1920s, market value of black drum exceeded the value of red drum and spotted seatrout combined. Between January 1926 and May 1927, more than 60% (432,000 lb) of the total landings were black drum (Pearson

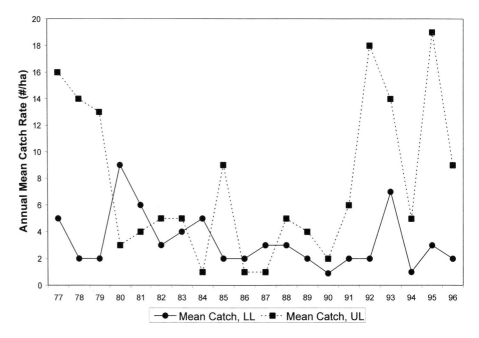

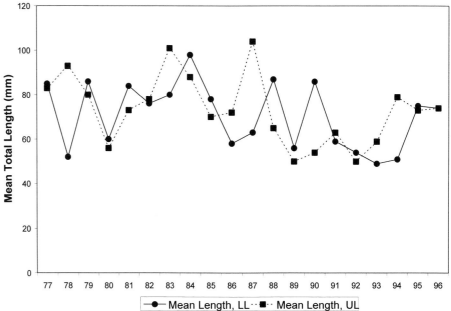

1929). Although Pearson (1929) advised placing size limits of 20.3–50.8 cm (8–20 in) on black drum to increase proportion of spawning adults, no size restrictions existed until 1988, when a slot limit of 35.6–76.2 cm (14–30 in) was adopted (Ponwith and Dokken 1996). However, Baffin and Alazan bays and the area of upper Laguna Madre known as The Hole, described by Pearson (1929) as "some of the best drum-fishing waters along the coast of Texas," were closed to seine fishing in the 1920s.

Gill net catch rates in upper Laguna Madre were low until after 1987 or 1988, when numbers began to increase (fig. 15.13). Overall, black drum catch rates for upper and lower Laguna Madre and for spring and fall seasons followed the same trends, with the exception of peaks in the fall of the late 1970s in the lower Laguna. Sizes of fish caught in gill nets varied little and have shown a steady upward trend since 1991. Bag seine catch rates have been fairly steady except for several peaks in

Fig. 15.13. Black drum mean catch rate (number/hour; top) and mean total length (millimeters; bottom) during spring (solid line) and fall (broken line) in gill nets (all mesh sizes combined) between 1975 and 1996 in upper Laguna Madre. LL = lower Laguna Madre; UL = upper Laguna Madre (Data from Hensley and Fuls 1998)

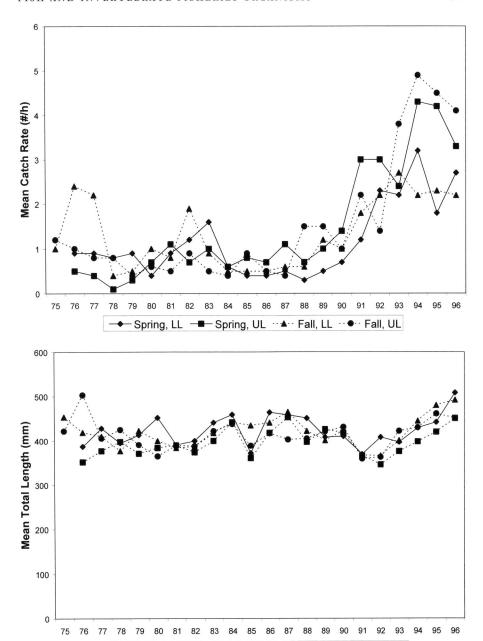

1987, 1990, 1995, and especially 1990, when 833 black drum were caught per hectare (fig. 15.14). Steadily increasing CPUE for modeled gill net catches was evidence of sustained population growth in upper Laguna Madre beginning in 1988 (Lacson and Lee 1997). Increasing subadult and adult populations were cited as evidence that brown tide was not adversely affecting reproductive populations of black drum. It is probable that size restrictions enacted during that year also played a role.

Penaeid Shrimp   Shrimp are a favorite among seafood lovers, and the shrimp fishery is the most valuable commercial fishery on the Texas coast. There is also a smaller, but important, bait fishery because shrimp are likewise a favorite food of red drum and spotted seatrout, favored sportfish among anglers. Much of the bait shrimp harvested in upper Laguna Madre is caught at night using push nets and

Fig. 15.14. Black drum annual mean catch rate (number/ha; top) and mean total length (millimeters; bottom) in 18.3 m (60.4 ft) bag seines between 1977 and 1996 in upper and lower Laguna Madre. Note the single very high value for 1990. LL = lower Laguna Madre; UL = upper Laguna Madre (Data from Hensley and Fuls 1998)

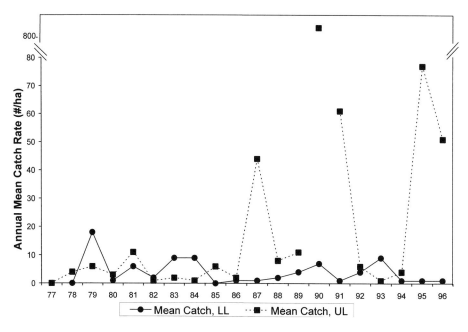

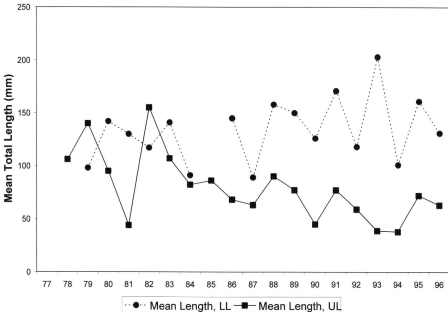

trawls. The push nets are mounted on small, shallow draft boats that are able to work the edges of grassbeds near the GIWW.

Shrimp stocks in the western Gulf of Mexico along the coasts of northern Mexico and South Texas probably represent a single entity and should be managed accordingly (Patillo et al. 1997). In general, the commercial fishery may cause large declines in parental stocks without affecting recruitment of young into the fishery the next year. However, both the brown and white shrimp fisheries are fully exploited, and the white shrimp fishery may be at the point where overfishing can occur. The pink shrimp fishery is not fully exploited, but annual catch is managed to prevent parent stocks from declining.

Shrimp represented the largest proportion of the commercial catch of all species from Rockport to Brownsville (Aransas and Laguna Madre districts) from 1942 to 1970 (Ponwith and Dokken 1996). Brown shrimp were the primary commercial

Fig. 15.15. *Brown shrimp annual mean catch rate (number/ha; top) and mean total length (millimeters; bottom) in 18.3 m (60.4 ft) bag seines between 1977 and 1996 in upper and lower Laguna Madre. LL = lower Laguna Madre; UL = upper Laguna Madre (Data from Hensley and Fuls 1998)*

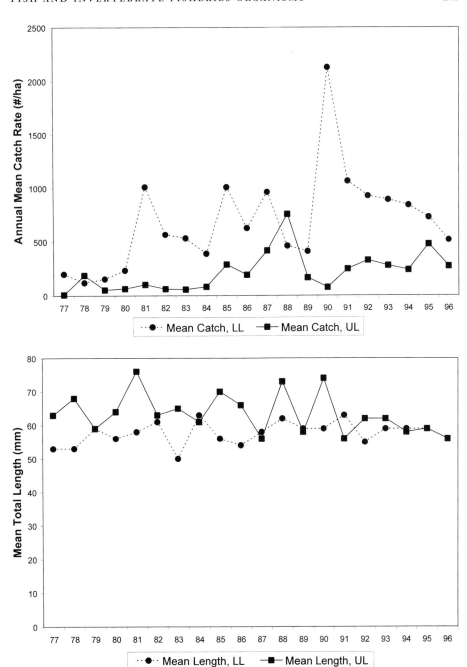

species in Texas from 1956 to 1959, particularly from the Coastal Bend south, where they constituted 96% of average annual catch in waters between Rockport and the Land-Cut and 99% in lower Laguna Madre (Gunter 1962). Brown shrimp dominated the live bait fishery in lower Laguna Madre in 1970 and 1972, but nearly equal numbers of brown and white shrimp were taken in 1971 (Stokes 1974). Brown and white shrimp remain the significant commercial penaeid species on the central and southern Texas coast (Lacson and Lee 1997).

Bag seine catch rates for brown shrimp throughout upper Laguna Madre were generally low (fig. 15.15), with a single well-defined peak in 1988 (Lacson and Lee 1997). Overall, bag seine catch rates in lower Laguna Madre were higher than in the upper Laguna; catch rates peaked in 1990 and have since sustained a steady downward trend. Mean length for brown shrimp collected in bag seines remained fairly

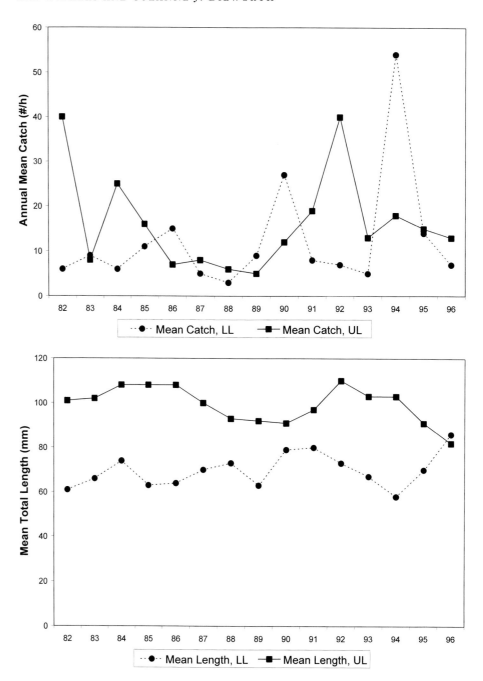

Fig. 15.16. Brown shrimp annual mean catch rate (number/hour; top) and mean total length (millimeters; bottom) in 6.1 m (20.1 ft) trawls between 1982 and 1996 in upper and lower Laguna Madre. LL = lower Laguna Madre; UL = upper Laguna Madre (Data from Hensley and Fuls 1998)

stable in the lower Laguna, while shrimp collected from upper Laguna Madre varied with an overall downward trend. Trawl mean catch rates varied widely over time, with peak intervals for the lower Laguna about every four years (fig. 15.16). Mean length of brown shrimp collected in trawls was higher in upper Laguna Madre; however, since 1994, a downward trend in size can be seen for upper Laguna Madre and an increase in size for lower Laguna Madre. Shrimp caught in bag seines were primarily juveniles, whereas shrimp from trawls were subadults (>80 mm) and of the size when offshore migration begins. Modeled trawl CPUE increased after 1990, which may have been caused by reduced fish predation due to brown tide causing low visibility conditions (Lacson and Lee 1997).

Yield of young-of-year (40–59 mm) and emigratory-sized (100–124 mm) pink shrimp improved in the early 1990s in upper Laguna Madre, suggesting that brown

Fig. 15.17. *Pink shrimp annual mean catch rate (number/ha; top) and mean total length (millimeters; bottom) in 18.3 m (60.4 ft) bag seines between 1977 and 1996 in upper and lower Laguna Madre. LL = lower Laguna Madre; UL = upper Laguna Madre (Data from Hensley and Fuls 1998)*

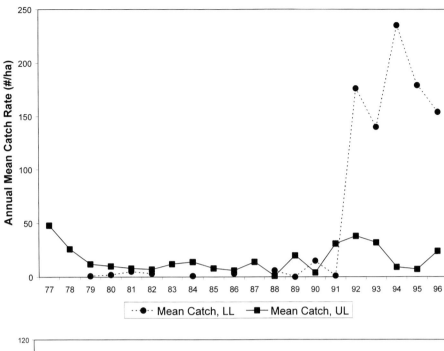

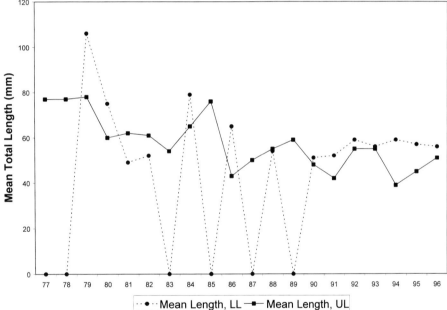

tide was not adversely affecting populations (Lacson and Lee 1997). Bag seine catch rate in upper Laguna Madre for pink shrimp was highest in 1977 (fig. 15.17), and average size has steadily declined since then, with one high peak in 1985. Bag seine catch rates in lower Laguna Madre were exceptionally low until 1992, when rates increased almost 200%. Total length for both upper and lower Laguna Madre displayed a downward trend. Trawl catch rates were low throughout the survey except in 1992, and mean total length was fairly stable except for declines noted from 1987 to 1989 (fig. 15.18).

Bag seine catch rates for white shrimp were much higher in lower than in upper Laguna Madre (fig. 15.19); however, both followed a similar trend. Mean length for bag seine catches for both upper and lower Laguna Madre were similar. Overall, trawl catch rates were higher in the upper laguna than in the lower, but both have been declining recently (fig. 15.20). Mean size of individuals collected by trawl

Fig. 15.18. *Pink shrimp annual mean catch rate (number/hour; top) and mean total length (millimeters; bottom) in 6.1 m (20.1 ft) trawls between 1982 and 1996 in upper and lower Laguna Madre. LL = lower Laguna Madre; UL = upper Laguna Madre (Data from Hensley and Fuls 1998)*

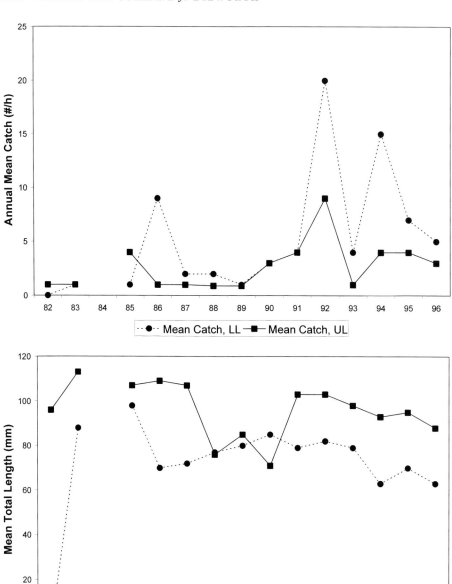

dropped in 1986 in lower Laguna Madre; however, white shrimp have increased in size, as in the upper Laguna, since that time. Overall, fewer white shrimp were caught in upper Laguna Madre than from Corpus Christi or Aransas bays, where salinities are optimal for recruitment of juvenile shrimp.

Effects of Freshwater Inflows on Commercial Harvest Freshwater inflows affect fisheries productivity through complex and poorly understood physical, chemical, and biologic pathways (TDWR 1983). Year-to-year variability in estuarine surplus production (i.e., the portion available for harvest) is affected by the timing and amount of freshwater inflows and their effects on salinity, nutrient types and availability, prey production, and habitat availability. Time-series analysis of Laguna Madre commercial inshore fisheries landings (1962–76) and shrimp harvests (1959–

Fig. 15.19. White shrimp annual mean catch rate (number/ha; top) and mean total length (millimeters; bottom) in 18.3 m (60.4 ft) bag seines between 1977 and 1996 in upper and lower Laguna Madre. LL = lower Laguna Madre; UL = upper Laguna Madre (Data from Hensley and Fuls 1998)

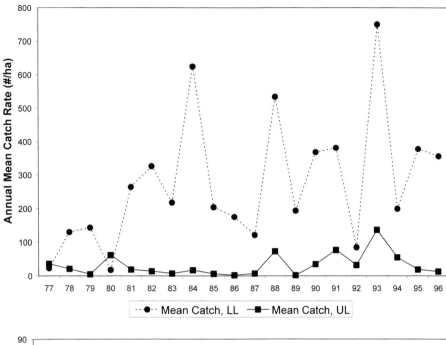

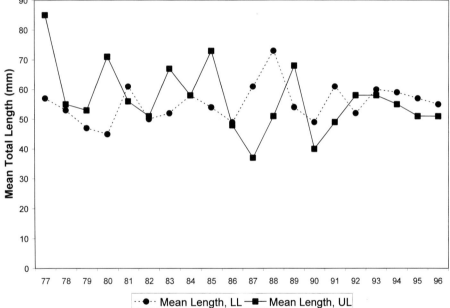

76) were used to estimate effects of freshwater inflow on harvest (table 15.3). Estimated effects for significant models were computed by holding all other correlating seasonal inflows constant at their mean values and varying the seasonal inflow of interest from its lower to upper observed value. All models were significant at $p \leq 0.05$; r^2 ranged from 0.49 (lower Laguna, bay oyster) to 0.99 (upper Laguna, all shrimp).

In upper Laguna Madre, harvest of most species appeared to respond positively to freshwater inflows between April and August. A notable exception was for black drum, which appeared to respond negatively to freshwater inflows during all time periods except July–August. In lower Laguna Madre, freshwater inflows during January–March and July–August had positive effects on most species. However, red drum appeared to respond negatively to freshwater inflows except during January–March and September–October.

Fig. 15.20. White shrimp annual mean catch rate (number/hour; top) and mean total length (millimeters; bottom) in 6.1 m (20.1 ft) trawls between 1982 and 1996 in upper and lower Laguna Madre. LL = lower Laguna Madre; UL = upper Laguna Madre (Data from Hensley and Fuls 1998)

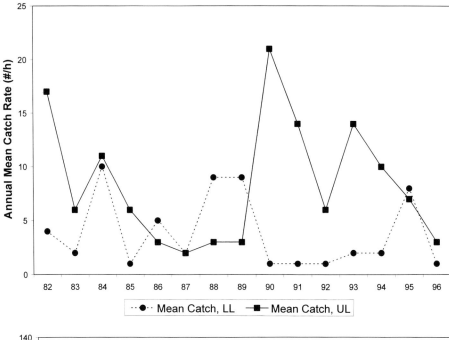

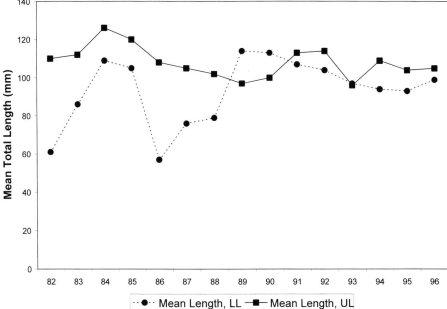

Fisheries Stocks and Commercial Harvest: Tamaulipas

Historical Perspective Historically, fisheries of Laguna Madre de Tamaulipas alternated between relatively short, productive boom periods, when salinities were marine or estuarine, and phases of increasing salinities that left the Laguna unproductive for years at a time (Hildebrand 1958, 1969, 1980). Major favorable changes resulted from singular, aperiodic, tropical storms that lowered salinities dramatically either by opening passes or because of associated heavy rainfall. Changes caused by the storms were short-lived, but organisms living within the Laguna responded rapidly to favorable conditions following storms. Very large increases in populations of both fish and shrimp occurred in subsequent months. As the duration of dry spells between major storms increased, the salt budget of the Laguna magnified; therefore, the magnitude of storms needed to cause changes also increased.

Over a period of about 100 years (1880–1980), almost half of these years (45) were

Table 15.3. *General effects of freshwater inflows on fisheries' harvests in Texas Laguna Madre based on time-series analysis of seasonal mean freshwater inflows and total commercial landings for 1959–76 (modified from TDWR 1983)*

Months of Inflow	UPPER LAGUNA MADRE					LOWER LAGUNA MADRE				
	J–M	A–J	J–A	S–O	N–D	J–M	A–J	J–A	S–O	N–D
Shellfish[a]	ns	ns	ns	ns	ns	–	ns	+	ns	ns
Penaeid shrimp[b]	–	+	–	ns	+	+	ns	ns	+	ns
White shrimp	ns	+	ns	ns	ns	+	ns	–	ns	–
Brown and pink shrimp	–	ns	ns	ns	ns	+	ns	ns	+	ns
Blue crab[c]	ns	ns	ns	ns	ns	ns	ns	ns	ns	ns
Bay oyster	nd	nd	nd	nd	nd	–	ns	+	ns	ns
Finfish	ns	+	+	ns	–	+	–	+	ns	ns
Spotted seatrout	ns	+	+	ns	ns	ns	ns	+	ns	ns
Red drum	ns	+	+	ns	ns	+	–	–	+	–
Black drum	–	–	+	–	ns	ns	–	+	–	ns

Note: Months of inflow: J–M = January–March; A–J = April–June; J–A = July–August; S–O = September–October; N–D = November–December. ns = not significant; + = significant positive correlation; – = significant negative correlation.

[a] Includes shrimp, crabs, and oysters.

[b] Lower Laguna Madre is offshore shrimp harvest in Gulf Area No. 21.

[c] Found in South Bay only.

not productive (Hildebrand 1969, 1980). From 1880 to 1909, passes were closed and water levels were low, and area inhabitants petitioned the government to reopen the passes in 1902 and 1907. Unfortunately, there were no records of the fisheries during this period. A 1909 hurricane reopened all the passes and the lagoon was productive from 1909 through 1914. The first record of commercial landings from Laguna Madre de Tamaulipas was in 1911, when the catch from a fishing camp at La Capilla was transported by mule team to Brownsville. Conflicting accounts for the period of 1914–26 suggested that passes were closed during 1916–17. The Laguna was moderately productive between 1919 and 1924. All passes were apparently completely closed in 1926, and the Laguna remained unproductive until 1933. During 1933, four hurricanes opened eight passes, and the laguna remained moderately productive until 1960, although the northern area was occasionally extremely hypersaline.

Gear   Harvest regulations and methods in waters off the coast of Mexico are quite different than those implemented and practiced in U.S. waters. The fishing method of choice in Laguna Madre de Tamaulipas is the shrimp trap, more commonly known as a *charanga* (Hildebrand 1980), and as many as 10,000 may be in use (Cruz-Nieto 2000). Charangas are V-shaped traps that terminate in a mesh-enclosed rectangular *yagual* or *matadero* and may be used individually or with as many as eight connected together (Hildebrand 1980). Charangas are set in channels, passes, or near shore and are set to shrimp on an ebbing current. Normally, they are fished only at night, but they may be used during the day as well, particularly when fishing for white shrimp.

Another common fishing device used in Mexican waters was the *chinchorro*, a large drag seine that effectively captures great numbers of white shrimp (Hildebrand 1980). These devices are now illegal (Cruz-Nieto 2000). Originally chinchorros were used exclusively to capture fish, but because of increases in shrimp populations in Laguna Madre de Tamaulipas and increased marketability, the nets were modified to harvest shrimp. These nets consist of two wings, up to 600 m (1,980 ft) in length, and a bag. They may be used as stop-nets across an ebbing current and periodically pulled ashore, or they may be dragged between two sailboats for several hours then closed and retrieved. At times these nets have been set across Gulf passes to harvest migrating fish, but they were primarily used for harvesting white shrimp.

Fishing methods used by commercial fishermen in Laguna Madre de Tamaulipas were being restricted by 1980 (Hildebrand 1980). Otter trawls were banned to prevent habitat destruction. Other concerns were illegal (small) mesh sizes on charangas and chinchorros, which result in the deaths of many unmarketable shrimp and fish. Charangas were also restricted because they contribute to closing of passes and silting of channels and hinder movement of small juveniles to nursery grounds. Historically, fishing regulations have not been strictly enforced.

Important Fisheries Organisms   Approximately 80% of fish species within Laguna Madre de Tamaulipas are characterized as having some commercial use (Leija-Tristan et al., in press). The shrimp fishery in Laguna Madre de Tamaulipas expanded rapidly after 1972 (Hildebrand 1980), and currently about 90% of the fishing effort is dedicated to harvest of penaeid shrimp (Gomez-Soto and Contreras Balderas 1987). Black drum was the principal commercial finfish species, although red drum and spotted seatrout were the primary fishes exported to the United States between 1944 and 1962 (Hildebrand 1969). Before some passes were open and maintained, fisheries in Laguna Madre de Tamaulipas were characterized as boom-bust resources because their productivity was dependent on salinities within the lagoon (Hildebrand 1980). The following discussion of the finfish and shrimp fisheries in Laguna Madre de Tamaulipas comes from the work of Hildebrand (1958, 1969, 1980).

Large-scale exploitation of the Laguna started around 1935, when it became feasible to haul fish to market. The fishery was entirely in the northern Laguna until 1947. Between 1935 and 1941, 8.8–13.2 million kg (19–29 million lb) of fish, mostly red drum and spotted seatrout, were harvested each year from Laguna Madre de Tamaulipas. Yields of both red drum and spotted seatrout were high during most years between 1944 and 1960 (figs. 15.21, 15.22). In general, red drum exports were only about 30–50% of the exports of spotted seatrout. Sportfishing was extremely good during those years. Hildebrand (1969) reports photographing 112 red drum weighing a total of 1,200 lb, caught by five fishermen in only six hours in the north-

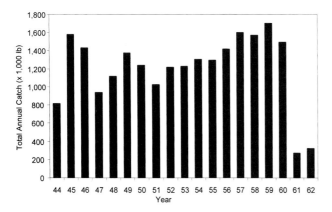

Fig. 15.21. Total red drum imports at Port Isabel and Brownsville, Texas, from the Laguna Madre de Tamaulipas, 1944–62 (Data from Hildebrand 1969)

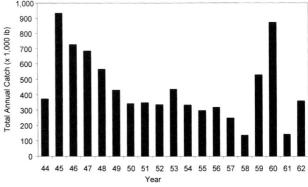

Fig. 15.22. Total spotted seatrout imports at Port Isabel and Brownsville, Texas, from the Laguna Madre de Tamaulipas, 1944–62 (Data from Hildebrand 1969)

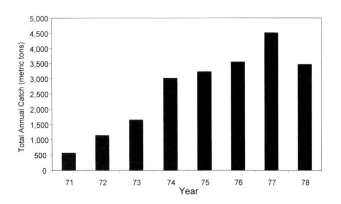

Fig. 15.23. *Total shrimp catch in the Laguna Madre de Tamaulipas for 1971–78 (Data from Hildebrand 1980)*

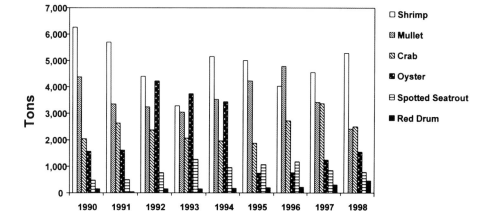

Fig. 15.24. *Commercial landings from Laguna Madre de Tamaulipas, 1990–98 (J. Brenner, pers. comm., data from Secretaria del Medio Ambiente, Recursos Naturales y Pesca)*

Fig. 15.25. *Comparison of Texas Gulf and Laguna Madre de Tamaulipas inshore shrimp landings, 1990–98*

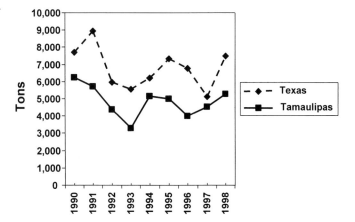

ern lagoon. Shrimp were not important fisheries organisms, with catches remaining small during the 1950s except during 1959.

From 1961 to 1967, passes were closed except briefly after Hurricane Carla in 1961. A dramatic decline in amount of fish imported was evident in 1961 (figs. 15.21, 15.22), when imports of both species declined by about 80% compared to the previous year. The good year for shrimp in 1959 led to a large number of charangas being placed in the Laguna, especially around Boca Jesús María, and these shrimp traps were thought to be the main reason the pass closed in 1960. Hurricane Beulah, accompanied by torrential rains, reopened passes in 1967. Productivity, especially of shrimp, was high between 1971 and 1978 (fig. 15.23). There was one report that as much as four tons of shrimp were caught in a chinchorro during one trip in 1972.

During this time, the goal of the Mexican fishery department appeared to be to maximize the shrimp fishery in Laguna Madre de Tamaulipas without regard for the offshore fishery. By 1975, most chinchorro fisherman had reduced the mesh size of their large bag seine nets and were fishing primarily for shrimp. By 1976, conversion of fishnets to shrimpnets was essentially complete and resulted in the large increase in catch of shrimp during 1977. Decline in shrimp landings in 1978 was attributed to actual shortages, possibly due to a combination of overfishing and environmental conditions rather than to changes in price or effort.

Between 1990 and 1998, inshore shrimp landings were generally higher than during the 1970s (fig. 15.24) and consistently lower than the Texas offshore harvest (fig. 15.25). The general trend of higher and lower shrimp harvests was the same inshore in Tamaulipas as it was offshore in Texas. Red drum and spotted seatrout continued to be harvested (fig. 15.24) but at relatively low rates. Of interest is the harvest of mullet, which generally increased through the mid-1990s, and of oysters, which in the Texas Laguna Madre are harvested only from South Bay in the lower Laguna. Oyster harvest in Laguna Madre de Tamaulipas peaked in 1992, four years after Hurricane Gilbert made landfall near La Pesca, possibly freshening the system, but dropped dramatically in 1995. Oyster harvest appeared to be beginning another increase in 1997, possibly due to freshening by tropical systems that came near the northern coast (Tropical Storm Josephine) and went in near Tampico (Hurricane Dolly) in 1996.

Part III   Special Issues and Concerns

16   *Red and Brown Tides*

KIM WITHERS

Both red and brown tides are classified as harmful algal blooms and occur worldwide. Red tides are typically harmful because the organisms that cause them produce toxins that can be deadly to fish and marine invertebrates and may cause health problems in humans either through ingestion of toxins contained in shellfish or via aerosols that may cause respiratory difficulties. On the other hand, brown tides may alter species abundance, distribution, and diversity due to allelopathy, light reduction, inhibiting organisms' ability to feed, or by replacing more nutritious food sources (Street et al. 1997), causing changes throughout the estuarine food web.

Historically, occurrences of reddish or brownish colored "bad water" in Laguna Madre have been noted (Gunter 1945a; Simmons 1957). Although the causative agent of this historical bad water cannot be known with certainty, dissolved iron, humic compounds from decaying vegetation, phytoplankton, and/or suspended clay particles have been suggested.

Brown Tide

An uninterrupted bloom of the "Texas Brown Tide" persisted from January 1990 to October 1997 in Laguna Madre and Baffin Bay (Buskey et al. 1996, 1997, 1998). Bloom conditions persist in some parts of the system and during some times of the year even at this writing. The alga causing the bloom is a very small (4–5 μ diameter), morphologically indistinct phytoplankton species in Division Pelagophyta (DeYoe et al. 1995), recently described as *Aureoumbra lagunensis* (DeYoe et al. 1997). This organism is not endemic to Laguna Madre and has been detected using immunofluorescence techniques in Nueces–Corpus Christi Bay, Matagorda Bay, and Lavaca Bay in Texas as well as in three South Florida bays (Lopez-Barreiro et al. 1998). Apparently the organism is present in low concentrations in coastal bays throughout the western Gulf of Mexico, and because it is both minute and visibly unremarkable, it is considered part of the "hidden flora" (Buskey et al., in press).

Aureoumbra lagunensis was first noted in water samples collected in August 1989 from the upper reaches of Laguna Salada, Cayo del Grullo, and Alazan Bay. Although bloom conditions had not previously been reported as having occurred until January 1990, more recent data indicate that the bloom may have started in these secondary bays as early as October 1989, and immunofluorescence suggests that bloom conditions were present within Baffin Bay proper on 19 December 1989 (Buskey et al., in press). The bloom was restricted to Baffin Bay and its secondary bays until May 1990, when a major flushing event washed the bloom out into upper Laguna Madre (Buskey et al. 1996). The organism spread into lower Laguna Madre when strong north winds associated with winter cold fronts pushed water south through the Land-Cut. Amazingly, this organism has been present in bloom concentrations in at least some parts of upper and lower Laguna Madre and especially Baffin Bay for more than nine years, the longest algal bloom ever recorded. It has also reached near bloom proportions in northern Laguna Madre de Tamaulipas (Lopez-Barreiro 1998). Earlier occurrences of bad water, which might have been caused by the same organism, were apparently neither long-lasting nor severe.

Initiation and Persistence   There is some evidence that the relative importance of seagrasses, macrophytic algae, and phytoplankton as primary producers in Baffin Bay may have shifted for decades at a time over the last few thousand years (Anderson et al. 1992). This suggests that persistent phytoplankton blooms in Laguna Madre may not be unusual but merely unknown in our limited experience and life span. The phenomenon may be characteristic of "blind estuaries," with the causative organisms remaining in the mouths of the few small streams flowing into the lagoons until conditions favor a bloom (H. Hildebrand, pers. comm.). A bloom of phytoplankton can only occur and persist if algal growth exceeds losses to sinking, mixing, flushing, disease, grazing, and other mortality (Buskey et al. 1997). The initiation of the brown tide was the result of an interaction of two climatologic events: drought with its associated hypersalinity and a severe freeze with its associated fish kill (DeYoe and Suttle 1994). The synergism of these conditions resulted from a unique set of biological and environmental circumstances that allowed algal growth to exceed mortality, setting the system up for a major change in the dominant primary producer. Unless otherwise noted, the following is a summarization of literature and data presented by Buskey and colleagues (1996, 1997, 1998, in press) concerning initiation and persistence of brown tide.

As a consequence of the extended drought that gripped South Texas in 1989, extreme hypersalinity (≤ 60 ppt) occurred within the upper reaches of Baffin Bay. In the months preceding the bloom, increased salinities corresponded to decreased populations of microzooplankton, major grazers of phytoplankton the size of the brown tide organism. Prior to the bloom, microzooplankton consumed as much as 98% of phytoplankton standing stock in upper Laguna Madre and Baffin Bay. Concomitantly in Baffin Bay, populations of dwarf surfclam *(Mulinia lateralis)*, a benthic filter feeder, were nearly extirpated. Populations of the filter-feeding polychaete *Streblospio benedicti* increased by four orders of magnitude in the months prior to onset of the bloom in both Baffin Bay and upper Laguna Madre but began to decline soon after the bloom began. In addition, large numbers of invertebrates were killed by high salinities in Baffin Bay during the year preceding the bloom.

Then, in December 1989, two severe cold fronts within seven days resulted in freezing conditions along the coast. After the second front, water temperatures in Baffin Bay dropped to 0.2°C (35.6°F) and remained below 5°C (41°F) for seven days, whereas in upper Laguna Madre water temperatures dropped to –1.6°C (29°F) and remained below 0°C (32°F) for 36 hours. These two severe freezes resulted in a fish kill estimated at 965,000 fish in Baffin Bay and upper Laguna Madre (DeYoe and Suttle 1994).

Mortality of invertebrates due to hypersalinity followed by a large fish and invertebrate kill resulting from freezing weather meant large inputs of nitrogen into the system. Concentrations of dissolved inorganic nitrogen (DIN) in Baffin Bay and upper Laguna Madre more than doubled between October 1989 and January 1990 and peaked in March 1990. As much as 95% of the DIN was ammonium (NH_4^+), which was beneficial to the brown tide organism since, unlike other algae, it is unable to use nitrate (NO_3^-) as a nitrogen source. However, hypersaline conditions and fish kills associated with freezing weather have occurred before in Laguna Madre without initiating major algal blooms (e.g., Gunter and Hildebrand 1951). Since there is evidence of bloom conditions prior to the freeze, nitrogen from the fish kill may not have initiated the bloom, but at the very least, these inputs of nitrogen probably intensified the growth phase of the bloom. A slight drop in silica levels prior to the bloom may also have contributed by preventing diatoms from competing successfully with the brown tide alga.

In Naragansett Bay, an outbreak of brown tide caused by a related pelagophyte species, *Aureococcus anophagefferens*, began under similar conditions of depressed microzooplankton populations (Smayda and Villareal 1989). However, once the bloom was established, grazer populations rebounded and phytoplankton populations decreased, suggesting that grazers affected the decline. It would be logical for microzooplankton populations in upper Laguna Madre and Baffin Bay to rebound in the presence of such an abundant food source, but this was not the case. After the bloom spread into upper Laguna Madre, both micro- and mesozooplankton populations declined, apparently because *Aureoumbra lagunensis* does not supply them with the nutrients they need, so it is not heavily grazed. Although dwarf surfclams are able to feed on *A. lagunensis* and appear able to derive from it adequate nutrition, populations had already declined to the point that they were unable to impact progression of the bloom. The only protozoan species found to grow well on a diet of *A. lagunensis* alone, the heterotrophic dinoflagellate *Oxyrrhis marina*, was adversely affected by hypersalinity. In addition, early in the bloom large amounts of algae coagulated and settled to the bottom, potentially interfering with surface deposit or suspension feeders, further impacting grazer controls.

Essentially, the bloom was initiated due to a breakdown in the factors that control algal growth. The physical controls of sinking, mixing, and flushing are always minimal in Laguna Madre due to its shallowness and a turnover time greater than one year. The breakdown of grazer controls coupled with abundant nitrogen set the system up for the bloom. The question of why it persisted for so long remains poorly understood. Long turnover times probably contributed, since small blooms attributed to the same species in both Nueces and Copano bays lasted approximately as long as the turnover times in those bays. Viral disease may also have contributed to the demise of the bloom in Nueces Bay. However, blooms do not persist for years in other water bodies with low flushing rates, such as lakes, so other factors must be at work. The crux of the explanation seems to lie in the inability of grazers to bring the bloom under control. The reasons for this failure are unclear, but *A. lagunensis* is somewhat toxic to some species of planktonic grazers, causing growth inhibition, and since it is a poor food source for those same organisms, predation pressure of mesozooplankton on microzooplankton has undoubtedly increased. Increased predation pressure on microzooplankton populations probably helped keep their numbers too low for grazing to impact the bloom significantly.

Another factor contributing to persistence of the bloom was hypersalinity. Hypersalinity provides conditions under which *A. lagunensis* thrives, but it causes reduced growth in many other algae and potential grazer species. In the laboratory, maximum growth rates of *A. lagunensis* were observed at 25°C (77°F) and salinities of 30–50 ppt, but the organism is able to continue growth at salinities between 15 and 80 ppt. In fact, decreased salinities (<30 ppt) as a result of heavy rains in late summer and early fall of 1997 coincided with declines in cell concentrations below bloom levels. Although lower salinities undoubtedly impacted growth of *A. lagunensis*, the favorable effect of lower salinities on both grazers and algal competitors likely contributed to the temporary demise of the bloom.

Effects   The persistence of the brown tide bloom in upper Laguna Madre and Baffin Bay has had two major effects: long-term light reduction and alteration of food webs. Significant declines in shoalgrass (*Halodule beaudettei* [= *wrightii*]) cover and biomass in upper Laguna Madre have been attributed to reduced penetration of sunlight (Dunton 1994; Onuf 1996b). Additional information on the effect of brown tide on seagrass meadows can be found in chapter 7. Production by benthic microflora also declined to nearly nothing due to shading (Blanchard and Montagna 1992).

Declines in abundance and diversity of a variety of organisms including micro- and mesozooplankton and benthic invertebrates have also been noted (Buskey and Stockwell 1993; Buskey and Hyatt 1995; Buskey et al. 1996; Street et al. 1997). The primary mechanisms thought to be responsible for loss of diversity are either the inability of grazing organisms to assimilate the brown tide organism or allelopathy (Street et al. 1997). The brown tide alga is toxic to young larval fish but does not appear toxic to adult fish or macroinvertebrates (Buskey and Stockwell 1993; Buskey et al. 1996).

Benthic diversity declined markedly in Alazan Bay, which is largely devoid of submerged vegetation and where brown tide dominated primary production (Street et al. 1997). Diversity also declined in upper Laguna Madre, but seagrasses remained the dominant primary producers, and the decline was not as severe. The food web of Alazan Bay was phytoplankton based, whereas the food web of upper Laguna Madre was based on seagrass detritus and phytoplankton. The six benthic species that remained in Alazan Bay appeared able to use brown tide or brown tide detritus as a food source, based on carbon isotope data. Some fish altered their diets, switching to those species that remained. In the more complex food web of upper Laguna Madre, brown tide supported a planktonic food web, but seagrass detritus remained the primary source of carbon for benthic organisms. However, if seagrass loss continues, there is potential for more dramatic alterations to the Laguna Madre food web. Adult fish appear unaffected by the brown tide, but because they are relatively long-lived, it may take years for changes at lower trophic levels to affect their populations.

Red Tide

Two dinoflagellates that cause red tides, *Gymnodinium breve* (= *Ptychodiscus brevis*) and *Alexandrium* (= *Gonyaulax*) *monilita*, are present in Laguna Madre phytoplankton communities (Gunter 1945b; Simmons 1957; Hildebrand and King 1978). Few occurrences of red tide caused by *G. breve* have been documented in Laguna Madre. A fish kill in late November 1990 alerted public health officials and marine scientists to a bloom in the Brownsville Ship Channel, which lasted until April 1991 (Buskey et al. 1996). In addition, South Bay was closed to shellfish harvesting in March 1991 as a result of the bloom. Red tide was also documented in upper Laguna Madre during September–October 1996, with some fish mortality, primarily pinfish *(Lagodon rhomboides)* and striped mullet *(Mugil cephalus)*. In addition, a moderate fish kill of striped mullet, Atlantic needlefish *(Strongylura marina)*, and hardhead catfish *(Arius felis)* during October 1996 near Green Island in lower Laguna Madre was attributed to red tide (Hensley and Fuls 1998). No red tides have been documented in Laguna Madre de Tamaulipas; however, several blooms have occurred in the nearshore waters around La Pesca and may have spread into lagoonal waters (H. Hildebrand, pers. comm.).

Blooms may be more common in Laguna Madre than is realized. Buskey et al. (1996) cited the many closures of shellfish beds by the Texas Department of Health due to short-lived, local blooms of *G. breve* as evidence that red tides may be more frequent in South Texas inshore waters than is generally known. However, no commercial shellfish beds are present in Laguna Madre other than in South Bay. Hence only a severe bloom resulting in fish kills would even be noticed. Prevailing hypersalinity may restrict *G. breve* from reaching bloom populations. Optimal salinity for *G. breve* has been documented as 27–37 ppt, although the organism was able to survive salinities of 46 ppt for 10 weeks (Aldrich and Wilson 1960).

17 The Laguna Madre: A Conservation Framework

JAMES F. BERGAN

Bounded by the Mississippi Delta in Louisiana and the Río Soto la Marina at the southern terminus of the Laguna Madre de Tamaulipas in Mexico is the Gulf Coast Prairies and Marshes (GCPM) ecoregion. Parts of it lie in two states within two countries, and it encompasses 22 primary bays, 19 major rivers, and nearly 1,000 km (1,600 mi) of shoreline.

Ecoregional Context

Estimates of total surface area of the GCPM ecoregion range upward of 6.4 million ha (Britton and Morton 1989). Biologically vast and complex as this ecoregion is, it faces equal or greater complexity in the threats to ecological processes that drive the productivity of the region. Humans have always been drawn to the Gulf of Mexico. Nomadic native peoples took advantage of the bounty of food resources—oysters, shrimp, fish, alligators, birds—available in nearshore waters and on the coastal prairies (Ricklis 1996). Today, the attraction is fueled by industrial development and distribution, business infrastructure, agricultural production, and the appeal of a coastal lifestyle with associated recreational and aesthetic attributes.

The Nature Conservancy (the Conservancy) recognizes the complexity of the GCPM ecoregion not only in a biological context but also in a socioeconomic setting. Just as there are unique species of animals, plants, and plant communities within the region, so too are there unique population, economic, cultural, and social attributes. To meet our the Conservancy's mission, which is to preserve the plants, animals, and natural communities that represent the diversity of life on earth by protecting the lands and waters they need to survive, we must frame our conservation action within the acceptable limits of each community in which we work. We must guide our site-based actions by the best available conservation science information. Where data are lacking or inconclusive, we must be proactive in filling information gaps to focus our actions better. Within the GCPM ecoregion, if the Conservancy is to be successful, we must facilitate the means by which people can live productively and sustainably while conserving biological diversity. This is especially pertinent in the Laguna Madre portion of the GCPM ecoregion within both Texas and Tamaulipas.

Before European settlement, the GCPM ecoregion was composed of a mosaic of tallgrass coastal prairie, riparian bottomland hardwood forests, ephemeral freshwater wetlands, canebrake swamps, extensive coastal forests, chenier woodlands, freshwater tidal wetlands, brush mottes and corridors, barrier islands, estuaries, saltwater marshes, hypersaline lagoons, lomas, and associated Tamaulipan thornscrub habitats. This integrated matrix of habitat types combined to form one of the biologically richest and most productive ecosystems in the world (Briggs 1974; Smeins et al. 1991). The ecoregion has been transformed dramatically since the early 1900s. Freshwater wetlands have been reduced by 50% (Moulton et al. 1997), coastal forests have been cleared and fragmented (Lange 1997), the chenier woodlands of the upper Texas coast are essentially gone (Gosselink et al. 1979), and less than 2% of the tallgrass coastal prairie is left (Smeins et al. 1991). Remaining representative pieces of most habitat types are generally small, fragmented, and degraded in some way (exotic plants, disrupted hydrology, overgrazing, channelization, etc.).

Large landholdings are also becoming less and less common due to inheritance taxes and development pressure. However, in the Laguna Madre portion of the GCPM ecoregion, large-scale land ownership is the norm. Many of the development pressures that have been felt along other portions of the ecoregion have not occurred within the Laguna Madre. This factor, along with a history of sound private land stewardship, provides the Conservancy a unique opportunity to develop well-leveraged conservation actions in this portion of the ecoregion. In other words, instead of being reactive to a rapid decline in biodiversity, we can be proactive.

Nonetheless, in conservation, the only constant is change. Laguna Madre was established as a high conservation priority for the Conservancy during the early 1990s, with recognition that it is an internationally important resource. The Nature Conservancy's counterpart in Mexico, Pronatura Noreste, has been leading conservation planning efforts for the Laguna Madre de Tamaulipas. Pronatura Noreste has adopted and adapted the Conservancy's ecoregional planning methodology and is presently working in parallel with efforts in Texas. Being proactive and working in partnership with other nongovernmental organizations, private landowners, and other entities, the Conservancy hopes to develop long-lasting and sustainable conservation strategies that will benefit the binational resource of Laguna Madre and its residents and visitors alike.

The Conservancy Approach to Conservation

Every journey starts with a single step. We thought our first step must be as big as possible. Thus, early in our conservation planning for Laguna Madre, we realized that ecological characterization information regarding the Laguna Madre of Texas and Tamaulipas was disjointed, with many vital portions of the literature not readily available. Substantial data were embedded within unpublished reports and in-house documents. We considered it imperative to develop a "one-stop shopping source" for biological information, not only to assist our own conservation planning efforts but for all private landowners, researchers, federal and state resource managers, and all those with a deep interest in Laguna Madre. This compendium captures the state of knowledge regarding Laguna Madre. Conservation strategies will be based in large part on the contents of this work.

As noted, the mission of the Conservancy is to preserve plants, animals, and natural communities that represent the diversity of life on earth by protecting the lands and waters they need to survive. To accomplish this mission, the Conservancy has launched an ambitious and innovative approach to focus on conserving the best examples of native species and plant communities. In essence, for biodiversity conservation to be successful, we must look at larger scales and along ecological boundaries instead of geopolitical lines. This new approach, termed "Conservation by Design," is centered upon our conservation goal of securing the long-term survival of all viable native species and community types through the design and conservation of portfolios of sites within ecoregions (TNC 1996). How we achieve this goal is through a focused process of conservation target delineation and identification upon the landscape. Each site in the portfolio is an area within which we or our partners can work at sustainable levels to conserve, or where necessary to restore, the ecological processes that maintain the elements for which that site was selected.

Fig. 17.1. The ecoregional planning process as defined by the Nature Conservancy

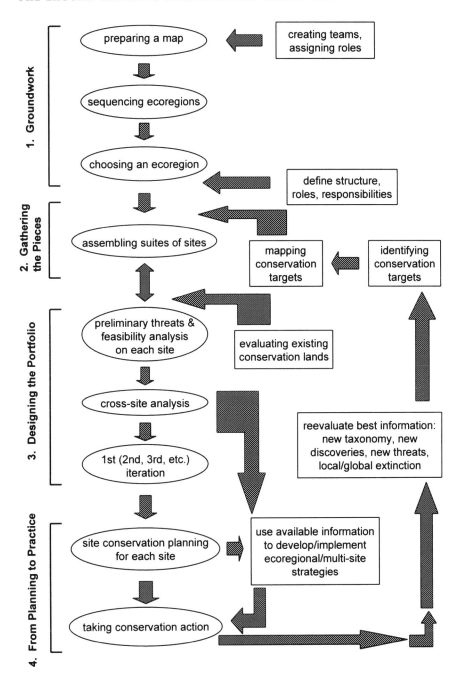

The Gulf Coast Prairies and Marshes Ecoregion is one of 63 ecoregions the Conservancy has delineated in the continental United States. Boundaries are based primarily upon patterns and distribution of species, communities, and associated biotic (plants and animals) and abiotic factors (e.g., soil type, climate; Bailey 1998). While many sites are yet to be selected for the ecoregional portfolio, the Laguna Madre megasite was formally designated as a phase I ecoregional portfolio site in 1996.

How the Conservancy carries out ecoregional planning is charted by *Designing a Geography of Hope: A Practitioner's Handbook for Ecoregional Planning* (Groves et al. 2000). Essentially, the process involves 13 steps, from mapping the ecoregions to taking conservation action (fig. 17.1). At the outset, conservation targets (species of animals and plants, plant communities) are selected, and site-specific ecological processes critical to long-term viability of those conservation targets are evaluated.

The next step involves formulating an assessment of conservation target vulnerability (i.e., threats, stresses, and their sources) and then evaluating the leverage and opportunity for conservation success, based in part on location upon the landscape and on genetic diversity and flow in relation to existing conservation areas possessing identified targets. Of utmost importance is the need to recognize that biodiversity exists at many levels of ecological scale, such as species, communities, ecosystems, and landscapes. Geographic scale can vary from several square meters to millions of hectares (Poiani and Richter 1999).

Historically, the Conservancy has usually worked at local scales (<800 ha, although there are exceptions). Such sites have included small-patch communities and ecological systems (e.g., bogs, individual wetland basins). Local-scale species (plants, invertebrates, desert spring fish species) generally have limited ranges. However, in recent years the Conservancy has been working at much larger scales, from intermediate to regional. Intermediate-scale species rely upon large-patch communities and ecological systems that are discrete and easily defined (e.g., coastal salt marsh). Intermediate-scale species could include wintering redheads *(Aythya americana)* and whooping cranes *(Grus americana)*. Depending upon the specific ecological system and regional context, intermediate-scale biodiversity occurs at 400 to 20,000 ha. Coarse-scale sites generally range from 8,000 to 400,000 ha and consist of terrestrial matrix communities. Examples include longleaf pine forests and the sky island forest matrix found in mountain ranges within the Chihuahuan Desert. The highest order of ecological scale is defined as regional, with 400,000 ha the minimum area required for sustainability for regional-scale species. Migratory animals and high-end predators (bats, fishes, bear) are examples of regional-scale species or animal groups (Poiani and Richter 1999).

The Laguna Madre megasite is defined as a functional landscape. This means that multiple ecological systems (barrier island, Coastal Sand Plains, hypersaline lagoon), multiple communities (Tamaulipan thornscrub, freshwater wetlands), and multiple species (ocelot *[Felis pardalis]*, reddish egret *[Egretta rufescens]*), occur at all scales below regional—that is, coarse, intermediate, and local. The total area of the Laguna Madre region far exceeds 400,000 ha, and indeed, our focus is upon the various scales at which conservation strategies will be applied. Functional landscapes possess a high degree of intactness and maintain (or can have restored) most or all of their key ecological patterns, processes, and components. Conservation targets selected within functional landscapes often represent other biodiversity at various scales. For example, selection of a shorebird guild as a conservation target would also capture ecological systems and communities such as wind-tidal flats, beach habitats, washover passes, and some freshwater wetland systems.

Site Conservation Planning for a Binational Resource

Conservation Target Selection   The Nature Conservancy has identified 40 zoological targets (species and guilds), 53 botanical targets, and 11 community targets that are documented from or thought to exist in the Laguna Madre region (table 17.1). Pronatura Noreste has identified 84 zoological targets, 30 botanical targets, and eight community targets for the Mexican portion of the Laguna Madre. Of these targets, 17 zoological species and guilds, five botanical targets, and four communities are common to both Texas and Mexico portions of the region (table 17.1).

While conservation strategies center around species of plants and animals and vegetation communities, we have selected a list of ecological systems and species as targets that capture multiple scales of biodiversity (table 17.1). Essentially, we think that if our focus is maintained upon this suite of systems and species, we will capture

Table 17.1. *Focal conservation targets (communities, guilds, or species) and associated nested conservation targets (communities, guilds, or species) within the Laguna Madre of Texas*

Conservation Targets	FOCAL TARGETS						
	Tamaulipan Thornscrub Matrix	Coastal Sand Plains Clay Dune and Prairie Complex	Hypersaline Lagoon–Seagrasses	Barrier Islands	Reddish Egret	Shorebird Guild	Ocelot
Plants							
Amelia's sand verbena (*Abronia ameliae*)		X					
Bailey ballmoss (*Tillandsia baileyi*)		X					
Bigflower bladderpod (*Lesquerella grandiflora*)		X					
Black mangrove (*Avicennia germinans*)				X			
Black-laced cactus (*Echinocereus reichenbachii*) var. *(albertii)*	X						
Bristle-free least daisy (*Chaetopappa imberbis*)		X					
Clovergrass (*Halophila engelmannii*)			X				
Coastal Bend greenthread (*Thelesperma nuecense*)		X					
Cory's croton (*Croton coryi*)		X					
Crestless wild onion (*Allium canadense*) var. *(eristatum)*		X					
Elmendorf's onion (*Allium elmendorfii*)		X					
Crown coreopsis (*Coreopsis nuecensis*)		X					
Hairy cutleaf evening primrose (*Oenothera mexicana*)		X					
Hooker's palafoxia (*Palafoxia hookeriana*)		X					
Jones' nailwort (*Paronychia jonesii*)		X					
Kleberg knotweed (*Polygonum striatulum*)		X					
Kleberg saltbush (*Atriplex klebergorum*)			X				
Large selenia (*Selenia grandis*)		X					
Leafless alkali weed (*Cressa nudicaulis*)			X				
Lemon beebalm (*Monarda citriodora*)		X					
Lila de los llanos (*Anthericum chandleri*)		X					
Lindheimer's tephrosia (*Tephrosia lindheimeri*)		X					
Lundell's nailwort (*Paronychia lundelliorum*)		X					
Manatee-grass (*Cymodocea filiformis*)			X				
Padre Island dropseed (*Sporobolus tharpii*)		X		X			
Plains gumweed (*Grindelia oolepis*)		X					
Roughseed sea-purslane (*Sesuvium trianthemoides*)		X					
Sand brazoria (*Brazoria arenaria*)		X					
Sand-belt bluet (*Hedyotis subviscosa*)		X					
Seaside beebalm (*Monarda maritima*)		X					
Shinner's rocket (*Thelypodiopsis shinnersii*)		X					
Shoalgrass (*Halodule beaudettei*)			X				
Shortcrown milkvine (*Matelea brevicoronata*)		X					
Slender rushpea (*Hoffmannseggia tenella*)		X					
South Texas clammyweed (*Polanisia erosa*)		X					

Table 17.1. (continued)

Conservation Targets	FOCAL TARGETS						
	Tamaulipan Thornscrub Matrix	Coastal Sand Plains Clay Dune and Prairie Complex	Hypersaline Lagoon– Seagrasses	Barrier Islands	Reddish Egret	Shorebird Guild	Ocelot
Plants (continued)							
South Texas phacelia (*Phacelia patuliflorida*) var. (*austrotexana*)		X					
Stinking rushpea (*Pomaria austrotexana*)[a]		X					
Texas stonecrop (*Sedum texanum*)		X					
Texas wilkommia (*Willkommia texana*)		X					
Texas windmillgrass (*Chloris texensis*)		X					
Texasgrass (*Vaseyochloa multinervosa*)		X					
Tharp's rhododon (*Rhododon tharpii*)[b]		X					
Turtle-grass (*Thalassia testudinum*)			X				
Velvet spurge (*Euphorbia innocua*)		X					
Welder machaeranthera (*Machaeranthera heterocarpa*)		X					
Invertebrates							
Blue land crab (*Cardisoma guanhumi*)			X				
Hypersaline fiddler crab (*Uca subcylindrica*)				X			
Mangrove crab (*Gecarcinus lateralis*)				X			
Mangrove periwinkle (*Littorina angulifera*)				X			
Fish							
Blackfin goby (*Gobionellus atripinnis*)			X				
Texas pipefish (*Syngnathus affinis*)			X				
Amphibians							
Black-spotted newt (*Notophthalmus meriodionalis*)	X	X					
Rio Grande lesser siren (*Siren intermedia*)	X	X					
Sheep frog (*Hypopachus variolosus*)	X	X					
White-lipped frog (*Leptodactylus fragilis*)	X	X					
Reptiles							
Atlantic hawksbill turtle (*Eretmochelys imbricata*)			X				
Black-striped snake (*Coniophanes imperialis*)	X						
Green sea turtle (*Chelonia mydas*)			X				
Keeled earless lizard (*Holbrookia propinqua*)		X					
Kemp's ridley sea turtle (*Lepidochelys kempii*)			X				
Loggerhead sea turtle (*Caretta caretta*)			X				

Table 17.1. *(continued)*

Conservation Targets	FOCAL TARGETS: Tamaulipan Thornscrub Matrix	Coastal Sand Plains Clay Dune and Prairie Complex	Hypersaline Lagoon–Seagrasses	Barrier Islands	Reddish Egret	Shorebird Guild	Ocelot
Reptiles *(continued)*							
Mexican blackhead snake (*Tantilla atriceps*)	X						
Speckled racer (*Drymobius margaritiferus*)	X						
Texas horned lizard (*Phrynosoma cornutum*)	X						
Texas indigo snake (*Drymarcon corais*)	X						
Texas tortoise (*Gopherus berlandieri*)	X						
Birds							
Aplomado falcon (*Falco femoralis*)		X					
Audubon's oriole (*Icterus granduacauda*)	X						
Botteri's sparrow (*Aimophila botterii*)		X					
Brown pelican (*Pelecanus occidentalis*)			X				
Cactus ferruginous pygmy owl (*Glaucidium brasilianum cactorum*)	X						
Northern beardless tyrannulet (*Camptostoma imberbe*)	X						
Peregrine falcon (*Falco peregrinus*)				X			
Piping plover (*Charadrius melodus*)				X		X	
Reddish egret (*Egretta rufescens*)					X		
Snowy plover (*Charadrius alexandrinus*)				X		X	
Mammals							
Coues' rice rat (*Oryzomys couesi*)	X						
Jaguarundi (*Felis yaguarondi*)	X						
Maritime pocket gopher (*Geomys personatus maritimus*)		X					
Ocelot (*Felis pardalis*)							X
Southern yellow bat (*Lasiurus ega*)	X						
Guild or Community							
Neotropical songbird				X			
Nesting sea turtle				X			
Texas ebony-snake eyes shrubland	X						
Wintering waterfowl			X				

[a] Simpson (1998)
[b] Turner (1995)

Table 17.2. *Identified threats to focal conservation targets within the Laguna Madre of Texas with associated threat rankings by threat for each target*

	CONSERVATION TARGETS						
	Tamaulipan Thornscrub Matrix	Coastal Sand Plains Matrix	Hypersaline Lagoon–Seagrasses	Barrier Islands	Reddish Egret	Shorebird Guild	Ocelot
Incompatible development	Medium	Low	Low	Medium	Medium		Very High
Conversion to agriculture		Low					Very High
Roads							Very High
Brush clearing	High						Low
Brown tide			High				
Dredging			Medium				
Agricultural runoff			Medium				
Unsuitable grazing practices	Low	Low					Low
ORVs				Low		Low	
RVs on beaches and mudflats				Low		Low	
Propeller scarring			Low				
Industrial discharge			Low				
Urban runoff			Low				
Wastewater treatment/septic discharge			Low				
Fire suppression		Low					
Threat status for targets and site	Medium	Low	Medium	Low	Low	Low	Very High

all biodiversity represented within the Laguna Madre region. For example, by selecting the Tamaulipan thornscrub matrix, we have captured numerous other botanical, zoological, and even community targets embedded within the matrix.

Stresses and Sources   Numerous stresses are acting upon Laguna Madre. From incompatible development to non-point source pollution, many factors are involved in impacting the ecological functions and processes operating within the Laguna. However, one can take solace in the fact that the level at which most of these stressors function is less than that documented for other coastal systems, such as Galveston Bay. The key to our conservation success is correctly identifying all the threats to the various targets and then formulating strategies to abate those threats. In table 17.2, the various stresses are listed, with a qualitative assessment as to how severe each one is for the conservation target (system or species) concerned. In addition, we have attempted to quantify overall critical threats across all systems (fig. 17.2). It is obvious that incompatible development, agricultural conversion, and roads are overarching threats for all systems within the Laguna Madre area. It should be clear that the Conservancy does not propose curtailing road construction in the region; however, perhaps there are ways to engineer and build roads so as to lessen their impact on specific conservation targets, such as the ocelot.

When evaluating critical threats for the seven conservation targets within Laguna Madre, overall scale must be considered. For example, off-road vehicles (ORVs)

Fig. 17.2. Critical threats rankings across all systems within the Laguna Madre. Degree of threat is a qualitative assessment based upon existing data and expert opinions.

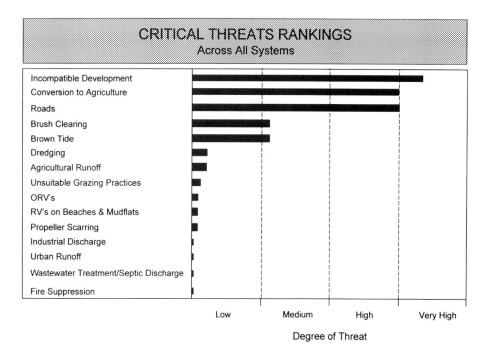

cause serious damage to dune systems on South Padre Island. However, when we consider the entire barrier island system fronting the Laguna Madre of Texas and Tamaulipas, we find that ORVs exert damage upon a relatively small portion of the system (see fig. 17.2). The National Park Service maintains a high level of control over ORVs within the boundaries of Padre Island National Seashore, thus abating the ORV threat there. This is not to say that ORV-caused dune destruction should not be addressed by means of abatement strategies. Site-specific plans for South Padre Island (barrier island system) include specific strategies for addressing problems associated with ORV use.

For the Laguna Madre de Tamaulipas, the conservation targets remain the same but the threats are different in type and severity. For example, overfishing is much more significant in Mexico, while dredging is much less of an issue at present. Grazing on barrier island areas in Tamaulipas is more severe than in Texas. In addition, development pressures are much less in Mexico than on South Padre Island and on the mainland fronting the lower Laguna in Cameron County. Expansion of the aquaculture industry and potential dredging projects could pose future threats to the Laguna Madre de Tamaulipas.

Strategies for Conservation

As already mentioned, the Laguna Madre region has not to date been subjected to the level of development (residential and industrial), shoreline hardening, and other impacts readily observed elsewhere on the Texas coast. Evaluation of the viability of conservation targets in the Laguna Madre region illustrates this well (fig. 17.3). The ocelot possesses by far the lowest viability ranking with less than 60 known individuals left in Texas.

The Tamaulipan thornscrub matrix has experienced extensive clearing on both sides of the border. Clearing continues today, especially for expanding residential and *colonia* development. However, in spite of the status of the aforementioned conservation targets, the remaining five are assessed as having good viability. Thus, the Conservancy has a unique opportunity to develop strategies in a more proactive

Fig. 17.3. Viability rankings for seven conservation targets within the Laguna Madre of Texas based upon size, condition, and landscape context

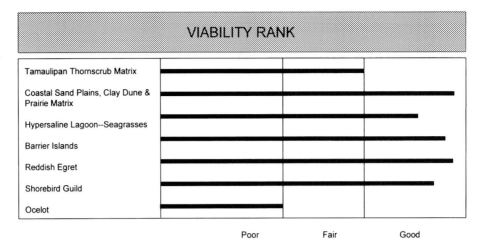

Fig. 17.4. Paradigm for the concept of community-based conservation. The success of community-based conservation rests on a holistic approach bringing together ecological, economic, and community interests.

manner to abate threats to conservation targets, rather than reacting to a declared conservation crisis.

Many strategies, most of which are site-based, must be developed to implement landscape-level conservation in the Laguna Madre region. All of our work must be developed through community-based conservation efforts that incorporate socio-economic concerns, the desires and interests of local community members, and sound application of ecological knowledge (fig. 17.4). Essentially, the Conservancy has identified several key conservation zones based upon local input from landowners, resource agencies, and community leaders. These zones are Baffin Bay watershed, South Texas Sand Plain, the Laguna itself (marine system), South Padre Island, Arroyo Colorado, the Boca Chica–South Bay complex, the Bahia Grande–Redhead Ridge complex, Rancho Rincon de Anacahuitas, and other sites to be determined by Pronatura Noreste in Mexico. Each zone will have its own set of discrete strategies addressing the most serious threats. Highest consideration will be given to strategies that can be applied at multiple sites to abate a common threat. For example, if meaningful partnerships could be developed with state and federal agencies, local agricultural interests, and other conservation groups to reduce non-point source pollution in the Arroyo Colorado watershed, that aquatic system would benefit along with the Laguna and the variety of conservation targets embedded within these two zones.

Other strategies already being implemented include site-based acquisition of habitats (e.g., recent purchase of 9,813 ha on South Padre Island), exploring conservation easement applications, and development of a native plant nursery to assist with the implementation of a large-scale Tamaulipan thornscrub restoration effort on private and public lands. Incorporating science into conservation strategies will be crucial. For example, conducting dune restoration research will assist efforts to address serious ORV damage that has been inflicted on dune systems of South Padre Island.

People who have experienced the aura of the Laguna Madre may not know the full biological and geographic significance of this unique ecosystem, but they do know that this is a special place, in and of itself and for all of the species of wildlife that depend upon it to survive. The Conservancy has long recognized these values, and now we are embarking on a plan of action to protect in perpetuity the unique biological richness and mostly intact landscape and marine functions and processes of Laguna Madre.

THE LAGUNA MADRE: A CONSERVATION FRAMEWORK

Selecting the right places to work is critical in conserving biodiversity. As this compendium attests, Laguna Madre is obviously such a place. Even more important is implementing a sound plan of action. Conservation actions taken outside the context of an overall ecoregion-based plan will not make lasting contributions to maintaining biodiversity. Finally, we must always strive to understand the sites we seek to conserve, and there is still much to be learned about the last Texas frontier, Laguna Madre.

18 *Information Gaps and Needs*

JOHN W. TUNNELL, JR.

From the earliest writings in the 1920s and 1940s, scientific knowledge about the Laguna Madre of Texas and Tamaulipas focused on hypersaline conditions and fisheries productivity. In Texas, interest then turned to the vast seagrass beds (almost 80% of Texas distribution) and the importance of this submerged vegetation as essential habitat. Most recently in Texas, concern over the brown tide and the impacts of maintenance dredging of the Gulf Intracoastal Waterway (GIWW) have stimulated extensive new research. In Tamaulipas, most recently, the idea of extending the GIWW from Brownsville, Texas, through the Mexican lagoon has stimulated both concern over its future environmental health (and protection) and much research. Unfortunately, much of the work in Mexico has not been published and is only available through the federal government with permission.

During the compilation of literature for this volume and the accompanying (electronic) comprehensive bibliography, more than 1,250 citations were listed for Laguna Madre and surrounding area (Padre Island, the Río Grande Valley, and adjacent mainland; table 18.1). About 86% of these citations concerned Texas. Of the nearly 350 citations that were specifically on the Laguna Madre only, about 75% concerned the Texas lagoon and 25% the Tamaulipas lagoon. Most studies were projects on a given topic, and most lasted only one or two years, which can be a problem in characterizing such a dynamic system. The only long-term biological data set available is the Coastal Monitoring Program conducted by Texas Parks and Wildlife Department for fishery species management. The Conrad Blucher Institute for Surveying and Science at Texas A&M University–Corpus Christi began collecting water level data at eight stations within the Laguna Madre of Texas in the early 1990s. At selected stations they also collected data on other physical parameters, such as temperature, salinity, pH, and dissolved oxygen. No published, long-term data sets were revealed for the Tamaulipas lagoon but the fisheries institute of Mexico does keep records of landings of selected commercial species.

No comprehensive synthesis of all Laguna Madre information has been compiled. However, extensive topical syntheses and characterizations have recently been completed for the northernmost part of the upper Laguna Madre system in the Corpus Christi Bay National Estuary Program (now Coastal Bend Bays and Estuaries Program). Reports include numerous topics (living resources, water quality, sediment quality, point source and non-point source discharges, seagrasses, wetlands, habitat distribution, marine debris, freshwater inflow, and more) within the Texas Coastal Bend geographic study area.

Information and knowledge gaps discovered during this compendium synthesis are presented in a matrix format for quick review (table 18.2). Overall, geological information seems to be more thorough and complete than biological data. A considerable amount of information about seagrass distribution and ecology is available for Texas, but much is still unknown about community dynamics and linkage to other ecosystem habitats. Little is known about seagrasses in Tamaulipas.

Table 18.1. Summary of literature listed in Laguna Madre Comprehensive Bibliography concerning the Laguna Madre (Texas and Tamaulipas) and surrounding areas by geographic area and type of literature

Location	Journal Articles	Proceedings	Reports	Theses	Dissertations	Books	Magazines	Total
United States								
Laguna Madre–Texas	80	22	106	26	4	0	22	260
Baffin Bay	12	3	3	9	1	0	1	39
Padre Island	25	12	27	4	1	1	3	73
Rio Grande Valley and Arroyo Colorado	40	1	72	7	2	7	0	129
South Texas Coast	36	9	40	2	2	1	3	93
South Texas	53	2	8	9	1	2	0	75
Texas Coast	75	8	75	3	3	6	10	180
Texas	22	1	23	0	0	13	1	60
United States	5	1	7	0	0	2	0	15
Total U.S.	348	59	361	60	14	32	40	924
Mexico								
Laguna Madre–Tamaulipas	13	35	31	3	0	0	6	88
Northeastern Mexico	7	1	2	1	0	0	0	11
Tamaulipas	12	1	0	2	0	0	0	15
Coastal Lagoons–Mexico	10	6	1	2	1	1	0	21
Mexico	11	1	1	0	0	3	1	17
Total Mexico	53	44	35	8	1	4	7	152
Combination Papers[a]	26	14	17	3	1	3	0	64
Miscellaneous Papers[b]	59	8	26	2	0	10	3	108
Grand Total	486	125	439	73	16	49	50	1248

[a] Includes papers concerning both sides of the border (e.g., South Texas and northeastern Mexico, Río Grande, Gulf of Mexico).

[b] Includes papers primarily on taxonomic groups or events (e.g., hurricanes) within the Laguna Madre area. Most concern Texas species or events.

Extensive multi-year data are available on fish and some invertebrates via the Texas Parks and Wildlife Department's Coastal Fisheries Monitoring Program, but most of the material is unanalyzed, except for regulated species. For wind-tidal flats, waterfowl, colonial waterbirds, and shorebirds, a moderate amount of information is available, and for the brown tide there is a currently expanding volume of literature.

The following itemization lists some specific information or knowledge gaps that were discovered during compilation of this compendium. The list is not prioritized, but it is listed by subject areas.

PHYSICAL CHARACTERISTICS

Accurate determination of areal coverage of Laguna Madre of Texas and its major habitats is needed.

A geological question needs addressing: Why are there so many natural islands in

Table 18.2. *"Information gap matrix" for selected aspects of knowledge concerning the Laguna Madre of Texas and Tamaulipas. ULMTex = Upper Laguna Madre of Texas, LLMTex = Lower Laguna Madre of Texas, NLMTam = Northern Laguna Madre de Tamaulipas, SLMTam = Southern Laguna Madre de Tamaulipas.*

	ULMTex	LLMTex	NLMTam	SLMTam
Climate	****	****	**	**
Hydrography	***	***	**	**
Geology	****	****	**	**
Tamaulipan biotic province	***	***	**	**
Ranching heritage	****	***	**	**
The environment	***	***	**	**
Seagrass meadows	***	***	**	**
Open bay	**	**	**	**
Wind-tidal flats	***	**	**	**
Barrier islands	****	****	**	**
Redhead and other waterfowl	****	***	**	**
Colonial waterbirds and rookery islands	***	***	**	*
Shorebirds and wadingbirds	***	**	**	*
Sea turtles	**	**	*	*
Fish and fisheries	***	**	**	**
Brown tide	****	**	**	*
Red tide	**	**	*	*

Notes: Rankings based on the amount of literature.

* = no information located or available

** = little information is available

*** = a moderate amount of information is available

**** = an extensive amount of information is available

Laguna Madre de Tamaulipas (approximately 200) and less than 10 in Laguna Madre of Texas?

Climate data are difficult to access for Tamaulipas; long-term, continuous stations adjacent to the Laguna are apparently lacking.

Tidal characteristics under today's conditions are not known for lower Laguna Madre in Texas or any of the system in Tamaulipas.

ECOLOGY, ECOSYSTEM

A comprehensive monitoring program is needed to track status and trends of major habitats, biota, and environmental quality.

Linkages of habitats (e.g., between tidal flats and seagrass beds, or between Laguna Madre and freshwater ponds for waterfowl) is lacking.

Ecology of Río Grande Delta ecosystems is practically unknown.

Little is known of the biology and ecology of certain habitats in Texas (Bahía Grande, Laguna Larga, San Martín Lake).

Cumulative impacts of tidal flat losses are unknown.

Information concerning ecosystem linkages between Laguna Madre, the mainland,

and the Gulf of Mexico are needed, along with an ecosystem model (although much research will be needed before an accurate model can be developed).

There is little information on population dynamics for most species except commercial fish and shellfish.

Mangrove distribution and importance in Laguna Madre de Tamaulipas need study. Black mangroves (*Avicennia germinans*) in the Lower Laguna Madre of Texas also need attention.

Little is known of wind-tidal flat and seagrass ecology in Laguna Madre de Tamaulipas.

The dynamics of invertebrate recruitment to and persistence of wind-tidal flats and its relationship to habitat quality for shorebirds is poorly understood.

BIODIVERSITY

No ecological or genetic information exists on oysters for Laguna Madre de Tamaulipas or Laguna el Catán.

No comprehensive (biodiversity) surveys or checklists are available for Laguna Madre systems.

Little information exists on distribution or abundance of annelids or epibenthic crustaceans in seagrass beds; the invertebrate nekton have been almost completely ignored.

HARD SUBSTRATES

No information is available on jetty habitat in Tamaulipas, and little is available for Texas.

Are there serpulid reefs in Tamaulipas (Laguna el Catán), as in Baffin Bay, Texas?

No biological or ecological information is available on coquina outcrops in Texas or Tamaulipas.

SEAGRASS BEDS

The effect of manatee-grass replacement by turtle-grass as succession proceeds is unknown. Effects of shoalgrass replacement by manatee grass is also poorly known.

No information exists about seagrass biomass decline and invertebrate communities associated with seagrass in Laguna Madre de Tamaulipas.

BARRIER ISLANDS

No information is available on the role of bacteria and fungi in barrier island vegetation dynamics.

Importance of invertebrates as part of the food web has not been quantified for Texas or Tamaulipas barrier island chains.

No quantitative studies have been made of invertebrate community structure on barrier islands.

BIRDS

No study has been conducted to identify and quantify the importance of dunes to resident and migrant herbivorous birds.

More study is needed on the role of barrier island grasslands in the wintering and migratory ecology of Neotropical migrant songbirds.

With the exception of redheads, limited information exists on population dynamics of wintering waterfowl in Laguna Madre of Texas or Tamaulipas, the Río Grande Delta, or coastal depressional wetlands.

Shorebird wintering populations and movements within and between Texas and Tamaulipas wind-tidal flats and adjacent habitats are not known well enough to allow management of either the birds or the habitats they frequent.

Knowledge of wading bird wintering ecology is inadequate in both lagoons.

Knowledge of shorebird nesting ecology is inadequate in both lagoons.

There is no information concerning the effects of droughts and wet cycles on shorebird, wading bird, and waterfowl use of either lagoon.

Relationships between colonial waterbird nesting guild dynamics and rookery island habitat availability is unknown.

19   *Conservation Issues and Recommendations*

JOHN W. TUNNELL, JR., KIM WITHERS, AND
ELIZABETH H. SMITH

A number of environmental and conservation issues have been raised in the preceding discussion of the Laguna Madre of Texas and Tamaulipas, identified by the Nature Conservancy as one of its four North American initiatives within its new Coastal and Marine Program, including 20 sites worldwide. These difficulties and others are grouped here for a regional overview. Most issues involve anthropogenic impacts due to increasing human population levels and consequent environmental stresses to natural resources and systems. Some seem rather benign or of small consequence when considered alone, but when they are considered together, their cumulative effects may cause widespread impact or alteration. Further, some issues may appear to have a minor present effect, but when a hurricane storm surge arrives, they can be responsible for significant magnified impacts. Where appropriate, after discussion of an issue, recommendations follow.

Most activities altering and impacting land and water are now governed by various regulatory agencies. For the sake of readers concerned about issues and their consequences but unfamiliar with administrative and regulatory structures, these are the major state agencies involved and their respective roles and responsibilities: Texas Natural Resources Conservation Commission (TNRCC), air and water quality; Texas General Land Office (TGLO), submerged lands and tidal shorelines; Texas Parks and Wildlife Department (TPWD), living natural resources; and Texas Health Department (TDH), aquatic public health. Relevant U.S. federal agencies and their roles include the U.S. Fish and Wildlife Service (USFWS), living natural resources; U.S. Environmental Protection Agency (EPA), environmental protection and regulation; U.S. Army Corps of Engineers (USACE), dredging and filling activity; and National Marine Fisheries Service (NMFS), federal fisheries and habitat utilization of fishery species. In Mexico, all fishing, ecological, and environmental regulatory issues fall under the Secretaria de Medio Ambiente, Recursos Naturales y Pesca (SEMARNAP).

Conservation Issues

Conservation-Based Development   The environmental health of the Laguna Madre of Texas and Tamaulipas is important to the economic health of the entire region, providing an estimated $250–400 million per year to the local economy (Cameron, Willacy, Kenedy, and Kleberg counties) through commercial fishing, sportfishing, recreation, and tourism (K. Chapman, pers. comm.). Increasingly, the Laguna Madre System is impacted by human activity and growth of coastal communities. In 1999–2000 the Texas Center for Policy Studies and Pronatura Noreste set out to define clearly what the Laguna Madre actually means to Texas and Tamaulipas in terms of economic and natural resources and to discuss what processes local communities might use to best protect both the ecology of the area and the livelihood of the people who use this resource. The two organizations jointly conducted the effort in three phases: a binational assessment of the current economic and environmental state of the region; research on local public perception of the links between the economy and the natural environment of the Laguna Madre; and a binational symposium to present the assessment and findings of the research.

The overall goal of the project is to foster binational discussion about opportunities for promoting economic activities that encourage conservation and enhancement of natural resources and that maintain a climate for providing living-wage jobs. The methodology for achieving this goal is educational in nature, and the information produced is intended to assist in planning for the future of the Lower Río Grande Valley and northeastern Tamaulipas (K. Chapman, pers. comm.). Separate draft reports on the binational project on the Laguna Madre of Texas (Chapman 2000) and Tamaulipas (Cruz-Nieto 2000) were made available at "The Future of the Binational Laguna Madre Economic and Natural Resources Symposium," held on 13–14 April 2000, at South Padre Island, Texas.

Protection of Lands and Waters   The remoteness of the Laguna Madre from human population and industrial centers has acted as a substantial means of protection and conservation of natural resources. In Texas, the Laguna Atascosa National Wildlife Refuge, large ranches along the mainland shoreline, and Padre Island National Seashore along the barrier island have limited access and development of the Laguna shoreline, so that nodes of development are primarily to the north near Corpus Christi and to the south near Port Isabel and the community of South Padre Island. Some access and development also occur in western Baffin Bay and at Port Mansfield. In Tamaulipas, lack of paved highways and utility infrastructure has limited access, and development consists of small fishing villages. In the 1970s, paved highways were completed to Mezquital in the north and La Pesca in the south. In the 1990s, two additional highways were completed to the western shoreline, first from San Fernando to Carboneras and Carbajal in the southern Laguna Madre de Tamaulipas, and most recently from Highway 180 to El Barancón in the northern Laguna. Rancho Rincon de Anacahuitas, along the northwestern lagoon shoreline, is a model for land conservation management and protection. Comprehensive conservation and protection of the entire Laguna Madre de Tamaulipas has recently been proposed (DUMAC 1996).

Habitat Restoration, Enhancement, and Creation   Losses of seagrass meadows in the Laguna Madre of Texas have resulted primarily from dredging and filling activities. Submerged areas have been dredged for navigation channels, and the dredged material has been deposited on seagrass meadow areas. Several restoration projects have been implemented as the result of compensatory mitigation. These projects include scrapedowns of dredged material islands to appropriate water depths for submergent vegetation establishment (e.g., in upper Laguna Madre, the Transco scrapedown site, Gulf Isles site, Central Power and Light Company site), and filling old channels to previous depths and revegetating the areas with seagrasses (Transco Pipeline site in upper Laguna Madre; Montagna 1993). In some cases, upland areas of the barrier island have been excavated to form shallow embayments and planted with seagrass (Dimit Pier Project site in upper Laguna Madre; Belaire Environmental, Inc. 1997b).

No long-term monitoring was implemented to evaluate success of these projects, but variable results have been observed, ranging from complete failures to completely revegetated seagrass meadows. Several factors may be responsible for observed responses in less successful projects: (1) excavation to improper depths, affecting depth of the photic zone (too deep) or producing temperature extremes (too shallow); (2) establishment of seagrass species compromised by turbidity created during restoration activity or by siting on inappropriate substrate material; or (3) planting at wrong time of the year (Cobb 1987). Recovery of selected restored sites within the upper Laguna Madre required 13–17 years to reach functional equivalency to natural areas (Montagna 1993).

The following recommendations should be followed to ensure success of habitat restoration, enhancement, or creation projects: investigate thoroughly the prevailing factors within and surrounding the reference site (water depth, substrate type, turbidity, species composition, adjacent land and water uses); closely adhere to recommended planting strategies and timing in relation to natural seasons—rather than being governed by project timelines; develop and implement a long-term monitoring strategy to evaluate project success, and modify future projects accordingly; and minimize future losses of remaining seagrass meadows through wise use of existing resources and alternate planning efforts that do not destroy seagrasses.

Texas Coastal Zone Management The Texas State Legislature established the Texas Coastal Management Program (CMP) to improve management of coastal natural resources. This program integrates efforts on a variety of issues among state, federal, and local agencies with jurisdiction in coastal areas. The CMP is part of the federal Coastal Zone Management Act as well as Texas' Coastal Coordination Act. Through the approval of the federal program, consistency is achieved between state- and federally funded projects. Also, approximately $2 million a year is available for coastal projects and planning efforts. The Coastal Coordination Council, consisting of several state agency members and others appointed by the governor, oversees CMP activities and reviews grant proposals. The Coastal Division of the Texas General Land Office serves as administrative staff and oversees the funded CMP projects. The CMP focuses on five primary issues of concern to coastal communities: coastal erosion, wetlands protection, water supply and water quality, dune protection, and shoreline access. A certain proportion of funding requested must be matched for each grant administered (Coastal Coordination Council 1998).

The following funding categories receive annual funding: (1) coastal natural hazards response; (2) critical areas enhancement; (3) shoreline access; (4) water quality improvement; (5) waterfront revitalization and ecotourism development; (6) permit streamlining/assistance and governmental coordination; (7) information and data availability; and (8) public education and outreach.

Endangered and Threatened Species For a complete listing of endangered, threatened, and rare species in counties adjacent to the Texas Laguna Madre, see table 4.8. The following species found in or near the Texas Laguna Madre (LM) and/or Laguna Madre de Tamaulipas (LMT; DUMAC 1993) are listed as endangered or threatened by both the U.S. Department of Interior and Texas Parks Wildlife Department or Mexico's bird conservation authority, Sección Mexicana del Consejo Internacional para la Conservación de las Aves (CIPAMEX):

ENDANGERED

Slender rushpea (LM)
Texas ayenia (LM)
Black-laced cactus (LM)
Star cactus (LM, LMT)

South Texas ambrosia (LM)
Atlantic hawksbill sea turtle (LM, LMT)
Kemp's ridley sea turtle (LM, LMT)
Leatherback sea turtle (LM, LMT)
Brown pelican (LM, LMT)
Peregrine falcon (LM, LMT; recently delisted by U.S. Dept. of Interior; still considered endangered by TPWD)
Aplomado falcon (LM, LMT)
Yellow-headed parrot (LMT)
Interior least tern (LM, LMT)
Jaguarundi (LM, LMT)
Ocelot (LM, LMT)
Jaguar (LMT)
West Indian Manatee (LM, LMT)

THREATENED

Green sea turtle (LM, LMT)
Loggerhead sea turtle (LM, LMT)
Piping Plover (LM, LMT)

Two protected animal species that may be found in either lagoon are the bottlenose dolphin *(Tursiops truncatus)* and opossum pipefish *(Oostethus brachyurus)*.

For most species, there is a need for baseline information on population dynamics and habitat use within the system. Most species recovery efforts use a single-species approach; however, habitat conservation and multi-species management would be more practical and effective strategies. There is a need to standardize regulatory efforts between the United States and Mexico, especially in regard to conservation of marine mammals and sea turtles. Incentives and education to encourage conservation at the grassroots level will be more effective than legislating conservation.

Anthropogenic Issues

Arroyo Colorado   The Arroyo Colorado is part of a natural drainage system for the Lower Río Grande Valley (Bryan 1971) and lies on the northern edge of the Río Grande Delta (Brown et al. 1980). Today it is part of a floodway system that begins south of Mission, Texas, and drains eastward, dividing into the North Floodway and the Arroyo Colorado at Mercedes, Texas. The system produces little natural flow except during rainfall runoff, but it receives treated wastewater from several towns across the Valley, providing essentially the only "freshwater" inflow into the lower Laguna Madre. In the late 1940s the lower 40 km (25 mi) were dredged to a depth of 4.3 m (14 ft) to accommodate barge traffic to the Port of Harlingen (Bryan 1971).

Environmental concerns for Arroyo Colorado include low dissolved oxygen, agricultural contaminants, and most recently impacts from aquaculture effluents. Low dissolved oxygen seems to be a long-standing problem (Bryan 1971; Davis 1983, 1984, 1985; Baker 1997). Intensive water quality monitoring surveys conducted by the Texas Department of Water Resources indicate that the Arroyo Colorado "is unable to assimilate the waste load it presently receives without development of depressed dissolved oxygen levels." Fish kills have been reported due to these low oxygen levels (Breuer 1962; Bryan 1971). Some of the highest contaminant levels along the Texas coast have been recorded from Arroyo Colorado, including DDT and its metabolites DDD and DDE as well as dieldrin and endrin (Childress 1966).

Elevated chlordane and total DDT concentrations were regularly reported from sediments collected along the Arroyo (Dick 1982). Fish and fish-eating birds collected along the Arroyo in 1978 and 1979 contained elevated DDE levels (White et al. 1983a). Additionally, water samples from agricultural drains into the Arroyo Colorado had elevated arsenic levels (Wells et al. 1988). Finally, the two largest shrimp farms in Texas discharge their effluent, which smells bad, attracts flies, and reduces water quality, into the Arroyo Colorado, causing concern not only for the waterway but also for residents, who report declines in adjacent property values, and for fishermen, who complain about declining sportfishing productivity (Baker 1997).

In order to address the long-term issues and problems within the Arroyo Colorado, in 1997 TNRCC began a project within their Total Maximum Daily Load Program that will be funded at over $1 million. In addition to the TNRCC personnel concerned, numerous state and federal agencies, two universities, and other entities have been involved in this program via a Science and Technical Advisory Committee. The final project report, due to the EPA in 2001, will outline a watershed action plan for future usage and recovery of this important waterway leading to the Laguna Madre (G. Rothe, pers. comm.).

Since some current problems are related to low flow and to former and current poor agricultural practices, present efforts should focus on achieving lower environmental impacts through use of "cleaner" technology in wastewater treatment, agriculture, and aquaculture. Implementation of Best Management Practices (BMPs) has also been suggested, via mathematical modeling predictions, to cause significant reductions in nutrient and pesticide loadings (Flowers et al. 1998).

Additionally, the Río Grande Coastal Impact Monitoring Program (Hutchinson and Smith 1995) identified four recommendations:

1. Conduct a comprehensive study to identify and quantify inputs for point and non-point sources of toxic materials.
2. Establish monitoring stations at the mouths of the Arroyo Colorado and North Floodway to allow calculation of the volumes of flow and loading of nutrients and toxic materials.
3. Conduct a study to establish seasonal variability of nutrient loads and eutrophication rates in the Arroyo Colorado.
4. Conduct a comprehensive study of the fishery in the Arroyo Colorado.

Island Inhabitation, Tamaulipas   The Laguna Madre of Tamaulipas contains nearly two hundred natural islands (INEGI 1994). A recent survey of all inhabited islands in Mexico (107 total) reveals that 22 are in Tamaulipas, more than any other state, and that all of the inhabited islands of Tamaulipas are in Laguna Madre. Their total population in the early 1990s was 1,354 people on all 22 islands, 20 of which are located in the northern laguna. Population size on individual islands ranged from single-family dwellings of several people to a village of 237 people on Isla Las Malvinas. Most of the people on the islands are there for the fishing industry (INEGI 1994; 1990 census data). On some islands there is concern over human cohabitation with and impact on nesting colonial waterbirds. Removal of vegetation for housing and firewood destroys critical habitat, and domestic dogs may severely impact nesting success.

Island management plans need to be developed that enable fishermen to utilize non-nesting colony islands and to stay clear of rookeries during nesting season. Some government assistance may be necessary to help transfer people from rookery to nonrookery islands.

Channelization The construction of intracoastal waterways, irrigation and drainage canals, and access channels has resulted in extensive channelization and attendant disposal of dredge material throughout the Texas Coastal Zone, including the Laguna Madre (Brown et al. 1976, 1977, 1980). In Texas, cuts have been made on land, in the lagoon, and across the barrier island, and land drainage systems are most extensive in the Lower Río Grande Valley, particularly the Arroyo Colorado and North Floodway. In Tamaulipas few cuts exist, and all are across the barrier peninsulas and islands; however, land drainage systems are extensive in the agricultural areas immediately south of Matamoros. Major environmental consequences of channelization and dredged material placement (see next item) include: (1) covering of vital coastal habitats; (2) inhibition of water circulation or drainage in water and on land, respectively, due to dredge material piles or banks; and (3) creation of areas of sediment that are easily eroded and redistributed by natural physical processes, notably storms (Brown et al. 1976, 1977, 1980). Beneficial aspects of channelization in the Laguna Madre include reduced extremes of hypersalinity (Simmons 1957; Breuer 1962; Hedgpeth 1967) and the creation of isolated island habitat for colonial waterbirds (Chaney et al. 1978).

Excessive channelization and dredged material placement should be avoided. Channels no longer in use should be closed and filled and should have vegetation replanted (if appropriate) to restore original land and lagoon-bottom configurations (Brown et al. 1976, 1977, 1980).

Dredged Material Placement During the early years of dredging (1940s–1960s) in the Laguna Madre of Texas, large quantities of dredged material were indiscriminately placed in open water (plate 45) and along shorelines, covering vital seagrass and wind-tidal flat habitats. In the upper Laguna Madre alone, when surveyed in the 1970s, there were 109 dredged material islands along the GIWW and an additional 40 located along privately maintained channels (Chaney et al. 1978). In the entire Laguna Madre of Texas, dredged material covered approximately 78 km^2 (30 mi^2) of lagoon bottom and 114 km^2 (44 mi^2) of adjacent land above sea level (Brown et al. 1976, 1977, 1980). During the 1970s, disposal of dredged material resulting from the creation and maintenance of navigation waterways and harbors became a matter of national interest and concern. One result was establishment of the Dredged Material Research Program at the U.S. Army Corps of Engineers Waterways Experiment Station in Vicksburg, Mississippi (Chaney et al. 1978). Through this program much scientific information was generated about the flora and fauna, in the Laguna Madre, particularly colonial waterbirds (see chapter 12).

Heightened concern about the impacts of maintenance dredging on vital seagrass habitat and how this affected the wintering population of redheads led to the establishment in 1987 of the Texas Gulf Coast Field Station of the U.S. Geological Survey, Biological Resources Division, in Corpus Christi, to conduct research on the issue. Further concern was raised about placement of dredged material on lands adjacent to the Laguna Madre (King Ranch and Kenedy Trust 1993) and whether additional dredging was a wise proposition, considering all the economic and environmental implications (Diaz and Kelly 1994). Subsequently, the Corps of Engineers established the Laguna Madre Interagency Coordination Team (ICT) to help prepare a 50-year Dredged Material Management Plan for the GIWW in the Laguna Madre. ICT members are representatives of both state and federal natural resource and transportation agencies: TNRCC, TGLO, TPWD, TWDB, Texas Department of Transportation, USFWS, EPA, NMFS, and the Corps of Engineers. Numerous studies recently completed or still under way under the oversight of the

ICT cover all aspects of Laguna Madre dredging operations and impacts: physical oceanography (Brown and Kraus 1997); piping plover (EHA 1997; Zonick et al. 1998); containment (EHA 1998); benthic macrofauna (EHA and BVA 1998); sediment budget (Morton et al. 1998); habitat utilization (P. Sheridan, in prep.); and seagrass modeling (K. Dunton, in prep.) Thus absolute answers regarding the best sites and manner of dredged material placement are still not available, but extensive new information should aid the ICT in making science-based management decisions.

Careful consideration should be given to dredge material placement, using all available information. Disposal in open water should be avoided, especially in areas of seagrass habitat. The best available technologies should be used for containment of dredged material to reduce or eliminate resuspension of sediments in the water column, which causes problems of reduced light for highly productive seagrass habitat.

Dredged Material Island Cabins and Houseboats The presence of cabins on dredged material islands and houseboats anchored in the Laguna Madre of Texas may have impacts on the ecosystem (plate 46). More than 400 cabins are registered under the Cabin Program managed by the Texas General Land Office (TGLO) (M. Freytes, pers. comm.). There being no registration program for houseboats, numbers and locations are not known. Since new cabins cannot be constructed, most TGLO regulations deal with repairs, modifications, or approved construction on existing structures. When cabins are located over water and when docks and piers extend over water, seagrass meadows can be shaded, affecting plant productivity. Some illegal dredging of channels occurs when cabin lessees "prop-wash" a shallow area for better access to piers, thus impacting seagrass meadows. Most toilet facilities are primitive, ranging from pit toilets on islands to dock facilities over the water. The TGLO does not have jurisdiction over these practices, and permits generally require that the lessee conform to local county health codes. Weekend household trash and debris from cabin or dock modifications often accumulate. TGLO usually notifies the lessee by letter of the problem, requesting immediate removal. Houseboats are not usually self-propelled, therefore transfer of waste materials to dump stations does not occur. Those houseboats that are not moved every 21 days may impact seagrass meadows by shading (D. Rocha, pers. comm.).

The following recommendations should be followed to minimize impacts from cabins and houseboats: support the TGLO Cabin Program for general oversight and consistency of cabin/dock modification requests and approvals as well as for enforcement of and compliance with regulations; contact TGLO regarding modifications prior to implementation; avoid prop-washing channels to docks and destroying seagrass meadows and nearshore habitat; upgrade toilet facilities to reduce potential water quality problems; remove all trash and debris from the island to a mainland disposal site; and move houseboats regularly to minimize seagrass shading and to pump out holding tanks into an approved dump station.

Shoreline Construction Construction of groins, piers (plate 47), jetties, and oil and gas wellsite peninsulas has altered water circulation and sediment transport patterns along Laguna Madre and Gulf shorelines in Texas. In Tamaulipas, jetties along Gulf beaches and *charangas* (fish traps; plate 48) in Laguna Madre have similar effects. Charangas, usually placed specifically to catch fish or shrimp on flood or ebb tide, have caused considerable shoaling and erosion of lagoon bottom (J. W. Tunnell, pers. observ.). The state of a shoreline, whether erosional, depositional, or in relative equilibrium, is primarily caused by natural processes, such as availability of source sediments and wave intensity (Brown et al. 1976, 1977, 1980). Shoreline construction alters the natural dynamics, and each alteration in one place is compensated for in another. For example, construction of a jetty or groin along an erosional shoreline will trap sediment on one side and possibly speed up erosion on the other.

In Texas, the Coastal Erosion Planning and Response Act was implemented in 1999. This new act is being managed by the TGLO with scientific guidance from the Bureau of Economic Geology of the University of Texas at Austin.

Proper management and use of shorelines along the open Gulf and Laguna Madre require recognition of the natural characteristics and processes governing each area. Any modification of a particular shoreline should take full account of these characteristics and processes and should avoid disrupting them (Brown et al. 1976, 1977, 1980).

Devegetation   Vegetated lands serve naturally to stabilize substrate, and destruction or removal of vegetation can lead to increased erosion. Destructive activities include development construction, road construction, and off-road trails (Brown et al. 1976, 1977, 1980; Judd et al. 1989). Devegetation of vegetated barrier island flats and foredunes renders these habitats highly susceptible to erosion by wind and water, especially during tropical storms and hurricanes, which can carry large volumes of sediment into the Laguna Madre.

Destruction of natural coastal vegetation should be avoided, especially on barrier islands and areas adjacent to Laguna Madre. Since vegetation stabilizes coastal land and minimizes land loss by island or shoreline erosion, vegetation should be restored when destroyed by construction or other activities (Brown et al. 1976, 1977, 1980).

Filling and Land Reclamation   Artificial filling of shallow lagoonal waters adjacent to land creates valuable shorefront development land or additional land for industrial expansion. But this process also permanently destroys important coastal habitats and alters shoreline configuration, water circulation, and sediment transport (Brown et al. 1976, 1977, 1980).

Filling and land reclamation projects should be considered not only in terms of economic value but also in terms of environmental impact to natural systems (Brown et al. 1976, 1977, 1980).

Artificial Passes   Artificial passes between Laguna Madre and the Gulf of Mexico have been dredged in both Texas and Tamaulipas. Others have been proposed or attempted without success. Besides increasing access between the Laguna and the Gulf, another long-standing reason for connecting the hypersaline Laguna Madre with the Gulf of Mexico has been to reduce or moderate high salinities in the lagoon. However, given high longshore drift of sediments, blowing sand, low tidal range, and no freshwater inflow, these dredging attempts have been a failure, costly to maintain, or both. Along the Texas coast, due to the low tidal range, generally only one pass per bay or lagoon system can be maintained by natural processes, and additional passes reduce the tidal exchange through existing ones, necessitating increased dredging to maintain them (Brown et al. 1976, 1977, 1980). In addition, artificial passes alter the natural circulation pattern and subject protected lagoonal waters to greater effects from storm surges.

In South Texas, only Mansfield Pass has remained open as an artificial pass, and it requires considerable maintenance dredging. Yarborough Pass and Fish Pass (= Corpus Christi Water Exchange Pass) are examples of failed artificial passes (Gunter 1946; Behrens et al. 1977). In Tamaulipas, all four currently dredged passes were artificially opened, although the one at Boca Ciega was the site of a natural washover pass. All four were strategically placed for access and water exchange, two in the northern and two in the southern Laguna Madre (see figs. 2.1, 2.4, and 2.5).

Before constructing artificial passes, their economic benefit should be weighed against the cost of additional maintenance dredging and increased potential damage from storm surges (Brown et al. 1976, 1977, 1980).

Oil Spills   Exploration for oil and gas and subsequent production are major revenue-generating activities in South Texas. Impacts from oil and gas navigation channelization, seismic activity, and other issues are addressed elsewhere in this chapter. Oil spills from exploration and production occasionally occur and can potentially cause major environmental damage, especially in sensitive coastal environments. No major oil spills have occurred in the Laguna Madre in Texas or Tamaulipas. However, the major *Ixtoc I* oil spill in 1979 in the Bay of Campeche heavily impacted Texas Gulf of Mexico beaches (plate 49), and some oil extended through Brazos Santiago Pass and Mansfield Pass, impacting adjacent lagoonal habitats (Hooper 1981; Tunnell et al. 1981; Rabalais and Flint 1983). Environmental Sensitivity Index (ESI) maps were created as a result of that spill (Hayes et al. 1980), and oil spill prevention and preparedness became a priority in Texas. Today the Oil Spill Prevention and Response Division of the Texas General Land Office maintains a ready force to prevent and combat oil spills, and the division also maintains a constantly updated Geographical Information System set of ESI maps for the entire Texas coast, including the Laguna Madre (TGLO 1997).

TGLO is providing excellent oversight, preventive measures, and clean up of Texas oil spills. Support for this system should be continued.

Contaminants   The Lower Río Grande Valley (LRGV) is one of the most intensively farmed areas in the United States, with over 425,000 ha (1,050,175 ac) of cultivated land receiving repeated pesticide applications throughout the year (Custer and Mitchell 1987a, 1993; Jahrsdoerfer and Leslie 1988). Runoff is transported to the lower Laguna Madre via the Arroyo Colorado and other agricultural drains. As already noted, elevated chlordane and total DDT concentrations (Dick 1982), DDE (White et al. 1983c), and arsenic (Wells et al. 1988) have been reported within sediment, fish and fish-eating birds, and water associated with this drainage system. At or near the outlets of these drainages into the lower Laguna Madre, DDE and some arsenic has been reported in wintering shorebirds (White et al. 1983b), breeding willets (Custer and Mitchell 1991), and nesting black skimmers and laughing gulls (White et al. 1983c, 1984; Custer and Mitchell 1987b). Within the lower Laguna Madre concentrations of mercury, arsenic, selenium, lead, cadmium, and organochlorine compounds appear to be generally at background levels in sediments and biota and do not suggest a threat to wildlife (Custer and Mitchell 1993). Higher concentrations of mercury and DDE recorded in some samples in lower Laguna Madre probably originated from agricultural runoff (Custer and Mitchell 1993). No data were found for Tamaulipas.

Some hydrocarbons have been found in sediments (Sharma et al. 1997) and biota (redhead; Michot et al. 1994) in the Texas Laguna Madre, but they were not at levels high enough to be toxic. No data were found for Tamaulipas.

Contaminant monitoring in sediments, water, and biota needs to be established at key localities in Laguna Madre in both Texas and Tamaulipas. Numerous recommendations for monitoring of contaminants and water quality are presented in Hutchinson and Smith (1995) for the Río Grande Valley area and could be applied throughout the entire system.

Impacts of Seismic Activity on Barrier Islands Vehicles used during seismic surveys have the potential to impact vegetated and unvegetated habitats on barrier islands by altering the substrate elevation and thereby impacting reestablishment of natural flora and fauna. Habitats most affected by both natural and human alterations include the beach, coppice dune, foredune, and tidal flat zones. Research on relative effects in these zones determined that unvegetated areas are more affected than vegetated areas (Drawe and Ortega 1996). After seismic vehicle activity in vegetated areas, plant cover was reduced for several months, although recovery was evident. It was estimated that complete vegetative recovery would take more than 18–24 months. The most obvious alteration detected in these zones was the setting back of plant succession, as more colonizing species were abundant during early recovery stages. Vegetated barrier flats and lateral dunes were the zones most impacted, and recovery was limited.

The following recommendations should be implemented to minimize damage to barrier island ecosystems: monitor all oil field activity to minimize damage; do not allow vehicles in sensitive areas, including marshes, foredunes, lateral dunes, vegetated barrier flats, and wet tidal flats (Withers 1996c); if access is necessary, plan a route through well-vegetated low coastal sands or shoregrass communities that are at an advanced stage of succession; reroute access areas if bare sands appear or vegetation is repeatedly impacted.

Seismic Impacts to Seagrass Meadows Seismic exploration impacts both habitats and organisms. Local scarring or destruction of seagrass habitats occurs when boats move into shallow areas to set charges or as a result of blasting. If bamboo survey stakes or PVC poles are not removed after exploration is complete, they may cause additional seagrass scarring when boaters mistake them for channel markers. Blasting also results in death of large numbers of invertebrates and small forage fish in the immediate area of the blast and stuns large numbers of small fish outside the immediate area of the blast (B. Hardegree, pers. comm.). Whether stunned fish recover is unknown. Large fish are only rarely affected. Airboat noise and blasting may disturb birds, especially wintering redheads, which feed in seagrass meadows, and colonial nesters using dredged material islands in the vicinity of exploration activities. Noise associated with exploration also disturbs boaters, anglers, and residents in waterfront or canal homes.

Since little quantitative study has been done on the effects of seismic exploration on aquatic organisms, there is a need to monitor effects on fish and invertebrates. It is also necessary to monitor effects on seagrass, especially cumulative destruction and recovery time. To reduce effects on birds, access to areas around spoil islands should be limited during the nesting season (February–August), and access to preferred redhead feeding areas should be limited during winter (October–March). In addition, to minimize airboat and blasting disturbance to residents, boaters, and anglers, these activities should be limited to weekdays and daylight hours.

Trash and Debris Most trash and debris cleanup and evaluation of sources (origins) is targeted toward Gulf shorelines, and Padre Island National Seashore has implemented a long-term effort in these areas. Bay debris data are more difficult to locate and quantify. Therefore, a recent report on incidence of bay debris in the Texas Coastal Bend identified potential areas where bay debris may originate or accumulate (Amos et al. 1997). Locations such as boat ramps, harbors, industrial boatyards, and marinas were designated as point sources, while roadways adjacent to the shoreline and storm runoff discharges were designated non-point sources. Eighteen boat ramps were identified in the upper Laguna Madre as potential point source areas. Few roads are located near the shoreline of either upper or lower Laguna Madre, so trash accumulation at boat ramps may be a significant source. Other sources of trash and debris may include illegal dumping in remote areas; trash left at campsites or cabins or blown out of boats; and debris that has floated in through Gulf passes.

The following recommendations have been made to understand trash/debris issues better in the Laguna Madre of Texas: properly design bay debris surveys that result in good quality information; train volunteers to collect and categorize trash and debris at regular intervals; use and maintain the database to assess status and trends of bay trash/debris; identify sources and implement a public educational program to reduce bay trash and debris (Amos et al. 1997).

Mariculture   Coastal shrimp farming practices typically divert estuarine water into culture ponds, later releasing the effluent back into the estuary. These discharges may have elevated nutrient loads from excess feed, fertilizers, and shrimp wastes and may contain pathogens or release exotic shrimp. Impacts to water quality and natural fisheries populations raise environmental concerns on the current regulation and practices of the shrimp farm industry. Efforts to feed at appropriate levels with improved feed are being researched (T. Samocha, pers. comm.). Fertilizers are often added to the ponds to increase algal growth. Currently, the combination of excess feed and fertilizers produces discharge waters with extremely high nutrient levels, particularly in relation to the low-nutrient receiving waters. These discharges result in elevated nutrients in the estuarine system and an increase in epiphytic growth on seagrass leaves. Diseases have plagued the shrimp farming industry in Texas, including the Taura Syndrome virus, which caused production losses upward of 90% at almost all farms during 1996 (Baker 1997). Most Texas coastal shrimp farms raise the Pacific white shrimp *(Penaeus vannamei)*, and some accidental releases have occurred in the Arroyo Colorado area. No persistent populations have yet been established (M. Ray, pers. comm., in Baker 1997), and it is unclear what ecological consequences there would be for native species if this were to occur (J. Lester, pers. comm., in Baker 1997). Most recently, holding ponds or ditches equipped with screen filters are successfully being used to allow suspended solids to settle and to prevent accidental shrimp releases (J. W. Tunnell, pers. observ.).

Several steps should be implemented to reduce environmental impacts to natural ecosystems from mariculture practices: study impacts of shrimp farm discharges and water use; no new discharge permit approval until environmental impacts are assessed; enforce Texas wastewater discharge permitting authority; implement a disease-monitoring and -control program; involve local government in policy and decisions; implement performance bonding—money put up by industry to cover when they do not "perform" well, i.e., have an accident—to provide emergency funds (Baker 1997).

Circulation and Salinity   Hypersalinity due to the combination of limited circulation between the Gulf of Mexico and Laguna Madre, low freshwater inflow, and high evaporation has been identified as a "problem" since at least the early 1920s (Higgins and Lord 1926). Despite overall high fisheries productivity, in the early part of the 20th century frequent summer fish kills, particularly in Baffin Bay, resulted in cries to do something, beginning nearly a century of engineering projects designed to decrease salinities in Laguna Madre.

Barrier Island Passes   One popular "solution" to hypersalinity has been dredging passes through the barrier islands. Passes opened by hurricanes, combined with torrential rainfall, have a major short-term impact on salinities in Laguna Madre (e.g., Behrens 1969; Hildebrand 1969, 1980), and there is evidence that permanent, jettied passes have ameliorated salinities within Texas Laguna Madre (e.g., Quammen and Onuf 1993). However, permanent passes also interrupt longshore sand transport, resulting in erosion down-current from jetties. Closed natural passes or washover passes are often chosen for stabilization, but these habitats are vital to many wintering birds. Jettied passes may completely destroy these habitats when channels are dredged, or the value of areas may be changed due to alteration of hydrology or of other natural processes.

Artificially maintained passes in Laguna Madre de Tamaulipas have ameliorated salinities there to a certain extent. These passes differ from those in Texas because they are not separated from one another by long distances. Since salinities were frequently extreme (>100 ppt), especially in the northern lagoon, any decrease would be "beneficial." In the Texas Laguna Madre, all but Mansfield Pass have been total failures from both water exchange and navigation points of view: they filled rapidly with sand, often within one year of completion. And even Mansfield Pass, with jetties nearly 1.6 km (1 mi) long, is kept open only by means of yearly maintenance dredging at a cost of over $600,000.

The idea that passes "benefit" the ecosystem needs to be dispelled, and managers and planners need to be encouraged to be realistic about the economic costs and benefits of pass stabilization as well as its ecological or environmental costs. Because passes are often dredged through habitats used by birds, there is a need to study local effects of passes on hydrology and ecology of tidal flats and other bay margin habitats.

Gulf Intracoastal Waterway (GIWW)   The engineering project with the most profound impact on salinity and circulation in Laguna Madre was dredging of the GIWW, completed in 1949. The impact of decreased salinity is still being felt and assessed today (Quammen and Onuf 1993). The GIWW connects upper and lower Laguna Madre through the Land-Cut, allowing exchanges of water on a more regular basis as well as additional connection to the Gulf of Mexico via Mansfield Pass and Aransas Pass. Decreased salinity in upper Laguna Madre has resulted in more extensive and persistent submerged vegetation (seagrasses) and few, if any, summer fish kills due to extreme salinities. In lower Laguna Madre, decreased salinity has caused succession of submerged vegetation to progress, with declines in shoalgrass, a pioneer species, and increased coverage of both turtle-grass and manatee-grass. A turtle-grass climax is predicted in the next 50 years (Quammen and Onuf 1993). The Land-Cut also provides an avenue for biological exchange, especially seagrasses. Increasing coverage of manatee-grass in upper Laguna Madre is evidence that the process of succession to a turtle-grass climax may be in its seminal stages.

Changes in seagrass community composition may have negative effects on both fish and birds (Quammen and Onuf 1993; Tolan et al. 1997). The majority of the U.S. population of redheads winters in the Laguna Madre of Texas and Tamaulipas, feeding almost exclusively on shoalgrass rhizomes. Declines in shoalgrass cover may impact redhead populations negatively because the lagoons of Texas and Tamaulipas are the last areas where extensive beds of shoalgrass remain. A number of juvenile gamefish also prefer shoalgrass nursery areas over areas with other species of seagrasses; there is potential for impacts to these populations as well, if shoalgrass becomes an uncommon species in the lagoon.

It is necessary to continue monitoring the effects of salinity declines on seagrass community structure and composition, to predict potential effects on both waterfowl and juvenile fish populations. In addition, there is a need to continue monitoring waterfowl population levels, especially for redheads. More study is needed on effects of seagrass succession on juvenile fish populations.

Seagrass Scarring   The most obvious cause of current seagrass loss in Laguna Madre is light attenuation, but other factors may also be important. Many seagrass meadows in upper Laguna Madre, especially near the JFK Causeway, have been scarred by boat propellers, although damage is currently not classified as severe (Dunton et al. 1998b). There has been no study of the extent of seagrass scarring in lower Laguna Madre. Depending on the length and depth of scars as well as the species of seagrass affected, damage can result in permanent loss. Deep, long scars tend to deepen and erode along the edges, causing greater local turbidity as well as increased water flow, often resulting in continuing seagrass loss after the initial damage. Some species, particularly shoalgrass, may begin almost immediately recolonizing scars that are small or shallow. Damage to turtle-grass meadows with their extensive, often massive rhizome systems is typically longer lasting than is damage to meadows of shoalgrass, an annual species. Many seagrass meadows are accidentally scarred when boaters misjudge depths or the location of channels, but some damage is deliberate as boaters try to maintain illegally marked, prop-washed channels into otherwise inaccessible shallow waters or take shortcuts between channels or other areas.

Accidental losses of seagrasses due to scarring could be avoided through more effective education of boaters and better channel markers, especially in privately maintained channels. Those engaged in deliberate damage should be prosecuted. In addition, preservation of seagrass meadows in shallow areas might be accomplished through establishment of "no boat zones." This concept has merit and has been suggested by the Coastal Conservation Association, a U.S. coastal organization of saltwater anglers. No boat zones are currently under consideration by Texas Parks and Wildlife Department for several areas in the Texas Laguna Madre.

Natural Perturbations

Brown Tide   A persistent, uninterrupted bloom of *Aureoumbra lagunensis*, known as the Texas brown tide, lasted from at least January 1990 through October 1997 and continued intermittently in some areas through 2001 (see discussion in chapter 16). Brown tide has caused two major changes in the Laguna Madre ecosystem: long-term light reduction and alteration of food webs. Seagrass cover and biomass have declined due to light attenuation, particularly in upper Laguna Madre (Onuf 1996a,b). The nearly complete loss of phytoplankton diversity, the poor nutritive quality of *A. lagunensis*, and declines in planktonic grazers and benthic filter feeders as a result of the bloom have altered food webs, especially in Baffin Bay (Street et al. 1997). There is no evidence that the brown tide of the 1990s was anything other than a natural occurrence.

Continued monitoring of the brown tide and its impact on seagrass populations and animal populations is necessary to elucidate the long-term effects of the bloom on laguna ecology and to understand the system's potential for "recovery," for want of a better word.

Hurricanes   Several kinds of major natural processes create potentially harmful conditions in the Texas coastal zone: hurricanes, shoreline erosion, inland flooding,

surface faulting, and land subsidence (Brown et al. 1976, 1977, 1980). Of these, as
has been indicated in several chapters in this volume, hurricanes and their associated
storm surges and heavy rainfall have the greatest influence on natural systems along
the South Texas coast (see chapter 2); the other processes listed are of minor concern
in South Texas, pertaining more to the middle and upper Texas coast. With hurricanes and tropical storms, passes open, lagoons are flushed, salinity changes, and
sand moves more than ever. When a hurricane strikes, stability of barrier islands
(plate 50), particularly via dune-stabilizing vegetation, is a critical factor.

Although prediction of the frequency and landfall location of hurricanes is difficult, eventual impact on any given part of the coast is certain at some point in the future, and land use should therefore be planned accordingly. Viewing hurricanes as
alarming and dangerous events can mask the fact that they are merely one among the
many dynamic forces driving the ecology of the Laguna Madre region. A hurricane
may destroy buildings and roads, but it cannot destroy Laguna Madre; on the contrary, hurricanes are natural phenomena and cause natural physical processes in the
Laguna Madre region. The best kind of hurricane protection is through management to ensure maximum stabilization and integrity of natural environments, particularly on barrier islands—our first line of defense.

Appendix I   Contacts

This list includes current Laguna Madre researchers and interested parties, many of them cited in the text as sources for personal communication or observation. Following the individuals' names are indications of their areas of geographic and research or management interests. Abbreviations for geographic areas are as follows:

LMTex   Laguna Madre of Texas
ULMTex   Upper Laguna Madre of Texas
LLMTex   Lower Laguna Madre of Texas
LMTam   Laguna Madre de Tamaulipas
NLMTam   Northern Laguna Madre de Tamaulipas
SLMTam   Southern Laguna Madre de Tamaulipas

Jorge Adame   LMTam
Universidad Autónoma de Tamaulipas   water quality, pollution
Ciudad Victoria, Tamaulipas
Mexico
email: jadame@brahma.uat.mx

Sandra Alvarado   ecosystem ecology and management
Texas Natural Resources
    Conservation Commission
P.O. Box 13087
Austin, TX 78711-3087
(512) 239-6643
email: salvarad@tnrcc.state.tx.us

Dr. Terry Allison   LLMTex
UT-Pan American, Biology Dept.   crustaceans, molluscs, seagrass ecol-
12101 West University Drive   ogy
Edinburg, TX 78539
Phone: (956) 384-5023
Fax: (956) 381-3657
email: tallison@panam.edu

Charlie Bellaire   LMTex
Energy Development Corp.   habitat restoration/creation
P.O. Box 741
Rockport, TX 78382
(361) 729-2948

Chris Best Rt. 2 Box 202A Alamo, TX 78516 (956) 787-3079, ext. 124	plants, plant communities
Gene Blacklock Coastal Bend Bays and Estuaries 　Program 1305 N. Shoreline Blvd. Suite 205 Corpus Christi, TX 78401 Phone: (361) 885-6247 Fax: (361) 883-7801 email: geneb@cbbep.org	birds
Dr. David Blankinship Santa Ana/Lower River Grande 　Valley National Wildlife Refuge-USFWS Rt. 2 Box 202A Alamo, TX 78516 (956) 787-3079, ext. 110 email: david_blankinship@fws.gov	wildlife, land acquisition
Randy Blankinship Texas Parks and Wildlife Dept. Coastal Fisheries-Olmito Fish 　Hatchery 95 Fish Hatchery Rd. Brownsville, TX 78520 (956) 350-4490 email: randy.blankinship@tpwd.state.tx.us	LLMTex fisheries monitoring
Ing. Jorge Brenner Guillermo Pronatura Noreste Garza Sada 2501 Sur C.P. 64849 Monterrey, N.L., Mexico Phone: 011-52-8-328-4033 Fax: 011-52-8-387-5815 email: jbrenner@pronatura.org.mx	LMTam GIS, Information Systems
Dr. Timothy Brush UT-Pan American, Biology Dept. 1201 West University Drive Edinburg, TX 78539 Phone: (956) 381-2921 Fax: (956) 381-3657 email: tbrush@panam.edu	LLMTex shorebirds

Dr. Edward Buskey   LMTex
UT-Marine Science Institute   red/brown tides
750 Channelview Drive
Port Aransas, TX 78373-5015
Phone: (361) 749-6794
Fax: (361) 749-6777
email: buskey@utmsi.utexas.edu

Paul Carangelo   environmental issues, seagrass
Port of Corpus Christi Authority   restoration
222 Powers St.
Corpus Christi, TX 78401
Phone: (361) 882-5633
Fax: (361) 882-3079
email: paul@pocca.com

Eduardo Carrera González   LMTam
Ducks Unlimited de México, A.C.   ducks, habitat, ecosystem
Av. Vasconcelos 209 Ote. Res. San Agustín
C.P. 66260 Garza García, N.L., Mexico
email: ecarrera@infosel.net.mx

Dr. Gerardo Ceballos González   LMTam
Centro de Ecología   coastal lagoons
Universidad Nacional Autónoma de México
Apartado Postal 70-275
04510 Mexico D.F., Mexico
email: gceballo@miranda.ecologia.unam.mx

Dr. Allan H. Chaney   LMTex
3000 Fall Creek Rd.   birds,
Kerrville, TX 78028   vertebrates, ecology
Phone/Fax: (830) 896-1946
email: larue27@ktc.com

Karen Chapman   environmental and socioeconomic
Texas Center for Policy Studies   issues
44 East Ave., Suite 306
Austin, TX 78701
Phone: (512) 474-0811
Fax: (512) 474-7846
email: kc@texascenter.org

Robyn Cobb   LMTex
USFWS-Ecological Services   federal management
6300 Ocean Drive, Campus Box 338
Corpus Christi, TX 78412
Phone: (361) 994-9005
Fax: (361) 994-8262
email: robyn_cobb@fws.gov

Dr. Armando Contreras   LMTam
email: arcontre@ccr.dsi.uanl.mx   birds

Dr. Salvador Contreras Balderas
Laboratorio de Ictiología
Facultad de Ciencias Biológicas
Universidad Autónoma de Nuevo León
Apartado Postal 504
C.P. 66450 San Nicolás, N.L., Mexico
011-52-8-376-2231 or 313-1641
email: scontrer@ccr.dsi.uanl.mx

LMTam
fish, fisheries

Gabriela De la Fuente DeLeón
Ducks Unlimited de México, A.C.
Av. Vasconcelos 209 Ote. Res. San
    Agustín
C.P. 66260 Garza García, N.L., Mexico
Phone: 011-52-8-378-6648
Fax: 011-52-8-378-6439
email: dumac@infosel.net.mx

LMTam
wetlands classification

Dr. Hudson DeYoe
UT-Pan American, Biology Dept.
1201 West University Drive
Edinburg, TX 78539
Phone: (956) 381-3538
Fax: (956) 381-3657
email: hdeyoe@panam.edu

LMTex
plankton, brown tides, tidal flats

Dr. Lynn Drawe
Welder Wildlife Foundation
P.O. Box 1400
Sinton, TX 78387
(361) 364-2643
email: welderwf@aol.com

barrier island vegetation

Dr. Kenneth H. Dunton
UT-Marine Science Institute
750 Channelview Drive
Port Aransas, TX 78373-5015
Phone: (361) 749-6744
Fax: (361) 749-6777
email: dunton@utmsi.utexas.edu

LMTex
seagrass

Dr. Bob Edwards
UT-Pan American, Biology Dept.
1201 West University Drive
Edinburg, TX 78539
Phone: (956) 381-3545
Fax: (956) 381-3657
email: redwards@panam.edu

fish

Dr. Ernesto Enkerlin Hoeflich,   LMTam
Director, Pronatura Noreste   environmental planning,
Garza Sada 2501 Sur   avian biology
C.P. 64849 Monterrey, N.L., Mexico
Phone: 011-52-8-387-5814
Fax: 011-52-8-359-6280
email: enkerlin@campus.mty.itesm.mx

Dr. Diego Fabian Lozano García   LMTam
Instituto Tecnológico y de Estudios   GIS
    Superiores de Monterrey
Laboratorio de Información
    Georreferenciada
Centro de Calidad Ambiental
Suc. de Correos "J"
C.P. 64849 Monterrey, N.L., Mexico
Phone: 011-52-8-328-4032
Fax: 011-52-8-359-6280
email: dlozano@campus.mty.itesm.mx

Manuel Freytes
Texas General Land Office, Field
    Operations
NRC Bldg., Suite 2400
6300 Ocean Drive
Corpus Christi, TX 78412
(361) 825-3030
email: manuel.freytes@glo.state.tx.us

Mike Farmer   reddish egret
3410 Bridlepath
Austin, TX 78703
(512) 474-7671

Dr. Tim Fulbright   rangeland
Animal and Wildlife Sciences
Texas A&M University-Kingsville
Campus Box 156
Kingsville, TX 78363
Phone: (361) 593-3714
Fax: (361) 593-2788
email: timothy.fulbright@tamuk.edu

Ma. Elena García Ramírez   LMTam
Laboratorio de Ictiología   fishes
Facultad de Ciencias Biológicas
Universidad Autónoma de Nuevo León
Apartado Postal 450
C.P. 66450 San Nicolás, N.L., Mexico
Phone/Fax: 011-52-8-376-2231
email: mgarciar@ccr.dsi.uanl.mx

Dr. Eugenio Gómez Reyes   coastal ecosystems
email: egr@xanum.uam.mx

Dr. Larry Hauck   environmental studies
Texas Institute for Applied
   Environmental Research
Tarleton State University
Stephensville, TX 76401
Phone: (254) 968-9561
Fax: (254) 968-9559
email: hauck@tiaer.tarleton.edu

Beau Hardegree   seagrass ecology/management
Texas Parks and Wildlife Dept.
Resource Protection Div.
NRC Bldg., Suite 2500
6300 Ocean Drive
(361) 825-3241
email: beau.hardegree@tpwd.state.tx.us

Rick Hay   LMTex
Center for Water Supply Studies   subsurface waters
Texas A&M University-Corpus Christi
NRC Bldg., Suite 3100
6300 Ocean Drive
Corpus Christi, TX
(361) 825-3347
email: rhay@falcon.tamucc.edu

Keene Haywood   LMTex
Geography Dept.   environmental history
University of Texas-Austin
210 E. 24th Street
Austin, TX 78712
email: khaywood@mail.utexas.edu

Dr. Henry H. Hildebrand   LMTam/LMTex
413 Millbrook   fisheries
Corpus Christi, TX 78418   ecosystem
(361) 937-4008

Don Hockaday   LLMTex
Coastal Studies Lab
UT-Pan American
100 Marine Lab Drive
South Padre Island, TX 78597
Phone: (956) 761-2644
Fax: (956) 761-2913
email: hockaday@panam.edu

Dr. Joan Holt and Scott Holt   LMTex
UT-Marine Science Institute   fish ecology
750 Channelview Drive
Port Aransas, TX 78373-5015
Phone: (361) 749-6716
Fax: (361) 749-6777
email: joan@utmsi.utexas.edu
    and scott@utmsi.utexas.edu

Dr. Frank W. Judd   LLMTex
UT-Pan American, Biology Dept.   barrier islands, lomas, vertebrates
1201 West University Drive
Edinburg, TX 78539
Phone: (956) 381-3537
Fax: (956) 381-3657
email: fjudd@panam.edu

Peter Jenny, Vice President   peregrine falcon
The Peregrine Fund
566 West Flying Hawk Lane
Boise, Idaho 83709
Phone: (208) 362-3716
Fax: (208) 362-2376
email: tpf@peregrinefund.org

Mary Kelley   environmental and socioeconomic
Texas Center for Policy Studies   issues
44 East Ave., Suite 306
Austin, TX 78701
Phone: (512) 474-0811
Fax: (512) 474-7846
email: tcps@igc.org

Walt and Nancy Kittleberger   LLMTex
Lower Laguna Madre Foundation   conservation, preservation
P.O. Box 153   education
Port Mansfield, TX 78598
Phone: (956) 944-2387
Fax: (956) 944-2278
email: llmf@vsta.com

Dr. Roy Lehman   algae
Texas A&M University-Corpus Christi
Department of Physical and Life
    Sciences
6300 Ocean Drive
Corpus Christi, TX 78412
Phone: (361) 825-5819
Fax: (361) 825-2742
email: rlehman@falcon.tamucc.edu

Dr. Bob Lonard
UT-Pan American, Biology Dept.
12101 West University Drive
Edinburg, TX 78539
Phone: (956) 381-3656
Fax: (956) 381-3657
email: rlonard@panam.edu

terrestrial vegetation

Dra. Ma. de Lourdes Lozano Vilano
Cerro de la Conformidad 115
Las Puentes 2d Sector
San Nicolás de los Garza, N.L., Mexico
Phone: 011-52-8-350-8627
Fax: 011-52-8-376-2231
email: marlozan@ccr.dsi.uanl.mx

LMTam
fishes

Sr. Jorge Martínez
Rancho Rincón de Anacahuitas
Jazmín no. 26
Av. de las Rosas
Col. Jardín
C.P. 87300 Matamoros, Tamaulipas,
    Mexico

LMTam

Larry McEachron
Texas Parks and Wildlife Marine Lab
702 Navigation Circle
Rockport, TX 78382
Phone: (361) 729-2328
Fax: (361) 729-1437
email: larry.mceachron@tpwd.state.tx.us

LMTex
fisheries

Dr. Russ Miget
Sea Grant College Program
Texas A&M University-Corpus Christi
6300 Ocean Drive
Corpus Christi, TX 78412
Phone: (361) 980-3460
Fax: (361) 980-3465
email: rmiget@falcon.tamucc.edu

LMTex
ecology, fisheries

Dr. Paul Montagna
UT-Marine Science Institute
750 Channelview Drive
Port Aransas, TX 78373-5015
Phone: (361) 749-6711
Fax: (361) 749-6777
email: paul@utmsi.utexas.edu

LMTex
benthos, ecosystem modeling

Lloyd Mullins	LMTex
Texas General Land Office	permit assistance, colonial waterbirds
NRC Bldg., Suite 2800	
6300 Ocean Drive	
Corpus Christi, TX 78412	
(361) 980-3050	
email: lmullins@wpgate.glo.state.tx.us	

Ismael (Smiley) Nava   LMTex
Texas Parks and Wildlife Dept.   state management, resource
NRC Bldg. Suite 2501   protection
6300 Ocean Drive
Corpus Christi, TX 78412
Phone: (361) 980-3244
Fax: (361) 980-3248
email: smiley.nava@tpwd.state.tx.us

Julie Noriega   LMTam
Instituto Technólogico y de   GIS
    Estudios Superiores de Monterrey
Laboratorio de Información
    Georreferenciada
Centro de Calidad Ambiental
Suc. de Correos "J"
C.P. 64849 Monterrey, N.L., Mexico
Phone: 011-52-8-328-4032
Fax: 011-52-8-359-6280
email: jnoriega@campus.mty.itesm.mx

Dr. Jim Norwine   climate
Geography/Geology Dept.
Texas A&M University-Kingsville
Kingsville, TX 78363
Phone: (361) 593-3589
Fax: (361) 593-3068
email: kfjrn00@tamuk.edu

Dr. Chris Onuf   LMTex
USGS-BRD   seagrass, wind-tidal flats
Texas Gulf Coast Field Station
6300 Ocean Drive, Campus Box 339
Corpus Christi, TX 78412
Phone: (361) 985-6266
Fax: (361) 985-6268
email: chris_onuf@usgs.gov

Leonardo Ortiz Lozano   LMTam
Instituto de Ciencias del Mar y
    Limnología
Universidad Nacional Autónoma de Mexico
Colegio de la Frontera Norte
Tijuana, Baja California, Mexico
email: ortizleo@hotmail.com

Mr. Gary Powell   water issues
Environmental Systems Section
Texas Water Development Board
611 S. Congress
Austin, TX 78704
(512) 912-7014
email: gpowell@twdb.state.tx.us

Dr. Jennifer Prouty   geology, coquinas
Department of Physical and Life Sciences
Texas A&M University-Corpus Christi
6300 Ocean Drive
Corpus Christi, TX 78412
Phone: (361) 825-2750
Fax: (361) 825-2742
email: jprouty@falcon.tamucc.edu

Dr. Warren Pulich   LMTex
Texas Parks and Wildlife Dept.   seagrass
Resource Protection Div.   ecosystem
3000 IH 35 South, Suite 320
Austin, TX 78704
(512) 912-7014
email: warren.pulich@tpwd.state.tx.us

Dra. Andrea Raz-Guzman Macbeth   LMTam
Av. San Jeronimo 1032   crustaceans
San Jeronimo Lidice
10200 Mexico D.F., Mexico
011-52-5-683-5299
email: andrea@mar.icmyl.unam.mx

Dr. Maurice L. Renaud   LMTex
National Marine Fisheries Service   sea turtle habitats
4700 Ave. U
Galveston, TX 77551
Phone: (409) 766-3517
Fax: (409) 766-3508
email: Maurice.Renaud@noaa.gov

Dennis Rocha   LMTex
Texas General Land Office   submerged lands
1700 N. Congress Ave., Rm. 620
Austin, TX 78701-1495
(512) 475-1412
email: drocha@glo.state.tx.us

Gail Rothe   Arroyo Colorado
Texas Natural Resources   LLMTex
    Conservation Commission   TMDLs
P.O. Box 13087
Austin, TX 78711-3087
(512) 239-4617
email: grothe@tnrcc.state.tx.us

Dr. Tzachi Samocha   mariculture
Texas Agricultural Extension Service
Shrimp Mariculture Research Facility
4301 Waldron Road
Corpus Christi, TX 78418
(361) 937-2268
email: samocha@falcon.tamucc.edu

Dr. Felipe E. San Martín   LMTam
Universidad Autónoma de Tamaulipas
Boulevard Adolfo López Mateos No. 928
Apartado Postal 186
87040 Ciudad Victoria
Tamaulipas, Mexico
email: biota@correo.tamnet.com.mx

Dr. Donna Shaver   sea turtles
USGS-Padre Island National Seashore
9405 S. Padre Island Drive
Corpus Christi, TX 78418
Phone: (361) 949-8173, ext. 226
Fax: (361) 949-8023
email: donna_shaver@nps.gov

Dr. Pete Sheridan   LMTex
National Marine Fisheries Service   seagrass habitat
4700 Ave. U
Galveston, TX 77551
Phone: (409) 766-3524
Fax: (409) 776-3508
email: pete.sheridan@noaa.gov

Dr. Elizabeth H. Smith   coastal wetlands
Center for Coastal Studies   habitat restoration
Texas A&M University-Corpus Christi
6300 Ocean Drive
Corpus Christi, TX 78412
Phone: (361) 825-6069
Fax: (361) 825-2770
Email: esmith@falcon.tamucc.edu

Kyle Spiller   LMTex
Texas Parks and Wildlife Dept.   state fisheries
Coastal Fisheries
NRC Bldg., Suite 2500
6300 Ocean Drive
Corpus Christi, TX 78412
Phone: (361) 980-3353
Fax: (361) 980-3370
email: kyle.spiller@tpwd.state.tx.us

Dr. Dean Stockwell   LMTex
School of Fisheries and   red/brown tides
    Ocean Sciences
University of Alaska-Fairbanks
P.O. Box 757220
Fairbanks, AK 99775-7220
Phone: (907) 474-7229
Fax: (907) 474-7204

Dr. Mike Tewes   cats
Caesar Kleberg Wildlife Res. Institute
Texas A&M University-Kingsville
Kingsville, TX 78363
Phone: (361) 593-4025
Fax: (361) 593-3924
email: michael.tewes@tamuk.edu

Dr. Jim Tolan   LMTex
Texas Parks and Wildlife Dept.   larval fish, seagrasses
Resource Protection Div.
Texas A&M University-Corpus Christi
NRC Bldg., Suite 2300
6300 Ocean Drive
Corpus Christi, TX 78412
Phone: (361) 825-3247
Fax: (361) 825-3248
email: james.tolan@tpwd.state.tx.us

Dr. J.W. (Wes) Tunnell, Jr.   benthos
Center for Coastal Studies   coastal ecology
Texas A&M University-Corpus Christi
6300 Ocean Drive
Corpus Christi, TX 78412
Phone: (361) 825-2736
Fax: (361) 825-2770
Email: jtunnell@falcon.tamucc.edu

Dr. Mario Alberto Vasquez   LMTam
Universidad Autónoma de Tamaulipas   environmental education, redhead
Fac. de Agronomía   duck
C.U. Adolfo Lopez Mateos
Apartado Postal 337
Ciudad Victoria, Tamaulipas, Mexico

Mary Ellen Vega
Texas Parks and Wildlife Dept.
Resource Protection Div.
NRC Bldg., Suite 2501
6300 Ocean Drive
Corpus Christi, TX 78412
(361) 825-3243
email: maryellen.vega@tpwd.state.tx.us

Dr. Tracy Villareal   LMTex
UT-Marine Science Institute   red/brown tides
750 Channelview Drive
Port Aransas, TX 78373-5015
Phone: (361) 749-6732
Fax: (361) 749-6777
email: tracy@utmsi.utexas.edu

Dr. José Ma. Villarreal G.   LMTam
Instituto Technológico de Estudios
    Superiores de Monterrey
Centro de Calidad Ambiental
Suc. de Correos "J"
C.P. 64849 Monterry, N.L., Mexico
Phone: 011-52-8-358-2000, ext. 4826
Fax: 011-52-8-358-2000, ext. 4827
email: jmvillar@campus.mty.itesm.mx

Dr. Richard Watson,   LMTex
Consulting Geologist   geology tidal flats,
P.O. Box 1040
Port Aransas, TX 78373
Phone/Fax: (361) 749-4152
email: rwatson@centuryinter.net

Dr. Terry Whitledge   LMTex
School of Fisheries and   nutrients, brown tides
    Ocean Sciences
University of Alaska-Fairbanks
P.O. Box 757220
Fairbanks, AK 99775-7220
Phone: (907) 474-7229
Fax: (907) 474-7204
email: terry@ims.uaf.edu

Dr. Kim Withers   tidal-flat ecology, invertebrates,
Center for Coastal Studies   shorebirds
Texas A&M University-Corpus Christi
6300 Ocean Drive
Corpus Christi, TX 78412
Phone: (361) 825-5907
Fax: (361) 825-2770
Email: kwithers@falcon.tamucc.edu

Dr. Marc Woodin   redhead duck
USGS-BRD
Texas Gulf Coast Field Station
6300 Ocean Drive, Campus Box 339
Corpus Christi, TX 78412
Phone: (361) 985-6266
Fax: (361) 985-6268
email: marc_woodin@usgs.gov

Dr. Roger Zimmerman   habitat ecology
National Marine Fisheries Service
4700 Ave. U
Galveston, TX 77551
Phone: (409) 766-3500
Fax: (409) 766-3508
email: roger.zimmerman@noaa.gov

Dr. Curt Zonick   shorebirds, piping plover, snowy
2144 NE 38th Drive   plover
Gresham, OR 97030
(503) 669-8919

Appendix 2 *Acronyms*

BEG	Bureau of Economic Geology
CBC	Christmas Bird Counts
CBBEP	Coastal Bend Bays and Estuaries Program
CCBNEP	Corpus Christi Bay National Estuary Program
CCS	Center for Coastal Studies
CINVESTAV	Centro de Investigaciónes y Estudios Avanzados
COE (USACE)	Army Corp of Engineers
CONACYT	Consejo Nacional de Ciencia y Technología
CMP	Coastal Management Program
D-J & W-B	Dingell-Johnson & Wallop-Breaux
DU	Ducks Unlimited
DUMAC	Ducks Unlimited de México, A.C.
EPA	Environmental Protection Agency
GIS	Geographic Information System
GIWW	Gulf Intracoastal Waterway
GLO	(Texas) General Land Office
HEART	Help Endangered Animals—Ridley Turtles
INEGI	Instituto Nacional de Estadística, Geografía y Informática
INP	Instituto Nacional de Pesca (of Mexico)
ITESM	Instituto Technolgico y de Estudios Superiores de Monterrey
LLMTex	Lower Laguna Madre of Texas
LMTam	Laguna Madre de Tamaulipas
LMTex	Laguna Madre of Texas
MARFIN	Marine Fisheries Initiative
MARPOL	Marine Pollution Treaty
MMRP	Marine Mammal Research Program
MSL	Mean Sea Level
NLMTam	Northern Laguna Madre de Tamaulipas
NMFS	National Marine Fisheries Service
NOAA	National Oceanic and Atmospheric Administration
NPS	National Park Service
NSF	National Science Foundation
PINS	Padre Island National Seashore
PN	Pronatura Noreste
SLMTam	Southern Laguna Madre de Tamaulipas
SPMA	Southwestern Parks and Monuments Association
STSSN	Texas Sea Turtle Stranding and Salvage Network
TAES	Texas Agricultural Experiment Station
TAMU-CC	Texas A&M University–Corpus Christi
TCPS	Texas Center for Policy Studies

TCWS	Texas Colonial Waterbird Surveys
TDWR	Texas Department of Water Resources
TED	Turtle excluder device
TGFC	Texas Game and Fish Commission
TGLO	Texas General Land Office
TMMSN	Texas Marine Mammal Stranding Network
TNRCC	Texas Natural Resource Conservation Commission
TPWD	Texas Parks and Wildlife Department
TSU	Tarleton State University
TWC	Texas Water Commission
TWDB	Texas Water Development Board
UAT	Universidad Autónoma de Tamaulipas
UANL	Universidad Autónoma de Nuevo León
ULMTex	Upper Laguna Madre of Texas
USACE (COE)	U.S. Army Corps of Engineers
USGS	United States Geological Survey
USFWS	United States Fish and Wildlife Service
UTMSI	University of Texas Marine Science Institute
UTPA	University of Texas–Pan American
WWF	Welder Wildlife Foundation
YBP	Years before present

Literature Cited

Adair, S. E. 1990. Factors Influencing Wintering Diving Duck Use of Coastal Ponds in South Texas. M.S. thesis, Texas A&M University, College Station. 201 pp.

Adair, S. E., J. L. Moore, W. H. Keil, and M. W. Weller. 1990a. Winter Ecology of Redhead Ducks in the Gulf Coast Region. Texas A&M University–U.S. Fish and Wildlife Service Wetlands Research Center Cooperative Agreement 14-16-009-87-909. College Station. No page numbers.

Adair, S. E., J. L. Moore, and W. H. Kiel. 1990b. Wintering diving duck use of coastal ponds: An analysis of alternative hypotheses. *Journal of Wildlife Management* 60:83–93.

Aldrich, D. V., and W. B. Wilson. 1960. The effect of salinity on growth of *Gymnodinium breve* Davis. *Biological Bulletin* 119:57–64.

Allen, J. A. 1892. The geographical distribution of North American mammals. *American Museum of Natural History Bulletin* 4:199–243.

———. 1893. The geographical origin and distribution of North American birds, considered in relation to the faunal areas of North America. *Auk* 10:97–150.

Allen, R. P. 1954. The reddish egret: Bird of colors and contrasts. *Audubon* 56:252–55.

———. 1955. The reddish egret: Part II. *Audubon* 57:24–27.

Aller, R. C. 1978. The effects of animal-sediment interactions on geochemical processes near the sediment-water interface. Pp. 157–72 in M. Wiley (ed.), *Estuarine Interactions.* New York: Academic Press.

Alvarado, S. A. 1996. Hard substrate. Pp. 111–50 in J. W. Tunnell, Jr., Q. R. Dokken, E. H. Smith, and K. Withers (eds.), *Current Status and Historical Trends of the Estuarine Living Resources within the Corpus Christi Bay National Estuary Program Study Area.* Corpus Christi Bay National Estuary Program CCBNEP-06A. Corpus Christi: Texas Natural Resource Conservation Commission.

Alvarez, T. 1963. The recent mammals of Tamaulipas, Mexico. *University of Kansas Publication of the Museum of Natural History* 14:363–473.

Amdurer, M. 1978. Geochemistry, Hydrology, and Mineralogy of the Laguna Madre Flats, South Texas. M.S. thesis, University of Texas, Austin. 172 pp.

Amdurer, M., and L. S. Land. 1982. Geochemistry, hydrology, and mineralogy of the Sand Bulge area, Laguna Madre flats, South Texas. *Journal of Sedimentary Petrology* 52:703–16.

Amos, A. F. 1989. Recent strandings of sea turtles, cetaceans and birds in the vicinity of Mustang Island, Texas. P. 51 in C. W. Caillouet, Jr., and A. M. Landry Jr. (eds.), *Proceedings of the First International Symposium on Kemp's Ridley Sea Turtle Biology, Conservation and Management.* Texas A&M University Sea Grant College Program, TAMU-SG-89-105. College Station. Abstract only.

Amos, A. F., A. R. Wickham, and K. C. Keplar. 1997. *Current Status and Historical Trends in the Incidence of Marine/Bay Debris in the Corpus Christi Bay National Estuary Program Study Area.* Corpus Christi Bay National Estuary Program CCBNEP-12. Corpus Christi: Texas Natural Resource Conservation Commission. 130 pp. + appendices.

Anderson, B., R. S. Scalan, E. W. Behrens, and P. L. Parker. 1992. Stable carbon isotope variations in sediment from Baffin Bay, Texas, USA: Evidence for cyclic changes in organic matter source. *Chemical Geology* 101:227–33.

Andrews, P. S. 1964. Serpulid reefs, Baffin Bay, southeast Texas. Pp. 101–20 in A. J. Scott (ed.), *Depositional Environments, South-Central Texas Coast: Field Trip Guide-*

book (October 30–31). Houston: Gulf Coast Association of Geological Societies.

Anonymous. 1967. *Estudio Preliminar para la Rehabilitación de la Laguna Madre de Tamaulipas, México.* Mexico, D.F. 458 pp.

———. 1976. Management of wetlands for wildlife habitat improvement. Pp. 226–33 in M. Wiley (ed.), *Ecological Processes,* vol. 1. New York: Academic Press.

———. 1993. Introduction. In King Ranch and Kenedy Trust, Environmental Impacts of the Plan to Dump Dredged Spoil from the Gulf Intracoastal Waterway on Lands Bordering the Laguna Madre. Kingsville, Tex.: King Ranch and John G. Kenedy Charitable Trust.

Armstrong, N. E. 1987. *The Ecology of Open-Bay Bottoms of Texas: A Community Profile.* U.S. Fish and Wildlife Service Biological Report 85(7.12). Washington, D.C. 91 pp.

Armstrong, N. E., and H. T. Odum. 1964. Photoelectric system. *Science* 143:256–58.

Auffenberg, W., and W. G. Weaver, Jr. 1969. *Gopherus berlandieri* in southeastern Texas. *Bulletin of the Florida State Museum* 13:141–203.

Bacak-Clements, P. 1988. A Survey of Avian Use and the Aquatic Fauna of Three Ponds, in Willacy County, Texas. M.S. thesis, Texas A&I University, Kingsville. 115 pp.

Bailey, R. G. 1998. *Ecoregions: The Ecosystem Geography of the Oceans and Continents.* New York: Springer-Verlag. 176 pp.

Bailey, R. O., and R. D. Titman. 1984. Habitat use and feeding ecology of post-breeding redheads. *Journal of Wildlife Management* 48:1144–55.

Baird, S. F., T. M. Brewer, and R. Ridgeway. 1884. The waterbirds of North America. *Harvard University Museum of Comparative Zoology Memorandum* 12:452–537.

Baker, K., and N. Rabalais. 1975. Manuscript for the Biological Survey of Padre Island. Unpublished manuscript on file at Padre Island National Seashore. Corpus Christi, Texas.

Baker, M. C., and A. E. M. Baker. 1973. Niche relationships among six species of shorebirds on their wintering and breeding range. *Ecological Monographs* 43:193–212.

Baker, P. 1997. Coastal shrimp farming in Texas. Pp. 117–30 in R. Goldburg and T. Triplett (eds.), *Murky Waters: Environmental Effects of Aquaculture in the United States.* Washington, D.C.: Environmental Defense Fund.

Baldassarre, G. A., and E. G. Bolen. 1984. Field-feeding ecology of waterfowl on the southern High Plains of Texas. *Journal of Wildlife Management* 48:63–71.

Baldassarre, G. A., A. R. Brazda, and D. R. Woodyard. 1989. The east coast of Mexico. Pp. 407–25 in L. M. Smith, R. L. Pederson, and R. M. Kaminski (eds.), *Habitat Management for Migrating and Wintering Waterfowl in North America.* Lubbock: Texas Tech University Press.

Barnes, D. 1971. Anatomy of a Spoil Island. M.S. thesis, Texas A&I University, Kingsville. 70 pp.

Bauer, D. W. 1993. Avian Use of Wetlands in Southern Texas during Nonbreeding Seasons. M.S. thesis, Texas A&M University–Kingsville. 156 pp.

Behrens, E. W. 1963. Buried Pleistocene river valleys in Aransas and Baffin bays, Texas. *Publications of the Marine Science Institute, University of Texas* 9:7–18.

———. 1966. Recent emerged beach in eastern Mexico. *Science* 152:642–43.

———. 1969. Hurricane effects on a hypersaline bay. Pp. 301–308 in A. Ayala Castañares and F. B. Phleger (eds.), *Coastal Lagoons: A Symposium.* Mexico, D.F.: Universidad Nacional Autónoma de México.

———. 1974. Holocene sea level rise effect on the development of an estuarine carbonate depositional environment: Baffin Bay, Texas. *Memorias Institucion Géologia Bassin Aquitaine* 7:337–41.

Behrens, E. W., and R. L. Watson. 1973. Corpus Christi Water Exchange Pass: A Case History of Sedimentation and Hydraulics during Its First Year. Coastal Research Center Contract DACW 72-72-C-0026. Springfield, Va.: U.S. Army Corps of Engineers. 135 pp.

Behrens, E. W., R. L. Watson, and C. C. Mason. 1977. Hydraulics and Dynamics of New Corpus Christi Pass, Texas: A Case History, 1972–1973. Report no. DACW-72-72-C-0026 and DACW-72-72-C-0027. Austin: Bureau of Economic Geology, University of Texas. 126 pp.

Belaire Environmental, Inc. 1997a. 1997 Seagrass Monitoring Survey Oleander Point Mitigation Unplanted Scrapedown Area Upper Laguna Madre, Texas. Rockport. 38 pp.

———. 1997b. Two-Year Seagrass Coverage Monitoring Survey 21.37 Acre Mitigation Site, Demit [*sic*] Pier Project. Rockport, Texas. 1 p. + maps.

Bellrose, F. C. 1980. *Ducks, Geese, and Swans*

of North America. Harrisburg, Pa.: Stackpole Books. 544 pp.

Bengtson, S. A., A. Nilson, S. Nordstrom, and S. Rundgren. 1976. Effect of bird predation on lumbricid populations. *Oikos* 27:9–12.

Benson, L. H. 1979. *Plant Classification.* 2nd ed. Boston: D.C. Heath and Company.

Bent, A. C. 1921. *Life Histories of North American Gulls and Terns.* New York: Dover Publications. 337 pp.

———. 1926. *Life Histories of North American Marsh Birds.* U.S. National Museum Bulletin no. 135. 392 pp.

Bergman, R. D. 1973. Use of southern boreal lakes by postbreeding canvasbacks and redheads. *Journal of Wildlife Management* 37:160–70.

Blair, W. F. 1950. The biotic provinces of Texas. *Texas Journal of Science* 2:93–117.

———. 1952. Mammals of the Tamaulipan biotic province in Texas. *Texas Journal of Science* 4:230–50.

Blanchard, G. F., and P. A. Montagna. 1992. Photosynthetic response of natural assemblages of marine benthic microalgae to short- and long-term variation of incident irradiance in Baffin Bay, Texas. *Journal of Phycology* 28:7–14.

Brager, S. 1993. Diurnal and seasonal behavior patterns of bottlenose dolphins *(Tursiops truncatus). Marine Mammal Science* 9:438–40.

Brenner, J. 1997. Estimación de Batimetría Utilizando Datos Multispectrales Caso de Estudio Laguna la Nacha, Tamaulipas. Tesis, Maestro en Ciencias, Instituto Tecnológico y de Estudios Superiores de Monterrey, Monterrey, Nuevo León, Mexico. 72 pp. + appendices.

Breuer, J. P. 1957. An ecological survey of Baffin and Alazan bays, Texas. *Publications of the Institute of Marine Science, University of Texas* 4(2):134–55.

———. 1962. An ecological survey of the lower Laguna Madre of Texas, 1953–1959. *Publications of the Institute of Marine Science, University of Texas* 8:153–83.

Briggs, J. C. 1974. *Marine Zoogeography.* New York: McGraw Hill. 475 pp.

Briggs, R. J., and D. D. Everett. 1983. Avian use of small aquatic habitats in South Texas. *Proceedings of the Annual Conference of the Southeast Association of Fish and Wildlife Agencies* 37:86–94.

Britton, J. C., and B. Morton. 1989. *Shore Ecology of the Gulf of Mexico.* Austin: University of Texas Press. 387 pp.

Brogden, W. B., C. H. Oppenheimer, and D. Bowman. 1977. Selected biological data, Mustang and north Padre islands. Chap. 4 in R. S. Kier and E. G. Fruh (eds.), *Environmental and Economic Impacts of Recreational Community Development, Mustang Island and North Padre Island,* vol. 2. Austin: University of Texas.

Broussard, A., and N. Martin (eds.). 1986. *Texas Coast Hurricanes.* Texas A&M University, Sea Grant College Program TAMU-SG-86-505. College Station. 24 pp.

Brown, C. A., and N. C. Kraus. 1997. Environmental Monitoring of Dredging and Processes in Lower Laguna Madre, Texas. Texas A&M University–Corpus Christi, Conrad Blucher Institute for Surveying and Science Technical Report TAMU-CC-CBI-96-01. Corpus Christi. 134 pp.

Brown, L. F., J. L. Brewton, T. J. Evans, J. H. McGowen, W. A. White, C. G. Groat, and W. L. Fisher. 1980. *Environmental Geologic Atlas of the Texas Coastal Zone: Brownsville-Harlingen Area.* Austin: Bureau of Economic Geology, University of Texas. 140 pp. + 9 maps.

Brown, L. F., J. L. Brewton, J. H. McGowen, T. J. Evans, W. L. Fisher, and C. G. Groat. 1976. *Environmental Geologic Atlas of the Texas Coastal Zone: Corpus Christi Area.* Austin: Bureau of Economic Geology, University of Texas. 123 pp. + 9 maps.

Brown, L. F., J. H. McGowen, T. J. Evans, C. G. Groat, and W. L. Fisher. 1977. *Environmental Geologic Atlas of the Texas Coastal Zone: Kingsville Area.* Austin: Bureau of Economic Geology, University of Texas. 131 pp. + 9 maps.

Brush, T. 1995. Habitat use by wintering shorebirds along the lower Laguna Madre of South Texas. *Texas Journal of Science* 47:179–90.

Bryan, C. E. 1971. *An Ecological Survey of the Arroyo Colorado, Texas 1966–1969.* Texas Parks and Wildlife Department Technical Series no. 10. Austin. 28 pp.

Bryant, D. M. 1979. Effects of prey density and site character on estuary usage by overwintering waders (Charadrii). *Estuarine Coastal Marine Science* 9:369–84.

Buroker, N. E. 1983. Population genetics of the American oyster *Crassostrea virginica* along the Atlantic coast and the Gulf of Mexico. *Marine Biology* 75:99–112.

Burr, J. G. 1930. A sail down the Laguna. *Year Book on Texas Conservation of Wildlife* 1929–30:54–58.

———. 1945a. Adventure on Laguna

Madre. *Texas Game and Fish* 4(4):8–9, 17–20.

———. 1945b. Nature wins. *Texas Game and Fish* 4(9):4, 16–17, 25–26.

———. 1947. The Laguna Madre sphinx. *Texas Game and Fish* 6(5):4, 21–22.

———. 1950. Pass cutting on Padre Island. *Texas Game and Fish* 9(3):22–23.

Buskey, E. J., and C. J. Hyatt. 1995. Effects of the Texas (USA) "brown tide" alga on planktonic grazers. *Marine Ecology Progress Series* 126:285–92.

Buskey, E. J., P. A. Montagna, A. F. Amos, and T. E. Whitledge. 1997. Disruption of grazer populations as a contributing factor to the initiation of the Texas brown tide algal bloom. *Limnology and Oceanography* 42:1216–22.

Buskey, E. J., S. Stewart, J. Peterson, and C. Collumb. 1996. *Current Status and Historical Trends of Brown Tide and Red Tide Phytoplankton Blooms in the Corpus Christi Bay National Estuary Program Study Area.* Corpus Christi Bay National Estuary Program CCBNEP-07. Corpus Christi: Texas Natural Resource Conservation Commission. 174 pp.

Buskey, E. J., and D. A. Stockwell. 1993. Effects of a persistent "brown tide" on zooplankton populations in the Laguna Madre of South Texas. Pp. 659–66 in T. J. Smayda and Y. Shimizu (eds.), *Toxic Phytoplankton Blooms in the Sea.* Proceedings of the Fifth International Conference on Toxic Marine Phytoplankton. Amsterdam, Netherlands: Elsevier.

Buskey, E. J., T. A. Villareal, and T. Lopez-Barreiro. In press. Reconstructing the initiation of the Texas brown tide bloom of *Aureoumbra lagunensis* from archived samples using an immunofluorescence assay. *Planktonic Biology and Ecology.*

Buskey, E. J., B. Wysor, and C. Hyatt. 1998. The role of hypersalinity in the persistence of the Texas "brown tide" in the Laguna Madre. *Journal of Plankton Research* 20:1553–65.

Bustard, H. R. 1972. *Sea Turtles, Their Natural History and Conservation.* London, England: Collins Publishing Company. 220 pp.

Caillouet, C. W., Jr., M. J. Duronslet, A. M. Landry, Jr., D. B. Revera, D. J. Shaver, K. M. Stanley, R. W. Heinly, and E. K. Stabenau. 1991. Sea turtle strandings and shrimp fishing effort in the northwestern Gulf of Mexico, 1986–1989. *Fishery Bulletin* 89:712–18.

Calvert, R. A., and A. DeLeón. 1990. *The History of Texas.* Arlington Heights, Ill.: Harlan Davidson. 479 pp.

Capone, D. G., and B. F. Taylor. 1980. Microbial nitrogen cycling in a seagrass community. Pp. 153–61 in V. S. Kennedy (ed.), *Estuarine Perspectives.* New York: Academic Press.

Carangelo, P., R. Heiser, M. Knight, J. Snodgrass, K. Allen, C. Hughes, and G. Penn. 1975. Final report: Plant and animal study group. Chap. 6 in C. P. McRoy (ed.), *Biology of Seagrass Ecosystems: Report of a Summer Field Course.* Seagrass Bulletin no. 1. Fairbanks: Institute of Marine Science, University of Alaska. No page numbers.

Carls, E. G., R. I. Lonard, and D. B. Fenn. 1990. Impact of oil and gas operations on the vegetation of Padre Island National Seashore, Texas, USA. *Ocean and Shoreline Management* 14:85–104.

Carpelan, L. H. 1967. Invertebrates in relation to hypersaline habitats. *Contributions in Marine Science* 12:219–29.

Carr, A. F. 1986. Rips, FADS, and little loggerheads. *Bioscience* 36:92–100.

Carr, B., N. Damude, and M. Lindsay. 1993. *Endangered, Threatened, and Watch List of Texas Plants.* Publication no. 9, 3rd Revision. Austin: Texas Organization for Endangered Species.

Carr, J. T., Jr. 1967. *The Climate and Physiography of Texas.* Report 53. Austin: Texas Water Development Board. 27 pp.

Carr, W. E. S., and C. A. Adams. 1973. Food habits of juvenile marine fishes occupying seagrass beds in the estuarine zone near Crystal River, Florida. *Transactions of the American Fisheries Society* 102:511–40.

Carrera, E., and G. De la Fuente. 1996. *Estudio Previo a la Declaratoria en el Área Natural de la Laguna Madre.* Ducks Unlimited de México, A.C., Technical Report. Monterrey, Nuevo León. 225 pp.

Carroll, J. J. 1927. Down Bird Island way. *Wilson Bulletin* 39:195–208.

Caudle, C. S. 1992. Population Dynamics of the Fish Fauna Found in Three Earthen Ponds on North Padre Island, Texas. M.S. thesis, Southwest Texas State University, San Marcos. 57 pp.

Chabreck, R. H., and A. W. Palmisano. 1973. The effects of Hurricane Camille on the marshes of the Mississippi River delta. *Ecology* 54:1118–23.

Chaney, A. H. 1981. A Study of the Bird Use of the Wetlands in the Middle Río Grande Valley. Report to U.S. Fish and

Wildlife Service Ecological Services Division, Agreement 20181-0885 FY 80. Corpus Christi, Tex. No page numbers.

———. 1988. An Analysis of the Nekton and Plankton around a Shoal Grass Bed in the Laguna Madre of Texas. Report to Padre Island National Seashore, Contract no. PX7490-7-0009. Corpus Christi. 156 pp.

Chaney, A. H., G. W. Blacklock, and S. G. Bartels. 1996. *Current Status and Historical Trends of Avian Resources in the Corpus Christi Bay National Estuary Program Study Area*. Corpus Christi Bay National Estuary Program CCBNEP-06B. Corpus Christi: Texas Natural Resource Conservation Commission. 120 pp. + appendices.

Chaney, A. H., B. R. Chapman, J. P. Kargas, D. A. Nelson, R. R. Schmidt, and L. C. Thebeau. 1978. *The Use of Dredged Material Islands by Colonial Seabirds and Wading Birds in Texas*. Waterways Experiment Station Report no. D-78-8. Vicksburg, Miss.: U.S. Army Corps of Engineers. 170 pp.

Chapman, B. R. 1984. Seasonal Abundance and Habitat-Use Patterns of Coastal Bird Populations on Padre and Mustang Island Barrier Beaches [following the *Ixtoc I* Oil Spill]. U.S. Fish and Wildlife Service FWS/OBS-83/31. Washington, D.C. 73 pp.

———. 1988. History of American White Pelican colonies in South Texas and northern Tamaulipas. *Colonial Waterbirds* 11:275–83.

Chapman, K. 2000. The Binational Laguna Madre—Texas. Draft Report, Texas Center for Policy Studies. Austin. No page numbers.

Chapman, S. S., and B. R. Chapman. 1990. Bats from the coastal region of southern Texas. *Texas Journal of Science* 42:13–22.

Cheeseman, B. S. 1994. Richard King: Pioneering market capitalism on the frontier. Pp. 86–91 in J. S. Graham (ed.), *Ranching in South Texas: A Symposium*. Texas A&M University–Kingsville. Kingsville, Tex.

———. 1997. "Let us have 500 good determined Texans": Richard King's account of the Union invasion of South Texas, November 12, 1863, to January 20, 1864. *Southwestern Historical Quarterly* 101:76–95.

Childress, U. R. 1966. An Investigation into Levels of Concentration, Seasonal Variations, and Source of Pesticide Toxicants in Some Species from Selected Bay Areas. Austin: Texas Parks and Wildlife Department. 53 pp.

Chin, J. L. 1978. Distribution of Marine Grasses in Southern Laguna Madre. Report to Texas Parks and Wildlife Department on file at Texas A&M University–Corpus Christi, Center for Coastal Studies Library. 45 pp.

Clark, T. L. 1961. Coastal Waterfowl Project: Ecology of Wintering Waterfowl in Lower Laguna Madre. Texas Parks and Wildlife Federal Aid Project, W-29-R-14. Job 16. Austin. No page numbers.

Clover, E. U. 1937. Vegetational survey of the lower Río Grande Valley, Texas. *Madroño* 4(2–3):41–66; 77–100.

Coastal Coordination Council. 1998. CMP Grants Program: Application Guidance. Texas General Land Office, Coastal Division. Austin. 35 pp.

Cobb, R. A. 1987. Mitigation Evaluation Study for the South Texas Coast, 1975–1986. Corpus Christi State University, Center for Coastal Studies Technical Report, USFWS Cooperative Agreement 14-16-002-86-919. Corpus Christi. 88 pp.

Coffey, G. N. 1909. Clay dunes. *Journal of Geology* 17:754–755.

Cole, R. M. 1981. The serpulid reefs of Baffin Bay, Texas. Pp. 63–74 in J. L. Russell and R. W. Shum (eds.), *Geology of Clay Dunes, Baffin Bay, and the South Texas Sand Sheet*. Field Trip Guidebook, 83rd Annual Meeting, Texas Academy of Science. Austin.

Collier, A., and J. W. Hedgpeth. 1950. An introduction to the hydrography of tidal waters of Texas. *Publications of the Institute of Marine Science, University of Texas* 1(2):121–94.

Colwell, M. A., and S. L. Landrum. 1993. Nonrandom shorebird distribution and fine-scale variation in prey abundance. *Condor* 95:94–103.

Conant, R. 1975. *A Field Guide to Reptiles and Amphibians of Eastern/Central North America*. Boston: Houghton Mifflin. 429 pp.

Conover, J. T. 1964. The ecology, seasonal periodicity, and distribution of benthic plants in some Texas lagoons. *Marine Botany* 7:4–41.

Contreras Balderas, A. J., J. A. García Salas and J. I. González Rojas. 1990. Aves acuáticas y semiacuáticas de la Laguna Madre, Tamaulipas, Mexico: Otoño-invierno 1988–1989, su aprovechamiento cinegetico. *Biotam* 2(2):23–30.

Cooke, W. W. 1910. Distribution and Migration of North American Shorebirds. U.S. Bureau of Biological Survey Bulletin 35. Washington, D.C. 100 pp.

Coover, J. R., and C. A. Rechenthin. 1965. Report of a Preliminary Investigation of the Wind Erosion and Salt Problem on the Salt Flats of Laguna Madre. U.S. Department of Agriculture, Soil Conservation Service. Temple, Tex. 32 pp.

Copeland, B. J. 1967. Environmental characteristics of hypersaline lagoons. *Contributions in Marine Science* 12:207–18.

Copeland, B. J., and R. S. Jones. 1965. Community metabolism in some hypersaline waters. *Texas Journal of Science* 17:188–205.

Copeland, B. J., J. H. Thompson, Jr., and W. Ogletree. 1968. Effects of wind on water levels in the Texas Laguna Madre. *Texas Journal of Science* 20:196–99.

Cornelius, S. E. 1975. Food Choice of Wintering Redhead Ducks *(Aythya americana)* and Utilization of Available Resources in Lower Laguna Madre, Texas. M.S. thesis, Texas A&M University, College Station. 121 pp.

———. 1977. Food and resource utilization by wintering redheads on lower Laguna Madre. *Journal of Wildlife Management* 41: 374–85.

———. 1984. An Ecological Survey of Alazan Bay, Texas. Technical Bulletin no. 5, Caesar Kleberg Wildlife Research Institute. Kingsville. 163 pp.

Coste, R. L., and M. K. Skoruppa. 1989. Colonial Waterbird Rookery Island Management Plan for the South Texas Coast. Corpus Christi State University Center for Coastal Studies Technical Report CCSU-1089-CCS. Corpus Christi. 77 pp.

Cottam, C. 1970. A commentary on endangered species. Mimeographed paper on file at Welder Wildlife Refuge Library. Sinton, Tex. 5 pp.

Cowardin, L. M., V. Carter, F. C. Golet, and E. T. LaRoe. 1979. *Classification of Wetlands and Deep-Water Habitats of the United States.* U.S. Fish and Wildlife Service, Office of Biological Services FWS/OBS-79/31. Washington, D.C. 103 pp.

Crimm, A. C. C. 1997. Introduction. Pp. xv–xxxvii in J. Monday and B. Colley (eds.), *Voices from the Wild Horse Desert: The Vaquero Families of the King and Kenedy Ranches.* Austin: University of Texas Press. 265 pp.

Cronin, L. E., R. B. Biggs, D. A. Flemer, G. T. Pfitzmeyer, F. Goodwin, Jr., W. L. Dovel, and D. E. Richie, Jr. 1970. Gross Physical and Biological Effects of Overboard Spoil Disposal in Upper Chesapeake Bay. University of Maryland Chesapeake Biological Laboratory, Natural Resources Institute Special Report no. 3. College Park, Md. 66 pp.

Crouse, D. T., L. B. Crowder, and H. Caswell. 1987. A stage-based population model for loggerhead sea turtles and implications for conservation. *Ecology* 68:1412–23.

Cruz, G. R. 1988. *Let There Be Towns: Spanish Municipal Origins in the American Southwest, 1610–1810.* College Station: Texas A&M University Press. 236 pp.

Cruz-Nieto, M. A. 2000. The Binational Laguna Madre—Tamaulipas. Draft Report, Texas Center for Policy Studies. Austin. No page numbers.

Curray, J. R. 1960. Sediments and history of Holocene transgression, Continental Shelf, northwest Gulf of Mexico. Pp. 221–66 in F. P. Shepard, F. B. Phleger, and T. H. van Andel (eds.), *Recent Sediments, Northwest Gulf of Mexico.* Tulsa, Okla.: American Association of Petroleum Geologists.

Custer, T. W., and C. A. Mitchell. 1987a. Exposure to insecticides of brushland wildlife within the Lower Rio Grande Valley, Texas. *Environmental Pollution* 45:207–20.

———. 1987b. Organochlorine contaminants and reproductive success of black skimmers in South Texas, 1984. *Journal of Field Ornithology* 58:480–89.

———. 1991. Contaminant exposure of willets feeding in agricultural drainages of the Lower Rio Grande Valley of South Texas. *Texas Environmental Monitoring and Assessment* 16:189–220.

———. 1993. Trace elements and organochlorines in the shoal grass community of the lower Laguna Madre, Texas. *Texas Environmental Monitoring and Assessment* 25:235–46.

Czerny, A. B. 1994. Growth and Photosynthetic Responses of Two Tropical Seagrasses, *Thalassia testudinum* and *Halodule wrightii* to in situ Manipulations of Irradiance. M.S. thesis, University of Texas, Austin. 83 pp.

Czerny, A. B., and K. H. Dunton. 1995. The effects of in situ light reduction on the growth of two subtropical seagrasses, *Thalassia testudinum* and *Halodule wrightii*. *Estuaries* 18:418–27.

Dahl, T. E., and C. E. Johnson. 1991. *Status and Trends of Wetlands in the Coterminal United States, Mid-1970s to Mid-1980s.* U.S. Department of the Interior, Fish and Wildlife Service. Washington, D.C. 28 pp.

Daniell, L. E. 1892. *Personnel of the Texas State Government, with Sketches of Representative Men of Texas.* San Antonio: Maverick Printing House. 210 pp.

Darnell, R. M. 1958. Food habits of fishes and larger invertebrates of Lake Pontchartrain, Louisiana, an estuarine community. *Publications of the Institute of Marine Science, University of Texas* 5:353–416.

Davis, A. M. 1942. A Study of Boscaje de la Palma in Cameron County, Texas and of *Sabal texana*. M.A. thesis, University of Texas, Austin. 111 pp.

Davis, J. R. 1983. Intensive Survey of the Arroyo Colorado Segment 2201. Texas Department of Water Resources no. IS-49. Austin. 58 pp.

———. 1984. Intensive Survey of the Arroyo Colorado Segment 2201. Texas Department of Water Resources no. IS-61. Austin. 43 pp.

———. 1985. Intensive Survey of the Arroyo Colorado Segment 2201, August 22–25, 1983. Texas Department of Water Resources no. IS-69. Austin. 66 pp.

Davis, W. B., and D. J. Schmidly. 1994. *The Mammals of Texas.* Austin: Texas Parks and Wildlife Press. 338 pp.

Dean, C. 1999. *Against the Tide: The Battle for America's Beaches.* New York: Columbia University Press. 270 pp.

den Hartog, C. 1977. Structure, function, and classification in seagrass communities. Pp. 89–122 in C. P. McRoy and C. Helfferich (eds.), *Seagrass Ecosystems: A Scientific Perspective.* New York: Marcel Dekker.

DePue, J. 1974. Nesting and Reproduction of the Black Skimmer (*Rhynchops niger* Linnaeus) on Four Spoil Islands in the Laguna Madre, Texas. M.S. thesis, Texas A&I University, Kingsville. 190 pp.

DeYoe, H. R., A. M. Chan, and C. A. Suttle. 1995. Phylogeny of *Aureococcus anophagefferens* and a morphologically similar bloom-forming alga from Texas as determined by 18S ribosomal RNA sequence analysis. *Journal of Phycology* 31:413–18.

DeYoe, H. R., D. A. Stockwell, R. R. Bida-

gare, M. Latasa, P. W. Johnson, P. E. Hargraves, and C. A. Suttle. 1997. Description of the algal species *Aureoumbra lagunensis* gen. et sp. nov. and referral of *Aureoumbra* and *Aureococcus* to the Pelagophyceae. *Journal of Phycology* 33:1042–48.

DeYoe, H. R., and C. A. Suttle. 1994. The inability of the Texas "brown tide" alga to use nitrate and the role of nitrogen in the initiation of a persistent bloom of this organism. *Journal of Phycology* 30:800–806.

Diamond, D. D., and T. E. Fulbright. 1990. Contemporary plant communities of upland grasslands of the coastal sand plain, Texas. *Southwestern Naturalist* 35:385–92.

Diamond, D. D., D. H. Riskind, and S. L. Orzell. 1987. A framework for plant community classification and conservation in Texas. *Texas Journal of Science* 39:203–21.

Diaz, A., and M. Kelly. 1994. *Subsidized Destruction: The Gulf Intracoastal Waterway and the Laguna Madre.* Austin: Texas Center for Policy Studies. 57 pp.

Dice, L. R. 1937. Mammals of the San Carlos Mountains and vicinity. *University of Michigan Studies and Scientific Series* 12:245–68.

———. 1943. *The Biotic Provinces of North America.* Ann Arbor: University of Michigan Press. 78 pp.

Dick, M. 1982. *Pesticide and PCB Concentrations in Texas: Water, Sediment and Fish Tissues.* Report no. 264. Austin: Texas Department of Water Resources. 77 pp.

Diener, R. A. 1975. *Cooperative Gulf of Mexico Estuarine Inventory and Study, Texas: Area Description.* NOAA Technical Report NMFS Circular 393. Seattle, Wash. 129 pp.

Dixon, J. R. 1987. *Amphibians and Reptiles of Texas.* College Station: Texas A&M University Press. 434 pages.

———. 2000. *Amphibians and Reptiles of Texas.* 2d ed. College Station: Texas A&M University Press. 421 pp.

Dobie, J. L., L. H. Ogren, and J. F. Fitzpatrick, Jr. 1961. Footnotes and records of the Atlantic ridley turtle *(Lepidochelys kempii)* from Louisiana. *Copeia* 1961:109–10.

Dodd, C. K., Jr. 1988. *Synopsis of the Biological Data on the Loggerhead Sea Turtle* Caretta caretta *(Linnaeus 1758).* U.S. Fish and Wildlife Service Biological Report 88(14). Washington, D.C. 110 pp.

Dokken, Q. R. 1981. Spatial and Temporal

Distribution and Species Composition of Larval Fish Populations within Alazan Bay, Texas. M.S. thesis, Corpus Christi State University, Corpus Christi. 61 pp.

Dokken, Q. R., G. C. Matlock, and S. Cornelius. 1984. Distribution and composition of larval fish populations within Alazan Bay, Texas. *Contributions in Marine Science* 27:205–22.

Doughty, R. W. 1984. Sea turtles in Texas: A forgotten commerce. *Southwestern Historical Quarterly* 88:43–70.

Douglas, C. L. 1968. *Cattle Kings of Texas.* Fort Worth: Branch-Smith. 376 pp.

Drawe, D. L., and K. R. Kattner. 1978. Effect of burning and mowing on vegetation of Padre Island. *Southwestern Naturalist* 23:273–78.

Drawe, D. L., K. R. Kattner, W. H. McFarland, and D. D. Neher. 1981. Vegetation and soil properties of five habitat types on North Padre Island. *Texas Journal of Science* 33:145–57.

Drawe, D. L., and I. M. Ortega. 1996. Impacts of geophysical seismic survey vehicles on Padre Island National Seashore vegetation. *Texas Journal of Science* 48:107–18.

Duarte, C. M. 1991. Seagrass depth limits. *Aquatic Botany* 40:363–77.

DUMAC (Ducks Unlimited de México, A.C.). 1990. Laguna Madre y Lagunas de Tamaulipas. *Ducks Unlimited de México, A.C. Magazine* 12(3):15–16.

———. 1993. Diagnóstico Eco-gráfico para el Manejo y Conservación de la Laguna Madre, Tamaulipas y Zonas de Influencia: Informe Final. Ducks Unlimited de México, A.C., Technical Report. Monterrey, Nuevo León. No page numbers.

———. 1996. Vegetación Acuática de la Laguna Madre de Tamaulipas (Pastos Marinos): Informe Final de Proyecto. Ducks Unlimited de México, A.C. and Instituto de Ecologia y Alimentos, de la Universidad Autónoma de Tamaulipas. Monterrey, Nuevo León. 44 pp.

Dunton, K. H. 1994. Seasonal growth and biomass of the subtropical *Halodule wrightii* in relation to continuous measurements of underwater irradiance. *Marine Biology* 120:479–89.

Dunton, K. H., A. Burd, L. Cifuentes, P. Eldridge, and J. Morse. 1998a. The Effect of Dredge Deposits on the Distribution and Productivity of Seagrasses: An Integrative Model for Laguna Madre. Draft Final Report to Interagency Coordination Team, Galveston District, U.S. Army Corps of Engineers. No page numbers.

Dunton, K. H., P. A. Montagna, and S. A. Holt. 1998b. *Characterization of Anthropogenic and Natural Disturbance on Vegetated and Unvegetated Bay Bottom Habitats in the Corpus Christi Bay National Estuary Program Study Area*, vol. 2: *Assessment of Scarring in Seagrass Beds.* Corpus Christi Bay National Estuary Program CCBNEP-25B. Corpus Christi: Texas Natural Resource Conservation Commission. 23 pp.

Dyer, K. R. 1973. *Estuaries: A Physical Introduction.* London, England: Wiley and Sons. 140 pp.

Dykstra, R. F. 1966. Investigation of Some Algae of the Texas Gulf Coast. M.S. thesis, University of Texas, Austin. 100 pp.

Ecoservices. 1993a. Laguna Madre Bird Project from Yarborough Pass to Mansfield Channel during July 1992 through April 1993. Report to Padre Island National Seashore, Contract no. 1443PX7000092582. Corpus Christi, Tex. 82 pages.

———. 1993b. Bird Use of the Padre Island National Seashore Gulf Beach from September 1992–August 1993. Report to Padre Island National Seashore, Contract no. 1443PX749092188. Corpus Christi, Tex. 85 pp.

Edwards, P., and D. F. Kapraun. 1973. Benthic marine algal ecology in the Port Aransas, Texas area. *Contributions in Marine Science* 17:15–52.

EHA (Espey, Huston and Associates, Inc.). 1977. Ecological Baseline Inventory (Appendix B) and Environmental Effects Assessment, Hidalgo and Willacy County Drainage Districts, Permit Application no. 11374. Report to U.S. Army Corps of Engineers, Galveston District. Galveston, Tex.

———. 1997. Piping Plover Habitat Survey of Dredged Material Placement Areas along the Gulf Intracoastal Waterway from Port Isabel Bay to the Mud Flats. Report to U.S. Army Corps of Engineers, Galveston District, EH&A Job no. 18383, Document no. 970507. Austin, Tex. 14 pp.

———. 1998. Laguna Madre, Texas Contaminant Assessment. Report to U.S. Army Corps of Engineers, Galveston District, EH&A Job no. 18798, Document no. 971410. Austin, Tex. 63 pp.

EHA and BVA (Barry A. Vittor and Associates). 1998. Benthic Macroinfaunal Analysis of Dredged Material Placement

Areas in the Laguna Madre, Texas, Spring and Fall 1996 Surveys. Report to U.S. Army Corps of Engineers, Galveston District, EH&A Job no. 15650-53, Document no. 970740. Austin. 112 pp.

Ehrhart, L. M. 1989. A status review of the loggerhead turtle, *Caretta caretta*, in the western Atlantic. Pp. 122–39 in L. Ogren, F. Berry, K. Bjorndal, H. Kumpf, R. Mast, G. Medina, H. Reichart, and R. Witham (eds.), *Proceedings of the Second Western Atlantic Turtle Symposium.* NOAA Technical Memorandum, NMFS-SEFC-226. Springfield, Va.

Eleuterius, L. N. 1987. Seagrass ecology along the coasts of Alabama, Louisiana, and Mississippi. Pp. 11–24 in M. J. Durako, R. C. Phillips, and R. R. Lewis, III (eds.), *Proceedings of the Symposium on Subtropical-Tropical Seagrasses of the Southeastern United States.* Florida Department of Natural Resources Marine Research Publication 42. St. Petersburg, Fla.

Ellis, M. J. 1986. *The Corpus Christi Hurricane Almanac, Texas.* Corpus Christi: Hurricane Publications. 128 pp.

Ernst, C. H., and R. W. Barbour. 1972. *Turtles of the United States.* Lexington, Ky.: University of Kentucky Press. 347 pp.

Evans, P. R., D. M. Herdson, P. J. Knights, and M. W. Pienkowski. 1979. Short-term effects of reclamation of part of Seal Sands, Teesmouth, on wintering waders and shelduck. *Oecologia* 41:83–206.

Evendon, F. G., Jr. 1952. Notes on Mexican bird distribution. *Wilson Bulletin* 64:112–13.

Everitt, J. H., and D. L. Drawe. 1993. *Trees, Shrubs and Cacti of South Texas.* Lubbock: Texas Tech University Press. 213 pp.

Everitt, J. H., D. L. Drawe, and R. I. Lonard. 1999. *Field Guide to the Broadleaved Herbaceous Plants of South Texas Used by Livestock and Wildlife.* Lubbock: Texas Tech University Press. 277 pp.

Everitt, J. H., F. W. Judd, D. E. Escobar, M. A. Alaniz, M. R. Davis, and W. MacWhorter. 1996. Using remote sensing and spatial information technologies to map Texas palmetto in the lower Rio Grande Valley of Texas. *Southwestern Naturalist* 41:218–26.

Farmer, M. 1991. Reddish Egrets of the Lower Laguna Madre, Texas. Report to U.S. Fish and Wildlife Service, Lower Rio Grande National Wildlife Refuge. Alamo, Tex. 54 pp.

———. 1996. Reddish Egrets along the Western Gulf of México. Report to U.S.

Fish and Wildlife Service, Ecological Services. Clear Lake, Houston, Tex. 51 pp.

Farmer, M., and E. Carrera González. 1993. Mid-Winter Surveys of Reddish Egret Foraging Habitat in the Laguna Madre, Mexico. Report to U.S.–Mexico Joint Committee of U.S. Fish and Wildlife Service and Secretaría de Desarrollo Social. Albuquerque, N.M. 18 pp.

Ferguson-Wood, E. J. 1963. A study of the diatom flora of fresh sediments of the South Texas Bays and adjacent waters. *Publications of the Institute of Marine Science, University of Texas* 9:237–310.

Fisk, H. N. 1949. Geological Investigation of the Laguna Madre Flats. Report to Humble Oil and Refining Company. Houston, Tex. 152 pp.

———. 1959. Padre Island and the Laguna Madre flats: Coastal South Texas. Pp. 103–52 in R. J. Russell (ed.), *Second Coastal Geography Conference.* Baton Rouge, La.: Coastal Studies Institute, Louisiana State University.

Flint, R. W., S. Rabalais, and R. D. Kalke. 1982. Estuarine benthos and ecosystem functioning. Pp. 185–201 in J. R. Davis (ed.), *Proceedings of the Symposium on Recent Benthological Investigations in Texas and Adjacent States.* Austin: Texas Academy of Science.

Flowers, J., N. Easterling, and L. Hauck. 1998. Prediction of Effects of Best Management Practices on Agricultural Nonpoint Source Pollution in the Arroyo Colorado Watershed. Tarleton State University, Texas Institute for Applied Environmental Research Report no. PR97-06. Stephenville, Tex. 54 pp.

Fonseca, M. S. 1994. Seagrasses: A Guide to Planting Seagrasses in the Gulf of Mexico. Texas A&M University Sea Grant College Program Technical Report TAMU-SG-94-601. College Station. 26 pp.

Ford, G. 1998. "Tio" Kleberg leaving King Ranch. *Corpus Christi Caller-Times* 116(125C):6, 10.

Frazier, D. E. 1974. *Depositional-Episodes: Their Relationship to the Quaternary Stratigraphic Framework in the Northwestern Portion of the Gulf Basin.* Geology Circular 74-1. Austin: Bureau of Economic Geology, University of Texas. 28 pp.

Fredrickson, L. H., and R. D. Drobney. 1979. Habitat utilization by postbreeding waterfowl. Pp. 119–31 in T. A. Bookhout (ed.), *Waterfowl and Wetlands: An Integrated Review.* Madison, Wis.: Wildlife Society, North-Central Section.

Freeman, T. 1962. Quiet water oölites from Laguna Madre, Texas. *Journal of Sedimentary Petrology* 32:475–83.

Fretey, J., and M. Girondot. 1989. L'activité de ponte de la tortue luths, *Dermochelys coriacea* (Vandelli, 1761), pendant la saison 1988 en Guyane Française. *Revue d'Écologie: La Terre et la Vie* 44:261–74.

Friedmann, H., L. Griscom, and R. T. Moore. 1950. *Distributional Check-list of the Birds of Mexico.* Pacific Coast Avifauna 29. Berkeley, Calif.: Cooper Ornithological Club. 202 pp.

Fritts, T. H., A. B. Irvine, R. D. Jennings, L. A. Collum, W. Hoffman, and M. A. McGehee. 1983. *Turtles, Birds, and Mammals in the Northern Gulf of Mexico and Nearby Atlantic Waters: An Overview Based on Aerial Surveys of OCS Areas, with Emphasis on Oil and Gas Effects.* U.S. Fish and Wildlife Service, Division of Biological Services, FWS/OBS-82-65. Washington, D.C. 455 pp.

Fry, B., and P. L. Parker. 1979. Animal diet in Texas seagrass meadows: ^{13}C evidence for the importance of benthic plants. *Estuarine and Coastal Marine Science* 8:499–509.

Fulbright, T. E., D. D. Diamond, J. Rappole, and J. Norwine. 1990. The coastal sand plain of southern Texas. *Rangelands* 12:337–40.

Fuls, B. E. 1974. Further Ecological Studies on the Macroichthyofauna of the Laguna Salada, Texas. M.S. thesis, Texas A&I University, Kingsville. 106 pp.

Fulton, K. J. 1976. Subsurface Stratigraphy, Depositional Environments, and Aspects of Reservoir Continuity: Rio Grande Delta, Texas. Ph.D. diss., University of Cincinnati. Cincinnati, Ohio. 314 pp.

Garcia, C. P. 1979. Padre Island and Padre Jose Nicolas Balli: Application for Historical Marker. Corpus Christi, Tex.: Grunwald Publications. 16 pp.

García-Cubas, A., Jr. 1968. *Ecologia y Distribución de los Micromoluscos Recientes de la Laguna Madre Tamaulipas, México.* Instituto de Geologia Boletín Numero 86. Mexico, D.F.: Universidad Nacional Autónoma de México. 44 pp.

García-Gil, G., J. Rendón-von Osten, J. García Guzman, E. Carrera González, C. Tejeda Cruz, F. E. Galán Amaro, and B. Ortiz Espejel. 1993. Diagnóstico ambiental de Laguna Madre, Tamaulipas. Pp. 535–52 in S. I. Sálazar-Vallejo and N. E. González (eds.), *Biodiversidad Marina y Costera de México.* Mexico, D.F.: Comisión Nacional para el Conocimiento y Aprovechamiento de la Biodiversidad y Centro de Investigaciones de Quintana Roo.

Gardner, L. R., W. K. Michener, E. R. Blood, T. M. Williams, D. J. Lipscomb, and W. H. Jefferson. 1991. Ecological impact of Hurricane Hugo: Salinization of a coastal forest. *Journal of Coastal Research* 8:301–17.

Gardner, L. R., W. K. Michener, T. M. Williams, E. R. Blood, B. Kjerfve, L. A. Smock, D. J. Lipscomb, and C. Gresham. 1992. Disturbance effects of Hurricane Hugo on a pristine coastal landscape: North Inlet, South Carolina, USA. *Netherlands Journal of Sea Research* 30:249–63.

Garrett, J. M., and D. G. Barker. 1987. *A Field Guide to Reptiles and Amphibians of Texas.* Houston: Gulf Publishing Company. 225 pp.

Garza, H., Jr. 1997. Habitat Use and Activities of the Piping Plover, *Charadrius melodus,* wintering on South Padre Island, Texas. M.S. thesis, University of Texas–Pan American, Edinburg. 49 pp.

Gomez Soto, A., and S. Contreras Balderas. 1987. Ictiofauna de la Laguna Madre, Tamaulipas, México. Pp. 8–17 in *Memorias del Congreso, IX Congreso Nacional de Zoologia,* vol. II. Villahermosa, Tabasco, Mexico.

Goss-Custard, J. D. 1970. The responses of Redshank (*Tringa totanus* [L.]) to spatial variations in the density of their prey. *Journal of Animal Ecology.* 39:1–13.

———. 1979. Role of winter food supplies in the population ecology of common British wading birds. *Verhandlungen Ornithologische Gesellschaft Bayern* 23:125–46.

———. 1980. Competition for food and interference among waders. *Ardea* 68:31–52.

———. 1983. Spatial and seasonal variations in the food supply of waders Charadrii wintering in the British Isles. Pp. 85–96 in J. Fjeldså and H. Meltofte (eds.), *Proceedings of the 3rd Nordic Congress of Ornithology, 1981.* Copenhagen, Denmark: Dansk Ornitologisk Forening–Zoologisk Museum.

———. 1985. Foraging behaviour of wading birds and the carrying capacity of estuaries. Pp. 169–88 in R. M. Sibly and R. H. Smith (eds.), *Behavioural Ecology.* Oxford, England: Blackwell Scientific Publishing.

Goss-Custard, J. D., and K. Charman. 1976. Predicting how many wintering waterfowl an area can support. *Wildfowl* 27:157–58.

Goss-Custard, J. D., and S. E. A. Le V Dit Durrell. 1990. Bird behaviour and environmental planning: Approaches in the study of wader populations. *Ibis* 132: 273–89.

Goss-Custard, J. D., D. G. Kay, and R. M. Blindell. 1977. The density of migratory and overwintering Redshank *Tringa totanus* (L.) and Curlew *Numenius arquata* (L.) in relation to the density of their prey in south-east England. *Estuarine Coastal Marine Science* 15:491–510.

Gosselink, J. D., C. L. Cordes, and J. W. Parsons. 1979. *An Ecological Characterization Study of the Chenier Plain Coastal Ecosystem of Louisiana and Texas.* U.S. Fish and Wildlife Service, Office of Biological Services FWS/OBS-78/9, 10, 11. Washington, D.C. 3 vols.

Gotto, J. W., F. R. Tabita, and C. Van Baalen. 1981. Nitrogen fixation in intertidal environments of the Texas Gulf coast. *Estuarine Coastal Shelf Science* 12:231–35.

Gould, F. W. 1969. *Texas Plants: A Checklist and Ecological Summary.* Texas Agricultural Experiment Station MP-585. College Station: Texas A&M University. 121 pp.

———. 1975. *The Grasses of Texas.* College Station: Texas A&M University Press. 654 pp.

Gould, F. W., and T. W. Box. 1965. *Grasses of the Texas Coastal Bend (Calhoun, Refugio, Aransas, San Patricio and Northern Kleberg Counties).* College Station: Texas A&M University Press. 186 pp.

Grant, M. L. 1998. A corporate end to a cowboy era. *Corpus Christi Caller-Times* 116(227A):1, 6–8.

Groue, K. J., and L. J. Lester. 1982. A morphological and genetic analysis of geographic variation among oysters in the Gulf of Mexico. *Veliger* 24:331–41.

Groves, C., L. Valutis, D. Vosick, B. Neely, K. Wheaton, J. Touval, and B. Runnels. 2000. *Designing a Geography of Hope: A Practitioner's Handbook for Ecoregional Planning.* Arlington, Va.: Nature Conservancy. 2 vols.

Gunter, G. 1945a. Some characteristics of ocean waters and Laguna Madre. *Texas Game and Fish* 3(10):7, 19–22.

———. 1945b. Studies on marine fishes of Texas. *Publications of the Institute of Marine Science, University of Texas* 1(1):1–90.

———. 1946. Problems of the Texas Coast. *Texas Game and Fish* 5(12):9, 25–28.

———. 1961. Some relations of estuarine organisms to salinity. *Limnology and Oceanography* 6:182–90.

———. 1962. Shrimp landings and production of the state of Texas for the period 1956–1959, with a comparison with other Gulf states. *Publications of the Institute of Marine Science, University of Texas* 8:216–26.

———. 1967. Vertebrates in hypersaline waters. *Contributions in Marine Science* 12:230–41.

Gunter, G., and H. H. Hildebrand. 1951. Destruction of fishes and other organisms on the South Texas coast by the cold wave of January 28–February 3, 1951. *Ecology* 32:731–36.

Haig, S. M., and J. H. Plissner. 1993. Distribution and abundance of Piping Plovers: Results and implications of the 1991 international census. *Condor* 95:145–56.

Haines, E. B., and C. L. Montague. 1979. Food sources of estuarine invertebrates analyzed using $^{13}C/^{12}C$ ratios. *Ecology* 60:48–56.

Hall, E. R. 1951. Mammals obtained by Dr. Curt von Wedel from the barrier beach of Tamaulipas, Mexico. *University of Kansas Museum of Natural History Publications* 5:33–47.

Hallam, A. 1965. Environmental causes of stunting in living and fossil marine benthonic invertebrates. *Palaeontology* 8:132–55.

Hardegree, B. 1997. Biological Productivity Associated with the Serpulid Reefs of Baffin Bay, Texas. M.S. thesis, Texas A&M University–Corpus Christi. 130 pp.

Hargrave, B. T., and G. F. Connolly. 1978. A device to collect supernatant water for measurement of flux of dissolved compounds across sediment surfaces. *Limnology and Oceanography* 23:1005–10.

Harrington, B. A., and R. I. G. Morrison. 1979. Semipalmated Sandpiper migration in North America. *Studies in Avian Biology* 2:83–99.

Harrington, R. W., and E. S. Harrington. 1972. Food of female marsh killifish, *Fundulus confluentus* Goode and Bean, in Florida. *American Midland Naturalist* 87:492–502.

Harris, R. V. 1988. The Mammals of Padre Island, Texas. Unpublished manuscript on file, Texas A&M University–Corpus Christi Center for Coastal Studies Library. 37 pp.

Harris, V. T., and R. H. Chabreck. 1958. Some effects of Hurricane Audrey on the marsh at Marsh Island, Louisiana. *Louisiana Academy of Science* 21:47–50.

Hayes, M. O. 1965. Sedimentation on a Semi-Arid, Wave Dominated Coast (South Texas) with Emphasis on Hurricane Effects. Ph.D. diss., University of Texas, Austin. 350 pp.

———. 1967. *Hurricanes as Geologic Agents: Carla, 1961 and Cindy, 1963.* Report Investigation 61. Austin: Bureau of Economic Geology, University of Texas. 56 pp.

Hayes, M. O., D. D. Domeracki, C. D. Getter, T. W. Kana, and G. I. Scott. 1980. *Sensitivity of Coastal Environments to Spilled Oil, South Texas Coast.* Research Planning Institute, Inc., Report no. RPI/R/80/4/11-12, prepared for NOAA Office of Marine Pollution Assessment. Columbia, S.C. 89 pp.

Hayes, M. O., and A. J. Scott. 1964. Environmental complexes, South Texas coast. *Transactions of the Gulf Coast Association of Geology Societies* 14:237–40.

Hedgpeth, J. W. 1947. The Laguna Madre of Texas. *North American Wildlife Conference* 12:364–80.

———. 1953. An introduction to the zoogeography of the northwestern Gulf of Mexico with reference to the invertebrate fauna. *Publications of the Institute of Marine Science, University of Texas* 3(1):111–224.

———. 1954. Bottom communities of the Gulf of Mexico. Pp. 203–22 in P. S. Galtsoff (ed.), *Gulf of Mexico: Its Origin, Waters, and Marine Life.* U.S. Fisheries Bulletin 89. U.S. Fish and Wildlife Service. Washington D.C.

———. 1967. Ecological aspects of the Laguna Madre, a hypersaline estuary. Pp. 408–19 in G. H. Lauff (ed.), *Estuaries.* Publication no. 83. Washington, D.C.: American Association for the Advancement of Science.

Heitmeyer, M. E., and L. H. Fredrickson. 1981. Do wetland conditions in the Mississippi Delta hardwoods influence mallard recruitment? *Transactions of the North American Wildlife and Natural Resource Conference* 46:44–57.

Hellier, T. R., Jr. 1962. Fish production and biomass studies in relation to photosynthesis in the Laguna Madre of Texas. *Publications of the Institute of Marine Science, University of Texas* 8:1–22.

Henry, W. K., D. M. Driscoll, and J. P. McCormack. 1980. Hurricanes on the Texas coast. Texas A&M University Sea Grant Program, Center for Applied Geo-

sciences Report TAMU-SG-75-504. College Station. 48 pp.

Hensley, R. A., and B. E. Fuls. 1998. *Trends in Relative Abundance and Size of Selected Finfishes and Shellfishes Along the Texas Coast: November 1975–December 1996.* Management Data Series no. 159. Austin: Texas Parks and Wildlife Department. 88 pp.

Herber, J. P. 1981. Holocene Sediments under Laguna Madre, Cameron County, Texas. M.A. thesis, University of Texas, Austin. 664 pp.

Hicklin, P. W. 1987. The migration of shorebirds in the Bay of Fundy. *Wilson Bulletin* 99:540–70.

Hicklin, P. W., and P. C. Smith. 1984. Selection of foraging sites and invertebrate prey by migrant Semipalmated Sandpipers, *Calidris pusilla* (Pallas), in Minas Basin, Bay of Fundy. *Canadian Journal of Zoology* 62:2201–10.

Hicks, D. W., and J. W. Tunnell, Jr. 1993. Invasion of the South Texas coast by the edible brown mussel *Perna perna* (Linnaeus, 1758). *Veliger* 36:92–94.

———. 1994. The Invasive Biology of the Edible Brown Mussel, *Perna perna* (Linnaeus, 1758), on the South Texas Coast: Year 1. Texas A&M University–Corpus Christi, Center for Coastal Studies Technical Report TAMUCC-9403-CCS. Corpus Christi. 31 pp.

Higgins, E., and R. Lord. 1926. *Preliminary Report on the Marine Fisheries of Texas.* Document no. 1009. Washington, D.C.: Bureau of Fisheries.

Hildebrand, H. 1958. Estudios biológicos preliminares sobre la Laguna Madre de Tamaulipas. *Ciencia* (Mexico) 17:151–73.

———. 1963. Hallazgo del área de anidación de la tortuga "lora" *Lepidochelys kempii* (Garman), en la costa occidental del Golfo de México (Reptila, Chelonia). *Ciencia* (Mexico) 22:105–12.

———. 1969. Laguna Madre de Tamaulipas: Observations on its hydrography and fisheries. Pp. 679–86 in A. Ayala Castañares and F. B. Phleger (eds.), *Coastal Lagoons: A Symposium.* Mexico, D.F.: Universidad Nacional Autónoma de México.

———. 1980. The Laguna Madre de Tamaulipas: Its Hydrography and Shrimp Fishery. Unpublished manuscript, submitted to National Marine Fisheries Service, on file at Texas A&M University–Corpus Christi, Center for Coastal Studies Library. 42 pp.

———. 1981. A historical review of the status of sea turtle populations in the western Gulf of Mexico. Pp. 447–53 in K. A. Bjorndal (ed.), *Biology and Conservation of Sea Turtles: Proceedings of the World Conference of Sea Turtle Conservation*. Washington, D.C.: Smithsonian Institution Press and World Wildlife Fund.

Hildebrand, H., and D. King. 1978. A Biological Study of the Cayo del Oso and Pita Island Area of the Laguna Madre. Final Report to Central Power and Light Company, vol. 1. Corpus Christi, Tex. No page numbers.

Hillestad, H. O., J. I. Richardson, and G. K. Williamson. 1978. *Incidental Capture of Sea Turtles by Shrimp Trawler Men in Georgia*. Athens, Ga.: Southeastern Wildlife Service, Inc. 24 pp.

Hirth, H. H., L. C. Klikorr, and K. T. Harper. 1973. Sea grasses at Khor Unaira, People's Democratic Republic of Yemen, with reference to their role in the diet of the green turtle, *Chelonia mydas*. *Fishery Bulletin* 71:1093–97.

Hobaugh, W. C., and T. G. Teer. 1981. Waterfowl use characteristics of flood-prevention lakes in north-central Texas. *Journal of Wildlife Management* 45:16–26.

Hoese, H. D., B. J. Copeland, F. N. Mosely, and E. D. Lane. 1968. Fauna of the Aransas Pass Inlet, Texas, pt. 3: Diel and seasonal variation in trawlable organisms of the adjacent area. *Texas Journal of Science* 20:33–60.

Hollandsworth, S. 1998. When we were kings. *Texas Monthly* 26(8):112–17, 140–44.

Hook, J. H. 1991. Seasonal variation in relative abundance and species diversity of fishes in South Bay. *Contributions in Marine Science* 32:127–41.

Hooper, C. H. (ed.). 1981. *The Ixtoc I Oil Spill: The Federal Scientific Response*. Boulder, Colo.: NOAA Hazardous Materials Response Project. 202 pp.

Huffman, G. G., and W. A. Price. 1949. Clay dune formation near Corpus Christi, Texas. *Journal of Sedimentary Petrology* 19:118–27.

Humm, H. J., and H. H. Hildebrand. 1962. Marine algae from the Gulf coast of Texas and Mexico. *Publications of the Institute of Marine Science, University of Texas* 8:227–68.

Hunt, W. G., R. R. Rogers, and D. L. Slowe. 1975. Migratory and foraging behavior of Peregrine Falcons on the Texas Coast. *Canadian Field Naturalist* 89:111–23.

Hunt, W. G., and F. P. Ward. 1988. Habitat selection by spring migrant peregrines at Padre Island, Texas. Pp. 527–35 in T. J.

Cade, J. H. Enderson, C. G. Thelander, and C. M. White (eds.), *Peregrine Falcon Populations: Their Management and Recovery*. Boise, Idaho: Peregrine Fund.

Hunter, R. E., R. L. Watson, G. W. Hill, and K. A. Dickinson. 1972. Modern depositional environments and processes, northern and central Padre Island, Texas. Pp. 1–17 in Corpus Christi Geological Society (ed.), *Padre Island National Seashore Field Guide*. Corpus Christi: Golden Banner Press.

Hutchinson, K. J., and C. B. Smith. 1995. *Río Grande Coastal Impact Monitoring Program (Final project report)*. Texas General Land Office no. X996069-01-1. Austin. 173 pp.

INEGI. 1980. Carta topográfica 1:250,000, Matamoros G14-6-9-12 Tamaulipas y Texas. Aguascalientes, Mexico: Instituto Nacional de Estadística, Geografía y Informática. 1 sheet.

———. 1994. *Atlas del Territorio Insular Habitado de los Estados Unidos Mexicanos, 1990 Anexo Cartográgrafico*. Aguascalientes, Mexico: Instituto Nacional de Estadística, Geografía y Informática. 146 pp.

———. No date. Carta estatal-fenómenos climatológicos, escala 1:2,000,000. Aguascalientes, Mexico: Dirección General de Geografía. Instituto Nacional de Estadística, Geografía y Informática. 1 sheet.

Jackson, J. 1986. *Los Mesteños: Spanish Ranching in Texas, 1721–1821*. College Station: Texas A&M University Press. 704 pp.

Jahrsdoerfer, S. E., and D. M. Leslie, Jr. 1988. *Tamaulipan Brushland of the Lower Rio Grande Valley of South Texas: Description, Human Impacts, and Management Options*. U.S. Fish and Wildlife Service Biological Report 88(36). Washington, D.C. 63 pp.

Javor, B. 1989. *Hypersaline Environments*. New York: Springer-Verlag. 328 pp.

Johnson, C. M., and G. S. Baldassarre. 1988. Aspects of the wintering ecology of Piping Plovers in coastal Alabama. *Wilson Bulletin* 100:214–15.

Johnston, M. C. 1955. Vegetation of the Eolian Plain and Associated Coastal Features of Southern Texas. Ph.D. diss., University of Texas, Austin. 167 pp.

———. 1963. Past and present grasslands of southern Texas and northeastern Mexico. *Ecology* 44:456–66.

Jones, F. B. 1975. *Flora of the Texas Coastal Bend.* Welder Wildlife Foundation Contribution B-6. Corpus Christi: Mission Press. 262 pp.

Jones, S. D., J. K. Wipff, and P. M. Montgomery. 1997. *Vascular Plants of Texas: A Comprehensive Checklist Including Synonymy, Bibliography, and Index.* Austin: University of Texas Press. 404 pp.

Judd, F. W. 1976. Food and feeding behavior of the keeled earless lizard, *Holbrookia propinqua. Southwestern Naturalist* 21:17–26.

Judd, F. W., R. I. Lonard, and S. L. Sides. 1977. The vegetation of South Padre Island, Texas in relation to topography. *Southwestern Naturalist* 22:31–48.

Judd, F. W., R. I. Lonard, J. H. Everitt, and R. Villarreal. 1989. Effect of vehicular traffic in secondary dunes and vegetated flats of South Padre Island, Texas. Pp. 4634–35 in Magoon, O. T. (ed.), *Coastal Zone '89: Proceedings of the Sixth Symposium on Coastal and Ocean Management.* New York: American Society of Civil Engineers (ASCE).

Judd, F. W., H. Nieuwendaal, and D. L. Hockaday. 1991. The leatherback turtle, *Dermochelys coriacea,* in southernmost Texas. *Texas Journal of Science* 43:101–103.

Judd, F. W., and S. L. Sides. 1983. Effects of Hurricane Allen on the nearshore vegetation of South Padre Island, Texas. *Southwestern Naturalist* 28:365–69.

Kaminski, R. M., and E. A. Gluesing. 1987. Density- and habitat-related recruitment in mallards. *Journal of Wildlife Management* 51:141–48.

Kantrud, H. A. 1991. *Wigeon Grass* (Ruppia maritima L.)*: A Literature Review.* Fish and Wildlife Research Report 10. Washington, D.C.: U.S. Fish and Wildlife Service. 58 pp.

Kapraun, D. F. 1980. Summer aspect of algal zonation on a Texas jetty in relation to wave exposure. *Contributions in Marine Science* 23:101–109.

Kattner, K. R. 1973. Secondary successional vegetation on Padre Island National Seashore. M.S. thesis, Texas A&I University, Kingsville. 71 pp.

Kelley, P. 1986. *River of Lost Dreams: Navigation on the Rio Grande.* Lincoln: University of Nebraska Press. 149 pp.

Kelsey, M. G., and M. Hassall. 1989. Patch selection by Dunlin on a heterogeneous mudflat. *Ornis Scandinavia* 20:250–54.

Kenworthy, W. J., and D. E. Haunert. 1991.

The Light Requirements of Seagrasses: Proceedings of a Workshop to Examine the Capability of Water Quality Criteria, Standards and Monitoring Programs to Protect Seagrasses. NOAA Technical Memorandum NMFS-SEFC-250. Beaufort, N.C. 181 pp.

Kiel, W. H., Jr. 1957. Coastal Waterfowl Survey: Ecology of Wintering Waterfowl in the Lower Laguna Madre. Texas Parks and Wildlife Federal Aid Project, W-29-R-10, Job 16. Austin. No page numbers.

Kieslich, J. M. 1977. *A Case History of Port Mansfield Channel, Texas.* U.S. Army Coastal Engineering Research Center, and U.S. Army Engineer Waterways Experimental Station Report GITI Report 12. Springfield, Va. 66 pp.

Kikuchi, T. 1980. Faunal relations in temperate seagrass beds. Pp. 153–72 in R. C. Phillips and C. P. McRoy (eds.), *Handbook of Seagrass Biology: An Ecosystem Perspective.* New York: Garland STPM Press.

Kikuchi, T., and J. M. Pérès. 1977. Consumer ecology of seagrass beds. Pp. 147–91 in C. P. McRoy and C. Helfferich (eds.), *Seagrass Ecosystems: A Scientific Perspective.* New York: Marcel Dekker.

King Ranch and Kenedy Trust. 1993. Environmental Impacts of the Plan to Dump Dredged Spoil from the Gulf Intracoastal Waterway on Lands Bordering the Laguna Madre. Kingsville, Tex.: King Ranch and John G. Kenedy Charitable Trust. 108 pp.

King, T. L., R. Ward, and E. G. Zimmerman. 1994. Population structure of eastern oysters (*Crassostrea virginica*) inhabiting the Laguna Madre, Texas, and adjacent bay systems. *Canadian Journal of Fisheries and Aquatic Science* 51:215–22.

Kitting, C. L., B. Fry, and M. D. Morgan. 1984. Detection of inconspicuous epiphytic algae supporting food webs in seagrass meadows. *Oecologia* 62:145–49.

Klima, E. F., G. R. Gitschlag, and M. L. Renaud. 1988. Impacts of the explosive removal of offshore petroleum platforms on sea turtles and dolphins. *Marine Fisheries Review* 50:33–42.

Koenig, R. L. 1969. A Comparison of the Winter Food Habits of Three Species of Waterfowl from the Upper Laguna Madre of Texas. M.S. thesis, Texas A&I University, Kingsville. 59 pp.

Kreuz, J. L. 1973. A Comparison of the Polychaete Fauna of Two Different Geographical Areas in South Texas. M.S. thesis, Texas A&I University, Texas. 63 pp.

Krull, R. M. 1976. The Small Fish Fauna of a Disturbed Hypersaline Environment. M.S. thesis, Texas A&I University, Kingsville. 112 pp.

Lacson, J. M., and W. Y. Lee. 1997. *Status and Trends of Selected Marine Fauna in the Corpus Christi Bay National Estuary Program Study Area.* Corpus Christi Bay National Estuary Program CCBNEP-24. Corpus Christi: Texas Natural Resource Conservation Commission. 283 pp.

Landry, A. M., Jr., J. A. Williams, and C. W. Caillouet, Jr. 1992. Sea Turtle Capture and Habitat Characterization Study. Unpublished report submitted to National Marine Fisheries Service, on file in Texas A&M University–Corpus Christi Center for Coastal Studies Library. 109 pp.

Lange, M. A. 1997. Austin's Woods Land Protection Compliance Document. U.S. Fish and Wildlife Service. Austin, Tex. 30 pp.

Lankford, R. R. 1977. Coastal lagoons of Mexico, their origin and classification. Pp. 182–215 in M. Wiley (ed.), *Estuarine Processes.* London, England: Academic Press.

Lassuy, D. R. 1983. *Species Profiles: Life Histories and Environmental Requirements (Gulf of Mexico): Spotted Seatrout.* U.S. Fish and Wildlife Service Biological Service Division FWS/OBS-82/11.4, U.S. Army Corps of Engineers Technical Report El-82-4. Washington, D.C. 14 pp.

Lea, T. 1957a. Captain King of Texas. *Atlantic Monthly* 199(4):40–46.

———. 1957b. *The King Ranch.* Kingsville, Tex.: Carl Hertzog Publishing. 838 pp. (2 vols.).

Leary, T. R. 1957. A schooling of leatherback turtles, *Dermochelys coriacea,* on the Texas Coast. *Copeia* 1957:232.

Leatherman, S. P., and P. J. Godfrey. 1979. *The Impact of Off-Road Vehicles on Coastal Ecosystems in Cape Cod National Seashore: An Overview.* Environmental Institute, University of Massachusetts/NPS Cooperative Research Unit UM/NPSCRU Report 34. Amherst, Mass. 34 pp.

Leber, K. M. 1985. The influence of predatory decapods, refuge, and microhabitat selection on seagrass communities. *Ecology* 66:1951–64.

LeBlanc, R. J., and W. D. Hodgson. 1959. Origin and development of the Texas

shoreline. *Transactions of the Gulf Coast Association of Geological Societies* 9:197–220.

LeBuff, C. R., Jr. 1976. Tourist turtle. *Florida Wildlife Management* July 1976:16.

Lee, M. C. 1995. Factors Influencing Shorebird Habitat Use and Interhabitat Movements on Mustang Island, Texas from September 1990 through September 1991. M.S. thesis, Texas A&M University–Corpus Christi. 49 pp.

Lehman, R. L. 1999. A checklist of benthic marine macroalgae from the Corpus Christi Bay area. *Texas Journal of Science* 51:241–52.

Lehmann, V. W. 1969. *Forgotten Legions: Sheep in the Rio Grande Plain of Texas.* El Paso: Texas Western Press. 226 pp.

Leija-Tristan, A., A. Contreras-Arquieta, M. E. García-Garza, A. J. Contreras Balderas, M. de Lourdes Lozano-Vilano, M. E. García-Ramirez, S. Contreras Balderas, D. Lazcano-Villarreal, J. A. de Leon-González, S. Martínez-Lozano, M. del Consuelo González-de la Rosa, J. O. Rosales, F. Segovia-Salinas, J. A. García-Salas, G. A. Rodriguez, G. A. Rodriguez-Almaraz, G. Guajardo-Martinez, M. A. Guzmán-Lucio, J. I. González-Rojas, A. Guzmán-Velazco, and F. Jimenez-Guzmán. In press. Taxonomic, bioecological and biogeographic aspects of selected biota of Laguna Madre, Tamaulipas, Mexico. *Ecovision.*

Leopold, A. S. 1959. *Wildlife of Mexico: The Game Birds and Mammals.* Berkeley: University of California Press. 568 pp.

Lockett, L., and R. W. Read. 1990. Extension of native range of *Sabal mexicana* (Palmae) in Texas to include central coast. *Sida* 14:79–85.

Lohse, E. A. 1958. Geochronology of mud flats through varve analysis. Pp. 1–47 in *Sedimentology of South Texas: Field Trip Guidebook* (Annual Meeting, October 27–November 1, 1958). Corpus Christi: Gulf Coast Association of Geological Societies.

Lonard, R. I. 1993a. *Guide to Grasses of the Lower Rio Grande Valley, Texas.* Edinburg: University of Texas–Pan American Press. 240 pp.

———. 1993b. Personal affidavit. Exhibit 6 in King Ranch and Kenedy Trust, Environmental Impacts of the Plan to Dump Dredged Spoil from the Gulf Intracoastal Waterway on Lands Bordering the Laguna Madre. Kingsville, Tex.: King

Ranch and John G. Kenedy Charitable Trust.

Lonard, R. I., J. H. Everitt, and F. W. Judd. 1991. *Woody plants of the Lower Rio Grande Valley, Texas.* Texas Memorial Museum Miscellaneous Publications 7. 179 pp.

Lonard, R. I., and F. W. Judd. 1980. Phytogeography of South Padre Island, Texas. *Southwestern Naturalist* 23:497–510.

———. 1985. Effects of a severe freeze on native woody plants in the lower Rio Grande Valley, Texas. *Southwestern Naturalist* 30:397–403.

———. 1991. Comparison of the effects of the severe freezes of 1983 and 1989 on native woody plants in the lower Rio Grande Valley, Texas. *Southwestern Naturalist* 36:213–17.

Lonard, R. I., F. W. Judd, and S. L. Sides. 1978. Annotated checklist of the flowering plants of South Padre Island, Texas. *Southwestern Naturalist* 23:497–510.

Long, D. T., and R. Gudramovics. 1983. Major-element geochemistry of brines from the wind tidal flat area, Laguna Madre, Texas. *Journal of Sedimentary Petrology* 53:797–810.

Longley, W. L., W. B. Brogden, and S. N. James. 1989. Texas Barrier Island Characterization Conceptual Models. U.S. Fish and Wildlife Service, National Wetland Research Center Open File Report 89-05. Lafayette, La. 418 pp.

Lopez-Barreiro, T. 1998. Detection and Distribution of the Texas Brown Tide Species *Aureoumbra lagunensis* in the Gulf of Mexico Using an Immunofluorescence Assay. M.S. thesis, University of Massachusetts, Boston. 67 pp.

Lopez-Barreiro, T., A. Villareal, and S. L. Morton. 1998. Development of an antibody against the Texas brown tide *(Aureoumbra lagunensis)*. Pp. 263–65 in B. Reguera, J. Blanco, M. L. Fernandez, and T. Wyatt (eds.), *Harmful Algae.* Viga, Spain: Xunta de Galicia and Intergovernmental Oceanographic Commission of UNESCO.

Lund, F. 1974. Marine Turtle Nesting in the United States. Report to the U.S. Fish and Wildlife Service. Washington, D.C. 39 pp.

Lutcavage, M., and J. A. Musick. 1985. Aspects of the biology of sea turtles in Virginia. *Copeia* 1985:449–56.

Mackin, J. G. 1971. A Study of the Effect of Oil Field Brine Effluents on Biotic Communities in Texas Estuaries. Texas A&M University Research Foundation Project 735. College Station. 73 pp.

Magnuson, J. J., K. A. Bjorndal, W. D. Du-Paul, G. L. Graham, D. W. Owens, P. C. H. Pritchard, J. I. Richardson, G. E. Saul, and C. W. West. 1990. *Decline of the Sea Turtles: Causes and Prevention.* Washington, D.C.: National Academic Press. 274 pp.

Marquez, M., R. A. Villanueva, and P. M. Burchfield. 1989. Nesting population and production of hatchlings of Kemp's ridley sea turtles at Rancho Nuevo, Mexico. Pp. 16–19 in K. A. Bjorndal (ed.), *Biology and Conservation of Sea Turtles.* Washington, D.C.: Smithsonian Institute Press.

Martin, F. D., and M. Cooper. 1981. A comparison of fish fauna found in pure stands of two tropical Atlantic seagrasses, *Thalassia testudinum* and *Syringodium filiforme. Northeast Gulf Science* 5:31–37.

Martin, J. J. 1979. A study of the feeding habits of the black drum (*Pogonias cromis* Linnaeus) in Alazan Bay and the Laguna Salada, Texas. M.S. thesis, Texas A&I University, Kingsville. 103 pp.

Martin, J. H., and L. W. McEachron. 1996. *Historical Annotated Review of Winter Kills of Marine Organisms in Texas Bays.* Coastal Fisheries Branch, Management Data Series no. 50. Austin: Texas Parks and Wildlife Department. 20 pp.

Martínez, M., and A. Novelo. 1993. La vegetación aquática del estado de Tamaulipas, México. *Anales del Instituto de Biología Universidad Nacional Autónoma Serie Botánica* 64(2):59–86.

Masson, P. H. 1955. An occurrence of gypsum in southwest Texas. *Journal of Sedimentary Petrology* 25:72–77.

McAdams, M. S. 1987. Classification and Waterfowl Use of Ponds in South Texas. M.S. thesis, Texas A&M University, College Station. 112 pp.

McCampbell, C. 1952. *Texas Seaport: The Story of the Growth of Corpus Christi and the Coastal Bend Area.* New York: Exposition Press. 305 pp.

McEachron, L. W., R. L. Colura, B. Bumguardner, and R. Ward. 1998. Survival of stocked red drum in Texas. *Bulletin of Marine Science* 62:359–68.

McGowen, J. H., L. F. Brown, Jr., T. R. Calnan, J. L. Chin, J. P. Herber, and C. L. Lewis. 1977. History and Processes Involved in Development of South Padre Island, Laguna Madre, and Los Bancos de en Medio. Report to Texas General Land Office. Austin: Bureau of Economic Geology, University of Texas. 141 pp.

McGowen, J. H., C. G. Groat, L. F. Brown, Jr., W. L. Fisher, and A. J. Scott. 1970. *Effects of Hurricane Celia: A Focus on Environmental Geologic Problems of the Texas Coastal Zone.* Circular 70-3. Austin: Bureau of Economic Geology, University of Texas. 35 pp.

McGowen, J. H., C. V. Proctor, L. F. Brown, Jr., T. H. Evans, W. L. Fisher, and C. G. Groat. 1976. *Environmental Geologic Atlas of the Texas Coastal Zone: Port Lavaca Area.* Austin: Bureau of Economic Geology, University of Texas.107 pp., + 9 maps.

McGowen, J. H., and A. J. Scott. 1975. Hurricanes as geologic agents on the Texas coast. Pp. 23–43 in L. E. Cronin (ed.), *Estuarine Research*, vol. 2: *Geology and Engineering.* New York: Academic Press.

McLendon, T. 1991. Preliminary description of the vegetation of South Texas exclusive of coastal saline zones. *Texas Journal of Science* 43:13–32.

McMahan, C. A. 1966. Ecology of Principal Waterfowl Foods of Laguna Madre. Texas Parks and Wildlife Department Job Completion Report, Federal Aid Project no. W-29-R-19. Austin. 23 pp.

———. 1967a. Ecology of Principal Waterfowl Foods of Laguna Madre. Texas Parks and Wildlife Department Job Completion Report, Federal Aid Project no. W-29-R-20. Austin. 6 pp.

———. 1967b. Coastal Waterfowl Survey: Ecology of Principal Wintering Waterfowl in Lower Laguna Madre. Texas Parks and Wildlife Federal Aid Project no. W-29-R-20, Job 16. Austin. No page numbers.

———. 1968. Biomass and salinity tolerance of shoalgrass and manatee-grass in the lower Laguna Madre. *Journal of Wildlife Management* 32:501–506.

———. 1970. Food habits of ducks wintering in Laguna Madre, Texas. *Journal of Wildlife Management* 34:946–49.

McMahan, C. A., R. G. Frye, and K. L. Brown. 1984. *The Vegetation Types of Texas Including Cropland. Wildlife Division.* Austin: Texas Parks and Wildlife Department. 40 pp.+ 1 map.

McMillan, C. 1975. Adaptive differentiation to chilling in mangrove populations. Pp. 62–68 in G. Walsh, S. Snedaker, and H. Teas (eds.), *Proceedings of the International Symposium on the Biology and Management of Mangroves*, vol. 1. Gainesville: University of Florida.

———. 1979. Differentiation in response to chilling temperatures among populations of three marine spermatophytes, *Thalassia testudinum, Syringodium filiforme* and *Halodule wrightii. American Journal of Botany* 66:810–19.

———. 1985. The seed reserve for *Halodule wrightii, Syringodium filiforme* and *Ruppia maritima* in Laguna Madre, Texas. *Contributions in Marine Science* 23:141–49.

McMillan, C., and F. N. Moseley. 1967. Salinity tolerances of five marine spermatophytes of Redfish Bay, Texas. *Ecology* 48:503–506.

McMurry, S. L. 1971. Nesting and Development of the Reddish Egret (*Dichromanassa rufescens* Gmelin) on a Spoil Bank Chain in the Laguna Madre. M.S. thesis, Texas A&I University, Kingsville. 78 pp.

McNeil, R., and J. Burton. 1977. Southbound migration of shorebirds from the Gulf of St. Lawrence. *Wilson Bulletin* 89:167–71.

McNulty, J. K., W. N. Lindal, Jr., and J. E. Sykes. 1972. *Cooperative Gulf of Mexico Estuarine Inventory and Study, Florida Phase I: Area Description.* NOAA Technical Report Circular 368. Washington, D.C. 126 pp.

McRoy, C. P., and C. Helfferich. 1977. Preface. Pp. iii–v in C. P. McRoy and C. Helfferich (eds.), *Seagrass Ecosystems: A Scientific Perspective.* New York: Marcel Dekker.

McRoy, C. P., and C. McMillan. 1977. Production ecology and physiology of seagrasses. Pp. 53–87 in C. P. McRoy and C. Helfferich (eds.), *Seagrass Ecosystems: A Scientific Perspective.* New York: Marcel Dekker.

Meire, P., and E. Kuyken. 1984. Relations between the distribution of waders and the intertidal benthic fauna of the Oosterschelde, Netherlands. Pp. 55–68 in P. R. Evans, J. D. Goss-Custard, and W. G. Hale (eds.), *Coastal Waders and Wildfowl in Winter.* Cambridge, England: Cambridge University Press.

Merkord, G. W. 1978. The Distribution and Abundance of Seagrasses in Laguna Madre of Texas. M.S. thesis, Texas A&I University, Kingsville. 56 pp.

Michot, T. C., T. W. Custer, A. J. Nault, and C. A. Mitchell. 1994. Environmental contaminants in Redheads wintering in coastal Louisiana and Texas. *Archives of Environmental Contamination and Toxicology* 26:425–34.

Miller, J. A. 1975. Facies characteristics of Laguna Madre wind-tidal flats. Pp. 67–73 in R. N. Ginsburg (ed.), *Tidal Deposits: A Casebook of Recent Examples and Fossil Counterparts.* New York: Springer-Verlag.

Milne, H. 1976. Some factors affecting egg production in waterfowl populations. *Wildfowl* 27:141–42.

Mills, E. L. 1975. Benthic organisms and the structure of marine communities. *Journal of the Fisheries Research Board, Canada* 32:1657–63.

Mitchell, C. A. 1992. Water depth predicts redhead distribution in the lower Laguna Madre, Texas. *Wildlife Society Bulletin* 20:420–24.

Mitchell, C. A., T. W. Custer, and P. J. Zwank. 1992. Herbivory on shoalgrass by wintering redheads in Texas. *Journal of Wildlife Management* 58:131–41.

Monday, J., and B. Colley. 1997. *Voices from the Wild Horse Desert: The Vaquero Families of the King and Kenedy Ranches.* Austin: University of Texas Press. 265 pp.

Montagna, P. A. 1992. Benthic Samples Taken from the Padre Island National Seashore. University of Texas Marine Science Institute Technical Report TR/92-002. Port Aransas. 11 pp.

———. 1993. Comparison of Ecosystem Structure and Functions of Created and Natural Seagrass Habitats in Laguna Madre, Texas. University of Texas Marine Science Institute Technical Report TR/93-007. Port Aransas. 72 pp.

Moore, J. L. 1991. Habitat-related Activities and Body Mass of Wintering Redhead Ducks on Coastal Ponds in South Texas. M.S. thesis, Texas A&M University, College Station. 97 pp.

Moore, R. H. 1976. Reproductive habits and growth of *Bufo speciosus* on Mustang Island, Texas, with notes on the ecology and reproduction of other anurans. *Texas Journal of Science* 27:173–78.

Morgan, D., and C. L. Kitting. 1984. Productivity and utilization of the seagrass *Halodule wrightii* and its attached epiphytes. *Limnology and Oceanography* 29:1066–76.

Morrison, R. I. G. 1984. Migration systems of some New World shorebirds. Pp. 125–202 in J. Burger and B. L. Olla (eds.), *Behavior of Marine Animals*, vol. 6: *Shorebirds: Migration and Foraging Behavior.* New York: Plenum Press.

Morrison, R. I. G., R. K. Ross, P. J. Guzman, and A. Estrada. 1993. Aerial surveys of Nearctic shorebirds wintering in Mexico: Preliminary results of surveys on the Gulf of Mexico and Caribbean coasts.

Canadian Wildlife Service Progress Notes 206:1–14.

Morton, R. A., and L. E. Garner. 1993. *Geological Investigation of the Wind-Tidal Flat Area, Kenedy County, Texas.* No. IAC (92-93) 2170. Austin: Bureau of Economic Geology, University of Texas. 99 pp.

Morton, R. A., and J. H. McGowen. 1980. *Modern Depositional Environments of the Texas Coast.* Guidebook 20. Austin: Bureau of Economic Geology, University of Texas. 167 pp.

Morton, R. A., and M. J. Pieper. 1975. *Shoreline Changes on Brazos Island and South Padre Island (Mansfield Channel to Mouth of the Río Grande): An Analysis of Historical Changes of the Texas Gulf Shoreline.* Report no. 75-2. Austin: Bureau of Economic Geology, University of Texas. 39 pp.

Morton, R. A., W. A. White, R. S. Kerr, and W. D. Kuenzi. 1977. Geological aspects of barrier island development: Mustang and north Padre islands, Texas. Chap. 3 in R. S. Kier and E. G. Fruh (eds.), *Environmental and Economic Impacts of Recreational Community Development, Mustang Island and North Padre Island*, vol. 2. Austin: University of Texas.

Morton, R. A., W. A. White, and R. C. Nava. 1998. Sediment Budget Analysis for Laguna Madre, Texas: An Examination of Sediment Characteristics, History, and Recent Transport. Report DACW64-96-C-0018. Austin: Bureau of Economic Geology, University of Texas. 194 pp.

Moulton, D. F., T. E. Dahl, and D. M. Dall. 1997. *Texas Coastal Wetlands: Status and Trends, mid 1950s to early 1990s.* Albuquerque, N.M.: U.S. Fish and Wildlife Service, Southeastern Region. 32 pp.

Mulhern, J. H., T. D. Nudds, and B. R. Neal. 1985. Wetland selection by mallards and blue-winged teal. *Wilson Bulletin* 97:473–85.

Murdy, E. O. 1983. Saltwater Fishes of Texas: A Dichotomous Key. Texas A&M University Sea Grant College Program TAMU-SG-83-607. College Station, Texas. 219 pp.

Murphy, T. M., and S. R. Hopkins-Murphy. 1989. *Sea Turtle and Shrimp Fishing Interactions: A Summary and Critique of Relevant Information.* Washington D.C.: Center for Marine Conservation. 52 pp.

Myers, J. P., R. I. G. Morrison, P. Z. Antas, B. A. Harrington, T. E. Lovejoy, M. Sallaberry, S. E. Senner, and A. Tarak. 1987. Conservation strategy for migratory species. *American Scientist* 75:19–26.

Myers, J. P., M. Sallaberry, A. E. Ortiz, G. Castro, L. M. Gordon, J. L. Maron, C. T. Schick, E. Tabilo, P. Antas, and T. Below. 1990. Migration routes of New World Sanderlings *(Calidris alba). Auk* 107:172–80.

Nelson, D. M. (ed.). 1992. *Distribution and Abundance of Fishes and Invertebrates in Gulf of Mexico Estuaries*, vol. 1: *Data Summaries.* ELMR Report no. 10. Silver Spring, Md.: NOAA/NOS Strategic Environmental Assessments Division. 273 pp.

Nelson, E. W., and E. A. Goldman. 1926. Mexico. Pp. 574–96 in V. E. Shelford (ed.), *Naturalist's Guide to the Americas.* Baltimore, Maryland: Williams and Wilkins Company.

Nelson, H. F., and E. E. Bray. 1970. Stratigraphy and history of the Holocene sediments in the Sabine–High Island area, Gulf of Mexico. Pp. 48–77 in J. P. Morgan and R. H. Shaver (eds.), *Deltaic Sedimentation, Modern and Ancient.* Special Publication 15. Tulsa, Okla.: Society of Economic Paleontologists and Mineralogists.

Nichols, J. L., and G. A. Baldassarre. 1990. Habitat selection and interspecific associations of Piping Plovers wintering in the U.S. *Wilson Bulletin* 102:581–90.

Nichols, M., R. J. Diaz, and L. C. Shaffner. 1990. Effects of hopper dredging and sediment dispersion, Chesapeake Bay. *Environmental Geology and Water Science* 15:31–43.

Nixon, J. 1986. *Stewards of a Vision.* Hong Kong: Everbest Printing Company. 42 pp.

NOAA (National Oceanic and Atmospheric Administration). 1989. *Final Environmental Impact Statement Listing and Protecting the Green Sea Turtle, Loggerhead Sea Turtle, and Pacific Ridley Sea Turtle under the Endangered Species Act of 1973.* Washington, D.C.: National Oceanic and Atmospheric Administration, National Marine Fisheries Service.

———. 1994. *Tidal Characteristics and Datums of Laguna Madre, Texas.* Silver Spring, Md.: Office of Ocean and Earth Sciences, Ocean and Lake Levels Division. 48 pp.

Norris, R. M. 1953. Buried oyster reefs in some Texas bays. *Journal of Paleontology* 27:569–76.

Norwine, J., R. Bingham, and R. V. Zepeda. 1977. Twentieth-century semi-arid and subhumid climates of Texas and northeastern Mexico. Pp. 30–41 in J. Norwine (ed.), *Climate and Human Ecology.* Houston: D. Armstrong Company, Publishers.

NPS (National Park Service). 1974. Padre Island National Seashore Master Plan. United States Department of the Interior, National Park Service. Washington, D.C. 39 pp.

O'Conner, R. J., and R. A. Brown. 1977. Prey depletion and foraging strategy in the oystercatcher *Haematopus ostralegus. Oecologia* 27:75–92.

Oberholser, H. C. 1974. *The Bird Life of Texas.* Austin: University of Texas Press. 530 pp.

Odum, E. D. 1971. *Fundamentals of Ecology.* Philadelphia, Pa.: W. B. Saunders Company.

Odum, H. T., and R. F. Wilson. 1962. Further studies on reaeration and metabolism of Texas bays, 1958–1960. *Publications of the Institute of Marine Science, University of Texas* 8:23–55.

Ogren, L. H. 1989. Distribution of juvenile and sub-adult Kemp's ridley turtles: Preliminary results from the 1984–1987 surveys. Pp. 116–23 in C. W. Caillouet, Jr., and A. M. Landry (eds.), *Proceedings of the First International Symposium on Kemp's Ridley Sea Turtle Biology, Conservation, and Management.* Program TAMU-SG-89-105. College Station: Texas A&M University Sea Grant College Program.

Olney, J. E., and G. W. Boehlert. 1988. Nearshore ichthyoplankton associated with seagrass beds in the lower Chesapeake Bay. *Marine Ecology Progress Series* 45:33–43.

Onuf, C. P. 1994. Seagrasses, dredging and light in Laguna Madre, Texas, USA. *Estuarine, Coastal and Shelf Science* 39:75–91.

———. 1995. Seagrass meadows of the Laguna Madre of Texas. Pp. 275–77 in E. T. LaRoe, G. S. Farris, C. E. Puckett, P. D. Doran, and M. J. Mac (eds.), *Our Living Resources: A Report to the Nation on the Distribution, Abundance, and Health of US Plants, Animals, and Ecosystems.* Washington, D.C.: U.S. Department of the Interior, National Biological Service.

———. 1996a. Biomass patterns in seagrass meadows of the Laguna Madre, Texas. *Bulletin of Marine Science* 58:404–20.

———. 1996b. Seagrass responses to long-term light reduction by brown tide in upper Laguna Madre, Texas: Distribution and biomass patterns. *Marine Ecology Progress Series* 138:219–31.

————. In press. Seagrass responses to and recovery(?) from seven years of brown tide. *Pacific Conservation Biology.*

Oppenheimer, C. H., and E. J. F. Wood. 1965. Quantitative aspects of the unicellular algal populations of the Texas bay systems. *Bulletin of Marine Science* 15:571–88.

Orlando, S. P., Jr., L. P. Rozas, G. H. Ward, and C. J. Klein. 1991. *Analysis of Salinity Structure and Stability for Texas Estuaries.* Strategic Assessment Branch, NOS/NOAA. Rockville, Md. 97 pp.

Orth, R. J., and K. A. Moore. 1983. Chesapeake Bay: An unprecedented decline in submerged aquatic vegetation. *Science* 222:51–53.

Ortiz, A. R. 1976. The Effect of Human Activity on the Insect Fauna of Padre Island. M.S. thesis, Texas A&I University, Kingsville. 71 pp.

Palmer, R. S. 1962. *Handbook of North American Birds,* vol. 1. New Haven, Conn.: Yale University Press. 567 pp.

Parker, R. H. 1959. Macro-invertebrate assemblages of central Texas coastal bays and Laguna Madre. *Bulletin of the American Association of Petroleum Geologists* 43:2100–66.

Patillo, M. E., T. E. Czapla, D. M. Nelson, and M. E. Monaco. 1997. *Distribution and Abundance of Fishes and Invertebrates in Gulf Of Mexico Estuaries,* vol. 2: *Species Life History Summaries.* ELMR Report no. 11. Silver Spring, Md.: NOAA/NOS Strategic Environmental Assessments Division. 377 pp.

Pearson, J. C. 1929. Natural history and conservation of the redfish and other commercial sciaenids on the Texas coast. *Bulletin of the U.S. Bureau of Fisheries* 54:129–214.

Pearson, T. G. 1922. Herons of the United States. *Bird Lore* 24:306–14.

Perales Flores, L. E., and A. J. Contreras Balderas. 1986. Aves acuáticas y semiacuáticas de la Laguna Madre, Tamaulipas, México. *Ciencia* (Mexico) 3(6):39–46.

Pfeiffer, W. J., and R. G. Wiegert. 1981. Grazers on *Spartina* and their predators. Pp. 87–112 in L. R. Pomeroy and R. G. Wiegert (eds.), *The Ecology of a Saltmarsh.* New York: Springer-Verlag.

Phillips, J. C. 1911. A year's collecting in the state of Tamaulipas, Mexico. *Auk* 28:67–89.

Phillips, R. C. 1960. *Observations on the Ecology and Distribution of the Florida Sea Grasses.* Professional Papers Series no. 2, Florida Board of Conservation. 72 pp.

————. 1974. Temperate grass flats. Pp. 244–99 in H. T. Odum, B. J. Copeland, and E. A. McMahan (eds.), *Coastal Ecological Systems of the United States.* Washington, D.C.: Conservation Foundation.

Phillips, R. C., and E. G. Meñez. 1988. *Seagrasses.* Smithsonian Contribution in Marine Science no. 34. Washington, D.C.: Smithsonian Institution Press. 104 pp.

PINS (Padre Island National Seashore). 1984. *Checklist of Reptiles and Amphibians: Padre Island National Seashore.* National Park Service Information Bulletin no. 12. Corpus Christi, Tex.: National Park Service. No page numbers.

Pitelka, F. A., J. P. Myers, and P. G. Connors. 1980. Spatial and resource-use patterns in wintering shorebirds: The Sanderling in central coastal California. Pp. 1021–44 in R. Nohring (ed.), *Acta XVII Congressus Internationalis Ornithologici,* vol. 2. Berlin, Germany: Verlag der Deutschen Ornithologen-Gesellschaft. (Congress in 1978).

Plotkin, P. T., M. K. Wicksten, and A. F. Amos. 1993. Feeding ecology of the loggerhead sea turtle *Caretta caretta* in the northwestern Gulf of Mexico. *Marine Biology* 115:1–15.

Poiani, K. A., and B. D. Richter. 1999. *Functional Landscapes and the Conservation of Biodiversity.* Working Papers in Conservation Science no. 1. Arlington, Va.: Nature Conservancy. 12 pp.

Ponwith, B., and Q. R. Dokken. 1996. Fisheries resources. Pp. 484–543 in J. W. Tunnell, Jr., Q. R. Dokken, E. H. Smith, and K. Withers (eds.), *Current Status and Historical Trends of the Estuarine Living Resources within the Corpus Christi Bay National Estuary Program Study Area.* Corpus Christi Bay National Estuary Program CCBNEP-06A. Corpus Christi: Texas Natural Resource Conservation Commission.

Powell, E. N., R. J. Stanton, Jr., H. Cummins, and G. Staff. 1982. Temporal fluctuations in bay environments: The death assemblage as a key to the past. Pp. 203–32 in J. R. Davis (ed.), *Proceedings of the Symposium on Recent Benthological Investigations in Texas and Adjacent States.* Austin: Texas Academy of Science.

Price, W. A. 1933. Role of diastrophism in topography of Corpus Christi area, South Texas. *American Association of Petroleum Geologists Bulletin* 17:907–62.

———. 1958. Sedimentology and quaternary geomorphology of South Texas. *Transactions of the Gulf Coast Association of Geological Societies* 8:41–75.

———. 1968. Abatement of Blowing Salt Conditions Inland from Laguna Madre, Texas. Report to Coastal Bend Regional Planning Commission. Corpus Christi. No page numbers.

Price, W. A., and G. Gunter. 1942. Certain recent and geological and biological changes in South Texas, with consideration of probable causes. *Texas Academy of Science Proceedings and Transactions* 26:138–56.

Price, W. A., and L. S. Kornicker. 1961. Marine and lagoonal deposits in clay dunes, Gulf Coast, Texas. *Journal of Sedimentary Petrology* 31:245–55.

Pritchard, P. C. H. 1969. Sea turtles of the Guianas. *Bulletin of the Florida State Museum* 13:85–140.

———. 1976. Post-nesting movements of marine turtles (Cheloniidae and Dermochelyidae) tagged in the Guianas. *Copeia* 1976:749–54.

———. 1982. Nesting of the leatherback turtle *Dermochelys coriacea*, in Pacific Mexico, with a new estimate of the world population status. *Copeia* 1982:741–47.

Prouty, J. S. 1996. Late Pleistocene–early Holocene karst features, Laguna Madre, South Texas: A record of climate change. *Transactions of the Gulf Coast Association of Geological Societies* 46:345–51.

Prouty, J. S., and D. W. Lovejoy. 1992. Remarkable cylindrical solution pipes in coquina south of Baffin Bay, Texas. *Transactions of the Gulf Coast Association Geological Societies* 42:599–606.

Prouty, J. S., and D. B. Prouty. 1989. Historical back barrier shoreline changes, Padre Island National Seashore, Texas. *Transactions of the Gulf Coast Association of Geological Societies* 39:481–90.

Pulich, W., Jr. 1980. Ecology of a hypersaline lagoon: The Laguna Madre. Pp. 103–22 in P. L. Fore and R. D. Peterson (eds.), *Proceedings of the Gulf of Mexico Coastal Ecosystem Workshop.* FWS/OBS 80/30. Albuquerque, N.M.: U.S. Fish and Wildlife Service.

———. 1985. Seasonal growth dynamics of *Ruppia maritima* L. *sensu lato* and *Halodule wrightii* Aschers. in southern Texas and evaluation of sediment fertility status. *Aquatic Botany* 23:53–66.

———. 1998. *Seagrass Conservation Plan for Texas.* Austin: Texas Parks and Wildlife Department. 79 pp.

Pulich, W., Jr., C. Blair, and W. A. White. 1997. *Current Status and Historical Trends of Seagrasses in the Corpus Christi Bay National Estuary Program Study Area.* Corpus Christi Bay National Estuary Program CCBNEP-20. Corpus Christi: Texas National Resource Conservation Commission. 131 pp.

Pulich, W., Jr., and J. Hinson. 1996. *Development of Geographic Information System Data Sets on Coastal Wetlands and Land Cover.* Coastal Studies Technical Report no. 1. Austin: Texas Parks and Wildlife Department, Resource Protection Division. 67 pp.

Pulich, W., Jr., and S. Rabalais. 1982. Primary Production and Nutrient Fluxes on South Texas Tidal Flats. Report to U.S. Fish and Wildlife Service, Office of Environment, Region 2. Albuquerque, N.M. 30 pp.

———. 1986. Primary production potential of blue-green algal mats on southern Texas tidal flats. *Southwestern Naturalist* 31:39–47.

Pulich, W., Jr., S. Rabalais, and S. Wellso. 1982. Food Chain Components on Laguna Madre Tidal Flats. Contribution no. 572. Port Aransas, Tex.: University of Texas Marine Science Institute. 20 pp.

Pulich, W., Jr., and R. S. Scalan. 1987. Organic carbon and nitrogen flow from marine cyanobacteria to semiaquatic insect food webs. *Contributions in Marine Science* 30:27–37.

Pullen, E. J. 1960. A Study of the Marsh and Marine Plants in Upper Galveston and Trinity Bays. Progress Report 1960–61. Austin: Texas Game and Fish Commission, Division of Marine Fisheries.

Quammen, M. L. 1984. Predation by shorebirds, fish and crabs on invertebrates in intertidal mudflats: An experimental test. *Ecology* 65:529–37.

Quammen, M. L., and C. P. Onuf. 1993. Laguna Madre seagrass changes continue decades after salinity reduction. *Estuaries* 16:302–10.

Rabalais, N. N. 1977. Gulf Beach National Environmental Study Area. Report on file at Padre Island National Seashore. Corpus Christi, Tex. 38 pp.

———. 1982. The ascidians of the Aransas Pass inlet jetties, Port Aransas, Texas. Pp. 65–74 in B. R. Chapman and J. W. Tunnell (eds.), *South Texas Fauna: A Symposium Honoring Dr. Allan H. Chaney.* Kingsville: Caesar Kleberg Wildlife Research Institute.

———. 1983. Adaptations of Fiddler Crabs, *Uca subcylindrica* (Stimpson, 1859), to Semi-arid Environments. Ph.D. diss., University of Texas, Austin. 335 pp.

Rabalais, N. N., and J. N. Cameron. 1985a. Physiological and morphological adaptations of adult *Uca subcylindrica* to semi-arid environments. *Biological Bulletin* 168:135–46.

———. 1985b. The effects of factors important in semi-arid environments on the early development of *Uca subcylindrica. Biological Bulletin* 168:147–60.

Rabalais, S. C., and R. W. Flint. 1983. *Ixtoc I* effects on intertidal and subtidal infauna of South Texas Gulf beaches. *Contributions in Marine Science* 26:23–35.

Rabalais, S. C., and N. N. Rabalais. 1980. The occurrence of sea turtles on the South Texas coast. *Contributions in Marine Science* 23:123–29.

Ramos, M. G. (ed.). 1995. *Texas Almanac 1996–1997.* Dallas: Dallas Morning News. 672 pp.

Rappole, J. H. 1993. Personal affidavit. Exhibit 7 in King Ranch and Kenedy Trust, Environmental Impacts of the Plan to Dump Dredged Spoil from the Gulf Intracoastal Waterway on Lands Bordering the Laguna Madre. Kingsville, Tex.: King Ranch and John G. Kenedy Charitable Trust.

———. 1995. *The Ecology of Migrant Birds: A Neotropical Perspective.* Washington, D.C.: Smithsonian Institution Press. 269 pp.

Rappole, J. H., and G. W. Blacklock. 1985. *Birds of the Texas Coastal Bend: Abundance and Distribution.* W. L. Moody Natural History Series no. 7. College Station: Texas A&M University Press. 126 pp.

———. 1994. *Birds of Texas.* College Station: Texas A&M University Press. 280 pp.

Rappole, J. H., M. A. Ramos, R. J. Oehlenschlager, D. W. Warner, and C. H. Barkan. 1979. Timing of migration and route selection in North American songbirds. Pp. 199–214 in D. L. Drawe (ed.), *Proceedings of the First Welder Wildlife Foundation Symposium.* Sinton, Tex.: Welder Wildlife Foundation.

Reagan, R. E. 1985. *Species Profiles: Life Histories and Environmental Requirements of Coastal Fishes and Invertebrates (Gulf of Mexico)—Red Drum.* U.S. Fish and Wildlife Service Biological Report 82/11.36, U.S. Army Corps of Engineers

Technical Report El-82-4. Washington, D.C. 16 pp.

Rebel, T. P. 1974. *Sea Turtles and the Turtle Industry of the West Indies, Florida and the Gulf of Mexico.* Coral Gables, Fla.: University of Miami Press. 250 pp.

Recher, H. F. 1966. Some aspects of the ecology of migrant shorebirds. *Ecology* 47:393–407.

Reese, P. 1938. The History of Padre Island. M.A. thesis, Texas College of Arts and Industries, Kingsville. 124 pp.

Reid, G. K., and R. D. Wood. 1976. *Ecology of Inland Waters and Estuaries.* 2nd ed. New York: D. Van Norstrand Company. 485 pp.

Reinecke, K. J. 1981. Wintering waterfowl research needs and efforts in the Mississippi Delta. *International Waterfowl Symposium Transactions* 4:231–36.

Renaud, M. L. 1995. Movements and submergence patterns of Kemp's ridley turtles *(Lepidochelys kempii). Journal of Herpetology* 29:370–74.

Renaud, M. L., J. A. Carpenter, S. A. Manzella, and J. A. Williams. 1993. Telemetric Tracking of Green Sea Turtles *(Chelonia mydas)* in Relation to Dredged Channels at South Padre Island, Texas, July through September 1992. Report submitted to U.S. Army Corps of Engineers, Galveston and New Orleans Districts. Galveston, Tex. 55 pp.

Renaud, M. L., J. A. Carpenter, and J. A. Williams. 1995. Activities of juvenile green turtles, *Chelonia mydas,* at a jettied pass in South Texas. *Fishery Bulletin* 93:586–93.

Renaud, M. L., J. A. Carpenter, J. A. Williams, and A. M. Landry, Jr. 1996. Kemp's ridley sea turtle *(Lepidochelys kempii)* tracked by satellite telemetry from Louisiana to nesting beach at Rancho Nuevo, Tamaulipas, Mexico. *Chelonian Conservation and Biology* 2:108–109.

Renaud, M., G. Gitschlag, E. Klima, S. Manzella, and J. Williams. 1992. Tracking of Green *(Chelonia mydas)* and Loggerhead *(Caretta caretta)* Sea Turtles Using Radio and Sonic Telemetry at South Padre Island, Texas. Report to Southeast Fisheries Science Center, National Marine Fisheries Service. Galveston. 47 pp.

Renaud, M. L., J. M. Nance, E. Scott-Denton, and G. R. Gitschlag. 1997. Incidental capture of sea turtles in shrimp trawls with and without TEDs in U.S. Atlantic and Gulf waters. *Chelonian Conservation and Biology* 2:425–27.

Rhoads, D.C. 1974. Organism-sediment relations in the muddy seafloor. *Oceanography and Marine Biology Annual Review* 12:263–300.

Richardson, A. 1995. *Plants of the Rio Grande Delta.* Austin: University of Texas Press. 332 pp.

Ricklis, R. A. 1995. Environmental and Human Adaptive Change on the Nueces Bay Shoreline: Phase I Archaeological Data Recovery at Koch Refining Company Middle Plant, Nueces County, Texas. Coastal Archaeological Research Inc. Report to Koch Refining Company. Corpus Christi. 190 pages.

———. 1996. *The Karankawa Indians of Texas: An Ecological Study of Cultural Tradition and Change.* Austin: University of Texas Press. 222 pp.

Ricklis, R. A., and M. D. Blum. 1997. The geoarchaelogical record of Holocene sea level change and human occupation of the Texas Gulf Coast. *Geoarchaeology* 12:287–314.

Rickner, J. A. 1979. The Influence of Dredged Material Islands in Upper Laguna Madre, Texas on Selected Seagrasses and Macro-benthos. Ph.D. diss., Texas A&M University, College Station. 57 pp.

Robertson, B. 1985. *Wild Horse Desert: The Heritage of South Texas.* Edinburg: New Santander Press. 309 pp.

Rocha, D. D., R. L. Lehman, S. A. Alvarado, J. W. Tunnell, Jr., and P. A. Montagna. 1995. A Comparison of the Benthic Community North and South of the John F. Kennedy Causeway, Upper Laguna Madre, Texas. Texas A&M University–Corpus Christi, Center for Coastal Studies Technical Report TAMU-CC-9504-CCS. Corpus Christi. 33 pp.

Rostal, D.C., J. S. Grumbles, R. A. Byles, R. Marquez-M., and D. W. Owens. 1997. Nesting physiology of Kemp's ridley sea turtles, *Lepidochelys kempii*, at Rancho Nuevo, Tamaulipas, Mexico, with observations on population estimates. *Chelonian Conservation and Biology* 2:538–47.

Rowe, G. T., C. H. Clifford, K. L. Smith, and P. L. Hamilton. 1975. Benthic nutrient regeneration and its coupling to primary productivity in coastal waters. *Nature* 255:215–17.

Rowe, G. T., and K. L. Smith. 1977. Benthic-pelagic coupling in the mid-Atlantic Bight. Pp. 55–66 in B. C. Coull (ed.), *Ecology of Marine Benthos.* Columbia, S.C.: University of South Carolina Press.

Rowe, J. 1953. History of the King Ranch.

Pp. 15–24 in *King Ranch: 100 Years of Ranching.* Corpus Christi, Tex.: Corpus Christi Caller-Times. 143 pp.

Rupert, J. R. 1997. The Brood-Rearing Habitat, Brood Home Range, and Fecundity of the Snowy Plover *(Charadrius alexandrinus)* in Coastal Southern Texas. M.S. thesis, University of Texas–Pan American, Edinburg. 39 pp.

Rusnak, G. A. 1958. Laguna Madre. Pp. 71–72 in *Sedimentology of South Texas: Field Trip Guidebook* (Annual Meeting, October 27– November 1, 1958). Corpus Christi: Gulf Coast Association of Geological Societies.

Rusnak, G. A. 1960. Sediments of the Laguna Madre. Pp. 153–96 in F. P. Shepard, F. B. Phelger, and T. J. van Andel (eds.), *Recent Sediments, Northwestern Gulf of Mexico.* Tulsa, Okla.: American Association of Petroleum Geologists.

Rzedowski, J. 1978. *Vegetación de México.* Mexico, D.F.: Limusa. 432 pp.

Salinas, M. 1990. *Indians of the Rio Grande Delta: Their Role in the History of Southern Texas and Northeastern Mexico.* Austin: University of Texas Press. 193 pp.

Sanchez, L. 1968. Variables superficiales fisico-químicas con prospección acuacultura en la Laguna Madre de Tamaulipas. Centro de Acuacultura (in-house report). Valle Hermosa, Tamaulipas. 31 pp.

Saunders, G. B. 1953. The tule goose *(Anser albifrons gambelli)*, blue goose *(Chen caerulescens)* and mottled duck *(Anas fulvigula maculosa)* added to the list of the birds of Mexico. *Auk* 70:84–85.

Saunders, G. B., and D.C. Saunders. 1981. *Waterfowl and their Wintering Grounds in Mexico, 1937–64.* Resource Publication 138. Washington, D.C.: U.S. Fish and Wildlife Service. 151 pp.

Schmidly, D. J. 1981. *Marine Mammals of the Southeastern United States Coast and the Gulf of Mexico.* U.S. Fish and Wildlife Service, Office of Biological Service FWS/OBS-80/41. Washington, D.C. 163 pp.

Schmidly, D. J., and S. H. Shane. 1978. A Biological Assessment of the Cetacean Fauna of the Texas Coast. Texas A&M University and Texas Agricultural Extension Service Report no. MMC074/05. College Station. 38 pp.

Schneider, D. 1973. Equalization of prey numbers by migratory shorebirds. *Nature* 271:353–54.

Schneider, D.C., and B. A. Harrington. 1981. Timing of shorebird migration in relation to prey depletion. *Auk* 98:801–11.

Scott, A. J., R. A. Hoover, and J. H. Mc-Gowen. 1969. Effects of hurricane "Beulah," 1967 on Texas coastal lagoons and barriers. Pp. 221–36 in A. Ayala Castañares and F. B. Phleger (eds.), *Coastal Lagoons: A Symposium*. Mexico, D.F.: Universidad Nacional Autónoma de México.

Scott, F. J. 1966. *Historical Heritage of the Lower Rio Grande*. Waco: Texian Press. 292 pp.

Segers, J. C., and B. R. Chapman. 1984. Ecology of the spotted ground squirrel, *Spermophilus spilosoma* (Merriam), on Padre Island, Texas. *Special Publications of the Museum at Texas Tech University* 22:105–12.

Selander, R. K., R. F. Johnston, B. J. Wilks, and Gerald G. Raun. 1962. Vertebrates from the barrier island of Tamaulipas, Mexico. *University of Kansas Museum of Natural History Publications* 12:309–45.

Senner, S. E., and M. A. Howe. 1984. Conservation of nearctic shorebirds. Pp. 370–415 in J. Burger and B. L. Olla (eds.), *Shorebirds: Breeding Behaviour and Population*. New York: Plenum Press.

Serie, J. R., and G. A. Swanson. 1976. Feeding ecology of breeding gadwalls on saline wetlands. *Journal of Wildlife Management* 40:69–81.

Shane, S. H., and D. J. Schmidly. 1978. *The Population Biology of the Atlantic Bottlenose Dolphin*, Tursiops truncatus, *in the Aransas Pass Area of Texas*. U.S. Marine Mammal Committee National Technical Information Service PB-283-393. Washington, D.C. 130 pp.

Sharma, V. K., K. Rhudy, R. Brooks, S. Hollyfield, and F. G. Vazquez. 1997. Petroleum hydrocarbons in sediments of upper Laguna Madre. *Marine Pollution Bulletin* 34:229–34.

Shaver, D. J. 1988. Sea turtles nesting on Texas beaches in 1987. *Marine Turtle Newsletter* 42:7–9.

———. 1990a. Sea turtles in South Texas inshore waters. Pp. 131–32 in T. H. Richardson, J. I. Richardson, and M. Donnelly (eds.), *Proceedings of the Tenth Annual Workshop on Sea Turtle Biology and Conservation*. NOAA Technical Memorandum NMFS-SEFC-278. Miami, Florida.

———. 1990b. Hypothermic stunning of sea turtles in Texas. *Marine Turtle Newsletter* 48:25–27.

———. 1990c. Sea Turtles in South Texas Inshore Waters. Padre Island National Seashore Report to U.S. Fish and Wildlife Service Contract no. 14-16-0002-89-919. Albuquerque, N.M.

———. 1990d. Kemp's ridley project at Padre Island enters a new phase. *Park Science* 10:12–15.

———. 1991. Feeding ecology of wild and head-started Kemp's ridley sea turtles in South Texas waters. *Journal of Herpetology* 25:327–34.

———. 1992. Kemp's ridley research continues at Padre Island National Seashore. *Park Science* 12:26–27.

———. 1994. Relative abundance, temporal patterns, and growth of sea turtles at the Mansfield Channel, Texas. *Journal of Herpetology* 28:491–97.

———. 1998. Padre Island National Seashore Kemp's Ridley Sea Turtle Project and Texas Sea Turtle Strandings 1997 Report. Report to National Park Service. Washington, D.C. 44 pp.

———. 1999. Padre Island National Seashore Kemp's Ridley Sea Turtle Project and Texas Sea Turtle Strandings 1998 Report. Report to National Park Service. Washington, D.C. 58 pp.

Sheire, J. W. 1971. *Padre Island National Seashore, Historic Resource Study*. Office of Archeology and Historic Preservation, United States Department of Commerce, National Technical Information Service PB-206-132. Washington, D.C. 93 pp.

Shelford, V. E. 1974. *The Ecology of North America*. Urbana: University of Illinois Press. 610 pp.

Shepard, F. P., and G. A. Rusnak. 1957. Texas bay sediments. *Publications of the Institute of Marine Science, University of Texas* 4(2):5–13.

Sherrod, C. L., and C. McMillan. 1981. Black mangrove, *Avicennia germinans*, in Texas: Past and present distribution. *Contributions in Marine Science* 24: 115–31.

Simersky, B. L. 1971. Competition and Nesting Success of Four Species of Herons on Four Spoil Islands in the Laguna Madre. M.S. thesis, Texas A&I University, Kingsville. 92 pp.

Simmons, E. G. 1957. An ecological survey of the upper Laguna Madre of Texas. *Publications of the Institute of Marine Science, University of Texas* 4(2):156–200.

Simmons, E. G., and J. P. Breuer. 1962. A study of redfish, *Sciaenops ocellatus* (Linnaeus) and black drum, *Pogonias cromis* (Linnaeus). *Publications of the Marine Science Institute, University of Texas* 8:184–211.

Simpson, B. B. 1998. A revision of *Pomaria* (Fabaceae) in North America. *Lundellia* 1:46–71.

Simpson, R. H., and M. B. Lawrence. 1971. *Atlantic Hurricane Frequencies along the U.S. Coastline.* NOAA Technical Memorandum NWS SR-58. Washington, D.C. 14 pp.

Sissom, S. L. 1990. A Baseline Study of Three Ponds within the Padre Island National Park. Southwest Texas State University, Department of Biology, Report to U.S. Department of the Interior, Padre Island National Seashore. Corpus Christi. 70 pp.

Smayda, T. J., and T. A. Villareal. 1989. The 1985 "brown tide" and the open phytoplankton niche in Narragansett Bay during summer. Pp. 159–87 in E. M. Cosper, V. M. Bricelij and E. J. Carpenter (eds.), *Novel Phytoplankton Blooms: Causes and Impacts of Recurrent Brown Tides and Other Unusual Blooms.* Coastal and Estuarine Studies 35. Berlin, Germany: Springer-Verlag.

Smeins, F. E., D. D. Diamond, and W. Hanselka. 1991. Coastal prairie. Pp. 269–90 in R. T. Coupland (ed.), *Ecosystems of the World: Natural Grasslands.* Amsterdam, Netherlands: Elsevier Press.

Smith, D. S. 1986. *The Armstrong Chronicle: A Ranching History.* San Antonio, Tex.: Corona Publishing Company. 358 pp.

Smith, E. H. 1986. Morphological and Karyotypic Variation of the Gulf Coast Kangaroo Rat, *Dipodomys compactus* (Rodentia: Heteromyidae). M.S. thesis, Corpus Christi State University, Corpus Christi. 46 pp.

Smith, E. H., and S. A. Cox. 1998. Status and Trends of Rookery Islands in the Corpus Christi Bay National Estuary Program Study Area. Report to Corpus Christi Bay National Estuary Program, Texas Natural Resource Conservation Commission. Austin, Tex. 100 pp.

Smith, H. M. 1939. *The Mexican and Central American Lizards of the Genus* Sceloporus. Zoological Series, vol. 26, publication 445. Chicago, Ill.: Field Museum of Natural History. 397 pp.

Smith, N. P. 1978. Intracoastal tides of upper Laguna Madre, Texas. *Texas Journal of Science* 30:85–95.

Smith, R. 1996. Temporal Variation in Intertidal Macroinvertebrate Assemblages Associated with the Invasive Mussel, *Perna perna* (Linnaeus, 1758), on a South Texas Jetty. M.S. thesis, Texas A&M University–Corpus Christi. 47 pp.

Smylie, V. 1964a. *Conquistadores and Cannibals.* Corpus Christi: Texas News Syndicate Press. 28 pp.

———. 1964b. *The Secrets of Padre Island.* Corpus Christi: Texas News Syndicate Press. 32 pp.

Soots, R. F., and M. C. Landin. 1978. *Development and Management of Avian Habitat on Dredged Material Islands.* Waterways Experiment Station Technical Report DS-78-18. Vicksburg, Miss.: U.S. Army Corps of Engineers. 96 pp. + appendices.

Soots, R. F., and J. F. Parnell. 1975. *Ecological Succession of Breeding Birds in Relation to Plant Succession on Dredge Islands in North Carolina Estuaries.* North Carolina Sea Grant Program Publication UNC-SC-75-27. Raleigh, N.C. 91 pp.

Sorenson, L. O., and J. T. Conover. 1962. Algal mat communities of *Lyngbya confervoides* (C. Agardh.) Gioment. *Publications of the Institute of Marine Science, University of Texas* 8:61–74.

Sprunt, A., Jr. 1925. An avian city of the South Carolina coast. *Auk* 42:311–19.

Sprunt, A., and C. E. Knoder. 1980. Populations of wading birds and other colonial nesting species on the Gulf and Caribbean coasts of Mexico. Pp. 3–16 in P. P. Schaeffer and S. M. Ehlers (eds.), *Proceedings of the National Audubon Society's Symposium on the Birds of Mexico, Their Ecology and Conservation.* Tiburon, Calif.: National Audubon Society Western Education Center.

Sternberg, J. 1981. *The Worldwide Distribution of Sea Turtle Nesting Beaches.* Washington, D.C.: Sea Turtle Rescue Fund, Center for Environmental Education. 7 pp.

Stokes, G. M. 1974. *The Distribution and Abundance of Penaeid Shrimp in the Lower Laguna Madre of Texas, with a Description of the Live Bait Shrimp Fishery.* Technical Series no. 15. Austin: Texas Parks and Wildlife Department. 32 pp.

Street, G. T., P. A. Montagna, and P. L. Parker. 1997. Incorporation of brown tide into an estuarine food web. *Marine Ecology Progress Series* 152:67–78.

Swanson, G. A., M. I. Meyer, and J. R. Serie. 1974. Feeding ecology of breeding blue-winged teals. *Journal of Wildlife Management* 38:396–401.

Talent, L. G., G. L. Krapu, and R. L. Jarvis. 1982. Habitat use by mallard broods in south central North Dakota. *Journal of Wildlife Management* 46:629–35.

Tamayo, J. 1949. *Geografía General de Méx-*

ico, vol. 2. Mexico, D.F.: Talleres Gráficos de la Nacion. 583 pp.

TCWC (Texas Colonial Waterbird Census). 1998. Texas Colonial Waterbird Census: 1972–1996, Database Summary, March 1998. Unpublished manuscript on file at Texas A&M University–Corpus Christi Center for Coastal Studies Library. No page numbers.

TCWS (Texas Colonial Waterbird Society). 1982. *An Atlas and Census of Texas Waterbird Colonies 1972–1980.* Kingsville: Caesar Kleberg Wildlife Research Institute. 358 pp.

TDA (Texas Department of Agriculture). 1983. *Texas Family Land Heritage: 1975 Registry*, vol. 2. Austin: Texas Department of Agriculture. 146 pp.

———. 1985. *Texas Family Land Heritage: 1983 Registry*, vol. 9. Austin: Texas Department of Agriculture. 157 pp.

TDWR (Texas Department of Water Resources). 1983. Laguna Madre Estuary: A Study of the Influence of Freshwater Inflows. Texas Department of Water Resources Report LP-182. Austin, Texas. 270 pp.

TERG (Turtle Expert Research Group). 1998. *An Assessment of the Kemp's Ridley (Lepidochelys kempii) and Loggerhead (Caretta caretta) Sea Turtle Populations in the Western North Atlantic.* NOAA Technical Memorandum NMFS-SEFSC-409. Washington, D.C. 96 pp.

Tewes, M. E. 1993. Personal affidavit. Exhibit 9 in King Ranch and Kenedy Trust, Environmental Impacts of the Plan to Dump Dredged Spoil from the Gulf Intracoastal Waterway on Lands Bordering the Laguna Madre. Kingsville, Tex.: King Ranch and John G. Kenedy Charitable Trust.

TGLO (Texas General Land Office). 1988. *Guide to Spanish and Mexican Land Grants in South Texas.* Austin: Texas General Land Office. 260 pp.

———. 1997. *Oil Spill Planning and Response Atlas: Lower Coast of Texas.* Austin: Texas General Land Office. 4 pp. + 101 maps.

Thayer, G. W., S. M. Adams, and M. W. LaCroix. 1975. Structural and functional aspects of a recently established *Zostera marina* community. Pp. 517–40 in L. E. Cronin (ed.), *Estuarine Research*, vol. 1. New York: Academic Press.

Thomas, G. W. 1975. Texas plants–an ecological summary. Pp. 7–14 in F. W. Gould (ed.), *Texas Plants: A Checklist and Ecological Summary.* Texas Agricultural Experiement Station MP-585. College Station: Texas A&M University.

Thomas, W. D. 1972. The mammals of Padre Island. Pp. 59–61 in Corpus Christi Geological Society (ed.), *Padre Island National Seashore Field Guide.* Corpus Christi, Tex.: Golden Banner Press.

Thompson, J. 1997. *A Wild and Vivid Land: An Illustrated History of the South Texas Border.* Austin: Texas State Historical Association. 206 pp.

Thornthwaite, C. W. 1948. An approach toward a rational classification of climate. *Geographic Review* 38:55–94.

Thurman, C. L., III. 1984. Ecological notes on fiddler crabs of South Texas, with special reference to *Uca subcylindrica. Journal of Crustacean Biology* 4:665–81.

Tinnin, R. K. 1974. A Trammel Net Survey of a Disturbed Hypersaline Environment. M.S. thesis, Texas A&I University, Kingsville. 75 pp.

TNC (The Nature Conservancy). 1996. *Conservation by Design.* Arlington, Va.: Nature Conservancy. 16 pp.

Tolan, J. M. 1994. Habitat Selection by Larval Fishes Immigrating into Estuarine Nursery Grounds. M.S. thesis, Texas A&M University–Corpus Christi. 123 pages.

Tolan, J. M., S. A. Holt, and C. P. Onuf. 1997. Distribution and community structure of ichthyoplankton in Laguna Madre seagrass meadows: Potential impact of seagrass species change. *Estuaries* 20:450–64.

Toland, J. 1996. Assault: A look back at Texas' greatest racehorse. *Corpus Christi Caller-Times* 114(122):18–19.

Tomasko, D. A., and K. H. Dunton. 1995. Primary productivity in *Halodule wrightii:* A comparison of techniques based on daily carbon budgets. *Estuaries* 18:271–78.

Tomkins, I. R. 1933. Ways of the black skimmer. *Wilson Bulletin* 45:147–51.

TPWD (Texas Parks and Wildlife Department). 1982. The Future of Waterfowl in Texas: An Issue of Habitat. Federal Aid Project W-106-R. Austin: Texas Parks and Wildlife Department, Wildlife Division. No page numbers.

———. 1998a. Special Species List, Kenedy County, rev. 3-27-98. Austin: Texas Parks and Wildlife Department, Endangered Resources Branch. 2 pp.

———. 1998b. Special Species List, Willacy County, rev. 3-31-98. Austin: Texas Parks and Wildlife Department, Endangered Resources Branch. 2 pp.

———. 1999a. Annotated County Lists of Rare Species, Cameron County, rev. 8-26-99. Austin: Texas Parks and Wildlife Department, Endangered Resources Branch. 5 pp.

———. 1999b. Annotated County Lists of Rare Species, Kleberg County, rev. 8-26-99. Austin: Texas Parks and Wildlife Department, Endangered Resources Branch. 4 pp.

———. 1999c. Annotated County Lists of Rare Species, Nueces County, rev. 8-26-99. Austin: Texas Parks and Wildlife Department, Endangered Resources Branch. 4 pp.

Trewartha, G. T. 1961. *The Earth's Problem Climates.* Oshkosh, Wis.: University of Wisconsin Press. 280 pp.

———. 1968. *An Introduction to Climate.* New York: McGraw Hill. 408 pp.

Tunnell, J. W., Jr., and S. A. Alvarado (eds.). 1996. *Checklist of Species within Corpus Christi Bay National Estuary Program Study Area: References, Habitats, Distribution, and Abundance.* Corpus Christi National Estuary Program CCBNEP-06D. Corpus Christi: Texas Natural Resource Conservation Commission. 298 pp.

Tunnell, J. W., Jr., Q. R. Dokken, M. E. Kindinger, and L. C. Thebeau. 1981. Effects of the *Ixtoc I* oil spill on the intertidal and subtidal infaunal populations along lower Texas coast barrier island beaches. Pp. 467–75 in *Proceedings of the1981 Oil Spill Conference.* Washington, D.C.: American Petroleum Institution.

Tunnell, J. W., Jr., Q. R. Dokken, E. H. Smith, and K. Withers (eds.). 1996. *Current Status and Historical Trends of the Estuarine Living Resources within the Corpus Christi Bay National Estuary Program Study Area.* Corpus Christi National Estuary Program CCBNEP-06A, B, C, D (4 volumes). Corpus Christi: Texas Natural Resource Conservation Commission. 1436 pp.

Turner, B. L. 1995. Synoptical study of *Rhododon* (Lamiaceae). *Phytologia* 78:448–51.

USFWS (U.S. Fish and Wildlife Service). 1987. Analyses of Selected Winter Waterfowl Survey Data (1955–1987): Central Flyway Portion. Albuquerque, N.M.: U.S. Fish and Wildlife Service, Region 2.

———. 1991. *The Five Sea Turtle Species of the Atlantic and Gulf Coast of the United States and Their Status under the Endangered Species Act (ESA).* Pamphlet. Washington, D.C.: U.S. Fish and Wildlife Service. No page numbers.

USFWS and NMFS (National Marine Fisheries Service). 1991. *Recovery Plan for U.S. Population of Loggerhead Turtle.* Bethesda, Md.: U.S. Fish and Wildlife Service and National Marine Fisheries Service. 64 pp.

———. 1992. *Recovery Plan for the Kemp's Ridley Sea Turtle* (Lepidochelys kempii). St. Petersburg, Fla.: U.S. Fish and Wildlife Service and National Marine Fisheries Service. 40 pp.

van Montfrans, J., R. L. Wetzel, and R. J. Orth. 1984. Epiphyte-grazer relationships in seagrass meadows: Consequences for seagrass growth and production. *Estuaries* 7:289–309.

Villarreal, J. M. 2000. Proyecto de Ordenamiento Ecológico de la Laguna Madre–Tamaulipas: Ordenamiento del Clima Regional. Technical Report, Centro de Calidad Ambiental. Monterrey, Nuevo León: ITESM Campus Monterrey–Pronatura Noreste.

Villareal, T. A., A. Mansfield, and E. J. Buskey. 1998. Growth and chemical composition of the Texas brown tide-forming pelagophyte *Aureoumbra lagunensis.* Pp. 359–62 in B. Reguera, J. Blanco, M. L. Fernandez, and T. Wyatt (eds.), *Harmful Algae.* Viga, Spain: Xunta de Galicia and Intergovernmental Oceanographic Commission of UNESCO.

Ward, G. H., and N. E. Armstrong. 1997. *Current Status and Historical Trends of Ambient Water, Sediment, Fish and Shellfish Tissue Quality in the Corpus Christi Bay National Estuary Program Study Area.* Corpus Christi Bay National Estuary Program CCBNEP 13. Corpus Christi: Texas Natural Resource Conservation Commission. 270 pp.

Ward, R., E. G. Zimmerman, and T. L. King. 1990. Multivariate analyses of terrestrial reptilian distribution in Texas: An alternative view. *Southwestern Naturalist* 35:441–45.

Warshaw, S. 1975. Water Quality Segment Report for Segment No. 2491 Laguna Madre. Texas Water Quality Board Report WQS-14. Austin. 37 pp.

Watson, R. L. 1971. Origin of shell beaches, Padre Island, Texas. *Journal of Sedimentary Petrology* 41:1105–11.

———. 1989. Sedimentation Rates, Kenedy Ranch Supratidal Flats. Unpublished manuscript on file at Texas A&M University–Corpus Christi, Center for Coastal Studies Library. 20 pp.

Weddle, R. S. 1985. *Spanish Sea: The Gulf of Mexico in North American Discovery*. College Station: Texas A&M University Press. 435 pp.

Weise, B. R., and W. A. White. 1980. *Padre Island National Seashore: A Guide to the Geology, Natural Environments, and History of a Texas Barrier Island*. Guidebook 17. Austin: Bureau of Economic Geology, University of Texas. 94 pp. + map.

Weller, M. W. 1964. Distribution and migration of the redhead. *Journal of Wildlife Management* 28:64–103.

Wells, F. C., G. A. Jackson, and W. J. Rogers. 1988. Reconnaissance Investigation of Water Quality, Bottom Sediment, and Biota Associated with Irrigation Drainage in the Lower Rio Grande Valley and Laguna Atascosa National Wildlife Refuge, Texas 1986–87. U.S. Geological Service Water-Resources Investigation no. 87-4277. Austin. 89 pp.

Wern, J. O. 1995. Nemerteans of the northwestern Gulf of Mexico. Ph.D. diss., Texas A&M University, College Station. 408 pp.

Whelan, T. 1975. Low-altitude aerosol distribution along a barrier island coast. *Contributions in Marine Science* 19:3–12.

White, D. H., and D. James. 1978. Differential use of freshwater environments by wintering waterfowl of coastal Texas. *Wilson Bulletin* 90:99–111.

White, D. H., C. A. Mitchell, and T. E. Kaiser. 1983b. Temporal accumulations of organochlorine pesticides in shorebirds wintering on the South Texas coast. *Texas Archives of Environmental Contamination and Toxicology* 12:241–50.

White, D. H., C. A. Mitchell, H. D. Kennedy, A. J. Krynitsky, and M. A. Ribick. 1983a. Elevated DDE and toxaphene residues in fishes and birds reflect local contamination in the lower Rio Grande Valley, Texas. *Southwestern Naturalist* 28:325–33.

White, D. H., C. A. Mitchell, and D. M. Swineford. 1984. Reproductive success of black skimmers in Texas relative to environmental pollutants. *Journal of Field Ornithology* 55:18–30.

White, T. L., and L. F. Elliott. 1998. Atlas of Piping Plover Sightings along the Texas Gulf Coast (1992–98). Report to Texas Parks and Wildlife Department, Resource Protection. Austin. 627 pp.

White, W. A., and W. B. Brogden. 1977. Descriptions of land and water resources.

Appendix A in R. S. Kier and E. G. Fruh (eds.), *Environmental and Economic Impacts of Recreational Community Development, Mustang Island and North Padre Island*, vol. 1. Austin: University of Texas.

White, W. A., T. R. Calnan, R. A. Morton, R. S. Kimble, T. G. Littleton, J. H. McGowen, H. S. Nance, and K. E. Schmedes. 1983c. *Submerged Lands of Texas, Corpus Christi Area: Sediments, Geochemistry, Benthic Macroinvertebrates, and Associated Wetlands*. Austin: Bureau of Economic Geology, University of Texas. 137 pp. + 6 maps.

White, W. A., R. R. Calnan, R. A. Morton, R. S. Kimble, T. G. Littleton, J. H. McGowen, and H. S. Nance. 1986. *Submerged Lands of Texas, Brownsville-Harlingen Area: Sediments, Geochemistry, Benthic Macroinvertebrates, and Associated Wetlands*. Austin: Bureau of Economic Geology, University of Texas at Austin. 138 pp. + 9 maps.

White, W. A., T. R. Calnan, R. A. Morton, R. S. Kimble, T. G. Littleton, J. H. McGowen, and H. S. Nance. 1989. *Submerged Lands of Texas, Kingsville Area: Sediments, Geochemistry, Benthic Macroinvertebrates, and Associated Wetlands*. Austin: Bureau of Economic Geology, University of Texas.137 pp. + 6 maps.

White, W. A., and W. E. Galloway. 1977. *Guide to Modern Barrier Environments of Mustang and North Padre Islands and Jackson (Eocene) Barrier/Lagoon Facies of South Texas Uranium District*. Research Note 7. Austin: Bureau of Economic Geology, University of Texas. 51 pp.

White, W. A., T. A. Tremblay, J. Hinson, D. W. Moulton, W. J. Pulich, Jr., E. H. Smith, and K. V. Jenkins. 1998. *Current Status and Historical Trends of Selected Estuarine and Coastal Habitats in the Corpus Christi Bay National Estuary Program Study Area*. Corpus Christi Bay National Estuary Program CCBNEP-29. Corpus Christi: Texas Natural Resource Conservation Commission. 161 pp.

Whitlach, R. B. 1982. *The Ecology of New England Tidal Flats: A Community Profile*. U.S. Fish and Wildlife Service, Office of Biological Services FWS/OBS-81/01. Washington, D.C. 125 pp.

Whitten, H. L., H. F. Rosene, and J. W. Hedgpeth. 1950. The invertebrate fauna of Texas coast jetties: A preliminary survey. *Publications of the Institute of Marine Science, University of Texas* 1(2):53–87.

Whorff, J. S. 1992. Physical and Biological

333

Interactions in the Midlittoral Zone along a Central Texas Inlet. Ph.D. diss., Texas A&M University, College Station. 253 pp.

Whyte, R. J. 1978. The Effects of Cattle on Shoreline Vegetation of Ponds and Tanks in South Texas. M.S. thesis, Texas A&M University, College Station. 59 pp.

Wilhite, H. S., T. C. Allison, and J. A. Rickner. 1982. The diversity and distribution of living mollusks in the lower Laguna Madre of Texas. Pp. 233–47 in J. R. Davis (ed.), *Proceedings of the Symposium on Recent Benthological Investigations in Texas and Adjacent States.* Austin: Texas Academy of Science.

Wilkinson, B. H., J. H. McGowen, and C. R. Lewis. 1975. Ingleside Strandplain sand of central Texas coast. *American Association of Petroleum Geologists Bulletin* 59:347–52.

Williams, T. C., J. M. Williams, L. C. Ireland, and J. M. Teal. 1977. Autumnal bird migration over the western North Atlantic Ocean. *American Birds* 31:251–67.

Williamson, C. J. 1980. Population Dynamics of Molluscs in a Seagrass Bed Surrounding a Dredged Material Island, Upper Laguna Madre, Texas. M.S. thesis, Corpus Christi State University, Corpus Christi. 81 pp.

Wilson, W. H., Jr. 1990. Relationship between prey abundance and foraging site selection by Semipalmated Sandpipers on a Bay of Fundy mudflat. *Journal of Field Ornithology* 61:9–19.

Withers, K. 1994. The Relationship of Macrobenthic Prey Availability to Shorebird Use of Blue-Green Algal Flats in the Upper Laguna Madre. Ph.D. diss., Texas A&M University, College Station. 117 pp.

———. 1996a. Seagrass meadows. Pp. 175–249 in J. W. Tunnell, Jr., Q. R. Dokken, E. H. Smith, and K. Withers (eds.), *Status and Trends of the Estuarine Living Resources within the Corpus Christi Bay National Estuary Program Study Area.* Corpus Christi Bay National Estuary Program CCBNEP-06A. Corpus Christi: Texas Natural Resource Conservation Commission.

———. 1996b. Tidal flats. Pp. 294–356 in J. W. Tunnell, Jr., Q. R. Dokken, E. H. Smith, and K. Withers (eds.), *Status and Trends of the Estuarine Living Resources within the Corpus Christi Bay National Estuary Program Study Area.* Corpus Christi Bay National Estuary Program CCBNEP-06A. Corpus Christi: Texas Natural Resource Conservation Commission.

———. 1996c. An Evaluation of Recovery of Benthic Invertebrate Communities in Vehicle Tracks and Restored Oil and Gas Impacted Areas on Wind-Tidal Flats in the Upper Laguna Madre, Padre Island National Seashore, Texas. Report to Padre Island National Seashore, Contract no. 1443PX749050162. Corpus Christi. 12 pp.

———. 1998. Biological Productivity of Southerly Wind-Tidal Flats within Padre Island National Seashore. Center for Coastal Studies, Texas A&M University–Corpus Christi Technical Report TAMU-CC-9810-CCS. Corpus Christi. 46 pp.

Withers, K., and B. R. Chapman. 1993. Seasonal abundance and habitat use of shorebirds on an Oso Bay mudflat, Corpus Christi, Texas. *Journal of Field Ornithology* 64:382–92.

Withers, K., and J. W. Tunnell, Jr. 1998. *Identification of Tidal Flat Alterations and Determination of Effects on Biological Productivity of These Habitats within the Coastal Bend.* Corpus Christi Bay National Estuary Program CCBNEP-26. Corpus Christi: Texas Natural Resource Conservation Commission. 171 pp.

Wolff, W. J. 1969. Distribution of nonbreeding waders in an estuarine area in relation to the distribution of their food organisms. *Ardea* 57:1–28.

Woodin, M. C. 1994. Use of saltwater and freshwater habitats by wintering redheads in southern Texas. *Hydrobiologia* 279–80:279–87.

———. 1996. Wintering ecology of redheads *(Aythya americana)* in the western Gulf of Mexico region. *Gibier Faune Sauvage* 13:653–65.

WRT (Writer's Round Table). 1950. *Padre Island.* San Antonio, Tex.: Writer's Round Table, Naylor Company. 222 pp.

Wunderle, J. M., Jr., R. B. Waide, and J. Fernandez. 1989. Seasonal abundance of shorebirds in the Hobos Bay estuary in southern Puerto Rico. *Journal of Field Ornithology* 60:329–39.

Yañez, A., and C. J. Schlaepfer. 1968. Composición y distribución de los sedimentos recientes de la Laguna Madre, Tamaulipas. *Universidad Nacional Autónoma de México, Instituto de Geología Boletín* 84 (parte 1): 5–44.

Yates, T. L., and D. J. Schmidly. 1977. Systematics of *Scalopus aquaticus* (Linnaeus) in Texas and adjacent states. *Occasional Papers of the Museum at Texas Tech University* 45:1–36.

Zehner, W. 1985. First record of *Pipistrellus subflavus* (Chiroptera: Vespertilionidae) on Padre Island, Texas. *Southwestern Naturalist* 30:306–307.

Zeitzschel, G. 1980. Sediment-water interactions in nutrient dynamics. Pp. 195–218 in K. R. Tenore and B. C. Coull (eds.), *Marine Benthic Dynamics.* Columbia: University of South Carolina Press.

Zieman, J. C. 1975. Seasonal variation of turtle-grass, *Thalassia testudinum* (König), with reference to temperature and salinity effects. *Aquatic Botany* 1:107–23.

———. 1976. The ecological effects of physical damage from motor boats on turtle-grass beds in southern Florida. *Aquatic Botany* 2:127–39.

———. 1982. *The Ecology of the Seagrasses of South Florida: A Community Profile.* U.S. Fish and Wildlife Service, Office of Biological Services FWS/OBS-82/25. Washington, D.C. 158 pp.

Zieman, J. C., and R. T. Zieman. 1989. *The Ecology of the Seagrass Meadows of the West Coast of Florida: A Community Profile.* U.S. Fish and Wildlife Service Biological Report 85(7.25). Washington, D.C. 155 pp.

Zonick, C. 1997a. Snowy Plover Breeding Ecology along the Texas Gulf Coast. Report to Texas Parks and Wildlife Department, Resource Protection and U.S. Fish

and Wildlife Service, Ecological Services. Corpus Christi, Texas. 8 pp.

———. 1997b. The Use of Texas Barrier Island Washover Pass Habitat by Piping Plovers and Other Coastal Waterbirds. Report to Texas Parks and Wildlife Department, Resource Protection, and U.S. Fish and Wildlife Service, Ecological Services. Corpus Christi. 44 pp.

Zonick, C. A. 2000. The Winter Ecology of Piping Plovers *(Charadrius melodus)* along the Texas Gulf Coast. Ph.D. diss., University of Missouri–Columbia. 171 pp.

Zonick, C., K. Drake, J. Thompson, and L. Elliott. 1998. The Effects of Dredged Material on Piping Plovers *(Charadrius melodus)* and Snowy Plovers *(C. alexandrinus)* in the Lower Laguna Madre of Texas: Final Report for the 1997–1998 Season. Report to Laguna Madre Interagency Coordination Team, U.S. Army Corps of Engineers, Galveston District. 15 pp.

Zonick, C., and M. Ryan. 1994. Ecology and Conservation of Piping and Snowy Plovers Wintering along the Texas Gulf Coast. Report to Texas Parks and Wildlife Department, Resource Protection and U.S. Fish and Wildlife Service, Ecological Services. Corpus Christi. No page numbers.

Zupan, A. W. 1971. Surficial Sediments and Sedimentary Structures: Middleground, Padre Island, Texas. Texas A&M University Department of Oceanography Report 71-12-T. College Station. 71 pp.

Contributors

James F. Bergan, Ph.D. Director of Science and Stewardship, The Nature Conservancy of Texas. Conservation Ecology. Conservation work at Mad Island Marsh, Laguna Madre, and Texas Barrier Islands. Statewide TNC Conservation, Science and Planning.

Susan A. Childs, M.S. Marine Biologist/Topographic Features Specialist, Minerals Management Service. Marine Ecology and Resource Management. Research in Reef Community Ecology, Marine Resource Policy, and Marine Public Education and Outreach.

Suzanne J. Dilworth, M.S. Natural Resource Specialist, Center for Coastal Studies, Texas A&M University-Corpus Christi. Wetland Ecology, Natural Resource Management. Research in Freshwater and Coastal Wetlands, Terrestrial and Riparian Habitats, and Natural and Artificial Reefs.

Nancy L. Hilbun, M.S. Ph.D Candidate, Dauphin Island Sea Lab and University Fellow, University of South Alabama. Research on Caribbean Coral Reef Ecology and Paleoecology. Gulf of Mexico Coastal Ecology.

Frank W. Judd, Ph.D. Professor, Department of Biology, The University of Texas-Pan American. Ecology. Research in Physiological Ecology, Population Ecology and Community Ecology. Remote Sensing of Coastal Vegetation and Oyster Reefs.

Amy E. Koltermann, M.S. Natural Resource Specialist, Center for Coastal Studies, Texas A&M University–Corpus Christi. Coastal Ecology. Research in Rockyshore Ecology, Coastal Wetlands, and Coral Reef Ecology.

Elizabeth H. Smith, Ph.D. Research Scientist, Center for Coastal Studies, Texas A&M University-Corpus Christi. Wetlands Ecology. Research in Wetlands Ecology, Natural Resource Management, and Remote Sensing. Development of Long-Term Conservation and Management Plans.

John W. Tunnell, Jr., Ph.D. Director, Center for Coastal Studies and Professor, Department of Physical and Life Sciences, Texas A&M University-Corpus Christi. Fulbright Scholar and Texas A&M University System Regents Professor. Marine Ecology. Research in Coastal and Coral Reef Ecology, Environmental Impacts, and Invasive Species.

Kim Withers, Ph.D. Research Scientist, Center for Coastal Studies, Texas A&M University-Corpus Christi. Coastal Ecology. Research in Tidal Flat Ecology, Seagrass Ecology, and Mangrove Ecology. Emphasis on the Invertebrate Community.

Index

Tables and figures are indicated with italicized *t* and *f*.

Acartia tonsa, 104–105

Acetabularia sp., 75, 88–89

Achnanthes, 103

Actinoptychus, 103

agriculture, 14–15, 15, 18, 22, 31. *See also* ranching history

Agua Dulce ranch, 64

Aix sponsa, 180

Ajaia ajaja, 186, 208

Alazan Bay: brown tide, 258; fish communities, 224, 231–33, 240; mollusc, 106; salinity patterns, 108; seagrass meadows, 88; zooplankton, 104–105

Alexandrium (=Gonyaulax) monilita, 258

algae: brown tides, 255–58, 287; jetty habitats, 79; open bay habitats, 103–104; red tide, 255, 258; seagrass meadows, 88–89, 99; wind-tidal flats, 114, 119, 122–23, 146. *See also* phytoplankton

Alice (town), 64

Allen (hurricane), 168

Ambrosia artemisiifolia, 190

Americamysis (=Mysidopsis) almyra, 105

American white pelicans *(Pelecanus erythrorhynchos)*, 162, 194–95

American wigeons *(Anas americana)*, 94, 178, 179

Amistad Dam, 22

amphibians/reptiles: barrier islands, 132, 136; biotic province perspective, 53–54, 56*t*; rare/threatened, 278; rare/threatened species, 264–65*t*; species totals, 83*t. See also* sea turtles

Amphora, 103

Amygdalum papyrium, 92

Anas acuta, 94, 172, 178–79

Anas americana, 94, 178, 179

Anas clypeata, 172, 176–77, 178–79

Anas crecca, 172, 179

Anas cyanoptera septentrionalium, 180

Anas fulvigula, 176, 177–79

Anas penelope, 181

Anas platyrhynchos, 180

Anas strepera, 176, 178, 179

anchovies *(Anchoa* spp.), 93, 191, 232–33

animal communities: barrier islands, 131–34, 135–36, 198–99; biotic province perspective, 39, 52–58; jetty habitat, 79–80, 94, 213; open bay habitats, 104–110, 113; research needs, 272–74; seagrass meadows, 90–95, 98, 101; species overview, 82–83*t;* wind-tidal flats, 120–22. *See also* bird habitat; fish communities; invertebrate communities; sea turtles

Anomalocardia auberiana, 105, 107

Aransas Pass, 78–79

Ardea alba, 122, 161, 163, 186, 207, 208

Ardea herodias, 122, 161, 186, 190–91, 207

Armstrong Ranch, 67

Arroyo Chorreras, 22

Arroyo Colorado: conservation recommendations, 278–79; drainage, 14, 21; geological characteristics, 31–32; photo, 141; wind-tidal flats, 118

Arroyo del Diablo, 22

Atlantic papermussel *(Amygdalum papyrium)*, 92

Atrina sp., 213

Atriplex spp., 32–33

Atwood, Nettie King, 67

Aureococcus anophageffereus, 257

Aureoumbra lagunensis, 255–58, 287

Avicennia germinans, 44, 84, 119

Aythya americana. See redheads *(Aythya americana)*

Aythya vasisineria, 169, 176, 178–79

baby-bubble *(Rictaxis punctostriatus)*, 113

back-island dunes, 128–30

backshore zone on barrier islands, 44, 46, 134

badgers *(Taxidea taxus)*, 133, 136

Baffin Bay: beach rock, 34, 80, 148; brown tide occurrence, 255–58, 287; fish communities, 223, 228, 229, 231–33, 240; freshwater inflows, 14, 21, 74; geologic history, 28–29, 33, 34; hurricane effects, 19; invertebrate families, 90–92, 120–21, 233; seagrass meadows, 87–88; serpulid reefs, 35, 80–81; shrimp, 233; wind-tidal flats, 118. *See also* open bay habitats

Ballí, José María, 61, 65

Ballí, Juan José, 65–66

Ballí, Padre José Nicolas, 65–66

Ballí families (Vallí), 61–62, 65–66, 67

banded plovers (*Charadrius* spp.), 121

barnacle larvae, 104, 105

Barra de San Pedro, 211

Barra El Conchillal, 12, 14

Barra Jesús María, 12, 14

Barra Los Americanos, 12, 14

Barra Soto la Marina, 12, 14

barrier islands: animal communities, 131–34, 135–36, 198–99; conservation recommendations, 282, 284; ecosystem processes, 135–36; geography, 12, 14; geologic history, 29; landform characteristics, 127–30; overview, 127; plant communities, 44–46, 131, 134–35; rainfall, 131; research needs, 273

bathymetry, 8–9, 16, 23, 28–29

Batis maritima, 119

bay squid (*Lolliguncula brevis*), 107

beach rock (coquina), 14, 34–35, 80, 148, 273

Beulah (hurricane), 19, 75, 172, 251

Big Bird Island, 195

biotic province approach, 38–39

bird habitat: barrier islands, 198–99; biotic province perspective, 54–58; conservation recommendations, 196, 279, 284, 285–87; dynamic character, 170–72; King Ranch, 69; open bays, 108; photos, 159–64; population estimates, 101, 172–79; rare/threatened species, 179–81, 206–10, 265t, 278; requirements, 169–70, 204–205; research needs, 273–74; seagrass meadows, 94, 98, 101; wind-tidal flats, 114, 121–22, 126, 199–202. *See also* rookery islands

Bird Island Basin, 93

birds (land-based): barrier islands, 133, 136; King Ranch, 68; rare/threatened species, 55–56t, 265t, 278. *See also* bird habitat; rookery islands

Bittium varium, 101

bivalves: open bay habitat, 104, 105–107, 113; seagrass meadows, 90–92, 101. *See also* invertebrate communities

black-bellied plovers (*Pluvialis squatorola*), 121–22, 201

black-bellied whistling ducks, 181

blackbrush communities, 46–47

black-crowned night herons (*Nycticorax nycticorax*), 186, 208

black drum (*Pogonias cromis*), 228–33, 234–35, 239–41, 247

black mangrove (*Avicennia germinans*), 44, 84, 119

black skimmers (*Rhynchops niger*), 162, 185, 186, 189, 195–96

blacktail jackrabbits (*Lepus californicus*), 133

Blucher Institute for Surveying and Science, 24

blue crab (*Callinectes sapidus*), 92, 107

bluestem grasslands, 46

blue-wing teal (*Anas discors*), 169, 178

bluewood communities, 47

boating impact. *See* recreation impact

Boca Chica, 12

Boca Ciega, 14, 26, 151, 282–83

Boca de Catán, 14, 26, 143

Boca de Santa Isabel, 14, 26, 154

Boca El Viborero, 27

Boca Jesús María (8th Pass), 27, 75

Boca Sandoval, 27

Borrichia frutescens, 190

bottlenose dolphin (*Tursiops truncatus*), 94–95, 108

Bourland, William, 62

Brazos Island, 12

Brazos Santiago Pass, 12, 25, 144

Bret (hurricane), 19–20

brine fly (*Ephydra*), 75

brine shrimp (*Artemia salinas*), 74–75

brittle stars (Class Ophiuroidea), 93

brown mussel (*Perna perna*), 79–80

brown shrimp (*Farfantepenaeus aztecus*), 107–108, 191, 233–34, 242–45

Brownsville, climate characteristics, 16, 18, 40

Brownsville Ship Channel, 12, 144, 258

brown tide, 98, 255–58, 287

brush-grasslands, 41–52

Bubulcus ibis, 186

Bucephala albeola, 180

Bucephala clangula, 180

bufflegrass (*Pennisetum ciliare*), 42

buffleheads (*Bucephala albeola*), 180

Bufo speciosus, 132

Bufo valliceps, 132

Butorides virescens, 208

cabins as conservation issue, 281

cactus ferruginous pygmy owl (*Glaucidium brasilianum cactorum*), 68

Caesar Kleberg Wildlife Research Institute, 68

Cairina moschata, 180

Calidris alpina, 122, 164, 201

Calidris mauri, 122, 201, 205

Calidris spp., 121–22, 200–201

Cameron County, 11–12, 18

Camone Indians, 65

Canis latrans, 133

canvasbacks (*Aythya valisineria*), 169, 176, 178–79

Carbajal, 152

Carboneras, 11, 152, 153

Caretta caretta. *See* loggerhead sea turtle (*Caretta caretta*)

Carla (hurricane), 19, 172, 251
carp *(Cypinus carpio)*, 75
Cartagena Convention, 222
Caspian terns *(Sterna caspia)*, 162, 186
Catoptrophorus semipalmatus, 201
cattle egrets *(Bubulcus ibis)*, 186
cattle ranching. *See* ranching history
Cavazos, José Narciso, 61, 67
Cayo Atascosa, 31
Cayo del Grullo, 88
Cayo del Infiernillo, 88
Celia (hurricane), 19
Cerithium lutosum, 105
channelization. *See* dredging effects; passes
Charadrius alexandrinus. See snowy plovers
    (Charadrius alexandrinus)
Charadrius melodus, 126, 198, 201, 202,
    206–207
Charadrius semipalmatus, 122
Charadrius wilsonia, 203
charangas (shrimp traps), 167, 249, 281
Chelonia mydas. See green sea turtle
    (Chelonia mydas)
chinchorro (shrimp net), 249–50
Chthamalus fragilis, 79
cinnamon teal *(Anas cyanoptera septentrional-*
    ium), 180
cities/towns, 11–12, 13*t*
Civil War era, 63–64, 66
clay dunes, 14, 32–33, 145–46, 151
climate, overview, 15–20, 39–40
clover grass *(Halophila engelmannii):* brown
    tide and, 98; distribution, 87–88, 89–90,
    99–101; overview, 85–87
Cnemidophorus gularis, 132
Cnemidophorus sexlineatus, 132
Coahuiltecan Indians, 59, 65
Coastal Sand Plains: biotic province per-
    spective, 48–50; clay dunes, 32; ecosys-
    tem overview, 15, 68; geologic history,
    33–34; photo, 147
colonial waterbirds. *See* rookery islands
colonization era, 59–62
common cattail *(Typha latifolia)*, 190
common golden-eye *(Bucephala clangula)*, 180
common mergansers *(Mergus americanus)*,
    181
common ragweed *(Ambrosia artemisiifolia)*,
    190
Conrad Blucher Institute for Surveying and
    Science, 24
conservation issues: projects, 220–222,
    276–277; recommendations, 196, 275–
    287; research needs, 270–274. *See also*
    Nature Conservancy project
copepods, 104–105
coppice dunes, 128–29, 134
coquina (beach rock), 14, 34–35, 80,
    148, 273
cordgrass marshes, 84, 119, 147

Corpus Christi: climate characteristics, 16,
    18; history, 66; population statistics, 11,
    12*t*
Corpus Christi Bay: fish communities, 225;
    harvest history, 229–31, 233, 234; salin-
    ity patterns, 73–74, 108; sediment
    effects, 109
Corpus Christi Pass, 125, 128
county geography, 11, 13*t*
coyotes *(Canis latrans)*, 133
crabs, 92, 107, 212–13
Crane Island, 9–10
Cygnus buccinator, 179
Cygnus columbianus, 179
Cygnus spp., 179
Cymodocea [=*Syringodium*], 89
Cynoscion nebulosus. See spotted sea trout
    (Cynoscion nebulosus)
Cypinus carpio, 75
Cyprinodon variegatus. See sheepshead min-
    now *(Cyprinodon variegatus)*

Deer Island, 32
Dendrocygna bicolor, 181
Dendrocygna spp., 181
Dermochelys coriacea. See leatherback sea
    turtle *(Dermochelys coriacea)*
Designing a Geography of Hope: A Practi-
    tioner's Handbook for Ecoregional Planning
    (Groves, et al.), 261
devegetation from grazing, 67–68
diatoms. *See* phytoplankton
Dice, L. R., 38–39
Dipodomys compactus, 133, 136
dowitchers *(Limnodromous* spp.), 121, 122
drainage: overview, 14–15, 20–22; waste-
    water, 278–79, 283. *See also* freshwater
    inflows
dredging effects: conservation recommen-
    dations, 280–83, 285–87; equipment
    photos, 165; gypsum crystals, 36–37;
    material placement, 10, 140–41, 160,
    166; salinity patterns, 76; seagrass mead-
    ows, 97–98, 102–103, 170; tides, 24;
    wind-tidal flats, 115, 126. *See also* passes;
    rookery islands
drought conditions: regularity, 16–18; salin-
    ity patterns, 75, 76*f*; waterfowl habitat
    in, 171–72, 173
ducks. *See* bird habitat; redheads *(Aythya*
    americana)
Ducks Unlimited of Mexico, 76
dunes. *See* barrier islands
dunlins *(Calidris alpina)*, 122, 164, 201
Dunn, Burton, 66
Dunn, Patrick, 66
Durst, John H., 67
dwarf surfclam *(Mulinia lateralis):* brown tide
    impact, 256, 257; clay dune deposits, 32;
    open bay habitat, 105, 106, 113

East, Alice, 67

East Potrero Grande, 194–95

echinoderms in seagrass meadows, 92–93

ecoregional planning process. *See* Nature Conservancy project

ecosystem overview: habitat types, 76–84; hypersaline characteristics, 73–76

Egretta caerulea, 186, 208

Egretta rufescens. See reddish egrets *(Egretta rufescens)*

Egretta thula, 164, 190, 208

Egretta tricolor, 163, 182, 190, 193, 208

8th Pass (Boca Jesús María), 27, 75

El Barrancón, 151

El Carrizal flats, 33, 126, 151

El Devisadero Ranch, 67

El Mezquital Pass, 11, 14, 26, 142

El Toro tide gauge, 20

endangered/threatened species: biotic province perspective, 54–58; birds, 179–81, 194–97, 206–10; information needs, 277–78; King Ranch area, 68–69. *See also* sea turtles

Environmental Geologic Atlases (Brown, et al.), 32, 37

Eolian Sand Sheet. *See* Coastal Sand Plains

Eretmochelys imbricata. See hawksbill sea turtle *(Eretmochelys imbricata)*

Escandon, José, 59

European wigeon *(Anas penelope)*, 181

evaporation effects, 16, 22–23. *See also* salinity effects/patterns

Falcon Dam/Lake, 22, 73

Falco peregrinus, 133, 136

false limpet *(Siphonaria pectinata)*, 79

Farfantepenaeus duorarum, 108, 233–34, 242, 244–45

feral hogs *(Sus scrofa)*, 133

fiddler crab *(Uca subcylindrica)*, 120–121

"finger" striped mullet *(Mugil cephalus)*, 121

fish communities: barrier islands, 131–32; brown tide and, 256–58; ecological values, 225–29; harvest history, 153, 234–41, 248–52; hurricane effects, 20, 75; jetty habitat, 79; rare/threatened species, 55*t*, 264*t*; red tide, 258; reef structures, 80–81; salinity effects, 73, 74–75, 158, 223–25; seagrass meadows, 85, 93–94, 95, 98; structures compared, 229–33; wind-tidal flats, 121

Fish Pass, 282

Florida, 216, 221

foredunes, 44, 46, 128–30

forest communities, 48–50

Forster's terns *(Sterna forsteri)*, 161, 186

fragile barnacle *(Chthamalus fragilis)*, 79

freezing temperatures, 18, 40, 84, 256

French Guiana, 216

freshwater inflows, 14–15, 20–22, 73, 246–47, 249*t*. *See also* hurricanes

fulvous pocket mouse *(Reithrodontomys fulvescens)*, 133–34, 136

fulvous whistling ducks *(Dendrocygna bicolor)*, 181

Fundulus similis, 121, 132

gadwalls *(Anas strepera)*, 176, 178, 179

Gambusia affinis, 75, 131–32

García, Abundio, 67

gastropods, 90–92, 101, 113. *See also* invertebrate communities

geography, overview, 7–15, 38, 138–39

geomorphology: conservation, 37; geochemical processes, 35–37; mainland features, 31–35; origins/development, 28–31, 35

Geomys personatus, 133

Gilbert (hurricane), 252

GIWW. *See* Gulf Intracoastal Waterway (GIWW)

glacial history, 28–29, 30*f*, 35

glasswort *(Salicornia* spp.), 119–20

Glaucidium brasilianum cactorum, 68

global warming effects, 16

goose populations, 176–77, 178

Gopherus berlandieri, 132

Grammatophora, 103–104

granjeno parklands, 47

grasslands-brush, 41–52

grass shrimp *(Palaemonetes* spp.), 92

grazing impact, 67–69, 267

great blue herons *(Ardea herodias)*, 122, 161, 186, 190–91, 207

great egrets *(Ardea alba)*, 122, 161, 163, 186, 207, 208

greater scaups *(Aythya marila)*, 180

great-tailed grackles *(Quiscalus mexicanus)*, 191

green herons *(Butorides virescens)*, 208

Green Island, 10, 31, 195

Green Island Cut Spoil, 193

green sea turtle *(Chelonia mydas):* appearance, 212; distribution, 211; feeding habits, 213; nesting history, 214–16; population trends, 217–19; seagrass habitat, 94, 213; threats, 219–20

green tree frog *(Hyla cinerea)*, 132

green-winged teal *(Anas crecca)*, 172, 179

Gulf coast kangaroo rats *(Dipodomys compactus)*, 133, 136

Gulf Coast Prairies and Marshes ecoregion, 259–60

Gulf coast toad *(Bufo valliceps)*, 132

Gulf Intracoastal Waterway (GIWW): conservation recommendations, 286–87; dredging materials/maintenance, 10, 69, 182; geography, 7; open bay habitat,

102–103; photo, 140; salinity patterns, 25–26, 76; seagrass meadows, 88, 97

Gulf menhaden *(Brevoortia patronus)*, 93–94, 229–33

Gulf Prairies and Marshes area, vegetation characteristics, 44–51

Gul killifish *(Fundulus similis)*, 121, 132

gull-billed terns *(Sterna nilotica)*, 161, 186, 189, 196

Gymnodium breve, 258

gypsum crystal formation, 36–37, 148

Halodule beaudettei[=wrightii]. See shoalgrass *(Halodule beaudettei[=wrightii])*

Halophila engelmannii. See clover grass *(Halophila engelmannii)*

Hawk Island, 10, 31

hawksbill sea turtle *(Eretmochelys imbricata):* appearance, 212; distribution, 211; feeding habits, 213; nesting history, 216; population trends, 217–18, 219; seagrass habitat, 94; threats, 219–20

Higuerillas, 11

Hildebrand, H., 73, 75

Hinojosa, Juan José de, 61

Hinojosa, Rosa María, 61

Hinojosa families, 61–62

hispid cotton rat *(Sigmodon hispidus)*, 133–34, 136

Hole, The, 88, 102, 240

Holocene period, 28–29, 34, 35

holoplankton, 104–105

hooded mergansers *(Mergus cucullatus)*, 180–81

Horse Island, 31

houseboats, 281

human habitation: clay dune archaeology, 32; as conservation issue, 276, 279, 280, 281

Humble Channel Spoil rookery, 191

Humble Oil and Refining Company, 64–65

humidity, 16, 40, 131

Hunt, Jack, 65

hurricanes: as conservation issue, 287–88; erosion effects, 168; fish communities and, 20, 75; as geologic history, 30; overview, 18–20, 21*t*; shrimp harvests, 251, 252; waterfowl populations and, 172

Hurter's spadefoot toad *(Scaphiophus holbrookii hurteri)*, 132

hydrography, overview, 20–25

hypersaline conditions. *See* salinity effects/patterns

Ingleside Barrier, 34

insects, 55*t*, 75, 120, 135

invertebrate communities: barrier islands, 131, 135; brown tide and, 256–58; clay

dune deposits, 32; food productivity role, 110–12, 191, 204–205; jetty habitat, 79–80; open bay habitats, 102, 105–10, 113; rare/threatened species, 55*t*, 264*t*; salinity effects, 74–75; seagrass meadows, 90–93, 101; wind-tidal flats, 114, 120–22. *See also* penaeid shrimp harvests

irrigation diversion, 14–15, 22, 31

Isla Blanca. *See* Padre Island

islands: geography overview, 9–11, 12, 14, 140; geologic history, 29, 31–32; human habitation impact, 166, 279, 281

Ixtoc I oil spill, 167, 283

jetty habitat: overview, 77–80; research needs, 273; turtle populations, 94, 213

John G. and Marie Stella Kenedy Memorial Foundation, 64

John G. Kenedy Charitable Trust, 64

Karankawa Indians, 59, 65, 218

keeled earless lizard *(Holbrookia propinqua)*, 132

Kemp's ridley sea turtle *(Lepidochelys kempii):* distribution/appearance, 94, 211–12; feeding habits, 212; nesting history, 213–14, 215*t*; population trends, 216–18; threats, 219–20

Kemp's Ridley Sea Turtle Restoration and Enhancement Project, 220–21

Kenedeños, 63

Kenedy, John, 64

Kenedy, Mifflin, 63–64, 66

Kenedy, Sarah J., 64

Kenedy Pasture Company, 64

Kenedy Ranch, 60*f*, 64

killifish, 93, 121, 132, 233

Kineños, 63

King, Alice Gertrudis, 64

King, Henrietta, 64

King, Richard, 62–64, 66, 67

King Ranch, 60*f*, 63–65, 68–69

Kinney, H. L., 66

Kleberg, Alice, 65

Kleberg, Cesar, 65

Kleberg, Richard, 65

Kleberg, Robert, 64–65

Kleberg, Robert, Jr., 65

Kleberg saltbrush *(Atriplex klebergorum)*, 32–33

La Becerra Ranch, 67

Laevicardium mortoni, 92

Lagodon rhomboides, 232–33

Laguna Almagre, 22

Laguna Atasco Wildlife Refuge, 31, 201–202

Laguna el Catán, 35, 80, 152

Laguna la Nacha, 15, 22

Laguna Morales, 22

Laguna Vista, 32

La Lunta Larga, 32

Land Cut area: geography overview, 7, 14; geologic overview, 28, 30–31, 33; gypsum crystals, 36–37, 148; photos, 140, 143, 146, 166; rookery islands, 194–95; seagrass meadows, 88; wind-tidal flats, 114–15, 116, 118, 120, 202

land grant system, 60–62, 65–66

La Parra Ranch, 64

La Pesca, 12, 16, 18, 155

La Pesca flat, 126

Larus atricilla, 186, 191, 193, 196–97

laughing gulls *(Larus atricilla)*, 186, 191, 193, 196–97

Laureles Ranch, 64

least terns *(Sterna antillarum)*, 161, 186, 196

leatherback sea turtle *(Dermochelys coriacea)*: appearance, 212; conservation management, 221; distribution, 211; nesting history, 216; population trends, 219; seagrass habitat, 94, 213; threats, 217, 219–20

Lepidochelys kempii. See Kemp's ridley sea turtle *(Lepidochelys kempii)*

lesser scaups *(Aythya affinis)*, 170, 179

Lewis, Gideon K. ("Legs"), 63

light levels: brown tide effects, 257–58; seagrass meadows, 86, 97–98

light pollution and turtles, 221

Ligia exotica, 79

Limnodromous spp., 121, 122

lined periwinkle *(Nodilittorina lineolata)*, 79

Litopenaeus setiferus, 108, 233–34, 242–43, 245–46

little blue herons *(Egretta caerulea)*, 186, 208

live oak *(Quercus virginiana)*, 44, 47, 135, 143

LM 63A (New Marker 127), 192

loggerhead sea turtle *(Caretta caretta)*: appearance, 212; distribution, 211; feeding habits, 212–13; nesting history, 214; population trends, 217–18; seagrass habitat, 94; threats, 219–20

lomas, 10

Los Bancos de en Medio, 32

Lucania parva, 93

Lyngbya confervoides (=Microcoleus lyngbyaceus), 119

macrozooplankton, 108

Malaquito Indians, 65

mallards *(Anas platyrhynchos)*, 180

mammals: barrier islands, 133–34, 136; biotic province perspective, 39, 52–53, 57t; jetty habitat, 79; open bay habitat, 108; rare/threatened species, 68, 265–

66t, 278; seagrass meadows, 94–95; species totals, 83t

manatee grass *(Cymodocea [=Syringodium])*: algae components, 89; distribution, 87–88, 89–90, 99–101; fish communities, 95, 98; overview, 85–86; photos, 156

mangroves, 44, 84, 119

Mansfield Pass: conservation recommendations, 282–83, 286; geography, 12, 128; gypsum crystals, 36–37; photos, 142, 146; salinity effects, 25

marine mammals, 79, 94–95, 108

Marker 63-65 Island, 192

Marker 81 (New Marker 163) Spoil Island, 192–93, 195, 197

Marsh-Barrier Island Vegetation Type, 44–46

Martinez, Jorge, 69

masked duck *(Oxyura dominica)*, 181

Matamoran Biotic District, 40–43

Matamoros, 11

Mendiola, Juan, 63

Menidia beryllina, 74, 224, 233

Menidia peninsulae, 93, 95

Menidia spp., 121, 232–33

mergansers *(Mergus* spp.*)*, 180–81

Mergus americanus, 181

Mergus cucullatus, 180–81

Mergus serrator, 181

Mergus spp., 180–81

mermaid's wine glass *(Acetabularia* sp.*)*, 75, 88–89

meroplankton, 104–105

mesquite *(Prosopis glandulosa)*, 46–47, 51, 190

Mexico-Texas conflict, 62, 63

Miller, James, 62

M. Kenedy and Company, 63

Mollie Beattie Coastal Habitat Community, 125

molluscs, 55t, 101, 105–107, 113. *See also* invertebrate communities

Morton eggcockle *(Laevicardium mortoni)*, 92

mosquito fish *(Gambusia affinis)*, 75, 131–32

mottled ducks *(Anas fulvigula)*, 176, 177–79

mud crab *(Neopanope texana)*, 107

Mugil cephalus, 121

Mulinia lateralis. See dwarf surfclam *(Mulinia lateralis)*

Mullet Island, 10, 31

Murdoch's Landing, 26

muscovy duck *(Cairina moschata)*, 180

mussel beds, 79–80. *See also* invertebrate communities

mysids, 105

naiad, 179

Naragansett Bay, 257

Nature Conservancy project: GCPM ecoregion overview, 259–60; planning background, 260–62; strategies, 267–69; target selection, 262–67

Negro Indians, 65

Neopanope texana, 107

Neritina virginea, 101

nesting of colonial birds. *See* rookery islands

New Marker 127 (LM 63A), 192

New Marker 163 (Marker 81) Spoil Island, 192–93, 195, 197

Nodilittorina lineolata, 79

North Bird Island, 10

northern pintails (*Anas acuta*), 94, 101, 172, 178–79

northern shovelers (*Anas clypeata*), 172, 176–77, 178–79

North Floodway, 14, 22

Nueces County, 11–12, 18

Nueces Strip, 62

Nuecian Biotic District, 43

Nyctanassa violacea, 208

Nycticorax nycticorax, 186, 208

oak: barrier islands, 135; biotic province perspective, 44, 47; photo, 143; savanna, 15, 68

ocelot (*Felis pardalis*), 68, 266

Odocoileus virginianus, 133

odostome (*Odostomia canaliculata*), 113

oil spills, 125–26, 167, 283

Onuf, Chris, 20

oolite formation, 35–36

open bay habitats: animal communities, 104–108; ecosystem processes, 110–12; overview, 76, 102–103, 112–13; plant communities, 103–104; salinity effects, 108; sediment effects, 108–10

Oryzomys palustris, 133–34

Ossorio y Llamas, José de, 60

Oxyura dominica, 181

oyster reefs, 81–82, 84, 107

oysters, 80, 252

Packery Channel, 128

Padre Island: animal communities, 131–34, 135; geography overview, 12; geologic history, 29–31, 35; landform characteristics, 128, 130; photos, 141–42, 146, 157, 167, 168; rainfall, 131; ranching history, 59, 65–66, 67–69; recreation development, 66–67

Padre Island National Seashore: creation, 66–67; fish communities, 131–32; sea turtles, 220–21; shorebird populations, 198, 201; tidal island flats, 124, 125; trash cleanup, 284–85

Padre Isles, 11, 141

Palacio, Juan Armando de, 60

Palaemonetes spp., 92

Paralichthys lethostigma, 121

passes: geography overview, 12, 14, 128; habitat overview, 77–80; hurricane effects, 18, 20; photos, 140–41, 142, 144, 146, 151, 154; salinity patterns, 25–26, 286; shorebird distribution, 199, 202–203; Tamaulipas lagoon, 14, 18–19, 142–43, 286. *See also* dredging effects; Land Cut area

patch reefs, 35, 80

Pearson, T. G., 235

penaeid shrimp ecology/habitat, 92, 107–108, 191, 233–34

penaeid shrimp harvests: history, 235, 241–47, 249–52; sea turtle impact, 217–18, 219, 221–22; waste products, 279, 285

Penascal Point, 34, 80, 148

peninsulas, geography overview, 12, 14

pen shells (*Atrina* sp.), 213

pregrine falcons (*Falco peregrinus*), 133, 136

pesticides, 278–79, 283

physiographic data, 7–9

phytoplankton: brown tide and, 256–57, 287; open bay habitats, 102, 103, 108, 110–12. *See also* algae

Pineda, Alonso Alvarez de, 59, 65

pinfish (*Lagodon rhomboides*), 232–33

pink shrimp (*Farfantepenaeus duorarum*), 108, 233–34, 242, 244–45

piping plovers (*Charadrius melodus*), 126, 198, 201, 202, 206–207

Pita Island, 9–10, 140, 191

plant communities: barrier islands, 44–46, 131, 134–35; biotic province perspective, 15, 41–52, 54–55; clay dunes, 32–33; as heron nesting materials, 190–91; King Ranch, 68–69; mangroves, 44, 84, 119; open bay habitats, 103–104; rare/threatened species, 263–64t, 267–68, 277–78; species overview, 82–83t; wind-tidal flats, 114, 119–20. *See also* algae; seagrass meadows

Plegadis chihi, 186

Pleistocene period, 28–29, 34, 35

Pogonias cromis, 228–33, 234–35, 239–41, 247

pointed venus (*Anomalocardia auberiana*), 105, 107

polychaetes: brown tides, 256; open bay habitat, 105–107, 110; seagrass meadows, 90–92; wind-tidal flats, 120. *See also* invertebrate communities

ponds: barrier islands, 130, 131; ranch, 68; salt, 150; as waterfowl habitat, 169, 170–71, 173, 174–75

population centers (human), 11–12, 13t

porciones (land grants), 60

Port Mansfield, 11, 167

potreros, 10

Powers, Stephen, 63

precipitation, 15, 16–18, 22–23, 40. *See also* drought conditions; hurricanes

Price, W. Armstrong, 28

primary dune zone on barrier islands, 134

Pronatura Noreste, 260, 275–76. *See also* Nature Conservancy project

Prosopis glandulosa, 46–47, 51, 190

Puerto Rico, 222

Punta Piedras, 34–35, 75, 80, 148, 152

Quercus virginiana, 13, 44, 47, 135, 143

Quiscalus mexicanus, 191

R. King and Company, 63

Rabb Ranch, 42

rain, 15, 16–18, 22–23, 40. *See also* drought conditions; hurricanes

rainwater killifish (*Lucania parva*), 93

Rana berlandieri, 132

ranching history: ecological impact, 11, 67–69; overview, 59–67

Rancho Nuevo, 211, 214, 216–17, 220, 221

Rancho Rincon de Anacahuitas, 15, 69

Rancho Santa Cruz, 66

Rattlesnake Island, 31

recreation impact: conservation recommendations, 281, 284–85, 287; dune systems, 266–67; reef structures, 35, 81; seagrass meadows, 99; sea turtles, 216; wind-tidal flats, 125

red-breasted mergansers (*Mergus serrator*), 181

reddish egrets (*Egretta rufescens*): distribution, 126, 182, 195; habitat/ecology overview, 122, 207–10; nesting patterns, 190–91; photo, 164

red drum (*Sciaenops ocellatus*): habitat/ecology overview, 93, 227–28; harvest history, 234–36, 250–52; population surveys, 229–33; salinity preferences, 75, 247

redheads (*Aythya americana*): feeding behavior, 170, 173–74; photos, 159; pond use, 174–75; population estimates, 172–73; seagrass meadows, 94, 98, 101, 286–87. *See also* waterfowl habitat

red mangrove (*Rhizophora mangle*), 84

red tide, 255, 258

reef structures, 35, 80–82, 106–107, 273

Reithrodontomys fulvescens, 133–34, 136

reptiles/amphibians: barrier islands, 132, 136; biotic province perspective, 53–54, 56t; rare/threatened species, 264–65t, 278; species totals, 83t. *See also* sea turtles research needs, overview, 270–74

Rhizophora mangle, 84

Rhodpalodia, 103–104

ribbon worms (Phylum Rhynchocoela), 93

rice rat (*Oryzomys palustris*), 133–34

Rictaxis punctostriatus, 113

Rincón de Santa Gertrudis, 63

Río Grande Coastal Impact Monitoring Program, 279

Río Grande Delta: drainage, 14, 21–22; geography, 7; geologic overview, 28–29, 31, 32, 33, 144–45; as waterfowl habitat, 171–72, 175–79

Río Grande leopard frog (*Rana berlandieri*), 132

Río Grande Plain, 15

Río San Fernando Delta, 7, 14–15, 22, 126, 151

Río Soto la Marina, 18, 22, 84, 155

Robertson, Sam, 66

rookery islands: human habitation, 279; nesting history, 182–88; nesting success factors, 188–91; photos, 162; species of concern, 194–97; specific islands described, 191–94. *See also* bird habitat

roseate spoonbill (*Ajaia ajaja*), 186, 208

royal terns (*Sterna maxima*), 161, 186, 189–90, 193–94, 198

Ruppia maritima. *See* wigeon grass (*Ruppia maritima*)

Sabal texana, 42–43

Salicornia spp., 119–20

salinity effects/patterns: brown tide, 256, 257; as conservation issue, 285–87; fish communities, 223–25; fisheries production and, 74–75, 247; hurricane impact, 19, 73; open bay habitats, 103, 105, 107, 108; oyster reefs, 81–82; photos, 158; pre/post channelization compared, 25–26, 27, 73–74, 76; red tide, 258; seagrass meadows, 85–86, 170, 286–87; waterfowl habitat, 170–72

saltbrush (*Atriplex* spp.), 32–33

saltflats, 46

saltwort (*Batis maritima*), 119

San Carlos Mountains, 38, 39

sanderlings (*Calidris alba*), 198, 203

sandpipers (*Calidris* spp.), 121–22, 200–201

sand plains. *See* Coastal Sand Plains

Sandwich terns (*Sterna sandvicensis*), 161, 186, 189–90, 193–94

San Juan de Carricitos, 61, 67

Santa Fe Ranch, 60f, 67

Santa Gertrudis Ranch, 64

Saunders, George B., 175

Sauz Ranch, 60f, 67

Scaphiophus holbrookii hurteri, 132

scarring, 99, 125, 287

scaups, 170, 175, 178, 179, 180

Sciaenops ocellatus. *See* red drum (*Scianenops ocellatus*)

sea cucumbers (Class Holothuroidea), 93

seagrass meadows: algae components, 88–89; animal communities, 90–95, 101, 170, 173–74, 213, 228, 234; brown tide effects, 98, 257–58; distribution, 14, 87–88, 99–

101, 102–103; dredging effects, 97–98, 280–81, 286–87; ecosystem processes, 95–96, 111–12; overview, 76, 85–87; photos, 149, 152, 154, 156, 157; research needs, 273; restoration projects, 276–77; seismic activity, 284; succession patterns, 86–87, 89–90; threats, 97–99, 287

sea oats *(Uniola paniculata)*, 134

sea-ox-eye daisy *(Borrichia frutescens)*, 190

sea purslane, 134

sea roach *(Ligia exotica)*, 79

seashore dropseed *(Sporobolus virginicus)*, 134

sea turtles: conservation management, 220–22; distribution/appearance, 94, 211–12; feeding habits, 212–13; jetty habitat, 79; nesting history, 213–16; population trends, 216–19; seagrass meadows, 94; threats, 219–20

Second Chain of Islands, 195

sediment effects, 30–31, 35, 108–10, 118. *See also* barrier islands

seismic activity, 284

semipalmated plovers *(Charadrius semipalmatus)*, 122, 201

serpulid reefs, 35, 80–81, 106–107, 273

sheepshead minnow *(Cyprinodon variegatus)*: barrier islands, 131; as egret/heron food, 191; population survey, 233; salinity tolerances, 74, 223–24; wind-tidal flats, 121

shoalgrass *(Halodule beaudettei[=wrightii])*: algae components, 89; bivalves, 92; brown tide impact, 98, 257–58; distribution, 87–88, 89–90, 99–101, 102–103; dredging impact, 97–98; fish survey, 231; nutrient cycling, 96; overview, 85–87; photos, 156; redhead consumption, 94, 98, 170, 173–74; salinity effects, 75, 286–87

shorebirds. *See* bird habitat

shoreline construction as conservation issue, 281–282

Sigmodon hispidus, 133–34, 136

silversides *(Menidia* spp.): population survey, 232–33; salinity tolerances, 74, 224; seagrass meadows, 93, 95; wind-tidal flats, 121

Singer, Isaac, 66

Singer, John, 66

Siphonaria pectinata, 79

six-lined racerunner *(Cnemidophorus sexlineatus)*, 132

smooth cordgrass *(Spartina alterniflora)*, 119

snowy egrets *(Egretta thula)*, 164, 190, 208

snowy plovers *(Charadrius alexandrinus)*: barrier islands, 198; overview, 207; washover passes, 202–203; wind-tidal flats, 121–22, 126, 201

songbirds and Sand Plains, 68

Soto la Marina, 16, 154

South Bay: fish communities, 93–94, 121, 233; geography, 12; oyster reefs, 81–82;

red tide, 258; seagrass meadows, 88; sea turtles, 94

South Bird Island, 10, 191–92, 194

southern flounder *(Paralichthys lethostigma)*, 121

South Floodway, 22

South of South Bird Island, 194–95

South Padre Island, 11, 44–46, 84, 142, 157, 206

South Texas Brush Country, 48–50

South Texas Plains area, vegetation characteristics, 44–51

Spanish influences, 59–62, 65–66

Spartina alterniflora, 119

Spermophilus spilosoma, 133

Spohn, E. A., 64

Sporobolus virginicus, 134

spotted ground squirrel *(Spermophilus spilosoma)*, 133

spotted sea trout *(Cynoscion nebulosus)*: Baffin Bay populations, 223; Bird Island Basin, 93; ecology/habitat overview, 225–27, 228; harvest history, 234–35, 237–39, 250–52; population surveys, 229–33; post-Beulah populations, 75

steamboat business (Kenedy/King), 63–64

Sterna antillarum, 161, 186, 196

Sterna caspia, 162, 186

Sterna forsteri, 161, 186

Sterna maxima, 161, 186, 189–90, 193–94

Sterna nilotica, 161, 186, 189, 196

Sterna sandvicensis, 161, 186, 189–90, 193–94

Strecker, John K., 211

stunted oak *(Quercus* spp.), 135

Sus scrofa, 133

swans *(Cygnus* spp.), 179

Tamaulipan biotic province: animal communities, 52–58; overview, 38–43; plant communities, 43–52, 54–55

Tamaulipan thornscrub, 267–68

Tamaulipas lagoon: barrier islands, 128, 130, 132, 133–34; biotic province perspective, 51–52; climate, 15–20; conservation issues, 267, 276, 279, 281, 282–83; ecosystem overview, 73, 74–75, 76–79, 82–84; fish communities, 225; geography, 7–15; geology, 32, 33, 34–35; harvest history, 248–52; hydrography, 22–25; open bay habitats, 112–13; passes, 14, 18–19, 26–27, 142–43, 286; photos, 139, 140, 148, 149–55; ranching heritage, 69; research needs, 270–74; rookery islands, 188, 194, 195; seagrass meadows, 99–101; shorebirds, 198, 203, 206, 207, 209; waterfowl population estimates, 101, 171–72, 173, 175–79; wind-tidal flats, 126

Tampa tellin *(Tellina tampaensis)*, 105, 106, 107
Taura Syndrome virus, 285
Taxidea taxus, 133, 136
Taylor, Zachary, 62
temperatures, 17*t*, 18, 40, 256
"Texas Brown Tide," 255, 287
Texas Center for Policy Studies, 275–76
Texas Coastal Zone Management Program (CMP), 277
Texas Land and Cattle Company, 64
Texas palmetto *(Sabal texana)*, 42–43
Texas pocket gopher *(Geomys personatus)*, 133
Texas spotted whiptail *(Cnemidophorus gularis)*, 132
Texas toad *(Bufo speciosus)*, 132
Texas tortoise *(Gopherus berlandieri)*, 132
Thalassia testudinum. See turtle-grass *(Thalassia testudinum)*
Three Islands, 10, 31
Three Island Spoil, 193–94
tidal flats. *See* wind-tidal flats
tides, 19–20, 23–25, 141
tidewater silversides *(Menidia beryllina)*, 74, 224, 233
tidewater silversides *(Menidia peninsulae)*, 93, 95
Total Maximum Daily Load Program, 279
Tovar, José María, 66
towns/cities, 11–12, 13*t*
toxic wastewater, 278–79, 283
trash cleanup, 284–85
Treaty of Guadalupe Hildalgo, 62
Tres Norias Ranch, 67
tricolored herons *(Egretta tricolor)*, 163, 182, 190, 193, 208
Trumpeter swans *(Cynus buccinator)*, 179
turbidity. *See* dredging effects
turtle excluder devices (TEDs), 219, 221–22
turtle-grass *(Thalassia testudinum):* boating impact, 99; distribution, 87–88, 89–90, 99–101; fish communities, 98; overview, 85–87; photos, 156; as sea turtle food, 213
turtles. *See* sea turtles
Typha latifolia, 190

Uca subcylindrica, 120–21
Uniola paniculata, 134
upland habitat, 15, 68. *See also* Tamaulipan biotic province

Valli families (Ballí), 61–62, 65–66, 67
variable bittiums *(Bittium varium)*, 101

variable cerith *(Cerithium lutosum)*, 105
vegetation. *See* plant communities
Vidal, Petra Vela de, 64
virgin nerites *(Neritina virginea)*, 101

wading birds. *See* bird habitat
Walworth, James, 63, 64
wastewater loads, 278–79, 283
Watson, Richard, 20
Wells, James, 63
western sandpipers *(Calidris mauri)*, 122, 201, 205
whistling ducks *(Dendrocygna* spp.), 181
whistling swans *(Cygnus columbianus)*, 179
white-faced ibis *(Plegadis chihi)*, 186
white shrimp *(Litopenaeus setiferus)*, 108, 233–34, 242–43, 245–46
white-tailed deer *(Odocoileus virginianus)*, 133
wigeon grass *(Ruppia maritima):* distribution, 87–88, 89–90, 99–101; nutrient cycling, 96; overview, 85–87; photos, 156
willets *(Catoptrophorus semipalmatus)*, 201
Wilson's plovers *(Charadrius wilsonia)*, 203
winds, 16, 19–20, 40. *See also* wind-tidal flats
wind-shadow dunes, 129
wind-tidal flats: animal communities, 120–22, 204–205, 207–210; distribution, 14, 114–15, 128; ecosystem processes, 122–23; environmental dynamics, 115–17; geologic overview, 31–32, 33, 118; gypsum crystals, 36–37; islands, 10; overview, 114; photos, 140, 143, 146, 157–58; plant communities, 114, 119–20; shorebird distribution, 199–202, 204–205; threats, 123–26, 210
wind-tides, 24–25
wood duck *(Aix sponsa)*, 180
woodland communities, 48–50

Yalima po-Les Hattes, French Guiana, 216
Yarborough, Ralph, 67
Yarborough Pass, 26, 122, 282
yellow-crowned night herons *(Nyctanassa violacea)*, 208
Yturria, Francisco, 67
Yucca Island, 10, 31

zooplankton, 104–105, 108, 256–57